P. O. Box 384
Reynoldsburg, OH 43068
614-864-8875

currencyquest@papermoneyworld.com

Specializing in Large-Size notes
Buying & Selling all U. S. paper money
Want Lists Serviced

Please consider us for all your collecting needs. We attend all major paper money shows and sales and promise knowledgeable and fair dealing.

Member: Professional Currency
Dealers Association
American Numismatic Association

U. S. Paper Money
Guide and Handbook

Carlson R. Chambliss, Ph. D.

Other current works from the same publisher:

Comprehensive Catalog of U. S. Paper Money Errors (Frederick J. Bart, 1994)
Comprehensive Catalog of Confederate Paper Money by Grover Criswell (1995)
Comprehensive Catalog and History of Confederate Bonds by Douglas B. Ball (1998)
U. S. Essay, Proof, and Specimen Notes (Gene Hessler, 1977)
Comprehensive Catalog of U.S. Paper Money (Gene Hessler, 1996)
Comprehensive Catalog of U.S. Large Size Star Notes (Doug Murray, 1996)
An Illustrated History of U. S. Loans 1776-1892 (Gene Hessler, 1988)
The Engraver's Line (Gene Hessler, 1993)
College Currency: Money for Business Training (Herb and Martha Schingoethe, Neil Shafer, editor, 1993)
Civil War Encased Stamps (Fred Reed, 1995)
Stocks and Bonds of North American Railroads (Terry Cox, 1995)
Prisoner of War and Concentration Camp Money, second edition (Lance Campbell, 1993)
World War II Remembered: history in your hands, a numismatic study (C. Frederick Schwan and Joseph E. Boling)
Military Payment Certificates (Fred Schwan, 1996)

copyright Carlson Chambliss and BNR Press 1999
ISBN 0-931960-59-2

BNR Press
132 East Second Street
Port Clinton, Ohio 43452-1115

phone   (419) 732-NOTE (6683)
         (800) 793-0683
         (419) 734-6683 (message service only)
fax   (419) 732-6683
         (800) 793-0683
e-mail   BNR Press@aol.com

TABLE OF CONTENTS

Acknowledgements	4
Preface	5
1. Introduction	10
2. Small-Size Notes: General Properties	28
3. Small-Size Notes: Non-Current Types	40
4. Small-Size Federal Reserve Notes	73
5. Fractional Currency	95
6. Large-Size Type Notes	120
7. National Bank Notes	199
8. Military Payment Certificates	268
9. Currency Errors	283
10. Fancy Serial Numbers	312
11. Paper Money in Sheets	318
12. Altered and Counterfeit Notes	325
13. Non-Federal Paper Money	337
14. Other Types of Fiscal Paper Collectibles	365
15. Sources of Paper Money	380
16. Care and Preservation of Paper Money	397
17. An Annotated Bibliography	406
18. Collections and Displays of Paper Money	426
Appendix	431
Resources	444
Hot Contact List	480

ACKNOWLEDGEMENTS

I have now been seriously collecting U. S. paper money for more than 20 years, and over those years I have acquired a large number of notes while learning a lot about the subject. I admit to having made a few mistakes along the road, but we all learn from our mistakes. I have probably learned more about paper money from some of the individuals from whom I have made substantial purchases than from any other persons. Thus I do wish here to acknowledge the insights that I have received from such currency professionals as Tom Denly, Lyn F. Knight, Allen Mincho, Leonard Glazer, Dean Oakes, David Koble, Don C. Kelly, and George Schweighofer persons from whom I have obtained numerous items as well as good advice on the building of my collection. I particularly wish to thank Martin Gengerke for providing me with much useful information, especially about large-size type notes. I also am indebted to the late John Hickman for the considerable amount of information that he supplied me concerning national bank notes. The proprietary data that Mr. Hickman made available enabled me to begin my sideline of numismatic writing, a pursuit that I have enjoyed doing for the past ten years or so. Thanks also to Bob Kvederas Jr. for supplying me with much useful information about web notes. I also wish to thank Dr. William Schulz, a professor of mathematics at Northern Arizona University in Flagstaff and a fellow classmate of mine (Harvard '62), for his careful reading of the manuscript of this book.

The illustrations that appear in this book are almost entirely of notes that are in my own collection. I wish to acknowledge the help of Fred Schwan in providing some of the illustrations of items that are not in my collection along with the historical photographs that appear in this book.

PREFACE

Paper money has had a very long history in the United States. The first issue of paper currency in what was later to become the United States was an issue of notes in four different denominations from the Massachusetts Bay Colony in 1690. By 1735 twelve of the original American colonies had issued some form of paper money, and the next half century was to see a great increase in the variety of issues and in the quantities of paper currency that were printed. The most famous of these was the Continental Currency that was issued by the Continental Congress. There were eleven different issues of this money between 1775 and 1779, most of which were issued from Philadelphia, but one issue was from Baltimore and another was issued in York, Pennsylvania.

Both the Continental Currency and the paper currencies of the various states were subject to severe inflation during the 1780s. There was also so much counterfeiting that some of these issues had to be recalled, among them the 1778 Yorktown issue of Continental Currency (i.e., the issue from York, Pennsylvania). The United States under the Articles of Confederation was in a state of almost complete monetary chaos, and thus such persons as Alexander Hamilton, the first Secretary of the Treasury under the new Constitution, were determined to put an end to the abuses that had arisen with the issuance of paper money during the 1770s and 1780s. As a result the states were specifically forbidden from issuing money, and the power of the Federal government to do so was severely curtailed. Almost all paper money issued in the United States between 1790 and 1860 was private in nature. The bulk of it was from banks chartered by the states, but several canal and railroad companies, as well as many private firms and individuals also issued paper currency.

Prior to 1861 the United States Federal government issued virtually no paper money. A number of issues of short-term interest bearing securities were emitted from time to time, but few of these have survived even in unissued or proof form. The sole exceptions are the notes made during the War of 1812 that were issued between 1812 and 1815. They were issued in denominations of $3, $5, $10, $20, $50, and $100, and many of these did not bear interest. There are a number of survivors that exist as issued, canceled, or unissued notes, but most standard catalogs of U. S. paper money have chosen to exclude them from their listings. The crisis of the Civil War, however, resulted in issues of paper money that were to become permanent, and thus from 1861 on, there is a continuous progression of different types of paper money issues.

Although I shall devote one chapter each to non-Federal paper money and to non-currency items related to paper money, this book is devoted very largely to what can be called Federal paper money. Unlike many countries of the world, the United States has printed its currency in uniform sizes. Most of the paper money issued between 1861 and 1929 was of the same size. In 1929 the size for paper money was reduced to that which we use today, and all money printed for the past 70 years has been of this uniform size. Small-size paper money also displays a much narrower range of designs than do the earlier large-size notes, and so nearly all collectors make a sharp distinction between small-size and large-size currency. Between 1862 and 1876 there were also five issues of Fractional Currency, which were notes of very small sizes in denominations of less than one dollar. All of these types of paper money continue to remain valid currency today. The United States is perhaps the only nation on earth that has never repudiated any of its former monetary issues. I also include in this book, however, a detailed discussion of a type of Federal paper money that is no longer valid as currency. These are the Military Payment Certificates that were issued between 1946 and 1973. In addition to no longer being valid currency, the MPCs differ from the other forms of Federal paper money in that they were exclusively used abroad. More cursory discussions are also given of the various types of non-Federal paper money and fiscal paper that have been used in what is today the territory of the United States.

I began seriously to collect U. S. Federal paper money in 1976, although I had been collecting stamps and coins for many years prior to that date. Over the past two decades I have formed a very large collection of paper money, and in this book I shall outline how this came about. One of the chapters concerns sources of paper money, and in it I shall examine auctions, numismatic shows, mail order sales, etc. Another chapter that should be of great interest concerns the care and preservation of paper money.

This book is not intended as a catalog of U. S. paper money. There are several good catalogs of this material presently on the market, and I shall be referring to these many times in my discussions. When discussing specific issues I do mention market prices on many occasions. Since prices are subject to change, it should be noted that they mostly refer to the years in which this book was written (1997 and 1998) unless I have stated otherwise. I have often used numerous recent auction realizations on many of the rarer items, and I do feel that auctions are a good way of obtaining rare notes. In the appendix of this book there is also a detailed price guide for the current values of most of the collectible types of U. S. Federal paper money.

Also included in this book is an annotated bibliography of the more important works on U. S. paper money. In this section I shall provide summaries of what each catalog or other reference work contains and does not contain. Before one gets seriously into paper money collecting he or she should have a good numismatic library. This is as true in paper money as it is in coins, medals, tokens, or any other branch of numismatics.

I feel that very careful thought should be given to just what a potential collector plans to collect in the paper money field. There are literally tens of thousands of different varieties of national bank notes and several thousands of different varieties of small-size Federal Reserve Notes, and so considerable restraint in acquiring new specimens is needed at least in these two areas regardless of the depth of one's pockets. It should also be noted that U. S. Federal paper money, like gold coins or ancient coins, is basically a fairly expensive area to collect. The very cheapest large-size notes cost about $65 today in uncirculated condition or about $25 in very fine condition. Small-size notes (especially the numerous varieties of $1 Federal Reserve Notes) are often very much less expensive than this, but substantial funds are still necessary for a sizable collection. I do not think that one can form a significant collection of any type of U. S. Federal paper money on a shoestring budget, but this does not mean that an enormous outlay of funds is needed to obtain a good collection of many of these items.

In this book I shall generally use the first person when I refer to my own collection or my own opinions, but permit me now to refer to you, the reader, in the second person rather than the awkward third person form. I think that you will find much of interest in this book even if you already have a substantial collection of U. S. paper money, but I have aimed much of my discussion at someone who is just beginning collecting in this field or who is considering the possibility of forming a collection of U. S. paper money. I think that you will find U. S. currency a most interesting area in which to get involved. In my opinion it is in a much healthier state than are most areas of coin and stamp collecting.

At the present time there seems to be an excessive emphasis on condition in coins, and this leads to attempts to overgrade them and to other abuses. The days when gold and silver were money are probably now in the past, and today they are commodities with a fairly limited demand. After the weird speculative excesses of the 1979-81 period, these two metals have not proven to be good investments in the subsequent 15 years or more, and the prices of many gold coins are now tied fairly closely to the bullion price for gold. If you to turn to foreign coins, you must also consider whether or not to collect any of the increasingly meaningless deluge of non-circulating coins from such entities as the Isle of Man or the Marshall Islands, to name just two of the worst offenders, but there are many others.

Stamps also have their problems. Although I find that few real philatelists are particularly concerned with whether or not unused stamps have been previously hinged, the never hinged craze has risen to absurd heights, particularly when it comes to selling stamps from several Western European and East Asian countries. There are also many reperfed and regummed stamps on the market, particularly among the earlier U. S. issues. The practice of regumming stamps has arisen because some persons are willing to pay absurd premiums for undisturbed gum. Today there are even expertization services for stamp gum. Isn't it a bit absurd for someone who wants only original gum to pay an additional sum to find out whether or not the glue that he so craves is indeed what it was when originally issued?

Stamps also suffer from a surfeit of new issues. No longer are there excessive issues from obscure sheikdoms in the Persian Gulf, but such former British colonies as Grenada, Guyana, and St. Vincent have in recent years flooded the market with literally thousands of new issues. When there were only a couple of hundred thousand different stamps for the entire world, one could contemplate forming a general world collection, but now there are millions of different varieties, and such a project would be absurd.

I also feel that stamps suffer a great deal from price gouging. In paper money and in most types of coins you can expect to get about 70% of the retail price from a dealer for an item that he wants to buy for stock. (Most bullion coins, of course, would have a much lower markup, and for rare bank notes sold on consignment the markup is more like 10% or 15%.) Many stamp dealers, however, will try to buy most stamps at only 25% or 30% of what they hope they can sell them for. This would not be true of the rarest or the very most popular issues, but in general the markup for stamps is quite high. Getting much higher prices for your stamps often necessitates that you become a stamp dealer.

In the 1950s a substantial percentage of 12-14 year-old boys (and many girls as well) collected stamps. Only a relatively small number became serious philatelists, but probably most serious collectors of today arose from their ranks. Today young people of this age collect sports cards, if they collect anything at all. Despite heavy promotion by agencies such as the U. S. Postal Service, the percentage of young persons who engage in stamp collecting is certainly very much lower than it was 40 years ago. I feel that the average age of stamp collectors is becoming progressively older, and thus it seems that more and more new issues are being printed to satisfy a steadily declining pool of collectors.

Paper money collecting is still a small field when compared with either coin or stamp collecting, but it strikes me as being a much healthier field than either of the latter. Most paper money collectors have come into this area from coin collecting, and thus they already have a fair amount of sophistication with respect to the importance of grading and other matters. But grading has never assumed the excessive importance that it has for certain types of U. S. coins such as Morgan silver dollars. This is especially true of national bank notes, where most collectors seek certain banks rather than particular states of preservation. Uncirculated notes are naturally preferred, but it is most unlikely that any collector would pay ten times as much for an uncirculated note from a particular bank than he would pay for a note from that same bank in only very fine condition.

One very interesting aspect of paper money collecting is that it is sometimes possible to obtain items that are extremely rare or even unique, often for fairly modest prices. Numerous national bank notes fall into this category. In my own collection I have at least two or three of these that are known to be unique, but the prices that I paid for them were tiny fractions of what one would have to pay for any of the major rarities among United States coins.

If you are new to paper money collecting, then welcome to it. If you have already been collecting for several years, I think that you will agree with many of the remarks that I have just made. In the first regular chapter of this book I shall introduce a variety of terminology, most of which will not be strange to anyone who is already collecting paper money. The next three chapters concern small-size paper money. Most books on U. S. currency begin with the large-size issues, often with the earliest of these, the Demand Notes and Interest Bearing Notes of 1861. But these items are very rare, and only advanced collectors can hope to have examples of these notes in their collections. Most persons will begin their collections with the notes most familiar to them, viz., the small-size notes that have been issued exclusively for the past 70 years. And, of course, these notes are also vastly more available and economical to collect than are any of the ephemeral large-size issues of the Civil War years. This book is about collecting paper money, and so there is no need to discuss the history of U. S. currency in a strictly chronological fashion.

One final thing that I should mention in this preface is the term syngraphics, which means that branch of numismatics that is devoted to paper money. The word numismatics is derived from the Greek-based Latin word *nomisma*, which means coin. But this field has been broadened to include medals, tokens, military orders and decorations, paper money, and fiscal paper as well. In Greek-based Latin (Latin like English borrowed numerous words from Greek.) the word *syngrapha* means a promissory note. The word syngraphics was coined about 25 years ago, but it is not yet very widely used. If you are a syngraphist, you are also a paper money collector. If you have not yet become one, I hope that this book may help persuade you to join this fraternity.

Kutztown, Pennsylvania

June, 1999

CHAPTER ONE

INTRODUCTION

Before discussing the specifics of any particular issues of Federal paper money we need to touch on several general topics such as basic terminology and the sizes, colors, and the sheet layouts for the notes. For coins one uses the term "obverse" for the "head" side and "reverse" for the "tail" side. For bank notes the terms "face" and "back" are much preferred. Although I do see fairly often the term "reverse" used for the back side, this term is not the preferred one for paper money. A note that is printed on only one side is termed uniface.

In many nations of the world bank notes are printed in a progression of sizes with the larger notes having higher face values than the smaller ones. The United States has always used uniform sizes for its dollar-denominated bank notes, but in 1929 a radical change was made in this basic size. Prior to that time almost all bank notes were about 190 x 80 millimeters (7.50 x 3.15 inches) in size. In that year the size of our nation's banknotes was reduced to 156 x 66 mm (6.15 x 2.60 inches), hence the distinction between the large-size notes of 1861-1929 and the current or small-size notes. The latter have just over two-thirds of the surface area of the former and thus require less paper to print. This is one of the major reasons why it was decided to reduce the size of our paper money.

I am an astronomer by profession, and in that field I work exclusively in metric units. In this book I intend to quote sizes of design elements and other features almost exclusively in millimeters or centimeters. Inches are normally divided into eighths, sixteenths, and thirty-seconds, and these are very awkward units to work with when one is dealing with the sizes of small design elements. The conversion factors between these units are 25.4 mm or 2.54 cm per inch, or conversely 0.3937 inch per centimeter and 0.03937 inch per millimeter.

Large-size notes are not all of precisely the same size, and a few differences are appreciable. For instance, the earlier national bank notes (i.e., the notes of the so-called First and Second Charter Periods) are several millimeters shorter than are nearly all other large-size notes. The very rare Interest Bearing Notes of the Civil War years are about 10 mm wider than are most other large-size notes. The excessively rare Three-Year Notes of these issues were printed with five attached coupons, and this feature made them much longer than any other large-size notes. Another issue of wide notes were the Series 1900 gold certificates, which were printed in sheets of three rather than the sheets of four that were used for almost all other types of large-size notes. Since large-size national bank notes were generally cut apart by hand, a fair amount of variation in size occurs depending upon how closely they have been trimmed. Aside from national bank notes all large-size notes were numbered sequentially in a sheet. Each note also had a plate position letter, which was most often A, B, C, or D, but sometimes the letters E, F, G, and H or higher sequences of letters were used. national bank notes were numbered by the sheet, and thus all notes on a given sheet had the same serial numbers.

Small-size notes do not show much variation in size, but many national bank notes from the smaller banks were again cut apart by hand, and this leads to a certain amount of size variation. Small-size notes have been printed in sheets of 12, 18, and 32 subjects, and the differences in the sheet layouts and serial numbering schemes will be covered in the next chapter. Although all small-size national bank notes were printed in sheets of 12, these were cut into two strips of six notes each before being sent to the banks that ordered them.

Fractional Currency comes in a wide variety of sizes, all of which are much smaller than any of the higher denomination notes. This I shall discuss in detail in the chapter on these notes. Military Payment Certificates were also issued in four distinct sizes, and they were printed in sheets that were much larger than those used for any of the regular issues of paper money. These details will be covered in the chapter on MPCs.

With the exception of Military Payment Certificates the faces of all U. S. government paper money have been printed in black. The backs of these notes have generally been printed in green, but there are several exceptions among the large-size notes. Almost all large-size gold certificates have bright orange backs to simulate the color of gold. The earliest issues of silver certificates (i. e., Series 1878 and 1880) featured dark brown backs. Other exceptions to notes with exclusively green backs were the earlier national bank notes. The so-called First Charter notes had black centers with green frames, while the Second Charter Brown Backs naturally featured brown backs with dark green numbering at their centers. The National Gold Bank Notes of the First Charter Period had black centers with brown frames. Among large-size notes with green backs, however, numerous shades of green ranging from yellow green to deep blue green are noted. Most collectors pay no attention to the shade variations that are found on the back sides of U. S. paper money, but a comparison of notes that were issued over several decades will reveal significant variations in the shades of green that are to be found on their backs.

All small-size notes have green backs except for the non-circulating Series 1934 gold certificates which have orange backs. Many fractional notes have backs printed in colors other than green, and these will be discussed in the chapter on Fractional Currency. As has already been noted, the MPCs have radically different color schemes from those of any other types of U. S. currency.

The face sides of the notes, however, are enhanced considerably by a distinctive Treasury seal and often with colored embellishments as well. The only series of large-size notes that do not bear a Treasury seal are the very rare Demand Notes of 1861. All seals that appear on large-size notes bear the Latin inscription, *Thesaur(i) Amer(icae) Septent(rionalis) Sigil(lum),* meaning Seal of the Treasury of North America. This seal was originally used by the Continental Congress in 1782, which was five years prior to the adoption of the U. S. Constitution. The seal presently used states in English, "The Department of the Treasury 1789." It has been used on notes only since 1966. On large-size notes Treasury seals are found in various shades of red, as well as brown, blue, and orange. One speaks of these seals as having plain, spiked, or scalloped edges, and their sizes range from 18 to 53 mm. The last two issues of Fractional Currency also featured seals, and two of these notes were the first U. S. currency to bear green Treasury seals.

Almost all Federal notes carry the facsimile signatures of two Treasury Department officials. All of the national bank notes carry these two signatures in addition to those of two bank officers, usually the president and the cashier of the bank in question. This type of signature combination is also used on the Federal Reserve Bank Notes. The first two issues of Fractional Currency carried no signatures, but the later issues all have a pair of signatures, some of which are autographed on a number of these notes. The Demand Notes of 1861 were the only issues of government paper money that were hand signed by various clerks at the Treasury Department.

Most collectors of large-size notes who go beyond type collecting attempt to obtain the various signature combinations that exist for a given issue, and all currency catalogs list the notes in this fashion. On the small-size notes the series was changed each time there was any change in the signatures, and nearly all collectors attempt to obtain at least one note from each series. Thus the Treasury signature combinations are an important factor in determining the distinctiveness of almost all issues of Federal paper money.

Among large-size notes the facsimile signatures that are usually found are those of the Register of the Treasury and the Treasurer of the United States. Prior to the formation of the Federal Reserve System the Treasurer was responsible for the issuance of nearly all forms of coins and paper money. The first Treasurer in the note-issuing period was Francis E. Spinner, who served from 1861 to 1875. Many currency collectors are attracted to his unusual and elaborate signature that appears on most government notes issued during this period. Spinner was a most innovative individual, who was also responsible for the invention of Fractional Currency, the development of the Secret Service, and the large-scale employment of women in government offices. His signature is found in combination with those of four different Registers of the Treasury who served during his term of office.

There are a total of 34 different Register-Treasurer signature combinations that were used on large-size notes. All of these were utilized on national bank notes, but the other currency types used a substantially smaller number of these. Collectors refer to these by the surnames of the two officials, and these signature combinations vary greatly in their relative scarcities. The signature combinations of Lyons-Roberts (from 1898-1905) and of Speelman-White (1922-27) are especially common, while those of Jeffries-Spinner and Rosecrans-Morgan are very rare on large-size notes. The former is also obtainable on Fractional Currency, but the latter exists only on a few national bank notes. The rarity of this combination is due to the fact that these officials had a joint term of office that lasted only 18 days in 1893. Another very rare signature combination on large-size notes is that of Jones-Woods. This appears on only a very few national bank notes that were printed in 1929. Ironically this combination is ultra-common on small-size notes, since all Series 1929 national bank notes carry it.

Federal Reserve Notes bear the facsimile signatures of the Treasurer of the United States and the Secretary of the Treasury. There are four such signature combinations that appear on large-size Federal Reserve Notes (all fairly common), but all small-size notes with the exceptions of national bank notes and Federal Reserve Bank Notes also follow this format for signatures. It would have been much more logical to have used the signature of the Chairman of the Federal Reserve Board for the second signature rather than that of Treasurer of the United States, especially since 1971, when all paper money other than Federal Reserve Notes ceased to the printed. Although the Treasurer had very significant functions during the 19th Century, this position has now declined hugely in importance, particularly since all currency is now issued through the Federal Reserve System. Since 1949 the Treasurer has always been a woman. In one case a change of marital status resulted in two distinct series of bank notes. In 1970 the Treasurer Dorothy Elston married Walter Kabis. Series 1969 notes have the Elston-Kennedy combination, while the Kabis-Kennedy combination appears on Series 1969A notes.

Paper money is not dated annually, as are nearly all coins. Most notes have a series designation, and this refers to the year of the design of the note rather than to the date that it was printed. Most Fractional Currency notes display no dates of design or printing, but there were five quite distinct issues of this type of paper money. Small-size notes and Military Payment Certificates carry series designations that will be discussed further in the chapters on these notes. Large-size national bank notes always contain two dates, a series year and a specific date that refers to the day on which the bank in question was chartered or rechartered. This matter will be more fully described in the chapter on national bank notes.

Let us now look at the various types of Federal paper money that have been issued since 1861. In terms of monetary legislation there was no change made in 1929 when the United States switched from large-size to small-size notes, but over the years there have been several important laws that have affected the issuance of the various types of paper money.

United States Notes: These notes, which are also often called Legal Tender Notes, were first issued in 1862. They continued to be issued throughout the large-size period and were also issued as small-size notes up to 1971. USNs had no specific backing in specie (gold or silver), and prior to 1879 they traded at a discount with respect to gold. In that year they became convertible into gold at par, but the total amount outstanding (either in circulation or in storage in the Treasury) had been fixed at $346 million in the previous year. These notes are the original "Greenbacks," although this term is a bit confusing since most other types of Federal paper money were printed with green backs as well. United States Notes continued to be regarded as current money until the 1990s, but by that time they constituted an utterly negligible portion of the nation's currency supply.

Large-size USNs were issued in all denominations from $1 to $10,000. The two ultrahigh denomination notes of this type (i.e., $5000 and $10,000 notes) were issued only in Series 1878, and all examples of these notes have long since been redeemed. The other denominations were issued in Series 1862-63, 1869, 1874-78, 1880, 1901, 1907, 1917, and 1923, although none of these series included all of these denominations.

Small-size USNs were largely confined to the $2 and $5 denominations. These were issued continuously from 1929 to 1967. In the following year small-size $100 USNs were issued for the first time, but these circulated only to a limited extent outside the U. S. Treasury. There was also a limited issue of Series 1928 $1 USNs that were actually printed in 1933. All small-size USNs have red seals and serial numbers.

Silver Certificates: Silver certificates were first issued under the provisions of the Bland-Allison Act of 1878, which also provided for the purchase of silver by the Treasury and its coinage into standard silver dollars. These notes were secured by silver dollars that were stored in the Treasury, and soon the public came to prefer these notes over the bulky silver dollars that backed them. Large-size silver certificates were printed in all denominations from $1 to $1000, but the great majority of the issues of these notes were in the lower denominations especially the $1, $2, and $5 notes. These notes exist in Series 1878, 1880, 1886, 1891, 1896, 1899, 1908, and 1923, although several of these series were confined to only the lower denomination notes. The Series 1878 and 1880 notes have dark brown backs, while those of Series 1886 and 1896 are noteworthy for their especially beautiful designs.

Small-size SCs were issued in denominations of $1, $5, and $10. Between 1929 and 1963 nearly all $1 bills in circulation were silver certificates. In 1934 these notes were made payable in silver rather than in silver dollars, and that freed the U. S. Mint from striking additional silver dollars to back these notes. Series 1934 $1, $5, and $10 silver certificates then appeared with this new obligation. In the previous year there had been a small release of Series $10 SCs that were made payable in silver coin. The ambiguous wording on these notes caused their recall, and Series 1933 $10 notes are very rare today. All regular small-size silver certificates have blue seals and serial numbers.

Silver certificates continued to be printed until 1963, but production of these notes then ceased. Between 1965 and 1968 they were worth a premium over their face value, since they continued to be redeemable in silver at a time when silver prices were rapidly increasing. In 1968 they ceased to be redeemable in silver, and as far as the government is concerned, they are now only worth their face value.

Treasury Notes of 1890: Treasury Notes, or coin notes as they are sometimes called, were issued under the provisions of the Sherman Silver Purchase Act of 1890. They were initially used to pay for silver bullion that was purchased according to this act. They were redeemable either in silver or in gold, and many persons on receiving these notes chose to redeem them for gold. This lead to a gold drain at the Treasury, and to the repeal of the Sherman Silver Purchase Act in 1893. Treasury Notes continued to circulate widely during the 1890s, but they rapidly fell out of circulation after 1900. They were issued only in Series 1890 and 1891. The former series included notes for $1, $2, $5, $10, $20, $100, and $1000. The latter series also included a $50 note, but all high denomination Treasury Notes are major rarities. The Series 1890 notes are noted for their elaborate and beautifully designed backs.

Gold Certificates: Gold certificates were first issued in 1865. There were three issues of these notes between 1865 and 1878 at a time when gold had a substantial premium over paper money. These notes functioned as warehouse receipts and were used to clear gold settlements between banks. After U. S. paper money became convertible into gold at par in 1879, these notes were withdrawn, and today all gold certificates issued between 1865 and 1878 are excessively rare.

Circulating large-size gold certificates were issued in Series 1882, 1905, 1906, 1907, 1913, and 1922. All of these notes have bright orange backs to simulate the color of gold. Gold certificates were issued in all denominations from $10 through $10,000. These notes were payable in gold coins that were held in the Treasury. In the 19th Century the amount of gold certificates in circulation was much less than the amount of gold coins publicly held, but by the 1920s the amount of gold notes in private hands far exceeded the amount of gold coins outstanding.

There were also two issues of gold certificates, Series 1888 and 1900, that were used exclusively for transfers between the Treasury and large banks or the Federal Reserve Board, once it had been established. A number of canceled $10,000 Series 1900 notes are presently in collectors' hands, and the status of these peculiar items will be discussed more fully in the chapter on large-size type notes.

Small-size gold certificates were issued to the public only in Series 1928 in denominations of $10 to $10,000. These notes have yellow-orange seals and serial numbers, but their backs are green in color, as are all normal small-size notes. Gold certificates were abruptly pulled from circulation in 1933, and their redemption was required up until 1964, when they again became fully legal to collect. These notes are no longer redeemable in gold, but they still are legal tender at their face value. Small-size gold notes also included Series 1934 gold certificates that were used exclusively within the Federal Reserve System. They were issued in denominations between $100 and $100,000, but none have ever been made available to the public.

National Bank Notes: National bank notes were first authorized by the National Banking Act of 1863, although the first NBNs appeared only late in 1864. These notes were secured by U. S. government bonds that were held on deposit at the Treasury. A national bank could then issue up to 90% of the face value of the bonds that it had deposited. These notes were treated as obligations of the bank that issued them, but if the bank in question failed, these notes continued to remain good money and were treated instead as obligations of the Treasury. Many thousands of different national bank notes still exist, since these notes were issued by about 12,000 different banks in the large-size era, and about 7000 different banks issued small-size NBNs between 1929 and 1935.

Large-size NBNs were issued in three so-called charter periods, and each of these was issued in a variety of different types. The First Charter NBNs were issued in two different series, the so-called Original Series and the Series of 1875. They were in production from 1864 to as late as 1902. The majority of these notes were in denominations of $5, $10, $20, $50, and $100, but notes of the $1 and $2 denominations were also issued between 1864 and 1878. National bank notes for $500 and $1000 were also issued up to 1885, but these notes are either excessively rare or non-existent today. First Charter NBNs are noted for their beautiful green and black backs which depict historical paintings that are to be found in the Rotunda of the U. S. Capitol.

A special issue of First Charter notes were the National Gold Bank Notes that were issued by nine different California banks during the 1870s. They were redeemable in gold coin at par at a time when most types of U. S. paper money traded at a discount with respect to gold. Although a fair number of these notes have survived, they are notorious for their generally low states of preservation.

Second Charter NBNs were printed in three different issues, but all of them are inscribed Series 1882. Thus the terms Second Charter notes and Series 1882 NBNs can be used interchangeably. They exist in denominations of $5, $10, $20, $50, and $100, as do all subsequent NBNs. The Brown Backs were issued between 1882 and 1908, and as their name implies they have brown backs, but with large charter numbers inscribed in dark green. The Second Charter Date Backs have green backs on which the dates 1882-1908 are featured predominantly. They were issued from 1908 up until the early 1920s. The Value Backs look quite similar to the Date Backs, but the 1882-1908 dates have been replaced with the denomination of the note. They were issued between 1916 and 1922.

The Third Charter NBNs were also printed in three different issues, and all of them are inscribed Series 1902. The so-called Red Seal notes were printed between 1902 and 1908, and they are much the scarcest of the three types. The Blue Seal Date Backs have the dates 1902-1908 printed on their backs, and these notes were printed between 1908 and 1926. The Blue Seal Plain Backs lack these dates on their backs, but otherwise they are quite similar to the date back issues. These notes were issued up to 1929, and they are by far the most common of the large-size NBNs.

Small-size NBNs are all Series 1929, and all have brown seals and serial numbers. There are two different types for each denomination - type 1 that were issued between 1929 and 1933, and type 2 that were produced between 1933 and 1935. Today roughly half of the known national bank notes are small-size notes with the balance being the numerous varieties of large-size types.

A collector might well ask why there are so many different types of national bank notes. National banks were originally granted charters that lasted no longer than 20 years, and it was not until near the end of the large-note period that these charters could be extended up to 99 years. Banks that began to issue Second Charter notes in 1882 would have switched to Third Charter Notes in 1902. If a bank received its charter in 1872, it would have issued First Charter Notes until 1892. It then would have issued Second Charter Notes from then until 1912, and it would have commenced issuing Third Charter Notes only in that year. An additional complicating factor was the Aldrich-Vreeland Act of 1908, which provided for the issuance of NBNs backed by securities other than government bonds. This act resulted in significant changes in the designs of NBNs in the year in which it was passed. The details of national bank legislation will be more fully explained in the chapter of this book on national bank notes.

National bank notes are among the most popular types of U. S. government currency. Many collectors collect only these notes, and often they collect only notes from a given state or even a given city. Since there are many thousands of possible varieties of these notes, it is absolutely impossible for anyone to form a "complete" collection of national bank notes. It is likely that no two collections of these notes are ever the same, and in each case a collection of NBNs reflects the interest and patience as well as the pocketbook of the person who formed it.

Federal Reserve Notes: Federal Reserve Notes were first authorized by the Federal Reserve Act of 1913, and they entered circulation in the year 1915. Within a few years they became the largest single component of our nation's currency supply, and this trend has continued ever since. Originally they required a 40% gold cover, and all large-size and

Series 1928 small-size FRNs state that they are payable in gold. In 1933 FRNs ceased to be payable in gold, and in 1945 the gold cover for their issue was reduced to 25% of their face value. In 1968 the gold cover for FRNs was removed altogether. By the late 1960s both silver certificates and United States Notes were effectively out of circulation, and today the FRNs constitute some 99.85% of the total paper money in circulation. FRNs are the only type of paper money that have been printed since 1971, and it does not seem likely that they will be supplemented by any other types of paper money in the foreseeable future.

Large-size Federal Reserve Notes were issued only in Series 1914 and 1918, but these notes were printed continuously from 1915 through 1929. For the first year or so, FRNs were printed with red seals and serial numbers, but these were subsequently replaced with notes having blue seals and numbers. The former exist only for the $5, $10, $20, $50, and $100 denominations, but the blue seal notes of Series 1914 were supplemented by the Series 1918 FRNs that were issued in denominations of $500, $1000, $5000, and $10,000. About 130 each of the large-size $500 and $1000 FRNs are presently known, but no issued $5000 or $10,000 Series 1918 FRNs are known to be in private hands. The Series 1914 notes come with four different signature combinations, but they also bear district seals for each of the 12 districts of the Federal Reserve System.

Although the blue seal Series 1914 FRNs are among the most common of the large-size notes, only relatively few syngraphists attempt to collect these issues by district and signature combinations. It seems likely that thus far no one has assembled a complete collection of all possible Series 1914 FRN varieties, and a definitive rarity scale for the many different varieties of these notes has yet to be worked out.

Between 1929 and 1963 all small-size FRNs were issued in denominations of $5 and higher. One-dollar FRNs made their appearance only in 1963, and $2 FRNs followed only in 1976. Before you attempt to get seriously into the collecting of small-size FRNs, I feel that you should think over very carefully just what you want to obtain. There are literally thousands of possible varieties. In addition to the varieties resulting from different series and districts, there are also several shades of green for the Treasury seals and serial numbers. One- and two-dollar FRNs are usually collected in district sets, but there is not much demand for the $5 through $100 notes in these sets. These five denominations are normally collected only by type or by series, although a few dedicated collectors may attempt to obtain these notes from all districts of a given series. Since small-size FRNs involve several factors that need not be considered with most other types of notes, I have included a special chapter on the collecting of small-size Federal Reserve Notes.

Among the small-size FRNs of the four high denominations there is a very sharp distinction between the $500 and $1000 notes on the one hand and the $5000 and $10,000 notes on the other. The former are rapidly gaining in popularity, and prices will doubtless rise as collectors continue to disperse the remaining supplies of these notes. Although these notes have not been printed since 1945, the Federal Reserve made them available until 1969, but for the past two decades they have been seen almost exclusively in numismatic circles. But moderately affluent collectors should be able to afford at least one note of each denomination, and they are still available in choice condition for less than double face.

The situation with the ultrahigh denominations ($5000 and $10,000) is quite different. These were last printed in 1944 and last available from banks in 1969. Twenty years ago these notes could be purchased for about a 40% premium over their face value, but today nice examples of these notes sell for at least four to six times their face value. There are probably about 200 examples of each denomination in private hands, but many of these are held by non-numismatists, and much of the demand for these notes seems to be coming from persons who cannot be seriously described as syngraphists. There is also a possibility that the current fad among a number of wealthy persons of holding "big bills" will vanish, and this would cause prices for these notes to drop should fair numbers of them hit the market.

Federal Reserve Bank Notes: When the Federal Reserve Act was passed, it contained provisions for the issue of Federal Reserve Bank Notes. The obligation on these notes was virtually identical to those of the national bank notes, and it was originally intended that the FRBNs should replace the NBNs, but that did not prove to be the case. Both large-size and small-size FRBNs were issued, but these two issues were for utterly different purposes. In both cases, however, the FRBNs were temporary money that was issued to deal with two different specific emergencies.

Large-size FRBNs were issued in Series 1915 and 1918. The former contains only notes of the $5, $10, and $20 denominations, while the latter series also includes $1, $2, and $50 notes. The Series 1918 $1 notes are by far the most common of the large-size FRBNs. All of these notes have four signatures - the two Treasury signatures plus those of the governor and cashier of the Federal Reserve Bank of issue. Many collectors attempt to get all possible signature combinations. In this case there are 39 different varieties of the $1 notes, 34 of the $2 notes, and 30 of the $5 notes. The $2 FRBN depicts a World War I battleship on its back, whence its nickname of "Battleship note." Complete sets such as these are very difficult to assemble, but it is possible to do this for each of these denominations.

Although the large-size FRBNs did not replace the national bank notes then in circulation, they did serve a very important purpose. In 1919 and 1920 silver prices rose to very high levels, and for some time in 1920 the bullion price of silver exceeded that at which silver dollars were coined ($1.293 per troy ounce). Some 370 million silver dollars were melted down and exported under the Pittman Act, and this measure necessitated the retirement of that amount of silver certificates. The large-size FRBNs were largely issued to serve as substitutes for the silver certificates that were removed from circulation. This seems to have been done on a one-for-one basis, and this would help explain why FRBNs are mostly found in the $1, $2, and $5 denominations. Silver certificates for $10, $20, and $50 had only very limited circulation by 1919, and so only a few FRBNs of these denominations were issued to replace them. By 1921 the price of silver had fallen to well under the value at which it was being coined, and this led to the removal of FRBNs from circulation and their replacement once more with silver certificates.

Small-size FRBNs are all Series 1929, and in physical appearance they closely resemble national bank notes. They were hastily printed in the spring of 1933, and they saw a fair amount of circulation during the 1930s. Unlike Federal Reserve Notes they did not require the 40% gold cover that was then necessary for circulation of the latter. They were backed by various government securities and were issued in denominations of $5, $10, $20, $50, and $100. Not all districts issued all five denominations, however, and so a complete set by denomination and district consists of 49 different notes. Although a denomination set of Series 1929 FRBNs can be easily assembled, getting all 49 small-size FRNs is a decidedly difficult task.

Other Large-Size Federal Notes: In addition to these seven major classes of large-size paper money, there also were a few ephemeral issues during and immediately after the Civil War. All of these issues are rare and valuable today, but some advanced collectors try to obtain at least a note or two from each series. The best known of these issues are the Demand Notes of 1861. They were issued in that year only, and they differ from all later Federal issues in that they are hand signed by clerks at the Treasury Department and bear no Treasury seal. The $5 and $10 Demand Notes are occasionally available, but the $20 notes of this issue are extremely rare.

There were four different types of interest bearing paper money that were issued between 1861 and 1865. These were the One-Year Notes, Two-Year Notes, Three-Year Notes, and the Compound Interest Treasury Notes, which also bore interest for three years. These notes were issued in denominations ranging from $10 to $5000, and the Three-Year Notes always bore five coupons when issued. By 1868 all of these notes had ceased to accrue interest, and they rapidly disappeared from circulation. All of these notes are rare to extremely rare today, and several of these issues exist only in proof form. The proofs of these notes are also rare and expensive, but they usually sell for considerably less than do the issued notes.

Most currency catalogs consider the $10 Refunding Certificate of 1879 as a type of paper money, although the Treasury Department has never viewed it in this light. It is actually a circulating bearer bond that was allowed to accrue interest for 28 years before interest payments were stopped in 1907. Although these notes are decidedly scarce, they are less rare and more affordable than are any of the ephemeral issues of the Civil War years.

World War II Issues: World War II also generated some ephemeral issues of American paper money, and these are vastly more affordable than are the short-lived issues of the Civil War years. Since the United States seriously considered the possibility of a Japanese invasion of Hawaii during the first year or so of its involvement in World War II, special paper money was issued for use by both the civilian and military populations in Hawaii and elsewhere in the Pacific. These notes were clearly marked Hawaii on both sides and came in denominations of $1, $5, $10, and $20. The $1 notes are SCs, but the higher denominations are FRNs from the San Francisco district. All of these notes have brown seals. If large numbers had fallen into Japanese hands, they could have been repudiated, but that never happened and they continue to remain valid money today.

A similar issue of notes was prepared for use in the European Theater of action. These were first used in North Africa, and so they are almost always referred to as the North Africa notes. They are silver certificates without special overprints, but the Treasury seal is lemon yellow in color instead of blue. They were issued in the $1, $5, and $10 denominations. The normal issues of these notes are common enough, but the $10 notes exist both in Series 1934 and in Series 1934A. The former had a very limited printing and is quite rare.

A third issue of special paper money were the experimental $1 SCs that were issued in 1944. They bore overprints of the letters "R" or "S" in red ink. These stood for the "regular" or "special" papers that were being studied for wear characteristics. Like two other paper experiments that the BEP had previously conducted, the results obtained for the special 1944 notes were inconclusive.

Fractional Currency: Fractional Currency was issued between 1862 and 1876, and for most of those years it was an essential component of our nation's currency. By the end of 1861 specie (i. e., gold and silver) payments had been suspended, and both gold and silver coins carried substantial premium over paper money. Various schemes for circulating currency items with face values under $1 were tried, but by far the most successful of these was Fractional Currency. This was issued for 14 years in five distinct issues. The first of these was inscribed Postage Currency, but these are always included with the other four issues. The denominations issued were 3, 5, 10, 15, 25, and 50 cents, although only the 10, 25, and 50 cent notes were printed for all five issues. Fractional Currency bore no serial numbers, but the last three issues bore the usual two Treasury signatures.

Despite its age a surprisingly large amount of Fractional Currency has survived, and it is not too difficult or expensive to assemble at least a basic type set of these notes in nice condition. There are numerous overprint varieties for these notes, particularly in the Second and Third Issues. There are also some major rarities, but all of these are of fairly minor type varieties having designs similar to much more common notes. It is also possible to obtain uniface specimen notes of the first three issues. These include the unissued 15 cent note of the Third Issue. This is the only example of an unissued type of U. S. paper money that is available without too much difficulty at the present time. All Fractional Currency continues to remain valid money today. I shall have much more to say in this book about this interesting type of Federal paper money in my chapter on Fractional Currency.

Military Payment Certificates: After the conclusion of World War II the United States found itself with numerous bases abroad, both in Europe and in Asia. Most of these were in nations with devastated economies and with very weak currencies. It was soon decided that U. S. military personnel serving abroad should use exclusively special notes that could be much more tightly regulated than could normal U. S. currency. Thus were born the Military Payment Certificates. These notes were issued only to authorized personnel, and they could only be used in specified locations. Their most significant property was that they could replaced with new issues of notes on very short notice. All MPCs that were issued have now been invalidated, and thus none remain redeemable today.

There were 13 different issues of MPCs that were issued between 1946 and 1973. They were issued in denominations of 5, 10, 25, and 50 cents, and $1, $5, $10, and $20. The $20 MPCs appear only in the last three series of these notes that were used exclusively in Vietnam, but the other denominations appear in all 13 series. There are also two issues of MPCs that were printed in the early 1970s but that never have been released. Presumably they are still in storage, and either or both of them may see use at some future date.

There are a total of 95 different MPCs with regular type serial numbers, but the fractional notes of Series 651 did not see normal usage and they are very rare today. All of the other fractional notes plus all of the $1 notes can be easily picked up in circulated condition, since a fair number of each were saved by many persons as souvenirs. But several of these are scarce in choice condition, and there are some rarities in this series particularly among the $5 and $10 notes. Since these notes could be invalidated on short notice, most persons did not save any of the higher denomination notes when they were still in circulation. Collecting a complete set of all 95 MPCs is a decidedly difficult task. This may seem surprising considering the modernity of these issues, but it is the fact that these notes were invalidated on short notice that has resulted in the rarity of several of the issues.

In addition to the regularly numbered MPCs there were also replacement and specimen notes that used distinctive serial numbers. All of these are scarce to extremely rare, and they are avidly collected today. Far more details on MPCs will be given in my chapter on these issues in this book.

This concludes our survey of the various basic issues of Federal paper money, but I shall be commenting frequently on some of the various items that syngraphists collect together with the normal notes of these series. Error notes are becoming very popular, and a wide variety of different types of currency errors are available. Although error notes exist for large-size notes, Fractional Currency, and MPCs, most of the error notes on today's market are on small-size notes that have been printed during the past two or three decades. Also of great interest to many collectors are fancy serial numbers. Very low numbers and certain other combinations can enhance enormously the value of an otherwise common note. The subjects of sheet layouts and serial number sequencing will be treated in detail in the following chapter that will deal exclusively with small-size notes.

As has already been noted, replacement notes for MPCs are now actively collected by several enthusiasts. On small-size notes replacements are indicated by stars either at the beginning or the end of a serial number. Small-size star notes range from very common to extremely rare, and all series of these notes are now being avidly collected. The use of star designators for replacement notes actually began in 1910, and there has now been a fair amount of research done on large-size star notes, but the scarcity of most of these has led thus far to a fairly low demand for these notes. This I shall touch on in my chapter on large-size type notes.

One other topic that should be touched on concerning Federal paper money are notes in complete sheets. Some issues, such as MPCs and most types of large-size notes other than national bank notes, are never available in sheet form, but both large-size and small-size NBNs can be collected in uncut sheets. A variety of other small-size notes issued between 1929 and 1954 are also available in full sheets. These are all rare and valuable today, but they do come up for sale in large auctions with some degree of regularity. Since 1981 the BEP has once again sold complete or partial sheets of current notes. Until very recently only $1 and $2 FRNs have been available, but $5 notes are now being offered in three different sizes of sheets. If these sell well, then notes of higher denominations will probably also be offered for sale in sheet form. At the present time there does not appear to be much of a secondary market in these items, despite the wide variety of issues (mostly of $1 FRNs of various series and districts) that are now available. This is undoubtedly due in part to the extremely large size for full sheets of these notes. In Chapter 11 I shall touch on some of the pitfalls to collecting paper money in this fashion.

To conclude this chapter I wish now to turn to a most important topic, viz., the subject of condition. The value of a bank note, like that of a coin or a stamp, is enormously affected by its state of preservation, but different criteria are needed for each of these items. Furthermore different considerations have to be given to the various issues of notes, and so this is a topic to which I shall be returning in many of the remaining chapters. Let us first consider the basic grades that are customarily used for describing paper money.

Crisp Uncirculated (CU): A note in CU condition should show no signs of circulation. It should be free of any folds, but there may be signs of light handling. The colors should be bright, and the note should show no signs of having been treated or processed in any manner. This grade more or less corresponds to BU in coins, but like that grade in coins, collectors are now differentiating sharply between different degrees of perfection in items that have not been in circulation. Today the following terms are in general use for differentiating uncirculated notes.

Gem Uncirculated: A note in this condition must be very bright, and the paper must show no sign of aging. It must be very well centered and with very good margins. The corners must be razor-sharp and show no trace of rounding. There must be no traces of smudging or handling.

Choice Uncirculated: Typically a note in this condition will show all of the criteria mentioned above, but it will have less than perfect centering or somewhat tight margins. It may show the tiniest signs of handling, and the paper may not have quite the "crackle" of a gem CU note. The embossing of the intaglio portions of the note may also be a little less sharp than it would be on a gem CU note.

Uncirculated or New: A note in this condition will show no obvious signs of circulation, but it might show a minor teller's crimp mark on one side. The paper may also be slightly aged, and one or two of the corners may be slightly rounded. This grade is also often used for CU notes that are fresh, but that have only average centering. If bank notes were coins, notes in this grade would be described as having a grade of MS-60.

About Uncirculated (AU): This is a very attractive grade for most notes, but notes in this grade will generally show a light fold when held up to the light. They also may have a minor corner fold or two. None of the folds should be heavy enough to break the design of the paper. Notes that have only extremely light folds and minimal signs of circulation are often graded AU-CU.

Extremely Fine (XF): Notes in XF condition will also be attractive in appearance, but they will typically show three light folds. There may also be some corner folds and a bit of surface dirt. The note should still retain full crispness, and it should be totally free of such defects as edge tears. The grade of XF-AU is often used for notes intermediate between XF and AU.

Very Fine (VF): A note in VF condition shows obvious signs of circulation, but it should retain much of its original crispness. There may be numerous folds, but they should not be very heavy. There will be some surface dirt, but at a casual glance a note in VF condition should appear to be nearly new. There should be no edge tears or other signs of damage. The grade of VF-XF is often used for notes intermediate between VF and XF.

Fine (F): A note in fine condition will show many signs of having been extensively in circulation. There will be numerous folds, and some of these may be heavy. It will be decidedly limp, and it may have some minor stains or edge tears. There will probably be a fair amount of surface dirt. This grade is not very attractive for most notes, but often rare notes are not generally available in higher grades. The grade of F-VF is often used for notes intermediate between fine and very fine.

Very Good (VG): This is not at all an attractive grade, but for collectors seeking rarities on limited budgets it may have to do. Notes in VG condition will be dirty and quite limp. There will be numerous folds, and some of them may be heavy. There will probably be a few edge tears, but the note should still be intact, i. e., there should be no missing corners or portions of the edge. Notes with fewer problems than these are often graded as being in VG-F condition.

Good (G): Notes in this grade are usually not collected unless they are of issues that are decidedly rare. The folds will be heavy, and some of these may be heavy enough to produce internal tears in the middle of the note. A note in good condition will be both limp and dirty. It may have a variety of stains. There may be several edge tears, but there should be no significant missing pieces, and the design should still be intact. If you wish to collect rare notes on a tight budget, this grade may still hold some appeal.

The grading scale, however, does not stop with good. Beneath it are fair and poor. For these grades substantial edge damage is to be expected, and pieces of the design may be missing. The folds may be heavy enough to produce several internal tears. There will also be edge tears, and some of these may be fairly long. Most likely notes in these grades will be quite dirty, and there may be some heavy stains. For the Federal paper money that is emphasized in this book, there are few notes that would be appealing in these grades. But Colonial paper money of the early 18th Century is sometimes only available in fragments, and collectors of this type of material must be prepared to consider these grades for some of the rarities that they hope to acquire.

Some currency auctioneers use terms such as 90% VF when describing certain notes. This does not mean that the note in question is at the upper end of the F-VF spectrum, but rather that 90% of the surface area of the note is in very fine condition, and there are serious problems with the remaining 10% of the note. This portion may be torn off, or it may have serious stains or abrasions. For any note so described, mention must be made of what the specific problems are.

In grading a note several other factors may need to be taken into consideration. One is the status of pinholes. In France bank notes are usually bundled together on wires, and almost all circulated notes of former years from this nation come with pinholes. This practice has been much less prevalent in the United States, but many Federal notes do have pinholes. I confess that I do not like pinholes, and I would prefer to have an XF note without pinholes than an uncirculated note with one or two pinholes in my collection. Some collectors feel the other way. I think that any note above VF condition that has one or more pinholes should be so described. A minor pinhole or two probably reduces the value of a note by about a grade (e. g., an XF note with a couple of pinholes should be worth about what a VF note without pinholes would be worth for the same variety), but this is clearly a matter for the buyer and seller to decide.

Bank notes in choice condition should have sharp corners, but sometimes corners are soft or somewhat rounded. Such characteristics would pull an otherwise choice CU note out of this class, although they may appear in notes that are only described as new. If the corner rounding is pronounced in a given note, it certainly should be mentioned for any note graded as XF or better.

In this book I shall occasionally use the words decent, nice, and choice to describe the condition of notes. The word choice is "officially" used as a qualifier to describe grades such as choice CU, but by itself this term is not used for a specific grade. My use of these terms is deliberately subjective. A note in VF condition may be very nice for you, but perhaps your standards are higher and you would not regard a note as nice or choice unless it is at least in XF or AU condition. Unless you plan to restrict your collecting to notes of a specific grade, it is often useful to talk about a general range of grades. When buying or selling notes, however, you do want to know the grade of what you are dealing with. Among current notes (especially $1 FRNs) one term that seems to be often used is the grade "circulated." In theory this could mean anything from G to AU. This term is rarely used except for the most recent of notes, but you will find it often used on pricelists of web notes, recent error notes, and other current items. The term is quite ambiguous, however, and I have not seen it used by any auctioneers when describing recent items.

Sizable edge tears are definitely not desirable, but what about minor edge splits? The United States Notes of Series 1862 and 1863 were printed in thin paper that is prone to edge splits. There are many examples of these notes that are in new or AU condition that have small edge splits. Any notes in this condition should be so described. An uncirculated note with edge splits plainly cannot be described as gem CU, but it can be described as new. The presence of minor edge splits, however, must be included in the description.

Centering has already been mentioned, and this is increasingly being taken into consideration for high grade notes. One currency dealer, David Koble of Bartlesville, Oklahoma, uses the grades VF, F, and A to describe the centering of notes as very fine, fine, and average, respectively. These are quite independent of the grades that he uses to denote the degree of wear. An average note will not be well centered. For some issues, of course, very fine centering is the rule rather than the exception. But there are a few issues that are notorious for their less than perfect centering. A good example of these are the Series 1928 $1 USNs. These notes are readily available in CU condition, but their centering often leaves much to be desired.

Most large-size national bank notes and many Series 1929 notes of these issues were cut by hand. These notes can often have wide and attractive margins, but they are sometimes also found cut into the design. Clearly the values of these notes are dependent upon the appearance of their margins or lack thereof. Many national bank notes from the New England states issued prior to about 1890 have very tight margins. Apparently boxes for storing bank notes in that part of the country were a bit too tight for the Federal currency, and this led to the notorious "New England trim." First Charter NBNs from the New England states are obviously much more desirable with adequate margins than without, but it you collect these, expect to acquire several notes with very tight or non-existent margins.

The black ink used to print the intaglio portions of Federal currency is a carbon-base ink that is little affected by light. The green inks that are used for printing the back sides of most notes are also stable, but the inks used to print seals and other features on various large-size and fractional notes were often sensitive to light or to various substances. How should one grade an uncirculated red seal note (e. g., a silver, gold, or Treasury note of the 1890s, or a Series 1902 red seal NBN) in which the Treasury seal has faded to light pink? Clearly it is much less desirable than the same note in which the seal is bright red. Such a note is best described as uncirculated, but with a faded seal. Its value depends upon what a buyer will pay for it, but a new note in such condition would probably sell for no more than an XF example of the same note with bright seal.

The presence of stains also affects the value of notes. Light brown toning of organic origin can be easily removed without any harm to the note, and I am often surprised that collectors even worry about it. Rust stains, however, are an entirely different matter. They are very difficult to remove and are quite annoying if they are heavy. Ink stains may or may not be easily removable. Stains or toning that is easily removable should have little no adverse effect on the value of a note, but heavy stains obviously reduce the value of a note to a considerable degree. In Chapter 16 I shall discuss some of the procedures that can be used with paper money. Some of what I write may engender controversy, but almost all of it is based on my own personal experience.

All collectors should be aware of the properties of strictly uncirculated notes. The term "cracking fresh" is sometimes used to describe the sound that a CU note will make when lightly waved, but this does not apply to MPCs. They were surface printed on a paper that does not "crackle." Most small-size notes of the early 1950s in CU condition have rough surfaces that make them seem as though they had been soaked and then carelessly dried. These notes were printed on wet paper, and unless they have been pressed they will show a degree of surface roughness. Many CU notes printed in the 1940s have a dirty grayish appearance. This seems especially true of the Hawaii notes. This is due to improper wiping of plates at the BEP and not to any external factors.

Bank notes are sometimes heavily washed or treated with laundry starch to improve either their appearance or their stiffness. Starched notes, however, seem stiff and heavy and do not have the crispness of fresh XF, AU, or CU notes. Notes that have been heavily washed will probably show signs of fading, and they also will lack the body found in higher grade notes. Such notes obviously should sell at substantial discounts from notes that are original. The word "original" is now coming into wide use to describe notes that have not been tampered with in any way.

I think that it is fortunate that grading in paper money has not been taken to the extremes that are now found for several series of coins (e. g., U. S. silver dollars). It strikes me as absurd that there are persons who are willing to pay hundreds of dollars each for such ultra-common coins as the Peace dollars of 1922, 1923, and 1925 which happen to be in very choice BU condition. Normal MS-60 examples of these coins can be purchased in large quantities for quite reasonable prices. Why pay vastly higher prices for coins that are only slightly better, when frequently the differences can only be seen under fairly high magnification?

In Federal paper money the price dependence on condition varies from series to series. In my opinion the two extremes of this scale at the present time are to be found for national bank notes at one end and Fractional Currency at the other. Most persons who seriously collect NBNs collect notes of specific banks or states. They may have a very great interest in a particular bank, because their grandfather served as an officer of that bank and signed some of the notes. To such individuals condition is of secondary importance. Notes in choice condition are obviously more desirable than are notes that are heavily worn, but the idea of huge price spreads between the better grades would seem absurd to them.

In Fractional Currency one is beginning to see quite large price spreads among the higher grade notes. Centering is often a problem with these notes, and they do show some variation in sizes for notes of a given type. Well centered CU notes with wide margins now sell for several times what typical notes in new condition of the same variety bring. Some of this price differentiation is certainly justified. The earliest fractional notes were perforated like postage stamps. Only rarely are these notes found well centered with perforations that are fully intact. Philatelists like their stamps to be free of short, nibbed, or pulled perforations, and stamps having these problems will sell at significantly lower prices than will those that are free of them. We should certainly expect a fairly wide range of prices for the perforated issues of Fractional Currency, but I am not convinced that it is fully justified for some of the other issues of fractional notes.

In the period from about 1977 to 1981 there was a huge amount of speculation in coins and postage stamps often by persons with lots of money but with little feeling for collecting. This market crashed severely in 1981-82, and prices on many stamps and coins are now much lower than they were at the peak of this speculative binge. A similar boom also occurred for Federal paper money, and it too was followed by a major correction at the same time. I expect that many of the novices who were getting into paper money collecting in the late 1970s were attempting to produce the same price spread with condition that had developed in stamps and coins. An examination of the 10th edition of the Friedberg Catalog of *Paper Money of the United States* shows a tendency that was then developing. In this book many of the Series 1914 Blue Seal $5 FRNs were listed at $20 in VF condition, but $250 in CU condition. Typical $10 notes of the same series were listed at $25 each in VF, but $275 in CU. A price spread of 11 or 12 to one between VF and CU for any type of large-size note is absurd. Today you can expect to pay about four or five times as much for a choice CU large-size note of most types as you might pay for a VF note. For XF notes the price spread between that grade and CU is no more than two or three to one at the most. And for national bank notes the price spreads are generally much less than this. It should be noted that the 10th edition of this standard catalog was published in 1981, just a few months prior to a severe downturn in the market for large-size notes in CU condition. The speculators who paid silly prices for these notes in the late 1970s or the beginning of the 1980s soon were rewarded for their foolishness when they began to liquidate their investments. It appears to me that since 1982 bank note collecting has been almost completely free of these sorts of speculative excesses.

Recently a professional grading service for paper money has been initiated by two currency dealers. This is similar to the various grading services that have been offered for coins for a number of years. When notes have been graded by this party, they are sealed in holders and breaking the seal invalidates their guarantee. Thus notes so sealed will closely resemble slabbed coins. It remains to be seen whether or not this form of marketing and of storing notes will catch on, but the PCDA (Professional Currency Dealers Association) has now taken an official position against "slabbing" and third-party grading for paper money. As I have already noted, few serious collectors of national bank notes are concerned with microscopic differences in grading standards. Personally I like to handle my notes, and despite the fact that I also have thousands of coins in my collection, I have no slabbed coins at all.

CHAPTER TWO

SMALL-SIZE NOTES: GENERAL PROPERTIES

Small-size notes were first placed into circulation on July 10, 1929, some 68 years after the first large-sized Federal bank notes intended for general circulation had been issued. During much of 1928 and the first half of 1929 a high percentage of the new currency printed was small-size, but it was decided not to release any of these notes into circulation until the after the beginning of the new fiscal year that commenced on July 1,1929. It is now about 70 years since small-size notes were first issued, but the numbers issued of small-size notes have exceeded by a vast amount the numbers of large-size notes that were ever issued. Only a few persons today are old enough to remember when large-size notes were in general circulation. Since small-size notes are by far the most familiar and frequently encountered form of Federal paper money, it seems logical to begin our detailed discussion with these issues.

Small-size notes have been printed in sheets of 12, 18, and 32 notes. Presently all notes are printed in sheets of 32 subjects, but between 1992 and 1995 a number of $1 FRNs were printed on the web press, an experimental press which allowed for a continuous feed of paper and printed both the faces and backs of the notes at the same time. Although more than 300 million notes were printed with this press, it did not prove capable of producing paper money as efficiently as did the Magna presses that have been in use by the BEP (Bureau of Engraving and Printing) since 1976.

The printing of paper money is today essentially a three-step operation. The green backs of the notes are printed first, and this is subsequently followed by the faces of the notes that are printed in black. Both of these are in intaglio, but the district seals and numbers, Treasury seals, and serial numbers are printed by letter press after both of the intaglio portions of the notes have been printed. Thus collectors speak of the first, second, and third printings when referring to these three stages of the printing process. Although the Federal Reserve seals and numbers are printed in black while the Treasury seals and serial numbers are in green, these overprints are applied at the same time and thus both of these overprints are referred to as the third printing.

All of the small-size notes printed between 1928 and 1952 were produced on 12-subject sheets, but in late 1952 and early 1953 there was a complete changeover to printing notes in 18-subject sheets. Notes printed in 12-subject sheets bear the plate position letters A through F in the first column and G through L in the second column. On most uncut sheets the notes are numbered sequentially from 1 - 12, 13 - 24, etc., but generally these sheets were cut in half before being serially numbered, and the serial numbers of the two halves of the sheet often were substantially different. Thus a pack of new notes of this vintage will normally show numerous half sheet sequences of six numbers each. These will always have plate letter sequences of either A through F or G through L. A few collectors attempt to obtain their notes in this fashion, but this becomes quite impossible for notes printed on 18-subject or 32-subject sheets.

The back design that had been prepared for all small-size $1 notes in 1928 was replaced by the Great Seal design in 1935. In 1952 this design was modified slightly by making it about 2 mm narrower. Series 1935D $1 SCs exist with both wide and narrow back designs.

Plates with 18 subjects were first introduced in 1952, and by 1953 all notes were being printed on sheets of this size. These sheets have a third column of notes, which have plate position letters of M through R. All Series 1950 type FRNs were printed in these sheets, as were all Series 1953 USNs and SCs. Some of the 1935D $1 SCs were printed in these sheets, but this series was also printed in the older 12-note format. All Series 1935E through 1935H $1 SCs were printed on 18-subject sheets.

On the 18-subject sheets an entirely different numbering scheme was used from what had been previously used on 12-subject sheets. The second note of a sheet would receive a serial number that was 8000 higher than that of the first note. This would continue throughout the sheet such that the 18th note would have a serial number that was 136,000 numbers higher than the first note of the sheet. An entire run of notes printed in this format would thus contain 8000 sheets or 144,000 notes.

Between 1957 and 1965 the back designs for all seven denominations then in print were modified to include the motto "In God We Trust." The most obvious difference is to be found on the $50 notes, where a large number of automobiles depicted as parked in front of the east side of the Capitol building on the older notes have been removed from the new design.

The 32-subject plates were introduced much more gradually than were the 18-subject plates. They first appeared with the Series 1957 $1 SCs that were released in that year. The higher denomination notes first appeared only in 1963, and by the end of 1965 almost all bank notes were being printed on 32-subject sheets. All of these notes have the motto "In God We Trust" on their back sides. This motto was also used on Series 1935G and 1935H $1 SCs that were printed in 18-subject sheets, but it was decided to continue printing the $2 through $100 notes in 18-subject sheets without this motto until the plates on hand were sufficiently worn for them to be retired from use. As things turned out, this phasing out of older plates lasted until 1968.

The notes printed on 32-subject sheets use position indicators to designate their position within a given sheet. Notes in the first quadrant are lettered A1 - H1 in their upper left portions. Notes in the second quadrant (lower left) are lettered A2 through H2, while those notes of the upper right and lower right portions of the sheets are lettered A3 - H3 and A4 - H4, respectively. The serial numbers on most sheets advance 20,000 numbers between the first and second notes of a given sheet. Thus a complete sheet will show a range of 620,000 numbers. An examination of the numbers of notes printed for each type reveals that most issues of bank notes since the later 1950s have been printed in multiples of 20,000 sheets. Thus typical runs for notes with smaller printings have often been done in editions of 0.64, 1.28, 1.92, 2.56, or 3.20 million notes each. The experimental web press that was in use between 1992 and 1995 did not use any sheet position indicators on the notes that it printed. The BEP had hoped to improve its rate of note output with this press, but that did not turn out to be the case.

In 1971 the BEP installed new state of the art equipment for overprinting and cutting notes. This is known as COPE (Currency Overprinting and Processing Equipment). Notes that were serially numbered with COPE first appeared in Series 1969B. The older machines for processing currency also continued in use for a few additional years, and there are some minor differences in the styles of the serial numbers between the notes processed with these two sets of overprinting equipment. It is sometimes difficult to distinguish these varieties except for the serial numbers themselves, and today there is not much interest among collectors as to which type of machine actually did the third printing for notes printed during the 1970s. The presses that do the first and second printings of the notes are officially referred to as Two-Plate Monocolor Intaglio Presses, but the alternate name of Magna press is generally used for the devices that the BEP has utilized for these printings since 1976.

The serial numbers on small-size notes fall into three different categories:
1) all notes other than Federal Reserve Notes, Federal Reserve Bank Notes, and national bank notes
2) Federal Reserve Notes and Federal Reserve Bank Notes
3) national bank notes

Small-size notes in first of these categories have a letter prefix followed by an eight-digit serial number which is followed by a letter suffix. A typical serial number for such a note would be E34672585B. The use of eight digits in the serial number allows for 100 million notes to be printed in this block. All letters of the alphabet are used in designating serial number blocks except for the letter "O" which is not used because of its similarity to the numeral zero. The first 25 blocks for notes of a given type, series, and denomination will all have the prefix "A," and the blocks will be AA, BA, etc., up to ZA. The next block will be AB, followed by BB, etc. The EB block would be the 30th block to be printed, and for the example given above, a note with that serial designation would be note number 2,934,672,585 in that series to be printed. The highest block designation that is found for notes of this type is EJ, which is found on $1 SCs of Series 1935H, notes that were actually printed in 1963. In order to get to this high a serial number block almost 23 billion notes had to be printed, but most of these were not Series 1935H. The numbering for this series began with Series 1935, which was first printed in the year 1935.

Although block collecting is not very popular among most collectors, it is catching on. For many of the scarcer notes only one block exists, but for some notes (especially $1 SCs and recent issue FRNs of various denominations) there may be literally dozens of different block varieties for notes of a given series and denomination. This is a matter that I shall return to in the next couple of chapters.

Closely related to the serial number blocks of the normally issued notes are the star or replacement notes. The practice of printing a special, auxiliary sequence of notes so that spoiled notes having normal serial numbers could be replaced without going to the very great effort of replacing the spoiled note with an identically numbered copy was begun in 1910. Not all types of large-size notes were designated in this fashion, and only recently has there been much research done on the large-size replacement notes. Small-size star notes, however, have been very popular and have been well documented for years. For small-size notes in the first category a typical star serial number would be *07864352A. Thus this note would be replacement note number 7,864,352 printed for that series of notes. Most small-size star notes have the block *A, since 100 million star notes were rarely printed for a given type of note. But for some 1935 type $1 SCs star blocks go as high as *G, which is found on Series 1935F, 1935G, and 1935H $1 SCs. The highest official number for such a star note is *21596000G, which is note number 621,596,000 among the replacement issues for Series 1935 through 1935H $1 SCs. Most star notes printed in sheets of 12 have solid stars, but for all notes printed with 18-subject and 32-subject plates serial numbers featuring hollow stars are used. Hollow stars were also used on all Series 1935 $1 SCs, regardless of whether they were printed on 12-subject or 18-subject plates. In the following chapter I shall have a considerable amount to say about the relative scarcity of these notes. Many star notes are now recognized as being rare, and very high prices are sometimes asked for star notes that are not at all scarce in normal serial number form.

The term group is used for a specific sequence of notes that arises when the normal sequencing within a given block is interrupted by other types of notes. The $1 Hawaii and North Africa notes did not have special block designations. Instead they were inserted among the regularly issued $1 silver certificates. For the block CC of Series 1935A $1 SCs the first seven million notes were Hawaii notes, and notes with serial numbers C60000001C to C62000000C and C780000001C to C79904000C were North Africa notes. All of the other notes of this block were normal $1 SCs, and thus they would include notes with serials 7 to 60 million, 62 to 78 million, and all notes higher than 79,904,000. Thus there would be one group of Hawaii notes, two groups of North Africa notes, and three groups of normal blue seal notes for this one block. Nearly all block collectors, however, would settle for just one note of each type in this block. There are at least a couple of serial number groups that are of great interest, however, and these I shall discuss in the next chapter of this book.

The Federal Reserve Notes and Federal Reserve Bank Notes use a different type of serial number designation. The prefix letter for any normal FRN or FRBN will be a letter A through L that designates the Federal Reserve Bank in question. The suffix letter will be used to indicate the sequential block designation for notes from that district. The first 100 million notes of a given type, denomination, and district will be designated A, the second such block will be B, etc. The prefix letters of the 12 Federal Reserve districts are as follows:

A Boston	E Richmond	I Minneapolis
B New York	F Atlanta	J Kansas City
C Philadelphia	G Chicago	K Dallas
D Cleveland	H St. Louis	L San Francisco

This numbering system can accommodate up to 2.5 billion notes of a given series, denomination, and district. This has not been a problem until very recent years, but large districts such as New York, Atlanta, Chicago, and San Francisco have almost used up their serial number quotas for notes in some of the recent most $1 FRN series. Today many serial number blocks for contemporary notes extend only to 96 million, an amount that is equivalent to 150 groups of 20,000 sheets or 640,000 notes each. As has already been noted, most notes are now printed and processed in batches of at least that size.

Replacement note FRNs and FRBNs have the district prefix letter followed by eight digits followed by a star. In the 1928, 1929, and 1934 series these stars are solid, but for Series 1950 and later the stars are hollow. One-dollar and two-dollar FRNs are often collected as district sets with either one star note or one regular note from each district. All FRBN star notes are scarce, and it is now clear that there are also many rarities among the higher denomination FRN star notes.

At the present time radical changes of design are being undertaken for all $5 through $100 FRNs. Thus far Series 1996 $100, $50, and $20 FRNs have been issued, and these are being followed by $10 and $5 notes in that order. By the turn of this century all of our money will be printed in these new types, at least for denominations of $5 and higher. The new notes employ a different serial number scheme from that used for previous FRNs. A typical serial number for a Series 1996 note would be AB46257483C. This note would be from the third block of notes issued for the New York district. The initial letter A is a reserve letter that allows for far more than 25 blocks of notes to be issued for a given district. If the AB - Z block is filled, then the next block to be printed would be BB - A, etc. At 96 million notes per block, it is possible to print 2.4 billion notes for the "A" series. This numbering system would allow one to go to ZB - Z before the numbers would be exhausted. At that point 60 billion notes would have been printed for a single district. This amount is far beyond the printing capacity of the BEP, but with this numbering system there is no possibility of running out of serial numbers, as is now often the case with $1 FRNs from some of the largest districts such as New York, Chicago, or San Francisco. The Series 1996 notes also exist in replacement form. These have a star suffix, as do all replacement FRNs.

Although Series 1929 national bank notes were printed in sheets of 12, they were always cut into two strips of six notes each before being distributed to the designated banks. On type 1 all notes on a given sheet will have the same serial number and letter suffix, but the notes will be differentiated by their letter prefixes, A through F. On a typical sheet of NBNs the serial numbers for that sheet might be A002638A through F002638A. Note that only six digits are used for the serial number. Each bank had its own set of serial numbers, and only for the largest banks were as many as one million notes of a given denomination issued. On only one issue of notes, the $5 type 1 note from the Chase Manhattan Bank of New York, were there more than 1,000,000 sheets, and in this case the B suffix was used for the last of the $5 notes printed for that bank.

On type 2 NBNs almost all notes have a serial letter prefix A followed by a six digit set of numbers. Thus the serial numbers for a typical type 2 sheet issued to a given bank might be A000721 through A000726. Only for the $5 type 2 notes of the Bank of America in San Francisco were more than one million notes issued. For those notes that exceeded this number the prefix B was used instead. Thus a note of this type with serial B004296 would actually be note number 1,004,296 printed for this bank and denomination.

There were no special designators for NBNs that had to be replaced. The serial numbers for notes that needed replacement were usually done with type set by hand, and typically these improvised serial numbers differed somewhat in alignment from those on the regularly printed notes. I shall return to these matters and to additional questions concerning the serial numbering of NBNs and of other types of paper currency in several of the later chapters of this book.

If you plan to collect small-size notes by serial number blocks, it is essential to obtain a copy of the *Standard Guide to Small-Size U. S. Paper Money* by Dean Oakes and John Schwartz. This catalog is now in its second edition, and it covers notes released as late as 1996. It gives far more detail on small-size notes than do the general reference catalogs that cover all types of U. S. Federal paper money.

Another item of interest to some collectors are the check numbers that appear on small-size notes. In addition to a plate number that does not appear on the printed notes, each plate bears a check number on each impression. Thus all notes will have a face check number and back check number. For most series of small-size notes there are far too many check numbers for one to attempt to collect all possibilities, but there is considerable interest among specialist collectors in the sizes of these check numbers. Originally the check numbers were about 0.5 mm high (the so-called "micro" numbers), but this was changed to about 1.0 mm (the so-called "macro" numbers) beginning in 1938. This change resulted in a number of possible varieties.

The signature combination Julian-Morganthau was used from 1934 to 1945, and thus it spanned virtually the entire duration of the Roosevelt administration. The first Federal Reserve Notes with this combination were Series 1934, but beginning in 1938 notes with the new, larger check numbers began to be printed. These were designated Series 1934A, and most collectors attempt to obtain notes of both of these series. For $1 SCs the transition was for Series 1935 / 1935A, while for $5 and $10 SCs it was for Series 1934 / 1934A. For $2 USNs it was for Series 1928C / 1928D, and for $5 USNs it was for Series 1928B / 1928C. A complication arose because back plates were used without regard as to whether they had large or small check numbers. Thus there are many mule notes, and these were printed as recently as 1953 for some series of $50 and $100 FRNs. A mule Series 1935 $1 SC will have large check numbers on its back, while a mule Series 1935A $1 SC will have small check numbers on its back. In both of these cases the mule notes are scarcer than their non-mule counterparts, but this is not always the case. For $50 and $100 FRNs of series 1934A, 1934B, 1934C, 1934D, and 1950 mules are definitely more common than non-mule notes. It is not even certain that non-mules exist for several series of these notes. In some cases, however, a mule note may be a true rarity. For Series 1928D $2 USNs mule notes are only somewhat scarcer than their non-mule counterparts, but for Series 1928C $2 USNs non-mule notes are fairly common, but mule notes for this series are extremely rare. Most collectors who distinguish between these varieties are also avid block collectors, so block collecting and mule collecting tend to go hand in hand.

A general property of small-size notes is that all notes of a given denomination have the same back designs, and these are always printed in green, at least for all notes that have been intended for general circulation. Nonetheless there have been some significant changes of design. The Series 1996 notes now being printed have radically new back designs, but if we consider only notes printed prior to this date, the most radical changes of back design occurred with the $1 and $2 notes. In 1935 the back design for all $1 notes was changed from an ornamental numeral design to the Great Seal design that is still in use. All $2 USNs have backs that depict Monticello, Thomas Jefferson's home in Virginia. When $2 FRNs were first issued in 1976, they depicted the *Signing of the Declara-*

tion of Independence, a design that had previously been used on the very rare $100 First Charter national bank notes. Another fairly major change in back designs was made when the motto "In God We Trust" was incorporated into the back designs of all notes then in circulation. All of the old style $1 notes are without this motto, and all of the $2 FRNs have it since this modification was made for most denominations in the early 1960s. Although the back designs previously in use were continued when this motto was added, there were a number of modifications. The most notable was for the $50 notes where the vignette of the U. S. Capitol was lowered to accommodate this motto. This resulted in the removal of a large number of automobiles that had been depicted parked at the bottom of the central vignette of these notes.

In 1948 the back design for all $20 notes was completely redrawn. In addition to the obvious differences in the central vignette, the legend was changed from "White House" to "The White House." Both of these designs were used for the $20 FRNs of Series 1934C.

There were also a few other changes of back design that are well known to most collectors of small-size notes. The Hawaii notes issued during World War II were overprinted Hawaii on their back sides. This overprint was printed by letter press with the word "HAWAII" appearing in large black capital letters. In 1952 the width of the back design of the $1 note was reduced by about 2 millimeters. This resulted in two varieties for the Series 1935D $1 SCs. The Series 1935G $1 SCs also exist with two varieties of back designs. This is the only series of notes to occur with both no motto and with motto types. There was no possibility of mule types occurring with most of the "motto" notes, since all non-motto notes at that time were printed on 18-subject sheets while almost all motto notes were printed on 32-subject sheets.

A third notable change of back design occurred in 1948, when the vignette of the White House that appears on $20 notes was radically modified. The Series 1934C $20 FRNs occur with both old and new backs, and almost all series collectors try to obtain at least one of each of these varieties.

There are also two much more subtle changes in back designs that are recognized by currency specialists. In about 1950 the backs of $5 notes were changed from a "wide" design" to a "narrow" design. There also was a change in the backs of $10 notes from a "narrow" design" to a "wide" design. Both of these changes were quite minor, and they are not given recognition in the standard currency catalogs, but the Oakes and Schwartz catalog of small-size notes gives full details. The notes affected by these changes are Series 1928F $5 USNs, 1934D $5 SCs, and 1950 $5 FRNs along with Series 1934D $10 SCs and 1950 $10 FRNs. Some specialists even distinguish between "wide I" and "wide II" designs for the $5 notes. These designs are in fact identical, and they differ only in that their check numbers are separated by a sequence of "narrow" back notes.

It is worthwhile to consider the ranges of check numbers for the back sides of the different denominations of small-size notes. For $1 notes these ranges are as follows:

$1 old design	1 - 3096
$1 Great Seal (micro)	1 - 929
$1 " (macro - wide)	930 - 5015
$1 " (narrow - no motto)	5017 - 6786
$1 " (narrow - motto)	6787 - 8648

These numbers refer only to the 12-subject and 18-subject plates. An entirely new sequence of check numbers beginning with #1 was initiated with the 32-subject plates that were first used in 1957.

For the $2 United States Notes the check numbers used for printing the back sides were as follows:

$2 micro numbers	1 - 288
$2 macro numbers	289 - 390
$2 macro - 18-subject	391 - 412
$2 motto - 32-subject	1 - 3

For the $5 through $100 notes I do not have full data on all back check numbers, but the following represent the important transitions:

$5 micro / macro	938 / 939
$10 micro / macro	584 / 585
$20 micro / macro (old)	317 / 318
$20 old back / new back	587 / 588
$50 micro / macro	162 / 163
$100 micro / macro	112 / 113

There was a smooth transition of back check numbers between the 12-subject and 18-subject plates, but the 32-subject plates were all numbered #1 from the beginning. On several occasions subsequent to that date the sequence of back check numbers has been rolled back to #1.

One peculiar group of notes are those printed with the so-called late finished plates. These were plates on which work was commenced in 1934-38 and which were assigned check numbers from the "micro" period. They were finished, however, as late as 1944, and thus the actual check numbers engraved on them were "macro" numbers. These plates included one $1 back plate, one $20 back plate, one $5 SC face plate, and two $10 SC face plates. Notes printed from these plates always have "macro" numbers, but these numbers are out of the normal ranges for such numbers. Specialists in small-size notes recognize a few varieties of notes that were printed with these plates. Among them are a number of the Word War II issues. These varieties are discussed in some detail in the Oakes and Schwartz catalog.

As for the high denomination notes, I have seen $500 notes with back check numbers of 1 through 12. All are of the "micro" variety. For $1000 notes I have seen back check numbers of 1 through 8. The first four check numbers are of the "micro" variety, but numbers 5 through 8 are "macro" numbers. Back check numbers, of course, are relevant to any discussion of mule and non-mule varieties for notes of all denominations.

Should you bother with mule and non-mule varieties in collecting those types of small-size notes for which both varieties occur? This decision is entirely up to you. But if you wish to obtain all possibilities for these varieties, there are several that are extreme rarities. I regard these varieties as fairly minor and have not distinguished between mules and non-mules in forming my own collection, but if you decide to get into block collecting, I expect that the mule varieties may also appeal to you.

In 1987 the Bureau of Engraving and Printing dedicated its western facility in Fort Worth, Texas. Full-scale production of $1 notes from this facility began in 1990, and since then $2, $5, $10, and $20 notes have been produced there as well. All notes printed in Fort Worth have the small letters "FW" in their lower right portions close to the check number designation for the face plate. Those notes printed in Washington lack this feature. Many syngraphists now collect both Washington-printed and Fort Worth-printed notes from districts for which both varieties occur. Notes printed in Fort Worth began with Series 1988A, and these have continued with Series 1990, 1993, and 1995. Generally the eastern Federal Reserve Districts (A through F) have been printed in Washington, while the western districts (G through L) have been printed in Fort Worth, but there has already been a substantial amount of overlap.

On recent Federal Reserve Notes I have also noticed a significant difference in the sizes of the back check numbers of the notes printed at the two facilities. The notes from the Washington facility have back check numbers that are about 0.9 mm high, while those printed in Fort Worth have numbers that are about 1.3 mm high. There are also quite different sequences of back check numbers that are used. These differences are deliberate. The face plates can be easily distinguished, since the plates used in Fort Worth have "FW" on each impression while those used in Washington do not. By making the back check numbers of not quite the same size and by using different ranges for these numbers, it becomes quite easy for the BEP to distinguish plates made at the two facilities, and this might prove useful as a control measure. It is also possible that a new series of mule notes will arise from these differences, and indeed that has happened for one issue of $1 Federal Reserve Notes, as I shall mention in chapter 4.

When small-size notes were first being printed in 1928, the two facsimile signatures were engraved on the plates, and thus they appeared in intaglio on the finished notes as part of the so-called second printing. This is also the way that all notes printed in Series 1966 or later have been prepared. But for many notes printed between the mid-1930s and the mid-1960s, these signatures were printed by letter press as part of the third printing. For $1 SCs all Series 1935 and 1957 notes were printed in this fashion, but for FRNs this practice commenced only with Series 1950 and it ended after Series 1963A. Series 1963B was the first series of $1 FRNs to once more have these signatures engraved directly onto the plates. All Series 1928 $2 and $5 USNs and all Series 1934 $5 and $10 SCs had the Treasury signatures printed in intaglio, but for Series 1953 these were changed to being printed by letter press onto the otherwise finished notes.

We have now surveyed the basic general properties of small-size notes. In the following two chapters I shall discuss the specifics of the various issues of small-size notes. All notes other than Federal Reserve Notes will be discussed in the first of these chapters, but I am devoting an entire chapter to small-size Federal Reserve Notes, since I feel that the collecting parameters for these notes should be quite different from those of any of the other series. Series 1929 national bank notes are small-size notes, but they are also NBNs. Although their basic characteristics will be examined in the next chapter, they will also be covered in substantially greater detail in the chapter in this book devoted to national bank notes.

Almost all collectors of small-size notes collect them at least by series. It is also possible to collect them by major type only, but this approach is trivially easy for most issues of small-size notes. For instance, there are only three major types each of the $2 and $5 USNs, all of which are extremely common. To acquire these six notes would require minimal effort and expense. In order for collecting to be interesting, it must impose some degree of challeng. Collections that can be completed in a matter of minutes with a minimal outlay of funds will soon lose their appeal. For small-size notes I feel that collectors should at least attempt to collect all series of a given class of notes, and in the following chapter which deals with the specifics on most issues of small-size notes I shall emphasize that mode of collecting. But if you wish to explore further in this field, block collecting or even mule collecting may appeal to you.

All notes currently produced by the BEP are printed in 32-subject sheets. The position of any note on a sheet is indicated by the letter and quadrant designators that appear in the upper left portions on the face side of these notes.

A_1 A	E_1 E	A_3 A	E_3 E
B_1 B	F_1 F	B_3 B	F_3 F
C_1 C	G_1 G	C_3 C	G_3 G
D_1 D	H_1 H	D_3 D	H_3 H
A_2 A	E_2 E	A_4 A	E_4 E
B_2 B	F_2 F	B_4 B	F_4 F
C_2 C	G_2 G	C_4 C	G_4 G
D_2 D	H_2 H	D_4 D	H_4 H

CHAPTER THREE

SMALL-SIZE NOTES: NONCURRENT TYPES

At the present time about 99.85% of the paper money in circulation consists of Federal Reserve Notes. Most of the balance is split roughly between silver certificates and United States Notes. The former were last printed in 1963, and production of the latter ceased in 1971, and thus for almost three decades no paper money other than Federal Reserve Notes has been printed by the BEP. In this chapter I shall deal with all types of small-size notes whose Treasury seals and serial numbers are printed in colors other than green.

UNITED STATES NOTES

Small-size United States Notes have only been printed in denominations of $1, $2, $5, and $100, and for most of the period between 1928 and 1971 only $2 and $5 USNs were printed. Let us begin our discussion with the $2 notes. There are three distinct issues of these notes; 1928, 1953, and 1963. Prior to 1933 USNs could not be used to pay customs duties or interest on the public debt, and this clause appears on the first three series of these notes. In 1933, this clause was eliminated, and these notes were made legal tender for all debts public and private. This new wording first appears on the Series 1928C $2 USNs, and it appears on all of the later issues of these notes. It is an extremely simple matter to obtain one each of the three (or four) major types of small-size $2 USNs, but most collectors attempt to obtain a complete set of all 14 different series varieties. This is much more of a challenge, but it also is not especially difficult to complete.

Four of the scarcest small-size USN star notes are depicted above. Note the difference in obligations between the Series 1928A $2 note and the 1928D $5 note. The Series 1966 $100 USNs were the first notes issued to portray the new Treasury seal.

Among the regular issue $2 USNs there are eight 1928 issues (Series 1928, 1928A, 1928B, 1928C, 1928D, 1928E, 1928F, and 1928G), four 1953 issues (Series 1953, 1953A, 1953B, and 1953C), and only two 1963 issues (Series 1963 and 1963A). The 1928 issues were printed in 12-subject sheets, the 1953 notes in 18-subject sheets, and the 1963 issues in 32-subject sheets. These last two series are the only $2 USNs to have the "In God We Trust" motto on their backs. All of the 1953 and 1963 issues are very common, and in CU condition they can be obtained for from $6 to $8 each. Among the 1928 issues Series 1928, 1928D, 1928F, and 1928G are also readily obtainable at $15 to $20 each in CU condition, or at about half this in the XF-AU grade. Series 1928C and 1928E are somewhat scarcer, and CU examples may sell for as much as $60, but attractive circulated examples of these two series can be had for only $15 or $20. Series 1928A $2 notes are a good deal scarcer, and CU examples sell for well over $100, but nice VF-XF examples of this note can be had for well under $50. By far the scarcest notes in this issue are the Series 1928B $2 USNs. A CU note of this issue will probably cost at least $600, but VF-XF examples should be obtainable for about $100 each.

There are relatively few normal block varieties for $2 USNs because these notes were printed in fairly small quantities, and Series 1928D was the only one of the 14 series to exceed a printing of 100 million copies. It is also the only one of these issues to appear in three different regular block varieties. Series 1928A, 1928B, 1928C, and 1928G are the only other series to appear in two different normal blocks. If you feel like collecting serial number blocks for these notes, none of them should be very difficult. Both the Series

1928C and 1928D notes exist as mules and as non-mules. The latter are easy enough to acquire, but Series 1928C $2 mules are very rare despite the fact that they exist in two different blocks.

Most collectors are undoubtedly much more interested in the star varieties for these notes than they are in the regularly issued block and mule variants. All 14 of the $2 USNs exist as star notes, but the rarities of these items vary enormously. The six notes of the 1953 and 1963 issues are readily obtainable in star form, and these range in price from about $15 to about $25 each in uncirculated condition. All of the various 1928 $2 star notes are fairly expensive in CU condition, and you might well want to consider grades no higher than VF or XF, if you want to acquire these. Five of these notes range from fairly scarce to fairly rare, but the other three star notes (Series 1928A, 1928B, and 1928E) are most definitely rare in any grade.

In terms of increasing rarity the five scarce star notes mentioned above are Series 1928G, 1928F, 1928D, 1928, and 1928C in that order. With the possible exception of Series 1928G, all of these notes sell for significantly more than $100 each when in new condition. The Series 1928D star notes exist both as mules and as non-mules, the latter being somewhat the more available. Of the five series mentioned above Series 1928C is by far the scarcest in star form. This note is very rare in CU, and it should cost at least a few hundred dollars when in XF condition.

Both Series 1928A and 1928E $2 USNs are major rarities in star form. Only little more than a dozen examples exist of each. A few examples exist in uncirculated condition, and these notes are very expensive in this grade. The auction of Lyn Knight that was held in Dallas in August, 1998 featured a 1928A star note in gem CU and a 1928E note that was also uncirculated. These items sold for $7700 and $5610, respectively. Only about five examples of the Series 1928B $2 star note are confirmed at the present time, and the condition for the majority of these is no better than fine. In 1995-96 there were two auction sales of this great rarity. Both notes were in only VG-F condition, and in both cases they fetched about $4000 each. Completing a set of all 14 $2 USN star notes is clearly a very great challenge.

This raises an interesting point of how you should collect star notes, or should you collect them at all? The cost of a single Series 1928C $2 star USN in high grade would be about the same as the cost of a complete set of all 14 regular $2 notes, all of which are in AU to CU condition. Small-size notes, for the most part, are relatively inexpensive, but large sums are required for the star note rarities that exist among these issues. One way to economize is to not bother with star notes at all. Another would be to acquire only the 10 or 11 most available of the $2 star notes and to forget all about the Series 1928A, 1928B, and 1928E stars. The Series 1928B $2 star is so rare that only a very few collectors can aspire to owning it regardless of the depths of their pockets. Hunting down the scarcer star notes can be challenging, but unless you wish to commit a large portion of your collecting budget to small-size star notes, you may wish to forgo the major rarities among these issues.

The $5 United States Notes closely parallel the $2 USNs, but there are two less series varieties since these notes were not issued with either the Tate-Mellon or Granahan-Fowler signature combinations. Only Series 1928 and 1928A $5 USNs carry the clause denying their use for customs duties and interest on the public debt, and only these two series plus 1928B have micro check numbers on their faces. Thus there are seven different notes of the 1928 type (Series 1928, 1928A, 1928B, 1928C, 1928D, 1928E, and 1928F), four different notes of the 1953 type (Series 1953, 1953A, 1953B, and 1953C), and only the single Series 1963 note for the last type of these issues.

It is very easy to complete a set of these twelve notes, since none of them can be described even as scarce. The least common of these issues is the Series 1928D note, and choice CU examples of this note now sell for about $150 each. Notes of this issue in XF condition, however, sell for less than $50 each. The Series 1928A note is also a bit uncommon, as CU examples are now worth at least $50, but XF examples of this note can be had for little more than $15 each. If you plan to obtain only a basic set of the 12 major varieties of this issue, I would recommend getting as many in CU as is possible. A couple of the scarcer notes could be in XF or AU condition, but several notes of this series are face value only items when in VF condition or less.

Although there are no rarities among the 12 major varieties of the $5 USNs, there are some very scarce notes in these issues. The Series 1928B, 1928C, 1928D, and 1928E notes all exist as mules. The 1928B and 1928C mules are uncommon, but they can be obtained without much difficulty. Both the 1928D and 1928E mules are very scarce, and these varieties are now bringing at least a few hundred dollars each when in XF or AU condition. The $5 USNs have more block varieties than do their $2 counterparts, and some of these are also scarce. Among the tougher varieties are the DA block of Series 1928 and the FA and GA blocks of the 1928C mules. Other varieties for specialists are the wide / narrow backs that occur on the Series 1928F notes. The narrow back notes are a good deal scarcer than are the wide back notes of this issue, but a few specialists even distinguish between wide I and wide II backs. The latter are identical to the former, but their higher back check numbers are separated from the wide I notes by a group of narrow back notes. The wide II notes are scarce, but demand for them is probably not very high in view of their extremely specialized (or should I say trivial?) nature.

It is less difficult to complete a set of 12 $5 USN star notes than it is to complete a set of the 14 $2 USN stars, but this is most definitely neither an easy nor inexpensive undertaking. The last five issues of these notes can be obtained in choice condition without too much difficulty, but all of the 1928 star notes are scarce to rare when in attractive condition. The least scarce of these is the Series 1928F star note, and uncirculated examples of this note sell for about $200 each with XF notes going at about one-third of this price. The Series 1928, 1928B, 1928C, and 1928E star notes are scarcer, but these four notes are all of comparable rarity and price. When available they can be had in XF condition for about $100 or a bit more per note, but CU examples are now selling for at least three times this figure. The two rarities of these issues are the Series 1928A and 1928D star notes. About 25 - 30 examples of each are known. The Series 1928A note is somewhat the rarer of the two, and CU examples of this note have recently fetched about $3000 each in auction. A CU Series 1928D note is a bit less expensive, but it still brings at least $2000 on those few occasions when this note comes up for sale. Both of these notes now sell for well over $1000 each in XF condition, and even in fine condition they are still worth significantly more than $500 each. But these high prices seem justified, when we take into consideration the rarity of these notes.

There also are a few minor varieties for the $5 USN star notes. Both the Series 1928B and 1928C star notes exist in mule form, and both of these are much scarcer than are their non-mule counterparts. The Series 1928F star note exists in wide and narrow form with the latter being the scarcer of the two. I regard the wide II variety as a trivial variant, but these also exist in star form. Before attempting to obtain all possible varieties of $5 USNs, you should again consider just what you plan to collect. It is very easy to acquire a set of the 12 major non-star varieties, and several of the star notes are also easy to obtain. But the Series 1928A and 1928D star notes are rarities that will cost a minimum of several hundred dollars each even in well circulated grades. There are also enough scarce and rare notes among the block and mule varieties of the $5 USNs to make you think whether or not you really want to try to obtain all of the possible minor variants.

Without doubt the Series 1928 $1 United States Note was the least necessary of all of the numerous types of small-size issues. These notes were printed in limited quantities in the spring of 1933, but the production of these notes was halted shortly after it had begun. It is my opinion that these notes were produced through ignorance of the law passed in 1878 that restricted to total amount of United States Notes outstanding to $346 million, an amount that was already covered by the $2 and $5 USNs then in circulation. The $1 USNs exist with 32 different face check numbers, and this indicates that sufficient plates were made to print at least 60 million of these notes yet only 1,872,000 were actually produced. This small quantity can be compared with the 4.296 b*illion* $1 silver certificates that were released for Series 1928 through 1934.

Also produced in 1933 were face plates for Series 1928 $10 and $20 United States Notes. A few impressions from these plates were produced, and it is believed that at least one pair of these is in private hands, but these two notes were never issued. As I have noted, it seems that production of the $1 USNs was halted and that for the $10 and $20 notes never commenced when it was discovered by the incoming administration that the law of 1878 prevented the issuance of additional United States Notes. The $1 USNs already printed were mostly put into storage, but 5000 of them were released in Washington during 1933. Many of these fell into the hands of numismatists, and thus notes with serials below 5000 are not especially uncommon.

The balance of the $1 USNs remained in cold storage at the Treasury for 15 years until 1,864,000 of them were released in Puerto Rico during 1948-49. The $1 USNs with serial numbers 5001 - 8000 have been somewhat of a mystery, since they were not accounted for in either of the two releases of this note. Recently, however, a heavily circulated note with a serial number in this range has turned up. It thus seems likely that these notes were also released in Puerto Rico in 1948 along with all of the other notes of this type that are known to have entered circulation there.

Although the normal issues of this note exist only in the AA block, there are two distinct groups, and I would recommend acquiring one note from each of these groups. The "Washington" notes have serials between 1 and 5000, and notes with serials between 1000 and 2000 are the most available of these. These notes almost always come in CU condition, although the centering on this issue is often far from ideal. This group is not as rare as you might expect, since the survival rate on these notes was very high.

The "Puerto Rico" notes have serials between 8001 (or is it 5001?) and 1872000, but most of the known examples have serials near the upper end of this range. These notes were first released on this then poverty-stricken island with little fanfare, and numismatists found out about them only late in their period of use. Many uncirculated notes were then saved, but the Series 1928 $1 USN shows a most peculiar distribution of grades. Most examples are in CU condition, but the balance are generally in VG-F condition or worse. Notes in VF, XF, or AU condition are decidedly scarce. Although they are less expensive than are the CU notes, they are much more difficult to find.

The Series 1928 $1 USN is among the most popular of all the small-size notes. Well-centered CU examples of either the "Washington" or the "Puerto Rico" issues now sell for about $200 each, but poorly centered notes can be had for not much more than $100, at least for the more common "Puerto Rico" issue. When available XF examples of this issue go for about $60 to $75, but these are not available for the "Washington" issue. If you require only a VG-F note, these now cost about $25 each. All of these will be "Puerto Rico" issues, and such notes would show a much wider range of serial numbers than will their CU counterparts.

The Series 1928 $1 star USN is one of the major small-size rarities. About 30 examples of this note are known, but the great popularity of this issue causes it to sell for more than the Series 1928A and 1928E $2 star USNs, which are actually substantially rarer. It is believed that 8000 $1 star notes were printed, and it seems that all of these were released in Puerto Rico late in 1948 or early in 1949. None were included in the large hoards of CU notes that later came to light. This note exists in a variety of conditions, but even VG-F examples now fetch at least $1500 each. The example in my collection is in XF condition, and it would be worth at least $5000 at the present time. There have been no sales of CU $1 USN stars in recent years, but I would expect that such an example would easily bring more than $10,000 in today's market.

I would recommend that you acquire one normal note from each of the two releases of this issue. Condition is no problem, since CU is the norm rather than the exception. In actual fact a well-centered XF note is probably more attractive than is a poorly centered CU note, but circulated notes are usually available only for the "Puerto Rico" releases of this note. You may also wish to acquire a star note of this issue, but these are high-priced rarities in all grades, and your budget for small-size notes may preclude the acquisition of this very scarce note.

The last deliveries of $2 and $5 USNs were made in 1967, and it was then decided to phase out both of these denominations of red seal notes. A logical measure would have been to repeal the 1878 act that required $346 million in USNs to be outstanding, but it seems that there is a great deal of inertia in monetary legislation where no major crisis is involved. Instead new $100 USNs were issued to replace the $2 and $5 notes that were being retired. A total of 768,000 Series 1966 $100 USNs were printed in 1968, and these were soon followed by 128,000 star notes of this same series and by 512,000 Series 1966A $100 notes. The last of these issues were delivered to the Treasury at the beginning of 1971. The notes were the first notes to bear the new Treasury seal and the last notes to have their seals and serial numbers printed in any color other than green.

A fair number of Series 1966 notes were released to the public, but the other two issues were mostly just held in the Treasury. Amazingly they were still counted as "currency in circulation" for many years. There was some debate as to what to do with these notes, but it was finally announced in 1996 that they had been destroyed. Thus USNs have now joined numerous other varieties of Federal paper money that are now termed "currency no longer being issued." Today only Federal Reserve Notes are counted as "currency in circulation."

The fact that the bulk of the $100 USNs have been destroyed has naturally increased the value of those notes in collectors' hands. Of the three varieties the Series 1966 regular note is by far the most common. CU examples now sell for about $350 to $400, but notes in XF condition carry only rather modest premiums over their face value. There are a fairly large number of these notes with very low serial numbers, and these sell at substantial premiums over the notes with higher serial numbers.

Until very recently the 1966 star and 1966A $100 USNs were selling for $700 or $800 each in CU condition and about half of this when in XF-AU condition. Auction sales for these items in CU condition at the beginning of 1998 were more like $1100 each. It seems that fewer 1966* and 1966A $100 USNs escaped destruction than had been previously assumed. Since only three notes are needed to complete this entire type, you may choose to get all three even if you don't plan to specialize in star notes.

SILVER CERTIFICATES

Small-size silver certificates were printed between 1928 and 1963. Three different denominations were issued, viz., $1, $5, and $10, and throughout this period almost all of the $1 notes in circulation were SCs. Although many of these notes are extremely common, there are also several major rarities among the notes of these issues.

One-dollar silver certificates were issued in 21 different series or major varieties excluding the experimental overprints and the wartime issues that were intended for use overseas. The notes of 1928 state that these notes were payable in silver dollars, but the issues of 1934, 1935, and 1957 state only that they are payable in silver. I shall consider this terminology further when discussing the $10 notes of these issues. The 1928 and 1934 $1 notes all have the so-called "old backs," but in 1935 the backs of all $1 notes were changed to the Great Seal design that is still in use today.

There are six different major varieties of the 1928 $1 SCs. These are the notes of Series 1928, 1928A, 1928B, 1928C, 1928D, and 1928E. The Series 1934 notes exist in only one major type, but there are numerous 1935 notes (Series 1935, 1935A, 1935B, 1935C, 1935D, 1935E, 1935F, 1935G, and 1935H). Both Series 1935D and 1935G exist with two different types of backs that are recognized as major varieties by collectors. The 1957 notes exist as Series 1957, 1957A, and 1957B. Of these notes Series 1928C and 1928D are decidedly scarce, while Series 1928E is rare. The other 18 varieties can be regarded as common, at least in their basic forms. The transition between micro and macro check numbers occurred between Series 1935 and 1935A, and both of these series exist in mule and non-mule form. All $1 SCs up through Series 1935C were printed in sheets of 12, but Series 1934D notes were printed both in sheets of this size and in sheets of 18. All notes of Series 1935E through 1935H used the latter format. All 1957 notes were printed in sheets of 32 subjects.

One-dollar silver certificates have become very popular with collectors, and even the most common of the notes with "old backs" are now selling for prices that are much higher than they were a few years ago, but the four most plentiful of these types (i. e., Series 1928, 1928A, 1928B, and 1934) are still readily available. Of these the 1928A notes are the most common, while the 1934 notes are the scarcest. At the present time notes of the former series sell for about $25 each when in CU condition, while those of the latter issue sell for about $45 each when in the same condition. In XF condition the cheapest "old back" ones sell for about $10 each, but the scarcer 1934 note only sells for about $15 in this condition.

Among these notes there are 12 regular blocks of Series 1928, 31 of Series 1928A, 15 of Series 1928B, and 7 blocks of Series 1934. Although all of the blocks of Series 1934 have about the same value, there are several serial number blocks that are scarce or rare for the earlier three series. Forming a complete set of all blocks of these notes would be a major undertaking.

In addition to these regular serial number blocks, there is also a special series of experimental blocks that were used on the Series 1928A and 1928B notes. In 1932 and 1933 an experiment was carried out by the BEP to test the wear characteristics of various compositions of paper. Notes were printed on paper with a 50% linen and 50% cotton rag content with the XB block, while another batch of notes on paper with a 75% linen and 25% cotton rag content were printed with the YB block. A third group of notes on the paper normally used was printed as a control using the ZB block. These notes could be easily distinguished, since the highest normal block used for any 1928 type notes was JB. About 10 million notes of each of these experimental blocks was printed, and these were more or less equally distributed among Series 1928A and 1928B notes. Despite all of these efforts the results of the experiments were inconclusive.

Collectors thus recognize six different varieties for the 1932-33 experimentals, and the XB, YB, and ZB blocks are more or less equally abundant for the Series 1928A and 1928B notes. A set of the three different blocks in CU condition sells for about $400 to $500, but VF-XF sets of three sell for prices of about $125 a set. In recent years there have been a number of the 1932-33 experimental sets with unusually low matched serial numbers that have come onto the market. Oddly enough all of these sets have been mixed as to series, i. e., one or two notes are of Series 1928A with the remaining note or notes of Series 1928B. These matched number sets of the 1932-33 experimentals, of course, sell at much higher prices (typically about $1500 per set of three) than do normal sets in CU with random serial numbers.

The $1 SCs of Series 1928C, 1928D, and 1928E were printed in much lower quantities than were the other earlier series of $1 silver notes. Although their respective mintages of 5.36 million, 14.45 million, and 3.52 million might seem fairly large, these must be weighed against a total of 4.296 billion notes for all of the 1928 and 1934 series. Thus only one note out of 801 in this grand total was a 1928C, one out of 297 was a 1928D, and one out of 1220 was a Series 1928E note. The 1928C note can be obtained for no more than $150 in XF condition, while a 1928D note in this grade still sells for less than $100. In CU condition, however, 1928D notes will probably cost about $250 while a CU 1928C note will cost more like $450. The 1928E note is much scarcer than either of these two notes. In VF condition this note will probably cost at least $300, but in choice CU it will cost more like $1500. Oddly enough several uncut sheets of this rarity have been recorded, and some of the notes presently on the market have been clipped from sheets that were originally sold intact.

The Series 1928E $1 SC is the rarest of the regularly issued $1 Silver Certificates. In 1934 an entirely new face design was introduced, but it was soon replaced by that of the Series 1935 notes. The Series 1928A $1 SC (YB block) is an experimental note that was printed late in 1932. The Series 1935 $1 SC (BB block) is from another experiment on paper characteristics that was conducted in 1937.

Despite the low productions for all three of these notes there are 9 normal blocks for the 1928C notes, 7 for the 1928D notes, and 5 for the 1928E notes. The reason that these notes exist in such a large array of serial number blocks is due to the fact that they were printed together with the much more common Series 1928A and 1928B notes. Many changeover pairs have been recorded for the various issues of 1928 $1 SCs. A changeover pair consists of two notes of different series but having adjacent serial numbers. Both "normal" and "reverse" changeover pairs exist. An example of the former would be a pair of 1928A / 1928B notes with the latter having the higher serial number, while the latter might be a 1928B / 1928A pair with again the latter note having the higher serial. Notes of these two series are among the most frequently encountered of the changeover pairs, and they typically sell for about $150 per pair when in CU condition, which is usually the case. Changeover pairs involving the three scarce series of $1 SCs are also known, but they are much scarcer than are the 1928A / 1928B pairs. It seems that the face plates of the various 1928 series were used fairly randomly, and so numerous changeover pairs were printed. The Series 1934 notes were treated as a different type by the BEP, and no changeover pairs involving this series are known. The scarcity of the three rare series can also be seen when we note that only 7, 49, and 10 face plates were used to print the Series 1928C, 1928D, and 1928E plates, respectively. The comparable figures for the face plates of the more common Series 1928, 1928A, 1928B, and 1934 notes were 1021, 1809, 566, and 838, respectively. Some of these numbers may be a bit high, since a few of the plates that were prepared may not have been used, but they do give some idea of how many plates were in use for each of these issues.

Most collectors recognize 14 major varieties of $1 SCs in the various 1935 and 1957 series. All of these are readily obtainable in normal form, and if you wish to obtain only one note of each of these types I would recommend that you acquire these notes in CU condition. Even then a complete set of these notes will probably only cost about $75 to $100. Such a classification takes into account the fact that Series 1935D notes exist both with wide and narrow backs, while Series 1935G notes exist both with and without the motto "In God We Trust."

If you wish to collect block and mule varieties of these notes, this simple situation becomes vastly more complicated. Both Series 1935 and 1935A notes exist in mule form, and these notes are significantly scarcer than are their non-mule counterparts. Series 1935A $1 SCs had a monumental printing of 6.11 billion notes, and this resulted in a total of 67 normal blocks for the non-mule notes and 18 normal blocks for the mule notes of this series. Very large printings were also recorded for the Series 1935D and 1935E $1 SCs, and these issues also exist in large numbers of different serial number blocks.

Although most serial number blocks of the Series 1935A notes are common, this is by no means true for all of them. The EB block of the 1935A mule variety is considered to be very rare, and the MA block of the non-mule variety of this issue is believed to be unique. If you decide to collect the serial number blocks of the $1 SCs, you will find it easy to acquire many of them, but you should forget about attempting to obtain a "complete" set of these notes. Although many of these notes will be obtainable in CU condition, you should be prepared to accept VF or XF notes when higher grades cannot be found. Many supposedly "common" notes will probably prove to be elusive. The best idea is probably to purchase an auction lot which contains a large number of different block varieties of these notes and then build from that beginning.

The Series 1935 $1 SCs contain three experimental blocks that were printed in 1937 to test once again different paper compositions and finishes. The blocks used were AB, BB, and CB, which are higher than any serials used for any normal Series 1935 notes, the last regular block of which ended with RA. There were 6,180,000 notes printed for the AB block, and 3,300,000 notes each for the BB and CB blocks. The results of the 1937 paper experiments again proved inconclusive. Although these notes were produced in smaller quantities than were the 1932-33 experimentals, the 1937 notes are comparable to the former series both in scarcity and in price. A nice CU set will probably cost about $400, while a VF-XF set will cost more like $150. The AB block is decidedly more common than are the BB and CB blocks, an a VF-XF example of this note should cost no more than $15. Notes in CU condition with very low serial numbers are known for this series, and surprisingly such notes are more frequently encountered for the BB and CB blocks than they are for the AB block.

These notes should not be confused with the two different types of Series 1935A notes that also were printed with the AB, BB, and CB blocks. These notes were printed in 1940, or about three years after the 1937 experimentals. The mule notes of Series 1935A having these blocks are fairly scarce, but the non-mule notes with these blocks are very common and thus are worth far less than are the Series 1935 experimentals.

The Series 1935D notes are a bit confusing, because these notes exist both with wide and narrow backs, and they were printed both with 12-subject and 18-subject plates. The wide back notes were printed only in sheets of 12, but the narrow back notes were printed with both types of plates. Both wide and narrow back plates were mixed freely in printing the Series 1935D notes in sheets of 12, and so changeover pairs are very numerous. Such pairs of these notes (either normal or reversed) can be easily obtained in CU condition for about $20 per pair.

Although most recent $1 silver certificate varieties are common, there is one rarity that is prized among specialist collectors. The Series 1935F note was regularly issued up to serial B54000000J, and thus the normal BJ block for this note is quite common. The Series 1935G note without motto then continued beginning with serial B54000001J, and so it is also very common in the BJ block. But in July, 1961 there was a small production run of 360,000 Series 1935F notes with serials between B71640001J and B72000000J. These were released with no publicity in New Orleans, and very few were saved. The B71J Series 1935F note is actually only a group variety, but it is avidly sought by block collectors of $1 silver certificates. Examples of this note usually fetch several hundred dollars each on the rare occasions when they are offered for sale.

The Series 1957 notes were printed on 32-subject plates that have quite different sheet position designations than do the Series 1935 notes, but otherwise they are of the same types as are their earlier counterparts. Although there are a few block rarities among the later issues of the 1935 notes, the 1957 issues are without any scarce notes. Putting together a complete block set of the 1957 notes will doubtless involve quite a bit of effort, but it should not involve much outlay of cash.

In my own collection of $1 silver certificates I have kept matters simple by obtaining only the 21 major varieties plus the 9 experimental blocks. Otherwise I have not attempted to collect these notes by serial number blocks. I have, however, also attempted to acquire one star note for each of the major varieties, and thus far I have obtained 19 of these including the rare Series 1928D star note. But block collecting may have its appeal, particularly if you have lots of time and patience but only relatively limited funds. Most of the serial number blocks of these notes are available at quite reasonable prices, but there are a large enough number of rarities to prevent you from ever obtaining a truly "complete" set. There is also a possibility, however, that you may be able to purchase a very rare note at a great bargain price. For instance, the UE block of the Series 1935D wide back note is very common, but this same block on a narrow back note is extremely rare. You just might be very lucky and obtain the latter rarity for the price of a common Series 1935D note. If you plan to engage in serial number block collecting, it is essential that you carefully study the Oakes and Schwartz catalog which gives all of the details on these varieties.

Thus far we have been speaking only of regular and experimental blocks for the $1 silver certificates. Many collectors, even if they do not collect block varieties, will want to obtain star notes for these popular issues. All 21 major varieties of the $1 SCs exist in star note form, and the scarcities of these notes more or less parallel the scarcities of the normal issues. The first five of the "common" $1 SCs (i. e., Series 1928, 1928A, 1928B, 1934, and 1935) are far from common as star notes, but they are not major rarities. The scarcest of these are the Series 1928B and 1934 notes, and these sell for at least $500 each in star form in today's market when in choice CU condition. The other three notes are less expensive, but they still should cost at least $175 to $250 each when in this grade. In XF condition these notes are considerably less expensive with prices ranging from about $40 for the Series 1935 note to about $100 for the Series 1934 star note. If you are willing to settle for only fine condition, the prices of these notes should range from about $15 to $25 each. The Series 1935 star note also exists in mule form, and this note is significantly rarer than is its non-mule counterpart.

As might be expected the Series 1928C, 1928D, and 1928E star notes are major rarities. Only about 15 examples each of the 1928C and 1928D notes are known in star form, and these sell for well over $1000 each in only fine condition. Sales of these notes in XF condition or better are infrequent, but the Dallas sale held in August, 1998 featured CU examples of each of these rarities. The 1928C note sold for $8250, while the 1928D star note in this sale realized $10,450. The Series 1928E star note is even rarer, as only about 8 or 9 examples are known, and one of these is badly damaged. An example of this note in CU condition was also offered in the Dallas sale. This note (probably unique in this grade) sold for $30,800, which is by far the highest price ever achieved for a small-size $1 note of any type.

The remaining 13 major varieties of $1 SC star notes are obtainable at much more reasonable prices. The scarcest of these is the Series 1935B star note, which sells for about $60 when in CU condition. The three 1957 star notes are all very common, and they sell for only a small premium over their non-star counterparts. If you wish to settle for only XF condition, then the Series 1935B star note should cost no more than $20, and several of the more common star notes should cost no more than about $3 each.

The $1 SC star notes are the only replacement notes for which various block varieties are possible. All other small-size star notes (other than FRNs and FRBNs) exist only in the block *A, but so many replacement $1 SCs were printed that blocks *B, *C, *D, *E, *F, and *G also exist for some series. The Series 1935A star note exists as a non-mule *A (the common variety), but it also exists as a *A mule and as a *B non-mule variety. Both of these are much scarcer than is the *A non-mule variety. Both the 1935D wide and the 1935D narrow notes exist in the *B and *C blocks, and for both notes the *C varieties are very much scarcer than are the *B notes. The Series 1935D replacement notes printed on 18-subject plates used the block *D, and these are also scarce. The replacement notes for Series 1935E through 1957B do not include any that are scarce, but there are a number of distinct block varieties.

So ends our discussion of small-size $1 silver certificates. These notes were printed in enormous quantities over a period of 35 years. Although many of these notes are very common, there are also several that are extremely rare. If you plan to collect small-size notes at all, you will certainly want to acquire several of these notes. A basic set of the 18 common normal issue notes can be easily obtained, and this is also true of these same notes in replacement form, provided one is willing to settle for grades of no higher than VF or XF for a few of the scarcer star notes. The three scarce series are fairly expensive in normal form, but they are still readily available. In replacement form, however, these three notes are major rarities. The $1 SCs are more amenable to block collecting than are any other series of small-size notes, but since there are so many varieties, much time and patience will be required. There are also a few extreme rarities here, as I have pointed out, and I doubt that a "complete" collection of all of these varieties has ever been formed.

Small-size $5 silver certificates were issued between 1934 and 1962. The notes printed with 12-subject plates are Series 1934, while those printed with 18-subject plates are Series 1953. These two types are quite different in their layouts, but both are very common. Almost all collectors will chose to collect these notes by series, and in that case there are eight major varieties, five for the 1934 notes (Series 1934, 1934A, 1934B, 1934C, and 1934D) and three for the 1953 notes (Series 1953, 1953A, and 1953B). If you plan only to obtain a set of these eight notes, I would suggest CU condition only. Even then this is a very easy task, and such a set should not cost you much more than $100.

If you decide to collect block and mule varieties, however, the $5 SCs do offer a few challenges. Mules exist for the Series 1934, 1934A, 1934B, and 1934C notes. The 1934A mule note is common enough, but the Series 1934 mule is decidedly rare. The 1934B and 1934C mules are also much scarcer than are their non-mule counterparts. The Series 1934D notes exist with both wide and narrow backs. The latter is less common than is the former, but a few specialists may also wish to consider the so-called wide II notes, which are scarcer than either the wide I or narrow back notes. There are far fewer block varieties for the $5 SCs than there are for the $1 notes and there are no great rarities among these for the $5 notes, but there are a few varieties that are definitely scarce. These include the KA and LA blocks of the Series 1934A mule notes and the MA block of the Series 1934B notes.

All eight of the major varieties of $5 SCs exist as star notes. Seven of these are readily available, but the Series 1953B star note is a major rarity. A total of 73 million normal notes and 3,240,000 star notes were printed for Series 1953B, but only 14,196,000 of these notes were issued. The normal notes were printed both in the FA and GA blocks, but only a portion of the FA notes were released and the GA notes are quite unknown to collectors. It appears that nearly all of the 1953B star notes were destroyed, but about 30 examples are presently known to collectors. All of these have been obtained from circulation, and their condition ranges from fine to XF. In late 1993 Stack's auctioned the important collection of small-size star notes formed by Dr. Bernard Schaaf. At that time this note in XF condition fetched only $690, but the price of this rarity has since escalated. The price for an XF note today is about $2000, and even in fine condition these notes now sell for something like $1000 each. The Dallas sale of 1998 also contained an example of this note in CU condition, a grade that had not previously been reported. It sold for $6875. I have recently acquired an XF example of this rarity at a fairly stiff price, but I admit that one must buy this note with some degree of trepidation. Since over three million of these notes were printed, there is always a chance that a hoard of them will appear on the market at some future date. Thus far, however, there is no evidence for such a hoard.

The other seven $5 SC star notes are obtainable at much lower prices. The 1934B star note is the scarcest of this group, and CU examples now sell for about $500 each. In XF condition, however, this note is much less expensive, and a nice example of this note should not cost much more than $75. The Series 1934 star note in XF should also cost about this much, but all of the others sell in the $10 to $30 range in XF condition. In CU condition their prices range from about $25 for the 1953A star note to about $200 for the Series 1934 replacement note. If you want to acquire a set of these seven star notes, I would suggest CU condition for the less expensive ones but VF, XF, or AU condition for the more elusive notes. The Series 1953B star is an entirely different matter, and if no further notes come onto the market, its present very high price will certainly hold.

For mule specialists there are also a few varieties for the $5 SC star notes. The Series 1934A, 1934B, and 1934C star notes all exist both in mule and non-mule form. The 1934C star mule is decidedly rare, and the 1934A star mule is definitely scarcer than its non-mule counterpart. For the 1934B star notes, however, the mule and non-mule varieties are about equally abundant. The Series 1934D star notes exist in wide and narrow varieties, the latter being rather the scarcer of the two. The so-called wide II variety is quite scarce in star form, but it my opinion this is an utterly trivial variant.

The Series 1953B $5 SCs were printed shortly before the removal of silver coins and certificates from circulation in the 1960s. Almost all examples of the star variety of this issue that were printed were subsequently destroyed.

The $5 silver certificates include one note that was printed but never issued. This was the Series 1953C $5 SC that displays the Granahan-Dillon signature combination. Numerous millions of these notes were printed in the GA, HA, and *A blocks in late 1963 and early 1964. At this time, however, the United States was undergoing an acute coin shortage, and silver certificates were being phased out. Soon these notes were to acquire a premium over their face value, since they continued to remain redeemable in silver at $1.293 per troy ounce until 1968. Consequently none of the Series 1953C $5 SCs were released, and almost all of them were destroyed. The BEP does display a canceled sheet of these notes at various numismatic shows, but no Series 1953C notes are known in private hands, and they would probably be ruled illegal to possess.

The Series 1933 $10 SC is a well-known rarity that arose because this note contained the ambiguous wording "in silver coin" rather than "in silver dollars" (as on Series 1928 notes) or "in silver" (as on Series 1934 and 1935 notes).

The small-size $10 silver certificates closely parallel the equivalent $5 notes, but there is one important exception. There is also a Series 1933 $10 SC, and this is probably the most famous of the small-size currency rarities. All large-size SCs and all Series 1928 $1 SCs state that these notes are payable in silver dollars to the bearer on demand. In 1934 the Silver Purchase Act was passed, and this obligated the government to purchase newly mined silver at a fixed price. It then began to stockpile large amounts of silver bullion, and in 1934 silver certificates were made payable "in silver" rather than "in silver dollars." The Series 1933 SCs are indicated as payable "in silver coin," and this created an ambiguity since silver dollars were coined at $1.29 per troy ounce whereas the subsidiary silver coins were minted at $1.38 per ounce. At the beginning of 1934 216,000 Series 1933 $10 silver certificates bearing the Julian-Woodin signature combination were printed and delivered. These were followed subsequently by 336,000 Series 1933A SCs with the Julian-Morganthau signature combination. In late 1935 government records indicate that 368,000 of these notes were destroyed, but the true number was clearly greater than this since no Series 1933A notes ever reached circulation, and most of the Series 1933 notes were destroyed as well.

The Series 1933 $10 note is a type rarity as well as a series rarity, since it differs radically in design from the other $10 SCs. Until 1996 only about 60 of these notes were known to be in collectors' hands, but in that year at least 20 more came onto the market. Many of these were from a collection of paper money formed by John and Opal Morris.

Although more Series 1933 notes were sold in 1996 than had been sold in the previous two decades, this note does remain a rarity. It is now believed that there are between 90 and 100 of these notes in existence. They show a peculiar distribution with respect to condition. They are more abundant in uncirculated than in circulated grades, but the majority of the CU notes have a very poor bottom trim which sometimes extends into the design. The notes which saw actual circulation tend to be better centered. The sudden appearance of so many of these rarities on the market within a few months did drop their prices a bit in 1996-97, but nicely centered CU notes have until very recently been selling in auctions with some consistency for about $8800 each. Until the summer of 1998 they had not broken the $10,000 barrier, but the Dallas auction held by Lyn Knight in August of that year included a perfectly centered CU example with serial number 27. It sold for $18,700, which is a record for a non-star small-size note of any type with a face value under $5000. A few notes of this issue are seen in well-worn condition, but these bring at least $1500 each when they come up for sale. Notes in XF condition or CU notes with a poor cut typically have been selling for about $3000 to $4000 when they come up at auction, but in view of the record high quoted above these prices are probably now obsolete. The Series 1933 $10 silver certificate is the only major type note that is a rarity among the small-size notes of the $1 to $100 denominations.

Much rarer than a normal Series 1933 $10 note is the unique star note of this series. The serial number of this great rarity is *00000002A, and the note is in XF condition. It sold for $29,700 when the Schaaf collection was auctioned in 1993. It is tied for rarity with another unique star note that I shall discuss in the section of this chapter on World War II issues.

No Series 1933A $10 notes are believed to have survived in issued form, but the BEP does have a canceled sheet of these notes that it sometimes exhibits. If an issued note of this series should turn up outside of government channels, it should be perfectly legal to hold since government records indicate that not all of these notes were destroyed. But it clearly does appear that all of these notes were destroyed, since no issued notes of this series have ever come to light.

Another decidedly scarce small-size silver certificate is the Series 1934B $10 star note that was printed in limited quantities in 1946.

The other eight series of $10 silver certificates are much easier to acquire. The 1934 type notes exist as Series 1934, 1934A, 1934B, 1934C, and 1934D, while the 1953 type notes exist as Series 1953, 1953A, and 1953B. Ten-dollar SCs were printed in far smaller numbers than were their $5 counterparts, and among these notes there are a couple that are difficult to acquire in choice condition. By far the most difficult is the Series 1934B note. This note is very scarce in CU condition, and truly uncirculated examples now sell for more than $1000 each. If you insist on getting all of your notes in CU condition expect to spend big bucks here, but this note is much more readily available in XF condition and should cost no more than $150 in this grade. The second most difficult note of these issues is the Series 1953A note, which sells for about $175 in CU. This note is rarely found in grades lower than XF-AU, and so you will find that you will probably have to spend almost $100 on an example of this note even if you like modern notes that show signs of substantial circulation.

The $10 SCs exist as mules only for the Series 1934 and 1934A issues. The Series 1934 mule is about as common as is its non-mule counterpart, but the 1934A is significantly scarcer in mule form. The Series 1934D note exists with wide and narrow backs, the latter being much the scarcer of the two. The BA blocks for the Series 1934 mule and Series 1934A notes are significantly scarcer than are the AA blocks for either of these issues, but neither variety is rare.

Only seven of the 1934 and 1953 $10 SCs exist as star notes, since the Series 1953B $10 star note was never printed. By far the scarcest of these is the Series 1934B star note, which is a rarity that is perhaps unique in CU condition. In only fine condition examples of this note sell for about $600 each. The Dallas auction of 1998 included an XF-AU 1934B star note and an example in gem CU condition. The former sold for $2200, while the latter brought $13,200. Although this note does appear to be somewhat less rare in circulated grades than does the Series 1953B $5 star, it is still a very difficult replacement note to acquire. The other $10 SC star notes are also fairly difficult to acquire in choice condition. The most abundant are the Series 1934C and 1953 notes, which sell for about $250 each in CU condition. In XF condition, however, these replacement notes cost more like $50 or $60 each. The Series 1953A star notes in CU condition sell for about $500 each. In earlier years they sold for little more than their non-star counterparts, but this series is now recognized as one of the hardest to find in replacement form. The Series 1934 star note exists both in mule and non-mule format, and both of these have about the same value. They are decidedly scarce and are worth at least $750 each in CU condition, but they should be available in XF condition for only about $150 each. The Series 1934D $10 SC is very scarce in replacement form, and I encountered more difficulty in acquiring one of these than I did for the more highly touted Series 1934B star note. A CU example would fetch at least $900, and even an XF example is probably worth $300 or so. These notes exist with both wide and narrow backs, but the latter variety is extremely rare in star form.

GOLD CERTIFICATES

Small-size gold certificates were issued for general circulation only in Series 1928. These bear the signatures of Woods and Mellon, and their Treasury seals and serial numbers are orange-yellow in color. The backs of these notes, however, are green rather than the bright orange color that was used on nearly all large-size gold notes. Most collectors concentrate on the four lower denominations, i. e., $10, $20, $50, and $100. These notes are available in a wide variety of conditions, and in fine condition only they can be obtained for roughly two or thee time face value. In choice CU condition, however, fifteen to twenty times face value is much closer to the truth. Attractive notes of this series in VF or XF condition are also available at prices that are more like five to ten times face value, but in these grades the price difference between a $10 note and a $20 note would be fairly small.

Series 1928 gold certificates were only in use from the summer of 1929 to the spring of 1933 when they were hastily removed from circulation. Among the more interesting of the collectible notes of this series are the $10 note from the BA block, the $100 star note, and the $500 and $1000 notes. The large blank area on the right side of the Series 1928 $1000 gold certificate was filled in with engraved numerals on the Series 1934 notes of this denomination that were never issued to the public.

There is one block variety that deserves special mention. The $10 gold note exists both in the AA and BA blocks. The latter is much scarcer than is the former, since many notes of this block were not put into circulation prior to 1933. In the spring of that year all gold certificates were withdrawn from circulation, and this action would have particularly affected the later printings of these notes, many of which were still in storage at the Treasury. I have this note in both the AA and BA blocks, but this is one of the relatively few block varieties that I have included in my collection.

Star notes exist for all four of the lower denominations of gold certificates. The $10 and $20 star notes are definitely uncommon, while the $50 and $100 replacements can be regarded as rarities. Previously it was thought that the $50 note in star form was rarer than its $100 counterpart, but it now seems that these two varieties are more or less equally scarce. Even in VF condition these two replacement notes should cost at least $2000 - 2500 each. In January, 1998 a CU example of the $50 gold note in star form sold for $6050, but this realization was topped by one of $12,100 for a $100 note in gem CU condition that was achieved at the Dallas sale held in August of that year. In my opinion this difference in realizations is more indicative of a rapidly rising market in these notes than in any significant difference in rarity between the $50 and $100 gold certificates in replacement form. The $10 and $20 gold notes in star form also have very nearly the same degree of rarity. In XF condition they should probably cost about $500 or $600 each, and in CU they would now sell for more than $1500 each when available. Although there are only four notes in this set, obtaining a complete set of gold certificate star notes even in well circulated grades is not at all an easy task.

In addition to the four lower denominations gold certificates were also issued in high denominations - 420,000 $500, 288,000 $1000, 24,000 $5000, and 48,000 $10,000 notes being printed for these denominations in Series 1928. The $500 and $1000 gold notes are rarities, but they are collectible for individuals with fairly adequate bankrolls. In CU condition both of these denominations are now selling for well over $10,000 each. In XF condition the $500 note should cost about $5000, while the $1000 note in this grade would probably sell for about $8000 or so. The $500 and $1000 gold notes in my collection are in XF and in XF-AU condition, respectively, but I obtained them several years ago when prices were much lower on these rarities than they are today. These notes also exist in fine condition, and in that grade one might expect to pay about $2000 for a $500 note and about $3500 for a $1000 note. It is difficult to make a good estimate of the numbers of these notes that are in existence today, but my guess would be that there are about 75 to 100 examples each of the small-size $500 and $1000 gold notes in all grades. No star notes exist for either of these denominations.

Although $5000 and $10,000 gold notes were issued in some quantity in Series 1928, it seems likely that none of these notes in private hands survived the forced redemptions of gold certificates that were required between 1934 and 1964. There certainly would have been little point in holding on to them at a time when they bore no interest and were subject to forced redemption if knowledge of their whereabouts reached certain government authorities. To my knowledge no Series 1928 $5000 or $10,000 gold certificates are known to be in private collections. Today they would be quite legal to possess, and such items undoubtedly would fetch very high prices if offered for sale. Hessler's catalog does provide color illustrations of these two notes, both of which have serial number 1, but these items are in government archives and not in private collections.

Also printed but apparently never issued were 2,544,000 $10 and 1,500,000 $20 gold notes of Series 1928A which bore the signatures of Woods and Mills. Although these notes were intended for general circulation, it seems that none were released prior to the ban on the circulation of gold coins and certificates that was proclaimed in 1933. It is sometimes stated that these notes are being held in storage for reserve purposes at the Treasury, but that is highly unlikely. These notes, like all Series 1882 through 1928 gold certificates, state that they are payable in gold coin to the bearer on demand. This would imply that they would be redeemed at the $20.67 per troy ounce rate at which gold coins were minted rather than the $35.00 rate that was established in 1934. Series 1934 gold certificates have entirely different obligations. It seems most likely that all examples of the Series 1928A gold notes were destroyed along with almost all of the earlier gold certificates that were returned to the government in the 1930s. If any were released prior to January, 1934 they would be legal to possess according to present statutes, but it seems much more likely that none were released and all were destroyed. The BEP does not own any sample sheets of these notes like those of various other unissued notes that it often displays at numismatic shows.

Thus small-size gold certificates fall into various categories. The regular $10 through $100 notes of Series 1928 are readily collectible and affordable for most collectors. The $500 and $1000 notes of this series as well as the replacement notes of the four lower denominations are also collectible, but they are rare and expensive. The $5000 and $10,000 notes are unknown outside of government archives because apparently they were all turned in and subsequently almost all were destroyed, and the Series 1928A $10 and $20 notes are also unknown because they were never issued and apparently were all destroyed. We now come to a fourth category of small-size gold notes, viz., the Series 1934 gold certificates.

Series 1934 gold certificates were a very special issue of notes that were intended exclusively for circulation within the Federal Reserve System. They are inscribed "payable in gold on demand to the bearer as authorized by law." All previously issued circulating gold certificates were "payable in gold coin to the bearer on demand." Thus only a person authorized by law (i. e., an agent of the Federal Reserve System or the Treasury Department) could use one of these notes, and they were payable in gold (at $35.00 per troy ounce) and not in gold coin (at $20.67 per troy ounce). These notes all have bright orange backs unlike any other issues of small-size notes. All bear the signatures of Julian and Morganthau, and all were printed in 1934 or 1935. The $100,000 note depicts Woodrow Wilson on its face, and this is the only series of Federal paper money that included a note of this denomination.

There were a total of 120,000 $100 notes, 84,000 $1000 notes, 36,000 $10,000 notes, and 42,000 $100,000 notes in this issue, and thus the total face value of these notes was $4.656 billion. Since Federal Reserve Banks needed to keep a gold cover that was not less than 40% of the amount of Federal Reserve Notes that were outstanding, these notes would have been quite adequate to cover all of the FRNs in circulation in the 1930s. By 1945 the amount of FRNs in circulation had increased substantially, but in that year the minimum gold cover was dropped to 25% of the amount of FRNs outstanding. The 1934 gold notes would then have been able to legally cover all FRNs outstanding until well into the 1950s.

The Series 1934 gold certificates apparently were never used to settle gold balances with foreign customers, for then some of them would have gone into outside channels. It seems that all such balances were handled with physical gold. Apparently these notes were held exclusively within the Federal Reserve System for as much as 20 years or even more, but then what happened to them? Most likely nearly all of them were destroyed. The BEP does have a set of unissued specimen sheets of these notes which it displays at various numismatic shows, and Hessler's catalog does provide color illustrations of the three higher denominations of this set (all with serial number 1). These notes, of course, are in government archives, and it is unclear how many additional normal Series 1934 gold certificates are presently in existence. In any case all such notes, whether issued or unissued, are regarded as government property, and they are most definitely not legal to collect under present regulations.

WORLD WAR II ISSUES

Between 1942 and 1944 there were three distinct issues of experimental and emergency notes, and these are generally lumped together by most currency collectors. In June, 1944 the third and final issue of experimental notes was printed. These notes differ radically from the experimental blocks of 1932-33 and 1937, since they have overprints and thus are distinctive types for currency collectors. The 1944 experimental notes are Series 1935A $1 SCs that have been overprinted "R" or "S" in red on their faces. These letters stand for "regular" and "special" papers, respectively. All of the regular notes are from the SC block of the Series 1935A notes. The "R" notes have serials S70884001C through S72068000C, while the "S" notes have serials S73884001C through S75068000C. Thus 1,184,000 normal notes were printed for each variety. There were also 12,000 star notes printed for each of these types. The exact ranges for their serial numbers are not known, but all have serials *911x - - - - A, and the digit that I have denoted by the letter x is always either 7, 8, or 9. In former years a number of fraudulent alterations of these notes were made by overprinting other blocks of the far more common Series 1935A notes with fake red letters, and so when purchasing these notes make sure that their serial numbers are in the correct ranges. There is an interesting group variety for normal Series 1935A notes. The serial numbers S72068001C through S73884000C lie between those used for the "R: and "S" overprinted notes. Although this group variety is not as well publicized as the aforementioned B71J variety for the Series 1935F $1 SCs, notes with these serial numbers command substantial premiums over their normal counterparts. The 1944 experimental notes are far scarcer than are most varieties of normal Series 1935A $1 notes. As for the experiment itself, once again the results were inconclusive. Although the BEP has changed paper compositions several times since 1944, it no longer issues special series of notes to test wear characteristics.

The regular "R" and "S" notes are readily available in a wide range of grades. If you are satisfied with notes in F-VF condition, these notes will cost about $40 a pair. A pair in XF condition will probably set you back about $100, and CU notes with average centering now sell for about $200 to $250 per pair. Gem CU notes, however, now fetch as much as $350 or $400 per pair. I am quoting these prices as pairs, because that is the way in which I would suggest that you acquire these notes.

Among the most interesting currency issues of 1944 are the "R" and "S" experimental notes that were yet another attempt to test the characteristics of two different compositions of paper. All of the regular notes of these types are from the SC block of Series 1935A, while the serial numbers of the rare star notes always commence with 911. Only 12,000 replacement notes for each of these varieties were printed.

Star notes of the 1944 experimentals are very much rarer. Furthermore they show an unusual range of grades. Normally these notes are available in VG-F, and in this condition a pair of these notes should fetch about $750. A number of CU pairs have also been sold in recent years, and prior to 1998 they sold for about $3500 to $4000 per pair. In February, 1998, however, a gem CU pair of these notes fetched the unprecedented price of $9350 in a Lyn Knight auction. A realization almost this high ($8250) was achieved in the Dallas sale held in August of the same year. For several years I tried to acquire a pair of these notes in VF-XF condition, but I have come to the conclusion that these notes are either nonexistent or else excessively rare in either VF-XF or XF-AU condition. I finally splurged and purchased an uncirculated pair for my collection, but at a price far less than what were realized in 1998. Clearly the 1944 experimental star notes are rare in all grades. Among the small-size $1 star notes they are exceeded in rarity and in price only by the Series 1928 USN, and by the SCs of Series 1928C, 1928D, and 1928E.

The Hawaii and North Africa notes are among the most distinctive of all the issues of small-size currency. Depicted above are the scarce FC block of a $1 Hawaii note that saw limited circulation in the mainland United States, and the back of a $5 Hawaii note.

The Hawaii notes were first delivered in June, 1942, and printing continued on these notes until July of 1944. The $1 notes are SCs, and the $5, $10, and $20 notes are FRNs on San Francisco. All of these notes have brown seals and black overprints on their faces. On their backs the word "HAWAII" appears as an overprint in large black capital letters. There are six different major varieties of these issues, since the $5 and $20 notes were printed in both Series 1934 and 1934A. All of the $1 notes are Series 1935A, and all of the $10 notes are Series 1934A. These notes were issued for both civilian and military use in Hawaii, and between 1942 and 1944 they were the only notes authorized for use in that territory. They were also used by military personnel further west in the Pacific Theater. Had the Japanese invaded Hawaii or had large numbers of these notes fallen into Japanese hands in the war zone, they could have been repudiated. Neither contingency occurred, and the Hawaii notes remain valid currency today.

All of the Hawaii notes are easy to obtain in F-VF condition, and in XF condition you should expect to pay about $20 for a $1 note, about $40 to $50 for the $5 and $10 notes, and about $75 to $100 for the $20 notes. The Series 1934 $5 and $20 notes are somewhat scarcer than their Series 1934A counterparts, but the price differences between these series are not very large. In CU condition most Hawaii notes have become expensive. The $1 notes in this grade cost only about $50 each, but the $5 and $10 Hawaii notes now sell for at least $200 each when in CU condition. The $20 notes are significantly more expensive, and a choice CU Series 1934 $20 note will probably cost at least $800 in today's market with the Series 1934A note selling at about half this price.

There are a number of block and mule varieties of the Hawaii notes, and some collectors are interested in these. The $1 Hawaii note exists in 8 different regular blocks - YB, ZB, AC, CC, FC, LC, PC, and SC. The FC was a special issue about which I shall have more to say in this section. The ZB and AC blocks are the scarcest of the normally issued blocks, and they sell for large premiums over the five more common blocks. All Series 1934A $5 and $10 Hawaii notes are non-mules, but the Series 1934 $5 note and both $20 Hawaii notes exists both in mule and non-mule format. For the 1934 $5 notes the mule variety is somewhat more common than is its non-mule counterpart. For the Series 1934 $20 notes the non-mule variety is very much rarer than is its mule counterpart, but for the 1934A $20 it is the non-mule note that is the more readily available.

Star notes were issued for all six major varieties of Hawaii notes, but assembling a complete set of these would be a most difficult task. The numbers of star notes printed for the $1, $5, $10, and $20 denominations were 204,000, 80,000, 68,000, and 52,000, respectively. These compare with the total printings for the non-star notes of 35.0, 9.42, 10.42, and 11.25 million examples, respectively. One-dollar Hawaii star notes are available in all grades, but the majority seem to be either CU or at least at the higher end of the circulated grades. In VF condition this note should cost about $150, but uncirculated notes now sell for $750 or so. The higher denomination Hawaii star notes are all very rare in CU condition, and I question whether either of the $20 replacement notes are even known in this grade. The Series 1934 $5 star note exists both in mule and non-mule varieties, as does the Series 1934A $20 replacement note. For the 1934 $5 note, the mule variety is the less rare of the two. The two varieties of the Series 1934A $20 replacement notes appear to be of comparable rarity, but both are decidedly scarce, as is the Series 1934 $20 Hawaii star note that exists in mule form only.

The greatest rarity among the Hawaii star notes is the Series 1934A $5 note. At the present time only some five examples of this rarity have been recorded. An XF example of this note appeared in the Schaaf collection which was sold in 1993. At that time this note brought $3575, but this note, if resold today, would certainly sell at a much higher price, since it is by far the finest known of this very rare item. Another example of this note in F-VF condition was sold on two separate occasions at auction during 1997. On average the price realized for this item was about $4000. In the Dallas auction of 1998 a newly uncovered 1934A $5 Hawaii star note in XF-AU condition sold for $7425.

It seems that the true rarity of most Hawaii star notes has been realized only in the last few years. At the Schaaf auction in 1993 I purchased a Series 1934 $5 mule star in XF for $330, but I just missed getting the $10 star note in XF-AU, which sold for $440. Both of these prices would be regarded as super-bargains by today's standards. At an auction run by R. M. Smythe in 1997 a 1934 $5 mule star in CU brought $2970, while a $10 star note, also in CU condition, sold for $7425. This auction also featured a Series 1934 non-mule $5 star in CU condition, and this note sold for $6050. The Dallas sale held in August, 1998 included Series 1934 $5 mule star and a non-mule star of the same series. Both of these notes were CU, and they sold for $3520 and $4180, respectively. This sale also had a gem CU example of the $10 Hawaii star note, and this item fetched $7150. If you want to assemble a set of Hawaii star notes, only the $1 note will prove fairly easy to obtain. The Series 1934A $5 star note is essentially noncollectible, and the other varieties definitely are rarities when in the higher grades.

This is the rare Series 1934 $10 North Africa note.

The third special issue of U. S. currency during World War II were the $1, $5, and $10 silver certificates that were issued for use in the European Theater. These were first used in North Africa, and so they are almost always referred to as the North Africa notes. They lack any special overprints, but the Treasury seals on these notes are lemon yellow in color rather than blue. Their serial numbers, however, are blue. Had large numbers of these notes fallen into Axis hands, they could also have been repudiated, and since they are very different in appearance from the Hawaii notes, the demonetization of one series would not have necessitated the demonetization of the other. The $1 notes are Series 1935A, and the normal issues of the $5 and $10 notes are Series 1934A. There was, however, a very limited printing of the $10 notes in Series 1934, and these notes are one of the classic rarities of small-size currency.

A basic type set of the North Africa notes consists of the $1 and $5 notes plus a Series 1934A $10 note. These are readily available in all grades. In uncirculated condition this set might set you back $300, but in choice AU it should cost not much more than $100. The $5 and $10 notes of this series in grades less than VF are little more than face value items, and any serious collectors of small-size currency should be able to afford better grade notes for these types. The $1 North Africa note exists in four serial number blocks that are common (BC, CC, IC, and RC) plus the scarce FC block. All series 1934A $5 and $10 notes are non-mules, and the $5 note exists only in the KA block while the $10 note exists in the AA and BA blocks, which are of equal abundance.

Star notes for the North Africa issue are much less of a problem for the collector than they are for the Hawaii notes. For the $1, $5, and $10 denominations there were total printings of 144,000, 100,000, and 276,000 star notes, respectively. These can be compared with total printings for the non-star $1, $5, and $10 notes of 26.9, 16.96, and 21.0 million examples, respectively. The $1 star note is probably the most difficult of this trio to acquire, and its value and range of available conditions is similar to that of the $1 Hawaii star note, although $1 North Africa stars are now selling for rather more these days than are their Hawaii counterparts. The $5 and $10 notes are substantially more common in replacement form, although they are still rather expensive when in CU condition. In VF condition, however, these replacement notes should cost little more than $75 to $100 each. These two notes are by far the most common of the World War II star notes.

Although the North Africa issue presents no problems for type collectors, most small-size currency specialists also collect these notes by series, and then for the North Africa issues there is one major rarity, viz., the Series 1934 $10 note. Apparently a few 1934 plates were used by accident among the large number of 1934A plates that were used for printing the faces of these notes. Series 1934 $10 North Africa Notes are always mules, and the face plates 116, 122-23, and 125-27 are known for this issue. Despite its rarity this note is known in both the AA and BA blocks.

At the present time the total number of these rarities known to collectors is about 60 or 70, and about a dozen of these are uncirculated. This note shows a fairly wide range of grades, but it does not have the centering problems that plague many of the Series 1933 $10 SCs. A nice XF example should cost about $3000, and a note in only VG-F condition will still probably fetch at least $1000. Uncirculated examples of this note are considerably rarer than they are for the Series 1933 $10 SC. A new price record for this note was set at the Dallas sale in August, 1998, where a gem CU example of this rarity sold for $16,500. A similar note, however, fetched only $9900 at a CAA auction held in St. Louis in October of the same year. There are a few fakes of this note on which someone has scraped off the "A" from a common Series 1934A note, but Series 1934 notes are always mules, while Series 1934A notes are always non-mules. Also the face check numbers on the 1934 notes are known, and these I have given above.

Even rarer than a normal Series 1934 $10 North Africa note is the unique star note of this issue. Its serial number is *01022388A, and its condition is F-VF. This note is in private hands, but it has not been on the market for many years. It can only be compared with the equally rare Series 1933 $10 star note. These two great rarities should be united in the same collection, and in May, 1999 I learned from an informed source that the unique 1933 $10 silver certificate star note and the equally rare 1934 $10 North Africa star have indeed by united in the same collection. It may be decades before these two ultra-rarities appear again on the open market, but I feel that they do belong together. Even very advanced collectors of small-size star notes will basically have to forget about owning this pair of notes.

In closing out this discussion of the World War II issues I should mention the FC blocks of the $1 Hawaii and North Africa notes. This was a special printing of these notes that was made in 1943. Almost all of the FC block was used for printing normal Series 1935A $1 SCs, but 12,000 examples of each of these wartime issues were printed in adjacent groups in the middle of this block. Thus the serial numbers of the two special varieties always differ by less than 24,000, the Hawaii notes having the higher serial numbers of the two. All of the complete sheets of these notes are from the FC block, but only 25 sheets were printed for each issue and this would account for only 300 each of these notes.

What happened to the other 11,700 examples of each issue? If they had been sent overseas for normal circulation, the FC varieties of these notes would be extreme rarities, since their printings are far less than they are for the star notes or any other blocks of these series. Although these notes are decidedly scarce, they are not extreme rarities. Thus it is obvious that they were not shipped abroad, but instead were distributed domestically in some special fashion. During the war years there was doubtless some talk of the "funny money" that our soldiers were using abroad, but hardly anyone saw any of it in the continental USA since it did not circulate there. It is my feeling that the FC block notes were printed as samples for distribution to persons interested in what this "funny money" looked like. This would also explain why the survival rate for these notes is fairly high.

Although I am not a block collector, I have included one of each of these special notes in my collection. Nice CU examples now sell for about $400 each. Notes in XF condition would sell for more like $150 each, but I imagine that notes in heavily circulated grades are quite uncommon, as these notes were clearly not intended for general circulation. Centering can be a problem on the FC $1 North Africa notes, since many of them are poorly cut.

The Hawaii and North Africa notes can be thought of as the predecessors of the Military Payment Certificates. Like the MPCs they were intended exclusively for circulation abroad or at least for remote territories of the USA. Unlike the MPCs, however, the wartime notes were never invalidated and they still remain good money to this day. Since they remained valid currency in all locations, the control that could be exercised on their circulation was less tight than what could be exercised on the MPCs that were issued in the postwar years.

FEDERAL RESERVE BANK NOTES

The FRBNs of Series 1929 are another example of emergency paper money. They were hastily printed in March, 1933 at the time of the banking crisis of that year. These notes were backed by government securities, and they did not require the 40% gold cover that was required for Federal Reserve Notes at that time. These notes were printed on plates that were modified from the plates used to print national bank notes. In addition to the government Jones-Woods signature combination they also carry the facsimile signatures of two officers of the Federal Reserve Bank in question. These signatures are usually those of the governor and cashier of that bank, but the New York, Chicago, and St. Louis used different combinations of bank officers. The Treasury seals are brown in color, as are those on all small-size NBNs, but the seals are slightly larger on the FRBNs than they are on national bank notes.

These FRBNs were issued in denominations of $5, $10, $20, $50, and $100. All 12 districts issued $10 and $20 FRBNs, and all districts other than Richmond issued $5 notes. The $50 and $100 FRBNs were issued by seven banks each, and of these New York, Cleveland, Chicago, Minneapolis, Kansas City, and Dallas are common to both denominations. In addition $50 notes were issued by San Francisco, and $100 notes were issued by Richmond. Thus a complete set of small-size FRBNs by denominations and districts consists of 49 different notes.

Fairly large numbers of some of these FRBNs have been preserved in choice condition, and it is a very easy matter to complete a set of the five denominations for which these notes were issued. It is also not difficult to obtain a note from each district. If you wish to try this for a single denomination, the $20 notes are by far the easier to complete of the two denominations that were issued from all 12 districts. Getting a complete set of all 49 notes, however, is very much more difficult. The $20, $50, and $100 notes are relatively easy to complete in this fashion, but this issue does include two very scarce notes (the $5 St. Louis and the $10 Dallas) and one note that is acknowledged to be a rarity (the $5 San Francisco).

The Series 1929 FRBNs were produced under emergency circumstances in March, 1933. Depicted above are normal $5 and $50 notes from Dallas and San Francisco, respectively, and a $100 replacement note from Kansas City.

The survival rates for these notes vary widely from issue to issue, and thus the numbers printed are not necessarily a good guide as to the present availability of a given issue. The smallest printing (36,000 examples) is that of the $100 notes from Dallas, and at one time these notes were thought to be rare, but a fair number of them turned up in the estate of Amon Carter Jr., who died in 1982. The $5 San Francisco note, however, is far rarer than its printing of 360,000 would indicate, and no strictly CU examples of this note are known at present. On the other hand, some of these notes are so common that they have no premium value when in only fine condition. This would include the $50 and $100 notes from the New York, Cleveland, and Chicago districts, and several districts of the $20 FRBNs. I have turned in a number of such notes at banks, and you should not really consider holding a common higher denomination FRBN in only fine condition when an XF-AU note of the same type is available at only 50-75% over its face value.

Several of these notes are now becoming quite scarce in CU condition, but few will pose much challenge in VF or XF condition except for the three notes that I have mentioned above. If you are planning only a denomination set, I would recommend getting all of the FRBNs in CU, but if you are planning to get a complete set of all 49 possibilities, then I feel that you should consider getting several of these in VF, XF, or AU grades, The $5 St. Louis and the $10 Dallas note are about equally scarce, and in F-VF condition they sell for about $125 each. In XF condition, however, they would easily cost three to four times this amount. Both of these notes are rare in CU, and several other notes of this series are also very uncommon in that grade. In my opinion there is not much point in trying to assemble all possible notes of this issue in CU condition, since the $5 San Francisco notes is presently unknown in that grade. This note is rarely available in better than fine condition, but I was able to obtain a nice VF example at auction several years ago. In VG-F this note can sometimes be obtained for about $250, but in a full VF grade it can easily sell for more than $750 in today's market.

Since the Series 1929 FRBNs were hastily printed under emergency conditions, it is surprising how little spoilage there seems to have been for this issue. As a result, only relatively few star notes were released. It appears that all 49 possible varieties were initially printed as star notes in editions that ranged from 4000 to 84,000 notes each, but these were then inserted into the regular packs of notes only when needed to replace spoiled notes. At the present time all possibilities except for the $5 notes from St. Louis and San Francisco and the $50 and $100 notes from Dallas are recorded as existing in star form. Several of these are either unique or excessively rare, however, and thus it is not really possible to complete a set of all 45 known replacement Series 1929 FRBNs. No FRBN star notes can be regarded as common, since the total number of these notes recorded for all denominations and districts is only about 300.

If you plan to collect star notes for the Series 1929 FRBNs, I would suggest that you limit yourself to one note only of each denomination. Amazingly there is not much spread in price for the star notes from the $5 through the $100 denominations. Kansas City is the only district that is normally available for the $100 notes in star form, but these are often found in choice condition. For the $50 notes New York is by far the most available of the "star" districts, while for the $5 notes the least scarce district is Chicago. For the $10 and $20 notes a somewhat larger array of possibilities exists. In high grades Kansas City is again the district most often encountered for the $10 and $20 notes, but for star notes in only fine or VF condition New York seems to be the district most often obtainable. Expect to pay at least $200 or $250 for a $5 through $50 replacement FRBN from the most common district in VF condition. These notes are hardly ever available in CU condition, and when they do come up for sale prices approaching $1000 are to be expected for even the most available of the replacement FRBNs. A few years ago there was a small "mini-hoard" of $100 star notes from Kansas City on the market. They have long since been dispersed, but you should expect to pay at least $750 each for one of this notes in AU condition. Kansas City is probably the only district for which it is possible to assemble a denomination set of FRBN star notes in high grade (XF or better), but this will most definitely not be an easy job.

Since it is essentially impossible for anyone to collect all 45 known varieties of replacement FRBNs and since the total supply of all of these notes totals only about 300 examples, I feel that all serious collectors of these notes should confine their interests to acquiring only one FRBN star note per denomination. This can also be seen as a courtesy toward your fellow collectors. If several collectors attempt at the same time to obtain many more star notes than this, far fewer notes will be left remaining in what is already a decidedly small pool of these varieties.

NATIONAL BANK NOTES

Small-size national bank notes in Series 1929 were issued between the summer of 1929 and the summer of 1935. These notes were issued in denominations of $5, $10, $20, $50, and $100, and all bear the government signatures of Jones and Woods. The Treasury seals and serial numbers are always printed in brown, but there are two distinct types of these issues. In the first type (issued between 1929 and 1933) the charter number of the bank in question appears only in black and the notes of each sheet bear the same serial number but each with a different prefix ranging from A through F. Type 2 notes were issued between 1933 and 1935, and these have the charter number of the bank repeated in brown ink with each note having its own serial number. For type 1 notes the suffix letter is almost always A, while for type 2 notes there is no suffix letter and the prefix letter is almost always A. Both varieties carry the facsimile signatures of two of the bank's officers. These were usually the president and cashier of the bank in question, but there are some interesting variations from this norm. Type 2 notes were issued in substantially smaller numbers than were type 1 notes, but large numbers of both varieties are still available.

In 1990 I published an article in the June issue of the *Bank Note Reporter* in which I examined the numbers of possible varieties of small-size NBNs that were actually issued. Subsequently I have detected a few minor modifications that are needed for the data that I published in 1990, but numbers given at that time are as follows:

	type 1	type 2
$5	3194	2721
$10	6182	4422
$20	5711	3956
$50	298	50
$100	288	37

These data refer to the numbers of distinct varieties of notes that were issued for each denomination and type of small-size NBN. These notes were issued by a total of 6925 different banks. A given bank is considered to be the same bank unless it changed its charter number as well as its title during the issuing period of 1929-35, but notes issued by those banks using more than one title are considered as distinct varieties in the data given above. I was not able to consider any variations due to a change of bank officers or of the type faces for notes from a given bank, since these modifications are not noted in the National Archives from where almost all of the original statistics on national bank notes have been obtained. If these numbers are added together, then the total is 26,859. Considering any possible changes in bank officers or in type fonts, I think that it is safe to say that not less than 27,000 distinct varieties of Series 1929 NBNs were actually issued.

Type 1 NBNs of Series 1929 were issued between 1929 and 1933, while type 2 notes of this series were issued between 1933 and 1935. The latter use an entirely different style and sequence of serial numbers, and the charter number appears twice on each note in brown and twice in black whereas on type 1 notes this number appears two times only in black.

It should be immediately clear to you that there is no possibility that anyone could even hope to obtain all of these varieties regardless of the depth of his pockets. Despite the fact that the numbers of known surviving notes is but a small fraction of the numbers of NBNs originally issued, more than 20,000 different varieties from over 6500 different banks are still believed to be in existence.

In the past three decades there has been a great deal of research done on national bank notes. Much of this work has been done by such individuals as Louis Van Belkum, Peter Huntoon, Don Kelly, and the late John Hickman. Several good reference works are now on the market including the *Standard Catalog of National Bank Notes* by John Hickman and Dean Oakes and *National Bank Notes, A Guide with Prices* by Don Kelly. The former book is now in its second edition, while the latter work is now in its third edition. If you plan to become seriously involved in the collecting of national bank notes, it is essential that you obtain one or both of these definitive works. They are the only books to contain complete listings of all the NBNs that were issued, and both give up to date listings of the approximate numbers of notes known for each national bank. It is now estimated that there are probably between 300,000 and 400,000 national bank notes still in existence. This total is believed to be roughly divided evenly between large-size and small-size notes, and thus 200,000 examples may be a fairly good estimate for the upper limit of the number of Series 1929 NBNs presently in collectors' hands.

If some 200,000 notes are distributed between about 20,000 different varieties and 6500 different banks, it follows that on average there are only 10 notes of each variety and 30 notes for each bank. Although these estimates are a bit crude, they are both probably fairly realistic. Since there are some varieties for which well over a hundred examples are known and some banks for which many hundreds of notes are known, it follows that there are many small-size NBNs that are either unique or at least very rare.

For type and series collectors of small-size notes the two great rarities are the Series 1933 $10 silver certificate and the Series 1934 $10 North Africa note. There are roughly 75 examples known for each of these notes, and yet we describe them as great rarities. A specific national bank note for which 75 examples are known would be described as fairly common. Why is there so great a distinction in these rarity classes?

The reason, of course, is that there are not many thousands of different varieties of silver certificates or of World War II notes. Many collectors will want to obtain complete sets of these notes, and thus they will require these two rarities. But no one attempts to obtain 20,000 or more different varieties of small-size NBNs. If there were only a few hundred known varieties, then a few affluent collectors would doubtless attempt to obtain all such varieties, but the scope of NBNs is so vast that this simply cannot be done. Despite the great appeal of national bank notes, no one can hope to assemble a collection that is even remotely complete in terms of the total numbers of varieties that do exist.

Over the past 20 years I have built up a substantial collection of national bank notes, and it now totals over 900 different small-size notes and about 750 large-size notes. Indeed this is a large general collection of these items, but numerous specialized state collections of NBNs have come on the market in recent years, and my holdings for a given state (e. g., California or Texas) are completely dwarfed by such collections as the Philip Krakover collection of California NBNs or the J. L. Irish collection of Texas NBNs, both of which have been sold at auction in the past few years.

National bank notes may well be the most popular of all types of U. S. Federal paper money. I have been a generalist, and my collection of NBNs is just part of my collection of Federal paper money. But many collectors of NBNs choose to limit themselves to a particular state or even to a particular county or city. This limits one's scope, but if all that person's interest and collecting budget is focused on the notes of a given state (e. g., Indiana), then it is likely that he will develop a very fine and comprehensive collection of Indiana NBNs after a few decades of patient search.

I shall return in greater detail to this subject in the chapter of this book that is devoted exclusively to national bank notes. Let us finish off this section by considering only a few salient aspects of Series 1929 NBNs. As type notes this is not a difficult group to complete. If you do not regard type 1 and type 2 notes as distinct major varieties, then it is easy to obtain one note for each of the five denominations. Type 2 notes are also easily acquired for the $5, $10, and $20 denominations, but type 2 $50s and $100s are decidedly scarce. After years of search I now have eight of the type 2 $50 notes and only four of the type 2 $100s. The type 2 $100 would be a rarity except for the fact that there are a fair number of survivors of this type from the Bank of America in San Francisco. These notes can still be obtained for about $400 - $500 in VF-XF condition, and type 2

$50s are available from a few banks for no more than this. None of the other note types should cause any problems. There are many small-size NBNs of the $20, $50, and $100 denominations that sell for little or no more than double face in VF condition or better. Thus these notes are selling at a fraction of what their buying power was in the early 1930s.

Another approach is to obtain one small-size NBN for each state irrespective of type or denomination. Including the District of Columbia Series 1929 NBNs were issued from 51 such jurisdictions. One of these, however, can be ruled out by all but the most affluent of collectors. Series 1929 NBNs were issued by only three different banks in Alaska (one each in Fairbanks, Juneau, and Ketchikan), and although these are not the rarest of small-size NBNs, they are probably the most expensive. Series 1929 NBNs from this state in decent condition are now selling for about $10,000 each, a sum which probably either matches or exceeds the cost of an entire collection of notes from the other 50 states or districts. You will find that about 40 of these states are easily obtained, but a few of the western states such as Arizona, Idaho, Nevada, and Wyoming are definitely hard to come by. Among the eastern states Delaware is without doubt the toughest to acquire. Hawaii only has one bank that issued small-size NBNs, the Bishop First National Bank of Honolulu, but it was a large bank and notes from this institution are not particularly uncommon. You may have to spend as much as $200 or $300 each on notes from four or five of the scarcest states, but many of the others can be had for prices of less than $50 per note. For notes in choice condition there is typically very little difference in the numismatic value of the $5, $10, or $20 notes of a given bank. The $5 notes were generally printed in larger quantities than were the $20 notes, but the rate of survival was substantially higher for the latter denomination.

At this point we close our discussion of noncurrent small-size notes. For the small-size Federal Reserve Notes other collecting parameters must be taken into consideration, and so I am discussing them in the following chapter.

CHAPTER FOUR

SMALL-SIZE FEDERAL RESERVE NOTES

Small-size Federal Reserve Notes are so abundant and there are so many different varieties that these notes require quite different collecting parameters from those used for any of the other types of small-size notes. In terms of denominations I feel that these notes fall into three fundamentally different groups - the small (i. e., $1 and $2 FRNs), the medium (i. e., $5, $10, $20, $50, and $100 notes), and the high denomination notes. This last group can also be subdivided into high (i. e., $500 and $1000) and ultrahigh (i. e., $5000 and $10,000) groups. Low denomination FRNs have only been issued since 1963, and all production of high denomination FRNs ceased in 1945. The middle denomination notes, however, have been in continuous production and circulation throughout the entire 70-year era of small-size notes. The designs of these notes have been extremely conservative, and major changes are only now being made. Series 1996 $20, $50 and $100 notes which have radically different designs from their predecessors are now in circulation, and they are to be followed soon by equally different $10 and $5 notes most likely in 2000. Thus by the turn of this century we should have notes of entirely new designs for these denominations in circulation. This is really the first time that this has happened since the changeover from large-size notes to small-size notes that was undertaken in 1929. Let us begin our discussion, however, with the $1 and $2 Federal Reserve Notes.

One-dollar Federal Reserve Notes were released into circulation late in 1963. Within a few months they completely supplanted the $1 SCs, particularly since the former notes would soon prove to be worth a premium over their face value and that situation was to continue until 1968. By that time almost all SCs had been removed from circulation. Thus far 18 different series of $1 FRNs have been issued. If you desire only one regular note from each series, it is extremely easy to buy a series set of these notes. One can also purchase a star set of these notes at a price that is only somewhat higher than that of a regular series set. Almost all syngraphists, however, collect these notes as district sets. Even then most of these notes are regularly available. Series 1988 was the last series in which there were no "complications," and so let us first consider what was issued up through that series. The following table gives the numbers of different varieties for the first 15 issues of $1 FRNs.

The first column lists the numbers of districts that issued these notes in non-star form, while the second column gives the same datum for star notes. The third column gives the total number of serial number blocks for a given series including both regular and replacement issues. All of these notes were printed at the Washington facility of the BEP, and this list includes a few blocks beginning with Series 1981 that were included only in complete sheets. There is also a minor complication for Series 1981A and 1985. The back check numbers appear almost always on the right sides of these notes, but check #129 was placed on the left side, and this variety exists on several Series 1981A and 1985 notes. The majority of collectors, however, regard these as plate errors rather than as normal notes. The total numbers of blocks listed above for these series do not include these varieties.

	regular	star	total
1963	12	12	34
1963A	12	12	69
1963B	5	4	13
1969	12	12	36
1969A	12	11	31
1969B	12	12	35
1969C	10	9	25
1969D	12	11	47
1974	12	12	68
1977	12	12	61
1977A	12	12	55
1981	12	12	87
1981A	12	5	48
1985	12	6	124
1988	12	7	54

For most of years covered by these issues it was easy for commercial banks to acquire large numbers of freshly printed notes from their respective districts, and star notes were almost as easy to acquire as regular notes despite their much lower printings. Currency dealers could then acquire these notes from their hometown banks, and by trading packs with dealers in other parts of the country it was relatively easy to assemble district sets of these notes in new condition. Since most dealers who specialized in such issues obtained their sets at least in packs of 100 notes each, it was easy to assemble individual sets with the last two digits matching. Fairly often one also finds sets with the last three digits matching. Such sets sell for only relatively modest premiums over their randomly numbered counterparts. This situation changed with Series 1981A, when star notes were no longer issued for all districts and when some of these notes became quite difficult to acquire. In Series 1981A the K* note is scarce, and in Series 1985 it is the H* note. Each of these notes is worth at least $30 to $40 in CU condition, and star sets for each of these series are fairly difficult to acquire. Another difficult item is the L* note of Series 1969C, which is of comparable value to the two scarce notes of Series 1981A and 1985. The most difficult note of all seems to be the F* note of Series 1988. Although BEP records indicate that 3,840,000 of these notes were printed, it now appears that far fewer may actually have been delivered, and of these many may not have been released from the Federal Reserve Bank to which they were shipped (presumably Atlanta). Despite their recent vintage complete star sets for Series 1988 are only infrequently offered for sale.

Series 1963B notes bear the signature of Joseph Barr, who was Secretary of the Treasury for only 28 days in 1968-69. Although these notes were issued for only a few districts, there was considerable advance notice and large numbers were saved. All of the 1963B notes can be acquired with little difficulty.

Although almost all collectors of $1 FRNs try to acquire these notes in district sets, only relatively few go in for complete block sets. These are occasionally available, at least for the earlier series, but there are a few blocks that are scarce. Included among these are the BC and DB blocks of Series 1963, the EH and JD blocks in Series 1981, and a few others. At one time there was a dealer (Leonard Bennett of Wichita, Kansas) who specialized exclusively in $1 FRNs and who carried a very comprehensive stock of these varieties. He has since passed away, and his stock has been dispersed. Although it is still possible to obtain simplified district sets of $1 FRNs from many sources, no one at the present time seems to be carrying good stocks of all possible block varieties.

The web notes of Series 1988A, 1993, and 1995 are very easy to distinguish from their counterparts printed in either Washington or Fort Worth on the 32-subject Magna presses. Note also that the forehead portions of Washington's portrait appears somewhat "underexposed" on the web note relative to the other notes.

Web notes are also easily identifiable from their backs, since the check number appears in the upper right rather than the lower right portion of the center. The streak (see arrow) is a printing artifact.

There is a difference in size of the check numbers printed in Washington and in Fort Worth.

Series 1988A has proven to be the most complex of all of the $1 FRN issues. The Fort Worth facility of the BEP was dedicated in 1987, and it went into full production of these notes at the beginning of 1991. Notes of this facility are easily identifiable, since they have a small "FW" near the check number in their lower right portions. A second complicating factor in Series 1988A was the introduction of the web press that was first used to print money at the Washington facility of the BEP in 1992. An additional aspect of this issue is that it was extended for an unusually long period of time. These notes bear the signature (as Treasurer) of Catalina V. Villalpando, who left office in January, 1993. But it was not until March, 1994 that Mary E. Withrow was appointed as her successor as Treasurer of the United States, and thus production of Series 1988A was continued well into 1994. Excluding web notes but including both facilities as distinct for both regular and star notes the number of serial number blocks equals 189 for this issue.

Regular Series 1988A notes were printed for all 12 districts at the Washington facility, but they were also printed for seven districts (F through L) at the Fort Worth facility. The last blocks printed for the four largest districts were BX, FY, GW, and LY, respectively, and so in each case the BEP almost ran out of serial numbers to use. What it did then was to begin printing large numbers of notes from smaller districts such as Richmond, St. Louis, and Minneapolis where the final blocks printed in this series were ER, HI, and IJ, respectively. The star notes of Series 1988A are relatively uncomplicated. There are seven possibilities from Washington and four from Fort Worth. The G* and I* blocks exist from both facilities, as do many of the non-star blocks. All of these notes are supposed to be fairly common, but assembling a complete block set of Series 1988A $1 FRNs would be a major undertaking in time and effort, if not in actual cash outlay. What about the web notes? Don't worry, we'll get to those later.

Series 1993 was a good deal less complex than was Series 1988A, because Lloyd Bentsen served as secretary of the Treasury for less than one year and was succeeded in this post by Robert E. Rubin, whose signature appears on the Series 1995 notes together with that of Mary E. Withrow. In Series 1993 $1 notes were printed for eight districts from Washington (A through G plus L), while this series was printed for five districts from Fort Worth (G, H, I, K, and L). No notes were printed for the Kansas City district. Star notes for Series 1993 exist as B*, C*, and F* from Washington, and G* and K* from Fort Worth. The C* note of Series 1993 is proving to be yet another one of the scarcer replacement notes. Excluding web notes but including both facilities and stars there are a total of 61 different serial number blocks for Series 1993.

Series 1995 notes have been printed for all 12 districts. Thus far substantial numbers of notes have been produced for eight districts each from the Washington and Fort Worth facilities. Additional overlap between the two facilities may occur, since notes for the Cleveland district have recently also been printed in Fort Worth while those for Kansas City and San Francisco have likewise been printed in Washington. Thus far A*, B*, C*, D*, E*, and F* notes have been printed in Washington, while G*, I*, J*, and L* notes have been produced in Fort Worth. As of March 1999, the number of different serial number blocks for Series 1995 (including stars but excluding the five web blocks) reached 200. This total includes a couple of enigmatic issues--an IA block from Washington that was issued only in complete sheet form and a printing of F* notes from the Fort Worth facility. In the summer of 1999 Robert E. Rubin was replaced by Lawrence H. Summers as secretary of the Treasury. Production of Series 1995 notes should continue a bit longer, but they will soon be replaced by notes bearing the Withrow-Summers signature combination. These can be expected to be in production at least until the end of the Clinton administration.

I would recommend that you collect these notes from both the Washington and Fort Worth facilities where both varieties exist for a single district. The difference on their face sides is obvious, but the back plates from the two facilities also use distinct sequences of check numbers. Furthermore these numbers are not quite of the same size. Those on current notes from the Washington facility are about 0.9 mm high, while those from Fort Worth are somewhat larger at about 1.3 mm in height. This recalls the distinction between the "micro" and "macro" numbers in earlier years. Recently there has been one "mule" or plate error reported. Check number 295 on the backs of $1 FRNs printed in Fort Worth is of the smaller size intended for the Washington facility rather than the larger size intended for Fort Worth. About a dozen block varieties have been reported with this interesting check number, and others may exist. Thus far no notes from the Washington facility have been reported with the larger back check numbers intended for Fort Worth, but that possibility also exists. The current edition of the Oakes and Schwartz catalog is less explicit than it should be about which block number groups are printed at which facility, but hopefully this confusion will be straightened out in subsequent editions of this book.

The web notes were printed intermittently on a single press at the BEP facility in Washington. This press printed both the front and back sides (i. e., the second and first printings) simultaneously on a continuously fed roll of paper. It was theoretically capable of printing notes at a rate substantially faster than that of the Magna presses, but this did not prove to be the case. In fact, the whole project was a fiasco which cost the BEP (and ultimately the American taxpayers) well over $30 million. About 309 million web notes (all $1 FRNs) were printed in Series 1988A, 1993, and 1995, but only one note in 60 was a web note in Series 1988A, and only one in 185 $1 FRNs was a web note in Series 1993. Production of web notes began in May, 1992, but the machine broke down so many times that it was only in use for a fraction of the time that it was supposed to be in operation. The Series 1988A web notes were printed between May, 1992 and October, 1993, while those for Series 1993 and 1995 were printed between May, 1995 and July, 1996. After that it was announced that no more web notes would be produced. Rather more than 50 million web notes were printed in Series 1995, but this amount will prove to be a tiny fraction of the total number of notes printed for this series.

Most collectors and dealers were caught sleeping on this issue. I now regret not putting aside large numbers of web notes at a time when they could be easily pulled from circulation. In 1992 and 1993 the BEP seemed so confident of its new toy that I suspect that nearly all of us thought that the new web notes would soon supplant the notes printed on sheet-fed presses much as had the $1 FRNs and cupronickel-clad dimes and quarters supplanted the earlier $1 SCs and silver coins in the 1960s. For those few persons who were closely following developments at the BEP, however, it soon became clear that was not what was happening. Still relatively few web notes were put aside, and all of them now sell at substantial multiples of their face value at least when in choice condition.

A total of 22 different blocks were issued for web notes in the three series in which they appear. The third printing for these notes was not done on the web press, but rather on the COPE machines as was the case for all other notes then being produced. There are two rarities among these notes (viz., the BL and F* blocks of Series 1988A), and these arose when some web-printed notes were inserted into larger numbers of sheet-printed notes as these notes were about to be overprinted. These two blocks were the first to be printed, the BL notes in May, 1992, and the F* notes in the following month. Although BEP records indicate that 1,920,000 BL web notes were printed in Series 1988A, the actual number may be less for this variety. These same records indicate a printing of 640,000 F* web notes in this series, but the serial number data available for notes known to be in collectors' hands indicate that this printing may have been only 160,000. Sheet-fed F* notes for this series were printed in large quantities (12,800,000 examples), and some sources indicate that the F* web note was an unintentional error caused when a few web-printed notes were accidentally inserted into a much larger batch of Magna press-printed notes for overprinting on the COPE machine.

Although the web press was a fiasco for the BEP, it did produce an interesting array of numismatic curiosities, and these web notes have sparked a great deal of interest among currency collectors. I think that it is safe to say the web notes are the most exciting thing to come along for collectors of small-size U. S. paper money in quite a few years. Today they are avidly collected, but this market is still young, and thus I feel that prices for these notes should be regarded as tentative at best. They may go higher, but many current prices may also come down as interest gradually wanes or as large supples of withheld notes possibly come onto the market. Web notes are very easily distinguished from normal notes, since they bear no sheet position indicators in their upper left and lower right corners, and the lower right corner contains only a small check number that is usually a single digit. On their back sides they bear a check number in the upper right rather than the lower right portion of the note. Another peculiarity of web notes is that the intaglio portions of their designs were often underinked. This gives many of these notes a decidedly washed-out appearance, even when they are uncirculated. Some specialists collect these notes by production runs (each of 6,400,000 notes) as well as by serial number blocks. Shown are the numbers of such groups for each block. The scarce BL and F* blocks of Series 1988A constituted only small portions of their respective runs.

Series 1988A - AE (3), AF (4), AG (3), BL, CA (2), EI (3), EK (3), FL (2), FM (1),
               FN (3), FU (3), FV (6), F*, GP (2), and GQ (1)
Series 1993 - BH (2) and CA (2)
Series 1995 - AC (2), AD (1), BH (2), DC (1), and FD (2)

     The actual numbers printed can be readily obtained by multiplying the numbers in parentheses by 6,400,000 in all cases except for the AD block of Series 1995. For this block only 5,760,000 notes were printed, the balance of this run being finished with notes produced from sheet-fed presses. For Series 1988A face check numbers of 1 - 5 and 8 - 10 were used, while the back check numbers were 1 through 8. It appears that back numbers 3 and 5 were little used in the printing of these notes, and notes with these back numbers are extremely difficult to locate. For the Series 1993 web notes only face check number 1 was used, and the back numbers were 8, 9, and 10. For the Series 1995 notes face numbers of 1 - 7 were used, while the back numbers employed were 8, 9, 10, and 12. The current Oakes and Schwartz catalog gives detailed data regarding the serial number groups for these notes, but collectors who specialize in these notes are usually more interested in the various check number combinations that exist for each block. In today's market it is a fair challenge just to assemble a set of the 20 different blocks of web notes that are supposed to be "common" in choice condition.

     Although $1 FRNs are usually collected almost exclusively in CU condition, it is obvious that any note that is rare and expensive in CU is also quite worthwhile in VF or XF condition. The F* web note is now selling for more than $1000 when in CU condition, and recent auction sales indicate that this note is worth about $300 to $400 when in VF-XF condition. The BL web note has sold at auction for about $150 in VF condition, but thus far I have not seen it offered in CU. I do know of the existence of a fairly large sequence of CU notes of this type with consecutive serial numbers, but these are presently off the market. Several of the other 20 blocks of web notes are also scarce in CU, but none of them should cost very much when in VF-XF condition. The least common of these other blocks appear to be the FL and FM blocks of Series 1988A. These also were among the earliest of the web notes that were printed, and thus they were placed into circulation at a time when they received little attention from the numismatic community. Please bear in mind that all prices on web notes are still rather tentative, since large numbers of them are probably being withheld from the market by persons hoping to obtain more money for them in the future.

     As this book goes to press, I feel that enough price data on web notes have come to light to state fairly well what an informed collector should pay for CU examples of these notes. Despite much higher quotes from some dealers in the past couple of years, it appears that four of the scarcer Series 1988A web blocks (FM, FN, GP, and GQ) can all be obtained for about $100 each or a trifle more. Web notes of the FL block in CU should cost about double this price. All of these notes are available in XF-AU for about one-quarter to one-third of these prices. The eight other "common" web blocks of Series 1988A (i.e., AE, AF, AG, CA, EI, EK, FU, and FV) are all selling for about $30 to $35 each in CU, and once again examples in XF-AU sell for about one-quarter to one-third of what the CU notes bring. The two web blocks of Series 1993 sell for less than $10 each in CU, and this is also true of four of the Series 1995 web blocks (AC, BH, DC, and FD). The AD block of Series 1995 is substantially scarcer as a web note, but CU examples should cost no more than $20 to $25 each. The only web note that is regularly offered in CU packs of 100 is the DC block of Series 1995. These are normally selling for about $500 to $600 per pack. Although inexpensive, circulated grades of common Series 1993 and 1995 web notes continue to remain popular, and one should expect to pay about $3 or $4 for a VF-XF example of any of these blocks. All of these prices, of course, refer to the least expensive check number combination for a given block. Several major rarities among these combinations are not acknowledged.

The interest among collectors in the products of this failed experiment has generated a number of people who specialize in web notes. If you want to go further than just assembling a set of the 22 different block varieties, then the next step would be to collect these notes either by production runs or according to their face and back check number combinations. According to Robert Kvederas Senior and Junior of Titusville, Florida the breakdown of these notes by such check number combinations is as follows:

Series 1988A				Series 1993	
AE	8	FL	6	BH	2
AF	9	FM	6	CA	3
AG	8	FN	8	Series 1995	
BL	1	FU	9	AC	6
CA	6	FV	11	AD	5
EI	6	F*	1	BH	10
EK	6	GP	5	DC	4
		GQ	6	FD	8

The scarce BL and F* blocks have check number combinations 1-1 and 1-2, respectively, and they are the only web notes that exist with only one such variety of each. According to the Kvederases, however, the rarest of these varieties are the Series 1988A AE block with 4-3 and 4-5 check number combinations and the FN block of this series with a 3-5 combination. Getting all 134 possible check number varieties for the web notes would prove to be a major challenge even for the most dedicated collectors. An even greater challenge would be to collect these notes both by check number combinations and by production runs. In that case the total number of possible varieties of web notes increases to 227, i. e., 174 for Series 1988A, 9 for Series 1993, and 44 for Series 1995.

An album for web notes is now being distributed which has spaces for all block, plate number, and run combinations. This may stimulate interest in collecting web notes in this fashion. Filling all 227 spaces, however, would be an extremely difficult task, however, since at least three of the combinations are acknowledged to be extreme rarities.

If instead you wish to collect current Federal paper money on a shoestring budget, an interesting project would be to go through large numbers of current, circulated $1 FRNs. Series 1988A and 1993 notes are still available in some quantity from everyday circulation, but they are becomingly increasingly well-worn as time passes. Many block varieties are available for the current Series 1995 notes, however, and assembling a collection of these by block would be an interesting undertaking. If you have no problems with these notes in only VF, XF, or AU condition, a large number of such varieties should be available to you at face value. And if you have a collector friend who lives in a different part of the country, obtaining districts that are not normally available from your hometown bank will also prove to be much easier.

The fate of the $1 FRN is again being considered in Congress and elsewhere. The USA is one of the very few western industrialized nations that has circulating notes for denominations as low as $US1.00 in value. Yet everyone agrees that the Susan B. Anthony dollar coin was a fiasco. I have gone on record in numismatic publications as favoring the cessation of printing of $1 FRNs. Two-dollar notes might be produced in quantity for a while, but I feel that both of these denominations should exclusively be coins as is now the case in Canada, Australia, New Zealand, and elsewhere. These nations all have circulating $1 and $2 coins that are made of aluminum bronze or some other gold-colored alloy or else are bimetallic in composition. We badly need such coins, but they must be completely different in size and appearance from such essential pieces of currency as our quarters. Although the American public still seems to favor $1 bills, most persons become much less enthusiastic when informed that the circulation of these notes costs the American taxpayers more than $400 million per year. One of the major problems, of course, is that the printing of vast numbers of these notes is taxing the production capabilities of the BEP. It had been hoped that the web press would make things easier, but that most definitely did not prove to be the case. One short-term solution would be to stop printing serial numbers on $1 FRNs. Only serial letter blocks (as on most Japanese occupation currency) or no serials at all (as on all U. S. Fractional Currency) could be used. Then at least the BEP would not run out of serial numbers, a situation that may arise with 1995 $1 FRNs in the not too distant future if production continues at the present rate. Another approach would be to use the numbering scheme that is now in use on Series 1996 $20, $50 and $100 FRNs. But these would only be interim solutions. Time will tell what is to be the eventual fate of the much used one-dollar bill.

Two-dollar Federal Reserve Notes have a shorter and less complicated history than do their one-dollar counterparts. The $2 FRN was originally issued in Series 1976 as a commemorative of our nation's bicentennial. On its back side it features an engraving of the Signin*g of the Declaration of Independence*, a vignette previously used on the very rare $100 NBNs of the First Charter period. Although intended for permanent circulation, these new $2 notes did not prove very popular with the public, and enough notes remained on hand from the original printing runs to satisfy public demand for many years. This note exists from all districts both as regular and as replacement note blocks. The printings from no district exceeded 100 million examples in the original printings, and thus all of these regular notes have A suffixes. A set of these 12 notes in CU condition can easily be purchased for well under twice its face value. The star set is a good deal scarcer, but these should cost no more than $100 or so. In recent years there have been some additional printings of Series $2 FRNs for the New York, Richmond, and Minneapolis districts, and these printings have produced five additional block varieties. Two-dollar FRNs have also been printed at the Fort Worth facility in Series 1995. Thus far all of these have been from the Atlanta district, and they currently exist with blocks FA, FB, and F*. If there is a cutback in the production of $1 FRNs, it is likely that the production of $2 FRNs will greatly increase, and thus many more varieties will become probable. In a later chapter of this book, I shall discuss notes in complete sheets, but I should note in passing that all of the $2 notes sold by the BEP in sheets of 16 or 32 subjects have come from replacement number blocks or from blocks not used for the regularly issued notes. The sheets of four for these notes have used non-star serial number blocks, some of which are different from those of the regularly issued notes.

The middle denominations of Federal Reserve Notes (i. e., $5, $10, $20, $50, and $100) are generally collected in a quite different fashion from their $1 and $2 counterparts. Hardly anyone collects these notes by district sets, and if a person chooses to collect in this fashion, he must form these sets on his own, since no dealers regularly carry stocks of district sets of FRNs for these denominations. Before forming a collection of these notes I feel that you should carefully consider just what you hope to obtain. A "complete" collection of FRNs of these five denominations can include only a few dozen notes (if by major type only) or several thousands of different varieties (if by series, district, and block as well). Budget considerations would probably preclude almost all collectors from attempting to obtain these notes by series, district, and block, and the amount of time required to hunt down the thousands of possible varieties necessary with so great a degree of specialization would also transform the completion of such a project into an impossible dream. There are several compromises, however, between these two extremes.

Let us first consider these notes by major types only. For FRNs of Series 1928 through 1995 there are seven types for each denomination for the $5 through $100 notes. These varieties are as follows.

1) Series 1928 and 1928A (1928 only for $50s and $100s). These notes carry the gold redemption clause and the district seal contains a large number.

2) Series 1928B, 1928C, and 1928D (1928A for $50s and $100s). These notes also have the gold redemption clause, but the large number in the district seal has been replaced by a large letter.

3) Series 1934 through 1934D. The gold redemption clause has been replaced by a statement promising payment in lawful money.

4) Series 1950 through 1950E. These notes have a much smaller district seal, and several of the legends have been rearranged.

5) Series 1963 and 1963A. The redemption clause has been simplified, and the phrase "will pay the bearer on demand" has been eliminated. The backs of these notes have been modified significantly, and they now carry the motto "In God We Trust."

6) Series 1969 through 1988A. These notes depict the new Treasury seal that was first used on Series 1966 $100 United States Notes.

7) Series 1990, 1993, and 1995. These notes contain a plastic security thread and microscopic lettering about the portrait.

The notes of major types 1, 2, and 3 were all printed in sheets of 12, while those of type 4 were printed in sheets of 18 subjects each. The notes of types 5, 6, and 7 were printed in 32-subject sheets. In 1948 there was a major modification to the back design for the $20 notes, and Series 1934C exists both with the old (White House) and new (The

White House) designs. I regard this as a major type change, and so for the $20 FRNs there are two different types in the 1934 notes. Thus a complete type set of the $5 through $100 FRNs for all of these series would consist of 36 different notes. None of these are rare, and so it is a fairly simple if rather expensive matter to put together a complete collection of FRNs by type in this fashion.

When I began to collect systematically the small-size FRNs of these five denominations, I decided on a much more ambitious plan. I have collected these notes by series as well as by type. After years of effort my collection of these items is now complete, but I can assure you that this is far from an easy task. The Series 1928C notes exist only for the $5, $10, and $20 denominations, and all of these are scarce, especially the $5 and $20 notes. Series 1928D exists only for the $5 notes, and this is the rarest of the lower denomination notes. Among the $50 and $100 notes there are several series that are very scarce. Foremost among these are the notes of Series 1934D and 1950E. I regard the Series 1950E $100 FRN to be the scarcest of the entire series despite the fact that the Series 1928D $5 note is much more highly touted. Several other $50 and $100 FRNs among the 1934 and 1950 types are also infrequently offered. But given lots of patience and fairly adequate funds it is possible to put together such a collection, which consists of 145 different notes.

Both the Series 1928 $10 FRN and the Series 1928D $5 FRN shown above have the gold redemption clause, but this was dropped from the Series 1934 notes. Only Series 1928 and 1928A FRNs for $5, $10, and $20 or only Series 1928 $50 and $100 FRNs display large numerals in their district seals.

For Series 1950 the district seals were made much smaller than they had been in previous series. The obligations were greatly shortened in Series 1963, and the new Treasury seal was used on FRNs commencing with Series 1969.

In terms of what is being acquired, both a collection of 36 different type notes and one of 145 different series notes can be regarded as "complete." The former can be easily completed, but the latter is really quite difficult to do. For these two approaches to collecting the FRNs of Series 1928 through 1995 the breakdowns by denomination are as follows:

	by type only	by type and series
$5	7	32
$10	7	31
$20	8	31
$50	7	26
$100	7	25
total	36	145
total face	$1315	$4890

For notes in choice condition (a minimum grade of XF, but mostly AU or CU) the type collection will probably cost you about $2000, which is not very much in excess of the face value of these notes. A collection of these notes by series will be very much more difficult to complete, and the actual cash outlay will be much higher, perhaps about $12,000 or so.

In forming my collection of FRNs for these denominations I chose to ignore any difference between star and non-star notes, i. e., either a star note or a non-star note of a given series would fill that slot. I began to collect these notes systematically in 1976 at a time when Series 1974 notes were current. Almost all of the 45 different notes in Series 1974 - 95 were obtained by me at banks in fresh CU condition. The total cost of these notes was $1530 (their face value) plus a small premium of $35.50 that I spent in obtaining a few star notes or notes of smaller districts from dealers. I even recovered one CU $20 star note from an ATM machine, but if you if you acquire your recent notes from banks it is unlikely that you will get many star notes or other interesting blocks. Of the 45 notes in this group only six are star notes, and five of these were purchased at modest premiums.

My collection of 57 different notes for Series 1950 - 69C is much more interesting. I had to purchase nearly all of these at a premium, but in my collection 22 of this group are star notes. Most of these were acquired in the early 1980s when the large premium values that are now associated with most pre-1974 FRN star notes had not yet developed. In fact, the only notes for which I paid more than double face from this group were the $20, $50, and $100 notes of the decidedly scarce Series 1950E. In today's market, however, many of the notes of this group would be worth large multiples of their face value. Thus the premiums I paid for nearly all of these notes were well worth the money. I obtained almost all of the 1974 - 95 notes in my collection at face value, but few of these notes are worth much more than their face value today. The moral of this story is that it may well be worthwhile to pay a small premium for a recent note that is somewhat unusual rather than to acquire a mundane note of the same series at face value from a bank.

I also have all 43 different FRNs of these denominations for Series 1928 - 34D. All of these are at least in XF condition, and the majority are in CU. At the time I was acquiring these notes, star notes of these series in choice condition were already selling at fairly high prices, and I chose to go for high grade non-star notes instead. As a result, I have no star notes in my collection of FRNs for these series.

Of the $5 to $100 FRNs for Series 1928 through 1995 a total of 142 out of the 145 different series varieties are known in replacement form. The only notes unknown as star notes are the $5 and $20 notes of Series 1928C and the $5 note of Series 1928D. Several notes of these issues, however, are extremely rare when in replacement form. The rarest of these are the Series 1928C $10, the $20 notes of Series 1928A, the $50 notes of Series 1928A, 1934B, and 1934D, and the $100 notes of Series 1928A, 1934B, 1934C, and 1934D. One of the highest prices paid in the Schaaf sale of small-size star notes in 1993 was $5775 for a CU example of a Series 1928C $10 star note from the Cleveland district. This same note was sold again at the Dallas auction held in August, 1998 for the unprecedented price of $25,300. One other note identical to this one is also known.

The Schaaf auction also featured Series 1934B and 1934D $50 star notes as well as Series 1928A and 1934B $100 star notes. Since that time the 1928A $50 star note and the 1934C and 1934D $100 star notes have also come to light. Despite their extreme rarity most of these notes have only sold in the $1500 to $3000 range. Among the 1950 issues Series 1950E $50 and $100 notes are also quite scarce in star form. It now seems that the very high prices obtained for a Series 1928C $10 star note are a bit of anomaly, since they are much higher than any of the prices that have been obtained for the various $50 and

$100 replacement note rarities. I expect that the market is not yet very well defined for the rare FRN star notes. Because of the extreme rarity of these notes acquiring all of the 142 series varieties of replacement FRNs from 1928 through 1995 would be exceedingly difficult if not an outright "impossible dream" similar to that of acquiring all 45 known varieties of Series 1929 FRBN star notes or all 88 known varieties of the MPC replacement notes, a topic that I shall discuss in some detail in the chapter on Military Payment Certificates.

Why do most of the small-size FRN star rarities sell for lower prices than do such well known non-FRN rarities as the Series 1928E $1 SC or the Series 1928B $2 USN in star form? This all hinges on how many varieties there are for a given series. The number of different small-size SCs or USNs is relatively small. Most collectors will try to acquire as many of these as is possible, and completing sets of these notes at least in non-star form is not particularly difficult to do. For Federal Reserve Notes, however, there are vastly more varieties, and consequently a number of the true rarities among these issues are submerged among the huge numbers of different possibilities that one can collect.

Let us now consider some of the complicating factors that result in there being so many different varieties for small-size FRNs. The non-FRN small-size notes have their Treasury seals and serial numbers printed in either red, dark blue, brown, or yellow. There are virtually no shade variations for these colors except for the yellow seals, but gold certificates always have orange-yellow seals while North Africa notes always have lemon-yellow seals. Federal Reserve Notes, of course, have their seals and serial numbers printed in green, but there are several shade variations. For the past three decades these features have been consistently printed in a vivid emerald green that has a faint bluish cast, but for the first 35 years or so of small-size FRNs there were several distinct shades of green. The earliest notes were printed with dark green (so-called forest green) seals. During the production of Series 1928B for $5, $10, and $20 notes or 1928A for $50 and $100 notes this shade was changed to light yellow green (so-called apple green). Notes of these series exist in both of these shades as well as in transitional forms. The apple green shade was used on all of the scarce Series 1928C and 1928D notes. It was also continued into Series 1934, but during production of this issue the seals began to be printed in a dull blue green (so-called dark green) shade. When compared side by side the so-called light green and dark green shades are quite distinct, but there are also transitional forms. The Series 1934 $10 note in my collection is one such example. The dull blue green shade was continued into the various 1950 issues, but by the late 1950s or early 1960s the Treasury seals were a good deal brighter than they had been in the Series 1934 or 1934A notes. As you can see from this discussion, the shade varieties for FRNs are a bit complicated, especially for Series 1928B/1928A and for Series 1934. If you want to try to obtain both shades for each of these issues, then I wish you good luck, but the transitional shades that exist will definitely complicate matters quite a bit.

Another major consideration concerns the status of the mule and non-mule notes. All of the $5 through $100 FRNs exist both in mule and non-mule form for various series beginning with 1934 and extending through 1950. All Series 1934 notes exist both as mules and as non-mules. The former have "micro" face numbers but "macro" back check numbers. For Series 1934A there are also mules for the $5, $10, and $20 notes, and mule notes also exist for Series 1934B $5 notes. All of these, of course, have "macro" face numbers but "micro" check numbers on their backs.

Mules most definitely exist for Series 1934A, 1934B, 1934C, 1934D, and 1950 $50 and $100 FRNs, but the question is do non-mules exist for all or even most of these series? All of the notes in my collection for these denominations and series are mules, and I think that it is likely that mules are the rule rather than the exception for all of these issues. Oakes and Schwartz claim that most of the notes for these series are mules including all of the various $50 notes. But since mule notes exist for both Series 1934 $50 and $100 notes (i e., with "macro" back check numbers), I find it a bit difficult to believe that "macro" back plates prepared most likely in the early 1940s and used to print Series 1934 mule notes at that time would then have gone unused until the "micro" back plates were finally phased out in 1953. If you do wish to collect various mule varieties, you may make some interesting discoveries, as I don't feel that the exact status of all mule and non-mule varieties for Series 1934A through 1950 has fully been resolved at the present time.

There is also the question of back designs. I have already discussed the major type change that was made on the $20 notes in 1948, resulting in two different major varieties for the Series 1934C notes of this denomination, but there are also the wide and narrow differences that exist for the $5 and $10 FRNs in Series 1950. These differences are quite trivial in comparison, and fortunately the two varieties are of about the same abundance and price for FRNs. If you really want to go to extremes, you can also acquire Series 1950 $5 FRNs with both wide I and wide II backs. Again the price differences between these varieties are small.

The major reason, however, why there are so many varieties of small-size FRNs is due to the fact that most series of these notes were issued from most or all of the 12 Federal Reserve districts. Thus there are up to 12 different notes for each series and denomination, if one chooses to collect these notes by series and district. Even greater numbers of notes would be required if these items are collected by serial number blocks as well. In recent years production of several denominations of FRNs has escalated to many times what it was in previous years. For instance, the Series 1985 $20 FRNs for the New York district were printed for the BA through BS blocks plus the B* block. This is a total of 18 regular blocks plus one star block for that series and district alone. The following data give some idea of the numbers of different varieties that are possible for small-size FRNs:

	series/district	regular blocks	star blocks
$5	347	595	325
$10	353	575	325
$20	347	635	305
$50	278	315	150
$100	273	360	160
total	1598	2480	1265

The data in the first column refer to the numbers of distinct series and district varieties for all FRNs from Series 1928 through 1995. Deleted from this list are Series 1928C $5 notes from the Cleveland and San Francisco districts and $10 notes of this series from Atlanta. Also omitted are $100 notes in Series 1934D from New York, for which the BEP quotes an absurdly low printing. Differences in shades of green and in mule varieties have not been considered. The differences between regular notes and star notes are also not taken into consideration, but the total given can be regarded as reasonably precise. The total face value for all of these notes would exceed $53,000.

The second and third columns give the total numbers of blocks both in regular and in replacement form for Series 1928 through 1993. For these tables shades of green and mule varieties have been considered for those series where these factors are relevant. These data are somewhat approximate, since it is still not clear in all cases just how many of such varieties do exist. In making these estimations I have used the listings given in the Oakes and Schwartz catalog. They list parallel mule and non-mule listings for $100 notes for most series of 1934 notes, but for the $50 notes they list only mule varieties for these issues. I strongly suspect that non-mule varieties also do exist for several of the 1934 series of $50 notes. Another distinction that has been taken into account is that between the notes printed in Washington and those printed in Fort Worth. Printing of $5, $10, and $20 notes at the Fort Worth facility began with Series 1988A, 1995, and 1990, respectively. Including the Series 1995 notes (not included in these two columns since production of these notes is still underway) it is clear that there are more than 2500 possible block varieties for the regular issues of the $5 through $100 FRNs and that the total number of possible star varieties approaches 1300. The total face value for all of these notes would be well over $100,000.

Could such a collection ever be assembled? I think that it is fair to say that it would be quite impossible to do this. Although most standard currency catalogs list small-size FRNs both by series and by district, no one carries a comprehensive stock of all of the possible varieties and assembling even a few district sets for all but the most recent issues would be a very difficult task. To do this for 25 or more series for each of the five denominations would not be possible for any collector to do regardless of the depths of his pockets.

What these data demonstrate is that it is pointless to attempt to collect all possible varieties of small-size Federal Reserve Notes. If you plan to collect small-size notes at all, you will certainly want to include some FRNs in your collection. Assembling a type set of the 36 major varieties of the $5 through $100 notes is a fairly challenging, but not too difficult project. Completing this for all series is very much more difficult, but I don't think that you should even consider expanding it to include all possible districts. If you have huge amounts of money to spend on small-size notes, I think that you will find collecting sizable numbers of national bank notes would be much more interesting than collecting endless varieties of FRNs. A problem with Federal Reserve Notes is that there are just too many varieties to collect. Decide what you want to acquire, and then stick within the boundaries that you have set for yourself with these notes.

The new Series 1996 $100, $50, and $20 FRNs have made their appearances, and the new $10 and $5 notes are now in the planning stage. The new Series 1996 $100, $50, and $20 FRNs have made their appearances, and the new $10 and $5 notes are now in the planning stages. It is likely that the first issues of the new $5 and $10 FRNs will bear the Withrow-Summers signature combination rather than Withrow-Rubin. Thus these notes will not be Series 1996. The new notes are radically different in design from any of their predecessors. Already there has been one highly publicized error for the $100 note, and I shall mention it in the chapter in this book on currency errors. By the turn of this century only "new style" FRNs will be in production, and within a decade or so the designs of Series 1928 through 1995 will be considered obsolete, and most people will look on them as being "funny money." But I imagine that adequate supplies of the older notes will remain available to collectors for many decades to come.

The high denomination notes can be split into two different groups. The $500 and $1000 FRNs are now affordable for many collectors, but the $5000 and $10,000 notes have become major rarities that command extremely high prices. All production of the two latter denominations ceased in 1944, and the last deliveries of $500 and $1000 notes took place on July 21, 1945. Up until 1969 the Federal Reserve banks maintained a stock of these notes, and they could be obtained on demand, but the issuance of these notes to all outside parties ceased on July 14, 1969.

Some BEP records indicate that $500 notes were printed in Series 1934B and 1934C, while $1000 notes were printed in Series 1934C. For the two ultrahigh denominations these same records indicate that a few of these notes were issued for both Series 1934A and 1934B. All of these entries, however, must be clerical errors. Series 1934B notes bear the signature of Fred Vinson as Secretary of the Treasury, while those of Series 1934C bear that of John Snyder in this same office. These gentlemen assumed the position of Secretary of the Treasury on July 23, 1945 and July 25, 1946, respectively. The first printings of Series 1934B notes for any denomination were made in November, 1945, while those for Series 1934C were made in September, 1946. Both of these were for $5 FRNs, but the first $50 and $100 notes were only delivered in July, 1946 (for Series 1934B) and July, 1947 (for 1934C). These dates are long after all production of high denomination notes was halted in July, 1945. Thus Series 1934B and 1934C high denomination FRNs do not and cannot exist in issued form. It also seems equally certain that no Series 1934A $5000 or $10,000 notes were released. The BEP did print a number of specimen notes in these series for all four of these denominations. These bear the serial numbers *00000000*, and the BEP does exhibit specimen sheets of these notes at many numismatic shows, but none of these notes were ever issued and all of them are in government hands.

Thus the $500 and $1000 FRNs were issued in Series 1928, 1934, and 1934A, while the $5000 and $10,000 FRNs were issued only in Series 1928 and 1934. The numbers of these notes outstanding on June 30, 1945 were as follows:

	in circulation	notes issued	ratio
$500	908,000	3,463,000	3.81
$1000	801,000	2,676,000	3.34
$5000	1,400	72,300	51.60
$10,000	2,400	62,630	26.10

Star notes are known for all three series and most districts of $500 and $1000 FRNs, but they are far from common. Depicted above are a Series 1934 $500 note from San Francisco and a Series 1934A $1000 note from Chicago. There are no known replacement notes for $5000 or $10,000 FRNs.

I have seen slightly different figures quoted as to the numbers of high denomination notes printed and released, but the numbers quoted in the second column can be regarded as more or less correct. The numbers in circulation refer to the numbers outside the Treasury and the Federal Reserve System. Already in 1945 there was a big difference between the two subsets of high denomination notes. The $500 and $1000 notes would have seen far more day-to-day use and thus would have required more frequent replacement, yet a much higher percentage of these notes printed were still in active circulation than was the case for their $5000 and $10,000 counterparts. It appears that the two ultra-high denomination notes were almost entirely kept on reserve within the Federal Reserve System, and many of these may have already been destroyed by that time.

The numbers of high denomination notes outstanding have been shrinking ever since. In 1997 it was reported that some 288,000 $500 FRNs and 167,000 $1000 FRNs are still in circulation. For the $5000 and $10,000 denominations these figures are 340 and 335 notes, respectively. Although $500 and $1000 FRNs are not major rarities, the numbers in numismatic hands do not even remotely approach the six-figure numbers quoted above. Many are still probably held abroad, but large numbers of them must also have become lost or destroyed. One problem with investing sizable sums of money in the collecting of $500 and $1000 notes is that new supplies may always come onto the market, and any large numbers hitting the market at more or less the same time would have a depressing effect on their prices.

Two or three decades ago the buying power of these notes was considered to be so high that they were generally regarded as noncollectible. That is certainly no longer the case, at least for the more affluent collectors. In actual fact, $500 and $1000 FRNs are much cheaper today than they were when they were in active circulation in the 1930s and 1940s given the much higher levels of prices and incomes that prevail today. There are two major type varieties for each note, but since there are only three series varieties for each denomination, there is not much distinction between collecting these notes by type or by series. Getting a complete set of all six series varieties is a relatively easy if decidedly expensive undertaking. This is how I have collected these two denominations. Series 1928 notes in choice CU condition now sell for about three times face or even more for either denomination, while Series 1934 and 1934A $500 notes in choice CU are now approaching double face. The $1000 notes in these two series now fetch something like $1600 to $1800 per item at auction. Attractive XF-AU examples of any of these notes, however, can still be had at prices much closer to their face value. One sometimes sees $500 and $1000 FRNs in fine or F-VF condition offered for sale at prices only very slightly in excess of their face value. I would strongly recommend holding out for higher grades, however, since the premiums for these notes in XF or AU condition are still fairly modest.

These notes were issued for all districts in Series 1928 and 1934, but for Series 1934A there were no $500 notes from Boston and no $1000 notes from Dallas. Thus a complete series and district set of these issues would consist of 35 notes of each of these two denominations. I wonder if anyone has ever attempted such a project! Star notes are known for all three series and for all 12 districts. All of the star notes sold at recent auctions have been for Series 1934 and 1934A notes, but the Oakes and Schwartz catalog records serial numbers for some districts of Series 1928 in replacement form for both the $500 and $1000 denominations. If you can afford high denomination star notes, expect to pay at least six times face for these star notes in CU and about triple face for such notes in VF-XF condition. I recently splurged and obtained a Series 1934 $500 star note and a Series 1934A $1000 star, the former from the San Francisco district while the latter is from Chicago. Both are in XF-AU condition. In the Dallas sale held in August, 1998 a Series 1934 $500 star note from San Francisco sold for an unprecedented $7975. This is much higher than any of the other recent realizations for high denomination star notes, and it may be indicative in a new trend on notes for which there was not much interest in previous years. The star notes of Series 1934 and 1934A appear to be of comparable abundance for both denominations, but judging from their absence from recent auction offerings, I expect that Series 1928 star notes of either denomination will prove very difficult and quite expensive to acquire.

The $500 and $1000 FRNs show peculiarities with regard to their back check numbers. On the $500 backs I have seen check numbers from 1 through 12, and all of these are "micro" numbers. On the $1000 backs I have seen check numbers of 1 through 8. Of these nos. 1 - 4 are "micro" numbers, but nos. 5 - 8 are "macro" numbers. Thus all Series 1934 $500 notes are non-mule notes, and all Series 1934A $500 notes are mules. For the $1000 FRNs both Series 1934 and 1934A exist as mules and non-mules. The faces of all Series 1934 notes of both denominations have "micro" check number 1, while all Series 1934A notes have "macro" check number 2. Usually the $500 and $1000 notes parallel each other very closely, but in this case there are many more possibilities for mules and non-mules with the $1000 notes than there are for the $500 notes. Personally I don't think that these denominations are good ones for seeking out all possible mule and non-mule varieties!

The $500 and $1000 FRNs show the same variations in the colors of their seals and serial numbers that are found on the lower denomination notes. The Series 1934 notes were produced both with light green and dark green seals. Some Series 1934 notes of these denominations were printed well into the 1940s, and thus they overlapped production of Series 1934A notes. As might be expected, changeover pairs are possible for these denominations.

If you are planning to form a large collection of small-size notes, I would include at least one $500 and one $1000 FRN in it. In terms of constant dollars they are now much less expensive than they were in past decades, but the prices that these notes are bringing in auction are also now showing signs of significant increases, doubtless because there is far more numismatic interest in these notes than was the case in past years. The premiums asked for these notes are now bringing some out of storage. In the summer of 1998 Spink America sold a large hoard that contained 360 $500 and 228 $1000 FRNs. Most of these were decidedly circulated, and a substantial percentage were even damaged. Although these notes in such condition still do not bring prices that are greatly in excess of their face value, paying a little extra for higher grades on these two denominations is definitely worth the price.

The two ultrahigh denomination FRNs are major rarities. According to current Treasury records there are 340 $5000 notes and 335 $10,000 notes outstanding, but the numbers known to collectors are about half of these totals. Of these, 100 of the $10,000 notes are in the famous $1 million currency display at Binion's Horseshoe Casino in downtown Las Vegas. All of these notes are Series 1934 issues from the New York district. If you are on vacation in Las Vegas, this display is well worth a visit. You can also obtain a complementary photograph of yourself standing by this famous collection.

In the late 1970s $5000 and $10,000 FRNs in choice condition sold at premiums of only about 40% over their face value, but these notes have experienced dramatic price increases in the past two decades. Today $5000 FRNs sell for about $35,000 - $40,000 each in AU - CU and about $20,000 - $25,000 when in VF-XF condition. Series 1934 notes are more common than are Series 1928 notes, but there doesn't seem to be much price differential between the two series for notes of this denomination. A totally unprecedented price of $82,500, however, was obtained for a Series 1928 $5000 note from the Boston district in gem CU condition at a CAA auction held at the beginning of 1999.

Most known $10,000 FRNs are of Series 1934. There was even some question as to whether or not Series 1928 $10,000 notes still existed, but a VF-XF note of this series from the Atlanta district was sold at a CAA auction in September, 1996 at a price of $46,750. In May, 1998 a Series 1928 $10,000 FRN from the Richmond district in CU condition sold for $126,500, a price that totally breaks all records for a small-size note of any type. In June, 1998 Spink America sold two Series 1934 $10,000 notes from the Boston district. Both were in AU-CU condition, and they sold for $71,500 each. In today's market it seems that at least $40,000 or $50,000 is necessary to obtain a decent example of a Series 1934 $10,000 FRN from any district.

Much of the demand for these notes has come from persons who are not collectors. It seems that some very wealthy persons have purchased these notes for the purpose of ostentatiously displaying (or should I say flaunting?) them. Although my collection of small-size notes is now quite comprehensive, I do not own examples of either of these two denominations, and I am not planning to acquire them at any time in the foreseeable future.

According to BEP records $5000 FRNs were printed for nine districts in Series 1928 and eleven districts in Series 1934. The $10,000 FRNs were printed for eleven districts each for both of these series. There are no star notes known for either of these denominations. Aside from the notes on display in Las Vegas there is no detailed census by series, district, and serial number of the ultrahigh denomination notes. At the present time, however, it is most unlikely that these notes still exist for all or perhaps even most of the districts for which they were originally printed. This would be especially true for several of the possible varieties of Series 1928 notes.

The $5000 and $10,000 FRNs should only be collected by persons who can easily afford them. They have proven to be very good investments for the past 20 years, but will that remain the case? It is always possible that Binion's Horseshoe Casino may someday come under new management, and the new owners may decide to liquidate this famous collection. This would dump a large number of $10,000 FRNs onto the market in a short period of time, and I expect that prices for $5000 notes would also be adversely affected, should such a happening occur. The notes that are presently being held by nonnumismatists may remain off the market for many years, but it is also possible that many of the persons now holding them will tire of these items and dump them back into the market in fair numbers. Before deciding whether or not to purchase one or both of these denominations such factors as these should be taken into consideration.

Thus we come to the end of our survey of small-size Federal Reserve Notes. If you collect small-size notes at all, you will doubtless acquire numerous examples of these issues. But since thousands of varieties of these notes are in existence, I feel that you should carefully consider in advance just what you want to collect. Without doubt the $1 and $2 FRNs are most often collected as district sets, but this form of collecting rarely extends to any of the higher denominations. I have collected both the $5 through $100 and the $500 and $1000 notes by series and it is possible to complete such a collecting project, although you will find that great patience and fairly ample funds are most definitely needed. Forming a type set of the major varieties of the $5 through $100 notes is an alternate and much less difficult approach that still offers some challenge to complete. If you really want to specialize in these issues, however, it is possible to collect them by districts and by serial number blocks, but then the numbers of notes required for completion runs into the thousands. You should also then consider whether or not you want to tie up this much capital in assets that do not pay interest. Although some small-size FRNs have risen sharply in price during the past two decades, this is probably not true for most of the notes with denominations of $5 and up that have been printed in the last 25 years. The investment potential of most recent FRNs is doubtless adversely affected by the huge numbers of different varieties that do exist, a factor that causes most collectors to assemble these notes only in a fairly simplified fashion.

CHAPTER FIVE

FRACTIONAL CURRENCY

Although Fractional Currency has not circulated for well over a century, it did play an essential role in our nation's money supply during the Civil War years and in the immediate post-Civil War period. Today it is one of the most popular forms of U. S. paper money particularly since sizable numbers of fractional notes are still available, and for the most part these items are not very expensive.

When the Demand Notes were first issued in August, 1861, it was intended that they should be a temporary issue only and that they should be fully convertible into specie (i. e., gold and silver). As things turned out, the Federal government was quite correct on the first assumption, but it was most definitely wrong on the second. By the end of 1861 all specie payments were halted, and for the next decade or more almost all government paper money was inconvertible into specie at par. The Demand Notes were very soon to be replaced by the much longer-lived United States Notes, and the circulation of the latter notes effectively removed all gold coins from normal circulation. But silver coins also disappeared from circulation, and this created a serious problem in conducting smaller transactions.

In the Northern states numerous municipalities and private organizations issued small-change notes. These were also augmented by vast issues of metallic tokens, which were generally in bronze and of the one-cent denomination. None of these items had legal tender status, and some of them were fraudulently issued by parties who had no intent of redeeming them. There was also an attempt to circulate unused postage stamps as money, and various private individuals printed special envelopes for holding stamps of a specified total face value. Although there were stamps for 5 cents and 10 cents, the contemporary higher value stamps of denominations 12, 24, 30, and 90 cents were not well suited as substitutes for the subsidiary silver coins that were needed for most transactions. In any case all stamps soon proved to be most unsuitable as a circulating medium. They readily stuck together and soon became quite tattered or dirty. A few attempts were made to mount a stamp onto a small piece of thin cardboard, but the idea for fractional notes apparently arose with the Treasurer of the United States, Francis E. Spinner.

Fractional Currency was first placed into circulation in August, 1862, and soon after its appearance the issue of small-change notes by municipalities or private individuals was made illegal. The issuance of Fractional Currency continued until 1876, and for most of these years it proved to be an essential component of our nation's money supply. During these 14 years there were five distinct issues of these notes, and thus numerous types of fractional notes can be distinguished.

The First Issue of Fractional Currency was printed by the National Bank Note Co. and by the American Bank Note Co. in New York. This issue is designated as being receivable for postage stamps, an obligation that was to appear on the next three issues of Fractional Currency as well. They also state that they are redeemable in United States

Notes when presented in sums of $5 or more. On the other four issues of these notes the minimum amount required for redemption was reduced from $5 to $3. The First Issue notes are designated Postage Currency, but for the other four issues the term Fractional Currency is formally used. Almost all collectors, however, refer to all five of these issues as Fractional Currency.

The face designs of the First Issue fractional notes depict the 5¢ and 10¢ postage stamps first issued in 1861. Since the 5¢ stamps were printed in brown and the 10¢ stamps in green, these colors were used for the faces of the notes for these denominations. The 25¢ notes show five of the 5¢ stamps, while the 50¢ notes depict the same number of 10¢ stamps. The 5¢ and 10¢ stamps are 65 x 45 mm in size and were printed in sheets of 20 subjects, while the 25¢ and 50¢ stamps are 78 x 48 mm in size and were printed in sheets of 16 subjects each. All of these notes have back designs printed in black, and the 5¢ and 25¢ notes are printed on buff-colored paper while the other two denominations are on white paper. These notes, like all other types of Fractional Currency, have no serial numbers.

The First Issue of fractionals were issued with or without a monogram of the American Bank Note Co. on their backs. The perforated example shown above displays perfs that are much sharper than what are usually found on these notes.

Most collectors and currency catalogs recognize 16 different major varieties for the notes of the First Issue. The earlier notes were perforated on all four sides (perforated 12, or 12 holes per 20 mm), just as were all of the postage stamps of that era. The later and more common notes of this issue were imperforate, as were all subsequent issues of Fractional Currency. The reason there are 16 major varieties of these notes and not just eight is that the American Bank Note Co. added an ABNCo monogram to the lower right of each note whose back was printed by them. Notes whose backs were printed by the National Bank Note Co. do not have this monogram. For the imperforate varieties these notes are much scarcer than are those having the ABNCo monogram. All 16 notes of this issue are obtainable, although perforated varieties are generally much more difficult to acquire in choice condition than are the imperforate notes.

As I noted in Chapter 1, the prices for fractional notes in very choice condition have risen substantially in recent years and there now is a wide spread in prices between notes that are in a superb CU grade and those that are merely in typical new condition. In the case of the perforated notes one must take into consideration both the centering and the quality of the perforations. Often the latter are clipped, pulled, or even trimmed off on one or more sides. Clearly such notes are much less attractive, and these sell for significantly lower prices than do gem CU notes. For the latter prices of between $200 and $400 per notes are now being realized for the three lower denominations, and in 1995 a superb 50¢ perforated note fetched almost $750. Examples with intact perforations but with substandard centering (as is usually the case) do sell for significantly lower prices than these. The notes without the ABNCo monogram on their backs are scarcer than are their monogrammed counterparts, but the price differential between these two varieties is not very great for the perforated varieties of any of the four denominations. In VF condition these notes sell for from about $35 to about $60 each, but such notes will probably have some problems with their perforations. In my opinion a well-centered note in XF condition with all its perforations intact is far more desirable than is a strictly new note with numerous perfs trimmed or missing, as is so often the case.

One rare variety that is often included with the regularly issued perforated notes is the 50¢ note with the ABNCo monogram on its back but perf. 14 rather than the normal perf. 12. It has now been established that these notes were privately produced by dealer Harlan P. Smith in about 1890, or ca. 28 years after the notes themselves were printed. It is believed that two sheets or 32 notes were thus perforated, but only about a dozen or so examples of this variety are presently known. They always are in AU or CU condition, and often these notes come with selvage from the edge of a sheet. In recent auctions these notes have sold for about $3000 to $4500 each. In view of the rarity of these items this price seems justified, but it may seem a bit high when we consider that this note is merely a private alteration that was produced years after these notes ceased to circulate.

The imperforate notes with the ABNCo monogram on their backs are much the most common of the First Issue notes. The firm Currency Auctions of America (CAA) estimates that the imperf varieties without monograms are about 35 times scarcer than their monogrammed counterparts for all four of the denominations, but the former notes only sell for about three times the prices of the latter when in comparable condition. When in choice CU condition the more common of the 5¢ and 10¢ imperforate notes sell for about $75 to $100 each, while the 25¢ and 50¢ notes are more like $125 to $150 each. In VF-XF condition these notes sell for about one-third these prices, and thus they should be affordable to almost all currency collectors. Complete sheets are known for all four denominations of the monogrammed imperforate notes, but these are rarely offered, particularly with wide margins on all four sides.

During the past four years there have been two major collections of Fractional Currency that have been sold at auction, both by Currency Auctions of America. In January, 1995 the collection formed by Martin Gengerke was sold, and two years later the collection of Milton Friedberg was auctioned. The Gengerke collection was the only holding of these notes thus far formed that contained all of the major varieties as listed in the standard currency catalogs. The Friedberg collection lacked a few of the greatest rarities among the regularly issued notes, but it was considerably more extensive, since it also contained many proofs, experimental notes, and other auxiliary items related to Fractional Currency. Three of the more unusual First Issue items in this collection were covers on which these notes had been used as postage. Two of these were contemporary (i. e., early 1860s), but the third was only canceled in the 1930s. Although these notes were never intended to be used as postage, it seems that this practice was tolerated to a limited extent.

Production of the First Issue fractional notes was halted in May, 1863, and by that time the printing of the Second Issue of fractional notes was already in its initial stages. These were produced by the Currency Printing Bureau of the Treasury Department in Washington. This office was shortly to become the Bureau of Engraving and Printing. These notes were produced at a substantially lower cost to the government than were the First Issue notes, a matter than Spencer M. Clark, the superintendent of the bureau and the man most responsible for their production was to emphasize.

For this issue, the notes of all four denominations were of the same size, viz., 66 x 48 mm, and all were printed in sheets of 20 subjects. Overprints in bronze ink were made on both sides of these notes, the faces having a large oval about a portrait of George Washington, while large numerals appeared at the center of each back design. The faces of all of these notes were printed in black, but the colors of the backs are different for each denomination. The 5¢ notes have reddish brown backs, the 10¢ green backs, the 25¢ purple backs, and the 50¢ notes have red backs. Although the 5¢ and 10¢ notes are fairly consistent in their coloration, the two higher denominations show several distinct shades. In addition to various shades of purple, the 25¢ notes are also known with slate-gray backs. The earlier issues of the 50¢ notes have light red backs, but later issues usually come with deep carmine red backs.

Although the First Issue notes were only in production for about ten months during 1862-63, the Second Issue was printed for a full two years between 1863 and 1865. As a consequence, significantly more varieties are known for the latter issue. The 5¢, 10¢, and 25¢ notes all have large "5," "10," or "25" numerals overprinted at the centers of their backs, and the most common variety for each of these notes has no additional overprints on their back sides. At one time it was felt that a small number of 50¢ notes were also printed in this fashion, but it is now believed that all such notes are either fraudulent alterations or a notes in which the corner letters have faded off.

Most of the Second Issue notes are printed on hard bank note paper similar to that which was used for the First Issue notes, but late in the production of the Second Issue some of the notes were printed on a thin, fragile fiber paper. This paper can be separated into even thinner sheets, since the fibers were placed between the two layers of this paper in its manufacture process. In terms of the percentages of notes issued about 0.5% of the 5¢ notes were on fiber paper, 0.7% of the 10¢ notes, 4.0% of the 25¢ notes, and 10.5% of the 50¢ notes for the Second Issue of Fractional Currency. There is one variety each of the 5¢ and 10¢ notes on fiber paper, but there are two different major varieties for the 25¢ notes and three varieties of the 50¢ notes on this type of paper.

Almost all of the Second Issue notes with overprints on their backs (in addition to the large numerals at their centers) have the control numerals 18 - 63 in their bottom corners. At their tops various control letters or numerals were used. The standard catalogs list four major varieties for the 5¢ notes, five fairly common ones for the 10¢ notes, seven for the 25¢ notes, and six for the 50¢ cents. These totals include varieties for both types of paper and for notes with no control letters or numerals. Often these letters are indistinctly printed, and sometimes one or more of them may be missing. Although missing letters or numerals were once thought to be significant errors, they are now regarded only as minor varieties. None of these notes will prove very difficult to acquire in VF or XF condition, but gem CU examples of some of the scarcer fiber paper varieties have fetched more than $500 each in recent auctions. Second Issue fractional notes are often poorly trimmed and/or poorly centered. Notes with wide margins and with very good centering will command large premiums over notes that have the centering and margins that are more typical for notes of this issue. Notes with very sharp overprints on their backs sell for more than notes with blurred overprints. The large premiums that were asked for notes with missing numerals or letter in their overprints are no longer there, and these items are now usually regarded as mere curiosities that command only nominal premiums over normal notes of the same type.

Shown above are the backs of two Second Issue fractionals, a 25¢ note overprinted 18-63-S (Fr. 1286 or H-1555) and a 50¢ note on fiber paper overprinted T-1-18-63 (Fr. 1322 or H-1585). The overprints on Second Issue notes are often blurred, and often some of the numerals in their corners are missing as is the case with the 25¢ note depicted above.

There is one significant rarity among the major varieties of the Second Issue fractional notes, and that is the 10¢ note on regular paper but with the overprint O - 63 on its back. Only about 30 examples are presently known. A poorly centered CU example in the Gengerke sale brought $2255 in 1995, while an AU specimen in the Friedberg sale fetched $1210 in 1997. Before purchasing one of these rarities it would probably be advisable to check with an expert on Fractional Currency such as Leonard Glazer (Currency Auctions of America) or Martin Gengerke (R. M. Smythe). Although I have not heard of fraudulent alterations for this note, it would be possible to manufacture one by overprinting the common 10¢ note that has no control numerals or letters in its corners.

Complete sheets are known for the 5¢, 10¢, and 50¢ notes of the Second Issue, but I do not know of any complete sheets of the regularly issued 25¢ Second Issue notes. Neither the Gengerke nor the Friedberg collections had any complete sheets for the Second Issue fractional notes, and all complete sheets of this issue can be regarded as being very rare. The Second Issue does abound in experimental and other types of unissued notes, and these I shall discuss later on in this chapter.

The Third Issue of Fractional Currency is by far the most complex of these notes. All of these items were printed by the Bureau of Engraving and Printing with production beginning at the end of 1864 and continuing into 1869. Various sizes and sheet formats were used for this issue. The sizes of these notes were as follows:

3¢	67 x 42 mm	15¢	90 x 48 mm
5¢	67 x 48	25¢	98 x 48
10¢	84 x 48	50¢	115 x 48

The 3¢ notes were printed in sheets of 25, the 5¢ notes in sheets of 20, the 10¢ notes in sheets of 16, and the 25¢ and 50¢ notes in sheets of 12 subjects each. As is normal for all fractional notes, there is some variation in the sizes of these items and notes with wide margins are now commanding substantial premiums over their more typical counterparts that often have very tight margins.

With the exception of the 3¢ denomination all notes of this series exist either with red or with green backs. The notes with green backs were printed in far larger quantities than were their red back counterparts, but the notes with red backs account for many of the distinct varieties. Sheets of the 5¢, 10¢, 25¢, and 50¢ notes of this issue were marked with position indicators, either "1" or "a," or with both of these. The left column of notes on the 5¢ and 25¢ sheets used the "a" designation, while the "1" designation was used on the left column of sheets of the 10¢ notes. For 5¢ notes those with "a" will be four times scarcer than those without it; for the 10¢ notes those with "1" will be three times scarcer than those without it, and for the 25¢ notes those with "a" will be twice as scarce as those without it. Despite these differences in scarcity, notes with these position letters or numerals generally sell for only fairly modest premiums over the prices asked for the same notes lacking these features.

For the 50¢ notes each sheet of 12 subjects contained six notes with no position indicators, three with "1," two with "a," and one with both "1" and "a." The notes with either "1" or "a" tend to be worth only somewhat more than those lacking these features, but the "1a" notes of the 50¢ denominations command large premiums. Several changes of style and of size are noted in these features for some of the 50¢ notes, but almost all collectors prefer to ignore these variations.

The 3¢ and 10¢ notes of the Third Issue depict George Washington and an allegorical representation of Justice was used on the earlier 50¢ notes of this issue, but the other notes of this series depicted persons living at the time. Spencer Clark appears on the 5¢ notes, the then Secretary of the Treasury William Fessenden on the 25¢ notes, and Francis Spinner on the later 50¢ notes of this issue. The use of Spinner's portrait was appropriate for a fractional note, since he is the person more responsible than any other for the development and circulation of these issues. Other U. S. currency had already depicted living persons, since Salmon P. Chase appeared on the Series 1862 $1 United

States Notes and Abraham Lincoln had appeared on both Demand Notes and United States Notes of the $10 denomination.

The 3¢ notes of the Third Issue occur in two well-known varieties, which have been termed the light curtain and dark curtain types.

Although no objections were voiced as to the use of Fessenden's or Spinner's portraits on U. S. currency, Clark's portrayal on the 5¢ notes met with strong opposition from some quarters. One reason for this was that while individuals such as Chase, Fessenden, and Spinner all had numerous political connections on the Washington scene, Clark did not. Other opposition probably also came from the bank note companies in New York, who resented the fact that Clark had moved the production of Fractional Currency to Washington from their facilities in New York. As a result of the outcry, Clark was forced to resign from the Treasury, but subsequently he did obtain a position with the Bureau of Mines. In 1866 the issue of 5¢ notes was discontinued and they were replaced with 5¢ cupronickel coins, the familiar nickels that were first struck in that year.

The 10¢ notes of the Third Issue are unusual in that the denomination (10¢) is not explicitly stated. Both of the notes above are autographed notes with the autographs of Francis Spinner together with the autographs of S. B. Colby (at top) and Noah Jeffries (bottom). The latter is extremely rare except on a few fractional notes.

Also in 1866 an act was passed that prohibited the further use of living persons on government securities. By this time plates for the Third Issue 15¢ notes had already been prepared. These depicted Generals U. S. Grant and W. T. Sherman, both of whom were very much alive at the time. Although these notes were never regularly issued, uniface specimen notes were prepared by the Treasury Department, and these are without doubt the most popular and available of the unissued types of U. S. currency. The 3¢ and 15¢ notes were largely prepared to make it easy to purchase 3¢ postage stamps at a time when this was the basic letter rate.

The 15¢ notes of the Third Issue depict Grant and Sherman. They could not be regularly issued due to the law passed in 1866 that forbade the depiction of living persons on U. S. government securities. These are by far the most collectible of the non-issued notes for any series of paper money.

The 3¢ notes are the smallest and simplest of all types of U. S. currency to collect. There are two major varieties, the so-called "light curtain" and "dark curtain" varieties, referring to the shading of the curtain behind Washington's portrait. The latter is the less common of the two, but both are readily available. Choice CU examples of either note can sell for well over $100 each, but nice VF or XF notes are more like $15 to $25 each in today's market.

The 5¢ note is also a very simple issue, but it does come with both red and green backs. Unlike the 3¢ notes that bear no signatures, the 5¢ notes of this issue always carry the printed signatures of Colby and Spinner. These notes exist both with and without an "a" position indicator, but all four of these varieties are fairly easy to obtain. Gem CU notes with red backs now sell for more than $200 each, and those with green backs in similar condition will fetch significantly more than $100 each, but attractive VF or XF examples of all of the 5¢ Third Issue notes should cost no more than $20 or $30 each.

The 25¢ notes of the Third Issue occur with two different types of overprints. The so-called "solid disk" varieties are very much rarer than are those with more open overprints at their sides.

    The 10¢ notes of this issue have a design peculiarity. On neither their faces nor their backs is the word "cents" used. Due to their small size it seems unlikely that they were ever successfully passed as $10 notes, but doubtless some individuals attempted to do this. There are six different collectible varieties of this note, four with red backs and two with green backs. The notes having printed signatures of Colby and Spinner (two of the red-back notes and both green-back notes) exist both with and without a "1" position indicator. The green-back 10¢ notes are probably the most common of all the Third Issue fractionals, and choice CU examples should cost no more than about $50 each. Their red back counterparts are less common, but they should sell for no more than the equivalent 5¢ notes of this series.

    The other two notes with red backs have autographed signatures either of Colby and Spinner or of Jeffries and Spinner. One of the peculiarities of the Third Issue fractionals is that there are several varieties with autographed signatures. These were printed in sheets with different layouts from those of the normally issued notes, and they always lack any sheet position indicators. Although the Jeffries-Spinner signature combination is extremely rare on national bank notes, the only type of large-size notes on which it exists, it is available to collectors in autographed form on some of the Third Issue fractionals. Both of the autographed 10¢ notes are scarcer than are the similar notes with printed signatures, the Jeffries-Spinner combination being the scarcer of the two, but in choice condition they should cost no more than $100 to $200 each in today's market. In VF-XF condition these two notes can probably be had for more like $40 to $60 each.

There is one extreme rarity among the 10¢ notes of the Third Issue. This variety has the autographed signatures of Colby and Spinner, but with a green rather than a red back. Only two examples are known at the present time. Both are uncirculated, but neither has perfect centering. The example in the Gengerke collection sold for $21,450 in 1995, while that in the Friedberg collection sold for an amazing $39,600 in 1997. This is by far the highest price ever paid thus far for a piece of Fractional Currency. It seems all the more amazing when we consider that this same note but with printed rather than autographed signatures is extremely common, and a nice XF copy can be had for no more than $15. A few years ago a price of over $10,000 would have been considered as excessively high for any fractional note, but this is clearly no longer the case.

As has been noted, the 15¢ fractionals of the Third Issue were never regularly issued. These exist as uniface specimens both with narrow and with wide margins. The most common of these varieties have the printed signatures of Colby and Spinner, and this is usually paired with a green back, but red backs are also encountered as are faces bearing the autographed signatures of Jeffries and Spinner and of Allison and Spinner. The notes are almost always in nice condition, either new or with signs of minimal handling, since they were never intended for normal circulation. A narrow margin pair of the Colby-Spinner notes sells for not much more than $200, but gem CU wide pairs of these notes typically bring more like $500 or a bit more.

There are also two notable rarities among the 15¢ Third Issue notes. These are the notes with the autographed instead of printed signatures of Colby and Spinner, of which only a few examples are known only with narrow margins. Even rarer is this note with no signatures at all. Only one example of this item is known, and it has fairly large margins indicating that it was trimmed from a wide margin specimen. In the Friedberg auction held in 1997, an example of the former in new condition fetched $1100, while the unsigned note in gem CU condition brought $3740. This price seems fairly low when compared to that obtained for the autographed 10¢ note in the same auction, but this large price differential may be explained by the fact that the 15¢ note was an unissued specimen whereas the 10¢ rarity is classified as an issued note.

Although 15¢ Third Issue fractionals are most often sold as pairs, single notes (either faces or backs) also are frequently offered. Occasionally one finds notes in which a face and a back have been glued together. Such a note would have passed for 15 cents in everyday commerce in the late 1860s, and thus this issue was far from being merely an essay or unissued design.

The 25¢ notes of the Third Issue come with both red and green backs. All of these notes bear the printed signatures of Colby and Spinner. Every third note of this group has an "a" position letter, but some variation exists in the sizes of these letters and this has caused much confusion in cataloging these notes. The 25¢ red-back note having the letter "a" exists as only one variety, earlier catalogs notwithstanding. The letter "a" on this note is always 1.0 mm high, and this size is also found on many of the 25¢ notes with green backs. There is some range of sizes for this letter on green-back notes, however, and I also have in my collection such a note with an "a" that is 1.4 mm high. Formerly this was considered as number 1296 in the Robert Friedberg catalog, but the true large "a" variety that has this catalog number displays this letter well down and 7 mm to the right of its normal location.

The regular red-back and green-back 25¢ notes are easy enough to acquire, and they should cost little more than do their 10¢ equivalents, but the true large "a" variety is very rare, as only about 15 examples are known to exist. Both the Gengerke and the Milton Friedberg collections contained this note, and both notes were in choice CU condition. The former sold for $1760 in 1995, while the latter fetched $1980 in 1997.

The 25¢ Third Issue fractionals also exist on thick fiber paper that is quite different from the very thin fiber paper that was used for printing some of the Second Issue fractionals. These notes exist only with green backs, but both unlettered and "a" varieties exist. All of these notes bear the overprint M-2-6-5 in the corners of their backs. Actually there are four varieties of this issue, since the faces exist either with the normal light overprint in bronze ink at either side or with a heavy, solid bronze overprint incorporating the numeral "25" in the same locations. The former notes are decidedly scarcer than are their counterparts printed on regular paper, but nice examples in XF-AU condition still should not cost more than $100 each.

The so-called "solid disk" varieties of this issue are very rare, as only about 30 of the unlettered notes are known and only about 12 of the "a" notes have come to light for this variety. The former note typically brings about $1000 when in XF or AU condition, but several of the known examples are damaged. One of the examples in the Friedberg collection, however, was in gem CU condition, and it sold for $3080. The example of the solid disk "a" note in both the Gengerke and the Friedberg collections was the same note, and its condition is AU, but there is some writing on its back. This note brought $3740 in 1995, but it was resold for only $2860 in January, 1997. In September of the same year a problem-free XF example of this rarity sold at auction for $1625. I would regard this latter example as the more attractive of the two, and so it seems that great rarities are not always the best of short-term investments.

The 50¢ notes of the Third Issue are by far the most complex of all the Fractional Currency issues, and majority of the great rarities in fractionals are among these notes. The earlier type of these notes depicted a figure of Justice on their faces, but later on a portrait of Francis Spinner was used. This change in design was adopted because of fairly extensive counterfeiting of the Justice notes. There are also two different back designs, the first of which comes in both red and in green and is used on both the Justice and the Spinner notes. The second is in green only and was used only on the Spinner notes. All 50¢ Third Issue notes have two vertical overprints in bronze ink incorporating the word "FIFTY" on their face sides, and in the centers of their backs the numeral "50" always appears as an overprint in the same bronze ink.

All fractional notes with bronze ink overprints (thus including all Second Issue notes and all 10¢, 25, and 50¢ notes of the Third Issue) can show a degree of aging with regard to these overprints. Although these overprints should appear in a bright golden bronze shade, they sometimes have aged to either green or black. Occasionally notes that are otherwise in new condition have aged overprints. Clearly such notes cannot be regarded as being in gem CU or choice CU condition, although they are still to be regarded as being in attractive condition. Fifty-cent Third Issue notes are also often prone to having ink smudges (either red or green) on their faces that have come from their back sides.

Personally I see nothing wrong with light smudges, but some collectors are willing to pay substantial premiums for notes that are free of any such smudges. One other thing to consider with regard to condition for these notes is that the Justice notes were very closely spaced. It is very difficult to find these notes with good margins on all four sides, and most collectors must accept some degree of close trimming for notes of this type. I would always prefer an XF note with good margins to a CU note with very tight margins, but for Justice notes good margins are very much the exception rather than the rule.

The reason that there are so many varieties of 50¢ Third Issue notes is that most of these issues have four different varieties of plate position numbers or letters. In each sheet of 12 subjects there were six without such features, three with a "1," two with an "a," and one with both the "1" and "a" features. All of the notes that used this sheet arrangement have the printed signatures of Colby and Spinner, and a careful examination of these notes will show that the "1a" and "a" notes should have no trace of a printed signature in their top margins, but all of the plain and the "1" notes should show a small loop from the "p" of Spinner's signature in their top margins provided these notes have at least some margin at their tops. There are some variation in the sizes and styles of the "1" and the "a" in the various series of notes that have these features. Although the plate position varieties could be regarded as minor variants, all of the standard catalogs consider them to be major varieties, and so most Fractional Currency specialists try to obtain examples of each. If these features are treated as major varieties, there are a total of 51 different for the 50¢ Third Issue notes, a total that includes a number of autographed notes as well.

Thus defined there are a total of 32 major varieties of the Justice notes. Of these, 15 have red backs with the balance having green backs. The red-back notes occur with no letters or numerals overprinted on their back sides, or with either the sequences A-2-6-5 or S-2-6-4 overprinted in their corners. Twelve of the notes have printed signatures, and these have the aforementioned varieties of plate position numbers or letters. Three of the varieties were autographed by Colby and Spinner, and these notes lack these features. These notes also come with plain backs, or with the sequences A-2-6-5 or S-2-6-4 overprinted in their corners. All notes with the S-2-6-4 overprints are printed on the same thick fiber paper that was used for some of the 25¢ notes.

Of the 15 different red-back Justice notes 11 are collectible, although both the "1a" varieties with plain backs and with backs having the A-2-6-5 overprint in their corners are very scarce. The autographed note with the S-2-6-4 overprint on its back is also very scarce. The extreme rarities of the group, however, are the four notes with printed signatures and S-2-6-4 overprints in their back corners. It is believed that these were the first 50¢ Third Issue notes to be printed, since production of this issue commenced only in late 1864. In the Robert Friedberg catalog this quartet is given numbers of 1351-54 (or 1593-96 in the Hessler catalog), these referring to notes with no plate position features, "1a," "1," and "a," respectively. At the present time 8-10 are known for the first of these, 2 for the second, 6-7 for the third, and 6-7 for the fourth variety of these notes. In the Gengerke collection these notes were in CU, fine, AU, and AU, respectively, and they brought $18,700, $29,700, $9350, and $12,600 when sold in 1995. The notes of this group in the Milton Friedberg collection were all different from those in the Gengerke collection. No. 1352 was lacking, but the other three numbers were in CU, XF, and XF condition, respectively. These fetched respective prices of $27,500, $11,000, and $11,000 when sold in 1995. Although the red-back Justice note can be easily obtained as a type note, clearly only persons with very deep pockets should contemplate the acquisition of these four major rarities.

Of the 17 different green-back Justice notes there is also one major rarity. This is the note on fiber paper with the S-2-6-4 overprint on its back side (Fr. 1373a or H-1608a). Only nine examples of this rarity are known, and four of these are in a block of four. The Gengerke specimen was in choice AU condition, and it brought $23,650 in 1995. The specimen in the Friedberg collection was in similar condition, and it fetched $19,800 in 1997. It was noted, however, that this example has a small edge repair, and that feature probably lowered its price a bit.

The other 16 Justice notes with green backs are for the most part much more readily obtainable. All of these come with the usual four varieties of plate position designators. These notes exist with no overprints in their back corners, overprinted on back with widely spaced A-2-6-5 on plain paper, this same overprint on fiber paper, and with narrow spaced A-2-6-5 on plain paper. The widely spaced overprint measures 102 x 39 mm, while the narrow spaced overprint measures 94 x 34 mm. The very scarce S-2-6-4 overprint (found only on Justice notes) is also widely spaced, but all of the Spinner notes that feature the A-2-6-5 overprint have the narrow spaced version.

Of these 16 notes the rarities, of course, are those with "1a" position letters. Only about 12 to 15 each are known of these varieties with plain backs, widely spaced A-2-6-5 on regular paper, or widely spaced on fiber paper. These sell for well over $1000 each when in choice condition, but the narrow spaced "1a" variety (Fr. 1363 or H-1602) is significantly less rare. All of the other dozen varieties are also available, but I should note again that Justice notes in any of the better grades with good margins on all sides should always be regarded as highly desirable.

Of the 19 different varieties of Spinner notes, 7 have red backs while the other dozen are printed with green backs. The red-back Spinner notes are all printed on regular paper and have the compact A-2-6-5 overprint on their backs. In addition to the four notes having printed signatures of Colby and Spinner (and thus with the four plate position varieties) there are also three different autographed notes which lack these position designators. These three notes have the signature combinations Colby-Spinner, Allison-Spinner, and Allison-New. Of these seven notes four are fairly easy to acquire, but the "1a" note of the first group and the note with the Allison-Spinner signature combination will pose some difficulty. In choice CU condition both of these notes will cost about $750 each, but they can be purchased for substantially less in somewhat lower grades.

The great rarity among the Spinner notes is the red-back note with the autographed signatures of Allison and New (Fr. 1330, H-1615). Only about a dozen of these are known, and they were produced very late in the fractional era well after any regular printings of Third Issue notes were being made. The recorded notes of this type are mostly in choice condition, and both Gengerke's and Friedberg's examples were described as gem CU. They sold for $5885 and $5500, respectively.

There are 12 different types of Spinner notes with green backs. The first quartet has the usual green back and with no overprints in their corners. The second group has the compact A-2-6-5 overprint in the corners of their backs. The third group uses an entirely different back design. All three issues, of course, have the usual four different plate position varieties. Of the three different issues the second group with the A-2-6-5 overprints on their backs is much the most difficult to acquire. Only about 20 examples of the "1a" variety of this series are known, and I have also found the "a" variety of this series to be very elusive. The other Spinner notes with green backs should be much less difficult to acquire. The "1a" variety of the type I back without overprints (Fr. 1332, H-1617) is by far the most "common" of the "1a" 50¢ Third Issue notes, and if you should desire just one example of this scarce plate position, a nice XF example of this note can be obtained for only about $100 or so.

Shown are four different 50¢ notes of the Third Issue. All of these are "1a" notes, whose respective catalog numbers are Fr. 1359, 1348, 1325, and 1340 (H-1598, 1587a, 1610, and 1621). Note the variety of styles in these two design features. Contrary to the way these notes are listed in some paper money catalogs, the Justice notes were issued prior to the Spinner notes.

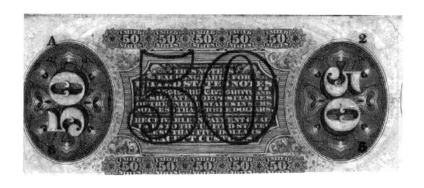

Many of the 50¢ notes of the Third Issue have overprints on their back sides. The compact A-2-6-5 overprints measure 94 x 34 mm, while both of the wide overprints measure 102 x 39 mm. The S-2-6-4 overprint is found only on Justice notes printed on thick fiber paper.

In my own collection I have attempted to get as many different major varieties of 50¢ Third Issue notes as is possible. Of the 51 possibilities I now have 43. Of the eight varieties that I lack, five are extreme rarities that I never expect to own. The Allison-New note is a bit less expensive than are the five S-2-6-4 rarities, but it is still a very rare item.

It would fetch an even higher price in choice condition were it not for the fact that all known examples are in this grade. There is no reason, however, why anyone should attempt to get all of the possible varieties of these notes. In my opinion there are just five major types for these notes, viz., the red-back and green-back Justice notes, and the Spinner notes with red backs, green type I backs, and green type II backs. It is not at all difficult to acquire one of each of these types, although Justice notes with nice margins are always fairly difficult, as I have already noted. If you should want to acquire additional notes of these types, most of the "1" and "a" notes carry only modest premiums over their plain counterparts, and most of the autographed notes are also fairly reasonable in price.

The only Third Issue fractional notes that are normally available in complete sheets are the 3¢ notes. Sheets of 25 notes appear at auction from time to time. The sheets of the dark curtain variety are encountered much less frequently than are those of the light curtain variety. Examples of the latter usually sell for little more than the price that 25 individual uncirculated copies of these notes would bring. A very few complete sheets are known for the other denominations of Third Issue notes, but all of these are extremely rare.

The 10¢, 15¢, and 25¢ notes of the Fourth Issue are noted for having either large Treasury seals (40 mm) or seals that are somewhat smaller (38 mm). The design elements of these seals are also not quite the same.

As was the case with the Postage Currency, the Fourth Issue of fractional notes was largely contracted to the New York printing companies. There are four denominations - 10¢, 15¢, 25¢, and 50¢ - but six major types, since the 50¢ notes of this issue appear in three radically different designs. The first notes of this denomination depicted Abraham Lincoln, but this note was counterfeited, and that led to the issuance of a second design featuring Edwin Stanton, Lincoln's Secretary of War. The Stanton note was also counterfeited, and so a third design featuring Samuel Dexter, an early Secretary of the Treasury, was issued. The sizes of these notes are as follows:

10¢	80 x 47 mm	50¢ Lincoln	105 x 47 mm
15¢	90 x 47	50¢ Stanton	103 x 47
25¢	97 x 47	50¢ Dexter	96 x 55

The Fourth Issue notes were printed between 1869 and 1875 at a time when there was much experimentation with security features on bank notes. All of these notes feature security devices of various types that include watermarks, silk fibers, localized blue staining, and colored seals. Despite the fact that this series is much less complex than is the Third Issue, there still has been confusion in the various catalogs as to just how many varieties there are for each note. In my opinion four or five distinct varieties can be recognized for each of the three lower denominations, but there is only one variety for each of the three major types of the 50¢ notes of this issue.

The Fourth Issue fractionals were initially printed on watermarked paper that contained only a very small number of pink silk fibers. The three lower denominations all exist in this form. Later on the number of silk fibers was considerably increased, and so it is possible to find these notes on watermarked paper but with a large number of silk fibers. Subsequently these notes were issued on heavily silked paper that was unwatermarked. Formerly the Robert Friedberg currency catalog distinguished the two varieties of silk paper, but it ignored the watermark differences. In more recent editions it has considered watermark varieties, but it has ignored the difference between lightly silked and heavily silked paper. For the 10¢ and 25¢ notes these three varieties are all more or less equally abundant, but the 15¢ note is very rare on unwatermarked paper. An uncirculated, but not well centered, example of this note sold for $440 in the Gengerke auction, and another much better centered CU example sold for $1210 in a September, 1997 auction. Note, however, that this note very closely resembles its counterpart on heavily silked but lightly watermarked paper. I feel that this note is not necessary for a "complete" collection of Fourth Issue notes, but if you want to purchase one of these rarities, be sure to very carefully examine the note for any trace of watermark. Most notes that are claimed to be this variety (Fr. 1268, H-1540) are actually Fr. 1267 (H-1539) printed on heavily silked paper.

There has also been confusion with regard to the 50¢ Lincoln note. All of these appear to be on watermarked paper, and the unwatermarked variety that was formerly listed in most catalogs has now been deleted. All of the notes that are printed with red Treasury seals (i. e., all notes of this issue except for the 50¢ Dexter note) are known with a pinkish cast on their faces. At one time these were regarded as distinct varieties, but it is now recognized that these variants arose when the plates used to print the seals were improperly cleaned.

The third type of security feature that was employed for the Fourth Issue notes was a localized blue stain. This feature appears only on the right side of the notes, since these notes were printed in a *tete-beche* fashion that facilitated the blue printing on only a portion of these notes. All of the notes printed with a localized blue stain are on heavily silked paper. The first issues of the 10¢, 15¢, and 25¢ notes with this feature depict a Treasury seal that is 40 mm in diameter. Later the design of this seal was modified somewhat and its size was reduced to 38 mm. These two varieties are treated as major varieties, and both are more or less equally common for all three denominations. The 50¢ Stanton note features a much smaller Treasury seal, but it always on heavily silked paper with a pronounced localized blue stain. The Dexter note was the first type of U. S. currency to feature a green Treasury seal. The blue staining on this note is always much more subdued than it is on the Stanton note.

A major item of controversy has arisen concerning the seal colors of the first group of blue-stained notes of this issue. These notes usually have red seals, but a few notes of each denomination (i. e., 10¢, 15¢, 25¢, plus the 50¢ Stanton note) are known with this seal in maroon or brown. Previously these were given numbers 1260, 1270, 1305, and 1377, respectively, in the Friedberg catalog. Although the prices quoted for these varieties were far higher than they were for their normal counterparts with red seals, experts on Fractional Currency have concluded that these varieties are actually chemical changelings that acquired their unusual seal colors after they entered circulation. When offered for sale these notes still sell for substantial premiums over the equivalent notes with red seals, but they need not be included in the collections of anyone who desires a "complete" collection of fractional notes.

The 50¢ Dexter note was the only note of the Fourth Issue to be printed in large part at the Bureau of Engraving and Printing. The face of this note has an imprint of the BEP, but its back features an imprint of the National Bank Note Company. This note carries both a plate number and plate position letter. The number of possible combinations of these features runs to several hundred, and this fact discourages collectors from attempting to form "complete" sets of this note that would include all possibilities for these design elements.

The Fourth Issue of Fractional Currency contains no true rarities, and the six major types of these notes can be obtained without much difficulty. By far the scarcest of these is the Lincoln note. A choice CU example may sell for as much as $300 or more, but this note is still available in VF or XF at prices significantly under $100. If you want to obtain all possible watermark, paper, and seal varieties of the 10¢, 15¢, and 25¢ notes, only the 15¢ note on heavily silked but unwatermarked paper is truly scarce, and much caution should be exercised in purchasing this note. But if you ignore that minor variant (in my opinion), the other possibilities should not cause you any major difficulties. The four varieties of "brown seal" notes have now been downgraded to color changelings, but if you desire them for your collection, you will find that they are decidedly scarce and difficult to acquire.

The Fifth Issue of Fractional Currency was issued between 1874 and 1876. Only three denominations were issued - 10¢, 25¢, and 50¢ - but the 10¢ notes come with both green and red Treasury seals. These notes depict William Meredith, Robert Walker, and William Crawford, respectively, all of whom were Secretaries of the Treasury during the first half of the 19th Century. Like the Dexter note of the Fourth Issue all of these designs were prepared at the BEP. The back designs for these notes, however, were subcontracted either to the Columbian Bank Note Co. of Washington or to Joseph R. Carpenter of Philadelphia. The 10¢ note measures 84 x 53 mm, the 25¢ note is 91 x 53 mm, and the 50¢ note is 112 x 53 mm in size.

The Fifth Issue is a very easy series of notes to collect. I would regard the green and red seal varieties of the 10¢ notes as distinct major types, but there are two other varieties that are also considered as distinct for this series. All of the green seal notes and the earlier printings of the red seal 10¢ and 25¢ notes of this issue have a Treasury seal that includes a thin key which is 5 mm long in its design. On later printings of the red seal 10¢ and 25¢ notes this has been changed to a thick key that is 4 mm long. Thus most syngraphists would include six different notes for this series in their collections. All of these varieties are common.

In past years there has been some confusion with regard to the notes of this series that have overall pinkish shades. Previously the Robert Friedberg catalog assigned special numbers for the pink shades of the "short key" 10¢ and 25¢ notes, and it also listed the 50¢ note of this issue both with and without this toning. Both the Friedberg and Hessler catalogs still continue to use two numbers (Fr. 1380-81 or H-1629-30) for the latter note, but all auctioneers and dealers use only number 1381 for this note. As I have already noted, an overall pinkish cast can occur with any of these notes that have red seals, and thus the so-called "pink" notes should not be regarded as distinct varieties.

All notes of the Fifth Issue have both plate numbers and plate position letters. Although these notes are readily available, the numbers of possible letter-number combinations runs into the hundreds for each of these notes, and thus almost no syngraphists attempt to collect these notes in this fashion. Although complete sheets are unknown for these notes, they are available in original bundles complete with the bands that were wrapped around such items. Usually the 10¢ notes are in bundles of 50, the 25¢ notes in bundles of 40, and the 50¢ notes in bundles of 20.

Although some collectors are now paying fancy prices for certain fractional notes in superb condition, I would not recommend this for any of the Fifth Issue notes. These notes are common in all grades, and with a little patience you should be able to find very choice examples for all of these notes at quite reasonable prices. If VF-XF condition is good enough for you, a set of all six of the major varieties of these notes should set you back less than $100.

One sideline of fractional note collecting are the so-called satirical notes. These are most often found on the 10¢ Fifth Issue notes, although the 25¢ notes of this issue were also sometimes used. On a typical note of this type the portrait of Meredith would be modified by including a hat, beard, moustache, or other features. These fall into the category of altered notes, and I shall discuss these items further in Chapter 12.

Many numismatic writers have concluded that a complete type set of fractional notes should consist of 24 different items. This set would include one note each of the four denominations of the First and Second Issues, seven notes of the Third Issue [one each of the 3¢, 5¢, 10¢, and 25¢ notes, plus one Justice and two Spinner notes (i. e., with both reverse designs)], six notes of the Fourth Issue, and one each of the 10¢, 25¢, and 50¢ notes of the Fifth Issue. Such a grouping, however, ignores the obvious differences between Third Issue notes with red and with green backs. The two designs for the 3¢ notes and the two seal colors for the 10¢ notes of the Fifth Issue are also major differences.

I feel that the total of 24 should be increased by at least 11 notes. There would then be eight First Issue notes (both perf. and imperf.), four Second Issue notes, both varieties of the 3¢ notes, both red and green back varieties for the Third Issue 5¢, 10¢, 25¢, 50¢ Justice, and 50¢ Spinner notes plus the second green back variety for the Spinner note, the six major types of the Fourth Issue notes, and four Fifth Issue notes including both seal colors for the 10¢ note. One should also consider adding at least three of the unissued 15¢ Third Issue notes (a face plus red and green backs) to such a collection. Additional varieties that might warrant major type status are the fiber paper varieties of the Second Issue, the thick fiber paper 25¢ and 50¢ notes of the Third Issue, the autographed 10¢, 15¢, and 50¢ notes of the Third Issue, and the blue end varieties of the 10¢, 15¢, and 25¢ notes of the Fourth Issue. Such additions would increase a collection of Fractional Currency to about 50 different items.

Thus far with one exception (the 15¢ note of the Third Issue) we have spoken only about the regularly issued fractional notes. Fractional Currency, however, also includes many items that were not intended for normal circulation, and it is the only type of U. S. paper money for which unissued items were ever made regularly available to the public.

Perhaps the most impressive display items of U. S. currency are the Fractional Currency shields that were prepared by the U. S. Treasury in 1866 and 1867. These consist of a large printed shield upon which 39 different uniface specimens of Fractional Currency have been mounted. In most cases this shield is printed in black ink, but since this printing is fairly light, it has the appearance of being printed in gray. Much scarcer are shields printed in red ("pink") or in green. Recently a shield was also sold in which the background was lilac brown in color. Gray shields in nice condition typically sell for about $4000 to $5000 each, although they are often affected by fairly serious aging or water stain problems. The purple back of the 25¢ Second Issue note is sensitive to light, and thus it is often faded or discolored to dull green on many shields.

The 39 notes mounted on these shields included the faces and backs for the First and Second Issues (8 of each) plus 23 different Third Issue specimens. This group includes both printed signature and autographed varieties for the faces of the 10¢, 15¢, and both types of 50¢ notes. Both face designs of the 3¢ notes are included, and both red and green back designs are included for the 5¢, 10¢, 15¢, 25¢, and 50¢ notes. The second back design for the 50¢ Spinner note was not used on these shields. According to Treasury Department records, 4500 of these shields were prepared but not all were sold. They were offered at a price of $4.50 each, which was slightly above the total value of the specimen notes with each note being figured at half its face value. Since sales were less than anticipated, a number of these were either dismantled or destroyed in 1869.

Contrary to a statement that is often made, there were no official frames for the Fractional Currency shields. It was up to the purchaser of a shield to frame it, if he so desired. Although they may have served some use as counterfeit detectors, it is far from clear that this was their major function. At least a few hundred of the gray shields still exist, and I have seen these in numerous places, especially in 19th century banks or in parlors or studies of historic houses of that era. When these items are sold in today's market, they generally come with a wooden frame and a glass overlay.

If you wish to acquire one of these shields, please bear in mind that they are fairly large. The shield itself measures 54 x 61 cm (21 x 24 inches), and the frame will increase its size significantly. Clearly it is not possible to store this item in a safety deposit box. It should not be exposed for long periods of time to bright light, but nearly all shields show some damage to the 25¢ Second Issue back, the most light-sensitive of the 39 specimens that are mounted on these shields. Nonetheless this shield does make a most impressive wall display.

The experimental notes of the Second Issue of Fractional Currency are among the earliest items actually printed by the Treasury Department in Washington. Shown are the back of a 10¢ note and the face of a 25¢ note. Both are overprinted SPECIMEN and have two semicircular holes, but the 25¢ note lacks the bronze oval overprint that is found on the faces of all issued notes of this series.

The uniface specimen notes of Fractional Currency exist for the first three issues only. These are clearly distinguished as narrow-margin and wide-margin notes. The latter are always the more valuable of the two, and in a few cases they are very much rarer and more expensive than are their narrow-margin counterparts. The specimens mounted on the Fractional Currency shields were always narrow-margin notes, but there are also many narrow-margin specimens that were never mounted on shields. All of these specimen notes are listed in the standard currency catalogs. In 1978 Milton R. Friedberg published *The Encyclopedia of United States Fractional and* Postal Currency, and in this book he distinguishes between the narrow-margin notes which he terms "specimens" and the wide-margin notes which he terms "proofs." There are also proofs for the Fourth and Fifth Issues of Fractional Currency, as well as a number of true proofs for the first three issues, but these were never issued to the public in the way in which the specimens of the first three issues were.

Although the uniface specimen notes did not circulate as currency, the narrow-margin specimens frequently have serious condition problems. Many of these have been removed from shields, and these often suffer from glue stains, adhering paper, edge tears and nicks, etc. The glue used is mounting them was not readily soluble in water as are most water-based glues today, and consequently it is not easy to remove adhering paper, etc., from their backs. For the most part, these specimen notes are relatively inexpensive, but finding notes in decent condition is quite a challenge.

Although specimens of the 15¢ Third Issue note was printed in no greater quantities than were any of the other specimen notes, I have found it to be the most available (but not the least expensive) of the narrow-margin specimen notes. In most cases these notes are also free of glue stains and other signs of having been mounted on shields. It is my opinion that many of the other narrow-margin specimen notes not used on shields were simply glued together and placed into normal circulation. Since the 15¢ notes were of a design that was not familiar to the public, not many of these were placed into circulation. When the face and back of given note were so attached, they had full legal tender status, and this may explain why one sees relatively few of the other narrow-margin specimens that are free of evidence of having been mounted on shields.

Aside from the 15¢ notes a complete set of narrow-margin specimen notes would consist of three 3¢ notes (both faces plus one back), seven 5¢ notes, nine 10¢ notes (including both varieties of autographed notes), seven 25¢ notes, and twelve 50¢ notes (including two varieties of autographed notes for both the Justice and Spinner notes). Excluded from this total, however, is the type II back for the Spinner note, for which only about a dozen examples are known, and the extremely rare Spinner face with the autographed signatures of Allison and Spinner. As I have noted, the former was never used on Fractional Currency shields. This item sells for about $750 in narrow-margin form. Only five examples of the Allison-Spinner specimen notes are known, and one of these was sold for $1375 in the Gengerke sale in 1995. This seems like a rather low price to pay for so rare an item, but clearly demand is less for specimens than it is for issued notes. In January, 1999 all three examples of the Allison-Spinner specimen notes not mounted on shields were sold at a CAA auction. These fetched prices that ranged from $2200 to $3740.

In addition to the 15¢ notes there are also two 50¢ notes that exist only in specimen form. These are the Justice and Spinner notes with the autographed signatures of Jeffries and Spinner. These are fairly scarce as narrow-margin specimens, but they are extremely rare as wide-margin specimens, since only two notes are known for each of these designs.

Narrow-margin specimens are generally very tightly trimmed, as this was the practice for the notes that were mounted on shields, but sometimes these notes are found with more adequate margins. Such items were probably trimmed from wide-margin notes. These notes are clearly worth substantially more than are the typical narrow-margin notes that are both very closely trimmed and that usually show evidence of having been mounted.

Condition is rarely a problem with wide margin notes, since they were never mounted on shields, but they tend to be much more expensive than are their narrow-margin counterparts. All of the 5¢ and 25¢ notes that exist as narrow-margin specimens also exist in wide-margin form, but typically they cost four or five times as much. All of the aforementioned 10¢ notes also exist in wide-margin form, but the Jeffries-Spinner autographed note is a major rarity in this form. As I have noted this signature combination is also excessively rare on wide-margin 50¢ Justice and Spinner specimens. The Allison-Spinner note that is extremely rare in narrow-margin form is even more rare in wide-margin form. Only very few examples of the 50¢ type II back specimen notes are known in wide-margin form. One of these sold for $3410 in the Gengerke auction. Another extreme rarity is the light curtain 3¢ specimen note in wide-margin form. Only three of these notes are believed to exist.

A variety of papers was used to print the Fractional Currency specimen notes. Some are on the normal paper that was used for the regularly-issued notes, but most are on a much thinner paper. Many of these are on paper that is watermarked "CSA." This is paper that was seized from blockade runners during the Civil War. Although specimen notes are often blank on their backs, many of these items come with the word "SPECIMEN" printed on their backs.

One additional set of items that is related to the Third Issue of Fractional Currency are the counterfeit detectors that were surface printed on thin cardboard and appeared in editions of *Heath's Infallible Counterfeit Detector* that were published between 1866 and 1872. These include the 5¢, 10¢, 25¢, and 50¢ Spinner faces of the Third Issue notes plus a counterfeit impression of a Spinner note. The individual impressions are often cut from the plates and typically they sell for about $25 each, although occasionally they are marketed as "proofs" and offered at substantially higher prices.

Another type of collectible directly related to Fractional Currency are the so-called experimental notes, most of which are of the Second Issue. It must be remembered that this issue of notes was the very first type of paper money that was actually printed by the Treasury in Washington. Numerous "experiments" were apparently carried out on designs, overprints, and paper characteristics. Since these notes were of low face value, sample notes were apparently distributed to interested parties since they would have involved little loss to the Treasury should some of them be redeemed. Most experimental notes are canceled with two semicircular hole punches, and they are usually overprinted "SPECIMEN" as well. The great majority of them are uniface, but some have partial designs on their "flip sides" as well.

Although Milton Friedberg assembled a sizable collection of normal and specimen fractional notes, it would be better to describe his holding of experimental fractional notes as both a collection and as a large accumulation. In fact, this was without question the largest holding of such notes ever assembled. When this accumulation was sold on January 10, 1997, much material that had not been seen in public for several decades came to light. It is most unlikely that we shall ever again see a holding of experimental notes that is even remotely as large as what was sold at that time. Thus the catalog prepared by Currency Auctions of America for this sale is an excellent reference as to what types of this material are in existence. Milton Friedberg also listed the experimental notes in his encyclopedia, and this is the other good reference for these items, since they are not listed in any of the standard catalogs.

The experimental notes are very specialized in nature, and I am not going to cover these in any detail. As I have noted, almost all are of the Second Issue but a few are Third Issue notes. By far the most common are the faces of the 25¢ Second Issue notes with the usual two hole cancellations and a handstamped SPECIMEN overprint. These exist both without and with the bronze oval overprint about Washington's head. Friedberg's holding included 123 of the former and 46 of the latter on normal paper, but there were also a number of others on special papers or with special overprints on their backs. If you would desire just one or two of the experimental notes, either of these varieties can now be obtained for about $100 to $125 each. The hole cancellations do not add to their attractiveness, however, and I would avoid purchasing a note in which one of the holes cuts into an edge. Although scarcer, three varieties of 10¢ notes, two 50¢ items, and the back of the 5¢ note are also collectible as experimental notes.

The Friedberg collection also contained experimental notes that are very much rarer than the above including several items that are believed to be unique. Of greatest interest were uniface color trials of the back designs of these notes for all four denominations in purple and in blue. Both of these sets are probably unique, and they brought $7700 and $8800, respectively, at this auction. Another set of four had their faces printed as the issued notes minus the bronze ovals, but their backs appeared in the issued colors but minus the central shields. This set fetched $5500 in this sale. Like almost all of the other experimental notes, these items had the usual two semicircular holes punched into their designs.

There are also a fairly large number of error notes that exist for the regularly issued fractional notes. Most of these involve inverted backs, and there are also several notes known with inverted overprints. These I shall discuss in the chapter devoted to currency errors. Aside from small-size notes, error notes are more readily available for Fractional Currency than they are on any other type of U. S. paper money.

During the 14 years in which fractional notes were in production a total of 1.819 billion notes with a total face value of almost $369 million was issued. This total breaks down to 124 million notes for the First Issue, 161 million for the Second Issue, 401 million for the Third Issue, 775 million for the Fourth Issue, and 357 million for the Fifth Issue. The maximum circulation of Fractional Currency occurred between 1873 and 1875 when about 838 million pieces were in circulation. This amount constituted almost five percent of our nation's currency supply at that time. Yet Fractional Currency went out more with a whimper than with a bang.

Once silver coins were again in normal circulation by the mid-1870s, the public soon expressed a preference for coins over small paper money, and this once vital component of our nation's currency soon lost all significance as a circulating medium. Yet many fractional notes did survive. Their small size and low face value contributed to the keeping of these items as souvenirs. If you plan to collect 19th Century paper money at all, almost certainly you will want to acquire at least a few fractional notes.

If you are just beginning with this series, I would suggest that you obtain a group lot that has many of the different types. Type sets containing 24 different notes are often available at auction including sets in a wide range of grades including uncirculated. As I have already noted, I do feel that there are more than 24 major types of these notes, and I think that a collection of about 50 of these items would be better representative of the different major types. You may want to try to acquire as many of the notes as possible that are given major number status in the three standard currency catalogs (i. e., Robert Friedberg, Gene Hessler, and Krause-Lemke). All six of the varieties of the Fifth Issue are extremely easy to obtain, but it is essentially impossible to obtain all 51 major varieties of the 50¢ Third Issue notes. A set of the five different major types might do quite nicely for the latter items. One of the nice things about collecting fractional notes is that all of the major rarities of this series are in reality just variants of type notes that are fairly common. Although there are about a dozen or so varieties of Fractional Currency given major number status in the standard catalogs that can be regarded as being very rare, all of the others can be acquired without too much difficulty or expense. You may also want to acquire a number of the specimen notes. The 15¢ Third Issue note enjoys a special status, since it is the only unissued type of U. S. government paper money that is normally available to collectors, but the other specimen notes may also be of interest to you particularly since they are listed in all of the standard catalogs. Items such as the so-called experimental notes may be largely of interest only to specialists, but at least there are a couple of varieties of these unusual items that should prove fairly easy to acquire.

    Of all the types of U. S. government paper money Fractional Currency is probably the series whose prices are most sensitive to condition. Getting well centered examples of the First Issue notes with perforations that are fully intact on all four sides will prove to be rather difficult, and you should expect to pay substantial premiums for such notes, but I would definitely not pay large premiums for any of the Fifth Issue notes regardless of condition since all of the latter are common in all grades. Most of the major currency auction firms feature numerous fractional notes in their sales, and I would become familiar with the way in which these notes are lotted and with the range of prices that they bring before sinking too much money into their acquisition. But since a comprehensive array of these notes can be obtained without a particularly large expenditure of money, I feel that Fractional Currency is one of the most rewarding areas of U. S. paper money to collect.

CHAPTER SIX

LARGE-SIZE TYPE NOTES

We now turn to the notes that are of greatest interest to a sizable number of currency collectors, viz., the large-size type notes that were issued between 1861 and 1929. In this chapter I wish to cover all of the various issues of large-size notes with the exception of national bank notes. These will be discussed in detail in the following chapter.

Before getting into the details of these issues there are a number of important things to consider, if you are planning seriously to collect large-size notes. Fundamentally these are fairly expensive items, and a nice collection of large-size notes cannot be formed on a shoestring budget. The least expensive large-size type note, the Series 1923 $1 silver certificate, costs about $25 in VF condition, or about $70 in CU condition. Most large-size notes, however, are considerably more expensive than this. The ten least expensive types of large-size notes are the $1 USNs of Series 1917 and 1923, the $2 USN of 1917, the $5 USN of 1907, the $1 SCs of Series 1899 and 1923, the $1 FRBN of 1918, and the $5, $10, and $20 blue seal FRNs of Series 1914. At the present time the cost of these ten notes would be about $500 in VF condition or about $1750 or a bit more in new condition. Although this group of notes can be easily assembled, I would hardly term such an assembly a "collection." If you have only a few hundred or for that matter just two or three thousand dollars to spend on paper money, there probably is not much point getting into large-size notes. A minimum of several thousand dollars is necessary to form even a basic type collection of these items.

Careful consideration must be given as to whether to collect these notes by type only, or by seal and signature varieties as well. There is far from complete agreement as to just what constitutes a "type" for several of these issues. The Bison notes (Series 1901 $10 United States notes) are clearly a single type, for which there are nine signature varieties, none of which commands prices much in excess of the least rare of these notes. Should you attempt to obtain all nine of these varieties, or should you settle for just one example? This depends a great deal upon the funds that you have available for collecting bank notes. At the present time Bison notes cost about $400 each in fine condition, about $900 each in XF, and about $2000 in CU. It is not particularly difficult to assemble a complete set of all nine Bison notes in choice condition, but the cash outlay for such a project would be about $10,000, and significantly more than this if you want all of your notes to be strictly in CU condition but less than this if several of them need be only VF or so. There now is a strong market for notes in VG-F condition, but I try in most cases to avoid notes that grade less than full VF since I do not find notes in less than this grade to be very attractive. I do have all nine Bison notes in my own collection, and the grades for these notes range from XF to CU. In forming sets such as these I have tried to keep the condition of the notes fairly uniform. I do not see much point in assembling a complete set of Bison notes in which two or three are in XF condition or better, but the other six or seven are in VG condition or worse. Given the high cost of these notes, you may well decide to forget about signature varieties altogether and settle for just one nice note of this type. That is probably what the majority of collectors are doing these days.

Although all collectors would regard the Bison note as being just one major type, this term is far from clear for many other large-size notes, particularly for the various issues of Unites States Notes that were printed over several decades. The $5 United States notes of Series 1875 - 1907 are all of the same basic type, but there were several significant differences in their designs. Initially these notes were printed with small red seals and with numerous floral embellishments in red ink. In Series 1880 the floral embellishments were dropped, but the notes of this series have several distinct varieties of Treasury seals and serial number colors. The Series 1907 notes of this type have an additional design feature, but these notes have a more streamlined and modern look than do their predecessors. In terms of seal and signature varieties there are a total of 28 different notes for this issue. But should you consider just one basic type for these notes, or are there more? One can recognize as many as seven distinct sub-types for this issue. How many notes you wish to collect may again depend upon how adequate your funds are for the purchase of bank notes.

Another way of streamlining the collecting of large-size notes is to collect only notes of a single face value or range of denominations such as $1, $2, and $5 notes. But you must consider that $10 and $20 notes, for instance, would be considered fairly high denominations for silver certificates, Treasury Notes, or FRBNs, but they would be only middle denominations for USNs or national bank notes, and they would be low denominations for gold certificates or Federal Reserve Notes. Notes of $50 and $100 denominations are often thought of as very high values, but they are readily available as FRNs, NBNs, or gold certificates. These notes, however, are major rarities as Treasury Notes, and both USNs and SCs are also very scarce to very rare for these values. If you limit yourself to notes of only a couple of denominations, you will not be able to collect a very wide range of large-size notes, since several series were issued only for a fairly narrow range of denominations, and that range depends upon which class of notes one is dealing with.

The three basic catalogs that list small-size notes and Fractional Currency also cover large-size notes in detail. These are *Paper Money of the United States* by Robert Friedberg, the *Comprehensive Catalog of U. S. Paper Money* by Gene Hessler, and the *Standard Catalog of United States Paper Money* by Chester L. Krause and Robert F. Lemke. At the present time these books are in their 15th, 6th, and 17th editions, respectively. Each of these catalogs uses its own numbering system, but the Friedberg numbers are those used almost exclusively by dealers and auctioneers. The Hessler numbers are also widely used, and so I am using both where these numbers are needed. I have already been using these numbers in my chapter on Fractional Currency, but I do not find any of the standard catalog numbers to be very satisfactory for small-size notes, and so I did not use them in those chapters in which I discussed small-size notes in detail. If you plan to collect large-size notes, be sure to obtain at least one copy each of these three catalogs. You will find yourself referring to them very often as your collection grows.

In addition to the three standard catalogs there also are a couple of more specialized works on large-size type notes. For many years Martin Gengerke has carried on research as to which large-size notes actually exist. He has attempted to obtain complete censuses both by serial number and by condition for all of the rarer notes. Mr. Gengerke previously worked for Stack's, but he now is employed by R. M. Smythe. Both of these firms are major auctioneers of U. S. paper money. Together with Douglas Murray he has produced a manuscript entitled *The Encyclopedia of United States Large Size Currency*. This book has not yet been published commercially, but some preprints are available. It gives far more data on serial numbers and on plate number and security features data than are found in the three standard currency catalogs. Another work of Mr. Gengerke is *United States Paper Money Records*, a book that was recently revised in 1997 and again in 1998. This book gives complete serial number and condition data for most of the rare large-size type notes. In many cases complete pedigrees are given for each of the notes in his census. Some of Gengerke's census data are highly reliable, while others are admittedly incomplete. This book is expensive (retail price $125.00), but if you plan seriously to collect the scarcer large-size type notes, you will find much of interest in this work.

So much for the preliminaries of large-size collecting. Let us now survey the details of each of the various issues of these notes.

UNITED STATES NOTES

United States notes, or legal tender notes as they are sometimes called, were first authorized by an act passed on February 25, 1862. These notes proved to be the longest-lived of all of the various issues of large-size notes, since they were still being printed at the time of the changeover of currency sizes in 1929. Initially these notes had no specific backing, and there was much controversy over how many should be issued. During the 1870s there were political groups such as the so-called Greenback Party that favored a large increase in their circulation, while others favored removing them from circulation altogether. As things turned out, a compromise was reached by the end of that decade.

On January 1, 1879 USNs became fully redeemable in gold at par. During the previous year, however, the total amount of USNs allowed to circulate had been fixed at $346.7 million, the amount outstanding at that time. This amount included both notes in public circulation and those in storage but available for immediate release at the U. S. Treasury. In 1879 USNs constituted about 48% of the total paper money in circulation, but this percentage fell rapidly as the money supply increased and as new forms of paper money were issued.

In dealing with large-size United States notes I feel that it is easiest to consider the Series of 1862 and 1863 separately from all later issues (i. e., Series 1869 through 1917). All Series 1862 and 1863 USNs were printed on thin, unwatermarked banknote paper by the American and National Bank Note Companies in New York. All of these notes bear a small Treasury seal and serial numbers in red, and all carry the facsimile signatures of Lucius E. Chittenden and Francis E. Spinner. Thus it would seem that these notes are free of complications, but that most definitely is not the case. In an article that I wrote for the *Bank Note Reporter* which was published in January, 1996, I reviewed these issues in detail and described the various factors which complicate their classification.

The United States notes of Series 1862 and 1863 were issued in all denominations from $1 through $1000. All of these notes bear two dates. The earlier date is the date of the act under which a particular set of notes was issued, while the later date (the script date) is that on which the die for a given issue was certified. These dates are as follows:
  $1, $2 notes - Series 1862: July 11, 1862 and August 1, 1862
  $5 - $100 notes - Series 1862: February 25, 1862 and March 10, 1862
  $5 - $100 notes - Series 1863: March 3, 1863 and March 10, 1863
Notes of the $100, $500, and $1000 denominations exist under the Act of 1863, but with a script date of 1862. These notes were also issued with the same 1862/1862 and 1863/1863 date combinations that were used for the $5 - $50 denominations.

All notes of these series carry on their backs statements concerning the government's obligation for their redemption. All $1 and $2 notes and all Series 1863 notes of the higher denominations carry the so-called second obligation, while most Series 1862 notes have the first obligation. The first obligation is much more specific as to which types of government bonds may be purchased with these notes than is the second obligation.

For the $50 and $100 notes the difference in the logos for these two obligations is not very pronounced at first glance, but for the $5, $10, and $20 notes the central logos for the two obligations are entirely different. The backs of the $500 and $1000 notes of these series use the same logos as are used on the $5, $10, and $20 notes. Today these high value notes are extremely rare, with only five $500 notes and four $1000 notes known (in addition to a few proof impressions of each). At the present time no Series 1862 $1000 USNs are known to collectors.

The notes of these series were issued at a time when it was still legal to use portraits of living persons on government securities. Accordingly the $10 notes carry a portrait of Abraham Lincoln, while the $1 notes portray Salmon P. Chase, the Secretary of the Treasury at that time. Both of these men were very much alive when these notes were issued, and the law forbidding the depiction of living persons on U. S. government securities was not passed until 1866.

The $1 and $2 notes have a most interesting design feature that implies that $3 notes were also planned for this series. Since the $3 denomination was very common among the state bank notes that were still circulating at that time, it seems logical that government would also have considered the issue of such notes, but no Federal $3 notes were ever issued.

In fact, the American Bank Note Co. did prepare both face and back designs for a $3 USN that bore a date of July 15, 1862, but that is as far as this work went. Given the large use of private $3 notes in the 1850s and early 1860s the failure of the Federal government to issue either USNs or NBNs for this denomination is a bit surprising. The designs that were used for the $1 and $2 notes were also prepared by the bank note companies in New York, but alternate designs were prepared for these two denominations at the Treasury. The unused $1 design depicts the *Landing of Columbus*, while that of the $2 note depicts the *Embarkation of the Pilgrims*. Soon these designs were to be used instead for the backs of the $5 and $50 national bank notes, respectively.

The Series 1862 and 1863 USNs abound in a variety of different minor design features that make these notes rather difficult to catalog or classify. The logos of one or both of the two companies that printed them - the American Bank Note Co. or the National Bank Note Co. - appear on all of these notes. There are also one or more patent statements that appear on most of these notes. Most frequently encountered is the June 30, 1857 date which is always in green and refers to the green underprint on these notes. All Series 1862 $1 and $2 notes carry an April 23, 1860 patent date in black ink on their faces, and all $50 and $100 notes carry this same date in green ink on both their faces and backs. The date April 26, 1863 was printed in green on the faces of a few Series 1863 $10 and $50 notes. This also refers to the green underprint, and it replaces the 1857 patent date that is normally found on these notes. There are also two types of the red Treasury seals. The type I seal appears only on some of the Series 1862 $2 - $100 denominations. It features a solid field about the central shield and is always light rose in color. The type II seal appears on all of the $1 notes and on most of the notes of the other denominations. It features a lined design about the central shield. Later printings (especially of Series 1863 notes) are often vivid carmine red in color.

Shown are the $1 and $2 United States Notes of Series 1862. Note the design features on both of these notes that imply that a $3 note was also to be issued. The $1 note depicts a portrait of the then-living Salmon P. Chase, but this was not permitted after 1866.

Most confusing are the series designations and the serial numbers. It should be noted that all of these notes were numbered in blocks of 100,000. The serial numbers themselves were printed in a bright orange-red color and appear either once or twice on a given note. The series or new series designations were printed in black ink, and these appear on nearly all of these notes. All Series 1862 $1 and $2 notes had the series designation, as did most Series 1862 $5 - $100 notes with first obligation backs. The first 100,000 of the $5, $20, and $100 notes of this issue, however, bore no series designations. The second 100,000 notes printed for each of these denominations bore a Series 2 designation. All of the Series 1862 notes with second obligation backs of denominations $5 and up as well as all of the Series 1863 notes of these issues have new series designations.

Confusion over the serial numbers for these notes has led to major number status being bestowed on a minor variant in the paper money catalogs. They list two varieties for the Series 1862 $5 notes with the first obligation back, the former with no series and the latter with a series designation. In the Friedberg catalog these are assigned numbers 61 and 61a, respectively, and in Hessler they are 243 and 243a. The former is extremely rare, but it is merely the first block of 100,000 notes that was printed for Fr. 61a (H-243a), a note that had an edition of about 7,200,000. The $20 note of this issue also exists without a series designation and it is even rarer than is the $5 variant, but the standard catalogs say nothing about this item.

In recording the serial number of one of these notes, a collector should always note the series or new series number. These numbers also tell us the sequence in which these notes were printed. For instance, Fr. 17a and 41a were printed before Fr. 16 and 41, respectively. (Hessler's catalog has the correct sequence for its numbers, but caution should always be used when describing Series 1862-63 USNs by catalog numbers.) It is unlikely that many collectors have ever attempted to obtain complete sets of these notes by series numbers. There are far too many of these, and the notes themselves are basically rare and expensive.

A much more significant variation is whether the serial number appears once or twice on a given note. All $1 and $2 notes have two serial numbers, as do the later printings of the $5, $10, $20, and $100 notes, but all of the $50 notes and all of the earlier notes of the $5 - $100 denominations have only one serial number. The higher denomination notes with two serial numbers were the last notes of these types to be printed, and probably as a result of this, they constitute a large percentage of the notes of these issues that have survived in choice condition. Also to be considered is where these various design elements are located on the faces of these notes. Several minor varieties can be distinguished depending upon where these features are placed.

Martin Gengerke has distinguished a total of 8 different varieties of $1 notes, 3 of the $2 notes, 8 of the $5, 11 of the $10, 8 of the $20, 5 of the $50, and 7 for the $100 notes of these issues. Since all $50 and $100 notes are major rarities, and since several of the lower denomination notes of these series also fall into this class, clearly no one should attempt to obtain all of these possible varieties. Ignoring the No Series $5 variety mentioned above the Friedberg and Hessler catalogs list four varieties for the $1 notes, 2 for the $2 notes, and five notes each for the $5, $10, and $20 denominations. The Krause-Lemke catalog lists four varieties for the $5 notes but only three each for the $10 and $20 notes. The extreme rarity of the $1 note listed as Fr. 17 (Hessler 4) is acknowledged in two of the catalogs, and this note should not to be confused with the more abundant Fr. 17a (H-2).

According to Gengerke only six examples of this rarity are known. For the average collector it is quite difficult just to acquire one note each of the five lower denominations in decent condition. If you want to add additional notes of these types to your collection, the two types of backs on the $5, $10, and $20 notes are so distinct that they are really separate major types. You may also want to obtain both of the major logo varieties for the $1 and $2 notes [Fr. 16 and 17a (H-3 and H-2) and Fr. 41 and 41a (H-153a and 153), respectively]. The five major varieties of the $5 notes (Fr. 61a, 62, 63, 63a, and 63b, or H-243a - 244b) are roughly of equal abundance, and if you have ample funds you can attempt to acquire one of each, but this is the only denomination (other than the uncomplicated $2 notes) for which it is really possible to obtain in nice condition all of the notes that are listed in the standard catalogs.

It almost goes without saying that Series 1862 and 1863 USNs are very expensive in choice condition. The most frequently encountered denominations are the $1 (usually Fr. 16 or H-3) and several of the $5 notes, but even these are now fetching $1000 each or more in choice CU condition. Nice XF examples of these notes can be had for about $500 each, but they are still expensive. I have already discussed one problem that plagues these issues. The paper on which they were printed is thin, and it is very prone to edge splits. Many notes that are otherwise choice have an edge split or two. These notes are often seen with repaired edge splits, but if such a note is repaired, this aspect should be mentioned in its description.

If you wish to obtain several examples of these notes, I would very strongly suggest that you acquire a copy of Martin Gengerke's *Encyclopedia* beforehand. It gives much information on the sequences of Series numbers and on the variations in the styles and locations of the various design features that complicate these issues. If you are seeking a particular variety of a given note, it is important that you should be familiar with the design characteristics of that particular variety. Often these notes are not very accurately described in dealer pricelists and in auction listings. One should not blame the vendors of these notes too much for this confusion, however, since the listings of these issues in the standard currency catalogs are all in need of improvement. I feel that these catalogs should list these notes using a sequence of major and minor numbers, much as is done by stamp catalog editors in distinguishing major from minor varieties of a given series of postage stamps.

Martin Gengerke lists a total of 41 known $50 notes of the 1862 and 1863 series and a total of 52 known $100 notes for all varieties of these issues. Two of the $50 notes in this list, however, are counterfeits. No notes of either denomination in Series 1862 with second obligation backs are believed to exist. The Friedberg catalog states that this is the case, but both the Hessler and Krause-Lemke catalogs claim that they exist. Gengerke feels that all claims for the existence of these two varieties are due to confusion in their descriptions.

After considerable effort and expense I succeeded in adding a Series 1862 $50 note in VF-XF condition and a Series 1863 $100 note in CU condition to my collection. The latter is from a small hoard of Fr. 167a (H-1121a) notes that have been on the market for several years. The former is the plate note in the 14th edition of the Friedberg catalog. For many years the earlier editions of that catalog used a Series 1863 $50 note that was counterfeit. (If you have an earlier Friedberg catalog, compare Hamilton's portrait on the counterfeit $50 with that of the genuine $2 note that is also illustrated. They should be identical, but they are not.). The counterfeits of the Series 1863 $50 notes are among the best that were made, but you stand little chance of being deceived. All of these notes come with pedigrees that are detailed in Gengerke's book on paper money records. Although low grade Series 1862-63 $50 and $100 notes are sometimes offered at "only" a few thousand dollars each, be prepared to pay well in excess of $10,000 each for nice examples of these notes. In January, 1998 a choice AU example of the Series 1863 $100 USN sold for $44,000 at a CAA (Currency Auctions of America) sale, a price more than double what these notes were bringing four or five years ago. An even higher price was obtained in December, 1998 for a CU example of the Series 1863 USN (Fr. 150a, H-927), which sold for an unprecedented $115,500 in the Levitan auction. Proof examples of the faces and backs of these notes, however, have occasionally been offered at prices that are well under those of the issued notes.

As you might expect, the $500 and $1000 notes of Series 1862-63 are extreme rarities. Only five examples of the former and four of the latter are recorded. Two of the $500 and one of the $1000 notes are in government hands, but the two best notes of each of these denominations are still owned privately. In the spring of 1998 a CU example of the Series 1863 $500 note was sold in a CAA auction for $233,750, the highest price paid up to that time for any item of paper money. This note has serial number 42223, and there is also a similar note with serial number 42227. In 1972 the former note sold for only $15,500 in a Kagin's auction. There are also two high-grade Series 1863 $1000 notes in private hands. These also have closely similar serial numbers, 99202 and 99206. The second of these was sold for $30,00 in a Hickman and Oakes auction in 1985. In December, 1998 both the $500 (serial number 42227) and the $1000 (number 99202) USNs were sold by Lyn Knight as part of the Levitan collection of U. S. type notes. These two items brought $363,000 and $451,000, respectively. The latter figure is the second highest price recorded thus far for any piece of paper money in a public sale. As things have turned out, these ultra-rarities have proven to be superb investments. Items of this quality have a tendency of passing from one great collection to another, since three of the four notes that I have mentioned by serial number were once in the collection of Amon Carter, Jr.

The later issues of United States notes are less confusing than are the issues of Series 1862 and 1863. The Series 1869 notes are all inscribed "Treasury Note," but these issues are not to be confused with the Treasury Notes that were issued in the 1890s. Like the latter notes they also have serial numbers that end with star suffixes, but these are not replacement notes. As I have already noted, the use of star prefixes or suffixes to indicate replacement notes was initiated only in 1910, which is more than 40 years after the Series 1869 USNs were printed. Another feature of these notes was their use of localized blue stains or green underprints as security features. These features make these notes among the most beautiful of all American currency, and this series of notes is often referred to as the "Rainbow Issue." Several values of this series also appear on watermarked paper, but most catalogs and collectors do not bother to distinguish between these notes with or without watermarks. The designs of the Series 1869 notes were radically different from those of the 1862-63 notes, but for most denominations the basic face designs that were first used with this issue were continued for a half century or more.

128/large-size type notes   U. S. Paper Money

The so-called First Obligation and Second Obligation backs are shown on $5 USNs that were issued in Series 1862 and 1863, respectively. Similar differences also exist for the $10 and $20 notes of these series. The differences are radical enough for one to consider these varieties as distinct subtypes or even major types.

The Series 1869 USNs were printed for all denominations from $1 through $1000. The four lowest denominations feature a green underprint, while the other five notes of this series have a localized blue stain. All have large red seals and bear the signatures of Allison and Spinner. These notes were printed in fairly large quantities, and notes of the five lower denominations often are seen at auctions. By no means, however, are they cheap. In choice CU condition the $1, $2, $5, and $10 notes are currently fetching about $1500, $2500, $1000, and $3000 each, respectively. Choice CU Series 1869 $20 notes now sell for at least $6000 each, and recently there have been auction realizations as high as $10,000 for gem CU examples of this note. Since none of these notes are especially rare, it is possible to obtain attractive circulated examples of this series at much lower prices. In VF condition the $1 - $20 notes of Series 1869 now sell for about $300, $700, $300, $700, and $1500, respectively. As can be seen, it is not really possible to collect this series on a tight budget. In buying any of these notes I would recommend that you closely examine them before committing yourself. All notes of this series have jute fibers in the paper, and sometimes these have been pulled out leaving blank spaces. Occasionally there are also small holes or weak spots in the paper itself that were already there when the notes were printed. I had to examine several uncirculated Series 1869 $5 notes before I found one that was "just right" for my collection.

The $50, $100, $500, and $1000 notes of this series depict Henry Clay, Abraham Lincoln, John Quincy Adams, and DeWitt Clinton, respectively. Well-made counterfeits of the $50 and $500 notes were produced within a few years, and this led to the abandonment of the $50 and $500 designs for the upcoming series of USNs of these denominations. Martin Gengerke has recorded 52 genuine examples of the $50 note and 22 examples of the $100 note.

A number of the $50 notes came to light when the vault of a defunct bank in St. Joseph, Missouri was opened in 1987. Despite the fact that this note cannot be regarded as an extreme rarity, it sells for very high prices in today's market. An attractive VF-XF example recently sold for $24,200 in the same auction in which the Series 1863 $500 USN was sold. A Series 1869 $50 note in fine condition with some minor restorations brought $9350 in a 1998 CAA auction, so not all decent examples of this note sell for more than $10,000, but this is not an item for collectors on tight budgets. A CU example of the Series 1869 $100 was one of the highlights of the currency collection formed by Andrew Shiva. It was sold for $41,800 by Spink America in a 1995 auction, and in 1997 an AU $100 note of this series sold for $30,800 in an CAA auction. In 1988 uncirculated examples of the $50 and $100 notes of this series sold for $93,500 and $44,000, respectively, in the Levitan sale that was held in December of that year. Clearly the $50 note, which was graded gem CU, was a sharper example than was the $100 note of this series that was in the Levitan collection. Both the Series 1869 $50 and $100 notes exist in a wide variety of grades, but they are very expensive in almost any form.

As for the $500 and $1000 notes of this series, forget it. There are only four genuine examples of the former and two of the latter. Two of the $500 notes and one of the $1000 notes are in government hands. One note of each of these denominations was in Amon Carter's collection, but they were sold privately with very little fanfare. There has not been a public sale of either of these notes in decades.

The United States notes from Series 1874 through Series 1917 showed the same basic designs for most denominations. Most of the notes of Series 1874, 1875, and 1878 contained the same jute fibers that were used in the Series 1869 notes. Localized blue stains and watermarks were also used on a few notes of these issues. In about 1880 the jute fibers were replaced with two horizontal silk threads that ran the length of the note. In the early 1890s these threads were replaced by two columns of vertically distributed silk fibers. This feature was continued on all subsequent issues of large-size notes until their production was terminated in 1929.

The faces of all of these notes carry the imprint of the Bureau of Engraving and Printing, but many of the earlier notes of Series 1874 - 1880 bear the imprint of the Columbian Bank Note Co. of Washington, D.C. After about 1890 all of these notes have the imprint of the BEP on their backs. Plate numbers appear on both sides of these notes, and there is some variation with regard to the placement of these numbers on some of the issues. Martin Gengerke's Encyclopedia discusses these varieties, but most catalogs and auctioneers have considered only the seal and signature varieties to be of significance. Let us consider these notes on a denomination by denomination basis.

The USNs of Series 1869 were inscribed "Treasury Note" but they are not to be confused with Treasury Notes of 1890. The stars suffixes do not indicate replacement status. The Series 1907 $5 USN bearing the Woods-White signature combination has the same basic face design as does its 1869 counterpart, but it was issued almost 60 years later.

There are 22 major varieties of $1 USNs from Series 1874 through 1917 plus a single note in Series 1923 that is of an entirely new type. Nearly all of these notes depict a portrait of George Washington that is flanked by a vignette of *Columbus Sighting Land* at the left. The back sides of these notes boldly state United States of America in a cross pattern that has led these items to be termed "Sawhorse" notes. The Series 1923 notes use much more modern design on both sides. The back sides of these notes have a "generic" design that is common also to the silver certificates of this vintage. There would be even more varieties of large-size $1 USNs if it were not for the fact that no $1 USNs were printed between 1896 and 1917. Among these 23 notes there are no extreme rarities, but obtaining a complete set of all varieties is a very difficult task.

Although the normal $1 USNs of Series 1874, 1875 (two signature varieties), and 1878 were printed in substantially smaller quantities than were the Series 1869 notes, they are all significantly less expensive. Although CU examples now sell for at least $500 each for any of these notes, decent VF examples should cost only about $100 each. There are, however, five much rarer varieties for the Series 1875 notes. Initially it was decided to designate the first million notes in the series as Series A, the second million as Series B, etc. This procedure was continued for the first five million notes, and thus the earlier notes of Series 1875 bearing the Allison-New signature combination exist with each of these possibilities. It was then decided to discontinue this type of designation, and the remaining 10 million notes with this signature combination are designated Series 1875 only.

Both the Friedberg and the Krause-Lemke catalogs list these notes out of sequence, since all five of the rare letter varieties were printed before the normal notes lacking this feature were produced. In my opinion all five of these varieties are roughly of equal rarity. Gengerke estimates that about 50 examples exist of each variety in all grades. Expect to pay at least $3500 for a choice CU example of any of these, and nice VF examples now sell for more than $1000 each when they do come up for sale. I succeeded several years back in obtaining four of these varieties, but I am still looking for a Series A $1 note.

There are eight different varieties of Series 1880 $1 USNs. The first three of these have large brown seals and red serial numbers. The last two have red scalloped seals and blue serial numbers. The first three notes were printed in editions of 16 to 20 million each. The last two notes were printed in much smaller editions, but their survival rate seems to be much higher since they are of comparable scarcity and value to the earlier Series 1880 brown seal notes. All five of these items sell for prices that are comparable to the normal Series 1874 - 78 notes. The three rare Series 1880 notes have blue serial numbers, but their seals are all large and either red (actually salmon) or brown in color. The first two of these notes bear the signatures of Rosecrans and Huston, while the last has the Rosecrans-Nebeker signature combination. They have Friedberg numbers 31, 32, and 33 (H-18, 19, and 20), and their respective printings were 704,000, 432,000, and 68,000, respectively. Gengerke estimates that about 75 each of the first two of these notes exist and about 50 of the last note of this group are known to collectors. In today's market these notes sell for well over $2000 each in CU and at least $500 in VF condition.

The Series 1917 $1 USNs were produced in vastly larger quantities than were the earlier series of 1874 through 1880. For all of these earlier series only about 117.6 million notes were printed, but for Series 1917 the total printing was 996.3 million. There are four normal signature combinations for Series 1917, and all of these are common. A choice CU example of any of these notes now sells for about $150, while a VF example will cost about $40 or so. About 400 star notes are reported for the Series $1 USNs, and these are known for all of the four normal signature varieties of this series. This series also contains a most unusual error. On face plate 1519 the signatures of the Register and Treasurer were accidentally engraved as Burke and Elliott, respectively, instead of the correct Elliott and Burke. Technically speaking, this is only an engraving or plate error, but it has been given major number status in all of the standard catalogs and it is avidly collected. Enough examples were put aside, so that it is not especially rare. Gengerke estimates that about 200 examples of this error note may be known. Today these notes sell for about $800 each in CU condition and about $250 per note in VF condition.

The Series 1923 $1 USN closely resembles the more abundant $1 SCs of that era. All Series 1923 notes (including the $10 USN and the $5 SC) had "generic" backs on which no reference was made as to the type of currency for a specific note. All of the $1

USNs of this series bear the Speelman-White signature combination that was also used on the last of the Series 1917 notes. This note is fairly common, since about 81.9 million examples were printed, Choice CU examples are now selling for about $300 each, while VF specimens should cost more like $70 each. This note is also available in replacement form, and about 130 star notes of this type have been recorded.

The first printings of Series 1875 USNs were given letter designations for each block of 1,000,000 notes that was prepared. Shown are a Series 1875C $1 note and a Series 1875B $2 note. These varieties are much scarcer than are the latter Series 1875 notes that lack these special letter designations.

The $2 USNs of Series 1874 through 1917 closely parallel their $1 counterparts, but there are only 18 major varieties this time instead of 23. All of these notes depict Thomas Jefferson and an 1860s view of the U. S. Capitol. Several of these notes are decidedly rare, and so obtaining a complete set of all 18 of these varieties is a major challenge. Like the $1 USNs, no notes of this denomination were printed between 1896 and 1917. There are no Series 1923 $2 USNs, but printing of Series 1917 $2 USNs was continued until the end of large-size notes in 1929.

None of the Series 1874 - 78 $2 USNs can be described as "common," but the $2 notes of Series 1874, Series 1875 with the Allison-New and Allison-Wyman signatures, and Series 1878 with the Allison-Gilfillan signatures are less rare than are the other three varieties. All four of the more abundant varieties now sell for at least $1000 each in choice CU condition, while in VF condition they should still bring about $300 each. Much rarer are the Series 1875 Allison-New notes with Series A and Series B designations. Although there are five varieties of these notes for the $1 denomination, there are only two such varieties of $2 notes. Both of these varieties are rare, and it is my feeling that they are even rarer than the corresponding Series A through E $1 notes of Series 1875. I was fortunate to obtain these notes prior to a time when their true rarity was recognized. Today these notes sell for not less than $3000 to $4000 each in CU condition, and in VF condition they should still cost at least $750 to $1000 apiece.

There is also one other notable early $2 USN, whose rarity has been recognized for many years. This is the Series 1878 note with the Scofield-Gilfillan signature combination (Fr. 49, H-159) instead of the more common Allison-Gilfillan combination that appears on most of these notes. It is likely that these notes were printed by accident. All of them were printed from face plate 52, and it appears that they were dispersed among the Allison-Gilfillan notes that were being produced at that time. Only about 20 examples of these notes are presently known, and recent auction sales have been very infrequent. In my collection I have a VF example that was obtained from a Kagin's auction in 1983, but there have only been two more recent auction sales of this note. In a 1998 CAA sale this note in VG condition sold for $4290, and in a Lyn Knight auction held later in the same year a note in VF-XF condition sold for $8800. One CU example is reported, and there are at least four or five of these notes in VF or XF condition, but this item is a major rarity in all grades.

There are seven different Series 1880 $2 USNs. These closely parallel the $1 notes, and the earliest trio of these notes have large brown seals and red serials while the last pair have scalloped red seals and blue serial numbers. These are roughly of equal abundance and value with CU examples selling for about $600 each, while VF notes can be expected to bring about $125 each. The two rarities of this group are the notes having the Rosecrans-Huston signatures and large red or large brown seals with blue serial numbers. These are numbers 53 and 54 in the Friedberg catalog (or nos. 163 and 164 in the Hessler catalog), and they closely parallel nos. 31 (H-18) and 32 (H-19) which are the same notes except for their denominations. According to BEP records 348,000 and 316,000 examples of these $2 notes were printed, respectively. Previously the standard catalogs listed these two notes at decidedly low prices, but they are definitely rare. Gengerke is now attempting to list all known examples of each, and thus far he has enumerated 27 examples of the former but only 13 of the latter. He feels, however, that these data are incomplete, and their real numbers may be at least 50 -75 examples for each note. Recent auction sales of these notes in choice condition have been few and far between, but a CU example of Fr. 53 sold for $9900 and a fine example of Fr. 54 fetched $5225 in a CAA auction held in May, 1998. In October, 1998 an example of Fr. 554 in CU condition sold for $22,000 in another CAA sale. Clearly these two notes should be considered as major rarities.

The last four $2 USNs are of Series 1917. All of these are common, as 332.3 million of these notes were printed in Series 1917 as compared with only 51.6 million notes in Series 1874 through 1880. This issue is notorious for the tight spacing on its upper and lower edges. Only relatively few notes have decent margins on their top and bottom sides, and these command a premium over more typically centered notes. You should expect to pay about $225 or so for a choice CU note of this series and about $60 for a decent VF note of this same type. Over 200 star notes have been reported for this series. These exist on all four signature varieties, but those with the Speelman-White signature combination are by far the most abundant as replacement notes.

The $5 USNs of Series 1875 through 1907 were in continuous production from 1875 through the late 1920s, and so these notes exist with more seal and signature varieties than do their $1 and $2 counterparts. There are a total of 28 different major varieties, of which at least two or three are quite scarce. All of these notes depict Andrew Jackson together with a vignette of a pioneer family. The man of this family is holding an axe, and these items are sometimes referred to as "Woodchopper" notes. The Series 1875 $5 notes with the Allison-New signatures exists both with Series A and Series B and without these overprints. There were 3.8 million printed of the latter variety, and one million each, of course, of the two letter series varieties. Although these two notes are scarcer than are their fellow note without any letter overprints, for the $5 notes far more Series A and Series B notes seem to have been saved than was the case with either the $1 or $2 notes.

The Series 1875 notes also exist with the Allison-Wyman combination, and there is a Series 1878 $5 note, but this time only with the Allison-Gilfillan signature combination. Of these five notes the Series A note of 1875 (Fr. 66, H-246A) is the most difficult to obtain, but it seems to be far more readily available than are its $1 and $2 counterparts. A CU example of this note might fetch as much as $2500 in today's market, but a VF example should cost no more than $600 or so. The other $5 notes of 1875-78 are more like $700 each in CU and about $125 to $150 in VF condition.

There are 13 different Series 1880 $5 USNs. The first three of these have red serial numbers and large brown seals. Like their $1 and $2 counterparts they exist with signature combinations of Scofield-Gilfillan, Bruce-Gilfillan, and Bruce-Wyman. For the $1 and $2 notes these three varieties are of more or less equal abundance, but for the $5 notes the Scofield-Gilfillan combination is very rare. According to BEP records there were 3.8 million, 7.2 million, and 6.6 million $5 notes printed, respectively, for these three different varieties. Thus we should expect that the Scofield-Gilfillan variety should be somewhat scarcer than the two others, but it should not fall into the rare category. Perhaps the records are wrong, and many of the notes recorded for Scofield-Gilfillan actually were printed with the Bruce-Gilfillan signature combination. In any case the former note is very rare, and Martin Gengerke has only been able to confirm 17 examples of this variety but he feels that there may be as many as 50 of these notes in existence. I was able to obtain a VF example in a Lyn Knight auction in 1995 for just under $1500, but an example in only fine condition sold for $2970 in a 1997 CAA auction. In another CAA auction held in May, 1998 an example of this note that was graded F-VF brought $4675.

The other ten Series 1880 $5 USNs include several varieties of Treasury seals. The first three of these notes have large plain seals that are red in color. The notes with the Rosecrans-Huston signatures exist both with large red (salmon) spiked seals and large brown seals. These notes are scarce, but they are not as scarce as are their $1 and $2 counterparts. The $5 note with the Rosecrans-Nebeker signatures and a large brown seal (Fr. 78, H-259) is rare, and it may be almost as scarce as is the aforementioned Scofield-

Gilfillan $5 note (Fr. 70, H-250). Gengerke has recorded 26 examples of Fr. 78, but their average condition is much higher than is typical for Fr. 70. For the former Gengerke has a record of 15 examples in AU or CU condition, whereas no examples of the latter are known in grades better than XF. The other four Series 1880 $5 USNs all were issued at the turn of the century with a small red scalloped seal and blue serial numbers as their distinguishing features.

For Series 1907 the $5 USNs again bore red serial numbers, and the notes were given a more modern design. There are eleven signature varieties of these notes, and they range from very scarce to very common. The scarcest by far of these notes is that with the Napier-Thompson signature combination. Carmi Thompson was only in office for four months during 1912-13, and his signature is generally quite scarce on paper money. Only about 1.6 million of these notes were printed, and this total can be compared with the huge printing of about 155.4 million notes of this series that bear the Speelman-White signature. The latter note is by far the most common of the 11 different varieties of this issue, but most of the others do not sell at especially large premiums over the abundant Fr. 91 (H-272). These notes are now selling about $250 each in choice CU condition, and in VF condition they should cost about $75 each. The Napier-Thompson note (Fr. 86, H-267) is considerably more expensive, and you can expect to pay more than $1000 for a CU example or about $250 for a VF specimen of this note. Another fairly scarce note of this series is the last of the issue, a note that bears the Woods-White signature combination. Signature combinations later than the very common Speelman-White variety were used only on relatively few issues of large-size notes. Harley Speelman retired in the autumn of 1927, but his signature continued to be used on many large-size notes until the end of the large-note period. The Woods-White combination is very common on $1 SCs, but it was infrequently used on other types of large-size notes.

There were a total 462.0 million $5 USNs printed in Series 1907. This can be compared with a total of only 88.2 million notes for all of the various issues of Series 1875 through 1880. The $5 USNs were one of the first issues of U. S. currency to have star numbers to indicate replacement notes. Of the eleven different varieties of this issue, star notes are known for nine. Production of the first of these issues (Vernon-Treat) was halted before star notes were introduced, and no Napier-Thompson star notes have been recorded for this series, which is hardly surprising considering the rarity of this variety. Quite possibly no Napier-Thompson star notes were printed for this series. About 130 star notes are reported for Series 1907 $5 USNs. As might be expected, more than half of these are Speelman-White notes. There are also about 25 known star notes with the Tehee-Burke signatures, but all seven of the other star note varieties for this series are decidedly rare.

The large-size $10 USNs of this era were issued in three radically different types. The first of these depict Daniel Webster together with a vignette of Pocahontas at the English court. There is a small eagle at their center bottoms, and when this is inverted the wings of the eagle look like the ears of a donkey. For this reason these items are often referred to as "Jackass" notes. These notes were issued until 1901, and there are 17 major varieties in Series 1875 through 1880. There is one extreme rarity among these notes, but most are fairly scarce and so few collectors attempt to obtain all of the possible seal and signature varieties for these issues.

There are three varieties of $10 USNs for Series 1875 and 1878. All Series 1875 notes have the Allison-New combination, but these exist both with and without Series A. The Series 1878 notes exist only with the Allison-Gilfillan combination. For some reason it seems that 1.5 million rather than 1.0 million notes were printed with Series A. An equal number of these notes were printed without this designation. The Allison-Gilfillan note was printed in a larger edition of 2.6 million copies, and it is the least rare of these three notes. All three of these notes, however, are very scarce, and CU examples easily bring $3000 or more in today's market. In VF condition all of these notes should cost at least $600 each.

The $10 USNs of Series 1869 -80 are referred to as "Jackass" notes, since the small eagle vignette at the bottom looks like a donkey when inverted. The Series 1880 $20 USN utilizes a design that was kept more or less the same for half a century.

The Series 1880 $10 notes contain the same three brown seal notes with red serial numbers that are found for the three lower denominations. The Scofield-Gilfillan note is the scarcest of the three, but this time it is only somewhat scarcer than are the other two varieties. The other eleven varieties of "Jackass" notes closely parallel the balance of the Series 1880 $5 USNs, but for the $10 notes the Rosecrans-Hyatt signature exists in two major varieties. The first of these has a large plain red seal, while the second has the spiked salmon-colored seal. This latter variety does not exist on $5 notes. The great rarity of this series is the Rosecrans-Nebeker note with a large brown seal (Fr. 109, H-478). According to BEP records 304,000 of these notes were printed, but only two have been thus far recorded. One is in VF-XF condition and was offered by Lyn Knight in 1991 for $16,000. The other in XF-AU condition was sold at a CAA auction in 1992 for $7250. Thus there does seem to be some disagreement as to the true value of this major rarity!

The last four "Jackass" notes have small red seals and are much the most "common" of these issues. Still these notes still cost something like $1250 each in CU condition, and you can expect to pay about $400 or so for a nice VF example of this issue. Aside from Fr. 109, none of the "Jackass" notes are rated as being especially rare, but all of them are expensive enough to deter most collectors from attempting to obtain all of the major seal and signature varieties. I have succeeded in obtaining 13 of these issues in addition to the Series 1869 note that has essentially the same face design, but this is not an easy set to complete, even if we ignore the one extreme rarity of this issue.

At the beginning of this chapter, I spoke in some detail about the Bison notes, (the $10 USNs of Series 1901). These depict the explorers Meriwether Lewis and William Clark at their sides with a large bison at their center. Without doubt this is one of the most famous and popular of all U. S. paper money designs. Although these notes are not especially rare, they are admittedly expensive. Choice CU examples are selling for about $2000 each, and nice VF examples should now sell for about $600 or so.

For some reason neither the Napier-Thompson nor the Elliott-Burke signature combinations were used, and so there are just nine signature varieties for an issue that spanned a quarter century of use. The first and the last of these, i. e., notes with the Lyons-Roberts and the Speelman-White combinations, are the most "common" of the Bison notes, but none of the others are rare enough to command an appreciable premium over a typical note. It is not difficult to complete a set of all nine Bison notes provided you are willing to shell out the rather substantial sums required. Star notes exist for the last six signature varieties of this issue. About 65 star Bison notes have thus far been recorded, and most of these have either the Elliott-White or Speelman-White signatures. The other four varieties are all extremely rare. There were a total of about 149.0 million Bison notes printed. This compares with a total of about 49.0 million $10 USNs of Series 1875 through 1880. Hessler's catalog has one error with regard to printings for Bison notes. Only 10.0 million of these notes with the Lyons-Treat signatures were printed, not the 101 million that he reports.

The Bison note and the rather similar Indian note (i. e. the $5 silver certificate of Series 1899) was first issued at a time when the western frontier was disappearing from American life. Although the bison herds once estimated to have numbered as many as 50 million individuals before the 1850s, by the turn of the century these animals were rapidly approaching extinction. During the 20th century, however, there has been a substantial increase in the bison population.

138/large-size type notes U. S. Paper Money

The Series 1901 $10 USN and the Series 1899 $5 SC are among the most popular of all Federal currency designs. They were intended to invoke images of the old West. This theme is even more appropriate for the two notes depicted above, since the bear the signature of Houston Tehee, a full-blood Cherokee, who served as Register of the Treasury from 1915 to 1919.

The last issue of $10 United States notes is an enigmatic one. Only 696,000 examples were printed in Series 1923. This note depicts a portrait of Andrew Jackson in a modernistic frame. The back is a "generic" back, as are those on all Series 1923 notes. All of these notes are from the AB block, and all have the Speelman-White signature combination. As might be expected for a note with so low a printing, this item is quite scarce, but it shows a most unusual range of conditions. There are several large runs of uncirculated notes known for this issue. At one time it was thought that these totaled only about 75 notes or so, but Hessler now estimates that at least 250 CU notes exist of this type. Nonetheless it is an expensive note, and choice CU notes are once more commanding over $3000 each. I paid more than $2000 for one of these notes back in 1981, just before prices on many currency items took a sharp dip, and there was a time at which these notes could be obtained in CU condition for little more than $1000 each. Despite the fact that there seem to be fairly adequate numbers of this note available, prices are again rising. At present auction realizations for this note in gem CU condition again exceed $4000. For type collectors it is still a very scarce type. It is also a difficult note to obtain in nice circulated grades. You can expect to pay at least $900 for one of these in VF condition in today's market. Only two star notes are reported for this issue and these, of course, should be regarded as extreme rarities.

The Series 1923 $10 USN has a much more modernistic frame design than does its predecessors. Its back design is both modernistic and "generic," i. e., it makes no reference as to what type of note is involved.

The $20 USNs of Series 1875 though 1880 use the same face design that was used on the Series 1869 notes. These depict Alexander Hamilton along with a vignette of an allegorical representation of Victory. There is one signature variety each in Series 1875 and 1878 and 18 major varieties in Series 1880. These designs of the 1860s continued to be printed until well into the 1920s, thus giving the later issues of these notes a distinctly "old fashioned" appearance.

The Series 1875 and 1878 $20 notes normally come with a localized blue stain, and they are occasionally also found on watermarked paper. The latter issue (Fr. 129, H-705) is the less scarce of the two, and actually this note is fairly common, although expensive. Gengerke has thus far recorded 106 examples of this note in VF condition or better, and it seems likely that there are at least 200 or more notes of this variety in collectors' hands. Nonetheless CU examples are now selling for about $3000 each, and even in VF condition this note still fetches about $750 or so. The 18 varieties of Series 1880 $20 USNs show the usual range of seal and signature varieties that are found for the similar $5 and $10 notes of this series. The printing of $20 USNs appears to have become very sporadic after about 1910, since the last three issues of these notes bear the signatures of Vernon-McClung, Tehee-Burke, and Elliott-White, respectively, thus leaving out numerous other signature combinations that were in use between 1911 and the early 1920s.

By far the most common of the $20 USNs is the Elliott-White variety (Fr. 147, H-723). Several hundred of these notes are known to collectors, and at least 120 are in XF condition or better. The total production of these notes was 4,580,000 out of a total of about 22.4 million for all Series 1875-80 $20 USNs, but easily half of these notes presently known to collectors are of this one variety. In the mid-1970s an example of this note in VF condition could be had for only about $75, while a CU item of the same would have cost about $300. Today this note sells for about $350 in VF condition, and CU examples are now fetching about $1250 or so. I feel that this note is an excellent barometer on what collectors of large-size notes are seeking to acquire. Despite the fact that all other $20 USNs are much less common than is Fr. 147, they usually sell for not very much more than does this note. This is what we would expect if most collectors are only attempting to get just one type note, but if collectors are going for the other varieties of this series, then much higher prices are to be expected for the scarcer notes.

None of the 20 different varieties of Series 1875-80 $20 USNs are regarded as major rarities, but this would be an extremely difficult group to complete. The lowest printing (184,000 examples) is for the Rosecrans-Nebeker note with a large brown seal (Fr. 139, H-715). This is the same variety that is rare in $5 notes and extremely rare in $10 notes. Gengerke has recorded 15 examples of this note, and he reports similar totals for two other Series 1880 notes. He has recorded only ten examples of this note with the Scofield-Gilfillan signatures (Fr. 130, H-706), a variety that we have already noted as being very rare in $5 notes. Including the similar Series 1869 note I have thus far obtained 18 different varieties of these $20 USNs. I was very pleased a few years ago to obtain an XF example of the very scarce Tehee-Burke note (Fr. 146, H-722) at a price that was only slightly more than one should pay for the much more common Fr. 147. Since relatively few collectors attempt to obtain all of the signature varieties for these notes, one sometimes can find truly rare notes of this series priced only slightly higher than what the readily available Fr. 147 brings. Fr. 146 and 147 are the only notes of this series that exist in star form. Three of the former and 19 of the latter have been recorded.

The $50 USNs of Series 1874 through 1880 are of an entirely different design from that of the Series 1869 notes. Depicted is Benjamin Franklin along with a vignette of a decidedly Amazonian version of Liberty. There are a total of 13 different varieties of these notes, and the first ten of these display a design feature that is peculiar to this issue. The Treasury signatures on these notes are reversed from their normal order, and thus these notes feature signature combinations such as Spinner-Allison, Huston-Rosecrans, etc. There is one variety for each of Series 1874, 1875, and 1878, but the Series 1875 note is excessively rare. Only three examples of this notes are known, and one of these is in government hands while a second example in the ANA Museum in Colorado Springs. The only example of this note known to be in private hands is in F-VF condition. In October, 1998 it sold for $60,500 in a CAA auction.

Although it is possible to obtain several varieties of this issue, it is unlikely that one could ever obtain a complete set, since among the Series 1880 notes of this denomination there are also two extreme rarities. Only six examples of the Rosecrans-Hyatt note with a plain red seal (Fr. 158, H-935) and only four examples of the Bruce-Roberts note (Fr. 163, H-940) are currently known. Of these notes two examples of each variety are presently in institutional hands. An uncirculated example of Fr. 158 sold for $19,800 in the St. Louis auction of October, 1998. By far the most abundant of the $50 USNs is the Lyons-Roberts variety (Fr. 164, H-941). To date Gengerke has recorded 132 examples of this note in all grades, and it seems likely that at least 200 notes of this variety are in existence. These exist in a wide variety of grades, and this note is available enough for at least a fair number of currency collectors to obtain a copy without too much difficulty. In fine condition this note should cost about $1500 in today's market. Examples of this note in XF condition are now bringing about $3500, and in CU condition this note currently sells for about $7500 or so. This is far from cheap, but at least you can obtain one if you feel like spending this sort of money on large-size notes.

The second least rare of the $50 USNs is the Rosecrans-Huston note with a large brown seal (Fr. 161, H-938). Almost 60 of these notes are known, but the vast majority of these are from one hoard of new notes having consecutive serial numbers. As of now Gengerke has recorded 40 notes with serials between A448521 and A448572, almost all of which are in CU condition. It is also highly likely that at least the eleven serial numbers that he has not recorded from this range also exist. In contrast, he has recorded only 13 examples of Fr. 161 outside of this range, and the conditions for these notes range from VG to AU. This note is readily available in CU condition, but circulated notes having serial numbers other than A4485xx are rarely offered. In CU condition this note is now selling for about $10,000, a price that strikes me as being rather high in view of the fairly large supply of CU notes that exist for this variety.

In addition to the earlier series $100 USNs were also issued in Series 1875, 1878, and 1880. As was the case with the $50 notes there are also 13 known varieties of these issues. Unlike the $50 notes, however, there are no hoard notes (such as Fr. 161) and no "common" notes (such as Fr. 164). All large-size $100 USNs are rare and very expensive. Including the similar Series 1869 note Gengerke has recorded thus far about 200 examples of these notes, and these exist in a wide range of grades from good to CU. The least rare of these notes is the Lyons-Roberts note (Fr. 181, H-1135) for which 40 examples are presently recorded with the second most abundant being the Tillman-Morgan note for which 23 examples are currently known. Either of these notes would sell for about $10,000 each in XF condition in today's market, and even in only fine condition these notes are still worth at least $4000 each. The rarest of the $100 USNs is the Rosecrans-Hyatt note with a plain seal (Fr. 175, H-1129). This note is quite noncollectible, since only two examples are known and both are in government custody.

By far the finest array of large-size $100 USNs to be sold in recent years were those in the Andrew Shiva collection that was sold by Spink America in 1995. In addition to the previously mentioned Series 1863 and 1869 notes, this auction also contained ten of the twelve collectible varieties of Series 1875-80 $100 USNs. Conditions range from fine to AU, and the prices realized ranged from $4950 to $19,800. I purchased the Lyons-Roberts note, but I subsequently returned it due to the presence of a tear at its bottom. This note has since been resold, and I expect that the defect that I found has now been repaired. I have subsequently acquired another example of this note, and I also have the Tillman-Morgan and Rosecrans-Huston red seal varieties in my collection, but adding additional examples of this type to one's collection involves a serious outlay of funds.

This Series 1880 $50 USN with the Lyons-Roberts signature combination was issued in the early 1900s, while the $100 note of the same series with the Tillman-Morgan combination was printed in the late 1890s. The former note is by far the most abundant of the higher-denomination United States Notes.

The $50 and $100 USNs were issued in substantially smaller quantities than were their lower value counterparts. According to Treasury records about 2.0 million $50 and abut 1.2 million $100 USNs of Series 1874-80 were put into circulation. All three standard currency catalogs also mention a $100 USN with the Napier-McClung signatures, and this combination was also used on $500 and $1000 USNs. BEP records indicate that 8200 $100, 8700 $500, and 13,400 $1000 Series 1880 USNs were printed in 1914-15 with this pair of signatures, but all of these items are today quite unknown. It is my feeling that these notes were printed to be held as a reserve should the amount of United States notes outstanding fall below the legally required $346 million. That did not happen, and so these notes were probably all destroyed when the changeover to small-size notes came in 1929.

It goes without saying that all $500 USNs are major rarities. Due to serious counterfeiting of the Series 1869 notes depicting John Quincy Adams, a new design was adopted for the notes of Series 1874 through 1880. These depict General Joseph Mansfield (killed at Antietam) on their right sides and an allegorical representation of Victory at their left. There were 13 different seal and signature varieties issued for these notes, and of these ten are still recorded today. Martin Gengerke has recorded a total of 36 known examples of this type, but 24 of these are in government hands. One additional note is at the ANA Museum in Colorado Springs, and thus only eleven examples with five different signature combinations are presently available to collectors. The range in condition of these notes is from VG-F to XF. As for current prices, a VF example of the Series 1874 note sold for $63,250 in a CAA auction in 1996, a Series 1878 note in VF brought $46,750 in a 1998 CAA auction, and an XF example of the Series 1880 Lyons-Roberts note sold for $46,200 in a Lyn Knight auction in the same year. At the end of the 1998 a Series 1878 $500 note in XF condition was sold for $88,000 in the Levitan auction. Needless to say, $500 USNs are not for collectors on tight budgets!

The Series 1869 $1000 USN was not seriously counterfeited, and so the same design was used for the notes of Series 1878-80 that was used on the earlier notes. It depicts DeWitt Clinton (a prominent New York politician) at its center and a vignette of Columbus seated with maps and charts at its left. There are 11 different varieties of the Series 1878-80 notes that were issued, and eight of these are still known to exist. Gengerke has confirmed the existence of 25 examples of these notes, of which 11 are in government hands and one is in the ANA Museum. This denomination is more "collectible," however, than is the $500 USN since there are ten notes having the Lyons-Roberts signatures (Fr. 187j, H-1389) in private hands. The conditions of these notes range from VG-F at the low end to XF-AU at the high. In 1995 two of these notes, both in VF or VF-XF condition were sold at auction, one by Lyn Knight and the other by Stack's. Both notes fetched about $20,000 each. One of these items was subsequently resold for $41,800 in the Levitan auction that was held by Lyn Knight in December, 1998. In the same year a VF example of the Vernon-Treat variety of this note (of which only four example are known) also sold for $41,800 in a Lyn Knight auction. In another auction held in 1998, the only known example of the Bruce-Wyman variety of this note (Fr. 187b, H-1381) which is in AU condition sold for $231,000, a price which exceeds by a wide margin any other achieved for a $1000 USN of the Series 1878-80 type.

There were even a few United States notes or items closely related to USNs that were issued in $5000 and $10,000 denominations. In 1878 there was an issue of 4000 examples each of $5000 and $10,000 USNs bearing the signatures of Scofield and Gilfillan. All of these notes have long since been redeemed, but collectors can obtain their designs in the form of four different souvenir cards that were issued by the BEP between 1984 and 1991. The die used for producing souvenir cards that depicted the back of the $5000 note, however, lacked many of the design elements found on the issued note.

Two other items closely related to USNs are the Currency Certificates of Deposit that were issued under the Act of June 8, 1872. A total of 18,002 $5000 notes and 134,098 $10,000 notes were issued in Series 1872 and 1875. The $5000 note depicts Edward Baker, while the $10,000 note portrays Stephen Douglas. Both of these individuals were prominent political figures from Illinois in the immediate pre-Civil War years. These notes could be purchased by National Banks and then deposited with the Treasury where they would be counted as security for the note issues of the banks. They were also used to a limited extent for interbank transfers. Today these uniface notes exist only as proof impressions, and all are in government custody. They are listed in Hessler's catalog, but not in the two other general references.

Although USNs continued to circulate throughout the large-size era, they became increasingly a less important component of the currency supply as time passed. By 1900 only 9.1% of the total face value of the paper money in circulation was in the notes, and by 1929 this amount had decreased to only 6.2% of the total. Even if you are on an extremely tight budget, you should be able to afford at least one example each of the Series 1917 $1 and $2 notes, the Series 1923 $1 USN, and the Series 1907 $5 note. With substantially more funds numerous other notes of these issues can be added to your collection. As I have already noted, however, getting almost all of the signature varieties of the "Jackass" notes or the Series 1880 $20 USNs would prove to be an extremely formidable challenge, but the large-size United States notes are among the most fascinating of all U. S. currency to collect.

SILVER CERTIFICATES

Silver certificates came into existence as a consequence of the Bland-Allison Act, which was passed early in 1878. Up until 1873 a parity of 16 to 1 was maintained between gold and silver with unlimited coinage of both metals at rates of $20.67 and $1.293 per troy ounce, respectively. Huge new discoveries of silver in the early 1870s in the state of Nevada and elsewhere resulting in a flooding of the silver market and the abandonment of bimetallism both in the United States and in most European countries. Coinage of silver dollars in the United States ceased in 1873, and for the next five years only trade dollars were coined. These were intended exclusively for circulation abroad where they were valued for their bullion content (equivalent to that of a Mexican peso) rather than for their face value. As a consequence of these measures, the price of silver began to fall significantly.

The Bland-Allison Act was intended as a compromise between those persons who favored a return to the free and unlimited coinage of silver and those who favored a total demonetization of this metal. This act authorized the Treasury to buy silver bullion at the market price in amounts of not less than $2 million nor more than $4 million per month and then coin this metal into standard silver dollars. Under the provisions of this act silver certificates were to be issued that were fully backed by silver dollars held in the Treasury.

The first issues of silver certificates were of Series 1878 and 1880. They differ in appearance from all other issues of U. S. paper money in that their backs are dark brown rather than green in color. Notes for both of these series were issued in denominations of $10, $20, $50, $100, $500, and $1000. All of the Series 1878 notes and a few of those of Series 1880 were countersigned by various government employees who were signing on behalf of the Assistant Treasurer of the United States. These notes were domiciled to either New York, Washington, or San Francisco, although they were, of course, valid currency anywhere in the United States.

All countersigned SCs are major rarities. According to Martin Gengerke there are currently 29 known $10 notes, 28 $20s, 6 $50s, 6 $100s, and only one $500 note of these types. No countersigned $1000 SCs are presently known, and the unique $500 note is in government hands as are several of the other notes. There are five different date or signature varieties for both the $10 and $20 notes, but collecting these major rarities in this fashion would be an impossible task. By far the largest offering of countersigned SCs to reach the market in recent years was from the Shiva collection that was sold by Spink America in 1995. It featured three different $10 notes, four $20 issues, and a single $50 countersigned note. The condition of these notes ranged from fine to CU. The least expensive of these notes, a $20 issue in F-VF brought $11,000, while the $50 note (in VF condition, but by far the finest of the three in private hands) fetched $46,200. An uncirculated $10 note (the only such item known in private hands) was sold for $35,200. It is unlikely that an offering of countersigned SCs of this range and quality will be seen again for many years to come.

The silver certificates of Series 1886 are characterized by their elaborately designed backs. The $5 notes of this series are especially popular, since their backs portray five Morgan silver dollars. The coin in the middle of this design, of course, bears the date 1886.

In 1997 a Series 1880 $10 countersigned note (Fr. 286, H-584) in fine condition sold for $7700 in a CAA auction, but a Series 1880 $20 triple signature note (Fr. 308, H-813) that was graded choice XF sold for $30,800 in a 1998 auction of the same firm. Although a few middle grade examples of these issues may still be available at prices under $10,000 each, countersigned silver certificates basically are very expensive items. There are, however, many collectible varieties of large-size silver certificates, and included among these notes are some of the most beautiful of all forms of U. S. paper money. If you plan to collect large-size notes at all, you will certainly want to acquire some of these. On August 4, 1886 an act was passed that provided for the issuance of silver certificates in $1, $2, and $5 denominations as well as new types of $10 and $20 notes. The issuance of SCs was soon dominated by these low denomination notes, both in numbers printed and also in the total amount of face value outstanding. Let us follow these notes by using the sequence that I used in describing the United States notes, i. e., by denomination rather than by series.

Large-size $1 SCs were issued continuously between 1886 and 1929, and during the years 1896 - 1917 they were the only $1 notes in production. They were issued in Series 1886, 1891, 1896, 1899, and 1923, and type collectors may chose to obtain just one note for each of these series. The Series 1886 and 1891 notes have quite similar face designs, but the back of the latter series is much less elaborate than it is for the Series 1886 notes. Martha Washington is depicted on these notes, and she is almost the only historic woman (as opposed to numerous allegorical designs) to appear thus far on our currency. In order to be quite correct with such comments, I should note that the Indian maiden Pocahantas appears in vignettes on both the $10 "Jackass" notes and the First Charter $20 NBNs.

148/large-size type notes U. S. Paper Money

The Series 1896 silver certificates, the so-called Educational series, are often regarded as the most beautiful examples of all forms of Federal paper money. Three different signature combinations were used on this short-lived series of notes, and each of the notes depicted above has a different pair of these.

    The Series 1886 notes were issued at a time when the Treasury was experimenting with different types of seals and silk fibers as security devices. Most of these notes have two horizontal silk fibers that run the length of the note. The seals come in small red (plain), small red (scalloped), large red (actually salmon), and large brown. Altogether there are seven varieties of the Series 1886 $1 notes and two varieties of the Series 1891 $1 notes. It is possible to collect all of these notes, but they are not cheap in today's market. Uncirculated Series 1886 $1 notes sell for about $1000 each, while notes in VF condition are more like $250 each. The Series 1891 notes are somewhat less expensive than are their 1886 counterparts. Although the two Series 1886 notes with Rosecrans-Nebeker signatures (Fr. 220 and 221 or H-41 and H-42) had the lowest printings of all of these notes, they sell at prices that are only slightly higher than are those of the other Series 1886 $1 notes.

    The Series 1896 $1 SC is the first of the famous Educational notes, so-called because it depicts an allegorical representation of *History Instructing Youth*. Its back side is also elaborate, and it portrays both George and Martha Washington. There are two signature varieties, Tillman-Morgan and Bruce-Roberts, the former being the more common but there is little price difference between the two. Educational notes have always been among the most popular of large-size paper money, and at various times this series has been subject to a fair amount of speculative price pressure. At the present time choice CU examples of the $1 note sell for about $1250 each, while a note of this type in VF will probably cost about $300 or so. The Series 1896 SCs proved to be short-lived. There was some fear that their elaborate designs would prove easier to counterfeit by photographic means than would more open designs, and there was also controversy over the design of the $5 note of this series, as I shall mention. In any case, the Series 1899 SCs returned to much simpler designs on both their faces and backs

The Series 1899 $1 SC depicts a large eagle together with small portraits of Lincoln and Grant on its face. Thus this note is generally referred to as the Eagle note, and it is a design that was in use for nearly a quarter century. Sometimes these items are referred to as Black Eagle notes to avoid any confusion with the Series 1918 $1 FRBNs that feature a large eagle vignette in green on their backs. Even if you are on a very tight budget, you should easily be able to obtain at least one of these notes. There are a total of 11 different signature varieties for this issue, but most catalogs also give major number status to two additional varieties. The first 100 million notes with the Lyons-Roberts signatures have no block letters with their serials, and the serials appear below the Series of 1899 designation. The remaining 450 million notes with this signature combination have a block letter (A through E) in front of their serials, and the serial appears above the engraved series date. The current edition of Hessler's catalog gives an absurdly low total printing for these varieties, but both were printed in very large quantities and neither is scarce. Later on, the Series of 1899 designation was placed vertically at the right end of the note. Two varieties are now recognized for these notes that have the Vernon-McClung signature combination. The "horizontal" variety is much the more common of the two, since the "vertical" variety was introduced only late in the printing of the notes with this signature combination. Gengerke estimates that 220 million of the former and 31.4 million of the latter were printed with these signatures. The latter is definitely worth a substantial premium over a "common" Eagle note, but this variety (Fr. 229a, H-51a) has only been given major number status in the relatively recent past and its market value is still a bit tentative. In October, 1998 a CAA auction featured two examples of this variety. Both were in CU condition, and they sold for $2200 and $1870, respectively. It seem thus that this variety should be regarded as a rarity. An even higher price for ths rarity was attained in the sale of the Bass collection that was held in May, 1999.

Typically Eagle notes should cost about $60 each in VF condition, or about $200 each in CU. Most of the different varieties of these notes are worth about the same except for the scarcer type with the Vernon-McClung signatures and the Napier-Thompson note (Fr. 231, H-53). The latter was printed in an edition of only 6.74 million examples, as compared with a total printing of 3.744 billion examples for all of the Eagle notes. Thus only one note out of 555 was a Napier-Thompson note for this series. This variety now sells for about $1000 in CU condition and about $200 in VF on those occasions when it is offered. If the 13 different major varieties of the Eagle notes are not enough for you, it is also possible to collect this note by serial number blocks. According to Gengerke and Murray the total number of regular blocks is 54 for the entire series. Numerous fancy serial numbers are also available for Eagle notes, and these I shall discuss in my chapter on notes with these features.

Star notes have been reported for seven of the signature varieties, thus excluding the first three that were printed prior to 1910 and the scarce Napier-Thompson combination. Both varieties of the Vernon-Mclung note exist in replacement form with 14 of the "horizontal" notes and 2 of the "vertical" notes being recorded according to Hessler. A total of about 375 replacement Eagle notes have been recorded thus far with most of them having either the Tehee-Burke, Elliott-White, or Speelman-White signature combinations.

The Series 1923 $1 SCs are by far the most common of all large-size notes. They feature a "generic" back that was also used on the $1 USNs of the same series. The face design of these notes is quite similar that which was adopted for the small-size Series 1928 $1 SCs. There are three different signature varieties - Speelman-White, Woods-White, and Woods-Tate - and the total printing for these notes exceeds 2.66 billion. Although far more Speelman-White notes appear to have been printed than was the case for the Woods-White notes, I find these two varieties to be more or less equally common. Either is available for about $25 each in VF or about $70 in CU. If you wish to collect this note by serial number blocks, there are 28 such normal varieties for the Speelman-White note and six for the Woods-White note.

The Woods-Tate note (Fr. 239, H-61) was printed at the very end of the large-size era, and it is fairly scarce since only 4.686 million examples were printed or one out of every 568 of the total for all Series 1923 $1 silver certificates. In CU condition this note now sells for about $250, while a VF example should cost about $75. Nonetheless there are four different serial number block varieties, since these notes were interspersed with the Woods-White notes. There was also a substantial amount of mixing between the Speelman-White and Woods-White notes, and so numerous changeover pairs should exist. As might be expected, star notes are known in some quantity for this series. Over 500 examples have been recorded for the Speelman-White note, and for the Woods-White note this total exceeds 200. The Woods-Tate variety is very much scarcer in replacement form, and thus far only eight examples have been recorded.

The $2 silver certificates closely parallel the $1 notes, but there is one less type since there were no Series 1923 $2 notes. Unlike the $1 SCs, however, the $2 notes used radically different face designs for Series 1886 and for Series 1891. The Series 1886 $2 SCs depict General Winfield Hancock on their faces and an elaborate green design on their backs. There are five different major varieties of this issue, but there is little difference in price between these. Several hoards of CU examples of the Rosecrans-Hyatt variety with a large salmon seal (Fr. 242, H-180) are known, and thus this variety is much the most available of these notes in top grade. They are not cheap, however, as choice CU examples now fetch about $1500 each and VF examples about $350 whenever these notes come up for sale.

Although the United States notes of this vintage mostly depicted very well-known personalities on their faces, with a few exceptions the silver certificates of this period honored much more obscure persons. The Series 1878-80 $10, $20, and $50 notes honored Robert Morris, Stephen Decatur, and Edward Everett, respectively, and this tendency was continued with later issues of silver notes. General Hancock died in 1886, and his portrait was replaced by that of William Windom who died in 1891. There are only two signature varieties of the Series 1891 $2 SCs, but both are very scarce in CU condition, since no sizable hoards of CU notes are known for this series. Windom notes in choice CU condition now sell for about $3000 to $4000 each. This note is much more reasonably priced in circulated grades, however, and prices for this note in VF or XF grades cost about the same as do the equivalent Hancock notes.

The $2 note of the Educational series depicts an allegorical version of *Science Presenting Steam and Electricity to Commerce and Manufacture.* On its back there are portraits of the inventors Robert Fulton and Samuel Morse. The same two signature varieties that exist for the Series 1896 $1 notes also occur with the $2 notes of this issue. In today's market these notes cost about $2500 each in CU and about $800 in VF condition.

The Series 1899 $2 SCs portray George Washington at the center of a more open design. This note exists in ten different signature combinations from Lyons-Roberts to Speelman-White, but notes with the Elliott-White combination were never issued. As on the $1 notes of this series, the location of the inscription Series of 1899 was changed on two separate occasions, but these changes did not overlap with different signature combinations, and so there are only ten major varieties for this issue. These notes are now selling for about $550 each in CU condition, but nice VF examples can be had for about $200 each.

As is the case with the $1 notes, the Napier-Thompson variety is by far the scarcest of this series. Only 1.816 million of these were printed out of a total of 540.2 million examples for all Series 1899 $2 notes. When available this note sells for about $1250 in CU or about $350 in VF condition. Star notes are recorded for six different signature combinations - Vernon-McClung through Speelman-White, but excluding once again the Napier-Thompson variety. Only about 75 replacement notes are presently known for this issue, and of these the Tehee-Burke and Speelman-White varieties are the least rare.

There are five different types of $5 silver certificates, since these notes were issued in Series 1886, 1891, 1896, 1899, and 1923. The notes of the first two series depict U. S. Grant, who had died in 1885. The backs of the Series 1886 notes depict five Morgan silver dollars, the center one of which is dated 1886. This is the famous "Silver Dollar" note, and it is one of the most popular of all currency designs. Despite the fact that it would be many decades before the motto *In God We Trust* would be legally required on all of our paper currency, this motto does appear on this note together with *E Pluribus Unum* and *Liberty*. These notes exist in the same seven major varieties that occur with the $1 Series 1886 notes. There is not much of a price differential between these notes, although the last of this group, the Rosecrans-Nebeker note with a small red seal (Fr. 265, H-355) is definitely the scarcest of the seven. Due in part to their very great popularity Silver Dollar notes are expensive. Expect to pay at least $3500 or so for a choice CU note, and in VF condition these notes still sell for at least $750 or more each. The two varieties of the Series 1891 notes are probably at least as scarce as are the Series 1886 notes, but this type has a much less dramatic back design. In CU condition a Series 1891 $5 note should cost about $2500, while the same note in VF condition would sell for about $400 in today's market.

The Series 1896 $5 SC is the only note of the Educational series to exist with three signature varieties, since the Lyons-Roberts combination is used in addition to the two others that were used on $1 and $2 notes. The face design of this note is entitled

Electricity Presenting Light to the World. The back of this note portrays Civil War generals U. S. Grant and Philip Sheridan. The face of this note engendered considerable controversy while it was in circulation, since it was felt by Anthony Comstock and others that it displayed too much "flesh" in the female vignette at its center. Comstock was head of the Society for the Suppression of Vice and was also a militant crusader against all forms of birth control. This is one of the reasons why the Educational notes were replaced after a short run of only about three years. A $10 design of this basic type was designed for Series 1897 by Walter Shirlaw, the designer of the $5 note. It depicts *Agriculture and Forestry,* and this design is available to collectors in the form of a souvenir card that was issued by the BEP in 1974.

It is easy to see why the Series 1923 $5 silver certificate has been called the "Porthole" note. Its back design is modernistic and it makes no reference to the fact that this note is a silver certificate.

Although $5 Educational notes are not great rarities, they are quite expensive. In today's market a choice CU note will fetch about $5500, and nice VF examples cost about $1250 to $1500 or so. During the speculative boom of 1980-81 these notes were even more expensive, and prices as high as $9000 were occasionally recorded for gem CU notes of this series. After this market crashed in 1981-82, prices returned to more sensible levels but quality Educational notes are now rising again in price due to their great popularity. Although the Tillman-Morgan variety is the least scarce of the group, there is little difference in price between the three signature varieties of this issue.

The Series 1899 $5 SC resembles to a considerable extent the Bison note with which it is contemporary. Both recall themes from the American West. Depicted is Chef Tatoka-Inyanka of the Hunkpapa Sioux, but its design is symbolic of American Indians in general. Sometimes this note is called the Oncpapa note, but it should never be called the "One Papa" note as I have occasionally heard. It can also be called the Indian note, and so for simplicity let us use that term. There are 11 signature varieties of this issue, the same number that appeared on the $1 Eagle notes. There are no varieties arising from the "migration" of the Series of 1899 designation, since that wording remains in the same two locations on all of these notes. In the 1970s Indian notes could be easily be obtained in fine condition for prices of only about $50 -75 each, but today they are very much more expensive. Choice CU examples now sell for more than $1000 each, and in VF condition these notes are still worth at least $400 apiece.

Once again the Napier-Thompson variety is the scarcest note of this type. There were only 2.234 million of these notes printed out of a total printing of 556.05 million for all Indian notes. These notes sell for about double what the other Indian notes bring, but for the other ten varieties there is very little differentiation in price from one variety to another. Fewer than 60 star notes have been recorded for this type, and these come in seven different signature varieties from Vernon-McClung through Speelman-White with the scarce Napier-Thompson combination once more being absent from this list.

The Series 1923 $5 silver certificate exists only with the signatures of Speelman and White. It features a dramatic portrait of Abraham Lincoln surrounded by a circular design feature. This has led this item to be called the "Porthole" note. The back side of this note features another "generic" design, as is the case for all Series 1923 notes. Only 6.316 million of these notes were printed, but pricewise they cost about the same as do Indian notes in today's market. All of these notes are from the AB block, as was the case with the Series 1923 $10 USNs. Thus far 36 star notes have be recorded for the Porthole note. Although these notes are hardly common in replacement form, there are more star notes for this type than there are for any one signature variety of the Indian notes.

Once low denomination silver certificates began to be printed in 1886, this type of currency soon dominated the issues of $1 and $2 notes. Denominations above $5 were printed in only fairly modest quantities, and consequently all $10, $20, and higher denomination SCs are decidedly scarce today. Normal (i. e., not countersigned) $10 SCs were issued in Series 1880, 1886, 1891, and 1908. There are three or four major types of these notes, depending upon one's point of view, and there are a total of 18 different seal and signature varieties. The Series 1880 notes depict Robert Morris, a signer of the Declaration of Independence. The later $10 notes honor Vice President Thomas Hendricks, who died in office in 1885. This note continues the "tradition" of several Series 1886 and 1891 SCs in honoring fairly obscure individuals who had recently passed away. In these notes Hendricks is depicted in a frame that resembles a tombstone, whence the popular name for these issues, the "Tombstone" note.

The normal Series 1880 $10 SCs occur with four different seal or signature varieties. Three of these (Scofield-Gilfillan, Bruce-Gilfillan, and Bruce-Wyman) have large brown seals, while the fourth (also Bruce-Wyman) has a red seal at its center. At the present time roughly 60 each of the first two varieties have been recorded. The Bruce-Wyman variety with a large brown seal is the most common with at least 120 examples on record, while the red seal variety of this issue being the scarcest with only about 30 examples on record. Some collectors may attempt to obtain all four of these varieties, but this is an expensive type. Uncirculated brown seal notes presently sell for about $5000 each, and these notes still bring at least $1250 or so in VF condition.

The Series 1886 $10 SCs come in the same seven varieties as do the $1 and $5 notes of this series. This is a very difficult set to complete, however, as only 13 examples have been recorded for the Rosecrans-Jordan variety (Fr. 291, H-590) and only ten examples for the Rosecrans-Nebeker red seal type (Fr. 297, H-596). In CU condition all of these notes are quite expensive, and it today's market they fetch about $3500 each. In VF condition they should still sell for $750 or so, with the two rare notes that I have already mentioned bringing a good deal more than this when available.

The Series 1891 $10 SCs use the same face design as their Series 1886 counterparts, but the back design is much more open and less elaborate, a deterrent feature for counterfeiting by photographic methods, or so it was hoped. The Series 1891 notes all have red seals, while the similar Series 1908 notes have blue seals plus an additional logo. In addition to the Series 1897 "Educational" design that was prepared but never used, there was also a Series 1899 design for a $10 SC that depicts an 1890s vintage battleship. The frame of this design closely resembles that of the $10 Bison note, but this battleship vignette was never used on an issued note. It is available to collectors on a souvenir card printed by the BEP in 1994. Only modest numbers of $10, $20, and $50 silver certificates were printed in the 1908-16 period, and for these the designs in use in the 1890s were continued.

There are four different signature varieties for the Series 1891 $10 notes and three varieties of the Series 1908 notes. None of these are especially rare, but obtaining all seven of these items requires quite a bit of patience and money. In CU condition these notes now sell for about $2000 each, and in VF condition they cost more like $500 per note. Presumably star notes were printed for all three of the varieties of the Series 1908 notes, but only one replacement note each is known for the $10 notes with the Vernon-Treat and Parker-Burke combinations. None have thus far been recorded for the Vernon-McClung variety of this series.

The $20 silver certificates closely parallel their $10 counterparts. Again there are four varieties of the normal Series 1880 notes. There are between 30 and 40 examples known for each of the Scofield-Gilfillan and Bruce-Gilfillan notes, and the Bruce-Wyman variety with a large brown seal is substantially more abundant with rather more than 100 examples now recorded. The Bruce-Wyman variety with a small red seal is significantly scarcer, as only 29 examples are known at present. These notes now cost substantially more than do the corresponding $10 notes. Expect to pay almost $10,000 for a CU $20 note with a large brown seal, and about $2000 or so for one of these notes in VF condition. In 1998 a choice XF example of the Bruce-Wyman note (Fr. 311, H-816) sold for an unprecedented $7150 in a CAA auction. The red seal variety of this issue is scarcer and would probably sell for prices that are even higher than these.

The Series 1886 $20 SCs depict Daniel Manning, a Secretary of the Treasury who died in 1887. Although inscribed Series 1886, these notes were not actually issued until 1888. The backs of the Series 1886 notes show an elaborate diamond design, and so these notes are often referred to as the "Diamond Back" notes. There are four major varieties of this type, and all are scarce. As a type note, this item is much harder to come by than is the Series 1880 $20 note. The scarcest of these varieties has the Rosecrans-Hyatt signatures with a large salmon-colored seal. Only 12,000 of these notes were printed, and only 14 examples are known at the present time. An AU example sold in a Lyn Knight auction in 1996 for $16,500, and in 1998 a CU example with a very low serial number (B16) sold for $50,600 in the Levitan auction.

Although the three other varieties of "Diamond Back" notes are not quite so rare, they are all decidedly scarce. There are about 60 known examples of the Rosecrans-Huston note, and this is the most available of this rare type, although none of the recorded notes are in CU condition. Expect to pay about $3500 for one of these in VF condition. Fewer than 20 examples are known for the Rosecrans-Nebeker brown seal variety, and these show a range of grades similar to that found for the Rosecrans-Huston note. An absolutely unprecedented realization was attained for an example of this note in gem CU condition when one sold for $93,500 in a CAA auction held in Chicago in May, 1999.

There are also about 20 known examples of this note with a small red seal (Fr. 316, H-821). I was fortunate in acquiring a nice XF example of this note at a bargain price in a Kagin's auction in 1983. This note does have one problem, however. The color of its seal has faded to pink, doubtless the result of having been exposed too much light in past years. Nonetheless it is a major rarity in this grade. If you insist on having all of your notes in CU condition, you can forget entirely about "Diamond Back" twenties. They hardly ever show up in this condition, and the very rare notes of this type that are in CU condition have proven to be ultra-expensive.

There are four different signature varieties for the Series 1891 $20 silver certificates with red seals and two with blue seals. For some reason the designation 1891 was continued with the blue seal notes rather than being switched to Series 1908 or some other later date, as was the case with the $10 notes. The red seal $20s have the same signatures as do their $10 counterparts, while the blue seal notes exist with the Parker-Burke and Tehee-Burke combinations. Since the blue seal notes have an additional design feature added to their faces, as do the Series 1908 $10 notes, one can consider the Series 1891 $20 notes as constituting either one or two major types. Getting all six signature varieties of these notes is a major challenge. At the present time about 200 notes are known for the four red seal varieties and perhaps as many as 250 notes for the two varieties of blue seal notes. The price differentials between these notes is not particularly large, but all are expensive. Examples of any of these notes in CU condition are at least $3000 each in today's market, and VF examples now sell for about $1000 each. Among the red seal notes the Tillman-Morgan variety is the most abundant, but the there is a small hoard of Lyons-Roberts notes in CU condition. The latter note, however, is very hard to come by in nice circulated grades.

The Parker-Burke variety is the most abundant of all of the $20 silver notes, and it is available in a wide range of grades, but demand for this item as a type note is high and they cost about as much as does any other note of this series. There are five known star notes for this type, all of which are of the Parker-Burke variety. Very recently it has been noted that the signature of Houston Tehee that appears on the Tehee-Burke issue of these notes (Fr. 322, H-827) occurs in two different sizes. The current editions of the various currency catalogs have not yet acknowledged this variation, but future editions may note this distinction. It may also exist on some other types of notes that bear the relatively common Tehee-Burke signature combination.

Shown above are the backs of Series 1880 and 1886 $20 silver certificates. The former, in common with all Series 1878 and 1880 SCs, has a dark brown back. The latter is the beautiful, but decidedly rare, "Diamond Back" note.

The regular issue $50 silver certificates were issued in Series 1880 and 1891. All of these notes depict Edward Everett, a prominent political figure of the 1850s and 1860s. Since there were no Series 1886 notes for the $50 and higher denominations, the issue of Series 1880 type notes was continued into the 1890s. There are five known varieties of normal Series 1880 $50 notes, but the note with the Scofield-Gilfillan combination is unique and in government custody. There are rather more than 60 of these notes known for the other four varieties. These occur in a variety of grades including CU. As you might expect, these notes are very expensive, and a VF example in today's market would be at least $12,500 or more. In VG-F condition the price would be closer to $5000, but brown back $50 silver notes are genuinely rare in any grade. The Levitan collection that was sold late in 1998 featured three different examples of this series. The Fr. 327 (H-1020) was in VF condition and sold for $18,700, the Fr. 328 (H-1021) was CU and brought $93,500, while the Fr. 329 (H-1022) was graded XF-AU and fetched $22,000.

All of the $50 silver certificates carry a portrait of Edward Everett, a noted statesman and orator of the mid-19th Century. Like all other silver certificates of Series 1878 and 1880, the back side of this note is printed in dark brown.

There are five different signature varieties of the Series 1891 $50 SCs with red seals and one variety only (Parker-Burke) with a blue seal. These notes are otherwise quite similar, and they have an open back design that is characteristic of all Series 1891 notes. With effort I have managed to acquire four of these varieties over the years, but that would not be an easy task today. The blue seal variety (Fr. 335, H-1028) is much the most abundant of these, and something like 120 examples are presently known. These occur in a wide range of grades including CU. This note is comparable in rarity and in price to the Lyons-Roberts $50 USN (Fr. 164, H-941). In fine condition these notes are now fetching at least $1000 each, and in XF condition you can expect to pay $4000 or so. Although the total number of red seal notes that are known is somewhat less than the number recorded for the single blue seal variety, the least rare of these sell at prices that are not much higher than those for Fr. 335.

Only five examples are recorded for the Series 1891 $50 Rosecrans-Nebeker variety, and so this note is virtually noncollectible. There are about 20 known examples each of the Tillman-Morgan and Bruce-Roberts notes, about 30 examples of the Lyons-Roberts note, and about 40 examples known for the Vernon-Treat note. The latter includes a small run of a dozen or so CU notes having serials H1662xx. I was most fortunate to acquire one of these in 1985 at a price that would seem very low by today's standards. This note (Fr. 334, H-1027) is much rarer in CU condition than is Fr. 161 (H-938), the brown seal $50 USN that is now fetching more than $10,000 in CU condition. After a lapse of several years, a CU example of Fr. 334 was sold at auction in October, 1998. It fetched a price of $13,750. In May, 1999 a CU example of the blue seal variety sold for $14,950. This note was from the collection of Harry W. Bass, Jr. that was sold by Bowers and Merena.

If you want to add a $100 silver certificate to your collection, be prepared to shell out serious money. All $100 SCs are rare and very expensive. The normal Series 1880 notes parallel the $50 SCs exactly, but this time there are no known Scofield-Gilfillan notes either in public or in private hands. According to Treasury records 16,000 notes with this signature combination were printed for each of these denominations, but the attrition rate has been very high since the $50 note of this variety is unique and the $100 note is unknown. About 50 examples are known for the other four varieties of the Series 1880 $100 SCs. Thus these notes are only slightly rarer than are their $50 counterparts, and the prices for Series 1880 $100 notes are comparable to or only somewhat higher than those of the $50 notes of this series. In a CAA auction held in June, 1994 there was a beautifully matched pair of Series 1880 $50 and $100 SCs. The $50 note (Fr. 328, H-1021) was in AU condition and sold for $15,675, while the $100 note (Fr. 341, H-1218) was in XF-AU condition and sold for $20,900. In today's market prices would be even higher. A VG-F example should still be less than $10,000, but this type is rare in all grades. The Levitan collection featured an example of the Fr. 340 (H-1217) in VF-XF, a Fr. 341 (H-1218), and a Fr. 342 (H-1219) in CU, as well as a Series 1891 Fr. 343 (H-1220) in AU condition. These four $100 silver certificates sold for prices of $30,800, $23,100, $104,500, and $27,500, respectively.

The Series 1891 $100 silver certificates have small red seals, and they exist in two different signature varieties, Rosecrans-Nebeker and Tillman-Morgan. The portrait of James Monroe that was used in the Series 1880 notes is continued with this series, but the back design and color are entirely different. At the present time only 18 examples of the first variety and 27 of the second have been recorded, and of these five of the former and seven of the latter are in institutional hands. One reason for the rarity of this note is that very good counterfeits were made of the Tillman-Morgan variety in the 1890s. This led to a withdrawal of these notes from circulation, and no $100 SCs with blue seals were issued in 1910-15 as was the case with $10, $20, and $50 notes. The Series 1891 $100 SC is actually rarer than is the Series 1880 note of this denomination, a situation that is quite different from that of the $50 silver notes. Despite this fact prices for Series 1891 $100 notes are currently no higher than they are for Series 1880 $100 notes, but both of these types are clearly rarities in all grades. Two recent auction realizations for this type were $27,5000 for an AU example of Fr. 343 (H-1220) and $16,100 for a VF example of Fr. 344 (H-1221). These notes were in the Levitan and Bass collections, respectively.

All $100 silver certificates carry a portrait of President James Monroe. This denomination of silver notes was not printed after the late 1890s due to the fact that some good quality counterfeits of the Series 1891 notes with the Tillman-Morgan signature combination were produced.

As one might expect, all $500 and $1000 silver certificates are ultra-rarities. As is characteristic of many SCs these notes portray relatively obscure individuals. Charles Sumner is on the $500 notes, and William Marcy is depicted on the $1000 notes. There were a total of 9300 countersigned $500 notes issued in Series 1878 and a total of 24,000 normal $500 SCs issued in Series 1880. For the $1000 notes there were a total of 14,490 countersigned notes issued in Series 1878 and 16,000 normal notes issues in Series 1880. There were also 5600 $1000 SCs issued in Series 1891. Among the countersigned notes only a single $500 example is known, and it is in government custody. Seven Series 1880 $500 SCs are presently known, but four of these are in institutional hands. There are five known Series 1880 $1000 SCs, but three of these are in government hands. Of the two known Series 1891 $1000 notes, one is in government custody. Amon Carter Jr. had one $500 SC and both types of $1000 SCs in his collection, but these were sold privately in the early 1980s. After a lapse of more than 15 years, one example each of the Series 1880 $500 and $1000 silver certificates appeared in the Levitan collection. The $500 notes was graded VF, and the $1000 was graded VF-XF. They sold for prices of $286,000 and $363,000, respectively. Basically you can forget about these notes even if your pockets are very deep. But if you want authentic replicas of the faces and backs of Series 1878 $500 and Series 1891 $1000 SCs, these are available on four souvenir cards that the BEP printed between 1989 and 1996.

When low denomination silver certificates were first issued in 1886, they proved to be much more popular as circulating items than did the bulky silver dollars that backed them. The numbers of SCs continued to grow as more silver dollars were minted, and in 1904 they represented 27% of the total face value of the paper money in circulation. Since no silver dollars were coined between 1905 and 1920, the quantity of SCs in circulation remained very nearly constant at about $350 million during these years. Although silver dollars were again coined in the 1920s, the number of SCs in circulation grew only very slowly. By 1929 these notes constituted about 10% of the value of the paper money then in circulation. Silver certificates were the dominant form of paper money for the $1 and $2 denominations for many years. The $1 SCs alone represented more than 80% of the total numbers of large-size silver certificates that were printed, and despite their low face value they totaled almost 50% of the face value of all silver certificates that were issued in the large-size era.

If you are a type collector, the $1, $2, and $5 SCs will cause you no problems, although most $5 silver notes are expensive in high grades. If you want to collect these notes by signature and seal varieties, then there are 27 different $1 notes, 19 $2 notes, and 24 $5 notes. None of these are major rarities, but this is not an easy project to undertake. I have succeeded in obtaining all of these notes, but completing this group took quite a few years and represented a considerable outlay of funds. The $1 SCs of Series 1899 and 1923 are more amenable to block collecting than are any other types of large-size notes, and the $1 Black Eagle notes also abound in low and fancy serial numbers should your interests lie along those directions. Ignoring the countersigned notes there are 18 major varieties for the $10 notes and 14 for the $20 SCs. Obtaining all of these would be extremely difficult to do, as several of these notes are now recognized as major rarities. You might want to settle for four notes of each denomination, thus including one each of the red seal and blue seal varieties of the 1891/1908 series. The Series 1891 $50 notes are also collectible, but the Series 1880 $50 SCs and all $100 silver notes are rare and very expensive in the higher grades.

TREASURY NOTES

The Treasury Notes of 1890 (as they are called in official sources) are not to be confused with more recent interest-bearing government securities of the same name. These notes, which are also sometimes referred to as Coin Notes, were non-interest bearing paper money that circulated extensively in the 1890s. Like the silver certificates that preceded them by 12 years, Treasury Notes were issued to pay for purchases of silver by the Treasury. During the 1870s and 1880s the world production of silver steadily increased, while that of gold decreased. In 1878 about 2.5 million troy ounces of gold were produced in the United States, while the corresponding silver production was about 35 million ounces. By 1890 domestic gold production had fallen to about 1.6 million troy ounces annually, while that of silver had risen to 54.5 million ounces. During this interval the gold/silver price ratio had changed from 18 to 1 to 22 to 1.

To provide for additional money and to appease the western silver interests the Silver Purchase Act of 1890 was enacted. This act was passed under the sponsorship of Senator John Sherman. Under the provisions of this act the Treasury was obliged to purchase 4.5 million troy ounces of silver each month at its current market price. This was to be paid for in newly printed Treasury Notes that were redeemable in either gold or silver at the discretion of the Secretary of the Treasury. Treasury Notes were issued in denominations of $1, $2, $5, $10, $20, $50, $100, and $1000. All of these denominations were issued both in Series 1890 and 1891 with the exception of the $50 notes that were issued only in Series 1891. A $500 note was also planned for Series 1891, but it was never issued.

With the sole exception of the $20 note, all of these notes depicted Union military or government leaders. The portraits on these notes are as follows:
$1 Edward M. Stanton (1814-1869) - Secretary of War under Lincoln and Johnson
$2 James B. McPherson (1828-1864) - Union general killed in 1864
$5 George H. Thomas (1816-1870) - Union Army general
$10 Philip H. Sheridan (1831-1888) - Union Army general and cavalry commander
$20 John Marshall (1755-1835) - Fourth Chief Justice of the United States
$50 William H. Seward (1801-1872) - Secretary of State under Lincoln and Johnson
$100 David G. Farragut (1811-1870) - Admiral in the U. S. Navy
$1000 George G. Meade (1815-1872) - Union commander at Battle of Gettysburg

Philip Sheridan had died only shortly before these notes were issued, and thus to some extent the $10 Treasury Notes can be regarded as commemoratives. William T. Sherman (1820-1891) died while these notes were in production, and his portrait was selected for use on the proposed Series 1891 $500 Treasury Notes, but only face and back proof impressions for this note are presently known to exist.

The Series 1890 and Series 1891 Treasury Notes differ from each other primarily in their back designs. The former have extremely elaborate backs that resemble to a fair extent those of the Series 1886 silver certificates. The Series 1891 notes have far more open designs which closely resemble those of the silver certificates of the same year. All Series 1890 Treasury Notes have an initial letter A in their serial numbers, while all Series 1891 notes have an initial letter B. The serial numbers for both series terminate with a star, but this star is merely an end designator for the serial number and not an indicator of replacement status. The serial numbers of all Treasury Notes are printed in red. The Treasury seals on these notes come in two styles. Large brown seals were used on Series 1890 notes bearing the signature combinations of either Rosecrans-Huston or Rosecrans-Nebeker. The smaller red scalloped seals were used on all Series 1891 notes plus some of the Series 1890 notes with the Rosecrans-Nebeker signature combination.

For the $1 through $10 denominations of Series 1890 all Treasury Notes exist with the Rosecrans-Huston signature combination (large brown seal only) and with the Rosecrans-Nebeker combination bearing either a large brown seal or a small red seal. Of these three varieties the Rosecrans-Nebeker notes with brown seals were printed in much the lowest quantities, and generally this variety is the scarcest of the three for each denomination. The abundances of the Series 1890 $10 notes are anomalous, however, since a small hoard of CU examples of the Rosecrans-Nebeker brown seal note (Fr. 367, H-613) does exist making this note about as common in high grades as is the Rosecrans-Huston note which has a printing almost ten times as large.

Series 1890 Treasury Notes are far from common in any grade. In VF condition the more readily available varieties of $1, $2, $5, and $10 Series 1890 notes would cost about $600, $1000, $750, and $1000 each, respectively. The Rosecrans-Nebeker brown seal varieties for the $1, $2, and $5 notes (Fr. 348, 354, and 360, or H-63, H-198, and H-374, respectively) are all very rare. Although Martin Gengerke does not assign a high rarity class to Fr. 348 (H-63), this note comes up for sale very much less frequently than do the other two varieties of Series 1890 $1 notes. It seems likely that his census data are incomplete, since Gengerke lists only 14 known examples of Fr. 354 (H-198) and only eight of Fr. 360 (H-374), the $2 and $5 notes, respectively, of this variety. The latter note hardly ever appears in public auctions, however, and it is doubtless the rarest of the lower denomination Treasury Notes.

The $1 through $10 Treasury Notes of Series 1891 were all issued with the Rosecrans-Nebeker, Tillman-Morgan, and Bruce-Roberts combinations, and the $5 note exists with the Lyons-Roberts signatures as well. In general these notes are substantially more abundant than are their Series 1890 counterparts. In VF condition the more common signature combinations of the $1, $2, $5, and $10 notes sell in today's market for about $150, $400, $300, and $500 each, respectively, while in CU their respective prices would be more like $700, $1800, $1250, and $2000. The Lyons-Roberts $5 note (Fr. 365, H-379) and the Bruce-Roberts $10 note (Fr. 371, H-617) are much scarcer than are the other Series 1891 notes of these denominations. Gengerke lists only 14 of the former and 23 of the latter in his current census, but both of these totals are undoubtedly incomplete.

For both Series 1890 and 1891 there are a total of 25 different major varieties of $1 through $10 Treasury Notes. I now have 24 of these, but this is a very difficult group to complete. I feel certain that Fr. 360 (H-374) is very rare, as I hardly ever see it offered for sale. It is probable that most collectors attempt to obtain these notes by type only, but the relative scarcities of the different signature combinations of these issues will probably become more apparent as more collectors attempt to obtain all of the possible major varieties for these denominations.

Guide and Handbook — large-size type notes\163

For the $20 notes all three combinations exist in Series 1890, but only the Tillman-Morgan and Bruce-Roberts varieties were issued for Series 1891. Three of these notes (ie., Rosecrans-Huston, Rosecrans-Nebeker red seal, and Tillman-Morgan) are collectible, but the other two varieties are extremely rare. In his current census Gengerke records for the three collectible varieties totals of 45 examples of Fr. 372 (H-843), 79 of Fr. 374 (H-845), and 77 of Fr. 375 (H-846). These data are probably much more complete than are his data for the scarcer low denomination notes, as all $20 Treasury Notes are decidedly scarce. A significant number of CU examples of Fr. nos. 374 and 375 have come from cut sheets. These notes are now often bringing prices in excess of $10,000 each. Nice circulated notes of the three varieties sell for substantially lower prices, but all $20 Treasury Notes are expensive. Even in VG-F grade these notes still sell for at least $1500 or more.

The Treasury Notes of Series 1890 are noted for having extremely beautiful back designs.

Only nine examples of the $20 Rosecrans-Nebeker brown seal note (Fr. 373, H-844) are recorded. The highest known grade for these is XF, and this variety in that condition would fetch well over $10,000 in today's market. The $20 Bruce-Roberts note (Fr. 375a, H-847) is much rarer, since only two examples (one in VG and one in CU) are known. The better of these is in government custody, and thus this variety is quite noncollectible in any attractive grade.

There is only one variety each of the Series 1891 $50, the Series 1890 $100, and the Series 1891 $100 Treasury Notes. All of these are major rarities. There are 20 known examples of the $50 note, of which seven are in institutional hands. A recent sale of this note was of an XF example in the Shiva collection that was sold by Spink America in 1995. It brought $26,400. More recent sale of the $50 Treasury notes were $57,200 for another example in XF condition that was part of the Levitan collection, and a record $170,500 for a CU example with a very low serial number (B7) that was sold in August 1998. The Bass collection also contained a CU example of this note that sold for $161,000.

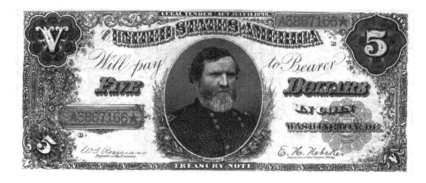

The Series 1890 $100 Treasury Note is the famous "Watermelon" note, so-called because of the two large green zeros on its back. There are currently 33 examples recorded for this note, of which nine are in institutional hands. In 1994 the note that had been in the Amon Carter Jr. collection was sold by CAA. This note is in VF-XF condition, and it brought $21,450. In 1998 another Watermelon note, this time in choice XF condition, sold for $52,250. The Watermelon note in the Levitan collection was in AU condition, and it sold for $99,000. The note in the Bass collection was in XF, but it sold for an even higher price of $138,000. To put it mildly, Watermelon notes are under a great deal of price pressure these days. The Watermelon note with serial number A93800 must have a most interesting history. In 1974 it was described as being "well circulated, soiled, laundered, and with pinholes." In 1975 this was upgraded to "VF with pinholes, rounded corners, and a light stain." In 1979 it was described as being "full crisp AU and free of pinholes." Clearly this note has been "improved" over the years. This is a matter that I shall discuss more fully in my chapter on the care and preservation of bank notes.

The Series 1891 $100 Treasury Note is substantially rarer than is the famous Watermelon note, since only eleven examples are presently recorded. Of these four are in institutional hands, and this includes the only known uncirculated example. An example of this note in F-VF condition was in the Shiva collection that was sold in 1995. It fetched $33,000 in this auction. The XF Levitan note sold for $88,000.

Four different varieties of $1000 Treasury Notes were printed. In Series 1890 there were 16,000 Rosecrans-Huston notes with brown seals and 12,000 Rosecrans-Nebeker notes with red seals, and in Series 1891 there were 8000 notes with the latter combination and 24,000 with the Tillman-Morgan signatures. Today only nine of these notes are known - five of the first variety and two each of the second and fourth varieties. Of these five are in government custody. To put it mildly, these notes are rare. The Series 1890 notes have been nicknamed the "Grand Watermelon" notes. There have been only three public sales of these notes during the past 25 years, and all of these were of the Rosecrans-Huston variety. In 1983 a VF example sold for $44,000, and in 1989 an AU example sold for $121,000. The latter realization was the highest price ever paid for a piece of paper money up to that time. This note was resold at the Levitan auction for $792,000, which again is a record for paper money in public auction, and it exceeds by a factor of four any price achieved for a single piece of paper money prior to the banner year of 1998.

The record price for a bank note did not stand for long. In late 1998 an AU example of the Grand Watermelon notes with a small red seal (Fr. 379b, H 1426) came into the market. This note, the only such example in private hands, was once in the famous Grinnell collection. it is reported that it sold for more than $1,000,000 in a private sale.

Although the Treasury Notes are "treasured" by today's collectors, they soon caused monetary problems in the years in which they were in circulation. Many persons on receiving them chose to redeem them for gold. This led to a serious drain of gold from the Treasury between 1893 and 1895. In 1893 the Sherman Silver Purchase Act was repealed, and from then on, the numbers of Treasury Notes in circulation ceased to increase. Treasury Notes had their maximum circulation in 1893, when they constituted about 13% of the total face value of the paper money in circulation. At this time some $141 million of these notes were in circulation, but this figure fell only gradually to about $75 million by 1900. In the next few years the circulation of Treasury Notes fell rapidly, but some new notes were being printed as replacements for worn notes almost to the end of the 1890s, since the Lyons-Roberts $5 notes could not have been printed any earlier than 1898.

Most collectors will probably have to be content with obtaining only an example or two of the four lower denominations - $1, $2, $5, and $10 - of the Treasury Notes. The back designs of the Series 1890 notes are among the most intricate of all U. S. currency designs, and they are truly beautiful on notes that are in nice condition. If you cannot afford the real items, several of the face and back designs of the Treasury Notes are available on souvenir cards that have been produced by the BEP using the original dies.

GOLD CERTIFICATES

Gold certificates were first authorized under the Act of March 3, 1863, but none were issued prior to late in 1865. Between 1865 and 1878 there were three different issues of these notes, but they were not intended for general circulation since gold was at a premium over most forms of paper money until January 1, 1879. The notes of the First Issue were printed in denominations of $20, $100, $500, $1000, $5000, and $10,000, while those of Series 1870 and Series 1875 (i. e., the Second and Third Issues) were printed in these same values minus the $20 note. The First Issue notes display an eagle on their faces, and their backs are bright orange to simulate the color of gold. The notes of Series 1870 and 1875 portray Thomas Hart Benton, Lincoln, Hamilton, Madison, and Jackson, respectively, on the $100, $500, $1000, $5000, and $10,000 denominations. Senator Benton was an appropriate choice for a gold note, since he was a strong advocate of hard money during the 1830s and 1840s. The notes of these two series are uniface.

The first circulating gold certificates appeared in 1882. The earliest issues were countersigned by Thomas Acton. The Series 1905 $20 gold notes are known as the "Technicolor" notes, since they have a beautifully colored underprint that was dropped on the much more common Series 1906 and 1922 notes of this basic type.

The gold notes issued between 1870 and 1878 included a space for the name of a payee to be filled in. Although these notes were transferable to a third party, they were clearly not intended for general circulation. Rather they were held to settle gold balances between banks and to function as certificates of deposit for gold. They were in fact inscribed as payable in gold rather than in gold coin, the latter clause being used only on the later issues of gold certificates intended for general circulation. These notes reached their maximum circulation of $32 million in 1870, but by 1882 they had fallen to only $5 million. Throughout this period they constituted only a small fraction of the total value of gold coins in circulation.

Today all gold certificates of 1865-78 are excessively rare. One of the $20 notes of 1865 in VF condition (serial number 41146) was sold at auction for $88,000 in 1990. A second note of this type (serial number 416) in XF-AU condition was sold at auction for $357,500 in 1999. This note was from the collection of gold certificates formed by Lawrence Cookson, which was sold by CAA at the beginning of 1999. These two $20 notes of 1865 are probably the only gold certificates of the 1865-78 issues that are outside of government custody. The current edition of Hessler's catalog provides illustrations of several other notes of these series, all of which are in government custody, but for all intents and purposes these notes are quite noncollectible.

Regular issue large-size gold certificates were issued in various series from 1882 to 1922. They were issued in denominations of $10, $20, $50, $100, $500, $1000, $5000, and $10,000, and all are inscribed as being payable in gold coin to bearer on demand. Unlike the earlier notes all of these issues are of the standard size used for large-size notes, and all have backs printed in bright orange. Once these notes came into general circulation the notes of 1865-78 were withdrawn, and this would account in part for the excessive rarity of the earlier gold notes.

The first issues of Series 1882 were countersigned and printed with brown seals. At the present time there are only 23 known $20 notes, 11 known $50, and 5 known $100 notes that have the Bruce-Gilfillan signature combination together with the countersignature of Thomas Acton. Of these three of each denomination are in institutional hands, as are the only two known countersigned $1000 gold notes. No countersigned $500 gold notes appear to have survived in either public or private hands. In a CAA auction held at the beginning of 1998 two outstanding countersigned gold certificates were featured. The $20 note in choice XF condition sold for $18,700, while the $50 in CU (and by far the finest known) sold for an unprecedented $82,500. For all intents and purposes the countersigned Series 1882 $100 gold note is noncollectible, but an example in AU condition sold for $253,000 in the Levitan collection.

The later issues of Series 1882 gold notes were first printed with brown seals, but later on small red scalloped seals were used. The $100 through $10,000 notes use the same portraits that were used on the Series 1870-75 notes, but new designs were introduced for the $20 and $50 notes. The former honors President James Garfield, who had been assassinated in the previous year and who also appears in Series 1882 $5 national bank notes. The $50 notes depict Silas Wright, a prominent New York political figure of the 1830s and 1840s.

There are four different major varieties of Series 1882 $20 gold notes that are not countersigned, three of which have brown seals. All brown seal gold certificates are very rare, and only about 50 examples are known for all three of these signature varieties. I was most fortunate to obtain an XF-AU example of the Bruce-Wyman note in the early 1980s, at a time when the true rarity of these notes was not realized. I have also acquired one of the countersigned $20 gold notes as well as the Rosecrans-Huston variety of this series. Sales are infrequent on these notes, but in XF condition any brown seal $20 gold note would probably bring about $10,000 or so in today's market. The red seal $20 note with the Lyons-Roberts signature combination (Fr. 1178, H-833) is much more readily available than are the brown seal notes. Today these notes sell for about $800 in VF condition, but in choice CU condition they now sell for several thousand dollars apiece.

Brown seal $50 gold notes are even rarer than are their $20 counterparts. There were three different issues of these without the third signature, and this note also exists with a large salmon-colored seal and the signatures of Rosecrans and Hyatt (Fr. 1191, H-1033). The only known example in private hands is in XF condition, and it sold for $165,000 in the Cookson collection sale held by CAA in January, 1999. Altogether there are about 30 known examples of these four varieties. A fine example of the Bruce-Wyman note (Fr. 1190) sold for $10,175 in a CAA auction in 1996, and in 1997 an XF example of the Rosecrans-Huston note (Fr. 1192) brought $33,000 in another CAA auction.

Rarest of all the $50 gold notes is an issue with a small red scalloped seal and the signatures of Rosecrans and Huston (now listed as Fr. 1192a, H-1034a). This note is unique, and it has only become recognized as a distinct variety in the past few years. It is in F-VF condition and was sold by Stack's in 1990 for $27,500. It is my opinion that this note was printed in error. Almost all of the type notes having the Rosecrans-Huston signature combination have either large brown seals or large salmon-colored seals (as is the case for some USNs and SCs). The small red seals were not used until after this signature combination was no longer in use. It is likely that an old plate with this combination was mixed into a production run of notes with one of the later signature combinations having small red seals.

The Series 1882 $50 red seal gold notes also exist with five different "normal" signature combinations. These are Lyons-Roberts, Lyons-Treat, Vernon-Treat, Vernon-McClung, and Napier-McClung, respectively. Of these five varieties the last is the most readily available. There are probably about 100 examples of this note available to collectors. There are only about 20 examples each recorded for the second and fourth varieties with the first and third varieties being of intermediate abundance. Getting all five of these notes is a major challenge. In today's market a Series 1882 $50 red seal note sells for at least $1250 in VF condition, but in CU condition these notes can bring as much as $4000 or more.

The Series 1882 $100 gold certificates exist in the same brown seal or large red seal varieties that are encountered for the non-countersigned $50 notes. But only 21 examples have been recorded for all four of these varieties, and 12 of these are in institutional hands. This makes these notes so rare as to be almost noncollectible. An XF example of the Rosecrans-Hyatt note was sold by Stack's in 1990 for $33,000. There were a couple of sales of brown seal $100 notes in VF condition in the early 1990s at prices not greatly in excess of $10,000 each, but prices are now much higher. The Levitan collection featured examples of the Bruce-Gilfillan and Rosecrans-Huston notes of this series. Both were in fine condition and they sold for $14,300 and $23,100 respectively. The Bass collection had a VF example of the latter variety. It sold for $43,700 in May, 1999.

The backs of Series 1882 gold certificates are noted for their heraldic eagle designs. The $20 note of this series also commemorates the completion of the Transatlantic Cable.

There are nine different signature varieties of Series 1882 $100 gold notes with small red seals. These range from Lyons-Roberts to Tehee-Burke. The Tehee-Burke variety (Fr. 1214, H-1240) is much the most "common" of these, and there are at least a few hundred of these known to collectors. A VF example of this note now sells for about $750, while a CU example of this variety sells for about $4000 or so. Although the other eight signature varieties are scarcer, relatively few collectors attempt to acquire all nine of major varieties of this subtype. As a result, prices for most of these are not greatly in excess of those for the Tehee-Burke variety in today's market. On gold certificates the Napier-Thompson signature combination exists on $10, $20, and $100 notes, but it is not particularly scarce on any of these. According to Martin Gengerke, the Lyons-Treat combination (Fr. 1207, H-1233) is much the scarcest of the nine notes of this subtype. He records only 11 examples, of which five are in government custody.

The Series 1922 $100 gold certificate is of the same basic design as are the Series 1882 notes of this denomination. It bears the signatures of Speelman and White and is even more abundant than is the Tehee-Burke $100 note. In the 1970s this note was worth about double face in VF condition, but today expect to pay at least $500 for one of these in that grade. A nice example in CU condition will probably cost about $3500 in today's market. This note also exists in replacement form, and thus far 18 of these have been recorded.

Let us next turn to the $10 gold certificates. These were introduced only with Series 1907. They bear the portrait of Michael Hillegas, the Treasurer of the United States during its pre-Constitution period. Hillegas was the person in charge of the production of Continental Currency. It is perhaps a bit ironic that this individual who supervised the printing of a type of paper money that soon became badly inflated was honored by being depicted on a "rock-hard" gold certificate. There are six signature combinations of this note in Series 1907 and one in Series 1922. Most collectors, however, recognize two or three additional varieties of these notes. The earlier notes of this series are inscribed Act of July 12, 1882, but this was later changed to Act of March 4, 1907. The Napier-McClung and Napier-Thompson combinations are found with both of these inscriptions. I find that the Napier-McClung note is about equally as common with either the 1882 or 1907 date, but it appears to me that the 1907 date is much more abundant on the Napier-Thompson notes than is the 1882 date despite the fact that the currency catalogs show no price differentials for the two date varieties of this note.

The Series 1922 $10 gold notes come in two different serial number varieties. The first 13.5 million of these notes were printed with serial numbers that are 3 mm high, while the remaining 147.1 million have serial numbers that are 4 mm high and much wider. Naturally the latter variety is much the more common, but none of the Series 1907 and 1922 $10 gold notes are rare enough to command large premiums over the more common varieties in today's market. In VF condition these notes sell for about $100 to $150 each, while in CU condition they are now fetching $400 and up. The Napier-Thompson variety was printed in smaller quantities than was any of the other signature varieties, but they usually sell for prices that are less than double those of the more readily available varieties. Star notes are reported for four varieties of the Series 1907 $10 notes and both varieties of the Series 1922 note. About 150 of these have been reported, and by far the largest number of these are for the Series 1922 note with large serial numbers.

The $20 gold certificates of Series 1905, 1906, and 1922 all depict George Washington on their faces. The same back design is used for all three series, but three different subtypes can be recognized. The Series 1905 notes have red seals, while the other two series have orange-yellow seals. The Series 1905 gold certificates are extremely beautiful, since their faces are also covered with yellow and orange tinting that is lacking on the 1906 and 1922 notes. These are known as the "Technicolor" notes, and they exist with two signature combinations, Lyons-Roberts and Lyons-Treat.

The Technicolor notes are extremely popular, and they have been subject to much speculative pressure in recent years. The two signature varieties appear to be about equally abundant, but they show a decidedly unusual distribution with respect to condition. There are a number of CU examples available, and these sell for extremely high prices. On occasion prices as high as $10,000 or more have been asked for these notes in gem CU condition, although neither variety can be termed a major rarity. These notes are also available in fine condition at much lower prices (about $800 each), but Technicolor notes are very scarce in choice circulated grades such as VF-XF or XF-AU. After years of search I located an XF specimen of the Lyons-Roberts variety and a nice AU example of the Lyons-Treat issue for my collection. In their price patterns these notes resemble other speculative issues such as the Educational notes and the Silver Dollar notes. Since the Technicolor notes are far from unique in CU grade, I question whether they are really worth as much as they have been fetching on some occasions. There are far rarer large-size type notes that sell for much lower prices than do CU examples of these issues.

There are six different signature varieties of the Series 1906 $20 gold notes. The Napier-Thompson note (Fr. 1184, H-839) has the lowest printing of these, but it is not a very scarce note. The Series 1922 $20 gold note exists in only one variety, and it is a common note. Examples of these notes in VF condition are now selling for about $200 each, while these notes can be expected to bring about $700 in CU condition. Although Fr. 1184 is definitely scarcer than are some of the other varieties of the 1906 and 1922 gold notes, it is not very much more expensive. Completing a set of all seven of these notes by signature combinations is relatively easy to do. About 100 star notes have been reported for $20 gold certificates. There are three known replacement varieties for the Series 1906 notes, but the great majority of the star notes for this denomination are for the Series 1922 type.

An entirely new design of $50 gold certificates was prepared for Series 1913 and 1922. These depict U. S. Grant on their faces. The Series 1913 notes exist with two different signature combinations, Parker-Burke and Tehee-Burke, while the Series 1922 notes exist in the same two serial number varieties as do the corresponding $10 notes of the same series. The two varieties of Series 1913 $50 notes are about equally abundant. In VF condition these notes are now selling for about $700 each, but in CU condition they would cost more like $3500 each. The small number variety of the Series 1922 note was printed in an edition of 800,000 examples, while 5,184,000 examples of the large number note were printed. The former is about as scarce as is either of the two Series 1913 varieties. The latter note is the most abundant of the $50 gold notes, and VF examples now sell for about $450 each. In CU condition these notes can be expected to bring $2000 or so. There are 13 star notes reported for $50 gold notes, and all of these are of the Series 1922 large number variety.

Gold certificates were also issued in higher denominations, and a few of the $500 and $1000 notes are at least collectible. There is one example each known for the Bruce-Wyman and Rosecrans-Hyatt varieties of the Series 1882 $500 gold notes, but both of these are in government hands. For the earlier Series 1882 $1000 gold notes there are the previously mentioned pair of countersigned notes, and also recorded are unique Bruce-Wyman and Rosecrans-Hyatt notes, all of which are in government custody. There are also three $1000 notes each of the Rosecrans-Huston combination with a large brown seal (Fr. 1218d, H-1419) and of the Rosecrans-Nebeker signatures with a small red seal (Fr. 1218e, H-1420). Two of each of these varieties are in government hands. There are eight examples reported for the Series 1882 $1000 note with the Lyons-Roberts signatures and four reported with the Lyons-Treat signatures. Only one of the former is presently in government hands, so this variety (Fr. 1218f, H-1421) is the most "available" of these major rarities, if that term can indeed be used. A few years ago this was not an impossibly expensive note. But in 1997 a newly discovered example of the Lyons-Roberts $1000 gold note in only fine condition brought $33,000 in a CAA auction. Unless you have very deep pockets forget all about owning one of these.

There are three varieties of Series 1882 red seal $500 gold certificates and one of Series 1922 than can be considered collectible. At the present time for the $500 gold certificates there are 23 known Lyons-Roberts notes, 27 of the Parker-Burke combination, 36 Tehee-Burke notes, and 42 of the Series 1922 (Speelman-White) notes. A few of these are only in fair or good condition, and according to Dean Oakes there is at least one additional note in really poor condition. Although the $500 gold certificates are major rarities, they are not impossible for collectors with sufficient funds. In today's market these notes have been selling for about $7000 - $8000 each in VF condition. At one time I was in possession of two of the Series 1922 notes, but I have since sold one of these. All four of the signature varieties are more or less equally abundant, and so they should sell at about the same prices. Despite the fact that over 125 large-size $500 gold notes are known, not one is recorded in CU condition. A grade of XF-AU is about as high as can be expected on any of these notes.

Although they are quite expensive, a fair number of $500 and $1000 gold certificates have survived. Shown above are Series 1922 $500 and $1000 notes.

The new design for the $1000 gold certificates was issued in Series 1907 and 1922. The Series 1907 notes are split between five different signature combinations, but the great majority of these are Tehee-Burke. At the present time there are 46 Series 1907 notes recorded plus 29 Series 1922 $1000 notes. Of the Series 1907 notes 28 are of the Tehee-Burke variety (Fr. 1219e, H-1423e). Fewer than five notes each exist of the Vernon-Treat, Napier-McClung, and Napier-Burke varieties in private hands, and so these should be worth a substantial premium over the less rare Tehee-Burke variety should affluent collectors decide to collect these notes by signature combinations. At one point I owned both a Series 1907 (Parker-Burke) and a Series 1922 note, but I am now down to just the latter note, which is well matched with my $500 note of the same series. The Tehee-Burke and Speelman-White $1000 gold notes in VF condition have been available for less than $10,000 each, but high denomination large-size notes are now becoming very popular. In the 1970s these notes typically sold for only about double face when in fine condition, but it seems that the $500 and $1000 denominations of both gold certificates and Federal Reserve Notes are being sought by an increasingly large number of collectors. If you feel that you can afford one of these notes, I would suggest that you get one soon before prices climb out of sight, as they already have done for the much rarer Series 1882 $1000 notes. Prices for all high denomination large-size notes have shown sharp increases in recent years. A CAA auction held in May, 1998 included very attractive Series 1882 $500 and 1922 $1000 gold notes that were in XF and AU-CU condition, respectively. These sold for $13,200 and $39,600, thus indicating that there is presently a very strong demand for high denomination large-size type notes of top quality.

The last of the regularly issued gold certificates are the Series 1882 $5000 and $10,000 notes. Although these notes were issued with several signature combinations, only those with the Tehee-Burke combination are known to exist. The $5000 note with serial M20625 and the $10,000 note with serial K31071 are both in VF condition, and they currently reside in the Federal Reserve Bank of San Francisco where a most impressive collection of rare bank notes is on display. The other pair of these notes, having serials M26080 and K56991, respectively, were illustrated in earlier editions of the Friedberg catalog and are presumably in private hands. In today's market either of these notes would certainly bring far into seven figures, but their present whereabouts are unknown.

The other types of large-size gold certificates that were issued were never intended for general circulation. Series 1888 notes of the $5000 and $10,000 denominations were issued as transfer documents either between the Treasury and a given bank or for interbank transfers. These notes are uniface, and physically the Series 1888 items closely resemble the Series 1870 and 1875 gold notes of the same denominations. All of these notes have long since been redeemed, and they are quite unavailable to collectors in any form. These notes were almost 10 mm wider than normal large-size notes, and they were printed in sheets of three rather than four subjects each.

The Series 1900 $10,000 gold certificates were yet another issue of transfer documents which closely resemble their predecessors of Series 1870, 1875, and 1888. Like the Series 1888 notes these items were not treated as currency in circulation. Rather they were transfer documents that were dated and issued to a specific payee, and they served to facilitate a one-time only transfer of gold from the Treasury to that payee. Once paid they were canceled and not reissued. But there is a very big difference concerning the survival of Series 1900 notes. At the present time about 400 to 500 of these notes are known in canceled form, and these are available to collectors who desire them.

The story of these unusual items is well known. On December 13, 1935 there was a fire in the Old Post Office Building at 12th and Pennsylvania Avenue in Washington. While this fire was going on, various paper items were tossed out of windows in this building and included among the documents were several hundred canceled Series 1900 gold notes. The government still regards them as their property, and officially they are not legal to collect. It seems, however, that they now have a quasi-legal status not unlike that of normal gold certificates in the years just prior to their full legalization in 1964. Some auction firms such as Stack's will not handle them, while others such as Currency Auctions of America have sold numerous examples in recent years. The government does not seem to mind the private ownership of test notes and proof items that occasionally leak from their custody, so it is most unclear to me why they should be concerned with these peculiar items. The obligations on these notes are totally different from those on normal gold certificates. They provide for the transfer of gold from the Treasury to a specific payee designated on the note. Even in uncanceled form they would have the status of third-party checks, which would be negotiable only when endorsed by the original payee. Almost all of the known examples, however, have punched cancellations of various types. There have been a few attempts to redeem these notes, but none of these have been successful.

The Series 1900 $10,000 gold certificates were intended only as transfer documents between the Treasury and large banks or the Federal Reserve System. All of the known examples are canceled and nonnegotiable. Note the numerous differences in overprints between the note that was issued late in 1915 and the second example which was issued early in 1917.

A total of 363,000 of these notes were issued in eight different signature combinations from Lyons-Roberts to Tehee-Burke. All except for the Napier-Burke variety have now been recorded, but the Tehee-Burke variety is by far the most common. Enough of these notes have been sold in recent years for one to assign market values fairly accurately for these items. In today's market they bring about $400 in fine condition, about $800 in XF, and at least $1500 in CU. Some of the notes have problems with water stains, and the earlier notes tend to be more brutally canceled than do the notes that were issued in the years 1916 and 1917. If you wish to obtain more than one of these items, several varieties are possible. The earlier notes were issued to different large private banks, and they are usually canceled with large punched holes in various parts of the design and signature blocks. Most of them have either the Vernon-Treat or Napier-McClung signature combinations. After the Federal Reserve System came into existence in 1914, it seems that almost all of these notes were made payable either to the Federal Reserve Board or to an individual Federal Reserve bank. They were canceled with punched letters that are more attractive than the larger holes that are found on their predecessors. All of the later notes bear the Tehee-Burke signature combination. On some notes the engraved word "Assistant" is retained, and on some it is blocked out. The dates of issue are found as late as mid-1917. Some of these notes also have a date of cancellation, and this is never more than a few months after the date of issue for a given note. This proves that these notes were used only as transfer documents and not as reserve currency.

Other varieties may exist, but a thorough census of these notes will not be possible until they have been declared completely legal to collect, as hopefully will soon become the case. At the present time many persons who own these notes are reticent to supply data on their holdings given the current status of these items. Other varieties of Series 1900 gold notes were probably prepared, but this is the only note for which the supply available to posterity was selected by having the survivors hastily thrown out of windows in a burning building. With that method of selection it is hardly surprising that some varieties would be much more common than others!

Once they began to circulate in the 1880s the normal gold certificates soon became a very important component of our nation's currency supply. The United States went fully on the Gold Standard only in 1900, and prior to that time there were far more gold coins in circulation than there were gold notes. But after 1900 the numbers of gold certificates in circulation rapidly increased. In 1907 the amount of these notes in circulation ($600 million) surpassed for the first time the amount of gold coins in circulation ($562 million). In that year these notes constituted about 30% of the total paper money in circulation. In the mid- and late 1920s the circulation of gold certificates considerably exceeded the amount of gold coins in actual circulation, and at the end of the large-size era these notes constituted about 24% of the total face value of the paper money then in circulation.

You will certainly want to include a few gold notes in your collection, if you collect large-size notes at all. The $10, $20, $50, and $100 notes of Series 1922, and their immediate predecessors in Series 1907, 1906, and 1913 are all readily available. The notes of these series are also amenable to being collected by signature varieties, if you are so inclined. Additional type notes that are obtainable are the small red seal varieties of the Series 1882 $20, $50, and $100 notes. If you are willing to settle for fine condition, the

Technicolor note is not too expensive, but this is a very tough item in high grades. In several instances a given type of note is dominated by a single variety. For instance, the only non-rare Series 1882 $20 note is Fr. 1178 (H-833), and nos. 1197 (H-1039) and 1214 (H-1240) are by far the most abundant of the $50 and $100 notes, respectively, for Series 1882. Although $500 and $1000 gold certificates may be beyond your means, the Series 1900 $10,000 note is often available. I feel that its present quasi-legal status need not deter you from obtaining one of these unusual items.

FEDERAL RESERVE NOTES

The United States was the last major industrialized nation to adopt a central banking system. This came about through the Federal Reserve Act of December 23, 1913. The Federal Reserve System established by this act began operations on November 16, 1914. Although this act called for the establishment of 12 separate reserve banks as well as several additional branch banks, control of the Federal Reserve System was maintained by the board of governors in Washington. The members of this board are presidential appointees, but they sit for 14-year terms of office and thus are much more independent of direct executive control than are such cabinet appointees as the Secretary of the Treasury.

Under the provisions of the Federal Reserve Act, Federal Reserve Notes were issued, and these began to see circulation in 1915. Until 1933 FRNs were redeemable in gold, and the obligation to redeem them was borne by the government itself rather than by the various Federal Reserve Banks. All large-size FRNs of the $5, $10, $20, $50, and $100 denominations are Series 1914, while the higher value FRNs of denominations $500, $1000, $5000, and $10,000 are Series 1918. All FRNs bear the signatures of the Treasurer of the United States and the Secretary of the Treasury. Once they began to circulate FRNs soon became a major form of currency in the United States. By 1920 these notes constituted over two-thirds of the total face value of all paper money in circulation. During the mid-1920s there were again heavy issues of gold certificates, but by the end of the large-size era in 1929 FRNs constituted 43% of the total amount of paper money then in circulation.

Large-size FRNs have relatively simple designs both on their faces and backs. The portraits used on the $5 through $100 denominations are the same as those in use today except that Andrew Jackson appears on the $10 notes and Grover Cleveland on the $20 notes. The back of the $5 note uses two historical vignettes, *Columbus Sighting Land* and the *Landing of the Pilgrims* that had previously been used on $1 USNs and $1 NBNs, respectively. The $10 notes use two vignettes depicting agriculture and industry, while the $20 notes use vignettes showing modes of transportation. The Panama Canal was opened in 1914, and this event was honored on the backs of the $50 notes.

The back of the $100 FRNs depicts a group of allegorical figures. This design had originally been proposed for use on all denominations of small-size notes. Serious consideration was being given in 1913 to the introduction of small-size currency, but the passage of the Federal Reserve Act and the beginning of World War I turned the attention of Treasury officials onto other matters. Fifteen years were to elapse before small-size currency actually went into production.

All large-size FRNs bear one of four different signature combinations: Burke-McAdoo, Burke-Glass, Burke-Houston, or White-Mellon. The first three were of persons who held office during the Wilson administration, while White and Mellon were in office during the Harding, Coolidge, and Hoover administrations. These notes also bear district seals as part of their designs, and all five denominations of the Series 1914 notes were issued for all 12 districts. The notes from the first issue of FRNs all bore red Treasury seals and serial numbers, but after about one year the color of these features was changed to blue. It has been claimed that this change was necessitated by the difficulty of importing red dyes from Europe under war conditions, but all USNs and the high value gold notes printed at this time continued to feature red Treasury seals, and so it seems that there may have been other reasons for this change.

The Series 1914 FRNs with red seals all bear the signatures of Burke and McAdoo, but there are two different types which differ in whether or not the district number and letter appear in small print in the upper left portion of the note. Shown above is a type a $100 note from San Francisco and a type b $50 note from St. Louis.

All red seal FRNs bear the signatures of Burke and McAdoo, but these come in two distinct types. In type "a" the plate position letter only appears in the upper left and lower right corners of the note. In type "b" these have been joined by small district numbers and letters in these corners. Both of these types carry large district numbers and letters in their lower left and upper right corners. Red seal FRNs were issued by all 12 districts for all five denominations issued in Series 1914. Furthermore all of the $5, $10, and $100 notes were issued in both the "a" and "b" varieties. For the $20 and $50 denominations only type "a" notes were issued for the Atlanta and Dallas districts. Thus a "complete" set of red seal FRNs would consist of 116 varieties.

By far the most comprehensive collection of large-size Federal Reserve Notes formed in recent years was that of James W. Thompson, which was sold by Stack's in 1991. It featured an unprecedented total of 95 different red seal FRNs - 21 $5, 20 $10, 20 $20, 18 $50, and 16 $100 notes. This is also a series that I have been working on diligently, and I now have 56 different of these issues - 17 $5, 13 $10, 10 $20, 7 $50, and 9 $100 notes. Through the efforts of Martin Gengerke and other researchers it is now estimated that total numbers of only about 150 and 230, respectively, of the $50 and $100 red seal notes are extant. The $20 notes of this issue do not appear to be significantly more abundant that are either of the two higher denominations. It is likely that these censuses are far from complete, but it is also clear that red seal FRNs are much scarcer than is sometimes realized.

Red seal FRNs are usually collected by denomination only, and it is not especially difficult to assemble a set of the five values of this issue. It is certain, however, that there are several major rarities in this issue when districts and types ("a" or "b") are also taken into consideration. Thus far only a few collectors have attempted this, but the supply of these notes will dry up very rapidly if several more persons try to collect red seal FRNs in this fashion. Despite the many rarities that exist in this issue, the price differentials between the different varieties of a given denomination are still relatively small. Prices of about $125, $150, $400, $650, and $800 would now be typical for the $5, $10, $20, $50, and $100 notes, respectively, of this series in VF condition. Red seal FRNs in gem CU condition, however, are now selling for very much higher prices. In a 1997 auction held by CAA a red seal $5 note (Fr. 835a, H-380D) in this grade sold for $852, while similar $10 (Fr. 893b, H-618B) and $20 (Fr. 959b, H-848H) notes brought $1045 and $1980, respectively.

The blue seal Series 1914 FRNs were issued in far larger quantities and over a much longer period of time than were the red seal notes. As type notes they are among the most common of all large-size notes, and until fairly recently heavily circulated examples commanded little or no premium over their face value. It is still a very easy matter to acquire a single note of each of the five denominations, but if signature and district seal varieties are taken into account, collecting these notes becomes very much more of a challenge.

All four signature combinations were used on these notes. Blue seal notes with the Burke-McAdoo signatures exist only as type "b." The Burke-Glass and Burke-Houston combinations are also without complications, but for several of the lower denomination notes there are three distinct varieties for the White-Mellon signatures. In the first (and most common) variety the district and Treasury seals are 120 mm apart (center to center), and there is a large district numeral and letter in the lower left corner. In the second variety the figures in the lower left corner have been greatly reduced in size. In the third (and scarcest) variety these figures are again large, but the seals are now only 100 mm apart rather than 120 mm as is the case for the other two varieties. These are referred to as types "a," "b," and "c," respectively.

In recent years there has been a considerable amount of research conducted by Martin Gengerke and others as to which varieties of blue seal FRNs were actually printed.

Although there is still no well established rarity scale for these notes, at least it is possible for collectors to know which notes exist and which do not. Since there are 12 different districts and four different signature combinations, it would be logical to assume that there should be at least 48 possible major varieties for each denomination. For many years this is the way that these notes were listed in the standard currency catalogs. Careful research has now proven that no Burke-Glass or Burke-Houston $100 FRNs were printed for several of the districts. A few of these possibilities for the $20 and $50 notes are also nonexistent. All of the $100 White-Mellon notes are of type "a," but for the $50 notes type "b" varieties also exist for the New York and Cleveland districts. The former seems to be quite scarce, but the latter is one of the more readily available $50 FRNs. For the $20 notes there are several type "b" possibilities, and type "c" notes are still being listed for the New York, Chicago, and San Francisco districts. It now appears, however, that this variety actually exists only for the San Francisco district (Fr. 1011c, H-849L4c), and this note is now one of the acknowledged rarities of the blue seal FRNs.

As my collection of blue seal FRNs grew over the years, I was puzzled as to why I had not been able to acquire a type "c" $20 note, since I had been able to purchase a number of the $5 and $10 notes of this variety. An example of Fr. 1011c in new condition finally appeared in the Thompson sale in 1991, but my bid was much too low since I was unaware of the true rarity of this variety at that time. It sold for $484 in this auction, but this note would doubtless bring a far higher price in today's market now that its distinctive status is confirmed.

The numbers of varieties of the $5, $10, and $20 blue seal FRNs are increased by the presence of several of the types for the White-Mellon notes. Type "c" varieties are now confirmed for seven of the $5 notes and six of the $10 notes. For the $5 notes type "b" notes exist for all 12 districts, but for the $10 and $20 notes these are known for six districts each. It now appears that there are a total of 68 major varieties for the $5 notes, 60 of the $10 notes, 53 for the $20 notes, 45 of the $50 notes, and 33 for the $100 notes. This is a total of 259 possible varieties for all Series 1914 blue seal FRNs. Both the Hessler and Friedberg catalogs also list type "c" $20 notes as possibly existing for the New York and Chicago districts. Friedberg still lists $20 Burke-Glass notes for the Atlanta and Kansas City districts, but they were probably not printed. The Friedberg catalog also lists a $50 Burke-Glass note for Dallas, but this variety probably does not exist. Both of these catalogs are in agreement as to 33 different varieties of $100 blue seal FRNs that were printed. For the $10 notes Hessler doesn't list a type "c" variety for the Kansas City district, but Gengerke has confirmed this variety. Both the Friedberg and Hessler catalogs are in agreement as to the existence of 68 varieties for the $5 blue seal FRNs.

In its new 17th edition the Krause-Lemke catalog no longer lists any of the nonexistent signature varieties for Series 1914 blue seal FRNs, but this book makes no distinction between the type "a" and "b" varieties of red seal notes or the three different types of White-Mellon notes. Hessler's catalog has a much more thorough listing of these notes than has Friedberg or Krause-Lemke, since it also lists star notes and gives the numbers of notes printed for each district and denomination. The latter data are quite interesting, so let us look at some of these.

There are three different varieties for some of the blue seal FRNs that have the signatures of White and Mellon. Type a was used for most White-Mellon notes, and it is much the most common. Type b was used in several districts for $5, $10, and $20 notes as well as two districts for $50 notes. Type c notes are much the scarcest, and nearly all of these are either $5 or $10 notes. Shown above are a type a $20 note from Minneapolis, a type b $10 note from Chicago, and a type c $5 note from New York. New York was the only district to issue Series 1914 FRNs with C or D suffixes.

There were a total of 81.7 million red seal FRNs issued and just under 2.0 billion blue seal notes for Series 1914. This gives a ratio of about 24.5 / 1 for blue seals to red seals, but I do not feel that red seals are as scarce as this datum would imply. By denomination the breakdown is as follows:

	Red Seal	Blue Seal	Ratio
$5	51,128,000	1,065,862,000	20.8
$10	24,132,000	597,440,000	24.8
$20	5,492,000	301,920,000	55.0
$50	540,000	25,253,000	46.8
$100	452,000	8,780,000	19.4

As can be seen from these data more than 100 times as many $5 notes were printed as $100 notes for both seal colors. In terms of examples in existence today, however, the ratios for these two denominations would be much smaller. The reason for this, of course, is that the $5 and $10 notes saw far more day-to-day use than did their $50 and $100 counterparts. Thus many more of the lower denomination notes required replacement while these notes were in circulation. Although Gengerke has attempted to do complete censuses for the higher denomination red seal FRNs, there are no good estimates for the total numbers of Series 1914 blue seal FRNs that are presently in collectors' hands. Certainly there are at least two or three thousand each of the $50 and $100 notes, and for the three lower denominations the numbers of available blue seal FRNs most definitely are in the tens of thousands.

How should one collect Series 1914 blue seal FRNs? The simplest approach is to obtain one of each denomination in decent condition. At the present time F-VF examples of the $5, $10, $20, $50, and $100 notes sell for about $30, $35, $45, $150, and $250 each, respectively. Even if you do not regularly plan to collect large-size $50 and $100 notes, one example of each of these notes will not strain your budget very much. Things get vastly more complicated, however, if you decide to collect these notes by district and signature varieties.

In my chapter on small-size FRNs I explained why I do not attempt to collect all district varieties of the $5 - $100 notes. For the large-size FRNs, however, this is precisely what I have attempted to do. At the moment I have 50 different $5 notes, 48 $10 notes, 42 $20 notes, 24 $50 notes, and 16 of the $100 blue seal notes. This total is now more than two-thirds of the 259 varieties that are known to have been printed. This is an interesting and very challenging project, which is possible in part because these notes are not especially expensive as far as large-size notes go and the total number of varieties is far less than it is for small-size FRNs. Thompson's collection contained several blue seal notes that I lack at present, but it does not appear that he pursued the acquisition of Series 1914 blue seal FRNs with quite the thoroughness that he did for some other series such as red seal FRNs, Series 1918 FRNs, and large-size FRBNs. Is it possible to obtain all 259 different varieties of blue seal Series 1914 FRNs that probably exist? That I do not know. I do not think that anyone has come extremely close to succeeding, although Thompson made a good attempt with over 200 different varieties of these notes by series and district in his collection.

In terms of serial numbers the Series 1914 FRNs follow a scheme which is quite similar to that adopted for small-size FRNs. For numbers under 10 million, however, no initial zeros were used. All of the low number Series 1914 FRNs are red seal notes, since the numbers for the blue seal notes began where those of the red seals left off. Only the $5 and $10 notes of New York and the $5 notes of Chicago had printings that exceeded 100 million, and thus for all other normal issues the serials have "A" suffixes. For New York $5 FRNs blocks of BA, BB, BC, and BD are known, but for New York $10 FRNs only BA and BB were used with the GA and GB blocks being used for the $5 Chicago notes. Compared with contemporary small-size FRNs, block collecting of large-size FRNs is extremely simple. As might be expected the issues of FRNs varied from district to district. The two largest, of course, were New York and Chicago with respective issues of 541.6 million and 301.3 million notes for all five denominations of the Series 1914 blue seals. The two smallest were Minneapolis and Dallas with respective issues of 50.5 million and 48.9 million notes for this series.

The back of the Series 1914 FRN commemorates the opening of the Panama Canal in 1914. The back design of the $100 FRN of this series was considered for a common design of a contemplated series of small size notes to be issued at about this time.

At the present time there is still remarkably little difference in the numismatic values for the different varieties of blue seal FRNs of a given denomination. In recent years there has been rather strong price pressure on these notes in gem CU condition, and such notes are now selling for significantly higher prices than are notes that are merely in "new" condition. At the present time gem CU blue seal $5, $10, $20, $50, and $100 FRNs are now selling for about $125, $175, $300, $1350, and $1250 apiece, respectively. The reason for $50 notes being higher priced that $100 notes in this condition is due to the fact that several dozen CU examples of the $100 Burke-McAdoo note from Atlanta (Fr. 1104, H-1245F1) are known, and these still frequently come up for sale. A significant hoard of CU notes with the same signatures but from Philadelphia (Fr. 1092, H-1245C1) has also recently come onto the market. In my collection there are several gem CU blue seal FRNs (including both Fr. nos. 1092 and 1104), but I am vastly more interested in the relative rarities of these varieties than I am in any nit-picking about whether the uncirculated notes in my collection are MS-62, MS-63, or MS-64, to use coin terminology. I have kept my minimum grade for blue seal FRNs at VF-XF, but most of my notes are better than this, and these notes are still available in AU-CU grades at prices well under what I have noted above.

    The big question with regard to blue seal FRNs, however, is what are the relative rarities for the notes of a given denomination? For instance, of the 3000 or so examples (my "guesstimate" but probably in the right ball park) of Series 1914 blue seal $100 FRNs that probably exist, how are their numbers distributed among the 33 different varieties that were printed? We know that some varieties (e. g., Fr. 1104) are common, but which ones are rare and how rare are they? Of all 259 different varieties of Series 1914 blue seal FRNs that probably exist, in my opinion the only one that commands a really large premium in today's market is the $20 type "c" note from San Francisco (Fr. 1011c, H-849L4c). It is likely that there are several other varieties among these issues that are equally rare, but thus far their rarity has not yet been recognized. For syngraphists who collect these notes only by denomination, there are no problems since all five of these are common. It is also fairly easy to obtain all four signature combinations for each of these denominations, and one can obtain without too much difficulty sets of one note from each district for the $5, $10, and $20 denominations, although you will find this to be very much more difficult to do for the $50 and $100 notes. Perhaps it is fortunate that not many collectors seek these notes by district and signature varieties. That would put huge pressure on certain varieties and cause their prices to increase sharply.

    By comparison, it is interesting to examine what has happened with certain series of coins. For instance, let us consider St. Gaudens $20 gold pieces. A collector in the late 1940s or early 1950s would have found that some dates of these (e. g., 1924 and 1927) were very common and could be had in substantial quantities at the then prevailing prices of $40 to $45 each. Certain other dates with large mintages (e. g., 1920S and 1921) would have proven to be much more elusive, but the true rarity of these dates did not become apparent until the very large holdings of $20 gold pieces existing in the United States and in European banks had been thoroughly searched. At the present time these two rarities sell for many thousands of dollars each, as do several of the late-date $20 gold pieces. This series even contains one ultra-rarity, viz., the 1927D double eagle, but fifty years ago it is unlikely that anyone would have offered a huge price for this coin. It is most improbable that any of the Series 1914 blue seal FRNs will ever command prices remotely comparable to what 1927D $20 gold pieces bring these days, but among the 259 different major varieties of these notes there may well be a few items that are of comparable rarity.

Detailed censuses of large-size star notes have been obtained by Douglas Murray, and these data are given by Hessler in his catalog for FRNs as well as for the other types of large-size notes. Although star replacement notes were first introduced in 1910, they were not used on Federal Reserve Notes until several years later. No red seal FRNs of this type were issued, but star notes are known for all four signature varieties of Series 1914 blue seal FRNs. These exist in quite a few different varieties. According to Hessler, there are currently 50 known varieties of star notes for the $5 notes, 44 of the $10 notes, 35 for the $20 notes, 8 varieties of $50 notes, and 9 for the $100 notes. In terms of recorded numbers there are presently 303 $5 notes, 185 $10 notes, 175 $20 notes, 21 $50 notes, and only 9 of the $100 star notes. Thus each of the $100 star note varieties is unique. I have not collected large-size star notes systematically, but my $20 Burke-McAdoo FRN from Dallas (Fr. 1004, H-849K1) is a star note that I purchased at the Thompson sale. The Thompson collection contained numerous other star notes for the Series 1914 FRNs including one each of the $50 and $100 notes. The latter was from Cleveland and had the unusual serial number D6*. Despite its unique status, this note sold for only $1155 in 1991. Since no red seal FRN star notes were issued, the blue seal issues of these varieties all began with serial number 1.

Series 1918 FRNs were issued in denominations of $500, $1000, $5000, and $10,000. Like their small-size counterparts these fall into two categories. The first two denominations are collectible at least for affluent syngraphists, but notes of the latter two denominations exist only in government hands. The $500 note depicts John Marshall on its face and De Soto Disco*vering the Mississippi* on its back. The $1000 note depicts Alexander Hamilton on its face and a large eagle engraving on its back. The $5000 FRN has James Madison on its face and *George Washington Resigning his Commission* on its back. The $10,000 note depicts Salmon P. Chase and the *Embarkation of the Pilgrims* on its back. The designs for the backs of the $500, $5000, and $10,000 FRNs had been previously used on First Charter $10, $1000, and $50 national bank notes, respectively.

A total of 283,600 Series 1918 $500 FRNs was issued, and for the $1000 notes of this series the total was 276,000. These notes were issued from all 12 districts. Most carry the Burke-Glass signatures, but a few notes are also known with the Burke-Houston or While-Mellon signatures. The Hessler and Krause-Lemke catalogs mention a Burke-McAdoo $500 note from Chicago, but this must be a typographical error since no Series 1918 FRNs could have been printed with this signature combination. The survival rate for these two denominations is almost exactly the same, about one in 2100 of the notes that were issued, but the numbers of notes known to collectors has steadily grown as more have turned up. In 1989 Martin Gengerke recorded just about 100 of each of these notes, but in 1997 he has now recorded about 130 of each denomination both in public and in private hands.

About 130 examples each of the Series 1918 $500 and $1000 FRNs are presently known. Shown are the backs of the $500 and $1000 denominations.

The Series 1918 $500 and $1000 FRNs are the most abundant of the high denomination large-size notes, the only other reasonably available notes of these denominations being the $500 gold notes of Series 1882 - 1922 and the $1000 gold notes of Series 1907 - 1922. In an article that I wrote for *Numismatic News* in late 1996 I stated that these two types were under a good deal of pressure, and I think that is still very much the case. In the present census all but four of the known $500 notes bear the Burke-Glass signature combination. New York is the most common district with Chicago being the second most abundant. For the $500 FRNs 22 are presently in institutional hands. The $500 FRNs show a wide range of conditions, but only about a dozen are CU. For the $1000 notes there are 12 that have either the Burke-Houston or White-Mellon signatures with the balance being Burke-Glass. San Francisco is the most common district with Chicago being second on the list. For these notes 19 are presently in institutional collections, and about 20 are in CU condition. No notes of either denomination are known from the Richmond district.

It is clear that James Thompson avidly sought these notes, since his collection contained 11 different varieties for each of these denominations. For the $500 notes conditions ranged from F-VF to AU with prices (in 1991) going from $1375 to $6600. For the

$1000 notes conditions ranged from F-VF to CU with prices in the range of $2090 to $11,550. No collection before or since has contained a selection of these notes that was even remotely this strong. I obtained Thompson's Chicago $500 note at this sale. I already had a $1000 note from Chicago in my collection, and since then I have added one of these from San Francisco. I am now in need of another $500 note to "balance" this group, but I think I will call it "quits" once this quartet is finished.

Although James Thompson attempted to obtain as many varieties of these notes as possible, most collectors settle for only one note each of the $500 and $1000 denominations. Thus the values of these notes depend almost entirely on condition and not on the relative scarcities of particular district or signature varieties. At one time $500 notes were significantly less expensive than were $1000 FRNs, but since these notes are equally abundant, that price distinction has almost disappeared for all but the lowest grades. In today's market nice XF notes are more than $10,000 each. A few years ago CU notes of either denomination sold for about this price, but a gem CU Series 1918 $1000 FRN from Cleveland sold for $24,200 in a CAA auction in 1997. This unprecedented price seemed temporarily to have been an anomaly, since more "reasonable" prices prevailed in the CAA auction held in early 1998. In that sale a CU $500 from Dallas brought $14,300, while a $1000 note in similar condition from Atlanta went for $15,400. Rather than decrease, however, prices for high grade Series 1918 $500 and $1000 FRNs have subsequently increased very sharply. In February, 1999 a $500 note from Dallas in CU sold for $31,900 in a Lyn Knight auction, while in May of the same year a $1000 note from Kansas City fetched $38,500 in a CAA auction. If you want a pair of these notes (I assume that every collector who wants one also wants the other.), I am afraid that they already have become extremely expensive. The remarks I wrote in 1996 about the heavy demand for these notes are most definitely still true today.

Only 6800 Series 1918 $5000 FRNs and 5600 $10,000 notes were issued. Given their extremely high face value, it is hardly surprising that almost all of them were eventually redeemed. At the present time 13 examples of the $5000 note and 10 examples of the $10,000 note are outstanding, but only five examples of each are known, all of which are in government hands. Of these notes four of each are in choice condition, but there is also one defective or low grade note for each denomination. Examples of these types are on public view at the Federal Reserve Bank of San Francisco. If you want intaglio prints of the back designs of these notes, they are available on souvenir cards that were issued by the BEP in 1986 and 1989.

For the collector who wishes to own the ultimate, however, there is one way by which more original samples of the Series 1918 notes can be obtained. In 1946 a unique set of face and back specimens of all nine denominations of large-size FRNs was sold in one of the series of seven auctions that featured the famous Grinnell collection. It sold for more than $4000, an amount almost unheard of for paper money at that time. In 1991 this set appeared again in the auction of the Thompson collection, where it brought $55,000. It has not been resold since that time, but it does remain in private hands and will undoubtedly appear once again on the market at some future date.

FEDERAL RESERVE BANK NOTES

Like the FRNs, the Federal Reserve Bank Notes (FRBNs) were envisioned by the Federal Reserve Act of 1913. Although the FRNs were issued by the Federal government itself, the FRBNs were issued through the various Federal Reserve Banks that were created by this act. The obligations on these notes are nearly identical to those of contemporary national bank notes, and initially the FRBNs were intended to serve as replacements for the NBNs. Beginning in 1913 many of the newly chartered national banks chose not to issue their own notes, and several banks that had previously issued NBNs decided not to continue with them. Federal Reserve Bank Notes, however, did not appear in circulation until 1916, and they never did serve their originally intended purpose of being replacements for the NBNs. As things turned out, large-size FRBNs circulated extensively for only five or six years, and during most of this period they served as emergency replacements for silver certificates rather than as substitutes for national bank notes.

Federal Reserve Bank Notes were originally envisioned to replace national bank notes, but that did not prove to be the case despite the fact that their obligations are virtually identical to those appearing on NBNs. FRBNs also resemble Nationals in the way in which the bank titles appear on their faces. Shown above is the face of a $1 note from Kansas City and the back of a $2 FRBN that depicts a battleship of the World War I period.

Large-size FRBNs were issued in Series 1915 and 1918. For the former series only $5, $10, and $20 notes were issued, but Series 1918 also included $1, $2, and $50 notes. All of these notes carry two pairs of signatures. The Treasury signatures are those of Tehee-Burke or Elliott-Burke. John Burke signed as Treasurer of the United States, while Houston Tehee (a full-blood Cherokee) or William Elliott signed as Register of the Treasury. All of these notes also contain the signatures of the Cashier and the Governor of the Federal Reserve bank through which a given note was issued. For some districts there are as many as three different combinations of bank signatures, and thus numerous signature varieties are needed to obtain truly complete sets of these issues. Let us examine these notes on a denomination basis, as I have done with most other large-size issues.

By far the most common of the large-size FRBNs are the Series 1918 $1 notes. These depict an eagle and flag vignette on their backs, a design that was not used on FRNs, since the latter series included no notes below $5. The $1 notes were issued by all twelve districts, but when the various signature combinations are taken into account, there are a total of 39 different varieties. About 470 million of these notes were issued. As might be expected, the district with the largest issue was New York, and the last variety from this district (Fr. 713, H-68B3) comes in both BA and BB block varieties. According to most authorities the rarest of the 39 major varieties of this type is the Minneapolis note with Tehee-Burke Treasury signatures and the bank signatures of Cook and Young (Fr. 735, H-68I2). In completing my set of these notes I also found one of the Atlanta notes (Fr. 724, H-68F2) and one of the Dallas notes (Fr. 741, H-68K2) to be quite elusive. There are also reports that one of the St. Louis notes is decidedly scarce.

As a type note, the $1 FRBN is one of the easiest of the large-size notes to acquire. Examples in VF condition are readily available for about $50 each. There are also numerous CU notes on the market, and typically these sell for about $175 each. Only about 20 examples are known for the rare Minneapolis note, and an XF example of this rarity now sells for about $1000. If you wish to obtain more than one example of the $1 FRBNs but don't feel that you can afford to obtain a complete set of all 39 varieties, a good compromise is to complete a district set of 12 notes. The smaller districts are naturally scarcer than are districts such as New York or Chicago, but there is at least one variety from each district that is obtainable without too much difficulty.

Although the printing statistics for this issue tell how many notes were printed for a given district, these data are not broken down by signature combinations. In his book on large-size paper money records Martin Gengerke regards all of the $1 FRBNs with the exception of Fr. 735 as being fairly common, but it is my feeling that several other varieties of this type are at least moderately scarce. The first issues of FRBNs from Cleveland are often available with low serial numbers, since a clerk at that bank put aside a number of these when they were issued. A total of about 250 star notes have been reported for 37 of the major varieties of this issue including the rare Minneapolis note. The Thompson collection included 14 of these. Prices of these ranged from about $130 for notes in VF condition to about $700 for CU notes when this collection was sold in 1991. One autographed star note from New York in CU condition brought $1210. Interest in large-size star notes has increased considerably since 1991, and I expect that the prices for all of these items would be very much higher on today's market. In the CAA auction held in January, 1998 two star notes from New York in XF sold for about $300 each, while a CU

$1 FRBN star note from Philadelphia brought $825. Also featured were two lower-grade star notes from Kansas City that sold for $350 in VG-F and $600 in fine condition.

The $2 note of this series is the famous Battleship note that depicts a vignette of a battleship of the World War I period on its back side. These notes were issued by all 12 districts, but for the $2 notes there are only 34 different signature varieties. This is a very popular type, and prices have risen substantially in recent years. At the present time Battleship notes in VF condition sell for about $250, while CU examples are now bringing more than $800 each. A total printing of about 70 million of these notes was made, but again there are no breakdowns for individual signature combinations.

According to Gengerke none of the 34 major varieties of the $2 FRBNs are especially rare, but there are some reports that one of the Philadelphia notes (Fr. 755, H-203C3) is very hard to come by. I acquired that note years ago, but I did have problems in securing one of the Atlanta notes (Fr. 763, H-203F2). Completing a set of all 34 major varieties of Battleship notes is most definitely not an easy thing to do. One can compromise by settling for a district set of 12 of these notes, but even this is much more difficult to do for Battleship notes than it is for $1 FRBNs. As is the case with $1 FRBNs, the first issue of Cleveland $2 FRBNs are often available with very low serial numbers, and I also have low serial numbers for the first issues of my $2 notes from St. Louis and Kansas City. Thompson's collection also featured $2 FRBNs with very low serial numbers from the New York, Richmond, and Dallas districts. At the present time a total of 63 star notes of this type have been reported. There are 20 known varieties of these, of which only three were in the Thompson collection. One of these, a note from Boston in XF condition with serial A422*, sold for only $605, a price that would be certainly very low by today's standards.

The $5 FRBNs were issued from all districts with the exception of Richmond. These notes were issued both in Series 1915 and 1918, and the face designs for these two series are slightly different. The backs of these notes are all the same, and their design is quite similar to that of the $5 FRNs. The obligations of FRBNs, however, are totally different from those of Federal Reserve Notes. The Series 1915 FRBNs all bear the Treasury signatures of Tehee and Burke, but the bank signatures have often been printed by the hectograph process rather than by intaglio, which would be the case if they had been engraved directly onto the plates. There are a total of 30 different series or signature varieties for the $5 FRBNs. The most abundant $5 FRBNs now sell for about $125 each in VF condition and about $500 in CU. Several notes of this type, however, are very scarce, and it is quite difficult to complete a set of all varieties. These notes are less common than are the Battleship notes, but generally $5 FRBNs sell at lower prices than do the more popular $2 notes. On their back sides the $5, $10, $20, and $50 FRBNs very closely resemble the vastly more common FRNs of these denominations, and this has been a factor in reducing the demand for these notes.

The statistics on the numbers of $5 FRBNs printed are rather spotty. Gengerke and Hessler quote a printing of 51,524,000 for notes from the St. Louis district, but this figure is certainly much too high. The highest serial that I have seen for $5 notes of this district is H1510506A, and thus I feel that the correct total for St. Louis is 1,524,000 rather than what is quoted in some sources. I expect that the total printing for all varieties of $5 FRBN's is only about 20 million examples. In passing, I should note that a few of the Atlanta and Kansas City notes are listed out of sequence in the Friedberg catalog.

Shown are a Series 1915 $10 FRBN from Dallas and a $20 note of the same series from Chicago. The face designs of these notes differ radically from those of the corresponding FRNs. They are also very much scarcer than are the latter notes.

The rarest of the $5 FRBNs are usually regarded as being the note from Boston (Fr. 781, H-382A1) and one of the notes from San Francisco (Fr. 809a, H-382L3). The latter carries a date of May 18, 1914, whereas all other FRBNs from San Francisco bear an engraved date of May 20, 1914. An AU example of the Boston note in the Thompson collection sold for $1540 in 1991, and a CU example of the Fr. 809a note sold for $2310 in a CAA auction in 1997. I have both of these notes in my own collection, but I lack one variety each of the Cleveland and Kansas City notes. I expect that these notes (Fr. 786 and 802, respectively) may be "sleepers" which are scarcer than is indicated in most currency catalogs. Thus far only 13 star notes have been reported for the $5 FRBNs. There are five different known varieties for these, but none were present in the Thompson collection.

The $10 and $20 FRBNs were also issued both in Series 1915 and 1918, but they were issued only from a few districts and in very limited quantities. About 1,650,000 $10 notes and only 508,000 $20 FRBNs were issued. There are twelve major varieties recognized for the $10 notes and eleven for the $20 notes. The Thompson collection contained all of these, and it is likely that this is the only collection formed in recent years that has been so complete for these types. A CU example of the relatively available Fr.817 (or H-620J1, a $10 note from Kansas City) brought $1375, while a CU example of Fr. 824 (or H-850G1, the $20 note from Chicago) fetched $1870 in the Thompson sale. Scarcer $10 and $20 notes in VF or XF condition sold for prices in the $1100 - $1400 range, but by far the highest price obtained was for an XF example of Fr. 822a (H-850F3) that sold for $5775. This note is believed to be unique. Over the years a few new varieties of these notes have become recognized, but this has resulted in some confusion in their listings in catalogs. Three different varieties of the Series 1915 $20 notes from Atlanta are now recognized, and these are listed as nos. 822, 822-1, and 822a in the Friedberg catalog, or 850F1, 850F1a, and 850F3 in the Hessler catalog. Some revisions in the numbering of these notes would definitely be useful. The only star note reported for these types is a unique example of the $10 note from St. Louis. This note was not present in the Thompson collection.

According to Gengerke and Hessler only about 240 examples of $10 FRBNs and 150 of the $20 FRBNs are presently recorded. My own collection now contains eight of the former and five of the latter, several less than that of Thompson but a good showing nonetheless. Some currency professionals feel that the true numbers of these types in collectors' hands are significantly higher than what have been recorded to date, but it does appear that both the $10 and $20 FRBNs are very scarce as major type notes. For the most part they are still fairly modestly priced, and it seems likely to me that these two types are the most underrated of all of the large-size type notes at the present time. On their back sides these notes are very similar to the vastly more common $10 and $20 FRNs. This has helped to limit demand for these notes in the past, but as type notes they are quite distinct from the Series 1914 FRNs. Although these notes are still available in VF or XF condition, they are generally quite rare in CU. The only run of uncirculated notes known for these types is of Fr. 817, a $10 note from Kansas City.

There is only one variety of the $50 FRBNs, a Series 1918 note from St. Louis. This note had an extremely small printing of only 4000 examples. Typically for the scarcer types of this vintage about one note in 2000 or 3000 issued has survived. If this were the case with this note, the $50 FRBN would be an ultra-rarity. But at the present time 50 examples are recorded, thus implying a survival rate of one note for every 80 issued. A survival rate this high is truly phenomenal; no other large-size type note comes even close to this figure. Given its fairly high face value and the similarity of its back design to that of the common Series 1914 $50 FRNs, it seems most surprising that this note was preserved in such numbers. The Series 1918 $50 FRBN is still a rarity, but enough examples are available for affluent collectors to include them in their collections.

The $50 FRBN is also probably the best documented of all the rarer types of large-size notes. Lists of the serial numbers of the known notes were published in currency catalogs long before Martin Gengerke began his current research on all rare large-size type notes. Of the notes of this type presently known 14 are recorded as being in CU condition, about a dozen or so are in XF or AU, and about 15 are in grades of fine or poorer. The example in the Thompson collection was in AU grade and sold for $4950. Recently (in 1997) a CU specimen of this note brought $12,100 in a CAA sale, and this seems the first time that an example of this note has sold for more than $10,000 at auction.

These notes are definitely not cheap, but since they are available in a wide range of grades, they are also available in fairly large range of prices.

As things turned out, Federal Reserve Bank Notes were used only as emergency money from 1918 into the early 1920s. In 1918 the price of silver rose sharply, and for a brief period in 1919 and 1920 it exceeded the $1.293 per troy ounce level at which silver dollars were coined. It then became logical to melt silver dollars, and under the Pitman Act of 1918 a total of 370 million silver dollars were melted. Since silver certificates were backed by silver dollars held in the Treasury, this major reduction in the numbers of silver dollars necessitated a cutback in the amount of SCs in circulation. This gap was largely filled by the FRBNs, whose circulation rose from $11 million in mid-1918 to $185 million by mid-1920. At that time FRBNs constituted about 4% of the total face value of the paper money in circulation. In 1921, however, silver prices declined sharply and the numbers of SCs in circulation rapidly increased. The numbers of FRBNs outstanding fell accordingly, and by the end of 1924 less than $10 million of these notes were in circulation.

The large-size FRBNs were issued as replacements for SCs on a one-for-one basis. Since the latter were dominated numerically by $1 notes, this was also the case for FRBNs. For the SCs the $2 and $5 notes were in much greater circulation than were the $10 and $20 notes, and this also is the case for the FRBNs. By 1918 only a fairly small number of $50 SCs were outstanding, and $100 notes for this series had already mostly been pulled from circulation. Designs for $100 FRBNs were prepared by the BEP, but no $100 notes for this series were issued.

Assembling a district set of 12 $1 notes is not very difficult to do, but fairly ample funds will be needed to form district sets for $2 and $5 FRBNs. I would strongly recommend obtaining at least one each of the $10 and $20 FRBNs, if you can afford them, since these notes seem to be far scarcer than their present prices would suggest. Some dealers continue to refer to the FRBNs as Federal Reserve Notes, but they are a totally different series from the latter, and there are enormous differences in the relative scarcities of the large-size $10 and $20 FRBNs on the one hand and Series 1914 blue seal $10 and $20 FRNs on the other.

OTHER LARGE-SIZE FEDERAL PAPER MONEY

In discussing the various types of large-size notes I have thus far omitted one extremely important category, viz., the national bank notes, but they will be examined in great detail in the following chapter. Let us conclude this chapter by considering the other types of large-size Federal paper money, all of which are notes that had an ephemeral existence and are quite rare today.

The Demand Notes were authorized by an act passed on July 10, 1861 that provided both for the issue of non-interest bearing notes of the $5, $10, and $20 denominations and for interest-bearing notes of higher denominations. There was a total of $60 million face value issued in Demand Notes including 4,360,000 $5 notes, 2,003,000 $10 notes, and 910,000 $20 notes. Each of these notes was domiciled to one of five cities (New York, Philadelphia, Boston, Cincinnati, and St. Louis). but the latter two cities are very much rarer than are the first three.

Demand Notes of 1861 were the first issues of Federal paper money intended for general circulation. Demand notes are the only forms of U. S. Federal paper money without Treasury seals and facsimile signatures of Treasury officials. The $10 note above depicts the then-living President Lincoln and is domiciled to New York.

The face designs of the Demand Notes are similar to those of the corresponding United States notes of Series 1862-63, but they have no Treasury seals and were handsigned by various clerks. At the present time about 280 $5 notes, 130 $10 notes, but only about 20 of the $20 Demand Notes are known. For notes of a given denomination the varieties from the first three cities are roughly equally as abundant, and consequently they all sell at about the same price. The first few issues of most of these varieties were printed without "for the" by the spaces used for signatures, but these were soon added. Only about 20 of all known Demand Notes have "for the" handwritten by the clerks, and only about 25 of the Demand Notes are domiciled to either Cincinnati or St. Louis.

These notes are printed on the same thin paper that was used for all United States notes of Series 1862-63. Thus the usual problems such as edge splits are normal for these notes. Typically they are also heavily worn, and all Demand Notes are very rare in conditions better than VF. In my own collection I have two $5 and one $10 Demand Note. The grades range between F-VF and VF-EF. There is little point in trying for grades much better than these. Only about 20 of the known $5 notes and less than ten of the known $10 notes are in XF condition or better. For the $20 Demand Notes there are two known examples in VF or XF condition from Philadelphia and one repaired note from New York that is basically in XF condition. All of the others are in less attractive grades.

As one might imagine, Demand Notes are expensive in nearly all grades. In fine condition a $5 note currently sells for about $1500 and a $10 note for rather more than $2000. In VF condition prices would be about double these. A sound $20 Demand Note in fine condition would probably cost at least $20,000 in today's market. Also extremely rare are any Demand Notes domiciled to Cincinnati or St. Louis and any with "for the" handwritten. Among the other great rarities in the Levitan collection was a $10 Demand Note from Philadelphia in AU condition with "for the" handwritten. It sold for $64,900.

The finest collection of Demand notes to be sold in recent years was that formed by Harry W. Bass, Jr., which was auctioned by Bowers and Merena in May, 1999. Included were six notes each of the $5 and $10 denominations, five $20 notes, and four proofs. The highest price realized was $86,250 for a $10 note in VF condition from Cincinnati with "for the" handwritten. A $5 note from New York in XF with "for the" handwritten sold for $33,350, while a $20 note from Cincinnati in VG condition sold for $55,200. Despite the fact that the Bass collection had the most comprehensive group of $20 Demand Notes to be seen in decades, all five of these notes were in relatively low grades. A high grade $20 Demand Note is an item of almost unparalleled rarity.

There were four different basic types of Interest Bearing Notes issued during the Civil War years. The Three-Year Notes were issued in 1861 and again in 1864 and 1865. These bore interest at 7.3% per year. Two-Year Notes were issued in 1863 and bore interest at the rate of 5% per annum. One-Year Notes were issued in 1864 and also bore interest at 5% per year. Compound Interest Treasury Notes were issued in 1864 and 1865 and bore interest at 6% compounded semiannually for three years. The Three-Year Notes were issued with five attached coupons, but all known examples of the other types of Interest Bearing Notes were issued without coupons. All of these notes are about 10 mm wider than are normal large-size notes, and the notes with coupons are also very much longer than the length (190 mm) that is typical for nearly all large-size notes. The circulation of Interest Bearing Notes reached a maximum in 1865, when these issues constituted almost 30% of the total amount of paper money in circulation. There was a very steep decline in their circulation by 1868, the last year in which these notes would have continued to accrue interest. Nearly all of these notes were redeemed by the early 1870s, and so it is hardly surprising that these items are major rarities today.

The One-Year Notes and Compound Interest Treasury Notes were both issued in $10 and $20 denominations as well as in higher values, and these are about the only types of Interest Bearing Notes that exist in any quantity today. About 35 examples each of the $10 and $20 One-Year Interest Bearing Notes are presently known. These notes exist with several different dates, all fairly early in the year 1864. There are two varieties of imprints for each denomination. Some were printed by the American Bank Note Co., but the majority were printed by the BEP. The $10 and $20 Compound Interest Treasury Notes are the least rare of the Interest Bearing Notes of the Civil War years. Rather more than 100 $10 notes of this type are presently known. They exist in two signature varieties and with several different printed dates in 1864. More than 50 of the $20 notes are known, and these have a variety of printed dates in 1864 and 1865. The Compound Interest Treasury Notes have a heavy overprint in bronze ink that has a high acid content. This is often discolored to green or black, and not infrequently these notes show some degree of ink erosion.

Shown are two of the rare types of interest bearing notes issued during the 1860s. The $10 note is a one-year note issued in 1864. Compound Interest Treasury Notes were one of the last issues of interest-bearing paper money that were issued during the Civil War years. Above is a $20 note of this series that was issued in 1865.

In fine condition a $10 compound interest note sells for about $2000 in today's market, while a $20 note in this condition would realize about $2500. Only about 30 of the $10 notes and about 20 of the $20 notes of this series are in VF condition or better. Virtually no compound interest notes are known in grades above XF. There are about a dozen each of the $10 and $20 One-Year Notes in VF condition or better, and these notes sell for higher prices than do the compound interest notes. I have managed to acquire one each of the $10 and $20 Compound Interest Treasury Notes as well as a single $10 One-

Year Note, all of which are in VF or VF-XF condition. In terms of major types the only other variety that can be considered reasonably collectible for advanced syngraphists is the $20 One-Year Note. Two attractive examples of this note sold in two different CAA auctions in 1997. An XF example sold for $14,300, while an AU note subsequently sold for $20,900. The latter item may be the highest grade Interest Bearing Note of any type in existence.

The $50 and $100 denominations for these two series do exist, but all four of these varieties are excessively rare. Of the $50 compound interest notes only about 15 genuine examples are known, while only about ten of the $100 notes are confirmed as genuine. In 1998 a CAA auction featured a $50 compound interest note in VF and a $100 note of the same series in XF. Both were free of edge splits or any problems in their signatures. These notes sold for $36,300 and $49,500, respectively. Although both of these notes were quite genuine, the $50 and $100 notes of this issue were extensively counterfeited, and several counterfeit examples are known for each of these denominations. The $50 and $100 One-Year notes are even rarer, since only three examples are recorded for each of these types. Notes for $500 and $1000 were issued for both of these series, but there are no known examples in either institutional or private hands.

All of the Two-Year and Three-Year notes are excessively rare. There are seven recorded examples of the $50 Two-Year note and two of the $100 note of this series. A VF-XF example of the $50 issue sold for $18,700 in a CAA auction in 1997, while a Series 1865 $50 Three-Year Note in similar condition brought $38,500 in another auction in that year. A number of other Three-Year notes of the $50, $100, $500, and $1000 denominations do exist in issued form. Only one $50 note and one $100 (both of the 1865 issue) are known with all five coupons still attached. Recently currency dealer William Youngerman of Boca Raton, Florida has offered $50 and $100 Three-Year notes of 1864 and a unique $500 note of 1861 for sale. These notes (all without coupons) are in VF, fine, and VF-XF condition, respectively, and have been offered at prices of $37,500, $49,500, and $150,000 apiece. The Bass collection included the unique $50 and $100 Three-Year notes of 1865 with all five coupons attached. The $50 note was in VF condition, but the $100 note had substantial damage. These items sold for $109,250 and $97,750, respectively.

Although all Interest Bearing Notes of $50 or higher are virtually noncollectible in issued form, a number of face and back proofs of these notes are known. These proofs of Interest Bearing Notes are very rare, but they sell for very much lower prices than do the issued notes. Several of these proofs were in the collection formed by Ambassador Middendorf that was sold by Christie's in 1993. Among the most impressive of these are the face and back proofs for the $5000 denomination of the Series 1861 Three-Year notes. The two sides are attached to a single card, and all coupons are intact. This item was more recently offered in a Bowers and Merena auction where it fetched $11,000. As might be expected, no $5000 Interest Bearing Notes have survived in issued form.

The final issue of interest bearing notes were the Refunding Certificates of 1879. Although they are listed in the standard currency catalogs, the Treasury has never considered them to be a type of currency *per se*. In actual fact they are circulating bearer bonds, all of which bear a date of April 1, 1879. They exist in two types - type 1 has a place for the name of the bearer to be entered while type 2 does not. Type 1 notes are excessively rare, since only two examples have been recorded, but something like 200 examples of the type 2 certificates are known. Although these notes were intended to accrue interest at 4% per annum indefinitely, this feature was terminated in 1907 at a time when the redemption value of a $10 Refunding Certificate was $21.30. All of these notes bear the signatures of Scofield and Gilfillan, but some of the type 2 notes were printed on watermarked paper with localized blue stains. These certificates exist in a variety of grades, and in VF condition they currently sell for about $1500 or so. In a grade of CU a price of about $6000 can be expected. Although expensive, the Refunding Certificates are the most readily available of all of the various series of interest bearing currency items.

Although type 2 certificates are available to advanced collectors, the type 1 rarity is essentially noncollectible. The Bass collection contained the only known example in private hands. It is in AU condition and sold for $230,000, the highest price achieved for any note in that collection.

Shown is a $10 Refunding Certificate of 1879. Although collected as paper money, these items were in reality circulating bearer bonds.

Thus we come to the conclusion of this extensive chapter on large-size type notes. If you become seriously involved with the collecting of U. S. paper money, it is likely that you will acquire many examples of these items. Since many types are rare, however, substantial funds will be necessary for the acquisition of comprehensive holdings of almost all of the various series of these notes.

CHAPTER SEVEN

NATIONAL BANK NOTES

National bank notes were issued initially under the National Banking Act that was passed on February 25, 1863 and supplemented by an act passed on June 3, 1864. Under the terms of these acts national banks were established, and these banks were allowed to circulate national bank notes up to 90% of the face value of the U. S. government bonds that they held on deposit at the Treasury. If a given bank should fail, its notes continued to remain good money throughout the United States, but they would then become obligations of the Federal government and not of an individual bank.

The creation of national banks did allow for a substantial expansion of the currency supply, but this legislation also contained a number of flaws. No provisions were made either for branch banking or for interstate banking, and the minimum capital requirement for establishing a national bank was just $50,000. In 1900 this was reduced to only $25,000 in cases of banks in small towns with populations under 3000. This virtually guaranteed the failure of many smaller institutions when times of adverse economic conditions arose.

Under the provisions of the acts passed in 1863 and 1864 a national bank was granted a charter that lasted for 20 years. Serious problems arose in the early 1880s, however, when the original charters granted to banks in the 1860s began to expire. Beginning in 1882 national banks were granted new charters that were also valid for 20 years. It seems strange that entirely new designs of currency were needed to acknowledge this administrative change, but that is what was done. All NBNs issued between 1864 and 1881 fall into what is called the First Charter period. Beginning in 1882 new series of notes were issued to the banks that were granted new charters, and these are referred to as Second Charter notes. A bank chartered in 1878 would have continued to issue First Charter notes until 1898, but a bank chartered in 1884 would initially have issued Second Charter notes.

The new charters first granted to banks in 1882 also lasted for 20 years, and thus these began to expire in 1902 when Third Charter notes were issued for the first time. These notes again have entirely different designs from those of the First or Second Charter periods. Once more these charters were valid for only 20 years, and thus many banks were rechartered again beginning in 1922. Notes issued by such banks are of the same type as those of the Third Charter period, but they may be distinguished by their different Treasury signatures and dates on their faces. Later in the year 1922 the charters of national banks were extended to 99 years, and so all large-size NBNs issued after this date are of uniform design. Small-size NBNs were first issued during the summer of 1929, but the charter provisions for banks issuing these notes were unaffected by this radical change of currency designs.

An additional complicating factor was the Aldrich-Vreeland Act of 1908. As a consequence of the so-called Panic of 1907, the Aldrich-Vreeland Act was passed in 1908 to allow for greater elasticity in national currency. National banks could now use a variety of securities to back their note issues. This act remained in effect for only seven years, since it expired in 1915. It is not clear to me why the passage of this act would have required the issuance of distinctly new types of currency, but that is again what happened. Both the Second Charter and the Third Charter notes then being printed were changed to reflect the provisions of this act. They now stated that they were secured by bonds or other securities rather than only by bonds of the United States. The backs of the Second Charter notes carry dates of 1882 - 1908, while those of the Third Charter carry dates of 1902 - 1908. The first of these dates refers to the beginning of that charter period, while the latter refers to the fact that this currency was issued under the provisions of the Aldrich-Vreeland Act of 1908. Beginning in 1915 yet new designs were used for both series of these notes. Once again NBNs could be secured only by U. S. government bonds, and the back designs of these notes were modified to remove any reference to the act of 1908.

BEP worker separating large-size national bank notes.

Once they began to circulate in 1864 national bank notes soon became a major component of our nation's currency. By 1866 the total circulation of NBNs had grown to

$276 million, or 34% of the Federal paper money then in circulation. For the next two decades or so, the amount of NBNs in circulation stayed at about $300 million, but it fell to as low as $160 million in the early 1890s. Since NBNs were secured by government bonds, their circulation would fall when it became unprofitable for the banks to tie up their assets in these bonds. By 1900 the circulation of NBNs was back to $300 million, and during the next decade it grew to about $700 million. It remained at about this amount for most of the remainder of the large-size era, and in 1929 NBNs constituted 16.6% of the total paper money in circulation. NBNs reached their maximum circulation in 1933 when they totaled more than $900 million, but none were issued after 1935 when the bonds that backed them were called in. After that the amount of NBNs in circulation dropped drastically, and by 1960 only about $50 million in these notes was outstanding. Since 1960 there has not been much change in the amount of NBNs reported by the Treasury as outstanding, but it is unlikely that more than about 10% of this amount are presently known to collectors or dealers. As I noted previously, there are probably about 200,000 small-size NBNs presently in existence, and the total number of large-size NBNs is likely to be almost as large as this. One must remember, however, that there are many thousands of different varieties of these notes, and so no single specific variety of a national bank note is ever extremely common.

In collecting NBNs please bear in mind two things. Since there are many thousands of different varieties, it is never possible for anyone to assemble a complete collection of all of these. I can also state categorically that no two collections of NBNs will ever be the same. Even if your collection contains numerous NBNs that are very rare, there will always be many common NBNs that you will lack. Before getting seriously into national bank note collecting, you should decide basically what you plan to do. Do you want to obtain these notes by major types with perhaps one note for each type? Although some types of NBNs are very easily obtained, others are quite rare. Do you want instead to collect these notes by state? There is a huge range of availability, however, between the different states. If you allow for several notes from each state, it will soon become obvious that states such as Ohio or Pennsylvania are vastly more plentiful than are Arizona or Nevada. Another approach is to concentrate just on the notes of a given state. Many of the finest collections of NBNs have been of this type. Note, however, that it is much easier to assemble a collection of 100 different notes from Pennsylvania than it is to assemble one of only ten notes from several of the smaller western states. You could tighten your geography even further by collecting only notes of a given city or county. There is a large array of NBNs available from New York City, and San Francisco heavily dominates the NBNs of California, so this form of collecting need not be a tight constraint on what you plan to collect.

There are several other approaches to collecting NBNs that are popular with many syngraphists. Although many collectors attempt to acquire at least one note from each of the state capitals, this is a project that can never be completed. No NBNs have been recorded from Carson City, Nevada, and notes from Tallahassee, Florida are effectively noncollectible. A few notes are known from Juneau, Alaska, but these are extremely expensive. Several other state capitals such as Annapolis, Maryland, Olympia, Washington, and Salem, Oregon are also decidedly elusive. Another approach is to form a collection of NBNs in an alphabetical sequence with at least one town for each letter of the alphabet. Most of the initial letters are easily acquired, but three are fairly scarce. The letter "Q" is best represented by Quincy, Illinois and Quincy, Mass., while "Z" is represented most often by Zanesville, Ohio and Zelienople, Pennsylvania The letter "X" is much the most difficult for such a sequence, since it is represented only by Xenia, Illinois (one very rare bank) and Xenia, Ohio (two collectible, but decidedly uncommon banks).

The charter numbers of the National Banks were first printed on NBNs in 1874, and they appeared on all subsequent issues. Collections have been formed of the first 100 charters (not all of these are possible due to the failure of several of the early banks) or of notes with unusual charter numbers such as those of the National Bank of the Republic of New York (Charter 1000), the FNB of Richmond, Va. (1111), or the FNB of Wilmerding, Pa. (5000), etc. The highest charter number that appears on a large-size note is from the City NB of Niles, Michigan (13307), while the highest on a small-size note is from the Liberty NB of Louisville, Ky. (14320). Rather more than 12,000 charter numbers were used on large-size NBNs, while somewhat fewer than 7000 numbers were used on Series 1929 NBNs.

All of the standard currency catalogs list NBNs according to the government signatures that appear on them. All of the Series 1929 Nationals bear the signatures of Jones and Woods, and so this feature is of no concern to collectors of these notes. For First Charter notes there are a total of 15 different combinations, of which the Jeffries-Spinner variety is the rarest. Noah Jeffries was in office for almost 18 months during 1867-69, but only a few new national banks were chartered during this period. This combination, however, can be obtained without too much difficulty on Fractional Currency. For the Second Charter notes there is a total of 18 different signature pairs, of which the Rosecrans-Morgan combination is the scarcest. These two individuals were jointly in office for only 18 days during 1893, and this combination is found only on a few national bank notes and on no other types of U. S. currency.

There are a total of 15 different Treasury signature combinations that are found on Third Charter NBNs. The Napier-Thompson, Woods-White, and Woods-Tate pairs are scarce enough to command substantial premiums on most types of notes. The rarest is the Jones-Woods combination that was used on only a small number of notes that were printed early in 1929. Ironically this signature pair is ultra-common on small-size notes, since all Series 1929 NBNs carry it. The Lyons-Roberts combination is much the most common on Third Charter NBNs and on many of the Second Charter issues as well.

Of much greater interest to many collectors are the bank signatures that are found on all NBNs. On large-size notes these were usually hand-signed, but the were also sometimes rubber stamped or applied with the hectograph process. A few Third Charter notes from very large banks had these signatures engraved on the printing plates. On small-size NBNs they were surface printed together with the name of the bank and its charter number. Usually the president and cashier of a bank would sign, but there are a fair number of vice presidential notes on which the vice president of the bank has filled in either for the president or the cashier.

Collectors who are descendants of one of the bank officers whose signatures appear on these notes are sometimes willing to pay extremely high prices for notes with just the right signatures. They view the acquisition of such items more as obtaining family heirlooms than as merely adding more notes to a currency collection. Some signers of

NBNs were justly famous in their own right. Brigham Young signed many of the First Charter notes of The Deseret NB of Salt Lake City, Utah Territory (2059), while the signature of J. P. Morgan appears on some of the Brown Backs issued by the National Bank of Commerce in New York (733) and that of Andrew W. Mellon on some of the Third Charter notes issued by the Mellon NB of Pittsburgh (6301).

If you plan to collect NBNs seriously, it is essential that you acquire at least a couple of the excellent books that are now available on these notes. There are two comprehensive catalogs that list all of these items that were issued. *The Standard Catalog of National Bank Notes* by John Hickman and Dean Oakes is now in its second edition. Another outstanding book is *National Bank Notes, A Guide with Prices* by Don C. Kelly. This catalog is now in its third edition, and it gives complete census data for the notes by bank in all cases except where more than 50 large-size or 50 small-size examples are known for a given bank. Another very useful book is *United States Large-Size National Bank Notes* by Peter Huntoon. It is actually a compilation of a series of articles that Dr. Huntoon wrote over a period of several years on this subject, but a huge amount of detail is provided. Also included in this book are illustrations of many proofs and other unissued items that are in government archives. Although now out of print *The National Bank Note Issues of 1929-1935* by Peter Huntoon and Louis Van Belkum is also very useful. There has been an enormous amount of research done on national bank notes by various individuals. Included among these are Peter Huntoon, Don Kelly, and Louis Van Belkum, together with the late John Hickman and Owen Warns. Must of this work involved the exhaustive study of reports by the Comptroller of Currency that are on file in the National Archives.

Since acquiring national bank notes by type is probably the most popular way in which the large-size NBNs are collected, let us examine the major type varieties in this fashion. The First Charter NBNs are the only types of these notes that were issued for all denominations from $1 through $1000. For all other types of NBNs, issues were restricted to denominations of $5, $10, $20, $50, and $100. The First Charter notes can be divided into three different sequences. These are the so-called Original Series notes, the Series 1875 notes, and the National Gold Bank Notes. I shall have much more the say about the last series of these notes shortly, but the other two issues have black faces with red Treasury seals combined with backs that are printed in green and black. The Original Series notes have small red seals with spikes, and they always carry the distinctive signature of Francis Spinner as Treasurer of the United States. The Series 1875 notes have scalloped seals and persons other than Spinner have signed as Treasurer. Aside from that, these two series are closely similar and they need not be regarded as separate types.

The back sides of the First Charter notes are among the most beautiful of all types of U. S. currency. The green borders include the seal of the state in which the bank in question was located, while the center designs in black feature various paintings that are located in the Rotunda of the U. S. Capitol in Washington. All of the Series 1875 notes and many of the Original series notes have the charter number of the bank in question overprinted in red. A very small number of notes are known with the charter number engraved on the face plate and thus printed in black. The best known of these are the $5 notes from the FNB (First National Bank) of Central City, Colorado Territory (2129). All First Charter NBNs carry two different serial numbers - a Treasury serial number and a sheet number that is sequential for the notes from the bank in question. A few of the earliest Original Series notes have their Treasury serial numbers printed in blue, but red ink was used for all subsequent issues of First Charter notes. All notes on a given sheet had the same serial numbers, but each note would have a different plate letter. During the 1870s a number of NBNs were printed on paper with localized blue stains much as was the case with United States Notes of the same vintage.

First Charter notes were issued in two different series that differ somewhat from each other. Shown above are a $1 Original Series note of the FNB of Springfield, Vermont and a $2 Series 1875 note of the National Revere Bank of Boston. Although the charter number of the former bank is 122, this did not appear on First Charter notes until 1874. All Series 1875 notes display these charter numbers. Note also the differences in the Treasury seals on these two notes.

First Charter notes show a much greater variety of sheet layouts than do any of the later types of large-size NBNs. The $1 and $2 notes were almost always printed in sheets of 1-1-1-2, although the combination 1-1-2-2 was also used very rarely. Five-dollar notes were always printed in sheets of 5-5-5-5. The $10 and $20 First Charter notes appeared in a variety of combinations. The 10-10-10-20 layout was the most common, but 10-10-10-10 was also widely used. Less common were 10-10-20-20 and 20-20-20-20 sheet layouts. For the higher denominations were such possibilities as 50-100, 50-50-50-100, 10-20-50-100, 20-20-50-100, and a few other rare combinations. The $500 and $1000 notes were often printed individually, but combinations such as 500-1000 were also used.

No $1 and $2 NBNs were issued after both national bank notes and United States Notes became redeemable into gold at par at the beginning of 1879. The last $500 and $1000 NBNs were printed in 1885, , but only 23,894 of the former and 7379 of the latter were issued. A total of 173 of the $500 notes and 21 of the $1000 notes were outstanding in 1940, but at the present time only three $500 notes and no $1000 NBNs are known to have survived. Two of the existing $500 items are Original Series notes from the Appleton NB of Lowell, Mass. (charter 986), but both of these are in government custody. The only $500 NBN in private hands is a Series 1875 note of the FNB of the City of New York (charter 29). This note, which is in VF condition, was in the Amon Carter collection. It was sold privately for $110,000 in the early 1980s. There is a remote possibility that an issued $1000 NBN will turn up, but at the present time only proof impressions are known and all of these are in government custody.

At present only about 80 $50 and $70 $100 First Charter NBNs are known in all grades. Even in only fine condition these notes sell for at least $6000 to $8000 each, and in XF condition or better prices of $20,000 or more would be typical. If you can settle for these notes in only VG-F condition, then $50 and $100 First Charter NBNs are obtainable for "only" a few thousand dollars each, but unless you have lots of patience and deep pockets you will have to forget about owning a nice example of either of these notes.

For most collectors it is quite a job just to acquire one First Charter note each of the $1, $2, $5, $10, and $20 denominations. The Original Series and Series 1875 notes differ so little in their designs that I do not even regard them as distinct subtypes. There is also very little price differential between these two series. In terms of abundance the $1 and $5 notes are the most "common," while the $2 and $20 notes are the scarcest of these issues. The $2 note features a very large reclining numeral "2" on its face, and so it is often called the "Lazy Deuce" note. A detailed census of these notes is presently being undertaken by Charles Dean and Don Kelly, and they estimate that the total number of Lazy Deuce notes in collectors' hands is about 1500.

In terms of basic prices expect to pay about $350, $1400, $400, $600, and $1500 each, respectively, for the $1, $2, $5, $10, and $20 First Charter notes from large big city banks in VF condition. A number of these notes are known in CU condition from small hoards that have been uncovered during the past few decades. Among the better-known hoard notes are those from Selma, Alabama (Charter 1537), Lincoln, Illinois (2126), Lebanon, Indiana (2057), Milford, Mass. (2275), California, Missouri (1712), Newark, Ohio (958), and La Crosse Wisconsin (1313). None of these hoards were large, however, and all have been widely dispersed. In CU condition all First Charter notes are very expensive. The most readily available $1 and $5 notes would now cost at least $800 - $1200 in this condition, while CU Lazy Deuce notes can easily bring $4000 each. There are no hoards of $20 First Charter notes in choice condition, and all notes of this denomination in XF condition or better should be considered as rarities. In terms of overall abundance Massachusetts is the most available state for First Charter notes, a distinction that it loses to such states as Pennsylvania, New York, and Ohio for the later issues of national bank notes. First Charter notes from the southern and western states tend to be very rare. The South was just recovering from the ravages of the Civil War when these notes were issued, and so only a few national banks were chartered in this region at this time. First

Charter notes from the western regions were often from territorial banks, and these I shall discuss further on in this chapter.

First Charter NBNs together with some of the earlier Second Charter Brown Backs have a few condition problems that are not usually found on later notes. The ink that bank officials used to sign their notes often had a fairly high acid content, and this frequently has resulted in a degree of ink erosion on examples of these notes. Another problem with these issues is the so-called "New England trim." Prior to about 1890 it appears that the boxes used by most banks in New England to store notes were a bit too small, and this led to close trimming of these notes. Tightly trimmed notes are found more frequently from the New England states than from other regions, whence the name for this unfortunate peculiarity. After about 1890 it seems that these notes were not generally tightly trimmed, but poor centering and irregular cutting are often encountered on NBNs of all issues and from all regions.

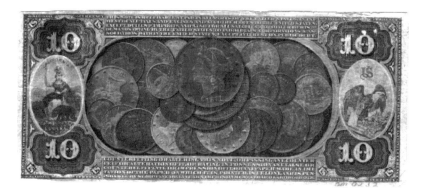

A $10 NGBN from the Farmers' National Gold Bank of San Jose (2158). Photo courtesy of BNR Press.

The National Gold Bank Notes of California were issued between 1871 and 1879 and closely parallel the normal First Charter NBNs. In California gold coins were in everyday circulation, and thus both USNs and normal NBNs traded at a discount and were not readily accepted in retail business transactions. The gold certificates issued between 1865 and 1878 were never intended for general circulation, but Californians were willing to accept a paper currency that was fully convertible to gold at par. The National Gold Bank Notes were issued by nine different banks in California (two each in San Francisco and in Oakland, and one each in Petaluma, Sacramento, San Jose, Santa Barbara, and Stockton). The bank in question rather than the Federal government guaranteed their redeemability in gold coin, and prior to 1879 they were almost the only type of paper money that circulated in California. A national gold bank could issue notes only up to 80% of the bonds that it deposited with the Treasury, and these banks had to maintain a minimum balance in gold coin equivalent to 25% of their note issue. Given these stiff requirements only one bank outside of California was granted this type of charter. This was the Kidder National Gold Bank of Boston (1699), but it chose not to issue any notes, although proof impressions of its $50 and $100 notes do exist. Once all U. S. paper currency became redeemable in gold at par, the National Gold Bank Notes lost their *raison d'etre*, and they were replaced by normal national bank notes.

A total of just over 200,000 National Gold Bank Notes were issued by the nine California banks. These have the normal face designs for First Charter notes, but their backs depict an assemblage of U. S. gold coins. These are printed in brown and black rather than green and black, as was used on the normal First Charter notes. Most National Gold Bank Notes were printed on yellow paper, although a few later issues are on white paper. Notes were issued both in the Original Series and in the Series of 1875. Denominations of the issued notes were for $5, $10, $20, $50, $100, and $500. Only 610 examples of the $500 notes were issued, and none are known today although four examples were reported as outstanding in 1915.

National Gold Bank Notes display two exceedingly peculiar survival characteristics. Of the approximately 200,000 notes that were issued, at least 510 are known today. This is a survival rate of better than one in 400. This is totally unprecedented for any other type of large-size NBN, where survival rates of about one in 5000 to 10,000 are much more typical. The number of known examples of these notes continues to increase, as new examples are uncovered. In 1986 the late John Hickman reported only 381 known examples . The problem with these notes, however, is in their typical degree of wear. Not one uncirculated National Gold Bank Note has thus far been authenticated. The normal grade for these notes is VG-F or worse. By far the most abundant of these items are the $5 notes from the First National Gold Bank of San Francisco (1741). Only 33,000 of these notes were issued, but about 240 are known today. That is a survival rate of one in 138, a rate exceeded among large-size notes only by the Series 1918 $50 FRBN from St. Louis. Of the known examples of this most abundant California gold note only about 10 are graded XF or better, and only about another 20 or so are in VF condition. In low grades this note is fairly common, and examples can be purchased for no more than a few hundred dollars each. In full VF condition, however, this note now sells for at least $4000, and realizations in excess of $6000 have recently be achieved for this note in XF condition. In June, 1998 a $5 note of the Farmers National Gold Bank of San Jose (2158) in XF condition sold for $22,000 in a Lyn Knight auction. Although charter number 2158 is much rarer than is number 1741, very high prices are to be expected for any of these notes in choice condition.

The condition situation is not better with any other of the National Gold Bank Notes. At the present time *in toto* almost 100 examples are known of the other five varieties of $5 notes and a similar total of the 11 known varieties of the $10 notes is also recorded. For the $20 notes there are 65 known examples, for the $50 notes the number known is seven, and for the $100 notes it is eight. The survival rate on the two higher denominations was lower than average, since 8047 examples of each were issued. All National Gold Bank Notes other than the aforementioned $5 note are very scarce to extremely rare, but prices are moderated somewhat by the generally low grades in which these notes are found. Nonetheless National Gold Bank Notes of the higher denominations are very seldom seen and are decidedly expensive. The Levitan collection contained a $20 note from San Francisco (1741) in fine condition, a $50 note of the same bank in G-VG, and $100 note from Petaluma (2193) that was also G-VG. These items sold for $8250, $27,500, and $25,300, respectively.

The National Gold Bank Notes were very popular in California when they were in general use, and it is clear that they continued to circulate long after they ceased to be printed in 1879. Although small hoards of high grade notes exist for other types of First Charter NBNs, none at all have been found for these notes. It is unfortunate that more examples of these notes were not pulled from circulation at a time when they were still current, but it seems that many were allowed to circulate until they were almost in tatters. If you wish to acquire one of these notes for your collection in VF condition or better, be prepared to spend very serious money. If you can put up with VG condition, then the $5 charter 1741 note is not at all difficult to acquire, but notes in this grade are never very attractive. In addition to the usual problems associated with VG or VG-F condition, these notes are often very closely trimmed (Did the New England banks send their surplus currency boxes to California?) and not infrequently they suffer from internal tears. Just getting a single National Gold Bank Note (usually the $5 charter 1741 issue) in decent condition is enough of a problem. Only a few advanced collectors attempt to obtain examples for several different banks or denominations.

The notes of the Second Charter period fall into three distinct issues. All are Series 1882, but the Brown Backs were issued between 1882 and 1908, the Date Backs between 1908 and 1915 (with many $50s and $100s issued into the 1920s), and the Value Backs between 1916 and 1922. The terms Series 1882 NBNs and Second Charter notes can be used interchangeably, since both refer to the same three issues of notes. The Brown Backs have red serial numbers with brown seals and charter numbers, whereas the other two series have blue seals with serial and charter numbers of the same color. All were issued in denominations of $5, $10, $20, $50, and $100. The face designs of these notes are similar to those of the First Charter notes, but the Columbus vignettes used on the $5 notes have been replaced with a portrait of President James Garfield, who had been assassinated in 1881.

The back sides of the Brown Backs feature the state seals that are also found on First Charter notes, but the central vignettes have been replaced with a large rendition of the charter number of the issuing bank in dark green. The Date Backs of this issue are printed in green and feature the dates 1882 - 1908 at their centers. The state seals have been replaced with designs that are uniform for each denomination. The back designs of the Value Backs are quite similar to those of the Date Backs, but the dates at the center have been replaced with their respective denominations spelled out. These notes occur in two subtypes. Some state on their faces that they are secured by bonds of the United States, while others (the great majority of these issues) state that they are secured by bonds or other securities.

Series 1882 (or Second Charter) NBNs were issued in three quite different series. The Brown Backs were issued between 1882 and 1908, the Date Backs between 1908 and 1916 (but up to 1922 for some $50s and $100s), and the Value Backs between 1916 and 1922.

Far fewer sheet arrangements were used for Second Charter notes than was the case with First Charter NBNs. Five-dollar notes were always printed in sheets of 5-5-5-5. The $10 and $20 notes were generally in sheets of 10-10-10-20, but sheets of 10-10-10-10 were also occasionally used. All $50 and $100 Brown Backs were printed in sheets of 50-100, and all $50 and $100 Value Backs were printed in sheets of 50-50-50-100, but for Second Charter Date Back $50s and $100s, both sheet layouts were used.

Only two banks (the Canal-Commercial NB of New Orleans and the Winters NB of Dayton) issued the ultrarare $50 and $100 Value Backs. Shown above are a $10 Brown Back of the immediate predecessor of the New Orleans bank and a $50 Date Back of the Dayton bank that issued these notes.

A complete type set of these notes would consist of 15 different items, but two of these are essentially noncollectible. Value Backs for $50 and $100 were issued only by the Winters NB of Dayton, Ohio (2604) and the Canal-Commercial NB of New Orleans (5649). Only 8571 $50 notes and 2857 $100 notes were issued for both banks combined. Only five of the $50 notes and four of the $100 Value Backs are presently known, and with one exception (a recently-discovered $100 note from Dayton), all of the $50 and $100 Value Backs i private hands are from the New Orleans bank. Not even the famous Grinnell collection that was sold in the 1940s had examples of either of these types. Sales of these notes have been few and far between. The *Currency Dealer Newsletter* (the so-called Green Sheet) has been listing both the $50 and $100 notes of this series in fine condition at $9000 each. This price is utterly absurd for these ultra-rarities. In Lyn Knight's sale of the Levitan collection that was held in December, 1998, an XF example of the $50 note from the New Orleans bank sold for $79,200 while a $100 note from the same bank in fine condition sold for $165,000.

As type notes all of the other 13 varieties of Second Charter notes are collectible, although both issues of $50 and $100 notes are very scarce and expensive. In my opinion there is not a huge difference in scarcity between the three different issues of these types. The Brown Backs were issued for the longest period of time, but the Date Backs were issued in comparable quantities and they seem to be of comparable rarity. The Value Backs are definitely the scarcest of the three issues, but it is my feeling that the rarity of the $5, $10, and $20 notes has been exaggerated in several of the currency catalogs due perhaps to the acknowledged ultra-rarity of the $50 and $100 notes of this series.

At the beginning of 1902 geographical letters were added to the faces of all NBNs to facilitate sorting of these notes when they were returned for redemption at the Treasury. The letters used were N, E, M, S, W, and P which stood for New England, Eastern, Mid-Western, Southern, Western, and Pacific states, respectively. Brown Backs exist both with and without these letters. At about this same time there also was a change in the composition of the ink used in the printing of the backs of these notes. The earlier ones usually have light reddish-brown backs, while the later notes are more often printed in sepia or chocolate brown.

Second Charter NBNs were issued in far larger quantities than were First Charter notes, and prices for these notes are generally much more reasonable for the more readily available banks. Typically $5 and $10 Brown Backs from common banks sell for about $250 to $300 each in VF condition, while the Date Backs for these denominations are slightly less expensive. Despite the fact that they were issued in much smaller quantities, $20 notes for these two issues are only a bit more expensive than are their $5 and $10 counterparts. Expect to pay about $350 - $400 for $20 notes of either of these issues in VF condition. The Value Backs are decidedly less common, but it is not difficult to obtain one of each of the $5, $10, and $20 denominations of this series. For Value Backs in VF condition prices of $350 for a $5 note, $400 for a $10, and $600 for a $20 note are typical in today's market. Second Charter notes in CU condition are not at all common, but as I have noted on several occasions minor differences in condition are not a major concern with most national bank note collectors. Thus most of these issues can probably be obtained for only about two or three times the prices that I have given above for notes that are basically in new condition. Well centered notes with wide margins will command premium prices in any of the higher grades, but the scarcity of a given bank is usually much more of a factor in determining the value of a NBN than is its precise degree of preservation.

Second Charter $50 and $100 notes are very much scarcer than are their lower denomination counterparts. A total of 1,429,587 each of the $50 and $100 Brown Backs were issued, and these figures can be compared with the issues of 459,974 Second Charter $50 Date Backs and 228,690 for the $100 notes of this series. We should therefore expect that the Brown Backs should be much more common than the Date Backs for these two denominations, but that does not appear to be the case. In fact $50 Date Backs seem to be almost as abundant as $50 Brown Backs, although for $100 Second Charter notes the Date Backs are definitely somewhat rarer. Based on the survival data that I have for specific states concerning $50 and $100 Second Charter Notes, my research indicates that about one in 5000 of the high value Brown Backs and something like one in 2500 of the corresponding Date Backs have survived. Extrapolating these figures to the entire nation and making some allowances for unrecorded notes we might expect about 300 each of the $50 and $100 Brown Backs together with about 250 of the $50 Date Backs and perhaps 150 $100 notes for this series. As of the beginning of 1998 Don Kelly has recorded totals of 218 $50 and 201 $100 Brown Backs and 139 $50 and 96 $100 Second Charter Date Backs. These two data sets can be regarded as being in fairly good agreement with each other, since detailed censuses will almost always miss a fair number of notes.

$50 and $100 Brown Backs and Red Seals were always printed in sheets of 50-100, and thus the two denominations should be more or less equally abundant. Depicted above are a $100 Brown Back of the Livestock NB of Sioux City, Iowa and a $50 Red Seal of the Third NB of Saint Louis. Both were in circulation during the first decade of the 20th Century.

If you wish to acquire any of these notes, you can expect to pay about $2000 to $2500 for a $50 or $100 Brown Back or a $100 Date Back in VF condition. A $50 Date

Back would cost a bit less at about $1500 for a common bank. Once there was even a mini-hoard of uncirculated $50 Date Backs from the Chase NB of New York (2370). Today these notes sell for about $3500 each. One telltale feature of these notes is that they almost always have minor smudges in black ink on their faces. Second Charter $50 and $100 notes in CU condition have done very well in recent auctions. A $50 Brown Back from Manhattan, Kansas (3782) sold for $7150 in a 1997 CAA auction, while a $100 Date Back from Sioux City, Iowa (5022) brought $11,550 in the same sale. In late 1997 a CU $100 Brown Back from the Union NB of Chicago (3278) sold for an unprecedented $20,350 in a Lyn Knight auction. Until very recently prices like these were quite unheard of for Second Charter $50 and $100 notes from any of the larger cities. Since the total supply of $50 and $100 Second Charter notes is quite limited, it follows that almost all examples are true rarities for which only a tiny number of individuals exist for a given type and a given bank. I now have four each of the $50 and $100 Brown Backs together with five $50 and four $100 Date Backs in my collection. This is a substantial holding, although far larger assemblies of these types have been put together in other collections.

The Third Charter NBNs were issued between 1902 and 1929. All are Series 1902. Like the Second Charter notes, they can be divided into three distinct issues. The Red Seal notes were issued between 1902 and 1908. The Blue Seal Date Backs were issued between 1908 and 1916, but some of the $50 and $100 notes of this type were printed as late as 1926. The Blue Seal Plain Backs were issued between 1916 and 1929, and they are by far the most common of the large-size NBNs. All notes of a given denomination for this series have the same back design, but the Blue Seal Date Backs carry the dates 1902 (the series date) and 1908 (the enactment of the Aldrich-Vreeland Act). The two issues of Blue Seal notes are so similar on their faces that there is little difference in their numismatic value despite the fact that the Date Back notes are decidedly scarcer for most issues of these types. All Red Seal notes state that they are secured by bonds only, and all Blue Seal Date Backs state that they are secured by bonds or other securities. For the Blue Seal Plain Backs both varieties of this inscription are found.

The Third Charter NBNs have portraits of persons who were not previously depicted on U. S. currency. President Benjamin Harrison died in 1901, and William McKinley was assassinated in the same year. They are depicted on the $5 and $10 notes, respectively. The $20, $50, and $100 notes depict Hugh McCulloch, John Sherman, and John J. Knox, respectively. All three of these individuals played important roles in fiscal and monetary policies during the latter part of the 19th century.

The sheet layouts of the Third Charter notes closely parallel those of the Second Charter issues. The $5 notes were always issued in sheets of 5-5-5-5, while the $10 and $20 notes were generally issued in sheets of 10-10-10-20 with some of the $10 notes issued in sheets of 10-10-10-10 instead. All Red Seal $50 and $100 notes were issued in sheets of 50-100, but the 50-50-50-100 arrangement was more popular for the later issues of Third Charter notes of these denominations.

Of the three issues of these notes the Red Seals are by far the least abundant. In VF condition the most readily available $5, $10, and $20 Red Seals should cost about $250, $275, and $350 each, respectively. In CU condition they would probably sell for about three times as much. Only 406,791 examples each of the $50 and $100 Red Seals were issued, a figure that is less than one-third that of the Brown Backs for these denominations. As a consequence $50 and $100 Red Seals are rarities in all grades. Thus far a total of 96 of the $100 Red Seals have been recorded, and for the $50 notes of this type the total is only 68. It is likely that there are a few additional notes of these types, but these data imply a survival rate of only about one note per 4000 that were issued for the $100 notes and one survivor per 6000 of the issued $50 Red Seals. An R. M. Smythe auction held in 1997 featured an unprecedented 31 different $100 Red Seal notes. These sold for a wide range of prices. The least expensive (a VG-F note from Pittsburgh) sold for $1430, while more typical prices for notes in F-VF condition were in the $2500 - $3000 range. The "stars" of this collection were a serial number 1 CU note from Bridgeton, New Jersey (2999) and a VF-XF example from Guthrie, Oklahoma Territory (7299). Both sold for somewhat over $30,000 each. Fifty-dollar Red Seals sell for about the same prices as do $100 Red Seals of comparable condition and rarity. It should be noted that all $50 and $100 Red Seals are essentially unique in that usually only one note is available for a given bank, and no hoards have been reported for either of these types. I have managed to acquire two of each denomination, and all four of these notes are from different banks.

The two series of Blue Seal notes are very much more common than are the Red Seal NBNs. I would estimate that there are about 150,000 large-size NBNs in numismatic hands, and of these easily two-thirds are Blue Seal notes of the $5, $10, and $20 denominations. As type notes they are very easy to acquire. The most common of the $5 and $10 notes sell for roughly $50 to $60 each in VF condition, while the $20 notes are more like $60 to $80 each in this grade. In CU condition these notes are more like $200 to $250 each for the most readily available banks. One could acquire just one note or two notes of each denomination (i. e., one of each of the Date Back and Plain Back issues), but most NBN collectors soon develop an interest in collecting these notes from various banks. The relatively low prices for the common varieties of these notes enable you easily to acquire several examples. Furthermore there is no need just to restrict yourself to the largest cities in the largest states. Most of the large currency auctions feature at least a few hundred examples of these notes, and so there is much material to choose from.

Third Charter $50 and $100 Blue Seals were issued by far fewer banks than were the three lower denominations, but they are much more readily available than are any of the earlier $50 and $100 NBNs. In past years enough were available for type collectors to readily acquire one or more notes of both denominations, but these notes are now under quite a bit of pressure. In VF condition "common" $50 Blue Seals now sell for about $450 each or more, while $100 notes are easily $500 to $600 at a minimum. Both of these denominations are very scarce in CU condition, and either would cost at least $1500 - $2000 or more in today's market. Since $50 and $100 Date Backs were issued as late as 1926, there is not much difference in availability or in price between the Date Back and Plain Back varieties for these denominations.

It is a bit dangerous to extrapolate survival data from one state to the entire nation, but based on what I know about NBNs from California and a few other states I would estimate that there are presently about 2500 $50 Blue Seal notes and roughly 1500 $100 notes in numismatic hands. There are no hoards of any of these notes, however, and thus any given $50 or $100 note is basically a rarity, since only a very few such examples exist for that particular bank regardless of which one it is. The census data compiled by

Don Kelly indicate totals of 584 $50 Date Backs and 592 $50 Plain Backs together with 348 $100 Date Backs and 307 $100 Plain Backs. These figures are only about half my estimates which are based on survival extrapolations. Since Third Charter Blue Seals are much more common than are Red Seal or Second Charter notes, I expect that the specific census data will be a good deal less complete, but note that a compromise between these two data sets indicates that only about 2000 $50 and not many more than 1000 $100 Blue Seals may be in existence.

Shown above are two Series 1902 Blue Seal $10 notes from the Commercial NB of Kansas City, KS. The former bears a script date of 1902 and the Treasury signatures of Lyons and Roberts. The latter is a so-called Fourth Charter note. It bears a script date of 1922 and the Treasury signatures of Speelman and White. Note also the differences in serial numbers and regional letters for these two notes. The so-called Fourth Charter notes exist only for the year 1922, since later in that year national bank charters were extended to 99 years, thus ending the concept of charter periods with 20-year durations.

In my own collection I have managed thus far to acquire 27 of the $50 notes and 30 of the $100 Blue Seal NBNs, but to do this I have lowered my usual minimum standard to a grade of fine rather than VF or better. Although $5, $10, and $20 Blue Seal NBNs will continue to be readily available as type notes for many years to come, it is my opinion that the supply of $50 and $100 Blue Seals is drying up. If you desire one or more examples of these notes, I would suggest that you try to acquire them in the not too distant future.

Although few collectors are interested in subtypes of Blue Seal NBNs, there were a few changes made in the 1920s that affected the appearance of these notes. In 1922 several of the banks that were chartered or rechartered in 1902 were once again rechartered. These new notes usually have dates of 1922 and the Treasury signatures of Speelman-White rather than dates of 1902 and the signatures of Lyons-Roberts. Such notes are often referred to as Fourth Charter notes, but they are identical in type to the Third Charter notes.

The Third Charter period for national banks actually ran only from 1902 to 1922, but there was no change of design for NBNs that were printed after 1922. All of the so-called Fourth Charter notes bear a date of 1922, but they are still Series 1902 NBNs. Late in the year 1922 national bank charters were extended for 99 years, and this rendered obsolete the concept of 20-year charter periods. Some researchers such as Don Kelly do not use the term Third Charter notes, preferring Series 1902 notes instead. Other experts such as the late John Hickman use the term Third Charter notes in preference to Series 1902 notes. In terms of note types, of course, it makes no difference which of these terms is used.

In 1924 the geographical letters ceased to be printed on NBNs, and in 1925 the serial numbering scheme was changed. Prior to that year all NBNs carried both a Treasury serial number and a sheet number that was peculiar to a given bank. After 1925 only the sheet number for the bank was used. Almost all Third Charter Date Back notes have both geographical letters and two different serial numbers, but some $50 and $100 notes of this type were issued as late as 1926. The $50 Date Back note from The Omaha NB (1633) in my collection has only the bank serial number and no regional letter. Thus obviously it is an issue of 1925 or 1926.

In this chapter we have discussed thus far the various types of large-size NBNs in substantial detail. In terms of their relative abundances by states the data on the values of NBNs outstanding in a given year can be useful. These data are available from government statistics, but they always refer to the total face value of the notes outstanding and not to the total numbers of notes. For June 30, 1929, the close of the last fiscal year in which only large-size NBNs were in circulation, the relative amounts of NBNs outstanding were as follows:

PA	TN	OK	MS
NY	MN	LA	MT
TX	IA	SC	UT
OH	AL	OR	SD
IL	WA	DC	WY
CA	WV	ME	ID
NJ	MO	FL	NM
IN	CT	NH	NV
MA	KS	CO	DE
VA	NC	VT	AZ
MI	GA	AR	HI
WI	MD	RI	AK
KY	NE	ND	

Since these data refer to mid-1929, they are much more relevant to Third Charter Blue Seal notes than they are to any of the earlier types of large-size NBNs, but they do give a fairly good idea as to the relative abundances of the various states for these notes. After reviewing the Series 1929 NBNs I shall return to the question of the relative abundances of NBNs on a regional basis.

In Chapter 3 Series 1929 NBNs were examined in some detail. As type notes, these are much the most common of the NBNs for all five denominations. Both type 1 and type 2 $5s, $10s, and $20s are readily available from many states, and the $50s and $100s are also common enough for type 1. Type 2 $50s and $100s are quite a bit more of a challenge, but I don't feel that the collector pressure on small-size $50 and $100 NBNs is anything like what it currently is on $50 and $100 Blue Seal notes. As I have already noted, there are probably something like 200,000 Series 1929 NBNs known to collectors at the present time. Although many scarce varieties are being keenly sought by enthusiasts, these items are extremely common as type notes, and you will have little difficulty in acquiring many dozens of different small-size NBNs from a wide variety of states. In CU condition the most common $5, $10, and $20 small-size NBNs are presently selling for about $60 - $75 each, but in VF condition prices equal to about half this are typical for many notes. Before getting seriously into national bank note collecting you should very carefully go over the advertisements in a publication such as the *Bank Note Reporter*, and it would also be most useful to check over the results of a large currency auction that features many Nationals. There are no fixed guidelines as to the prices for many NBNs, since some collectors are seeking only a few of these for types or as representatives of a given state whereas others may have been searching for a particular bank for many years.

Before examining NBNs on a regional basis let us consider the relative availability of Series 1929 notes by state. Although tables of the relative scarcities of these notes appear in many catalogs, I find myself in disagreement over a few entries. During the early 1930s there were many failures of National Banks (1428 between 1930 and 1935, to be exact), and this distorts the statistics on the amounts of NBNs outstanding. When a National Bank failed, its notes ceased to be liabilities of that bank but instead became liabilities of the U. S. government. Thus the notes of that bank were no longer listed as obligations of that bank in the comptroller's reports. A good example is the state of Michigan, where the amount of NBNs outstanding took a huge drop between 1932 and 1933. This was due to the failure of the FNB of Detroit (10527) in May of 1933. Prior to its failure this was by far the largest bank in that state. (Note that all of these statistical data refer to June 30th of a given year, i. e., the end of a particular fiscal year.) Michigan notes are fairly common, but using data for 1933 or later would indicate that they are scarcer than actually is the case. On the other hand, the amount of NBNs outstanding from California took an enormous jump from 1932 to 1933 due to a huge issue of notes from the Bank of America (13044). I feel that the following list is fairly reliable as to the relative scarcities of Series 1929 national bank notes.

PA	TN	NE	ND
CA	WA	LA	SC
NY	GA	CO	MS
TX	AL	RI	MT
OH	CT	MD	SD
NJ	MO	NH	WY
IL	KS	ME	NM
IN	OK	NC	DE
MA	KY	DC	ID
WI	IA	VT	AZ
MN	WV	AR	NV
MI	OR	HI	AK
VA	FL	UT	

This list differs from many of the published abundance lists for several states. Iowa often appears at near the top of many of these lists despite the fact that far fewer notes were issued from there than was the case in Illinois or Indiana. But Iowa NBNs are extremely well documented. It is the home both of the late John Hickman and of the Higgins Museum in Okoboji. The latter has by far the largest collection of Iowa and Minnesota NBNs extant. Wyoming is definitely a scarcer state than is Montana, but it is the home of Peter Huntoon, another major researcher of NBNs. Hawaii does not appear to be as scarce on this list as you might think, but this list refers to face value outstanding and not to the number of notes. The most readily available small-size note in choice condition from Hawaii is the $50 denomination. Although some states are much more frequently encountered than are others, the first forty or so states on the list given above are common enough for Series 1929 Nationals from any of them to be acquired without much difficulty.

During the past 20 years I have built up a decidedly large collection of national bank notes. Included are about 750 large-size notes (of which about 475 are Third Charter Blue Seals) and over 900 different Series 1929 notes. By far my largest holding (over 300 different notes) is from Pennsylvania. It is my home state, but it also has the largest number of notes for both the Third Charter and Series 1929 issues. With adequate funds and a good amount of diligence substantial collections can be obtained from almost any of the larger states. For some of the smaller states, however, acquiring just a half dozen or so notes can be quite a challenge.

It is possible to spend many years researching national bank notes, and in this book I can only touch on some of the information that is available on these items. If you plan to collect NBNs seriously, let me again remind you to acquire the major works in this field that are available. I would also advise you to carefully look over auction listings and dealers' pricelists before plunging in. Attending a major show such as those held annually in Memphis or St. Louis would also be most useful before getting very deeply into this type of currency.

Let us close out this chapter by examining national bank notes on a regional basis. There are various ways of subdividing our nation geographically, but I shall first consider territorial notes. Then let us examine the New England, Mid-Atlantic, Mid-Western, Southern, Great Plains, Rocky Mountain, and Pacific states in that order. I shall restrict discussion of territorial notes to large-size only, but for the other categories both large-size and small-size NBNs will be examined together.

Territorial Notes

All territorial NBNs are both very scarce and very expensive. There are total of 15 different jurisdictions that are usually considered as territories in the context of NBNs, but technically speaking, two or three of these did not have that status at the time that some of their NBNs were issued. Puerto Rico (Porto Rico on the notes) was never a territory of the United States. First Charter notes from three different banks in Nebraska were initially inscribed Nebraska Territory, but most of these were issued after Nebraska became a state in 1867. Alaska became a territory only in 1912, and its large-size NBNs are inscribed either District of Alaska, Ter. of Alaska, or just plain Alaska. Dakota Territory was split into two states in 1889, but Indian Territory and Oklahoma Territory were united into one state in 1907. There were no NBNs for Nevada Territory, since it became a state (prematurely, as things turned out) in 1864.

One of the supreme achievements in NBN collecting is to obtain at least one note from each of these 15 territories. Thus far the only individual to have done that was J. L. Irish, whose collection of these items was auctioned by Lyn Knight in 1997. In one of the sales there were a total of 35 large-size territorial notes. There have been larger offerings in the past of some of the more "common" territories such as Indian and Oklahoma Territories, but no other collection has featured some of the extreme rarities that were found in this sale.

In terms of the numbers of known notes the breakdown at present is about as follows:

Hawaii	175	Colorado	61	Wyoming	13
New Mexico	125	Dakota	41	Porto Rico	12
Indian Terr.	120	Utah	40	Washington	8
Okla. Terr.	100	Arizona	36	Nebraska	7
Alaska	68	Montana	33	Idaho	6

These data are based on information suppled by Peter Huntoon and by Lyn Knight. Overall there has been a survival rate of one note for every 7000 that were issued, a rate that is typical of early national bank notes. The survival rate, however, is much better than this for Alaska notes but much poorer for Nebraska and Washington Territories. The first Idaho Territory note was discovered only in the late 1970s Undoubtedly additional notes will be discovered as time passes, but no territorial notes can be described even remotely as "common."

I have already mentioned the $5 First Charter note from Central City, Colorado Territory (2129) with its charter number engraved in black. For Utah Territory the most available note is the $1 Original Series from Salt Lake City (2059) signed by Brigham

Young. For Dakota Territory it is the $1 Original Series from Yankton (2068). These notes brought between $3000 and $6000 each in the Irish sale.

In terms of specific varieties by far the most "common" territorial note is the $5 Red Seal from the FNB of Fairbanks, Alaska (7718). There are about four dozen of these, almost all of which are in CU condition. Despite its relative abundance this note is exceedingly expensive. Typically an example of this note sells for about $14,000 these days. The ultimate price in the Irish sale was for a serial number 1 note of this type which sold for $93,500. This is the highest price paid thus far for any national bank note excluding only Amon Carter's $500 First Charter note from New York and the $100 Value Back from New Orleans that was sold in 1998. A price of $93,500 strikes me as too high, since the note is not even unique. There are three other notes extant from the number 1 sheet.

Hawaii notes are completely dominated by the FNB of Hawaii at Honolulu (5550). These exist as Second Charter Brown Backs, Date Backs, and Value Backs, plus Third Charter Plain Backs. Prices start at about $1500 each for notes in VF condition. There were also four other National Banks, all of which were situated on the island of Maui. Only a total of seven notes are known for three of these banks, the bank from Paia being unknown, and four of these were featured in the Irish sale. The prices realized ranged from $14,300 to $27,500.

All notes of the Indian and Oklahoma Territories are either Brown Backs or Red Seals. Both of these types are more abundant as territorial notes than they are as state notes. Although Tulsa and Oklahoma City were the largest cities in these respective territories, notes from banks in these cities are no more common than are notes from smaller towns. Quite a few towns are available among the existing notes, and these items start at about $1000 each for notes in fine condition.

The other reasonably "common" jurisdiction is New Mexico Territory, which is much more abundant both as a territory and as a state than its sister state of Arizona. There are several New Mexico territorial notes that should cost no more than $1000 each in fine condition, but the best New Mexico note in the Irish collection was a $50 Brown Back from Albuquerque (2614) in VF-XF condition that sold for $12,100. In my opinion the greatest pair of NBNs of any type is from this bank. They are the unique $50/$100 and $100/$50 double denomination (i. e., one value on the face and another on the back) Brown Backs that were originally in the Grinnell collection. These were acquired by Aubrey Bebee, the Omaha coin dealer, who donated them to the ANA in Colorado Springs. It seems unlikely that this unique pair of notes will ever again come onto the public market.

Jurisdictions such as Idaho, Nebraska, and Washington Territories together with Porto Rico (sic) are so rare as to be essentially noncollectible. The Irish collection featured one note from each of these. By far the nicer pair of this quartet were the $10 Brown Back from Lewiston, Idaho (2972) in XF and the $5 Brown Back form Seattle (2966) in XF+. These sold for $52,800 and $50,600, respectively. The $10 Red Seal from San Juan (6484) was heavily circulated but basically in fine condition, yet it still sold for $37,400. The $2 Lazy Deuce from Nebraska City (1417) was only in good condition, but even in such shape it still fetched $19,800. Unless you can afford to put really serious money into national bank notes, there are several territorial jurisdictions that must be removed from all consideration.

New England States

The six New England states were all designated by the letter "N" during the period in which regional letters were in use on NBNs. In terms of national bank notes this region includes one large state (MA), one medium-sized state (CT), and four relatively small states (ME, NH, RI, and VT). All began issuing notes early in the NBN era, and so New England features an abundance of First Charter notes. Massachusetts, in fact, has the largest number of First Charter notes. Its only rival in this regard is New York, but Mass. presently offers a better variety of these notes than does New York.

As one might expect, more NBNs were issued from Boston banks than from any other towns or cities in the state, but Boston does not dominate Mass. in the way that San Francisco dominates California in its NBN issues. Such cities as Fall River, New Bedford, Springfield, Worcester, etc., are all readily available for NBNs of all periods. As I have already noted, many First Charter notes from this state are tightly trimmed, but fortunately there were several banks that did not employ this practice. Of the 62 First Charter notes that are presently in my collection, 20 are from Mass. I did not deliberately seek them out in this fashion, but if you plan to concentrate on First Charter notes this state is one of the very best to collect. The best known "hoard bank" for First Charter notes from Mass. is the Home NB of Milford (2275). Numerous uncirculated Series 1875 $1 and $2 notes have been recorded from this bank.

Second Charter notes are also frequently encountered from Mass. Among the more interesting issues of this vintage are the Brown Backs of the Pacific NB of Nantucket (714), which is most readily available of the three banks that issued notes in the two island counties of the state. Among Second Charter Date Backs issues of the National Shawmut Bank of Boston (5155) are seen with some degree of regularity. There is also an abundance of Third Charter notes including several banks that issued Red Seals in some quantity.

A total of 145 different banks in Mass. issued small-size NBNs. At the present time only two of these are unrecorded. Included among the common banks is the FNB of Easthampton (428). Several hundred type 2 $10 notes of this bank in CU condition appeared on the market a number of years ago. This hoard was so large that this is one of the very few Series 1929 NBNs that can still be obtained in quantity in CU condition. It is a popular note, however, and these items typically sell for about $60 each.

The NBNs from Connecticut parallel those of Massachusetts, but they are not dominated by a single city in the way that the latter state is. One of the best known charter numbers for this state is that of the FNB of New Haven (2). This bank was originally chartered in 1863, but it had to take another charter number (2682) when its original charter expired in 1882. It was allowed to retake its original number in 1909. All of the known notes of this bank bear the lower number, but two different titles are found on the Series 1902 Plain Back notes - the FNB of New Haven and the FNB and Trust Co. of New Haven. Another Conn. bank with a very low charter number is the FNB of Stamford (4). Despite two changes of title it continued to use the same charter number from Original Series right through to type 2 Series 1929 notes.

A total of 93 different banks from Conn. issued small-size NBNs, and all of these are known today. There are no hoards, but many different banks are available to collectors. In early 1998 the largest collection of Connecticut NBNs ever formed (about 340 notes) was sold in a CAA auction. This brought much material that had not been seen for years onto the numismatic market.

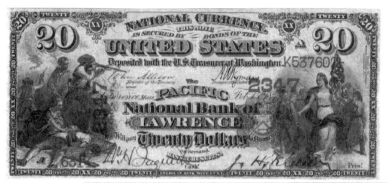

Massachusetts banks included the Pacific NB of Lawrence and the Pacific NB of Nantucket, odd titles for an Atlantic coast state. The top note is a Series 1875 $20, while the bottom note is a $5 Brown Back. The backs of the First Charter $20 notes depict the *Baptism of Pocahantas,* and these notes are the first Federal currency designs to honor an historical woman.

The NBNs of Rhode Island are heavily dominated by issues from the capital city, Providence. First Charter notes exist in some quantity, but these were generally subjected to the "New England trim." One of the notes in my collection is a $2 Series 1875 Lazy Deuce from Newport (1492). An interesting thing about this note is that only 83 examples are reported as having been issued, but 23 of these have been recorded by Charles Dean and Don Kelly as being in present-day collections. These are in a wide variety of conditions, and so this is not a typical First Charter period hoard note. A rate of survival of one note in four that were issued is vastly higher than for that of any other individual national bank note. I also own a Series 1875 Lazy Deuce from the FNB of New Bedford, Mass. (261). The earlier editions of the Hickman-Oakes and Kelly catalogs both list this note as being printed in the Original Series only. It appears, however, that all of the $1 and $2 notes from this bank were from Series 1875 instead, and this has been duly noted in the current edition of Don Kelly's catalog.

Only 12 banks issued Series 1929 NBNs from Rhode Island. All of these are recorded, but this is a difficult state for which to collect these notes, since Series 1929 notes are usually seen only from Providence and Newport. Some of the Providence banks do have rather odd names. The Blackstone Canal NB (1328) is common both in large and small size. The Rhode Island Hospital NB (13901), which is still very much in business today, was a late entrant that issued small quantities of type 2 $50s and $100s in addition to larger amounts of $5, $10, and $20 type 2 notes.

The three northern New England states offer a wider variety of notes than does Rhode Island. None are dominated by single cities, and thus a good variety of towns and banks is possible. The CAA auction held in January, 1994 included about 190 NBNs from Maine, and this was the largest selection of these notes to be offered in many years. Maine is a fairly difficult state from which to obtain First or Second Charter notes, but it does feature a wide variety of Third Charter Blue Seals and Series 1929 notes. It seems that demand for Maine NBNs in the early 1990s was not very heavy, since I was able to obtain quite a few notes for my collection at fairly modest prices from that sale. I have resold a couple of these notes more recently at much higher prices, so I expect that demand is picking up for a state that probably has few local collectors.

There were a total of 56 different banks that issued Series 1929 notes from Maine, but none of these issued any $50 or $100 notes. These notes have been recorded from all banks, but the note from the FNB of Fort Fairfield (13843) is unique. The town of Thomaston is unusual in that there were two different Thomaston National Banks. The first (charter 890) closed in 1931. It was taken over by the Georges NB (1142), but this bank then began to issue notes in the name of the bank that it had taken over but with its own charter number (1142).

Although far from common, First and Second Charter notes from New Hampshire are more readily available than are those from Maine. No major collections of NH notes have come up for sale in recent years, and patience is definitely required to build a good collection from this state. I also know of no sizable hoards of NBNs of any vintage from New Hampshire. The earliest notes encountered for this state are the Original Series notes of the FNB of Portsmouth (19). The history of this bank is not unlike that of the aforementioned New Haven bank. After being reorganized in 1883 and given a new charter number (2672), it was again permitted to use its original charter number in 1910.

Unlike the New Haven bank, however, at least a few notes are known from this bank from all the various issues from Original Series to Series 1929. A total of 58 different banks issued Series 1929 notes from New Hampshire. Only two of these, both situated in Concord, issued $50 and $100 notes. All New Hampshire banks issuing small-size NBNs have been recorded.

Despite its small population Vermont issued First Charter notes in larger quantities that did either of the other two northern New England states. A fairly decent production of notes was continued into the Second and Third Charter periods, and so among the small states Vermont is one of the easier ones for which it is possible to obtain at least a note or two from each of the different charter periods. Like New Hampshire there have been no major collections of Vermont notes that have come up for sale in recent years and there are no hoards of notes from specific banks, so patience is again needed to build up a good holding of Vermont notes.

There were two National Banks in Montpelier (charters 748 and 857). Both issued notes throughout the entire NBN era, but neither is common. If you want to collect a set of state capital notes for the six New England states, Montpelier, Vermont will prove to be much the most difficult to acquire. A total of 48 different banks issued Series 1929 NBNs from Vermont. All but one of these have now been recorded.

Mid-Atlantic States

Between 1902 and 1924 the NBNs of NY, NJ, PA, DE, MD, and DC were printed with the letter "E" as a regional indicator. The Mid-Atlantic region includes two states (NY and PA) with enormously large productions of NBNs, one (NJ) with a large number of notes, two states or districts (MD and DC) with fairly modest numbers of notes, and one (DE) with an unusually small number of national bank notes. When one looks at all periods for NBNs from 1864 through 1935 New York and Pennsylvania emerge as the two most prolific of all the states. Far more national banks were chartered in Pennsylvania than in any other state, and throughout this period New York City was the financial capital of the United States. The big New York banks were the largest in the nation, and most were major issuers of national bank notes.

It is hardly surprising that New York City had far more national banks than did any other city in the nation. There were about 154 different charter numbers used for New York banks including Brooklyn and other parts of the city that were merged in 1898, but since there were numerous takeovers and bank mergers the total number of different titles for these banks is significantly larger. No other city comes close to New York in terms of the total numbers of NBNs issued, and the issues for New York City alone exceeded all but a few of the largest states. Some collectors specialize in just the NBNs of this city, but there is always plenty of material to go around for even the most avid enthusiasts. Such charters as 29, 733, 891, 1250, 1393, 1394, 1461, 2370, 10778, and 11034 were held by very large banks that issued huge quantities of NBNs. Not all New York banks were large, however. As originally envisioned by the National Banking Act the first bank to be chartered in a given city would become the First National Bank, while the next one would be the Second National Bank, etc. The First National Bank of the City of New York (charter 29) is still very much in business, and presently it is one of our nation's largest banks, but the Second through the Tenth National Banks in New York either folded fairly soon or else changed their titles. Soon newly formed banks came up with more imaginative titles than things like the Ninth National Bank.

One of the most popular of the early New York banks is the Saint Nicholas NB (972) that was in business as a national bank from 1865 to 1882.

Occupational titles are common for many New York banks, and these were also used for banks in many other cities. Typical examples are the Grocers NB (1371), the Hide and Leather NB (4567), the Importers and Traders NB (1231), the Leather Manufacturers NB (1196), the National Butchers and Drovers Bank (1261), the National Shoe and Leather Bank (917), etc. There were also numerous neighborhood banks that functioned in only a small portion of the city. Included among these were the Maiden Lane NB (7107), the Kingsboro NB of Brooklyn (13304), the Staten Island NB and Trust Co. (6198), etc. The Brown Backs of the National Bank of the Republic (1000) are of great interest since they feature a large numeral "1000" on their back sides. It is rumored that these notes were passed as $1000 bills to unwary persons, but that seems somewhat unlikely in view of the huge buying power of $1000 at the turn of the century.

Needless to say, there are numerous NBNs from New York City in my collection. Among the more interesting are notes from neighborhood banks such as the Ozone Park NB (12280) and the Dunbar NB (13237). The latter bank was one of very few national banks that was run by Afro-Americans. It was chartered in August, 1928, and its large-size notes bear the signatures of Woods and Tate, a very scarce combination that was one of the last to be used on large-size NBNs. I also have a $100 Blue Seal note of the Bank of America National Association (13193). This was the only bank to issue $50 and $100 Blue Seal notes with the Woods-White signature combination.

It is possible to assemble a collection containing several hundred different NBNs from New York City, but it would be quite impossible to obtain a note from every one of the banks, since there are numerous banks that issued large-size notes that remain unknown. All of the several dozen New York City banks that issued small-size notes, however, have now been recorded.

By no means were the NBN issues of New York State restricted to its largest city. For the entire state there were 901 national bank charters that were used to issue notes, and of these 522 were used for Series 1929 notes. Included are major cities such as Albany, Buffalo, Rochester, and Syracuse, each of which had several national banks. The town of Rondout had three banks, but the town itself was merged into Kingston early in this century. Among the more unusual smaller banks there are the FNB of Horseheads (8301), the FNB of Painted Post (13664), and most especially, the FNB of the Thousand Islands in Alexandria Bay (5284).

In recent years the NBNs of Long Island (i. e., Nassau and Suffolk counties) have been avidly collected. Prices for almost all Long Island banks tend to be much higher than they are for notes of comparable rarity from other parts of New York State. The CAA auction held in October, 1998 featured the largest offering of Long Island NBNs that has ever been sold. There were 284 lots of notes included 20 complete sheets. Notes from Brooklyn and Queens were also included in this collection. In my collection there is a very nice $5 First Charter note from the FNB of Port Henry (1697), but alas, Port Henry is on Lake Champlain and not on Long Island Sound.

Occupational titles are frequently encountered on NBNs. Depicted above are a $1 First Charter note of the Importers and Traders NB of New York, a $5 Third Charter note of the Mechanics and Metals NB of the same city, and a $10 note of the same series from the Drovers and Mechanics NB of Baltimore.

In any case there is a tremendous variety of notes to collect from New York. Its issues of First Charter notes are exceeded only by those of Mass., and only Pennsylvania exceeds it in numbers and variety for the later issues of NBNs. If you collect these notes at all, you will doubtless acquire several notes from New York. Almost any auction that features NBNs at all will doubtless have several New York notes, and so there is no need to wait for a really big collection to come along to begin your own collecting of this state.

In terms of numbers of national banks and total output of NBNs Pennsylvania stands first in the nation for almost all issues. It stands far behind Massachusetts or New York in the production of First Charter notes, and the $1 and $2 notes of this period are quite difficult to acquire from Pennsylvania, but for almost all other types of NBNs Pennsylvania leads the nation by a wide margin. There were a total of 1196 charters that were used to issue NBNs in Pennsylvania, and of these, 899 were used to issue small-size notes. All but five of the latter banks have now been recorded. Although Philadelphia and Pittsburgh each had several large banks, these banks did not dominate the state in the way that the big San Francisco banks dominated banking in California. Pennsylvania also has numerous smaller cities (e. g., Allentown, Erie, Johnstown, Lancaster, Reading, Scranton, York, etc.), and all of these cities had banks that issued numerous NBNs. The scope of Pennsylvania is so large that many syngraphists choose to collect only specific counties, of which there are 67 in the state.

The late John Hickman recorded only about 9000 NBNs for Pennsylvania, but the total number of notes known from this state is definitely very much larger than this. It is my feeling that there are at least 25,000 to 30,000 Pennsylvania notes presently available to collectors. In my own collection there are about 330 notes, of which 200 are Series 1929 with the balance being large-size of the three charter periods. Naturally the majority of latter are Series 1902 Blue Seals, but I do have a nice selection of Second Charter notes together with a few First Charter and Third Charter Red Seal notes. This is a fairly large collection, but it is far from being the largest collection of Pennsylvania notes. Attempts have been made to obtain as many of the small-size charter numbers as is possible, and some persons have come within a few dozen of doing this. There have also been intense efforts to collect specific Pennsylvania counties, with Lancaster County probably having received the most thorough scrutiny in recent years.

Pennsylvania abounds in usual names for banks and for towns on its NBNs. Depicted above are a $5 Third Charter Blue Seal from the Cement NB of Siegfried at Northampton and a $20 Second Charter Date Back from the Gold Standard NB of Marienville.

In many parts of Pennsylvania it seems that there was an extreme degree of decentralization with regard to banking. I don't know why so many tiny hamlets needed their own national banks, but that is what happened in many parts of this state. In my collection there is a Series 1929 $100 note from the FNB of Stoystown (5682). In 1930 the total population of this village was 447 persons, and this bank issued 204 of these notes along with 516 $50 notes for this issue. It is unclear to me why the residents of this hamlet needed so many $50 and $100 notes at the bottom of the Depression, but indeed they were issued. I also have a Series 1929 $100 note from the FNB of Delta (1930 pop. = 762) and a $20 note of this series from Lake Ariel (1930 pop. = 408). The residents of Delta could also do their banking at the Peoples NB (5198), and both of the national banks in Delta functioned side by side for more than three decades.

Gap, Pennsylvania was one of very few three-letter towns to issue NBNs. Also depicted is a type 2 $50 NBN from the NB of Brookville. Only four banks in Pennsylvania issued the scarce type 2 $50 or $100 notes of Series 1929.

Pennsylvania is also a great state for banks and towns with strange names. Recently I acquired a $20 Second Charter Date Back from the Gold Standard NB of Marienville (5727). This bank was chartered in 1901, shortly after the nation went fully on the Gold Standard in 1900. As for banks in towns with strange names, the most famous is the FNB of Intercourse (9216). This is not an especially rare bank, but due to the "X-rated" name of its location small-size notes from this town in choice condition sell for as much as $800 each. There are also eight known large-size notes from Intercourse, and these fetch prices well over $1000 when in decent condition. In Pennsylvania there are also the towns of Black Lick (8428), Blue Ball (8421), Fawn Grove (9385), Hop Bottom (9647), Scenery Hill (7262), Shingle House (6799), and Slippery Rock (6483, 8724). The NBNs from all such places command high prices whenever they come onto the market. Slippery Rock is a big enough town to have a state university and to have two national banks, as these charter numbers imply. The town of Mauch Chunk together with its suburb of East

Mauch Chunk had five national banks over the years. The change of name of this town to Jim Thorpe occurred only after the NBN era had ended.

Among the large banks of the state the FNB of Philadelphia has charter no. 1. The Bank of North America (602) in the same city is the only national bank to omit the word "National" from its title. The Mellon family is from Pittsburgh, and the Mellon NB (6301) is one of the best-known sources for Third Charter Red Seal notes. Among the smaller cities the Allentown NB (1322) and the FNB of Scranton (77) both issued large numbers of notes. The United States NB of Johnstown (5913) used one of the so-called "forbidden" titles. After the Federal Reserve Act was passed in 1913, legislation was enacted to forbid national banks from using words such as "United States" or "Federal" in their titles, but those banks already using these words were permitted to continue using them.

Almost all types of NBNs are available from numerous Pennsylvania banks. As I have already noted, First Charter notes are not common from this state and $1 and $2 notes of this period are quite scarce. Pennsylvania also lacks any of the small hoards of First Charter notes in choice condition that have been uncovered in a few other states. But it is extremely rich in all types of Second and Third Charter large-size NBNs and in Series 1929 notes. There were 38 different varieties of $50 notes and 36 $100 notes that were issued in Series 1929. The last of these to be issued were type 2 $50 and $100 notes from the NB and Trust Co. of Erie (14219). These notes do exist, but they are very hard to come by in choice condition. I presently have 7 small-size $50 Pennsylvania notes and 9 of the $100 notes in my collection. The latter is a pretty good record for these, since several of the issued notes are not now believed to exist. Like the NBNs of New York, there are always a number of Pennsylvania notes in any currency auction or show, and so you need not wait for a large collection to appear before acquiring a few notes from this major state.

New Jersey was also a major producer of NBNs, but its production was more on a par with a state such as Indiana rather than New York or Pennsylvania for most periods in the NBN era. There were a total of 342 different charters that were used to issue notes in New Jersey, and of these 257 issued small-size notes. Of the latter four are still unreported. It is an easy state from which to obtain at least a few notes, although First Charter notes from New Jersey are difficult to acquire in nice condition, as is so often the case. It is an extremely easy state from which to acquire a capital city note, since the First-Mechanics NB of Trenton (1327) is probably the most common bank in the state, at least for small-size notes.

I have become interested in how the gaming industry has developed in Atlantic City since 1976, and this has led me to pursue Atlantic City NBNs with some degree of diligence. There were five different charters in Atlantic City between 1881 and 1935, and all are at least collectible. By far the most abundant are notes of the Boardwalk NB (8800). The building of this institution is still standing on the Boardwalk, but it hasn't been used as a bank for many years. Although the notes of this bank are fairly common, interest in Atlantic City as a modern-day gaming resort has caused their prices to rise sharply, and you can now expect to pay at least $200 for a small-size note from this bank in choice condition. I also have one note each from the Atlantic City NB (2527) and the Chelsea NB (5884), and both of these are Second Charter Value Backs, of all things. One of the three other towns on Absecon Island, Ventnor City, also had a national bank (10248). Notes from this bank are less expensive than are those from the Boardwalk NB, despite the fact that they were issued in far smaller quantities.

Perhaps the most sought after notes from New Jersey are from the FNB of Cape May Court House (7945), the only note-issuing town in the entire nation with four words in its name. These notes are none too common. According to Don Kelly only seven large- and ten small-size notes are known from this bank. To my knowledge no major collections of New Jersey NBNs have come on the market in recent years, since Christie's had a major sale of these notes more than 15 years ago. But there are always a few New Jersey notes around, since a number of its banks are decidedly plentiful.

Of all the eastern states Maryland is dominated by a single city to a much greater extent than are any of the others. Unless you deliberately try to seek out just one note from each town, you will find that most of your Maryland NBNs will be from Baltimore. There were a total of 138 issuing charters from this state, and 91 of these issued small-size notes. There are no known small-size notes from five of the latter. Although it is extremely easy to obtain a state capital note from New Jersey, just the opposite is true for Maryland. For Annapolis only the Farmers NB (1244) is normally available, and it issued only large-size notes. Don Kelly reports only 13 of these as presently recorded, so Maryland is one of the most difficult states from which to get a capital city note, if this form of collecting is your cup of tea.

In my own collection I do have a few nice Baltimore notes, the best of which are a Series 1875 $5 First Charter from the National Union Bank (1489) and a $50 Third Charter Blue Seal from the Citizens NB (1384), but I am amazed by how difficult it is to get Series 1929 notes from Maryland. For many years no major collections of Maryland NBNs reached the public market, but in 1998 CAA sold a very fine collection of these notes that had been formed by Armand Shank Jr. Record prices were obtained for many of these, the highest being $15,400 for a $10 Series 1902 Blue Seal note of the Pokomoke City NB (4191) that was only in F-VF condition. Although a few Maryland notes are easy to acquire, this is a very difficult state to collect in depth.

Notes of the District of Columbia are definitely much less frustrating to collect than are those of Maryland. There were a total of 27 issuing charters for the District, and of these 11 probably issued small-size notes. The Farmers and Mechanics NB of Georgetown (1928), was one of the two banks domiciled to Georgetown rather than Washington, the other being an ephemeral bank that closed down soon after it opened in the 1860s

Of the banks that issued small-size notes in DC, ten are collectible. The eleventh bank, the Federal-American NB (10316) is recorded as issuing a total of 1134 Series 1929 notes, but none of these have turned up. Although this is not a large printing, it is somewhat surprising that none of these notes have been found. Many Series 1929 notes of different banks were canceled before being issued, and perhaps that might have been the case with these notes. Small-size NBNs from DC were issued in denominations of $5, $10, and $20 only. The easiest banks to obtain are the NB of Washington (3425) and the Riggs NB (5046). A complete collection of Series 1929 notes from DC by type and denomination as well as by bank (excluding Charter 10316) would consist of 36 notes. This would be a most interesting project to attempt, but I don't know if anyone has succeeded in doing it.

Large-size notes from DC are usually Series 1902 Blue Seals. Earlier notes including First Charter notes are occasionally offered, but there hasn't been a really good collection of DC notes on the auction block for several years. The best collection from which I purchased anything was sold by Hickman and Oakes in 1985. In addition to national bank notes from the District, this collection also featured a number of private pre-Civil War bank notes from DC.

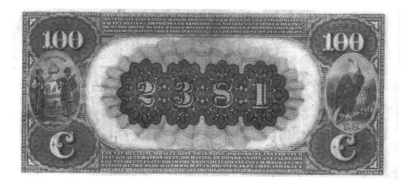

We now turn to Delaware, the scarcest of the eastern states. Although its population has grown substantially in recent decades, during the 1920s it was much less populous than Vermont and its issues of NBNs were also correspondingly low. All of the statistical data indicate that Delaware should be one of the scarcest states for national bank notes - about at a par with Idaho or New Mexico. It is a state that I have worked on with some diligence, and fortunately there have been some fairly good offerings of Delaware notes in recent auction sales. There were 28 issuing charters for this state, and of these 16 issued Series 1929 notes. All of these banks have been recorded, and for the large-size note issues only the Sussex NB of Seaford (3693) is presently unknown. Delaware also poses no problems for the state capital collector. There is a hoard of type 2 $5, $10, and $20 notes in CU condition from the FNB of Dover (1567), and these appear on the market from time to time.

In my own collection I now have a dozen small-size notes from six different banks. My holdings of large-size Delaware notes are fewer in number, but they include one great rarity. I was fortunate in purchasing at a Stack's auction in 1992 a $100 Brown Back in XF-AU condition from the NB of Smyrna (2381). I regard this as the greatest of all my national bank notes. I can only dream about Brown Backs from Idaho or Washington Territories, but a $100 Brown Back from Delaware is not a bad consolation. Incidentally the other bank from Smyrna has less exciting notes, but it does have a more interesting name, the Fruit Growers National Bank (2336). If you want a Delaware note, I would suggest acting fairly soon. The supply is definitely not very large, and they may soon vanish from the scene.

Mid-Western States

The letter "M" was used by the BEP to designate the large Mid-Western states, i.e., OH, IN, IL, MI, WI, MN, IA, and MO. All of these issued NBNs in huge quantities, and there are large numbers of surviving notes for each of these states. It is therefore very easy to acquire a few Series 1929 notes for any one of these states and to obtain at least a couple of Third Charter Blue Seal notes for each. For specialists all of these states are amenable to being collected in depth. There are differences of opinion as to the relative abundances of notes from each of these states, but next to Pennsylvania, New York, and Massachusetts they are probably the easiest of all the states to collect intensively. Space considerations prevent me from covering each of these states in as much detail as I did for New York and Pennsylvania, but let us look at some of the more interesting aspects of each.

Port Clinton Ohio had one national bank operating under three titles. Notes of the First National Magruder Bank (second title) were not reported in any collection until this note was found in 1998. Photo courtesy of BNR Press.

Of the first 100 charter numbers 29 went to Ohio banks. This appears to have been due to the influence exerted by Salmon P. Chase, a former state governor who was Secretary of the Treasury at the time. Although Ohio was not as prolific an issuer of First Charter notes as were Mass. and New York, a fairly large number of these notes do exist. Ohio is extremely rich in Second and Third Charter notes, however, and given sufficient funds a syngraphist can assemble an impressive array of large-size notes from this state. There were a total of 648 issuing charters for Ohio, and of these 346 issued small-size notes. For the latter notes from all but two are known to collectors. With one exception all of the major cities of the state are well represented by banks that issued numerous NBNs. This one exception is Akron, which had eight different national banks at various times, but these issued only large-size notes, none of which are very plentiful today. Among the smaller cities Xenia is of interest, since it is the only reasonably collectible town in the nation to have an initial letter beginning with "X." There is also a Xenia, Illinois, whose notes are very rare. Notes from Xenia, Ohio are less rare, but they are far from easy to come by. Ohio lacks towns with the sort of weird names that delight Pennsylvania collectors, but Washington Court House had two banks (4763 and 13490) and is an avidly sought location.

The Winters NB of Dayton (2604) was chartered early in 1882, and its first issues were Series 1875 notes. It subsequently issued $50 and $100 Brown Backs, Second Charter Date Backs, and Third Charter Plain Backs, as well as $50 and $100 small-size notes. It also issued $5, $10, and $20 notes for most of these issues. It is most noted, however, for issuing $50 and $100 Value Backs. For these, four survivors are presently known, and all but one are in government custody. My own collection of Winters NB high denomination notes is rather good, since it contains a Series 1882 $50 Date Back as well as $50 and $100 notes of the 1902 and 1929 issues. Needless to say, it lacks either of the Value Backs, but my $50 Second Charter Date Back is a nice substitute for the famous ultra-rarities of this bank.

One of the most famous Ohio banks was the Brotherhood of Locomotive Engineers Co-Operative NB of Cleveland (11862). This bank was chartered in 1920, shortened its title to the Engineers NB in 1928, but failed in 1930 as did almost all other union banks during the Great Depression. Its first title is the longest used on any NBNs, but these notes were issued as $5 Plain Backs only. This is not a rare note, but demand is very high because of its long-winded title. If you want one of these, expect to pay about $1000 for one in choice condition, as generally is the case. If you enjoy union banks, the Brotherhood of Railway Clerks NB of Cincinnati (12446) had a similar history and is also available to collectors.

Indiana was also a prolific issuer of NBNs. There were a total of 409 issuing charters for Indiana, of which 224 issued small-size notes. Of the latter all but three are presently known to collectors. Although Indianapolis is the state capital and by far the largest city, it does not dominate Indiana in the same way that Baltimore or Providence dominate their respective states. Indiana NBNs are readily available from all periods. One of the best known hoards of $1 and $2 Original Series notes are from the FNB of Lebanon (2057). Although these notes are quite expensive, they are almost always available in very choice condition.

Among the issuers of Second Charter notes from Indiana was the FNB of Marshall County at Plymouth (2119). The Brown Backs and Date Backs issued by this bank are the most readily available notes to feature the very rare Rosecrans-Morgan signature combination. I have a $10 Brown Back and a $20 Date Back from this bank, and I also have a $20 Red Seal from Indiana that Don Kelly claims is unique. It is from the Aurora NB (2963), a much smaller bank than the more prolific FNB of Aurora (699). One of the best known small hoards of CU Third Charter Blue Seal notes from Indiana is from the Citizens NB of Cicero (10720), which not to be confused with Cicero, IL, the town that gained notoriety during Prohibition days.

The Brotherhood of Locomotive Engineers Co-Operative NB of Cleveland was the longest title used on any National Bank Note. Another interesting labor-oriented bank title is that of the Brotherhood of Railway Clerks NB of Cincinnati. Both of these union controlled national banks went out of business in 1930.

For Series 1929 collectors Indiana offers a wide variety of notes. Two of the better-known hoard notes are the type 2 $5 and $10 notes from the Citizens NB of Evansville (2188). Ten times more of each of these notes were issued in type 1 than in type 2, but the available CU notes are usually of the second type. If you prefer your Series 1929 notes in higher denominations, South Bend (4764) and New Castle (9852) are the most readily available cities. The only Indianapolis bank to issue $50s and $100s in this series was the American NB (13759), and all the issues of this late entrant are of the scarce type 2 variety.

Ohio and Illinois are the only two states for which it is possible to form complete "alphabet sets" from the different towns and cities. Shown are a Series 1875 $5 note of the Ricker NB of Quincy, Illinois and a $10 Brown Back of the Old Citizens NB of Zanesville, Ohio. There are a fair number of survivors for each of these banks, but notes of the Second NB of Xenia, Ohio are very rare. This bank failed in 1888, and only two notes (including this Series 1875 $10 note) have thus far been recorded.

Illinois is another big Mid-Western state that was also a very prolific issuer of national bank notes in all periods. Throughout the NBN era Chicago was the second largest city of the nation, and it was also a major financial center. In terms of numbers of NBNs issued, however, it falls well short of San Francisco. The reason for this is that Illinois had very restrictive banking laws. The state legislature in Illinois was generally controlled by rural interests who feared that the big Chicago banks would totally dominate the economic life of the state unless they were restricted to that city alone. As a result, these banks were not allowed to set up branches in other parts of the state. Although there were numerous national banks in Chicago, their issues do not dominate the NBN issues of Illinois in the way in which a few other big cities do in some other states of the nation.

For Illinois there were a total of 769 issuing charters, of which 469 issued Series 1929 notes. Of the latter all but three are presently known to collectors. Illinois is a rather good state for syngraphists who desire First Charter notes in choice condition. Small hoards of choice notes from the Alton NB (1428), the Greene County NB of Carrollton (2390), the FNB of Kansas (2011), and the FNB of Lincoln (2126) are all well known. The Ricker NB of Quincy (2519) also issued numerous First Charter notes, and for collectors of alphabet sets it is one of the more available banks for the letter "Q."

Second and Third Charter notes were issued from a wide variety of Illinois banks. My one and only serial number 1 NBN is a $50 Brown Back for the aforementioned FNB of Lincoln. One of the best known hoards of $10 Value Back notes is from the La Salle NB (2503). Although I have found Red Seals to be fairly scarce from Illinois, there is a huge array of Third Charter Blue Seals available from this state. If you desire a $50 or $100 Blue Seal, you will find that the Commercial NB of Peoria (3296) is one of the more readily available banks for these issues.

Although the issues of Chicago are neither as numerous nor as diverse as are those of New York City, there are plenty of notes to keep collectors happy. A few of these incorporate the words "Live Stock" or "Stock Yards" in their titles to indicate a major economic activity of this city. One of the best known banks in the Chicago suburbs was the National Stock Yards NB of National City (12991). It issued Series 1929 notes with this title and charter and Series 1902 Blue Seals with a slightly different title and a different charter (9118). Both the bank and the town of National City were wholly owned by a big meat packing firm.

The banks of Illinois issued quite a few varieties of $50 and $100 Series 1929 notes. Again it is the Peoria bank (3296) rather than any large Chicago bank that dominates the issues for these denominations. These notes were also issued by three different banks in Danville (Charters 113, 2584, and 4731). Although the $100 notes of these banks are scarce, the $50s have survived in fair amounts. It is not clear to me why this denomination should be so popular in a fairly small city during the Great Depression, but for Danville that was indeed the case.

Michigan is another major state with prolific NBN issues. There were a total of 278 issuing charters in Michigan, of which 145 issued small-size notes, and all of these are now known to collectors. Although Detroit, of course, is the largest city, its banks do not dominate the NBN issues of this state. In fact, I have found that the sparsely populated Upper Peninsula of Michigan is well represented among the issues of this state. There are no hoards of CU First Charter notes for Michigan such as there are for several other states, and so these notes are decidedly scarce for this state. There are significant hoards of later issues, however, for a few banks in the state. The best known of these is from the FNB of Cassiopolis (1812). A fair number of Third Charter Blue Seals are known for this bank, but there are also several dozen uncut sheets of type 1 $5 Series 1929 notes. The City NB and Trust Co. of Niles (13307) has the distinction of being the last bank to issue large-size notes. These items are $10 notes that bear the very rare (for large-size) Jones-Woods signatures. Unfortunately they are extreme rarities, since only two examples are presently known.

The most prolific issuer of Third Charter Blue Seals and Series 1929 notes in Michigan was the FNB in Detroit (10527). This bank is noted for its wide variety of titles - two for Blue Seals and three for Series 1929 notes. The bank failed in 1933, and it did not issue any type 2 notes. But there are 15 possibilities for the type 1 notes of this bank, since all five denominations were issued with the three titles. Only very limited amounts of the $5, $50, and $100 notes were issued for the third title, however, and so it would be a difficult task to assemble a "complete set" of all 15 of these possibilities, but amazingly enough all of them do exist in complete sheet form. The major rival of this bank was the Guardian NB of Commerce (8703). This bank issued numerous small-size notes, and the $50s and $100s for this charter are readily available. It also failed in 1933, and thus its issues ceased to be recorded as obligations of this bank. By 1935 the amounts of outstanding Michigan NBNs were rather low compared with those of several other big states, but in considering the scarcity of Michigan notes one must take into consideration the major bank failures that took place in Detroit in 1933 and the numerous survivors of the two big banks that failed.

Missouri is another state that issued many notes in all charter periods. There were a total of 265 issuing charters in the state, and of these 119 issued small-size notes. All but one of these are known to collectors today. Missouri has two major cities, St. Louis and Kansas City, and both were substantial issuers of NBNs, but there were also many banks in other parts of the state as well. Among the 114 counties or independent cities in the state there were 36 that had no national banks, and so the custom of having at least one bank in every town of any size was followed to a much lesser extent in Missouri than it was in Pennsylvania and several other states.

Missouri is not an easy state for First Charter notes, but there are a number of CU notes from the Moniteau NB of California (1712). Missouri does have a rich legacy in Second and Third Charter notes, however. The NB of Commerce in St. Louis (4178) was a prolific issuer of $5, $10, and $20 Brown Backs, and the Merchants-Laclede NB (5002) and State NB (5172) of this same city also issued them in substantial amounts. There are presently only two Missouri Red Seals in my collection, but both of them are knockouts. My note from the Third NB of Saint Louis (170) is a $50 in AU condition, while my $100 note is a VF-XF example from the Fourth NB of St. Louis (283). Note that both spellings for the name of this city are used on the NBNs that were issued in St. Louis.

Occupational titles are much less frequent for St. Louis banks than they are for New York banks, but two very good ones are the Boatmen's NB (12916) and the Telegraphers NB (12389). Both of these banks are relatively common on Series 1929 notes. One absolutely great title for a St. Louis bank is the Bankers World's Fair NB (7179). As you might guess, it was chartered in 1904, the year of the Louisiana Purchase Exposition, but it lasted less than one year and issued only 334 notes each of the $50 and $100 Red Seals. Regrettably none of these are known to exist today. An interesting Kansas City bank was the Inter-State NB (4381). Prior to 1911 this was a Kansas bank; after that date it was a Missouri bank. Four different Missouri banks issued small-size $50 and $100 notes. Two of these were in Joplin and two were in Kansas City with none at all in St. Louis.

In 1917 and 1918 all of the national banks that had "German" or similar terms in their titles changed them as a result of America's entry into World War I. In the case of the German NB of Ripon this change was made on June 1, 1918. The charter number of the bank remained the same, but a new sequence of serial numbers was used on its notes.

For Wisconsin there were 240 issuing charters, of which 157 issued small-size notes. Of the latter only one bank is presently unknown to collectors. Like Missouri, the output of First Charter notes was fairly modest, but there are several dozen known notes of this series from the La Crosse NB (2344), most of which are in high grade. This is a bit unusual, since this bank issued only First Charter notes. In 1896 it was taken over by the NB of La Crosse (5047), and apparently the notes of the earlier bank remained in the vault of the latter bank for numerous years before eventually falling into numismatic hands.

As might be expected, Milwaukee had the largest number of charters, and Second and Third Charter notes plus Series 1929 are readily obtainable from several of these. Wisconsin has numerous citizens of German descent, and this was reflected in the names of several of the National Banks of that state. In 1917 and 1918 the titles of these banks were changed; thus the Germania NB of Milwaukee (6853) became the NB of Commerce, the German NB of Ripon (4305) became the American NB, etc. In each case there were no change of charter number, but the sequence of serials on the new notes was begun again with number 1.

Among the small-size Wisconsin notes, the $5 notes of the FNB of Wausau (2820) are available in some quantity in CU condition. Series 1929 notes from numerous other Wisconsin banks are common enough, but the Wausau note is the only one that can be termed a hoard note. Notes for $50 and $100 were issued from six different banks in five towns, but these did not include either Milwaukee or the state capital, Madison, which is otherwise quite common in small-size notes.

Numerous NBNs were issued from Iowa, but I feel that their overall abundance has been exaggerated somewhat due to the fact that they have been so thoroughly researched. Although a native of Georgia, the late John Hickman was a long-term resident of Iowa and he served as curator of the Higgins Museum in Okoboji for many years. This museum has by far the finest collection of Iowa notes ever formed, and its collections of Minnesota, Missouri, and South Dakota national bank notes are also outstanding. I expect that the data for Iowa are much more complete than they are for nearly all other states, and since Iowa was a prolific issuer of NBNs, it is not surprising that they appear to be quite common. In any case there were a total of 496 issuing charters for Iowa, and of these 249 issued small-size notes. Of these five banks have not been reported. Unlike Missouri there were national banks in all 97 of the counties of the state, and this explains partially why there were so many more charters for Iowa than there were for Missouri.

The first national bank in the nation to open for business was the FNB of Davenport (15). In 1882 this bank was reorganized with a new charter (2695). In 1911 it retook charter number 15, and so Third Charter Date Backs for this bank exist with both charter numbers. All later issues, however, again bear the original charter number. In my collection of Iowa there are two outstanding notes. One of these is a $100 Red Seal in XF from this bank (charter 2695 in this case). The other is a $100 Brown Back of the Live Stock NB of Sioux City (5022) in AU condition. As is typical of most states, far more $50 and $100 Brown Backs and Second Charter Date Backs were issued than was the case for Red Seals of these denominations.

Most of the available Iowa notes, however, are either Third Charter Blue Seals or Series 1929 notes. Although Des Moines is the state capital and largest city, there were numerous other cities such as Cedar Rapids, Davenport, and Sioux City that produced comparable numbers of notes. One factor, of course, that affects the number of Iowa notes available to collectors is the very large number that are permanently tied up in the Higgins collection. If you plan seriously to collect Iowa NBNs, then you must visit the Higgins Museum to see what a truly first class collection of these notes looks like. And as I have noted, this museum also features collections of all of the adjacent states and these are also of exceptional quality.

The final state under consideration in this section is Minnesota. There were 434 issuing charters for this state, and of these 248 issued Series 1929 notes. Of the latter five banks are at present unknown to collectors. Despite the fact that northern Minnesota is quite sparsely populated in many places, there were national banks in almost every country. This state is well known for towns with interesting names. Included are Blue Earth (5293, 7641), Good Thunder (11552), Grey Eagle (12607), and Sleepy Eye (6387). There are a number of $10 Red Seals from the FNB of Sleepy Eye, and typically these sell for about $1500 each in VF condition. This title came into use in 1904, but when this bank was originally organized in 1902 the name of the hamlet was Sleepy Eye Lake. The one and only known note with this title (also a $10 Red Seal) is on exhibit at the Higgins Museum.

Minnesota is a very tough state for First Charter notes, but one of the most interesting banks from this period is the FNB of Faribault (1686). This bank was organized in 1868, and its First Charter notes bear the very rare Jeffries-Spinner signature combination. For Third Charter notes the best known hoard is from the FNB of Starbuck (9596). The two biggest banks of the state are from its two largest cities, the FNB of Minneapolis (710) and the FNB of Saint Paul (203). The former comes with three different titles in large-size and two in small-size. The Saint Paul bank retained its same title, although it did absorb another large bank, the Merchants NB (2020), at the end of the large-size period in 1929. Duluth also had a couple of banks that were major issuers of Series 1929 notes. Small-size $50 and $100 notes were issued for a number of Minnesota banks, but only those of the Northern NB of Duluth (9327) are usually encountered. By far the largest collection of Minnesota NBNs to be sold in recent years was that formed by Marco Biondich. It was sold by Spink America in June, 1998. Although there was a substantial amount of duplication, the Biondich collection contained about 900 notes from this state.

Southern States

The regional letter "S" was used by the BEP on a the notes of 13 different states. One of these (Texas) I shall consider in the next section, but the other 12 (VA, WV, KY, NC, SC, TN, GA, FL, AL, MS, LA, and AR) display many similar properties. One might question the inclusion of Kentucky or West Virginia among these states, but their national bank issues have much more in common with the other Southern states than they do with those of the Mid-Western or Mid-Atlantic states. In almost all cases First Charter notes tend to be very rare for any of these states. Although a few Southern national banks were organized during the 1860s, there were no sizable issues of First Charter notes from any of them, and Second Charter and Series 1902 Red Seal notes are in general also quite uncommon for most Southern states. None of these states are anything like as common as are the big Mid-Western states, and although comprehensive collections have been formed for several states of this region, they tend to be much smaller than do those of the large states that we have been previously considering. Let us consider the Southern notes by series rather than by state, although I do wish to comment on the decidedly peculiar nature of the NBNs of Florida.

Almost without exception the First Charter notes of the Southern states are rarities. There is, however, one hoard of these notes in choice condition from the City NB of Selma, Alabama (1736). Although this bank issued these notes in all values from $5 through $100, only the $5 notes have survived in any numbers. Today these notes sell for at least $1000 each in nice condition, but this is by far the most available of the Southern First Charter notes. Although all of the other Southern First Charter notes can be described as very scarce at a minimum, the most available of these are from Kentucky or West Virginia. This is hardly surprising in view of the fact that the economies of these two border states were the least affected among this group by the ravages of the Civil War. Although all 12 of the Southern states issued First Charter notes, only three notes each are known from Arkansas and from Florida and none at all are known from Mississippi.

Type 2 notes from the Commercial NB of Spartanburg, SC are among the more available of notes from this state. The charter number 14211 indicates a late arrival for this bank, and this is also apparent from the modernistic type font used for the black overprints on this note. Another interesting small-size NBN from a Southern city is the $100 type 1 note from the Union Planters NB of Memphis. A small hoard of these was on the market during the 1970s, but the supply seems largely to have dried up.

There are far more Series 1882 notes and Third Charter Red Seals available for the Southern states, but these notes are always very rare from Florida, Arkansas, Mississippi, and South Carolina. The most famous Southern issues of these types are the $50 and $100 Value Back notes of the Canal-Commercial NB of New Orleans (5649). There are six known examples of these notes, five of which are in private hands. All $50 and $100 Value Backs are extremely rare, but in 1998 and 1999 one each of the $50 and $100 notes from New Orleans together with a recently discovered $100 note from Dayton were offered at public auction. The charter number 5649 was previously used by the Commercial NB, a bank which issued Brown Backs and Second Charter Date Backs of the three lower denominations. These are the most available of the Second Charter notes for Louisiana, and so notes of both the New Orleans and Dayton banks that issued the famous $50 and $100 Value Backs are at least obtainable without too much difficulty. My two best Southern notes are of this vintage. I have a $50 Brown Back of the State NB of New

Orleans (1774), which is one of seven New Orleans banks that issued $50 and $100 Brown Backs. Among Second Charter notes I also have a $100 Date Back from the NB of Kentucky of Louisville (5312), a major issuer of all three series of Second Charter notes.

As is the case with almost all states, Third Charter Blue Seals are much more readily available for the Southern states than are the earlier types of NBNs. It is not difficult to obtain a few examples for each of the states of this region. One of the very best titles is the Day & Night NB of Pikeville, Ky. (11944). This is a rare bank, however, since only seven Blue Seal and two Series 1929 notes are presently known. I know of no large hoards of Blue Seal notes for any of the Southern states, but among the more readily available are $20 notes of the FNB of Crowley, La. (5520). Although uncirculated, these usually lack the bank signatures. Another group of CU $20 Plain Backs that appear with some regularity are from the First and Citizens NB of Elizabeth City, NC (4628). Without doubt, Mississippi is the scarcest Southern state for Third Charter notes, but at least there are a few towns of this state that are collectible for Blue Seal notes.

You will not encounter any difficulty in acquiring at least a few Series 1929 notes from any of the Southern states. Several well-known hoards of CU notes exist. The largest of these is from the FNB & Trust Co. of Lexington, Ky. (906). Another bank that is common for CU notes is the Commercial NB of Spartanburg, SC (14211). NBNs with charter numbers over 14000 are avidly collected, and the notes of this bank are the most readily available notes for this type for any state. Another well-known group of Southern notes are the $5 notes of the Delta NB of Yazoo City, Miss. (12587), but most of these are not in CU condition. For high denomination notes there once was a small hoard of CU $100 notes from the Union Planters NB of Memphis (13349), but these have now largely been dispersed. With regard to $50 and $100 small-size notes there were none of these types issued from Alabama, Georgia, or South Carolina. For a while it was thought that no $50 or $100 Series 1929 notes were issued from Arkansas, but both of these were indeed issued from the FNB of Lawrence County at Walnut Ridge (11312). Thus far a single type 2 $100 note of this bank has been uncovered. Series 1929 $50 and $100 notes are also extremely rare from MS, NC, VA, and WV. There are numerous examples, however, from LA and TN, and from time to time FL and KY notes of these denominations do appear. One of the best known issues of small-size NBNs are the $10 type 2 notes of the Liberty NB and Trust Co. of Louisville (14320). They are not rare, but the fact that they carry the highest of all charter numbers gives them a large premium value.

For collectors of capital city notes, some Southern states are easy while others are not. As might be expected, notes of Atlanta, Nashville, and Richmond are very easy to acquire. There also will be no major difficulties in acquiring notes from Columbia, Raleigh, Montgomery, Jackson, or Baton Rouge. Frankfort, Ky. does have two collectible banks (4090 and 5376), and for Little Rock there are three collectible banks. One of these, the Commercial NB of Little Rock (14000) is obviously of interest both to collectors of state capital notes and to those who go in for charter 14000 notes. Arkansas is not a very easy state to collect, however, and for this state notes from Fort Smith are far easier to come by than are those from Little Rock. Finally we have Tallahassee, Florida. The only bank in this city that issued notes was the FNB (4132), but it released only very limited numbers of Second and Third Charter $50 and $100 notes. Three of these notes are pres-

Guide and Handbook   national bank notes\245

ently known to syngraphists, but for all intents and purposes Tallahassee is a noncollectible capital city.

The NBNs from Florida have such peculiar characteristics that some comments are needed especially for this state. Although Florida has a huge population today, the number of inhabitants of this state reached 1,000,000 only in the 1920s. For most of the NBN era there was only comparatively limited economic activity, and the banks of the state were generally fairly small. There was a good deal of land speculation in Florida during the 1920s. You might think that this would have resulted in a large production of Third Charter Blue Seal notes, but that was not the case. There were a total of 109 issuing charters for the state, of which 54 issued Series 1929 notes. Of these all but one are presently known, but collecting a sizable number of notes will prove to be extremely difficult. It may well be that many of the Florida notes are in private collections that are presently off the market, but for the time being only a decidedly limited variety of Florida NBNs is available to most collectors.

All Second Charter and Red Seal notes from Florida are very rare, and so the large-size NBNs of this state are basically restricted for most collectors to Series 1902 Blue Seal notes. The only city of the state that can be considered as "common" in large-size is Jacksonville, for which there are three collectible charters (6888, 8321, and 9049). A $5 or $10 Blue Seal note in VF condition from any one of these banks can be obtained for about $250, but large-size notes from any cities in Florida other than Jacksonville and Tampa sell at much higher prices.

For small-size notes the American NB of Pensacola (5603) is by far the most readily available for the entire state. Notes can also be obtained from Jacksonville, Miami, and Tampa, but from then on the going gets rough. Although the Hickman-Oakes and Don Kelly catalogs give the impression that notes from numerous Florida towns and cities are available in quantities, they simply are not on the market. Another problem with Florida notes is their overall condition. I choose to have nearly all of my Third Charter and Series 1929 notes at least in VF+ condition or better. You will soon discover that many Florida notes are in no better than fine condition, if that, and so it is probably advisable to lower one's minimum grading standards a bit before getting deeply into the collecting of NBNs from this state.

The best collection of Florida to be sold in recent years was a group of 86 notes that was sold by CAA in 1992. The only Second Charter note in the sale, a $10 Date Back of the FNB of Pensacola (2490) sold for $4895 in VF-XF condition. The "star" of this auction was a $100 Red Seal from the Atlantic NB of Jacksonville (6888) in F-VF condition, which sold for $6050. The only other known example of this type, also in F-VF condition, was sold by R. M. Smythe in 1997 for $8250. Another good collection of Florida NBNs consisted of 44 single notes and 5 uncut sheets. It was sold by Lyn Knight in June, 1999. Almost all of these were Series 1929 notes in stop condition. It is my guess that large numbers of Florida notes are still being held off the market, but time can only tell whether this state will become more collectible than it is today.

Great Plains States

The 100 degree meridian of longitude cuts through the six states (ND, SD, NE, KS, OK, and TX) that straddle the Great Plains. This is a rather heterogeneous bunch of states, but I shall consider them together in this discussion. On NBNs printed between 1902 and 1924 the BEP used the letter "W" for the first five of these, but for Texas it used the letter "S." In terms of their NBN issues there are two states that are small (ND and SD), three that are medium sized (NE, KS, and OK), and one (TX) that is extremely large.

An interesting thing about North and South Dakota is that they have had essentially zero population growth for the past 70 years. The populations of these states in 1910 were almost as large as they are today, and in 1930 they actually exceeded their current values. North Dakota had rather more than 200 issuing charters (223 to be exact), while South Dakota has somewhat less than this figure (177). Many of these banks were very small, and this was a region that was hit very hard by bank failures especially during the Great Depression. Only relatively small numbers of NBNs were issued for each of these states. The numbers of notes available to collectors for these two states are roughly equal, but in my opinion South Dakota is much the more interesting of the two. For both states the available supply of notes is largely restricted to Third Charter Blue Seals and Series 1929 notes.

For North Dakota the most common bank both for large- and small-size is the FNB of Grand Forks (2570). Although Third Charter notes from this bank are not very common, they are more plentiful than those for any other North Dakota bank, and thus a collection of notes from this state will probably consist very largely of Series 1929 notes. A most interesting issuer of Blue Seal notes was the FNB of Van Hook (10966). This town no longer exists, because it was flooded out during the creation of reservoirs along the Missouri River in the 1930s.

Series 1929 notes from North Dakota are found from a wide variety of towns. The only bank to issue $50s and $100s in this series was the FNB and Trust Co. of Fargo (2377), and occasionally these do come up for sale. Among the most available towns are Dickinson, Grafton, Valley City, and Wahpeton in addition to Fargo and Grand Forks. The state capital, Bismarck, is represented by two collectible banks. With a good deal of persistence it is possible to build up a modest collection of North Dakota notes, but nothing is really common. According to Don Kelly only the biggest Grand Forks bank (2570) is known to have more than 50 small-size notes, and no more than a couple of dozen large-size examples are known for a given bank anywhere in the state.

South Dakota shows a wider variety in its notes. Second Charter notes of the FNB of Deadwood (2391) sometimes come up for sale at rather stiff prices. These were issued long after the days of Wild Bill Hickock, but they do evoke images of the Wild West and are very popular with collectors. Series 1882 notes are more available from South Dakota than from its sister state. Probably the most "common" bank for notes of this vintage is the FNB of Mitchell (2645). Another bank from this town, the Mitchell NB (3578) along with the Home NB of Dell Rapids (9693) are among the more frequently seen for Third Charter Blue Seals. The Dakota NB of Yankton (9445) issued only $50 and $100 notes, and these are occasionally seen. For Series 1929 notes there were many issuers, but none are especially common. The most available are from the Security NB and Trust Co. of Sioux Falls (10592), but only about 60 of these are presently known to collectors. The state capital, Pierre, had four different banks. Although collectible, this is one of the rarer state capital cities. The Higgins Museum has a very good collection of South

Dakota notes, and if you are interested in this state a visit to view their holdings would be most worthwhile.

National bank notes from Nebraska were issued in much larger quantities than they were for the Dakotas, and this is a state that is readily available to collectors, at least for Third Charter Blue Seals and Series 1929 notes. In actual fact both Kansas and Nebraska have struck me as having far more NBNs that one might expect in view of their relatively small populations. It is possible to collect both of the states in depth, since there does seem to be a fairly ample supply of their notes on the market. In the case of Nebraska there were 349 issuing charters, of which 152 issued small-size notes. Only three of the latter remain unreported.

There are a few hoard notes that appear for Nebraska notes. The two best known of these are Otoe County NB of Nebraska City (1417) and the FNB of Wood River (3939). In both cases the notes in these hoards are Third Charter Blue Seals. Although Nebraska is a fairly tough state for early NBNs, a very nice selection of Third Charter Blue Seals of all five denominations is available. Two of the Blue Seal Date Back $100s in my collection are from Nebraska, and neither of these is from Omaha. Although the state is not as rich in towns with interesting names as is Minnesota, Weeping Water is represented by two banks. The town is noted as being the birthplace of populist presidential candidate William Jennings Bryan.

There are no particularly large hoards of any Series 1929 Nebraska notes, but numerous examples often do come up for sale. The state capital is extremely easy, since the FNB of Lincoln (1798) is perhaps the most readily available note in the state for small-size. The issues of this bank are a bit peculiar, since only $20 notes (both types) were issued. Usually banks issued both $10 and $20 notes, or $5, $10, and $20 notes for this series. There were seven banks that issued $50s and five that issued $100s in small-size. Oddly enough, my collection presently lacks a $100 note from the relatively common Omaha NB (1633), but it does include this denomination for the much scarcer FNB of Pender (4791).

Kansas is another relatively small state for which there is a fairly large supply of NBNs. Like Nebraska it is not an easy state for early NBNs, but it does have a wealth of Third Charter Blue Seals and Series 1929 notes. There were a total of 400 issuing charters for the state, of which 212 issued small-size. Only three of the latter are unreported at the present time, but a large number of the earlier banks are still unknown.

There is one small hoard of First Charter notes for Kansas, and this makes this state easier to obtain than Nebraska for notes of this vintage. These notes are from the FNB of Emporia (1915). The Series 1875 $1 note of this bank in my collection has a most attractive localized blue stain, a security feature that was only used infrequently on NBNs of the period. Another Kansas note in my collection of which I am proud is a Second Charter $50 Date Back from the Baxter NB of Baxter Springs (5952). The great majority of the available large-size Kansas notes are Third Charter Blue Seals, but for these a wide variety of banks is possible. In 1995 Lyn Knight sold the collection of Kansas notes that had been formed by Dale Lyon. In his collection Mr. Lyon typically attempted to obtain just two notes for each bank, one small-size and one large-size, but he did succeed in collecting 600 NBNs from Kansas including 197 different of the small-size charters. In addition to some 275 Third Charter Blue Seals his collection also contained 23 First Charters, 84 Second Charters (including 4 $50s and 3 $100s), and 25 Red Seals (including 3 $50s and one $100).

Although there are no large hoards for any large-size notes from Kansas, a very large number of CU $5 small-size notes from the FNB in Wichita (2782) are available. Another well-known issue of Series 1929 notes for Kansas are from the Chandler NB of Lyons (14048). In addition to being "14000" notes, these items are also vice presidential notes, since they feature that notation in their facsimile signatures. Notes from the state capital, Topeka, are very easy to come by, as are those of many other cities and towns of the state.

Depicted above are two so-called vice presidential notes of Series 1929. On the note from the Chandler NB of Lyons, KS the word "VICE" appears beneath the appropriate signature. On the note from the FNB of Tyndall, SD the letter "v" is subtly worked into the signature on the right side of the note.

Oklahoma became a state only in 1907, and for this state Brown Backs and Red Seals are rarer with state designations than with territorial designations. Although they are far from common, Second Charter notes from Oklahoma are more readily available as Date Backs and Value Backs than they are as Brown Backs. I have also found this state to be much more difficult for Third Charter Blue Seals than is either Kansas or Nebraska. Small-size Oklahoma notes, however, are readily available.

Including the two territories there were a total of 557 issuing charters for Oklahoma, and of these 214 issued Series 1929 notes. Of the latter 11 banks remain unreported. Many of the banks chartered in the late territorial and early statehood periods in Oklahoma had insufficient capital to function effectively, and the casualty rate for these was extremely high. Needless to say, there are many banks that issued large-size notes in this jurisdiction for which there are today no known survivors.

For small-size notes, however, there is a wide variety of issues for Oklahoma. One of the interesting factors for these is the ready availability of $50 and $100 notes from banks in Muskogee, Oklahoma City, and Tulsa. For the Oklahoma City bank (4862) there were both type 1 and 2 $50s, but for the $100s only type 1 notes were issued. The type 2 $50s of this bank are one of the more available issues for this scarce type. Both the Muskogee and Tulsa banks issued $50s and $100s only in small-size. The FNB of Muskogee (4385) is also a fairly easy bank from which to obtain $50 and $100 Third Charter Plain Back notes, and the FNB of Tulsa (5171) also restricted its later issues of large-size notes to these two denominations. Across the nation there were a number of banks that preferred to issue only $50 and $100 notes, and for Oklahoma these are the two best examples.

The state of Texas is a category unto itself. In terms of its national bank note issues, the earlier issues of Texas resemble those of the other Southern states. Texas notes were designated with an "S" between 1902 and 1924, but they totally dwarf the issues of any one of the other twelve Southern states that we previously examined. For Texas there were 917 charters that were used for the issue of NBNs, and of these 510 were used for issuing small-size notes. In terms of numbers of issuing banks Texas is quite similar to New York, and thus it is exceeded only by Pennsylvania in terms of the diversity of its note output.

When the Fort Worth collector Amon Carter Jr. died in 1982, I was expecting to see a large number of Texas Nationals come onto the market. As things turned out, however, Amon Carter did not own that many Texas notes. The truly large collection of these items was owned by J. L. Irish, and there was also a very impressive collection of large-size Texas NBNs that were owned by Jack and Mary Everson. Both of these were auctioned by Lyn F. Knight in 1997. In the Irish collection there were about 1600 individual notes plus 21 uncut sheets, of which one was a sheet of Blue Seal $5 notes while the others were 1929 issues. For the single notes there were only seven First Charter issues. Texas shows the typical "Southern" characteristic of being extremely rare for this period. For instance, thus far only a single $2 Lazy Deuce in well-worn condition has been recorded for this state. The Irish collection also contained about 120 Second Charter notes, of which there were approximately 65 Brown Backs, 40 Date Backs, and 15 Value Backs including six each of the $50 and $100 notes for this period. The best four of these brought between $7150 and $9900 each with conditions ranging from VF to AU. There were also some 30 Red Seals in this collection. The balance consisted of about 500 Third Charter Blue Seals and about 950 Series 1929 notes. J. L. Irish was prepared to accept lower grade notes from rare banks from which he could not find better copies, but there were also many choice examples in his collection. For the First Charter notes, for example, three of the $1 notes were in VF, one each of the $5 and $10 notes were in fine condition, while the other $1 and $10 notes were only in good condition. There was some duplication in the Irish collection, but there were no excessive quantities of notes from any given bank. For the Everson collection there were about 350 Texas notes, almost all of which were large size and for which there was virtually no duplication. Most of these were Third Charter Blue Seals, but there was one $5 First Charter note, 36 Second Charter notes, and eight

Red Seals. The Second Charter group included five $50 or $100 notes, while the latter included two $100 notes, which is half of the $100 Red Seals known for the state. The highest price realized was $9900 for Everson's $100 Red Seal of the FNB of Corsicana (3506) in VF condition.

As this book was being finalized, the collection of bank notes formed by Harry W. Bass, Jr. came onto the market. Included in this collection were 15 First Charter NBNs from Texas. Twelve of the 23 banks in Texas that issued First Charter notes were represented in the Bass collection. Most of the other Texas banks that issued these notes remain unknown for First Charter nationals. The highest prices was obtained for a $100 Original Series from Jefferson (1777) in fine condition. It sold for $62,100. There were also two $20 notes, a Series 1875 from Dallas (2455) and an Original Series from Waco (2189). The former was in fine condition and sold for $14,950, while the latter was VF and fetched $23,900. Another very nice note in this collection was a Series 1875 $10 from Galveston (1566) that was i VF condition and sold for $14,950. Most of these notes had previously been in the collections of William Philpott, Jr. or Robert Schermerhorn. Along with Amon Carter, Jr., these gentlemen were two of the pioneer collectors of paper money from the state of Texas.

The data that I quote for these collections become of interest when we consider the total supply of NBNs that is most likely available for all of Texas. Earlier in this chapter I estimated the total number of Pennsylvania Nationals as being at least as much as 25,000 to 30,000 notes. For Texas I would expect this total to approach 20,000 notes. Thus it seems likely that J. L. Irish succeeded in acquiring almost 10% of all the Texas NBNs in existence. Furthermore his collection would have shown a much greater range of diversity on a sample basis than would have been the case for the total population, since the latter would contain very large numbers of common small-size notes from a number of the big banks in Dallas, Houston, San Antonio, etc. Texas lacks any large hoards of CU notes similar to those for the $5 notes of Wichita (2782) or the $10 notes of Easthampton, Mass. (428), but some of the notes of its largest banks are very plentiful. If you want a detailed study of Texas NBNs, the catalogs that Lyn Knight prepared for the Everson sale (in February, 1997) and for the Irish sale (in August, 1997) are excellent references as to what is actually available for Texas Nationals. The Bass collection that was sold by Bowers and Merena (in May, 1999) contained far fewer Texas notes, but detailed writeups for each of the First Charter notes are included in the catalog.

If you collect NBNs at all, you will certainly want to acquire a few Texas notes. The First Charter notes for this state, however, will have to be excluded by almost all collectors. The two best $1 notes in the Irish collection (one each from Galveston and Houston, both of which were in full VF condition) brought $8800 each. The other First Charter notes went for somewhat lower prices, but their condition was in each case inferior to this pair. The least expensive of the First Charter notes in the Bass collection, a $5 note from Dallas in VG condition for $4600. Second Charter notes are collectible for all three series, but the $50 and $100 Brown Backs and Date Backs are very expensive if in high grade. Of these only the Brown Backs have the "Lone Star" emblem in the state shield on their back sides, and this makes them rather more interesting than the Date Backs and Value Backs. Oddly enough, the only two Second Charter notes that I own from Texas at the present time are Value Backs, the type that appears to be much the scarcest of the three Series 1882 issues for this state. As is typical for many states, Red Seals are scarcer than Brown Backs or Series 1882 Date Backs for Texas.

Thus it seems likely that a typical collection of Texas notes will consist very largely of Third Charter Blue Seals and Series 1929 notes. The largest cities of the state (i. e., Austin, Dallas, Fort Worth, Houston, San Antonio, etc.) all issued large numbers of NBNs, and many of these are readily available. Some of the smaller Texas cities (e. g., Galveston, Waco, or Wichita Falls) are quite common while others of similar size (e. g., Amarillo, Corpus Christi, or Lubbock) are not. In this respect Texas differs from a state like Pennsylvania where all of the smaller cities are relatively easy to obtain. Among the smaller towns of Texas there are several that are relatively obtainable, but many are extremely scarce. In any case the diversity of notes from Texas is matched or exceeded only by those of New York or Pennsylvania.

Texas is a good state from which to obtain examples of the scarce type 2 $50 and $100 notes of Series 1929. At the present time I have two for each denomination from this state. Although my type 2 $50 notes are from big Dallas banks, my $100 notes are from the much smaller communities of Bryan (4070) and New Braunfels (4295). In theory there are a total of 41 different $50 notes and 40 $100 notes for Series 1929 (including both types 1 and 2), but several of these are unrecorded. These totals are larger than for any other state, and for the three lower denominations the numbers of possible varieties of Series 1929 notes for Texas is exceeded only by those of New York and Pennsylvania.

Rocky Mountain States

Our next group of states includes eight states that are small or at least relatively small. Of these states four (CO, MT, NM, and WY) were designated with the letter "W" by the BEP, while the other four (AZ, ID, NV, and UT) were designated with the letter "P." Of the states Colorado and Utah are relatively common, three (Idaho, Montana, and New Mexico) are fairly scarce, while the remaining three (Arizona, Nevada, and Wyoming) can be classed as very scarce in terms of the numbers of NBNs that are presently available to collectors. With the exception of Nevada all of these jurisdictions issued NBNs as territories prior to becoming states.

Although a number of Second Charter notes are available for Colorado, this state is definitely much easier to collect as Third Charter Blue Seals. There were three large banks in Denver (1016, 1651, and 7408), all of which issued fairly decent quantities of NBNs. Fort Collins is the next most abundant city in Colorado for large-size, although numerous other towns are also collectible. Colorado, however, does not show the great diversity in its Third Charter issues that is found for either Kansas or Nebraska.

At the Memphis show in 1998 extremely high prices were obtained for a number of Third Charter Blue Seal notes from Colorado. The two highest prices achieved were $30,800 for a $5 note from Gill (9697) and $26,400 for a $10 note from Center (9743), both of which are in VF condition and are believed to be unique. Prices of well over $5000 each were also obtained for similar notes from Cripple Creek (4845), Hugo (10786), and Julesburg (9603).

Shown above are a scarce type 2 $100 note from the Exchange NB of Colorado Springs and a $10 type 1 note from the United States NB of Red Lodge, Montana. The latter is one of the so-called "forbidden titles" that were no longer to be used for newly chartered national banks after the passage of the Federal Reserve Act at the end of 1913.

The small-size NBNs of Colorado are found from numerous towns and cities, but only Denver can be described as very common. This state is a good one for $50 and $100 notes of this series. The FNB of Pueblo (1833) issued only $50 and $100 notes for this series, but the Colorado NB of Denver (2520) is a bit peculiar in that it issued $5, $10, and $100 small-size notes, but $20 and $50 notes were not issued. The Exchange NB of Colorado Springs (3913) issued the scarce type 2 $50 and $100 notes, and I was able to secure a $100 note from this bank in 1995. Thus far this is the only Series 1929 note for any state for which I have paid more than $1000.

Notes from Utah are available from a smaller range of towns than is the case of Colorado, but both Salt Lake City and Ogden are fairly common in large size. The FNB of Ogden (2597) used a total of four different titles on its Third Charter Blue Seal issues, although one of these is extremely rare. For Salt Lake City there are four or five fairly common banks that issued Third Charter Blue Seal notes. All Red Seal notes, however, are very rare from Utah. This state also has another peculiarity. There were only 34 issuing charters, compared with 185 for Colorado.

Small-size Utah notes were issued by only 17 banks, and all of these are known. Series 1929 Utah notes, unlike those of Colorado, are very largely confined to $5, $10, and $20 issues, and no $100 notes at all were issued for this series. Title changes are typical for a few of these issues. The Deseret NB (2059) became the FNB of Salt Lake

City, while the National Copper Bank (9652) became the Security NB. The previously mentioned Ogden bank also had a final title change in 1931 that affected its small-size issues.

National bank notes were issued in smaller quantities in Montana than was the case for Utah, but they were issued by a much larger total number of banks. Montana is not an easy state for Second Charter notes, but my best note for this state is one of these. It is a $10 Value Back from the NB of Montana in Helena (5671), which is one of only two banks to issue this series for the state. The FNB of Butte (2566) confined its issues almost exclusively to $50 and $100 notes from Brown Backs through to small-size. This bank is the only one in Montana that issued these notes for Series 1929. Among the most prized town names for Third Charter issues in Montana are Grass Range (10939) and Roundup (9165), but both of these are rare. Although no Series 1929 notes are very common for Montana, they are known for 42 of the 44 banks that issued them. The most abundant town is Missoula, but Billings, Great Falls, Helena, Kalispell, and Red Lodge all appear with some regularity.

The capital of Idaho is Boise, and the three banks of this city (Charters 1668, 3471, and 10083) dominate the issues of this state. Idaho is an extremely difficult state for Second Charter notes, and thus its large-size issues are very largely confined to Third Charter Blue Seals. There is, however, a cut sheet of $5 Red Seals from the FNB of Rexburg (7133), and these are available to collectors at very stiff prices. Not only are these notes uncirculated, but they also have serial number 1. There are also two uncut sheets of Blue Seal notes from this bank. No large-size Idaho NBNs can be described as common, but the three Boise banks at least do appear from time to time. The Pacific NB (10083) confined its issue to $10 and $20 notes, but for Third Charter notes the FNB of Idaho (1668) issued only $50s and $100s. In my collection there is a $50 Date Back together with $50 and $100 Plain Backs. The $100 note has boardwalk margins, and I regard it as my finest Third Charter Blue Seal note from any state. According to Don Kelly there are only about 315 large-size notes from Idaho for the entire state period, and so this is definitely not an easy state to collect in large-size.

There were a total of 28 issuing charters for small-size notes in Idaho, and all of these are presently known. Two of the banks in Boise plus one in Lewiston issued $50 and $100 notes. There are no hoards for any small-size Idaho notes. Kelly's census data indicate only a few more than 250 Series 1929 notes for Idaho including a few in uncut sheets. Idaho appears more available on my list for small-size notes than do some of the other Western states, but these data reflect total face value outstanding and thus are distorted for states like Idaho that issued numerous $50 and $100 notes. I feel, however, that this total is too low by a factor of about two, at least for the small-size notes of Idaho. The notes of this state are certainly no rarer than are those of Wyoming, a state for which the documentation is particularly good.

Depicted are notes from the capital cities of two of the Rocky Mountain states, a $10 Value Bank form the NB or Montana in Helena and a $100 Third Charter Blue Seal from the First National Bank of Boise, Idaho.

In the November, 1991 issue of the *Bank Note Reporter* I published a detailed survey of the NBNs of Wyoming. I had obtained my data from John Hickman, but his material, in turn, had largely come from Peter Huntoon, a Wyoming resident and a major collector and researcher of NBNs. The state of Wyoming has an interesting anomaly for a small Western state, a collectible First Charter note. It is the Series 1875 $5 note of the Stock Growers NB of Cheyenne (2652), for which 13 examples are known. This note is far from cheap, however, since nice examples presently sell for about $5000 - $6000 each, or about the same as the prices asked for high-grade examples of the more "available" territorial First Charter notes such as the $1 Original Series notes from Yankton (2068) or Salt Lake City (2059), or the famous $5 black charter note from Central City (2129).

New NBNs do turn up, and the data that Kelly gives in his new catalog indicate somewhat larger numbers of notes for Wyoming than I reported in my 1991 article. At the present time there are approximately 20 known First Charter notes from the State of Wyoming, 55 Second Charter notes, and 15 Red Seals, of which four are in one uncut sheet. For Third Charter Blue Seals there are about 275 notes. This totals about 365 large-size notes, as compared with only 315 for Idaho, but I expect that the data for Wyoming are far more complete than they are for the latter state. All Wyoming large-size notes are scarce, but there are banks in at least two or three towns including the state capital of Cheyenne for which two dozen or so examples are known.

There were a total of 23 issuing charters for Series 1929 notes from Wyoming, and all of these are known. In 1991 I reported a total of 572 small-size notes for this state. In 1997 Kelly is reporting about 680, or almost 20% more. No Wyoming notes are common, however, and in my opinion it is the third scarcest Western state next to Arizona and Nevada. A sizable number of Wyoming notes, however, are tied up in the collection of Peter Huntoon, and this is one reason why this state appears to be quite scarce.

The importance of mining in the Rocky Mountain states is emphasized by such titles as the National Copper Bank of Salt Lake City, Utah and the American National Bank of Silver City, New Mexico. Despite its name, however, the economy of Silver City is dependent on copper rather than silver mining.

New Mexico became a state at the beginning of 1912, and thus its NBN issues as a state begin with Second and Third Charter Date Backs. During 1997 Lyn Knight auctioned the New Mexico portions of the collections formed by the Eversons and by J. L.

Irish. The former contained 44 New Mexico notes including 15 from the Territory. The latter consisted of 57 notes with 14 from New Mexico Territory. Although the highlights of both collections were from the territorial period, the other notes in these collections showed what can be done with a fairly scarce Western state.

In my opinion New Mexico is about as difficult a state to acquire as is Montana. For large-size notes Albuquerque is the most common city, and its largest bank is the FNB (2614). The second most available town of the state in large-size is Silver City, where some 48 Blue Seal notes are reported for the American NB (8132). All of the other towns are scarcer, although about two dozen notes each are reported for Las Vegas, Roswell, and Santa Fe.

There were 23 charters that issued small-size notes in New Mexico, and all of them have been recorded. The two most available banks are the FNB (2614) and the National Bank (12485), both in Albuquerque. There was a small hoard of about 50 notes of the FNB of Belen (6597), but these have long been dispersed. There also are a couple of dozen notes each from Raton, Roswell, and Santa Fe. Some of the other larger towns of the state (e. g., Clovis, Farmington, and Las Cruces) are very poorly represented with NBNs.

Although the population of Arizona was comparable to that of New Mexico during the NBN era, it is a much more difficult state from which to obtain these notes. Only about one-third as many Arizona notes are reported for the Territorial period as is the case with New Mexico, and this tendency also continues for the state issues. Don Kelly reports 176 large-size notes for the state. In addition to his Wyoming collection Peter Huntoon also owns a large collection of Arizona notes, and so I imagine that given his exhaustive research efforts this figure is fairly complete. That would make Arizona notes about twice as scarce in large-size as is Wyoming. The most abundant towns are Arizona's two biggest cities, Phoenix and Tucson, but neither is common in large-size. Even the most readily available Third Charter Blue Seal note from Arizona would now cost about $2000 or so in VF condition.

There were only 11 issuing charters for Series 1929 notes from Arizona, and all of them are reported. By far the most common is the Consolidated NB of Tucson (4287). Enough notes are available from this bank to make it possible for most collectors to obtain at least one Arizona note. For Phoenix there are two banks with fairly large issues, the NB of Arizona (3728) and the Phoenix NB (4729). Notes from Mesa, Nogales, and Winslow are also sometimes seen, but they are far from common. Flagstaff, the third largest city in the state, is represented by a single bank, but notes from here are very rare.

The boom years of the Comstock Lode and Virginia City were too early for the NBN era in Nevada, and the development of Las Vegas as a world center for gaming and entertainment really only got going only after 1946. Thus no NBNs were issued for either Virginia City or for Las Vegas, Nevada. During the period of NBNs the economy of Nevada was precariously dependent upon ranching and small-scale mining. As one might expect, Nevada is a very difficult state for NBNs.

Two banks, one in Austin and one in Reno, issued First Charter notes, but all trace of the former has long since vanished. The only bank to issue Second Charter notes, the FNB of Winnemucca (3575), issued a few Brown Backs, and one of these (a $10 note) survives today. A few more banks issued Red Seals, and 11 of these notes are presently known to collectors. One bank that issued Red Seals was the FNB of Rhyolite (8686). Not only did all NBNs from this bank vanish, but so also did the town, today a total ghost in the desert. The state capital of Carson City is still very much alive, but its one and only National Bank (charter 9242) closed after only two years of operations, and no notes are known today from this institution. Most of the surviving large-size notes from Nevada are Third Charter Blue Seals, but all large-size notes from Nevada are very scarce to very rare. According to Don Kelly, there are about 165 large-size notes known from Nevada. This makes this state even rarer for large-size notes than is Arizona, the second rarest Western state. The great majority of Nevada notes, both large- and small-size, are from two different Reno banks, the FNB in Reno (7038) and the Reno NB (8424).

By far the largest collection of NBNs from Nevada ever formed was sold by Heritage Numismatic Auctions in August, 1995. This collection had been assembled by Harvey's Resort Hotel. There were a total of 101 single notes plus four uncut sheets of small-size issues. The "star" item was the unique $10 Brown Back from Winnemucca that sold for $55,000, a price slightly higher than those of the ultra-rare Brown Backs from Idaho and Washington Territories that formed part of the J. L. Irish collection. Other spectacular items included a $10 Red Seal in XF-AU from Reno (7038) and a $10 Blue Seal from the Nevada FNB of Tonopah (8530). These sold for $13,200 and $15,950, respectively.

Although Series 1929 notes have survived from all ten of the Nevada banks that issued them, getting a note from each bank would be a very difficult and expensive task. Only the two Reno banks are normally available, and for all eight of the other banks Don Kelly reports only a total of 153 notes including the notes in uncut sheets. The most "available" of these are the $10 notes of the FNB of Winnemucca (3575), for which 26 examples exist in choice condition. One of these will set you back at least $1250, but that is a cheap price by the standards of notes for the other small Nevada towns. The high end of the scale for a small-size note in the Heritage auction was achieved by a serial number 1 $5 note from the FNB of Elko (7743). It sold for $16,500, a price previously unheard of for any Series 1929 note from any state.

The Reno NB (originally the Nixon NB) was headed by George Wingfield, a big developer in Nevada during the 1910s and 1920s, but one whose banking empire collapsed in the early 1930s. His rival was the FNB in Reno (originally the Farmers and Merchants NB), a more conservative institution that survived the Great Depression. Today it does business as the First Interstate Bank of Nevada. Both issued fairly generous amounts of Third Charter notes, but Wingfield's issues included $50s and $100s, while his rival issued only $5, $10, and $20 notes. In small-size Wingfield issued type 1 $5, $20, $50, and $100 notes (but no $10s), while the rival bank issued type 1 and type 2 $5, $10, and $20 notes. For most collectors these are the only available Nevada notes.

Examples of the Wingfield $5 and $20 small-size notes can be obtained in XF condition for about $300 or $400 each. There are 18 known $50 and 12 known $100 notes. These sold for about $1200 and $1400 each, respectively, in the Heritage auction. The type 1 notes of the other Reno bank exist in VF condition, and in the Heritage auction these sold for about $200 to $300 each. The type 2 notes for this bank, however, are most peculiar. Large numbers of these exist as uncut CU sheets. There are more than 300 examples of the type 2 $5 note, thus making it comparable to the previously mentioned $5

Wichita and $10 Easthampton notes in abundance. If these notes were from a big state, they would be worth about $60 each. But typically the $5 and $10 notes are selling for about $400 each. There were also uncut sheets of these two denominations in the sale, but these sold for only about $1500 each, i. e., about $250 per note. By no means, however, are all of the type 2 notes of this bank in numismatic channels. Most are still in the vaults of the First Interstate Bank in Reno. Although I do not generally favor the cutting up of intact sheets, there are so many of these that there would certainly be no loss to the numismatic community if one or two dozen each of the $5 and $10 sheets were cut apart. The $20 notes are available in smaller quantities, and perhaps most of the existing sheets for this denomination should be preserved. At their present prices, I do not think that these notes make very good investments. Only a fraction of them are presently in numismatic channels, but more will certainly come onto the market from time to time. Although these notes are from a very scarce state, they are individually among the most common of Series 1929 notes for CU condition.

Although I did obtain a couple of items from this sale, I regret not being more aggressive on a few others. The type 1 notes of the FNB in Reno do not exist in the hoard, and they are very much scarcer than are the type 2 notes. Yet these notes (in VF or VF-XF condition rather than CU) sold for less than did the quite common hoard notes. There were also two examples each of the $50 and $100 Blue Seals of the Wingfield bank. The VF examples of these notes sold for only about $2400 - $2900 each. In retrospect I would have bid higher, since any "non-rare" large-size Nevada note (i. e., a $5, $10, or $20 Blue Seal from either of the two Reno banks) sells for more than $1000 when in VF condition.

Thus we come to the end of our discussion of the eight Rocky Mountain states. For small-size notes Utah and Colorado are easily acquired. Montana and New Mexico will be more difficult, but notes in decent VF condition from these states should cost not much more than $100 each. Idaho, Wyoming, Arizona, and Nevada will be increasingly difficult, and probably in that order. If you just want a single Series 1929 note from each of these states, however, none should set you back more than about $250 to $300 in VF condition. For Third Charter Blue Seal notes, however, notes from Nevada will cost at least $1000 each in VF condition, and those from Arizona will be even tougher to acquire. Notes from Idaho and Wyoming should cost more like $500 each in the same condition. Montana and New Mexico will again be less difficult with Colorado and Utah being the easiest of this region to acquire. As recent auction sales indicate, however, there is a huge demand for NBNs from the smaller towns of Colorado, and the most frequently encountered notes of this state are from Denver, its largest city and state capital.

Pacific States

Quite naturally the NBNs of the three Pacific Coast states (CA, OR, and WA) all were printed with a regional letter of "P" in the days when these were used, as were the two offshore states (AK and HI). We have already examined the large-sized issues of the latter two, since they are territorial issues, and technically speaking the Series 1929 notes for these states should also be regarded as territorial issues, although they are not so inscribed.

As I have already noted, large-size notes for Alaska were issued from two different banks, the FNB of Fairbanks (7718) and the FNB of Juneau (5117). The FNB of

Ketchikan (12578) was chartered in 1924, but it issued only small-size notes. Although Alaska notes are not ultra-rare, they are ultra-expensive. The $5 Red Seal from Fairbanks is actually one of the most abundant $5 red seals. Since nearly all of these are in CU condition, it is quite possibly the most common Red Seal note in high grade. Were it from a large state, it would sell for about $600 or a bit more. But these notes now sell for about $14,000 each. This price is well up from $3000, which is about what they sold for in the 1970s. They have proven to have been very good investments for the past two or three decades, but in my opinion the price for this rather common note is already too high.

As for the Series 1929 notes from Alaska, there are presently 17, 10, and 24 examples known from the banks in Fairbanks, Juneau, and Ketchikan, respectively. These data include the individuals in one uncut sheet of type 2 $5 notes from the Fairbanks bank. Aside from a very few notes from small towns in Nevada or other remote locations, almost no Series 1929 notes from other states sell for more than about $3000 each. All of the small-size Alaska notes, however, are extremely expensive, and even heavily circulated examples are now selling for about $10,000 each. If you want one, they are available, but again I feel that there are far more interesting small-size Nationals that can be obtained for much lower prices.

The NBNs of Hawaii are completely dominated by a single bank. On large-size notes the title of this bank is the FNB of Hawaii. On small-size notes it appears either as the Bishop FNB or the Bishop NB of Hawaii.

The NBN issues from Hawaii were totally dominated by a single bank, and the issues from the three small towns on island of Maui that are still known (Kahului, Lahaina, and Wailuku) so all so rare as to be almost noncollectible. The large-size notes from Honolulu are also scarce, and Third Charter Blue Seal notes from this bank cost about the same as do comparable notes from Arizona or Nevada, i. e., about $1500 each in VF condition.

In small-size this bank issued notes either as the Bishop FNB or the Bishop NB of Hawaii. The first of these titles was used on $5, $10, $50, and $100 notes of type 1, and it was also used on type 2 $5 and $10 notes. The second title was used on $5, $10, $50, and $100 notes of type 2. There are no $20 notes, and this is a major peculiarity of the notes from Honolulu. The notes with the first title are much more readily available than are the later notes. In strictly CU condition the $50 note is probably the easiest of the set to obtain, but the other three denominations are also not very difficult to acquire in circulated grades. The type 2 $50 and $100 notes are very scarce, and the $100 note of this issue may even be unique. In 1999 a F-VF example of the type 2 $50 note sold for $2860 in a CAA auction. It is thus an easy matter to acquire one note from this state, but it is a major challenge to acquire all ten possible varieties of the small-size notes from this bank.

Oregon became a state in 1859, but for Washington statehood did not come until 1889. Within a decade after statehood, however, the population of Washington overtook that of its neighbor to the south. Both states issued NBNs in substantial quantities, but Second Charter notes and Red Seals are decidedly rare for both Oregon and Washington. Most collections of these states are limited to Third Charter Blue Seals and Series 1929 notes, but there is a good variety of these for both states. For those who collect notes from the state capitals, Oregon and Washington are perhaps more difficult than any others save the ultra-expensive Juneau, the ultra-rare Tallahassee, and the nonexistent Carson City. There are two known banks each for Salem and for Olympia. But Don Kelly has recorded totals of only 12 notes for the Salem banks and 23 notes for the Olympia banks. For Annapolis, Maryland, by the way, there are only 17 known notes, and so these three cities will probably thwart all but the most determined of state capital collectors.

For Oregon there were a total of 127 issuing charters, of which 79 were used for small-size notes. Many of these banks are unknown in large-size, and several of the banks that issued small-size notes are also still unaccounted for. One characteristic for the NBNs of Oregon is that they are dominated by the banks of Portland, the largest city of the state. Two of the Portland banks, the FNB (1553) and the United States NB (4514) are quite common both in large-size and in Series 1929. In Portland there was also a union bank, the Brotherhood Co-operative NB (12613) and one for an occupation most appropriate for the Northwest, the Lumbermans NB (9180), but notes from the latter bank are quite scarce. Outside of Portland NBNs from Oregon are generally uncommon. Small-size notes from the FNB of Klamath Falls (7167) and the FNB of Medford (7701) are seen more often than are any other non-Portland notes, but neither of these banks can be described as common. Only a small number of $50 and $100 notes were issued in Series 1929 from Oregon banks, and these are rarely seen. Thus Oregon is an easy enough state from which to acquire a few notes, but an extremely difficult one for which to form a comprehensive collection.

During the state period in Washington there were 180 issuing charters, of which 84 issued small-size notes. Of the latter four remain unreported, but there are still numerous banks from Washington that issued large-size notes from which no examples are presently known. Unlike Oregon, however, Washington is not dominated by a single city. Although NBNs are more frequently encountered from Seattle than from elsewhere, there are numerous other towns and cities in Washington for which there are sizable numbers of notes.

The title of the Lumbermans NB of Portland, Oregon denotes an industry that is very important in the American Northwest. The Wells Fargo Nevada NB of San Francisco evokes a company that played a prominent role in the early days of the Old West. Unlike the vast majority of Value Backs, this note carries the designation "secured by bonds" rather than the more typical "secured by bonds or other securities."

One of the largest banks in Seattle went through a confusing change of titles. It began business as the Union NB (11280) and changed to the Dexter Horton NB in 1924. It then became the First Seattle Dexter Horton NB and wound up as the FNB of Seattle having absorbed the original FNB of Seattle (2783) in the process. Series 1929 notes appear with no less than three of the titles of the Dexter Horton bank. Another interesting merged title is that of the Old NB and Union Trust Co. of Spokane (4668). The former bank acquired the latter institution in 1926, but the Union Trust Co. did not have a charter for the issuance of NBNs. In this case the two different titles are found on Third Charter Blue Seals. In Tacoma they favored simpler names for their banks, the largest being the NB of Tacoma (3417). Small-size notes are also frequently encountered from such cities as Bellingham, Everett, and Yakima. The NB of Commerce of Seattle (4375) was the only bank to issue Series 1929 $50s and $100s in any quantity, but these can be obtained without too much difficulty. Thus Washington is a much easier state from which to collect a wide variety of notes than is Oregon.

We conclude our regional survey with California. I have already discussed the National Gold Bank Notes of this state in some detail, and I need not repeat these details here. Regular First Charter notes were issued for the first time only in 1879, and the total issue of these notes (214,686) actually exceeded those of the previous gold notes (200,308). Far fewer regular First Charter notes are known for California than is the case with the gold notes, however, for as I have already noted, the survival characteristics of the National Gold Bank Notes are extremely peculiar.

Throughout the NBN era the state of California was dominated by the banks of a single city, San Francisco. Although Los Angles became a much larger city than San Francisco well before NBNs ceased to be issued in 1935, it was the big San Francisco banks that dominated economic activities in most of the other parts of the state. Since I shall often refer to San Francisco in this discussion, permit me to use the abbreviation, S. F. As I have already noted, the banking laws of California were very different from those of states such as Illinois. In Illinois legislation restricted the big Chicago banks from setting up branches elsewhere in the state. In California just the opposite was true, and towards the end of the NBN era the Bank of America absorbed many dozens of smaller banks eventually growing to become the largest bank in the nation. In terms of the total numbers of NBNs issued S. F. is second only to New York as a city. Chicago ranks third, but it doesn't even remotely come close to S. F. in terms of the total numbers of notes that were issued by its banks.

Collectors of NBNs from California should feel most thankful to William K. Raymond of Fresno. He has compiled a thorough documentation of California NBNs of all vintages and has documented more than 10,000 notes for the state. In the June, 1992 issue of the *Bank Note Reporter* I published an article that detailed the survival characteristics of the NBNs of California, and it was the data supplied by Mr. Raymond that enabled me to undertake the statistical analyses that I made. There are large numbers of very common Third Charter Blue Seals and Series 1929 notes, and his data for these series are almost certainly not complete. In my opinion California is probably about as abundant a state as is Texas in terms of NBNs. Thus something like 20,000 notes are probably available for the entire state.

For California there were a total of 415 issuing charters, and of these 172 issued small-size notes. At present six of the latter are unknown. A fairly good variety of notes can be obtained from both the Second and Third Charter periods provided one is willing to stick to a fairly small number of towns and cities, headed most naturally by San Francisco. In California a total of 60 banks issued Brown Backs, and of these 28 issued Date Backs, and of these 14 issued Value Backs. These sort of ratios are typical of any state, since the two later series of Second Charter notes would only have been issued by banks that had already issued Brown Backs. Although there was a range of dates over which these notes were issued, the survival ratio did not differ very widely for the three different series. Based on the data that Raymond had assembled by the mid-1980s, about one note for every 15,000 that was issued had survived. One of the most readily available banks for these types is the Wells-Fargo Nevada NB of S. F. (5105). This bank issued all three series of Second Charter notes, and it had previously issued Brown Backs using the title of the Nevada NB. The Wells Fargo Bank also issued Third Charter Plain Backs, but it ceased to hold a national charter after 1923, thus becoming the largest bank in the nation not to issue NBNs at that time. Another good bank for Second Charter notes is the FNB of Los Angeles (2491).

The First National Gold Bank of San Francisco was much the largest of the nine national gold banks that operated in California, and the $5 note of this bank is by far the most abundant of these issues. Despite an unusually high survival rate (almost 250 notes out of 33,000 issued), these notes have the same condition problems that are found on all of these issues.

For California a total of 113 banks issued Third Charter Red Seals. This is one type of notes for which the large S. F. banks did not dominate the production. Most of them were issuing Brown Backs at this time. Since most California Red Seals were issued by relatively small banks, they are not common and only about 150 of them are known at the present time. Oddly enough, the catastrophic earthquake of April 18, 1906 did not result in the closure of a single national bank anywhere in California despite the huge amount of property loss.

Third Charter Blue Seals were issued by more than 300 of the banks in California, but once again their issue was dominated by the big banks of San Francisco. Two big issuers of these notes were the Crocker NB (3555) and the FNB (1741). These merged at the end of 1925 to form the Crocker FNB, which used the lower charter number of these two on its notes. Two other major issuers were the Bank of California (9655) and the oddly-named London Paris NB (9174). The name of the latter was changed to the Anglo & London Paris NB, and it also issued small-size notes with this title and as the Anglo-California NB. Subsequently it was acquired by the Wells Fargo Bank.

Although there were 172 different banks in California that issued Series 1929 notes, about 40% of these were issued by a single bank, the Bank of America (13044). This bank was chartered only in 1927, and it issued Blue Seals and its first series of small-size notes as the Bank of Italy. It changed its title to the present one in 1930. The founder of this bank, Amadeo P. Giannini, was a very dynamic individual who took over large numbers of banks during the Depression years. For Series 1929 this bank issued almost 11 million notes, an amount that was exceeded only by the Chase NB of New York (2370). In terms of dollar volume, however, the issues of the Bank of America exceeded those of the Chase NB by a substantial margin.

The Bank of America issued Series 1929 notes in all five denominations but in three different series. Both the Bank of Italy and its later title were used on type 1 notes, and the present title was also used on type 2 notes. A 16th variety is also possible for this bank, since the type 2 $5 notes exist with either A or B prefixes, the latter being the only issue among the several thousands of different varieties of type 2 $5 NBNs to have this serial number prefix. Although all type 2 $50 and $100 NBNs are scarce, there are at least enough type 2 $100s from this bank around to keep this type out of the rarity class. These were the only type 2 $50 and $100 notes issued from California, but there are a total of 16 different notes for each of these denominations in Series 1929 for the entire state. Three of the Los Angles banks (2491, 5927, and 6617) were also major issuers of these notes.

California is an interesting state to collect provided you are more interested in the different types of notes and in changes in bank titles than you are in notes from numerous small towns. Aside from San Francisco and Los Angeles only a few varieties of notes from Oakland and Sacramento can be described as genuinely common. Several large cities of the state (e. g., Bakersfield, Fresno, Long Beach, San Diego, San Jose, etc.) are actually very scarce. But next to New York City, San Francisco is probably the most interesting and diverse city in the nation to collect in terms of national bank notes. The present-day enormous population of California means that there is heavy demand for all but the most common notes of this state, and so it is not an easy state from which to assemble a collection that emphasizes diversity in its representation of towns and cities.

In May, 1999 CAA auctioned the collection of California national bank notes formed by Charles Colver, who died in the previous year. This collection, which consisted of more than 500 notes, emphasized diversity in its number of different banks and towns. Although a fair number of notes from San Francisco were present, they did not dominate this collection as is os often the case with offerings of NBNs from California. The auction catalog itself was beautifully prepared, and it contained much auxiliary information about the towns and their banks together with many old photographs. I would think that this sale attracted almost every serious California NBN collectors in the nation, and the prices realized were very firm in almost all cases. The most expensive items was an uncut sheet of $5 Brown Backs from Covina (5830) that sold for $77,000. Ten of the individual notes sold for more than $10,000 each including a Series 1875 $20 from Los Angeles (2491) in VF, a $10 Brown Back from San Louis Obispo (3826) in VF+, and a $20 Blue Seal from National City (9512) that was only in fine condition. These notes for $16,500, $17,600, and $17,600, respectively. The great majority of the notes in the Colver collection were Series 1902 Blue Seals or Series 1929 notes, as might be expected from a collection that emphasized geographical diversity. With its huge present-day population California can be excepted to be an extremely popular state for NBN collectors. High prices can be expected for notes from most localities in this state, which is so heavily dominated by the big San Francisco banks.

Having completed my geographical survey of national bank notes, I wish to conclude with a few general remarks. Before acquiring many NBNs I think that you should have some idea of what you plan to do. The three most popular approaches are to collect them on a type basis, or on a state by state basis (e. g., a couple of notes from each state), or on an in depth basis for a particular state or closely related group of states. As you can see from this detailed survey, some states are much easier to collect than are others. Some states that are fairly small (e. g., Kansas or Nebraska) have a large diversity of available notes, whereas others that are comparable in size (e. g., Florida or Maryland) only have a limited variety of notes that are readily available.

Before doing anything serious with NBNs you should definitely acquire the current edition of the Don Kelly catalog, and I would also recommend the Hickman-Oakes catalog as well. In this chapter I have given numerous data on the prices of NBNs, but you should be very cautious about any of the prices that appear for specific banks in any of the catalogs. These are computer generated, and they fail to take all of the relevant factors into account. For instance, the Brotherhood of Locomotive Engineers $5 note from Cleveland that was previously mentioned is of a common type from a major city in a big state. But its unique title results in a very heavy demand for this note, and it is far more expensive than any other big city Ohio note of comparable abundance. The price quoted in the Hickman-Oakes catalog for this note is absurdly low. Experience is probably the best guide as to what to pay for a given note.

In a later chapter of this book I shall discuss the sources of currency in detail. Since many NBNs are common and fairly inexpensive, I would suggest starting off by buying them at shows or mail order from dealers. You will soon probably also be obtaining them from auctions. Some of the auction catalogs that have been prepared for the major collections of these notes are valuable references in themselves. For the major NBN collections that he has sold in recent years, Lyn Knight has included much auxiliary information about the towns and the banks including old photos of some of the banks and street scenes from these towns during the NBN era.

Most auctioneers either do not allow or are very reluctant to accept "buy" bids. I do not recommend this form of bidding for any lots, but it is particularly inappropriate for NBNs. As I have already noted, there are some collectors who have been waiting for years to acquire a note from a specific bank or town or with a particular set of bank signatures. They may be willing to pay a price far higher than normal market for a note that they have been seeking for years. Occasionally bids on NBNs go completely runaway. I acted as agent on a group of notes that were sold by CAA in their May, 1996 sale. One of the notes I sent them was a $5 Blue Seal from the FNB of Cheraw, SC (9342). The note was in fine condition, but with some obvious rust stains. According to Don Kelly, there are five known examples. To be sure it is a scarce note, but not an outstanding rarity. It was sold for $1265, which is about $1000 more than I think it was actually worth, but there was the ideal vendor situation at this auction, i. e., two individuals who were not good friends hotly bidding against each other for the note.

In forming my large collection of NBNs, I have generally used a "shotgun" approach. I have submitted large numbers of relatively conservative bids on many of the notes in a sale that met my minimum condition standards (usually VF or better). Using this approach I am rarely successful on a high percentage of the notes on which I submit bids, but overall I do win quite a few. I collect notes by variety, and so I consider major type and denomination in forming my collection. I do distinguish between type 1 and type 2 Series 1929 notes and between Date Back and Plain Back Third Charter Blue Seals, as do the specialized catalogs. I have not bothered with the differences that these catalogs generally ignore such as the presence or absence of regional letters on Brown Backs and Third Charter Plain Backs or the two varieties of serial numbers on the latter issues. The different type fonts that appear on some of the Series 1929 notes might be interesting, but there is very little information about them in the standard catalogs so I generally ignore them. As I have already noted, I am little interested in bank signatures, but there are a few collectors who are immensely interested in these. I have also had no interest thus far in trying to trace my relatives on NBNs. On my mother's side I am of Swedish descent, but my father was descended from French Huguenots who came to Virginia in the 1600s and then dispersed to numerous Southern locations. As least one of them must have had something to do with the Munroe and Chambliss NB of Ocala, Florida (10578), but given the frustrating nature of NBNs from Florida I haven't tried very hard to chase that bank down.

I have tried to keep the types of NBNs that I have roughly in parallel with each other. It is no accident that I have four each of the $50 and $100 Brown Backs and two each of the $50 and $100 Red Seals. I have more $100 Blue Seals than I do $50 notes of this type (or types if you regard the Date Backs and Plain Backs as distinct), but that is largely due to a large collection of $100 Blue Seals that Lyn Knight made available some years ago. Naturally I have far more of the $5, $10, and $20 notes of all of these issues, but even here my collection is roughly balanced in numbers between these three denominations. For Series 1929 notes I have more $10 and $20 notes than $5 notes, largely because the rate of survival was much better for the $10s and $20s than it was for the $5 notes of this series. As I think you may have realized, I have an interest in the $50 and $100 notes of this series. They are under much less pressure than are the large-size $50 and $100 NBNs, and many are still readily available. Unlike the many thousands of varieties that exist for $5, $10, and $20 notes of Series 1929, there are only a total of 348 possibilities for the $50 notes and 325 for the $100 notes, but a fair number of these are quite unknown. In my collection there are presently 66 different $50 and 46 different $100 notes for Series 1929 NBNs. Although far from complete, these are fair percentages for each of these issues.

Let me close this chapter with a remark on buyer courtesy. You should recognize that some collectors have been searching for years for a particular NBN, and you should acknowledge their desire for that note. When I add a new Third Charter Blue Seal to my collection of NBNs from Ohio (for instance), it is just one more note in my already fairly respectable holding of notes from this state. If I am a floor bidder at an auction, I would set a fairly modest limit as to what I would pay for such a note. It could be, however, that I might be bidding against a collector who has been seeking that particular note for years because it bears his grandfather's signature, or it is from the town in which his mother was born, or the bank is the one that granted him a mortgage when others refused, etc. Then by all means, let him have the note at a reasonable price. You should neither want to pay an inflated priced for a note, nor should you want to have a fellow collector pay an inflated price just because you have a less than compelling interest in the same item.

CHAPTER EIGHT

MILITARY PAYMENT CERTIFICATES

Military Payment Certificates (MPCs) differ substantially from all other types of U. S. paper money in several respects. They were intended exclusively for circulation abroad, and they were issued through the Department of Defense and not through the Treasury Department or the Federal Reserve System. While other types of American paper money are printed by intaglio engraving on silk paper, MPCs are surface printed on paper containing small planchettes, a feature that has also been used on the bank notes of Canada and several other nations for many years. Unlike all other types of U. S. government paper money, all series of MPCs thus far issued have been retired and thus none remain valid today.

MPCs were intended for use exclusively by U. S. military personnel stationed abroad in nations in which the local economies and currencies were relatively weak. In order to make it difficult for black markets to operate, American military personnel in these countries were paid cash exclusively with MPCs, which in theory could only be used on base. To further discourage speculation, the issue of a new series of MPCs and the invalidation of an old one were made on very short notice. As a result of these practices, however, many of the MPCs are today quite scarce. This is particularly true of some of the higher denomination notes.

As I stated previously, during World War II there were two special issues of U. S. currency intended for use in or near areas of military operations. These were the Hawaii notes and the so-called North Africa notes. Had appreciable numbers of either of these fallen into enemy hands they could have been demonetized, but since that did not happen, these notes continue as valid currency. Unlike these two issues the MPCs were issued as a type of money over which the U. S. military could exercise exclusive control. At the same time the circulation of other types of U. S. currency could be restricted, as often was the case.

Thirteen different series of MPCs were issued between 1946 and 1973. The designation on the first issue, Series 461, stands for the first series to be designed in 1946. The second issue was Series 471, while the third issue was Series 472, i. e., the second issue to be designed in 1947. In several instances series of MPCs were designed and printed well before they were actually issued. All series of MPCs contained four fractional denominations (5¢, 10¢, 25¢, and 50¢) plus $1, $5, and $10 notes. The last three series also included $20 notes in addition to the seven lower denominations, but $2, $50, and $100 MPCs were never issued.

The first seven series of MPCs (Series 461 through 591) were printed either by the Tudor Press Incorporated or the Forbes Lithograph Corporation, both of which are located in Boston. The Forbes firm was also actively involved in the production of Allied Military Currency in the later years of World War II and in the immediate postwar era. Indeed the first three issues of MPCs resemble to a fair extent several of the Allied military notes. The last six issue of MPCs (Series 611 through 692) were printed by the BEP in Washington, DC.

The sizes of the MPCs are as follows:

fractionals	110 x 54 mm
$1 notes	110 x 66 mm
later $5 notes	135 x 66 mm
$10, $20, and earlier $5	156 x 66 mm

The sizes of the $10, $20, and the first four issues of the $5 MPCs are the same as those of the normal small-size notes. The last nine series of $5 MPCs, however, are a bit shorter, and all of the $1 MPCs are very much shorter than are normal American paper money. The fractional notes were printed in sheets of 84 subjects, the $1 notes in sheets of 70, and the higher denominations in sheets of 50 subjects each. All MPCs contain a sheet position number in addition to an individual serial number. Sometimes this number is referred to as a plate number, but that designation is incorrect. Plate numbers do not appear anywhere on MPCs.

A fresh pack of 100 notes will contain consecutively numbered MPCs, all of which have the same sheet position number. Even for the most common MPCs it would be extremely difficult to assemble a complete group of all possible sheet position numbers, and almost no collectors attempt to collect these notes in such a fashion. The normal MPCs of Series 461 all have an eight-digit serial number preceded and followed by the letter A. Series 471 uses the BB block, while Series 472 has the CC block, etc. This way of designating notes continues through the letter H (Series 611), which is then followed by J (Series 641), but for the issue that follows this one (Series 651) the AA block is again used. The last three issues (Series 661, 681, and 692) use the BB, CC, and EE blocks, respectively.

It appears that all issues of MPCs were printed, cut, and numbered in batches or units of 8000 sheets each. Thus there were 672,000 notes in each unit of fractional MPCs, 560,000 examples in each unit of $1 notes, and 400,000 notes in each unit of the higher denomination MPCs. The first example of a fractional note having sheet position # 1 would indeed have serial number 1, but the first note having sheet position # 2 would have serial number 8001. The serial number of the last note on the first sheet (i. e. the note having position # 84) would be 664001, and the serial number of the first note on the second sheet (again having position # 1) would be 00000002. The serial numbers of the position #1 notes in this unit thus would range from 1 to 8000, while those of the position # 84 notes would be from 00664001 - 00672000. The serial number 00672001 would then appear on the position #1 note of the first sheet to be printed in the second batch or production unit of these notes to be manufactured. To further investigate the numbering system for MPCs, let us consider the Series 461 $10 note that is in my collection. It has serial number A25062447A and sheet position # 33. Dividing the serial number by 400,000, the size of a production unit of $10 MPCs, yields 62.6561. Thus this note was in the 63rd unit of these notes to be printed. Taking the fractional part of this quotient (0.6561) and multiplying this amount by 50 (the number of notes in each sheet for this denomination) we come up with 32.805. Since this result lies between 32 and 33, the sheet position number must be 33, as indeed it is.

270/military payment certificates · U. S. Paper Money

The four scarcest of the regularly issued MPCs are the $5 notes of Series 471, 521, 541, and 591. All of these series were issued and used during peacetime years, but only small quantities of the higher values of each of these series were either put aside or escaped destruction by accident.

Replacement notes for normal issues of U. S. paper money are designated with stars that appear either at the end of a serial number (for Federal Reserve Notes or for FRBNs) or at the beginning of this number (for almost all other types). Regular issues of MPCs have the same block letter both at the beginning and at the end of the serial number, while MPC replacement notes have a series letter only at the beginning of their serials. Replacement MPCs are of great interest to many collectors, and these I shall discuss in substantial detail later.

In my opinion a complete set of normal (i. e., non-replacement) MPCs consists of 95 different notes. This includes two different varieties of Series 481 $1 notes (more or less equally abundant) and the four fractional notes of Series 651 that were in use for only a few days. All of the other 48 fractional notes and all 14 of the $1 MPCs are readily available in at least F-VF condition, and most of these are easily obtained in AU or CU, although a few of the earlier notes are decidedly scarce in the highest grades. Among the higher denomination notes there are several that are very scarce, especially in choice condition. It is possible to obtain a complete set of all 95 of these notes, but this is not at all an easy task.

Series 461 (issued 1946-1947), 471 (1947-1948), 472 (1948-1951), and 481 (1951-1954) were used in many countries of Europe and in Asia (Japan, Korea, and the Philippines). All four of these series feature "generic" designs, in which basically the same design and color scheme is used for all denominations of a given series. Series 461 and 471, in fact, differ only in their color schemes, the former having gray black and light blue faces, while for the latter series the colors are red and light blue. Although they were in use for only about six months, all notes of Series 461 are readily available, although most of the denominations are a bit hard to come by in the highest grades. The $5 and $10 notes of Series 471, however, are very scarce. The $5 notes of this series has often been regarded as the rarest of the normal-issue MPCs, but it is now clear that the Series 541 $5 note is definitely much rarer, at least in circulated grades. The $5 and $10 notes of Series 472 are also scarce, but not as scarce as are those of Series 471. For most of the earlier series of MPCs (up through Series 591) the $5 note is decidedly scarcer than is its $10 counterpart in the same series.

Series 481 MPCs were produced in two distinct varieties based upon the location of the position number either right or left.

Series 481 was produced in four distinct printings. For all but the $1 notes the differences among the printings are quite trivial, but the $1 notes of this series can be found in two readily distinguished varieties, those with position numbers on their right sides are from the first and fourth printing, while notes of the second and third printings have these numbers on their left sides. I chose to regard this as a major type difference, and since both varieties are readily available, obtaining both of these varieties for a collection should pose no problems. The $5 and $10 notes of Series 481 are easy to obtain in VF condition, but they are very much scarcer in CU. The faces of these notes feature a reclining male figure that was adapted from the backs of Series 1902 $50 national bank notes. Series 481 was the issue of MPCs that was most widely used during the Korean War.

A wider range of colors and more imaginative designs appear on the MPCs of Series 521 (in use 1954-1958), 541 (1958-1961), and 591 (1961-1964). Series 541 was the last issue of MPCs to be used extensively in continental Europe. Outside of Asia the use of MPCs continued for a bit longer only in rather isolated countries such as Iceland and Libya (pre-Qadhafi, of course). Despite the fact that these series were used in comparatively peaceful times, the $5 and $10 values of all three series are very scarce to very rare.

The Series 541 $5 note is without doubt the rarest of all normal issue MPCs, and this note is only infrequently offered for sale. Although a VG-F example of this note can be obtained for about $400 or so, an example of this item in AU condition or better would sell for more than $2000 in today's market. The $10 note of this series along with the $10 note of Series 591, and the $5 notes of Series 521 and 591 are also in the very scarce to rare categories, especially in high grades. Even the fractional notes and the $1 note of Series 591 are very hard to come by in choice condition, this series being by far the most difficult to acquire for the regularly issued low denomination MPCs. The notes of these three series (521, 541, and 591) depict allegorical female portraits on their faces (and sometimes backs as well), although the face depicted on the fractional notes of Series 591 is clearly that of the Statue of Liberty. The rare $5 note of this series depicts a geisha girl on its face.

The Series 611 $10 MPC depicts a portrait that resembles Marilyn Monroe,

The notes of Series 611 (in use 1964-1969) were the first to be printed by the BEP. They continue to feature female portraits on their faces, as do the next three series (641, 651, and 661). Although intended as allegorical, the portraits on the $1, $5, and $10 notes of Series 611 closely resemble Grace Kelly, Kim Novak, and Marilyn Monroe, respectively. These notes were designed in 1961 when all three of these movie stars were still living, but they were not actually issued until after Marilyn Monroe's death in 1962.

Beginning in 1965 there were two parallel series of MPCs in use at the same time. Series 611 and 651 (1969-1973) were used in Japan and Korea, while Series 641 (1965-1968) was the first series to be used exclusively in Vietnam. Series 641 and 651 have identical designs, but the color schemes are different and notes of the latter series all have a depiction of the Minuteman statue at their left ends. By 1970 the economies of Japan and Korea had strengthened to the point where there was no real reason for using MPCs. They were out of use in Japan by this time, but the use of the higher denomination MPCs of Series 651 continued in Korea until late in 1973.

Series 641 MPCs were used exclusively in Vietnam between 1965 and 1968, while Series 651 notes were used in Japan and Korea (but very largely in the latter country) between 1969 and 1973. The designs of these two series are quite similar, but notes of the latter series depict a Minuteman at their left sides and their colors are quite different from those of Series 641. The Series 651 fractionals are rare, since they were removed from circulation almost immediately after being released.

The $1, $5, and $10 notes of Series 651 are readily collectible, although the two higher denominations are scarce in choice condition. The fractional notes of this series, however, were put into use for only a few days and these are presently very rare. At first it was felt that none of these notes had been released, but then a single circulated 50¢ note came onto the market. In recent years several CU sets of all four of these fractional notes have sold either at auction or in private sales.

Without doubt the Series 651 fractionals are the most controversial of all of the MPCs. The total printings of these notes were large - 4,032,000 each for the 5¢ and 10¢ denominations, 2,688,000 for the 25¢, and 2,016,000 for the 50¢ notes, these numbers corresponding, respectively, to six, four, and three production units of 672,000 notes each. The first of these items to be discovered was a single 50¢ cent note that sold for the extremely high price of $6000 in the early 1980s. At that time it was thought that this one note was the only fractional of this series to have escaped destruction. It is now clear that these notes, although very rare, are far from being unique.

At the present time about two dozen notes for each denomination have serial numbers that have been recorded, but it is likely that the true number of notes already known for each denomination may be as much as double this figure. Almost all of these notes are in CU condition. The serial numbers of these notes fall into compact ranges, and this makes it seem possible that all notes within such ranges may exist. In that case there could be something like 150 notes for each denomination. The known 5¢ notes have sheet position numbers of 63 or 74, the 10¢ notes numbers of 66, 69, or 82, the 25¢ notes numbers of 59 or 78, and the 50¢ notes numbers of 7, 72, or 84. The colors of these notes are as follows: blue and violet for the 5¢ note, dark red and green for the 10¢ note, blue green and dark red for the 25¢ note, and dark brown and orange for the 50¢ note.

In 1990 a set of these four notes was sold by Stack's for $4400. More recent sales by other auctioneers have been closer to $3500 per set, but a price of $4400 was again achieved for a set of these fractionals at a Lyn Knight auction in June, 1998. Although the standard currency catalogs continue to list these items at much higher prices, it seems unlikely that prices much higher than those quoted above will prevail now that it is known that at least three or four dozen sets of these notes are in existence. Indeed prices could fall, if it turns out that there are at least 100 or more examples of each note in existence. At one time these four notes were regarded as noncollectible, but that is no longer the case. In fact, a set of the four rarest of the $5 MPCs (i. e., those of Series 471, 521, 541, and 591) in AU or CU condition would sell for much more in today's market than would a CU set of the four rare fractionals. I have recently acquired a set of these notes at a price that is somewhat less than any of the recent auction realizations. I confess, however, that buying these notes is a bit of a gamble. Since very few of these notes have been sold thus far, it seems certain that they do not exist in quantities of multiple hundreds or thousands. But only during the past few years has it become clear that there are at least a few dozen of these sets in existence. Each set that is sold reveals more information about the ranges of serial numbers that are probable, and these data in turn allow us to form better estimates of the total numbers of these notes that are in existence.

Together with Series 641, Series 661 (1968-1969), 681 (1969-1970), and 692 (1970-1972) were used exclusively in Vietnam. These last three series include $20 notes as well as all seven of the lower values. All denominations of Series 641 are easily acquired, although the $5 and $10 notes of this series are a bit expensive when in CU condition. The 5¢ through $5 notes of Series 661 are very readily available in CU, but the $10 and $20 notes of this series are very scarce in all grades. Series 681 is especially military in its designs. All branches of the U. S. armed forces are honored on these notes, although the fractional notes depict an astronaut in space on their backs. The design of the $10 note is particularly evocative of the nation in which it was used. It is fairly easy to obtain complete sets of Series 681 in CU condition, and at one time large numbers of the $20 notes of this series in circulated condition were available for well under their face value. In recent years, however, it seems that the supply of these notes has largely dried up.

The $10 note for Series 681 depicts a Vietnamese war scene and Series 692 $20 note depicts Chief Ouray of the Utes. Note also that both pieces are replacements.

Series 692 is probably the most beautiful of all the MPC issues. The $1 and $5 notes again depict female portraits on their faces, but their backs depict a bison and a family of elk, respectively. The bison vignette used on the $1 note of this series was taken from that used on the Series 1901 $10 United States Note. The $10 and $20 notes of Series 692 depict American Indians, but neither uses the portrait that appears on Series 1899 $5 silver certificates. Complete sets of Series 692 appear from time to time in CU condition, but they are expensive at about $1000 per set. The $5, $10, and $20 notes of this series are also fairly difficult to find in circulated condition, but in 1997 Lyn F. Knight offered small wholesale lots of the $10 and $20 notes of this series in F-VF condition in two of his auctions, and so it now seems likely that new supplies of these notes may be coming onto the market. It seems logical to me that a few black marketeers in Vietnam must have been stuck with quantities of these notes when they were invalidated in 1973.

Perhaps the controls for MPCs were so tight by the early 1970s that this situation did not arise to any extent.

Series 691 and 701 MPCs were also designed and printed over 20 years ago. Series 691 notes use the serial number block DD, and their designs closely resemble those of Series 541. This issue was intended as a replacement for Series 651, and apparently it exists only in denominations of $1, $5, $10, and $20. The $20 note, which was not printed in the original Series 541, depicts an allegorical female portrait in keeping with the other designs of this issue. Series 701 has entirely new designs and uses the serial number block FF. All eight denominations from 5¢ through $20 are included, and these depict famous American writers and inventors such as Mark Twain, Thomas Edison, and Robert Fulton. Presumably both of these series are in storage, and one or both of these issues may be put into use at some future date. The U. S. military has been very secretive about releasing any information on these notes, and even the designs of these notes have only been gleaned from rather cryptic information. There was some consideration given to putting at least one of these issues into use during Operations Desert Shield and Storm in 1990-91, but that action was not undertaken. It is also possible that these issues have in large part been destroyed. Unfortunately, the Department of Defense is not forthcoming about the present status of these two series of MPCs.

As I have already noted, it is not an easy matter to complete a collection of the normal MPCs. Many are quite common, and these can be easily obtained at low prices. Some issues are very easy to obtain in CU condition, but other issues are very rare in this grade. Excluding the Series 651 fractionals the five lower denominations (i. e., 5¢, 10¢, 25¢, 50¢, and $1) for all issues from Series 611 through 692 are readily obtainable in CU condition. Series 661 $5 notes are also very abundant in this grade, and the higher values of Series 641, 651, and 681 can be obtained in high grades without much difficulty. The $10 and $20 notes of Series 661 and the $5, $10, and $20 notes of Series 692 will all pose challenges, but more notes in circulated grades of the latter issue seem now to be coming onto the market. The $5 and $10 values of Series 611 are decidedly rare in CU condition, but nice XF or AU examples of these notes do appear for sale fairly often.

Although none of the notes of Series 461 (i. e., the first issue of MPCs) are scarce in circulated grades, this is not at all an easy issue to complete in AU or CU condition. The same can be said for Series 481, where the $5 and $10 notes are readily available in VF condition, but they are very scarce in AU or CU. The 5¢ note of Series 472 exists in large quantities in CU condition, but some of the other denominations of this issue are difficult to acquire in high grades. As is typical of the earlier MPCs, it is the $5 note of this series that is the scarcest of the set. Both the $5 and $10 notes of Series 471 are very scarce in choice condition. Although the Series 471 $5 was once regarded as the rarest of all MPCs, it is offered for sale far more frequently than is the Series 541 $5 note. A strictly CU Series 471 $5 note would cost at least $4000 to $5000 in today's market, but attractive VF examples of this rarity can be obtained for about $750 or so.

Series 521, 541, and 591 all contain notes that are very scarce. The fractional notes of Series 521 and 541 are easy to acquire in choice condition, and there are sizable quantities of Series 541 5¢ notes available in CU condition. For the $1 values of these two series, that of Series 521 is the more readily available in high grades, but neither of these two notes are very difficult. As I have already noted, however, all notes of Series 591 are scarce in choice condition and a set of the five lower values of this issue will presently cost at least $500 in the CU grade. The $10 notes of these three issues are in each case significantly less rare than are their $5 counterparts, but all six of these notes are rarities in CU condition. In general the printings for $10 MPCs were substantially larger than they were for the corresponding $5 notes. Since there were no $20 (prior to 1968), $50, or $100 MPCs it was necessary to print fairly large numbers of $10 notes for each series to take care of transactions where large amounts of cash were needed. I would suggest that you settle for VF or XF condition only on the $5 and $10 notes of these issues unless you have substantial funds and lots of patience. The Series 591 $5 note is probably at least as rare as is the more highly touted Series 471 $5 note. The Series 521 $5 note is somewhat more "common," but both of these notes are very scarce even in VF condition. As noted on more than one occasion, the Series 541 $5 note is the rarest of all of these issues. It is very scarce even in VG-F condition, and expect to pay at least $1500 or more for this note in VF-XF condition. In CU condition it is almost as rare as is the Series 471 $5 note that is often considered to be the great rarity among MPCs in this grade.

Thus I would suggest going for a variety of grades, if you want to obtain a complete collection of the normal MPCs. A few notes (such as the $5 note of Series 661) are probably more readily obtainable in CU condition than they are in any other grade, but many of the earlier issues are very elusive in this condition. From Series 611 on, most notes can be obtained in CU, but for the earlier notes it is probably much better to settle for VF or XF condition in many instances. Big savings can be had if you are willing to settle for VG-F condition on a few of the rarest notes, but MPCs in this condition are definitely not very attractive. I would prefer to be patient and wait for better copies to come along. Almost all of the Series 651 fractionals are available only in CU condition, and they are still quite expensive. Time will tell how much these four notes are really worth, but these notes may eventually sell at prices that are somewhat lower than their present market value of about $4500 per set. Although current editions of all of the catalogs that list MPCs price these notes at $10,000 or more per set, do not believe these prices! We now know that at least two or three dozen sets exist for these notes, and more may come onto the market within the next few years.

In January, 1998 Stack's auctioned the largest collection of uncirculated MPCs that had been seen on the market for many years. Almost all of the regular issue varieties were offered in this grade. During the previous month Spink America also sold a number of significant MPC items, and together these sales provide good indicators as to what top grade MPCs are bringing in today's market. By series the results were as follows:

Series 461	$616	Series 541	$4483	Series 661	$1287
471	5067	591	3630	681	495
472	1419	611	1061	692	880
481 (8)	1507	641	385		
521	2321	651 (3)	209		

This list is somewhat hybrid, since the Series 471 $5 note in the Stack's auction was only in XF condition. Thus for this series alone I have combined realizations from the Stack's and Spink's sales. All other data are exclusively from the Stack's sale. The total for all of these series was $23,360 (including, of course, the 10% buyer's charge). As might be expected, the two most expensive items were the Series 471 $5 note and the

Series 541 $5 issue. They sold for $3520 each, but the Series 471 $5 in the Spink sale was closer to AU-CU than to gem CU and the Series 541 $5 uncirculated note in the Stack's auction was not well centered. It seems that buyer demand on a few of the rare items that were available in the Spink sale had been partially satisfied by the time of the Stack's sale a month later. In the former auction CU examples of the Series 471 $10 note and the Series 521 $5 and $10 notes fetched $1320, $2200, and $1430, respectively. In the latter sale quite similar notes of these types sold for only $963, $1320, and $688, respectively. The market for rare MPCs is still fairly thin, and the addition of more items to the supply available to collectors can affect the prices that one can expect to pay for these notes.

We now turn to the replacement notes for MPCs. If you plan to acquire any of these, it is absolutely essential that you obtain a copy of the *Comprehensive Catalog of Military Payment Certificates* by Fred Schwan. This book contains an enormous amount of information about MPCs in general, but the exquisite detail that Schwan reveals on replacement MPCs in his catalog is found nowhere else. For many years Mr. Schwan has diligently studied these notes, and he has compiled censuses of all the notes that have become known to him. At the present time he knows of rather more than 2109 of these notes as of early in early 1999.

Within a few weeks of the deadline for this book two electrifying discoveries in MPC replacements were made. The first examples of Series 472 25¢ and Series 541 $5 were reported in collections! Obviously discoveries such as these are very important to the fraternity of MPC collectors, but they are also interesting to less specialized collectors as well. It had been ten years since such a discovery had been made so it was quite amazing when two were found in such a short time. Fred Schwan arranged for the illustrations of these great replacements to appear here.

Excluding the fractional notes of Series 651, for which no replacements are known, replacement notes are now recorded for 88 out of the other 91 possible varieties of the normal MPCs. At the present time only the $5 notes of Series 481, and 651 and the 25¢ note of Series 591 have not been recorded in replacement form by Fred Schwan. Six of the replacement notes are presently believed to be unique, and there are several other MPCs that can be regarded as excessively rare in replacement form. See the accompanying table sumarizing the survery of MPC replacements.

MPC replacements reported in collections

Series	5¢	10¢	25¢	50¢	$1	$5	$10	$20	Total
461	21	21	7	5	19	9	10		92
471	6	9	7	4	12	3	3		44
472	34	25	1	7	19	1	3		90
481	24	38	21	2	11	0	4		100
521	26	18	12	9	10	8	6		89
541	45	70	24	89	20	1	8		257
591	31	6	0	3	7	1	5		53
611	127	145	7	1	170	10	19		479
641	84	22	27	17	16	7	52		225
651	*	*	*	*	1	0	5		6
661	16	59	19	5	66	14	9	14	202
681	38	24	4	32	27	11	17	45	198
692	86	75	29	20	32	3	6	23	274
							Grand total		2109

*Possibly not issued, unlikely to be found. For the 481 $1 eight are the" left variety," and three are the "right variety."

If you wish to include replacement notes in your collection of MPCs, clearly you cannot hope to obtain a "complete" set of all 88 known varieties. The best collection of replacement MPCs to be sold in years was offered by Currency Auctions of America in September, 1997, but it only contained about three dozen varieties of these notes. The rarest of these was the unique example of the Series 591 $5 note in F-VF condition. It was sold for $5500. In his catalog Fred Schwan reports on a few larger collections that were formed in earlier years, the largest of these having 76 different examples. Clearly it takes both great patience as well as substantial funds to form a major collection of these notes.

In discussing the star notes of the Series 1929 FRBNs I indicated that it is not possible to obtain a "complete" set of all 45 varieties that have been recorded. One can obtain, however, a set of star notes that contains one note for each of the five denominations. This approach could be used for replacement MPCs, but it probably does not have much appeal since the designs for the various issues of MPCs are so different. For a denomination set of eight values you will almost certainly find that the $5 replacement notes are the most difficult to obtain. Another approach would be to obtain one replacement note for each of the 13 different issues, but Series 651 notes are excessively rare and Series 471 and 591 replacement notes are also very difficult to acquire. I expect that most collectors just try to obtain these notes as they come along. Condition can be a problem on some of these issues, but several of the more common replacement MPCs are from hoards of uncirculated notes. At the present time I have about 35 replacement MPCs in my collection. This includes two notes that are true rarities (the Series 461 $10 and Series 521 50¢ notes), but my collection lacks a few replacement notes that regarded as being fairly "common," if that term can be used for any of these scarce items.

It is believed that at least one batch (or unit) of replacement MPCs was printed just prior to commencing the bulk production of an issue of normal MPCs. Substitutions could then be made directly into the packs for all normal notes that were found to be spoiled. Typically about 1% of a normal unit of notes would have been printed in replacement form, but the numbers put into circulation would depend upon how many notes were found to be spoiled among the normal notes that were released. In all cases replacement notes are scarcer than are their normal counterparts, but the ratio of relative scarcities varies radically for issue to issue. For instance, the 50¢ note of Series 541 is relatively common in replacement form, and a CU example of this note sells for only about three times the price of a normal note of this issue in the same condition. On the other hand, the $1 replacement note of Series 651 is excessively rare; in fact, only one example has thus far been recorded. Normal Series 651 $1 notes, however, are extremely common, and VF examples of this note can be easily had for only $2 or $3 each.

Using the serial number data that Fred Schwan gives in his catalog it is possible to determine how many units of replacement notes were prepared for each issue. By unit I am referring to the lots of 8000 sheets each that were used as production units for all series of MPCs. For most issues only one or two units of replacement notes were prepared, but for Series 481 and 541 replacement notes from the third and fourth units of these issues have also been recorded. All known Series 481 $1 replacement notes with position numbers on their right sides are from the first unit, while the known replacements of the left number variety are from the second or third units of these notes that were printed for this issue. Series 521 replacement notes are known both from the first and second units and also from the seventh unit of the issues for the 5¢, 10¢, 25¢, and $1 notes. No replacement notes are known for the third through sixth units of this series, however, and perhaps these sequences of serial numbers were not used. The most unusual serial numbers of all MPC issues are to be found on some of the replacement notes of Series 541. Very high serial numbers appear on most of the relatively common 50¢ replacement notes of this series, and they are also recorded on a small number of the much rarer $1 and $10 Series 541 replacement notes. It is still far from clear why these numbers were used, as they exceed even the total printings of all notes that are known to have been produced for this issue.

In his catalog Schwan gives detailed tabular summaries of the data that he has acquired on replacement MPCs. All of these notes can be regarded as scarce, but a few issues at least are affordable for most collectors. The most "common" of the MPC replacement notes are the 5¢ and 10¢ notes of Series 611, for which well over 100 CU examples of each have been recorded. The $1 note of this series is also known in similar quantities, but most of these are presently off the market. Also fairly common are the 5¢ notes of Series 641 and 692 and the aforementioned 50¢ note of Series 541. The 5¢ and 10¢ replacement notes of Series 611 sell for about $75 each in today's market, and the other notes mentioned above are worth more like $100 to $150 in CU condition, while well circulated replacement notes for a few of the more common issues can be obtained for as little as $25 each. Most other replacement notes, however, bring at least a few hundred dollars each in choice condition, and obtaining as many as a dozen or more different varieties of these notes is quite a challenge.

Closely related to the replacement MPCs are the specimen notes with these types of numbers. The earlier issues used replacement serial numbers and were perforated "SPECIMEN," while most issues printed by the BEP used zero serial numbers for specimen notes. These notes were usually distributed in sample books to authorized personnel who would be issuing MPCs to persons under their command. Most of the known specimen notes are from the first three issues of MPCs, i. e., Series 461, 471, and 472. Fred Schwan has recorded about 400 examples of these notes, but most of them are in government hands and thus are not available to collectors. In 1997 a specimen book containing all seven notes of Series 461 was sold for $2310 in an R. M. Smythe auction, and a similar item sold a few weeks later in an Spink America auction fetched $2860. A specimen book of the even rarer Series 471 MPCs (but lacking the $5 note) brought $3300 in a CAA auction in 1998.

A few progressive proofs are known for Series 641 and 661 of the MPCs. Since all of the MPCs involved printings in two colors or more, proof impressions were made at the BEP for several of the stages of production and a number of these have come to light. It is likely that progressive proofs were made for nearly all of the multicolored issues of MPCs that were printed at the BEP, but only for Series 641 and 661 are such items available to collectors. These proofs are very scarce, and all such items are worth a minimum of several hundred dollars each on those rare occasions when they are offered for sale.

Military Payment Certificates are the only types of modern U. S. government paper money for which it is possible collect counterfeits without a great deal of hassle. Since MPCs are no longer valid money, the Secret Service appears to be little concerned with the private ownership of fakes of these issues. At the present time the prohibition against the holding or collecting of counterfeits of small-size notes is vigorously enforced, although more latitude seems to be tolerated for counterfeit large-size and fractional notes. A number of counterfeit MPCs are known, especially for the $10 notes of Series 471 and 641.

There are relatively few errors on MPCs, but one type of error that does occur with MPCs but not with other types of U. S. currency are notes lacking their underlying tinting. Since MPCs are printed by multicolor lithography, several different inks were often used for each side, and sometimes one of the more obscure shades was left out. I shall have more to say about error and counterfeit MPCs in Chapters 9 and 12, respectively.

There are also a number of different items that are related to MPCs but that definitely cannot be classed as U. S. government currency. Allied Military Currency was printed for use in Austria, France, Germany, Italy, and Japan. The last issue was also used in South Korea and the Ryukyu Islands. Much of this money physically resembles the earlier issues of MPCs, but some of the notes for Austria were printed in Great Britain and many of the German notes were printed in the Soviet Union. The fact that the Soviet

Union printed large numbers of German notes caused many problems for the Americans and British in their respective zones of occupation. The various issues of Allied currency are usually considered to be notes of the countries in which they were used, but many collectors of MPCs also collect these items. Some additional information on these notes is provided in Chapter 13.

More directly related to MPCs are the auxiliary coupons that were used by Korean and Thai soldiers serving in Vietnam in the early 1970s. Despite their recent issue all of these are scarce. Also of some interest are the sample notes that were used as training "money" for personnel learning to handle large transactions in MPCs. There are also a wide variety of checks that were payable exclusively in MPCs, and special gasoline coupons that functioned to some extent as currency for U. S. military personnel in a few western European countries. All of these items are treated in detail in Schwan's catalog, but they are far removed from what can be termed U. S. government paper money.

Although MPCs themselves are often overlooked by collectors who are interested only in U. S. paper money that still has retained its valid currency status, I regard these items very much as a type of U. S. government currency that should be seriously considered by all collectors of American paper money. For notes of such recent issue, it is amazing how many varieties of MPCs are scarce today. Doubtless that stems from the fact that MPCs could be invalidated on short notice, and very few persons were willing to put aside $5 or $10 notes that soon would be considered worthless paper by their government were they not promptly turned in for redemption. Although all MPCs are nonnegotiable at the present time, most of them are far from worthless.

			regular issue printings in millions					
	5¢	10¢	25¢	50¢	$1	$5	$10	$20	Total
461	7.6	8.1	4.7	4.0	14.6	5.4	40.8		85.2
471	8.3	7.6	4.5	4.0	14.6	5.4	13.6		58.0
472	8.0	8.0	4.8	4.2	11.8	4.2	11.6		52.5
481	24.0	23.1	14.8	10.0	25.5	8.6	24.8		130.7
521	27.2	26.9	14.4	11.1	28.0	6.4	24.4		138.4
541	18.8	18.8	12.1	8.1	20.2	6.0	21.2		105.2
591	7.4	8.4	4.7	3.7	10.1	2.4	6.8		43.5
611	9.4	10.1	5.4	4.7	10.6	2.8	8.4		51.4
641	22.8	23.5	12.1	11.4	33.0	6.8	20.4		130.1
651	4.0	4.0	2.7	2.0	6.7	1.6	3.6		11.9
661	23.5	23.5	13.4	10.1	33.0	7.2	4.8	8.0	123.6
681	14.1	14.1	8.7	6.7	22.4	4.8	3.2	6.4	80.5
692	14.1	14.1	8.7	6.7	22.4	4.8	3.2	6.4	80.5

This chart gives the total number of regular issue MPC printed for each issue in millions. Approximately 1% of the total should be replacements. Multiply the number in the table by 10,000 for an estimate of the number of replacements issued. Take the Series 461 5¢ certificate for example. Approximately 76,000 replacements were issued (7.6 x 10,000).

CHAPTER NINE

ERRORS

For some collectors error notes are the most fascinating and sought after of all paper money items. An error note can be defined as an item that is produced unintentionally by the BEP or other printing agency. Such notes are not supposed to enter circulation, and there are numerous stages in the production process that check for defective notes, but leakages do occur. When released into circulation such notes are fully legal to posses and collect, and they do retain their full face value as legal tender (subject to some considerations on such items as double denomination notes, etc.). The vast majority of error notes in today's market are small-size notes, but error large-size notes, Fractional Currency, and MPCs also exist.

In at least one case an error note has achieved major number status in the standard catalogs. The is the Series 1917 $1 USN with a Burke-Elliott signature combination (Fr. 37a, H-25) instead of the correct Elliott-Burke. I have already discussed this note in the chapter on large-size type notes, and almost all syngraphists who collect these notes by signature combination desire one of these for their collections. Among the non-Federal issues there is another famous error that has achieved major type status, and that is a $2 note from the Confederate States which is dated September 2, 1861 instead of the correct June 2, 1862. The former date is that used on all Confederate notes of the Third Issue, but no $1 or $2 notes were authorized at that time. This error note is actually a part of the Fourth Issue but with an incorrect date.

Although both the Hessler and Krause-Lemke catalogs provide some discussion of error notes, if you plan to collect these notes by all means acquire copies of the Comprehensive *Catalog of United States Paper Money Errors* by Frederick J. Bart and the *U. S. Error Note Encyclopedia* by Stephen M. Sullivan. These catalogs give a good idea of what to expect in errors. Since the vast majority of paper money errors are small-size notes, let us consider these first. It is perhaps surprising that far more paper money errors are being produced today than was the case several decades ago. One would expect far tighter quality control would be exercised at the present time than was the case in former years, but two factors have combined to increase the production and leakage of errors. One is the vastly greater production of notes. Large-size error notes are uncommon in part because far more time was allotted for the hand inspection of these notes while they were in production. The second factor is the much higher degree of automation than was the case in former decades. With automatic cutting and packaging of notes errors can slip by that would have attracted the notice of inspectors in previous years.

At the present time the backs of all notes produced by the BEP are printed first, and this is followed by the face printings. Both of these processes are done in intaglio on the Magna presses. The numbering and cutting of the notes is done on COPE-PAK machines. Errors can occur at any stage of these operations. Let us now consider the various important types of errors that are most frequently encountered by collectors.

BEP employee inspects notes.

Offsets: Offset printings occur when an impression from a printing plate is transferred onto an impression cylinder rather than onto a sheet of notes. This will result in a mirror-reversed image of the other side of the notes that are printed on the sheets that follow, and this may be transferred to either the face or back of the note. The offset printings, or wet ink transfers as they are sometimes called, may be either full or partial. It can range from quite heavy to very light. Typically the first sheet of notes printed with an offset impression will display the heaviest degree of inking, and this will become progressively lighter for the next half dozen or so sheets. Extremely light partial offsets are frequently encountered, but these are not usually classified as error notes. In fact, such offsets are likely to occur whenever large numbers of notes are stacked together under pressure. Such notes are of little interest to collectors of error notes and they have little, if any, premium value. Although a few offsets are known for large-size notes and the earlier series of small-size notes, the vast majority of offset notes in today's marketplace are on fairly recent issues of FRNs.

      Both back-to-face and face-to-back offsets occur. Generally speaking, the face-to-back offsets are rather more common than are their back-to-face counterparts. The values of these notes depend on the degree of darkness of the offset printing (the darker

the better), the completeness of the printing (full offsets are worth more than are partial offsets), as well as the denomination and condition of the note, etc. Typically heavy full offsets are selling for about $150-200 each in CU condition in today's market. Such notes would have about the same value irrespective of whether they are $1, $5, $10, or $20 notes. This type of error on $50 or $100 notes would be more expensive, but the values of most error notes are determined on a premium basis over the face value of the note. If a particular error enhances the value of an otherwise normal contemporary note by $100, then this error on a $20 note would be worth about $120 while the same error on a $100 note would be worth about $200, etc. An exception to this "rule" occurs with $2 notes. Of the seven different denominations currently being printed by the BEP, $2 notes are usually the most difficult to find in error form and these notes sometimes sell at prices that are significantly higher than are achieved for $50 or $100 notes with similar errors in comparable condition.

Partial offsets and offsets that are fairly light sell for prices that are substantially less that those asked for full heavy offsets. Typically such notes might sell for about $50 each in CU condition and perhaps no more than $20 or $25 if in VF or XF condition (provided that their face value is no more than $10, of course). Condition is rarely a problem with offset notes, since most notes with obvious offsets are pulled from circulation before they have much time to circulate.

286/errors   U. S. Paper Money

Offsets of the green and black overprints (i. e., the serial numbers, Treasury seals, district seals, and district numbers) are known, but they are significantly rarer than are face-on-back or back-on-face offsets. These features will appear mirror-imaged (as is always is the case with offsets) on the back sides of the notes. A small number of double denomination offsets are known. In this case the mirror image of a second denomination appears on either the face or back of an otherwise normal note. Such notes, however, are not to be confused with the even rarer double denomination notes in which the printed face and back of a given note are of different denominations. Another rare category of offset notes are the so-called double offset notes. These have partial offset impressions on both sides, i. e., the face of such as note has a partial back offset while the back of the same note has a partial face offset.

Underinked Notes: An underinked note will have a very weak impression on either its face or back side. A wide variety of possibilities exist for these notes. The overall impression may be too light, but frequently only a portion of the design is either very light or absent altogether. Such notes are apt to display progressive characteristics in a given sequence. The underinking will become progressively more pronounced as the ink runs out in such a run of notes. The ultimate in underinked notes are notes that lack either their entire face or back designs. On notes with unprinted face designs, the overprints of the third printing are almost always present. Underinkings can also occur with the overprints, and thus quite a few different types of errors fall into this general category. Most collectors draw a sharp distinction between notes that show underinking on either their face or back intaglio printings and those that show this deficiency in the third printing.

Generally the least expensive of the underinked notes are those with a weak overall face or back impression. Typical prices would be in the $50 to $100 range, but notes in which a large portion of design is missing due to underinking sell for more. Notes with either the face or back intaglio printing entirely missing typically sell in the $200 to $600 range when in CU condition. All denominations from $1 to $100 are known with the $2 note being the most elusive of the set. In 1998, however, a vastly higher price was achieved for a $10 FRN that had a blank face but with a normal third printing. This note, however, was a star note, and as a consequence it sold for $6600, a price far higher than normal for this type of error. Since star notes are printed as replacements for notes that were rejected because of defects, errors are not expected to occur on them, and consequently, star note errors are always very much in demand.

Board Breaks: Broad breaks arise when the impression cylinder becomes damaged. This will result in portions of either the face or the back intaglio designs being absent. It is often easy to confuse some board break errors with partially printed notes due to underinking, but these types of errors arise in quite different fashions. Generally only a relatively small portion of either the face or back design of a note with be affected by a board break. Prices for board break errors are usually fairly low, typically $25 to $50 or so, although scarcer notes obviously can sell at much higher prices. Almost all board break notes are FRNs that have been printed in Series 1963 or later. This type of error would not arise with notes that are printed on flat presses, and thus no board break errors at all are known for large-size notes. They should also be most unlikely for all small-size notes printed in either 12-subject or 18-subject sheets.

Ink Smears: The opposite of underinked notes are notes that are printed with too much ink. Usually these take the form of ink smears that can appear on either the faces or backs of the notes. These smears can range from very light (in which case they have hardly any premium value) to quite heavy. Heavy smears, however, lack eye appeal, and this helps hold prices down for this type of error. Typical prices on contemporary FRNs of the lower denominations are in the $15 to $50 range, although smear notes of special interest will doubtless attract higher prices.

Overinking is sometimes also encountered in the third printings of contemporary notes. The black district seal or the green Treasury seal may be so overinked as to be almost illegible. Although these notes are less frequently encountered than are notes with ink smears in their intaglio portions, examples of such notes should be available for not much more than $50 each or so.

You should exercise caution when purchasing ink smear notes. Without doubt these are the easiest of the error notes to fake. At the end of this chapter I shall discuss the general topic of fake error notes. It should be noted that errors are one of the few areas of U. S. Federal paper money in which fakes pose something of a problem. Unlike counterfeits, which are illegal both to manufacture and to possess, fake error notes are illegal to make only if an attempt is made to alter or raise the denomination. Before getting seriously involved with the collecting of paper money errors it is very important that you become thoroughly familiar with what the genuine products look like.

Solvent smears are another type of error note that are closely related to the ink smears. These arise when excess solvent reaches a printing plate. A heavily blurred or fuzzy portion of either the face or back design is the result. Solvent smears are less common than are ink smears, and so prices for these errors sometimes exceed $100. A characteristic of all smear errors, however, is that they are of generally unattractive appearance, and this helps keep both demand and prices fairly low.

Obstructed Printings: These errors arise when a foreign object (such as a small piece of wrapping paper) gets onto a sheet of currency paper that is being printed. This will result in an absence of that portion of the design on the printed note. In some cases it is possible to acquire the foreign paper object that was printed with a portion of the note design. Obstructed printings occur not only for the face and back designs, but also for the third printings of the notes.

Most notes with obstructed printings lack the foreign piece of paper on which a portion of the design (face, back, or third printing) was printed. Notes with small obstructed zones are fairly common, and premiums for these notes in uncirculated condition start at $25 or so. Notes with large obstructions are worth much more, however. Far rarer are notes on which the foreign body that retains a portion of the original printing has been preserved. Even if this piece is small and printed on low-quality paper, it should always be carefully preserved with the obstructed note since the value of the combination far exceeds the value of the constituent parts. All such obstructed combinations are worth a minimum of several hundred dollars each.

Although I do not collect error notes *per se*, in 1996 I acted as agent for the sale of a fine collection of these items. These were sold by CAA in their May sale of that year. By far the most unusual item in my consignment was an obstructed printing of a type that is most rarely seen. This was a Series 1985 $20 FRN from the Philadelphia district. Attached to this note was a BEP shipping form printed on thin cardboard that was almost as large as the note. The front and back intaglio printings of the FRN were normal, but almost all of the third printing was on the attached form and not on the note itself. Only one district numeral "3" was printed on the note, although this note also showed a number of albino impressions. How this "sandwich" ever got through a COPE machine without jamming it I do not know, but this is close to the ultimate in obstructed printings. This combination sold for $2310 at this auction, and it is presently illustrated on the front cover of Stephen M. Sullivan's error book. Most obstructed printings are not this dramatic, but all such errors that include the foreign piece of paper than caused the obstruction are highly desirable.

Missing Printings: As I have already noted, it is possible for error notes to lack entirely their face or back intaglio printings. In a certain sense such items represent the ultimate in underinked notes, although they are actually generally rather more common than are most notes with severe underinking on either their face or back sides. Notes with missing face printings usually have normal third printings on this side, but it is also possible for notes to be missing their third printings, either partially or in *toto*. For contemporary FRNs it is

possible for both the green and black overprints to be absent or for only the green or the black overprints to be missing. For recent $1 FRNs examples with no third printing at all sell for about $200 in CU condition. Notes with either the green or black overprints missing are about as scarce, but typically they sell at lower prices. All other denominations from $2 through $100 are also known with these types of errors. Missing third printings are also encountered on a few of the earlier issues of $5, $10, and $20 FRNs.

One-dollar silver certificates are also sometimes encountered with missing third printings. The notes of Series 1935 and later had overprinted rather than engraved signatures and series designations, and these features are generally missing on notes that lack the blue Treasury seals and serial numbers. A number of $1 SCs lacking both the blue and the black overprints have be sold in recent years, and in CU condition these sell for about $250 each. Both $5 and $10 SCs and $2 and $5 USNs of the 1953 types also exist that are lacking both their Treasury seals and serial numbers, as well as their signatures and series indicators. These would sell at prices that are substantially higher than those fetched by $1 SC error notes of this type.

For earlier small-size notes the facsimile signatures and series designations were engraved directly onto the face plates, and thus they were not included as part of the third printing. For notes of this vintage missing serial numbers and Treasury seals are known on $1 SCs of Series 1928, 1928A, and 1928B, $2 USNs of 1928 and 1928A, $5 USNs of 1928, $5 SCs of 1934, and $10, $20, and $50 gold certificates of Series 1928. One of the better notes in my 1996 consignment was a Series 1928 $5 USN of this type in F-VF condition. It sold for $468. Three years later CAA offered a Series 1928 $20 gold error

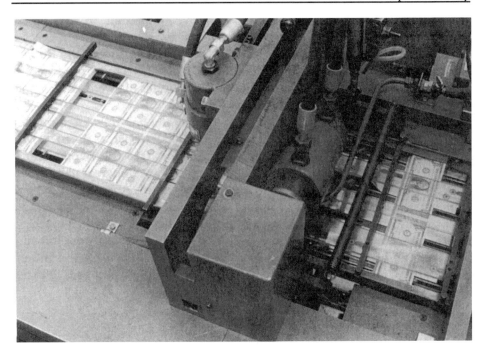

note of this type in CU. It sold for $17,600, a price that is far higher than any previously recorded for a note with a missing third printing.

Misaligned Overprints: A commonly encountered type of error are the notes with misaligned overprints. Typically the entire third printing is shifted to the left, but shifts to the right, as well as up, down, and sideways are also known. The latter are usually referred to as skewed overprints. Minor overprint shifts are among the most common of errors, and most collectors are not much interested in these errors unless the shift is large enough for either the serial number or a seal (district or Treasury depending upon which way) to touch or cover part of the portrait area. Such notes typically have premiums of $25 or so, but very large shifts can sell for as much as a few hundred dollars each. Intermediate cases fetch intermediate prices, and thus the degree of misalignment clearly is a major factor in determining the value of this class of error notes.

Contemporary FRNs exist in which either the green or black overprint is properly spaced, but the overprint of the other color is improperly aligned. Examples of recent $1 FRNs in which the green overprint is properly spaced but the black overprint is seriously out of line typically sell for about $100 each in CU condition. Notes on which the black overprint is properly spaced but the green overprint is misaligned are much scarcer and sell for significantly higher prices. As with any overprint alignment error, however, the value of such notes depends to as large an extent upon the degree of misalignment as it does on the condition, denomination, and scarcity of the note in question.

Inverted Overprints and Overprints on Back: An important class of error notes are those which have the third printing either inverted or on their back sides. Inverted overprints on small-size notes were known for only a few series prior to the introduction of the COPE-PAK machines in the mid-1970s. Since then these notes have been produced with some regularity on most FRN issues from Series 1974 to date. On the more recent FRNs all denominations from $1 through $100 are known. In CU condition a $1 note should cost about $150, and the $5, $10, and $20 notes will not cost a great deal more. Inverted overprints of the $2, $50, and $100 denominations are more expensive, but they are available. The $2 note is probably the scarcest of the set, and a nice CU $2 FRN with the third printing inverted now sells for about $700 or so. Some collectors attempt to complete a set of all seven denominations of these errors, and that is not especially difficult to do. Condition is rarely a problem with these notes, since they are almost immediately pulled from circulation once they are discovered.

Inverted overprints also exist on numerous earlier issues of small-size notes, but in general they are much less common than are notes that have been incorrectly processed on the COPE machines. By far the most common of these are $1 SCs of the various 1935 and 1957 series, and typically these sell for about $200 each in CU. Other notes such as pre-1974 FRNs, $2 and $5 USNs, and $5 and $10 SCs are known with this error, but they are far from common. The most treasured small-size notes with inverted overprints are probably the Hawaii notes with either their face or back overprints inverted. In 1996 a Series 1934 $20 Hawaii note in XF with its back overprint inverted sold for $4400 in a CAA auction. This error also exists on the $10 Hawaii note. An even more impressive Hawaii error exists on the Series 1934A $5 note on which the brown Treasury seal and serial numbers are inverted but the black overprints are normal. In 1995 three $1 Hawaii notes were sold in which the black face overprint was both shifted and skewed. All of these were in CU condition, and they sold for about $1000 each.

Closely related to the error notes with inverted overprints are those with their overprints on back. Prior to the introduction of the COPE machines these errors were virtually unknown, but all denominations from $1 through $100 except for the $2 have been seen with some regularity in FRNs printed since the mid-1970s. The values for these notes are comparable to those of the notes with inverted third printings. In 1996 CAA sold a $50 double error note in XF that combined two major error types. The third printing was on the back side, but the face of this note was entirely blank. It sold for $1870, a price far above what a blank back $50 or inverted overprint note of this type would bring.

A few notes are also known with inverted overprints on their back sides. Such notes also generally show misaligned centering of this side as well. These errors are much rarer that are notes with upright overprints on their back sides. They can easily sell for well over $1000 each whenever they come up for sale.

Inverted Backs: By far the most important category (in terms of numbers known) of error notes among the earlier issues are notes with inverted backs. Since the backs are actually printed prior to the faces for nearly all issues of notes, these errors should more properly be called inverted faces, and some authors indeed do use that term. As I shall indicate, they are far more abundant on large-size notes and on Fractional Currency than are any other classes of errors for these issues. They also exist for a wide variety of small-size notes, but it seems that current procedures for printing paper money now preclude the possibility of manufacturing many more of these notes.

Most known small-size inverts are $1 SCs of Series 1928 through 1935A, $2 and $5 USNs of Series 1928, and FRNs of various denominations from 1928 to 1934 series. The CAA auction held in May, 1996 featured a nice selection of invert notes. Typically the $1 SC (Series 1928 to 1935A) inverts in AU to CU condition sold for about $500 each. The $5, $10, and $20 FRNs of various series from 1928 to 1950A sold for comparable prices. Among the best notes in this group was an inverted Series 1928C $2 USN in XF, a 1934 $10 SC in XF-AU, a 1929 $5 FRBN from Chicago in VF, and a 1934 $100 FRN in CU. These inverts sold for $962, $781, $550, and $2090, respectively. Although notes with inverted backs are largely confined to the earlier series of small-size notes, occasionally a few have been printed in more recent times. This auction also featured a Series 1985 $20 FRN whose back was both inverted and seriously misaligned. This CU note sold for $1265 in this auction.

This Tigerton note has mismatched charter numbers. This error is so rare that it does not fit into a category. In addition, it represents a great collector story. It was found by a collector in the 1990s who bought it for his collection of Wisconsin nationals. It was only when he was entering the note in his collection inventory that he realized the error. Photo courtesy of Fred Bart.

Mismatched Serial Numbers: This is an important class of errors, and today about 100 different varieties are known for this type of error on small-size notes. At first glance this is not as obvious error as is a heavy offset or a missing third printing, and thus these notes exist in a fairly wide range of grades, since they may be used for some time once they enter circulation. In a few cases large numbers of mismatched notes have been discovered in a given bank, and the majority of such notes have quickly fallen into numismatic hands.

The majority of varieties of mismatched notes predate the introduction of the COPE machines in the mid-1970s, but mismatched notes continue to be produced, although they are far less a characteristic of contemporary error notes than are notes with inverted third printings or with these overprints on their back sides. Most of the mismatched notes are $1 bills, but $2, $5, $10, $20, and $50 notes are also available. Among the most common of the $1 SCs of this type are Series 1957 notes with serial G55———A on the left and G54———A on the right and Series 1957B notes with U37———A on the left and U47———A on the right. Both of these errors are available for about $75 each in CU condition, and they do come up in circulated grades as well. These notes are examples of one-digit mismatches, but numerous notes are known with two or more digits mismatched. The most recorded for a single note appears to be five, but several different three-digit and four digit mismatches have been recorded. Among the $1 FRNs the most common mismatch is probably the Series 1969D B44———E / B43———E error note that is about as common as are the two $1 SCs mentioned above.

There are two mismatched $2 notes in Series 1976 that appear with some frequency, and this is a boon for collectors who are seeking major errors of this denomination. The serial number mismatch is of the type B5920x—A / B5920y—A, where the mismatch is in the fifth digit. The second variety is a mismatched block letter variety with H454———A on the left and B454———A on the right. These notes are from the New York rather than the St. Louis district, since they carry the seal and number designation of the former bank. Both of these varieties sell for about $150 each in CU condition. Mismatched block letters are clearly very closely related to mismatched serial numbers, but fewer varieties of these have been recorded. It is fortunate that these two $2 FRN errors are available to collectors, since no mismatched $2 USNs have thus far been recorded.

There are also numerous varieties of $5 notes (mostly FRNs but also some USNs and SCs) with mismatched serial numbers or block letters. Mismatched $10 and $20 notes are much less frequently encountered. In 1996 a Series 1928 $20 gold certificate with a mismatched digit in the seventh place was sold at a CAA auction. Despite the fact that this note was only in VG condition, it brought $1320. Mismatched digits on gold notes are extremely rare, and this is perhaps the only recorded example. This type of error is also excessively rare, or perhaps nonexistent, on Series 1929 FRBNs and all World War II emergency issues.

In this chapter I have thus far said nothing about errors on $500 and $1000 notes. Although a number of minor errors do exist for these denominations, the only truly significant error known for a high denomination note is a Series 1934 $1000 FRN from the St. Louis district with serial number H00010367A on its left side and H00010337A on its right. No other similar examples are known.

Misaligned Digits: These errors are also often referred to as stuck digit notes. They occur when a single digit on one of the two serial numbers is out of alignment with the others. If portions of two digits are present, this is referred to as a rolled digit. These can occur with almost any type of note. Unlike the mismatched serial numbers, these will not be consistent from note to note in a given pack. This error, however, is common enough for these notes to be classified as minor errors. On recent FRNs in choice condition misaligned digits typically command premiums of only $15 to $20 or so. Rolled digits, in which portions of two digits are visible command somewhat higher prices, but they also are far from being rarities. Although various interesting examples of these errors can be purchased at auction or from dealers, it is also possible to find them among the notes encountered in everyday circulation.

Inverted Digits: Inverted digits are a much rarer and more significant class of error notes. On these notes only a single digit of the serial number is inverted, and usually this is a block letter or a star. The letter "M" can be easily confused with an inverted letter "W." On Series 1957 $1 SCs of the MA block a number of notes are known in which the right serial number begins with an inverted "W" rather than an "M." On Series 1935G $1 SC star notes a few notes are also known in which the star is inverted in the left serial number. On all star notes, both hollow and solid, the top of the star should have a single point while the bottom should have two points. For inverted stars the opposite is true. In a CAA auction in 1995 a CU example of the 1935G star note invert sold for $424. A few other varieties of these errors are known, but all are very scarce. Although inverted digits are not very obvious at first sight, they should be classed as major errors, and they do attract keen competition whenever they come onto the market.

Although star notes are prepared as replacements for regular notes that have been rejected because of faulty printing, errors do appear on these replacement notes with some regularity. Almost all classes of errors thus far discussed can occur on star notes. Star note errors usually command substantial premiums over their normal counterparts. It is a bit ironic, however, that the majority of known inverted digit notes are star notes, items that were printed to replace error notes that were detected and subsequently destroyed during the course of production.

Double Printings: This is an important class of errors that are also decidedly scarce. It sometimes happens that either the first or second printing of a sheet of notes will be fed through the press a second time. Since the alignment is not perfect, this will result in two distinct impressions that are shifted somewhat with respect to each other. The overall effect can range from fairly subtle to very dramatic. The value of a double printed note depends to a large extent upon how dramatic is its appearance. The majority of double printed notes are recent FRNs, but notes that were printed in the early 1950s are also known with this error. A doubly printed note will almost always show two distinct check numbers on the side that has been printed twice. Frederick Bart has also recorded a couple of doubly printed notes in which the second impression (backs in both cases) is inverted with respect to the first. In no way should these notes be confused with offsets.

In 1996 CAA in one of its auctions sold a number of doubly printed notes. The most dramatic were a Series 1976 $2 FRN and a 1977 $5 FRN, both of which were CU and had doubly printed faces. They sold for $1925 and $2090, respectively. A less dramatic Series 1950 $10 with a doubly printed back, and a 1974 $20 with a double face sold for $688 and $550, respectively. There were also a Series 1977 $100 with a double face and a Series 1950 $100 with a double back, both of which were in XF condition. These sold for $688 and $1128, respectively. It is also possible to have double third printing notes. These are even rarer than are notes with double first or second printings. In 1997 a spectacular Series 1976 $2 FRN from the Cleveland district was sold at a CAA auction. Both the black and the green portions of the third printing were doubled, and the serial numbers differed in the last place. This note sold for $2420. Doubly printed notes are most definitely not the least expensive types of error notes to collect.

Double Denomination Notes: We now come to the most dramatic of all the paper money errors, notes which have justly be termed the "king of errors." From either side a double denomination note appears to be quite normal, but once it is turned over its unique status is immediately revealed. Apparently the BEP makes very great efforts to prevent the printing and release of double denomination notes, and thus far only five different varieties of small-size notes of these great errors have been recorded. The five small-size double denomination notes that are known are as follows:

$5 1928B FRN face / $10 back BA block
$5 1934D FRN face / $10 back JA block
$10 1950A FRN face / $1 back BD block
$10 1928A FRN face / $5 back EA block
$20 1974 FRN face / $10 back KB back

A total of about 60 of these notes have been recorded. The 1928B "$15 bill," however, is unique and essentially noncollectible. In 1995 CAA sold examples of the other four varieties as part of the Doovas collection of error notes. The 1934D $5/$10 in CU sold for $5610, the 1950A $10/$1 in AU fetched $5225, the 1928A $10/$5 in CU brought $5170, and the 1974 $20/$10 was sold at $5445. In 1997 the same firm sold a 1934D $5/$10 Kansas City note for $5775 and a 1928A $10/$5 Richmond note for $6325. In 1998 a 1974 $20/$10 Dallas note was sold for $12,650 in a CAA auction, and a $5/$10 Kansas City note was sold for $9350 in a Lyn Knight auction that was held in the following month.

The Levitan collection featured another "complete set" of the small-size double denomination notes. The 1928A $10/$5 error in CU sold for $27,500, the 1934D $5/$10 note in CU brought $16,500, the 1950A $10/$1 in XF fetched $30,800, and the 1974 $20/$10 in CU went for $12,100. As can be seen, there has been a major change in the price structure of these notes from the time of the Doovas sale three years earlier.

Although these prices achieved prior to 1997 seem fairly high, what amazes me is how little they changed over the past two or three decades. In the mid-1970s these notes typically sold for between $3000 and $4000 each. Thus they not quite doubled in value over a period of 25 years. A doubling in value over 25 years is equivalent to 2.8% interest per annum, compounded annually. When compared with almost all types of large-size type notes (or good quality, no-load mutual funds for that matter) double denomination notes have not proven to be good investments for most of these years. The sales results achieved in 1998, however, indicate a significant new interest in the double denomination errors.

Officially a double denomination note has a legal tender value equal to the value expressed on its face side. This rule would also apply to notes with blank backs. It is unclear what the redemption value of a note with a blank face should be, but I doubt that any are being turned in for redemption in any case. Several decades ago a man showed a $10/$20 national bank note to government officials and inquired about its nature. His note was seized and forcibly redeemed for only $10 in normal currency. The officials were afraid that he might try to use it for a $20 note! As we shall see, there is a much wider range of double denomination notes among the large-size issues.

Wrong Overprint Notes: Perhaps the most impressive of all small-size paper money errors are two $5 notes of the 1950s that are best termed wrong overprint notes. Both have the intaglio faces of Federal Reserve Notes of the 1950 type, but in each case they received the wrong overprints. One of the two varieties has the third printing of a Series 1953 silver certificate complete with a blue Treasury seal and serial numbers. Two examples of these notes are presently known, and one in F-VF condition was sold for $3960 in an 1993 CAA auction. The second variety has the third printing of a Series 1953B United States Note complete with a red seal and serial numbers. It is also in F-VF condition and is believed to be unique. This note was sold for $5775 in a 1995 CAA auction. Although these errors are most impressive, they are so rare as to be virtually noncollectible.

Since the third printing is done in both black and green inks on Federal Reserve Notes, it is possible for the wrong color ink to be used in this process. Sullivan's book illustrates Series 1990 $20 and $50 FRNs in which the district seals and numbers have been printed in green rather than black ink. Such errors are extremely rare, and I do not know of any recent sales of these. It seems logical that if notes can have green district seals and numbers, notes with black Treasury seals and serial numbers should also be possible. As far as I know, however, none of these have ever been reported.

Frequently one sees so-called "errors of color" on a number of notes. In almost every case, however, these are private fabrications. I shall briefly discuss these in my section on fake errors at the end of this chapter.

Plate Errors: Plate or engraving errors have appeared on only a very few small-size notes. By far the most famous of these errors on large-size notes is the aforementioned Series 1917 $1 USN with the Burke-Elliott signature combination that has been given major number status in all of the standard paper moneycatalogs. On small-size notes these errors are much more subtle and do not warrant major number status.

A number of Series 1928 $2 USNs were printed with back plates that lacked any check numbers. This variant occurs on all 12 positions on a sheet of this note, and it is the only such plate error that appeared during the first half century in which small-size notes were in production. Although this variety is decidedly uncommon, a few star notes are known of this variant in addition to the normal notes that show it.

About three million $1 FRNs were printed in Series 1981A and 1985 using back plate 129. On this plate the check number appears on the left side of the plate rather than on the standard right side. The Krause-Lemke catalog treats these notes as distinct major varieties, but they are probably best regarded as check number variants. For each of these series normal notes were issued for all 12 districts, but it is not quite certain how many different varieties exist with the check number 129. It does not appear that any star notes were printed with this plate. The prices given in the Krause-Lemke catalog for these notes are much too low ($8 each in CU). Sullivan's estimate of $40 for a CU is more realistic, although I have recently seen them priced at about $20 to $25 per note. Collectors of normal $1 FRNs, however, need not regard these variants as major varieties that are needed for a complete collection of $1 FRN district or block sets.

In recent years two other plate errors have come to the attention of syngraphic researchers. A number of Series 1985 $1 FRNs are known with no back check number, all of which are from plate position E3. Also Series 1977A and 1981 $1 FRNs from the Richmond district exist with check number 7273. These were in 32-subject sheets sold to the public, and they should have had check number 3273. All such notes are from plate position H1 in the sheet. Since the sequence of check numbers for $1 FRNs of this vintage did not go as high as 7000, these can also be regarded as plate errors.

In 1998 a number of Series 1995 $1 FRNs were printed in Fort Worth with a small-size back check number that was intended only for notes from the Washington facility. All of these notes have check number 295, and they exist for several different serial number blocks.

Should any of these varieties be regarded as true error notes? One can regard them so, but they fail on one essential criterion for defining error notes. A good working definition of an error note is a note that would not have been released by the BEP had it been caught in the inspection process. Although most large-size notes have check numbers on their back sides, many do not. Thus nothing unusual would have been thought about a few $2 USNs that lacked back check numbers. Certainly the unusual position of check number 129 on $1 FRNs in the 1980s came to the attention of BEP officials before all three million of them were released. This "error" would not have been noted by the general public, however, and doubtless the BEP officials thought it prudent and economical to use a back plate that was otherwise perfect for the production of notes for its full lifetime.

"New" Errors: Major changes in the designs and printing of money have resulted in the release of a few new error types that have not been recorded on earlier issues. Many notes now printed by the BEP have zones in which magnetic-sensitive ink is used. Occasionally this does not print on a note. The result is a note in which there are numerous blank places on the faces of the notes that are printed in part with this type of ink (mostly $20, $50, and $100 notes of Series 1990 and later). To some extent these errors resemble notes with board breaks and/or obstructed printings or notes that are severely underinked in certain sections only, but the reason for these errors are quite different for any of the above. A fair number of these notes have come onto the market in recent years, and the premiums are typically about $100 or so for a CU note. In 1999, however, a particularly impressive example of this type of error on a Series 1990 $100 FRN sold for $1980 in a CAA auction.

When the Series 1996 $100 notes first were released, a number appeared with a major error. These had been printed inverted with respect to the special paper such that the plastic strip was on the wrong (i. e., right) side and the watermark was both on the wrong (i. e., left) side and inverted. The error notes detected thus far have all been from the New York district. These were duly noted in the popular press, and numerous examples were acquired by numismatists. In recent auctions they have been selling for about $700 to

$800 each. This price strikes me as decidedly high, since it is known that several thousand such notes were printed, but it is far from clear how many of the error notes were released. In a CAA auction held in May, 1999, one of these errors sold for only $40, a significant reduction from what these notes were bringing a couple of years earlier. It should also be noted that a substantial majority of the $100 FRNs now in circulation are in foreign nations. Many of these errors could be sitting in various banks abroad.

A few notes of Series 1990 and later are known to have their security threads on the right instead of the left sides. These have not proven to be common, and thus far errors of this type in Series 1990, 1993, and 1995 have been selling for several hundred dollars each in CU condition. One type of "error" that I would definitely not recommend collecting, however, are these notes without their security strips. It is a very easy matter to remove the security strips from these notes. Although this leaves a disturbed area where the strip was formerly located, authentication would most definitely be required for a true error note of this type, if indeed any such notes exist. Although it is easy to remove a plastic strip from one of these notes, it is not easy to put one back in. The possibility exists for $20 notes with $10 strips, etc., but no such genuine errors have thus far been confirmed. If a strip (of another denomination) can be clandestinely inserted outside the BEP, however, authentication of such an error would be an absolute must.

When the Series 1996 $50 notes were first released, it was noted that many of them had missing or broken lines in Grant's portrait. The more pronounced cases were scheduled for destruction, but many notes with very minor disturbances in this zone were released. Most of these are much too trivial to be considered as error notes, but perhaps a few notes with very obvious problems in Grant's portrait did escape.

Alignment Errors: Alignment errors are a large class of error notes in which one or both sides of a note are very badly centered. In general a poorly centered note is worth less than a well centered note. To qualify as an error, the centering must be truly bad on at least one of the sides. A note that does not show any portions of an adjacent note on its badly centered side is classed as a minor alignment error. Such notes may command premiums of $10 to $20 on common notes, but on scarce items they are probably worth less than is a well centered non-error example. As is the case with offsets, the value of an alignment error note is dependent upon the severity of the misaligned side. If a fairly small portion of an adjacent note shows on the misaligned side, then the premium jumps to something like $50 to $75 on a common note in CU condition. Essentially there are two different classes of these errors - notes on which only one side is badly aligned and notes of which both sides are similarly misaligned. The latter type of notes are a type of cutting error, and they are often considered together with other types of cutting errors in which the notes in question no longer have normal shapes or dimensions.

Major alignment errors can easily sell for several hundred dollars each. In this case a large portion of another note must be displayed on the error side. These errors exist on many different notes of numerous vintages, although the bulk of the notes presently available, of course, are FRNs and SCs with a scattering of USNs or other series. More ephemeral issues such as Series 1928 gold notes, 1929 FRBNs, or the various World War II issues are always in heavy demand as error notes, and these fetch much higher prices than do comparable errors of other series.

Before buying an alignment error, I would look the note over to decide if it is what you want. Remember than minor alignment errors are little more than poorly centered notes. Non-error collectors will find them less attractive than they will normal notes with better centering.

One type of alignment error to avoid are recent $1 and $2 FRNs that have been cut from the sheets that are sold by the BEP. Be especially careful about any $2 FRN star notes or any $1 FRN notes having serials near the top end of a given block. These should be checked against the listings given in the Oakes and Schwartz catalog. Such clandestinely trimmed notes will show major alignment problems on both sides. Genuine cutting errors will show similar misalignments, and so the serial numbers of any purported recent FRN $1 or $2 cutting errors should be compared with those of the notes known to have been issued in uncut sheets. It is pointless to attempt to list the various types of small-size notes for which alignment errors occur, since literally hundreds of different varieties are available, but if they appeal to you it is possible to form an impressive collection. If I collected alignment errors, however, I would concentrate on obtaining a relatively few major errors rather than a large number of very minor errors. To many collectors the latter might look like just an accumulation of poorly centered notes.

Gutter Folds: Although gutter folds may not be the ugliest types of errors, they are certainly not the prettiest. They retain accidental creases that appeared in the paper, generally during either of first two printings. The result is a white streak where there is no printing on one side together with a heavy crease in that zone. Gutter folds are common errors, and for the most part they sell for only fairly modest premiums over their face value. Typically the premiums on these notes are only $5 to $15 each unless they are quite dramatic or on scarce types of notes. Although notes of this class in CU condition command a premium over notes in VF-XF condition, I am not quite sure why, since all gutter fold notes have heavy creases. Sometimes there is only a single crease, but often there are multiple creases. On notes with very heavy creases there will often be a sizable area of the note in which there is no printing on at least one side.

Only rarely do gutter folds achieve premiums much higher than $100 on small-size notes. The exceptions would be very wide gutter folds or for these errors on the less encountered types such as Series 1928 gold notes, 1929 National Bank notes, and most especially some of the World War II issues. The Doovas collection that was sold by CAA in 1995 included a Series 1934A $5 Hawaii note in AU that had a pronounced gutter fold. It sold for $880, a price that would be regarded almost as absurd for most types of gutter folds on more typical small-size notes.

Each gutter fold is apt to be somewhat different from every other such error, since the creases will rarely be in the same places even if the same type of note is involved. If you enjoy this type of error, go ahead and buy a few. It is unlikely that they will strain your pocketbook in most cases. But gutter folds are basically rather unattractive notes, and I expect that a dozen or so samples of these items in one's collection should be adequate in nearly all cases to satisfy the appetites of most error enthusiasts.

Foldover Errors: This includes a wide group of errors that are broken down into several different classes by error specialists. One of the most common types are known as butterfly folds. These occur when there is a fold fairly near the corner of a note. This fold will be maintained during the first or second printing, and it will also be retained during the cutting process. The result is an extra wing tip to the note. When it is folded out, a blank portion of the corner design on that side will be revealed. Some caution should be observed in handling these notes, since folded corners can be easily torn off. Error catalogs and auction catalogs that illustrate these notes usually depict these notes with their butterfly folds extended, but they should be stored with these features folded over in the manner in which they were printed.

Butterfly folds can be found on all vintages of small-size notes, but the great majority of them are on recent issue FRNs. Typically these errors with relatively small corner folds command premiums of only $25 or so, but notes with multiple folds or with much larger folds may command premiums of $100 or more.

Some of the other types of foldover errors have the same appearance on one side as does a normal note. In some cases the portion that is folded over is left blank, while in others it picks up a portion of the printing that is intended for the other side. One of the scarcest small-size FRNs in my collection (a Series 1950E $100 from San Francisco) is of the former type. A portion of the first printing is missing due to a fold, but the second and third printings for this note are quite normal. This note is quite scarce in normal form, and I purchased it to complete my series of small-size $100 FRNs, but I can feel confident that a foldover error of this type will do nothing to reduce its value. It is easy to distinguish this type of error from an obstructed printing. In the former there will be a sharp crease at the junction of the printed and unprinted zones, but in an obstructed printing there will be no such crease.

Frequently the foldover may result in a portion of the third printing winding up on the wrong side. Both the first and second printings may be quite normal, but there will be a sharp crease on the note and the third printing features will be split between the two sides. Catalog illustrations usually depict these notes showing a normally spaced third printing, but when they are folded back or out these notes take on quite a different appearance since some of the third printing will wind up on the back side and there will be blank portions of the overprints on the face side. Premiums on such foldover errors will start at about $50, but dramatic examples can sell for several hundred dollars each. Before getting seriously into the collecting of foldover errors, I would recommend that you carefully examine various examples of this class. By all means fold them out to see how they look when so treated. For most notes only the front side or the back side can be displayed. For many foldover errors, however, a note can take on quite different appearances depending upon whether it is folded open or folded closed.

Another category of foldover errors are notes in which there are serious tears that developed somewhere in the printing process. Frankly I find this type of error to be decidedly ugly, but if you go in for notes that were damaged at the BEP rather than after they entered circulation, these may be of considerable interest to you. There are numerous illustrations of notes with printed tears in the error catalogs of Frederick Bart and Stephen Sullivan, but I would strongly recommend handling several examples of the real thing before committing much money to these items. A wide variety of possibilities exist. One of the more available (and least ugly) are the so-called accordion or pleat folds. Typically these sell at premiums of about $100 or so. Simple printed tears will sell at substantially lower prices, but complex mutilations may run to several hundreds of dollars. Frankly I prefer all my notes to be undamaged, but some collectors are willing to shell out serious money for these eyesores. The really seriously damaged error notes are rare, since they are usually detected and disposed of long before they leave the BEP.

Notes with BEP Rejection Markings: When error notes are detected by a BEP inspector, they are often marked with a red crayon or are indicated with a small adhesive rejection sticker. In numerous cases, however, a note with these markings survives the inspection process and is shipped out as an acceptable piece of currency. The presence of these indicators on an error note enhances its value, and they can be found on a wide variety of different types of paper money errors.

National Bank Note Errors: Although national bank notes exist with several of the aforementioned errors, other errors are possible for these notes as well. Basically all NBN errors are rare, and they are actively sought both by specialists in national bank notes as well as those who concentrate on errors.

National Bank Notes were in effect subject to a dual inspection process. They were subject to the usual control processes at the BEP, but then they were also carefully examined at the banks through which they were issued. Less attractive errors such as ink smudges or gutter folds would have often been returned for fresh notes, but major errors such as double denomination notes would frequently have been carefully preserved by the banks to which they were sent. Although no double denomination errors exist on 1929 Nationals, the majority of these errors on large-size notes occur on the various issues of NBNs.

The catalog of national bank notes written by Don Kelly provides a good idea of the types of errors that are known on NBNs. Gutter folds and butterfly folds do exist on a few 1929 Nationals, but they are decidedly rare. What would call for a premium of only $20 or $25 on a common FRN or SC would be worth a minimum of several hundred dollars on a 1929 National. Offsets of the black overprint of the backs of 1929 Nationals are known for several banks. Kelly's catalog lists two of these, and two others are illustrated in Sullivan's book. Sales of these errors are so infrequent that it is difficult to estimate values for them, but a minimum price of $1000 for a 1929 NBN offset in nice condition seems likely.

Series 1929 Nationals also exist with either the black or the brown overprints shifted or skewed. Notes from at least two banks are known with the brown overprints on their back sides. Turned digits are also known on a few notes of this series. Another class of error are obstructed printings in which a portion of either the brown or the black overprint is missing. One bank that shows these errors is the huge Chase NB of New York (2370). Such errors would be regarded as fairly minor on most common FRNs or SC's, but on 1929 Nationals they can bring big prices.

The following can be classed as major errors, and all are very rare.

Inverted Backs - This error is known on eight different banks for 1929 Nationals. Among these notes are a cut sheet of $10 type 2 notes from the Ohio NB of Columbus (5065). Recent auction sales for 1929 Nationals with inverted backs have been about $1000 to $1500 per note.

Inverted Overprints - Only three different varieties of these are known on 1929 Nationals, and all of them are on $5 type 1 notes. The error from The Farmers and Merchants NB of Tyrone, PA (6499) has an inverted black overprint, while those of The FNB of Belleville, IL (2154) and The Liberty NB & TC of New York (12352) have inverted brown overprints.

Mismatched Charter Numbers - This error is recorded only on a $10 type 2 note of the FNB in Tigerton, WI (14150). One of the two brown charter numbers is 12150.

Mismatched Serial Numbers - This error is recorded only on a $5 type 1 note of the Millikin NB of Decatur, IL (5089).

Missing Brown Overprint - This error is reported only on $10 notes of the Staten Island NB & TC (6198).

These major overprint errors are of the greatest interest and are worth a minimum of several thousand dollars each.

One type of "error" that must be treated with considerable skepticism are 1929 Nationals with their black overprints missing. A strong laundry detergent is capable of removing the black overprints on 1929 NBNs or FRBNs, but it will leave the intaglio printings and the brown overprints essentially intact. I do not know of any genuine error notes that are missing their black overprints, but any substantially worn 1929 National that lacks its black overprint is almost certainly a private alteration.

By far the most famous of the errors on large-size Nationals are the double denomination notes. Since most $10 and $20 notes were printed in sheets of 10-10-10-20, if one of these sheets were inverted prior to the second printing the net result would be a sheet consisting of one $10/$20, one $20/$10, and two $10 error notes with inverted backs. When such items were sent on to the banks, they were usually saved. These errors are known for both Second Charter and Third Charter notes. No $1/$2 or $2/$1 First Charter errors are known, and a $10/$20 Original Series error reported for the NB of Middlebury, VT (1195) is probably spurious. Second Charter $10/$20 or $20/$10 errors are presently known from nine different banks. If a $10/$20 error is known for a given bank, one would expect that its $20/$10 counterpart would also be known, but that is not always the case. All three issues of Second Charter notes (i. e., Brown Backs, Date Backs, and Value Backs) are known with these errors.

Series 1902 double denomination notes are presently also known from eight different banks. All of these are either Blue Seal Date Backs or Plain Backs, as no Red Seals are known. One of the best known examples of these errors are the notes from the FNB Parkers Prairie, MN (6661), an example of which is on display at the Higgins Museum in Okoboji, Iowa. The collection of Albert Grinnell, which was sold in the 1940s, contained most of the known varieties of double denomination NBNs, but today these notes are widely scattered and are offered for sale only infrequently. Expect to pay more than $10,000 for any of these notes in nice condition, which is usually the case. Even in the old days, "$30 bills" did not circulate very long before they were picked up by interested parties!

The Levitan collection featured the finest selection of double denomination NBNs since the auctions of the Grinnell collection. In the auction of the Levitan collection there were a total of seven of these notes. The notes together with their grades and prices realized were as follows:

1882 Dates $10/$20 FNB of Northport, NY (5963) VF+	$25,300
1882 Value Back $20/$10 Lowry NB of Atlanta, GA (5318) CU	$17,600
1882 Value Back $10/$20 FNB of Barry, Ill (5771) CU	$25,300
1882 Value Back $20/$10 FNB of Barry, Ill (5771) CU	$24,200
1882 Value Back $10/$20 Citizens NB of Houghton, MI (5896) AU	$18,700
1902 Dates $20/$10 Bank of North America, Phila, PA (602) XF	$13,200
1902 Plain $20/$10 FNB of Parkers Prairie, MN (6661) XF	$17,600

It will certainly be many years before we again will see an offering of these errors that is comparable to this one.

An additional pair of double denomination notes has only recently been reported and came into the market. These notes are Value Backs from the First National Bank of Smithton, PA (5311). The $10/$20 note in VF sold for $18,700, while the $20/$10 companion in VF-XF brought $17,600 in a CAA auction held in October, 1998. The Bass collection, which was sold in the spring of 1999, contained yet another $10/$20 error. The note in question was a Series 1902 Date Back from Lumberton, North Carolina (10610). It was in CU condition and sold for $36,800. This note was most unusual in that the $20 back was not inverted with respect to the $10 face. If arose when a 10-10-10-20 back plate was used instead of the 10-10-10-10-10 plate that should have been used for printing these notes.

The most impressive of all errors and also the most impressive of all national bank notes are two different pairs of $50 and $100 notes that were once in the collection of Albert Grinnell. The first consists of $50/$100 and $100/$50 Second Charter Date Backs from the Columbia NB of Buffalo, NY (4731). Even more spectacular is the $50/$100 and $100/$50 pair of Brown Backs from the FNB of Albuquerque, New Mexico Territory (2614). The notes in the latter pair are in CU condition. When these notes were sold in 1945, the Buffalo pair brought $730 while the New Mexico pair fetched only $830! Eventually the latter pair was acquired by Omaha coin dealer Aubrey Beebee, and he subsequently donated this set to the ANA Museum in Colorado Springs. In my opinion these are the finest and most valuable national bank notes in existence. When we consider that lower denomination Brown Backs in only VF or XF condition from Idaho Territory, Nevada, and Washington Territory have recently sold for more than $50,000 each, it seems certain that this pair of unique errors would be worth well into six figures, but unless the ANA decides at some future date to release this fabulous duo, they will remain institutionalized for many decades to come. The other pair of these ultra-rarities, i.e., the $50/$100 and $100/$50 notes from Buffalo were in the Bass collection that was sold in 1999. These notes are in AU condition, but each of them has a few pinholes. This unique pair sold for $109,250, a price that strikes me as rather low in today's hot market for double denominations notes, but I have been informed that the buyer was prepared to go quite a bit higher on this lot.

One would expect that $10 NBNs with inverted backs would be known for all of the banks for which double denomination notes are known, but these is not the case. Only two different varieties of $10 NBN inverts are known - a Second Charter Date Back from the FNB of Northport, NY ((5936) and a Value Back from the Old Citizens NB of Zanesville, Ohio (5760). A $5 Value Back from the latter bank is also known with an inverted back, as is a Third Charter Blue Seal $5 from the Commercial NB of Shreveport, LA (3600). Although large-size $5 NBNs were always printed in sheets of 5-5-5-5, inverted backs would have been possible even if double denominations were not. Although inverted backs are a major class of errors for large-size notes, they are extremely rare on national bank notes. Although "$30 bills" were often treated with much respect soon after they were issued, it seems that the $10 inverts that went with them were generally allowed to circulate and fade into obscurity.

Another extremely rare type of error that is known on large-size Nationals are mismatched charter numbers. A $5 1902 Date Back from the NB of Savannah, GA (3406) and a $10 1902 Date Back from the FNB of Bay Shore, NY (10029) are each known to have one of their charter numbers incorrectly printed. A $5 1902 Date Back of the Mechanics and Metals NB of New York (1250) is known overprinted with charter number 3557, a number used by a Philadelphia bank. Another unusual error is a $20 1902 Date Back from the FNB of Oxnard, CA (9481). This is supposed to have the Vernon-Treat signature combination (Fr. 644, H- 778), but Treat's signature was engraved twice on the plate while that of Vernon was not included. Oddly enough, the $10 notes on this plate all had the correct Vernon-Treat signature combination.

A few large-size NBNs are known with shifted or skewed overprints, transfers of these overprints, obstructed printings, or portions of overprints printed on back. All of these are quite rare and valuable. Errors involving the signatures of the bank officers were possible, and a fair number of these are known. Most of these involve misplaced or repeated signatures, etc. These notes command premiums over normal notes of the same types and banks, but they are much more reasonably priced than are any of the other classes of large-size NBN errors mentioned above.

Errors on other Large-Size Notes: Errors on large-size notes are vastly less common than they are on small-size notes, and several categories that are common on the latter do not even exist on large-size notes. Let us begin this discussion with double denomination notes. In addition to national bank notes, large-size errors of this type are also known on SCs, FRBNs, and FRNs, but the list of varieties is not a long one, as we shall see. No double denomination errors are known on USNs, gold certificates, or Treasury Notes. All of the non-NBN large-size errors of this type have their backs right-side up in contrast

with the NBN errors which always have their two sides upside down with respect to each other. The confirmed varieties are as follows:
    SC Series 1899 $2 (Fr. 258, H-196) / $1
    FRBN Series 1918 $2 Boston (Fr. 747, H-203A1) / $1
    FRBN Series 1918 $2 New York (Fr. 751, H-203B2) / $1
    FRBN Series 1918 $2 Chicago (Fr. 765, H-203G1) / $1
    FRN Series 1914 $5 Chicago (Fr. 868, H-381G1) / $10
    FRN Series 1914 $20 Boston (Fr. 964, H-849A1) / $10
    FRN Series 1914 $20 Chicago (Fr. 988, H-849G1) / $10

According to Martin Gengerke, only 31 examples of these errors have been confirmed to date. The $20/$10 FRN errors are all from cut sheets, and thus are still in choice condition. The other varieties all exist in a range of grades. If the term can be used, the most "common" of these errors is the $5/$10 FRN note. A total of seven examples of this item have been recorded. Prices on large-size double denomination notes are comparable to those of their small-size counterparts. The Levitan collection contained examples of the $2/$1 FRBN from New York in VF, the $5/$10 FRN in CU, and the $20/$10 FRN from Chicago in AU. These sold for $9900, $27,500, and $17,600, respectively. In 1999 a CU example of the Series 1899 $2/$1 silver certificate error was sold for $55,000 in a CAA auction. There have been rumors of a few other varieties of double denomination large-size notes, but they are unconfirmed.

    By far the most characteristic major error on large-size notes are those with inverted backs. In addition to NBNs these errors are noted on all six other classes of large-size notes that saw long-term circulation, i. e., USNs, SCs, gold certificates, Treasury Notes, FRBNs, and FRNs. In his book on errors, Stephen Sullivan lists a total of 68 different major varieties of non-NBN large-size notes that are known with inverted backs. His total census is 168 examples, of which 8 are star notes. All denominations from $1 through $100 are represented, and a full range of grades from AG to CU are found. Higher grades predominate, but the presence of numerous well circulated inverts indicates that these notes often circulated for several years before they were pulled from everyday use.

    The Ray Burns collection of errors that was sold by CAA in 1996 and 1997 featured a total of 21 different large-size inverts. Included were two different Bison note inverts in XF that sold for about $3000 each. A $5 Indian note in CU sold for $4125, while a Series 1908 $10 SC sold for $4675 in F-VF and a Series 1922 $20 gold note brought $1760 in VF. Even the most "common" $1 inverts in VG-F condition still brought about $500 each. Although less expensive than double denomination notes, large-size inverts are still important rarities that are being actively pursued by error enthusiasts.

    Inverted overprints are known on large-size notes, but they are far rarer than are notes with inverted backs. Only about a half dozen of these errors have been reported on various types of large-size notes, and all of these can be regarded as extreme rarities. Large-size notes with mismatched serial numbers are almost as rare, and thus far no large-size notes with seriously misplaced overprints (left, right, or skewed) have been confirmed. For all intents and purposes these types of errors are noncollectible on large-size notes. Oddly enough there are a number of large-size notes with missing overprints. In his catalog Frederick Bart lists 23 different major varieties of large-size notes (USNs, SCs, FRBNs, and FRNs) in all denominations from $1 through $20 that lack Treasury seals and/or serial numbers. Nonetheless these notes are still very rare, and prices of well into four figures can be expected for choice examples of these errors.

As I have noted in my chapter on large-size type notes, the red seals on most notes printed prior to 1900 are light-sensitive, and examples are often found in which this seal has faded to a dull pink. Prolonged exposure to strong light could remove a red seal altogether while leaving the carbon-base black intaglio printing intact. One should exercise considerable caution when purchasing an alleged missing overprint note that shows obvious signs of circulation.

Why are notes with inverted backs so much more common on large-size notes than are such errors as misaligned overprints or mismatched serial numbers? Just the opposite is true on small-size notes. Clearly large-size notes were hand inspected much more often during their production than has become the case with small-size notes in recent years. But if a note is not turned over, then the fact that its back is inverted would not be noted. Apparently the inspection procedures used by the BEP in processing large-size notes emphasized only the front sides of these notes. This would have readily caught such errors as misaligned overprints, but many inverted backs would have escaped detection.

Minor errors such as gutter folds and obstructed printings also exist on large-size notes, but they are very much less common than they are on their small-size counterparts. Other cutting errors such as butterfly folds are also occasionally encountered, but ink smears and offsets are virtually unknown on large-size notes. Even the most minor error would probably enhance the value of a large-size note in choice condition by at least $100 or $200.

Errors on Fractional Currency: A fair number of errors are known on the first three issues of Fractional Currency, and the great majority of these fall into one class, viz., inverts. The major collection of fractionals formed by Milton Friedberg featured a total of 90 inverts - 23 of the First Issue, 29 of the Second, and 38 of the Third. These were sold in a CAA auction early in 1997. Since the notes of the First Issue have no overprints, the inverts are straightforward, i. e., the back is inverted with respect to the face. For Second Issue notes, however, the back printing may be normal but the numeral overprint may be upside down. It is also possible for the numeral overprint to be normal with the back printing upside down or for both features to be upside down with respect to the face. On the 10¢, 25¢, and 50¢ notes of the Third Issue various possibilities also exist. For the common (in normal form) Third Issue 10¢ notes with green backs (Fr. 1255-56, H-1524-25) the Friedberg collection contained notes in which all overprints (face and back) were inverted but the intaglio back was normal, or these overprints were inverted and the back intaglio printing was also inverted, or the face overprint only was inverted, and the back intaglio printing was inverted but the overprints were normal.

No Fractional Currency inverts are common, and many of them can be classed as extremely rare. The highest price achieved for an invert in the Friedberg collection was $1870 for a 10¢ Third Issue note in superb condition. There was also a nice array of inverts for the complex 50¢ notes of the Third Issue, and typically sold for about $1000 to $1500 when in XF condition or better. Aside from a few low grade examples, hardly any of the inverts in this sale sold for less than $200 each. The least expensive of the fractional inverts appear to be the 5¢ and 10¢ imperf. notes of the First Issue (Fr. 1230 and 1242 or H-1504 and 1516).

The Friedberg collection also contained two major errors that were not inverts. A Second Issue double denomination note was offered that had a 5¢ face but a 50¢ back of one of the thin fiber paper varieties (Fr. 1322, H-1585). Although it is possible physically to separate the thin fiber paper on which these notes are printed, this note was in AU condition and appeared to be entirely genuine. It sold for $9625, which was by far the highest price paid for any of Milton Friedberg's error notes. Another impressive error was an XF example of the Third Issue 10¢ note (Fr. 1255, H-1524) that had no overprints at all on either side. It sold for $2200.

Miscut fractional notes also exist, but some caution must be exercised in purchasing these. Since full sheets or large blocks of various First and Second Issue notes as well as both varieties of the Third Issue 3¢ notes are available, it is possible to cut these into strange formats that resemble major cutting errors. On most alignment errors, however, one side with be badly out of alignment with the other side. Caution should be exercised in purchasing any so-called cutting errors of these notes. As I noted in my chapter on Fractional Currency, many fractional notes - and most especially notes of the Second Issue - are generally poorly centered on one or both sides. Do not confuse notes that are merely poorly centered with notes that are true alignment or cutting errors. Notes that very well centered on both sides and have good margins will command premiums over all but the most extreme of the notes with alignment problems.

Early editions of the Robert Friedberg catalog used to list a number of varieties of Second Issue notes in which some of the letters or numbers were missing. Today these are regarded as trivial variants. As I have noted, the overprints that appear on the back sides of the Second Issue notes are often indistinct. Some features are occasionally missing, but there isn't much interest in these variants at the present time. If you would like to collect these varieties, however, feel free to do so. They sell for not much more than do the normal notes of the equivalent major types.

Although the Milton Friedberg collection contained just about every conceivable variety of Fractional Currency, there were no genuine errors of the Fourth or Fifth Issues. Despite the unusual tete-beche sheet arrangements used for printing several of these notes, it appears that almost no inverts were made. Notes are known in which the red seals are absent, but like all red overprints found on pre-1900 paper money, they are subject to fading when exposed to strong light. Any Fourth or Fifth Issue fractional note that lacks its Treasury seal is probably an alteration.

Errors on MPCs: Despite the fact that there is a great deal of interest in replacement notes for MPCs, there does not appear to be much interest in error notes for this series. The chief reason for this apparent lack of interest is that MPC errors are basically very rare, and thus the supply is very limited. After leaving the BEP these notes were subjected to additional inspections by military authorities, and this tended to remove most errors before they could be released. Both alignment errors and shifted or skewed overprints have been reported, but they are far from common. MPCs with missing overprints are known, but they are extremely rare. A Series 541 5¢ note is known with a blank face, and a Series 471 fractional is known with serial numbers but with no design printing on its face, but both of these errors are excessively rare. Although mismatched serials are not possible on any of the fractional or $1 MPCs, they would be possible on the $5, $10, and $20 denominations, but I know of no such errors having been reported. No MPCs with inverted backs or with inverted overprints have been reported. Notes with ink smears or gutter folds also seem to be very rare for this series.

A spectacular misalligned overprint on a military payment certificate.

One error that does arise with MPCs but is absent from all other forms of Federal paper money are notes in which the printing from one of the underlying tint colors is absent. Unlike other forms of government paper money, MPCs are printed with multicolor surface printing that usually employs a number of different underlying tints. Often the shading imparted by one of these tints is rather subtle, and so its absence on an error note is not immediately obvious to the eye. One of the best known examples occurs with a small number of the $20 notes of Series 692, the last issue of MPCs.

Bookends, etc: To conclude this extensive discussion of error notes I should mention the term "bookend" that is often used in describing a sequence of error notes. A bookend note is an entirely normal note that is found either immediately in front of or immediately behind an error note. It is especially desirable to collect error notes with bookends in sequences that involve rolled digits or other numbering problems.

In a few important classes of errors the individual notes of a sequence may be quite normal. There are cases known in which a pair of notes (of the same series and denomination, of course) have identical serial numbers. This is a very rare type of error, and it helps to have bookends at either end to determine just what happened. The premium value of such a pair of notes, of course, is lost if they are ever separated. Another type of error sequence is what has been termed mixed denominations. This occurs if a $10 note were to be inserted and numbered into a sequence of $20 notes or vice versa. The authenticity of this type of error can be confirmed only if one of the denominations lies outside its normal serial number range for that district and series, but this type of error has been known to occur in recent production runs.

Fake Errors: At various times I have mentioned fake or altered errors in this chapter. In his book Stephen Sullivan wrongly asserts that manufacturing fake errors violates the counterfeiting laws. This is true only if there is an attempt to alter the denomination of the note, something that is virtually impossible to do with small-size U. S. paper money. It is not illegal to possess or collect fake error notes, but caution must be exercised before purchasing certain types of errors.

Almost all color errors are guaranteed to be fakes. I have seen USNs with seals and serial numbers in various shades of yellow or orange, but these never left the BEP in those colors. Oxalic acid is capable of changing many green-colored inks into blue, and so all FRNs with blue Treasury seals but black district seals can be dismissed as chemical changelings. Strong laundry detergents can remove the surface-printed black overprints from Series 1929 NBNs and FRBNs, so one must exercise great care in purchasing any so-called errors of these series that have missing or very light black overprints. I expect that the black overprints on Hawaii notes can be similarly treated. Almost all Hawaii error notes are scarce and command large premiums, but before you lay out serious money for a Hawaii error, make sure that you are getting the real thing.

Although most errors of color are alterations that have been produced after the notes left the BEP. There is one example that is unique and appears to be completely genuine. This is a Series 1922 $100 gold certificate (H-1241, Fr. 1215) on which the Treasury seal (which should be red) is in the same yellow-orange color that is used for the "GOLD" underprint. This note does not appear to have been altered in any way. It is in XF condition and was part of the Cookson collection that was sold by CAA early in 1999. The price realized was $10,450.

Fake offsets are not easy to make, but I have seen an attempt in which someone was able to get a normal note to go through a copying machine. The opposing side of a similar note was printed on top of one side, but the copied side was not mirror-reversed, as all offsets must be. Fake ink smears are much more of a problem. Before purchasing any ink smear error notes, become familiar with the genuine articles. I would strongly advise attending a large show or an auction that features numerous error notes before shelling out much money on these types of errors. Generally it is not advisable to purchase any heavily worn note that has a missing overprint. The surface printed overprints will go before the intaglio printings, but a lot of treatment is required. This is not possible on new or almost new notes. One other type of fake error that one must be careful about are so-called cutting errors for recent $1 and $2 FRNs. These may have been clipped from the uncut sheets that the BEP sells to collectors. Before buying any cutting errors of these notes, learn the sequence of serial numbers that were used on the printings of intact sheets.

If you have questions about the nature or authenticity of an error on a small-size note, I would consult with an expert on errors such as Frederick Bart, Stephen Sullivan, or Allen Mincho. I do not recommend sending an error note to the BEP for verification. Many agencies assume that if you supply them with a defective product that they have produced or sold to you, it should be replaced with a new intact specimen. When news about the Series 1996 $100 inverted errors reached the press, spokesmen from the BEP went on the air to assure the public that the error notes were good money and that anyone turning one in would be given a normal $100 bill in exchange. Selling an item now worth several hundred dollars for only $100 is not a good way to find out that the error note that you discovered is still acceptable as legitimate money!

Even if you plan to collect errors seriously, it is unlikely that you will attempt to acquire all of the various categories that I have described. Most errors that involve printed tears are downright ugly. The illustrations of mutilated notes depicted in the Bart and Sullivan books do not inspire me to want to acquire examples of these eyesores. Most likely you will want to specialize in only one or two categories of errors. I would avoid acquiring very many minor gutter folds or minor offsets. If you look through a pack of freshly printed notes, you will probably find a few that have light partial offsets. Unless these offsets, however, are decidedly obvious, they are probably not worth retaining in a collection, particularly if they are $20, $50, or $100 notes. Remember that the values of most recent error notes are figured as premiums over their face value. Collecting trivial errors on recent $100 notes is tying up a lot of capital on items in which there is not much collector interest. A good working definition of an error note is one that would have been rejected by the BEP if it had been detected during processing. Very minor misprints are tolerated on notes that are officially released, and these should properly not be regarded as errors.

As I have emphasized, the vast majority of available errors are on small-size notes. Errors on the other types of Federal paper money are basically rare and expensive. Perhaps you will want to collect only small-size errors. Small-size notes also feature error types (e. g., blank faces or backs, board breaks, overprints on back, ink smears, etc.) that are either nonexistent or are just about unheard of on other categories of Federal currency.

The truly spectacular errors, of course, are always expensive, but even these tend to be less expensive than are such items as Territorial national bank notes, Interest Bearing Notes, high denomination large-size notes, etc. The most treasured are probably the double denomination notes, and since there are only four different collectible varieties of small-size double denomination notes, this is a set that it is actually possible for an advanced collector to complete. Prices on these items now seem to be rising on this type of error after having been for many years in the doldrums. It also appears that in the last year or so much higher prices for some other types of dramatic errors are now being achieved. A few years ago hardly any errors sold for more than about $2000 each with the exception of the double denomination notes that typically brought about $5000 or $6000 each. For the first time we are now seeing prices in five figures for the most dramatic types of errors.

If you decide to add some large-size or fractional notes to your error collection, your range of categories for these is rather limited. Most of the significant errors for either of these are inverts. The great diversity of error types that is available for small-size notes is not available with these older forms of currency. Error collecting is a decidedly individual field. Some varieties may fascinate you, while others may leave you cold. If you go into this field, collect what appeals to you.

CHAPTER TEN

FANCY SERIAL NUMBERS

Collectors will differ as to what can be termed a fancy serial number, but I think that a good working definition is any note whose serial number is sufficiently unusual to impart a significant premium value to that note over what that same note would be worth if it had a normal or uninteresting serial number. Excluded from this definition, however, are star or replacement numbers and scarce blocks. These I have already discussed in detail in the earlier chapters of this book. For simplicity let us refer to notes with unusual serial numbers as "fancies." Since fractional notes have no serial numbers, "fancies" are not possible with these. MPC with fancy numbers is so rare that there does not seem to be much interest in MPC fancy numbers. Thus almost all interest in "fancies" focuses on large-size and small-size issues, and as usual, by far the vast majority of the existing "fancies" are small-size notes. Small-size notes also have a more uniform numbering system, so let us begin our discussion of "fancies" with these issues.

Aside from Series 1929 NBNs all small-size notes have eight-digit serial numbers. This allows for up to 100 million notes per block, although in recent years most blocks have been completed with only 96 million notes. Within a given block the notes are always numbered sequentially. For a block of 100 million notes there will be nine different solid numbers or "solids" as they are usually called. Examples would be 11111111, 22222222, etc. Since there is only one "solid" for roughly every ten million notes that are printed, these items are clearly highly desirable and worthy of very large premiums. Although it would be virtually impossible to assemble a set of "solids" from the notes in everyday circulation, enough have been put aside over the years for these items to be fairly readily available. In 1997 CAA auctioned the set of all nine solid numbers that had been assembled by Malcolm Thompson. All were on $1 SCs of various series from 1928 to 1957A, and all were in choice condition. The 33333333 through 77777777 notes sold for about $800 each, while the 22222222 note sold for a bit more and the popular 11111111 note brought $1100. The number 88888888 has become very popular, and that note in this set sold for $1485. Not unexpectedly, the 99999999 note brought the highest price at $1870. In August, 1998 another complete set of "solids" was sold by Lyn Knight in his Dallas auction. All of the notes in this set were $1 SCs ranging from Series 1935D to 1957A, and all were CU. The 11111111 note sold for $1870, the 88888888 for $2090, the 99999999 for $3080, and the prices on the six others ranged from $1210 to $1430. Note that all of these prices were significantly higher than what had been achieved for the similar set in the previous year. Although the "solid 9" notes are available on $1 SCs and the earlier $1 FRNs, most blocks that the BEP completes these days do not go past 96 million notes, thus eliminating the possibility of this serial number on recent notes. Solid numbers for recent $1 FRNs cost somewhat less than do the silver certificates that I have discussed above, but one can expect to pay at least $500 to $750 for a recent "solid" note in CU condition, as is nearly always the case.

You might think that notes with 7 digits the same or 6 digits the same would sell for healthy fractions of these prices, but that is most definitely not the case. For each solid number there are 72 possibilities for notes with 7 digits the same and one unmatched digit. For every solid number there are 4536 possibilities for notes with 6 digits the same. As a consequence recent $1 FRNs with 7 digits the same are only worth about $25 each, while note with 6 digits the same sell for only about $5 each.

Although I have stressed auction sales for the more expensive currency items, dealers are often good sources on these as well. They are particularly good sources for "fancies," especially those that are only moderately priced. A well-known dealer in "fancies" is Mike Abramson of Duluth, Minnesota, and his price lists give a lot of information about the pricing and availability of these items. Although a single solid number note would cost at least $500, Mr. Abramson offers progressive 7-digit sets of nine notes at prices that range from only $200 to $275 per set. Each set consists of nine notes having the same matched seven digits. If this digit is 6, then the unmatched digit is progressively 0, 1, 2, 3, 4, 5, 7, 8, and 9, and these digits are always in the same place in the serial number. Yet such an intriguing set costs only about half as much as does a single solid number note.

Other types of progressive number sets are those in which a given digit "migrates" between the zeros of the serial numbers. A complete set would consist of eight notes. If the migrating digit is 5, then the numbers of such a set would be 00000005, 00000050, 00000500, 00005000, 00050000, 00500000, 05000000, and 50000000. These sets are much harder to come buy, and generally they are available only with mixed series of $1 notes that include both FRNs and SCs. Typically such a set would cost about $1500, and the most difficult of these notes to acquire is almost always the last note of the set, i.e., the note with the highest serial number.

Number one notes are clearly in very great demand. For a full block only one note in 100 million can have this number. For a recent $1 FRN a #1 note typically sells for about $1500-2000. Although equally scarce, the other single-digit serial numbers sell for very much less. Typical prices for recent notes with the other single-digit numbers are between $100 and $200 each. Other highly desirable notes are the "ladder" notes. These have progressive sequences of eight numbers going either up or down. Sequences such as 12345678, 98765432, or 01234567 would be examples. These are worth a few hundred dollars each. "Round-the-corner" ladders such as 78901234 or 43210987 are less popular and sell for substantially less.

A much less expensive class of "fancies" are the repeater numbers. Typical three-digit repeaters would be 35253525 or 06070607, etc. Abramson sells these for $8.00 each. Two-digit and four-digit repeaters also exist. An example of the former would be 64646464, while the sequence 15461546 would be an example of the latter. If you are a tax accountant, a note with the number 10401040 would make a nice addition to your collection. Such notes are significantly less common than are the three-digit repeaters.

Another popular class of "fancies" are the radar or palindrome notes. On these notes the serial number will read the same way from left to right or from right to left. Ideally the block letters should also be the same at either end, but these are generally ignored on radar notes. The value of a radar note depends to a good extent upon how many digits are involved. A number such as 11166111 would be more desirable than would 15488451. Radars on recent notes begin at premiums of only $5 or so per note, but dramatic examples can sell for $100 or more.

Although notes with single digit serial numbers are very scarce, notes with two digit numbers are much less rare and command much smaller premiums. Notes with three or four digit serial numbers are readily available, and these are worth premiums of only a few dollars each on common $1 SCs or FRNs.

Some "fancies" can sell for well into four figures. In 1992 Lyn Knight offered a Series 1950C $10 FRN in XF with the serial A11111111* and a 1981A $10 FRN in AU with serial F00000001*. Solid numbers or number 1 serials on star notes such as these are of the highest rarity. Even rarer are the nine-digit notes (i. e., the last note of a 100 million note block). Prior to 1935 the last note of a given block was given the number 100000000 (one followed by eight zeros). Only five such examples have been confirmed on small-size notes. There are three known Series 1934 $1 SCs and one each of Series 1928A and 1928B. One of the former is the middle note in an incredible sequence of three notes - 99999999, 100000000, and 00000001. The first two notes of this trio are from the BA block that precedes the CA block for the #1 note. This sequence of three notes was originally in the famous Grinnell collection. It was last sold for $19,800 in a CAA auction in October, 1998.. The serial number 100000000 has also been recorded on eight individual large-size notes - $1 SCs of Series 1899 and 1923, a $2 USN of 1917, and a $5 FRN of 1914. All of these can be regarded as rarities of the highest order.

As I noted in Chapter 9, there are a few pairs of notes known that have identical serial numbers. These are classed as errors, and they are decidedly rare. Far more common are notes of two different blocks having identical eight-digit serial numbers. Also of interest would be notes of two different series having identical blocks and numbers or identical numbers only. One could also have FRNs of different districts but of the same series and having identical serial numbers aside, of course, from the initial district letters. Although the numbers themselves might not be interesting, such pairs are of some interest to a number of fancy serial number collectors.

A decidedly unusual fancy number in an unexpected place.

There is probably no field of paper money collecting that is as individualized as is that of fancy serial numbers. With the exceptions of extreme rarities such as 100 million number notes, the rarest and most desirable "fancies" are the number 1 notes and the solid number notes. Almost all other possibilities are much less expensive. If you cannot afford to collect "solids," try collecting 7-digit notes instead. A full progressive set of nine of these notes sells for only about half what is asked for an individual "solid" note. "Fancies" are very much like error notes in their valuations. A particular number sequence will command a certain premium that can then be attached to the face value of that note. If a certain 7-digit sequence is worth a premium of $30, that sequence on a current $1 note would be worth about $31 while the same sequence on a recent $20 note is worth about $50. The majority of "fancies" collectors concentrate on $1 notes. Although a few $50 and $100 "fancies" may be acquired, most of them are not very popular. Until recently printings for most $50 and $100 FRNs did not exceed 10 million per district. This did not allow for any eight-digit solid numbers for these denominations. These are now being printed, and the premiums on eight-digit "solids" are such that $50 and $100 notes with these numbers are now avidly collected.

Fancy serial numbers on large-size notes are also actively collected. If you plan to acquire any of the #1 notes or very low serial number notes of these, it is important that you acquire a copy of Martin Gengerke's paper money records. Serial #1 notes exist for a fairly wide variety of notes. The United States Notes of Series 1862-63 were numbered in "series" of 100,000 each. With these relatively short numbering sequences several #1 notes of this period have survived. In addition to some relatively common notes, the #1 notes for the very rare Series 1875A and 1875B $2 USNs (Fr. 45-46 or H-155A-B) both are known to exist. The serials 1-4 and 5-8 of all three of the Educational Notes still exist in uncut sheet form, although the first set of these is institutionally impounded. No very low serial numbers exist for Series 1914 blue seal FRNs, since the numbering of these notes continued from the red seal notes of this series. FRN star notes with low number serials do exist, however, since no red seal star FRNs were printed.

If you wish to collect large-size notes with very low serial numbers, the most interesting notes are probably the Series 1899 $1 SCs, the so-called Black Eagle notes. These exist with a wide variety of signature combinations, block letters, and low serial numbers. There are enough on the market such that most Black Eagle notes with two-digit serial numbers are only worth about a 50-100% premium over what the same notes in identical condition but with uninteresting serial numbers would be worth. There also are a fairly large number of low number $1, $2, and $5 Series 1918 FRBNs from the Cleveland district on the market. An astute teller in the Federal Reserve Bank of Cleveland is responsible for putting these aside. FRBNs with low numbers from a few other districts are also sometimes available.

Large-size notes were numbered in a different fashion from small-size notes. An eight-digit solid number note would be possible only if more than 10 million notes were printed for that block. Since the serial numbers on large-size notes were not preceded by zeros, notes with serial numbers such as 555, 4444, 77777, or 333333 can also be termed solid number notes, but these would be of substantially less value than would eight-digit solid notes.

Another category of fancy serial numbers are those found on NBNs. Since only six digits were used for numbering Series 1929 NBNs and since many issues of these notes had total printings that were only in the hundreds or even dozens, there is nothing at all unusual about notes with two-digit serial numbers. Even single-digit notes do not usually command much of a premium unless that digit is a "1." Oddly enough type 2 #1 notes do not sell for much more than do type 1 #1 notes. On type 1 notes there will be six #1 notes on the first sheet, whereas there will be only one #1 note on the first sheet of type 2 notes. For type 1 notes the #1 notes of all six blocks are worth about the same. For type 2 notes the notes with numbers 2, 3, 4, 5, and 6 are worth significantly less than is the #1 note. Many of the uncut sheets of 1929 Nationals are the first sheets of these notes to be issued from a given bank, and thus there are many varieties of #1 Series 1929 NBNs that are available. Number 1 notes also exist for many varieties of large-size NBNs. On notes that have both bank serial numbers and Treasury serial numbers, the #1 notes almost always have this number for their bank serial. Notes with the Treasury serial equal to unity would be excessively rare; perhaps there are none at all. Since I do not collect #1 notes *per se*, I have only very few of these in my NBN collection. The only large-size #1 note that I have in my collection is, of all things, a $50 Brown Back from the FNB of Lincoln, Illinois (2126). For large-size $5 NBNs there should be four #1 notes if this number is known to exist at all. For the majority of $10 NBNs there should be three notes of a given number, but only one $20 note. Serial number 1 large-size NBNs are less rare than one might think, because these notes were often retained by the banks that issued them. Another type of NBN fancy number collecting that could be pursued is to collect notes whose serial numbers matched their charter numbers. Although this pursuit could be undertaken on either large-size or Series 1929 NBNs, few collectors of Nationals seem to be much interested in acquiring such curiously numbered notes.

    Some of the other notes in my collection can probably qualify for either fancy or near fancy serial number status. My $1 Tillman-Morgan Educational (Fr. 224, H-45) has serial #643 together with plate numbers of "1" on both sides. This note would command a modest premium over more typically numbered notes. Fancy serial numbers do not necessarily enhance the value of a major rarity, however. For instance, the Series 1933 $10 SC in my collection has serial #44. If this were a common note such as a Series 1934 $10 SC, this number would be worth a substantial premium over a typical note, but for a major rarity a two-digit serial number is of not much significance. A couple of my 1937 experimentals (on Series 1935 $1 SCs) have very low serial numbers. The BB block note of this issue in my collection has serial #47, an interesting number on a silver certificate since 47 is the atomic number of silver. On the other hand, it is unlikely that collecting SCs with serial numbers ending in 47 or gold certificates with numbers ending in 79 (the atomic number of gold) would appeal to many persons who were not physical scientists. Notes with serial numbers that end a given sequence or series of notes are of much greater significance. The Series 1928 $1 USN with serial #5000 is in private hands. This would have been the last of the 5000 notes of this issue that were released in Washington in 1933, and as a consequence it is of great interest to specialist collectors of that enigmatic issue of notes.

    All sorts of serial number collecting is possible. If you want to collect "fancies," try to acquire as many different dealer price lists as is possible. Bear in mind that even rather inexpensive notes will usually only be one-of-a-kind, so if you want that note, telephone the dealer right away as to your wishes. If you are willing to settle for a variety of radar or repeater notes, then there will always be quite a bit of material available, but if you want a particular number sequence, you may have to wait quite a while, even if the note in question is inexpensive. By all means try to attend as many large currency shows as is possible. Much patience in searching for the serial numbers that appeal to you is required if you plan to collect "fancies" in depth. As is the case with error notes, I would concentrate more on a relatively small number of decidedly interesting "fancies" rather than assemble large numbers of notes whose serial numbers are only of very modest interest. For regular issue small-size FRNs, I stated in Chapter 4 that you should first carefully define your collecting parameters before you acquire many notes. For fancy serial numbers and for error notes as well, I expect that your collecting parameters will change as your collection grows.

CHAPTER ELEVEN

SHEETS

Although most varieties of U. S. Federal paper money are not available in complete sheet form, many uncut sheets do exist. For Fractional Currency a small number of First Issue and Second Issue uncut sheets do exist, but the most readily available of the fractional sheets are those of the 3 cent value of the Third Issue. This exists for both the light curtain and dark curtain varieties in uncut sheets of 25, although the dark curtain variety is quite scarce in this form. All of the later issues of Fractional Currency, however, are either excessively rare or nonexistent in complete sheet form. As for MPCs, none at all exist in uncut sheet form. Thus most uncut sheets of Federal money are of either large-size or small-size notes, and the great majority of these are of the latter varieties.

Some uncut sheets, such as those of all large-size notes and all Series 1929 NBNs, are of formats that cause relatively few problems concerning their storage and preservation. Sheets of some of the small-size notes, however, are very large, and their size often makes it difficult to store them properly. Before getting seriously into the collecting of uncut sheets, I would suggest that you familiarize yourself with each of the different formats of the sheets that are available. These are as follows:

Large-size notes:	1 x 4 notes	19 x 35 cm	$7^{1}/_{2}$ x 14 inches
Small-size NBNs:	1 x 6 notes	16 x 40 cm	$6^{1}/_{4}$ x $15^{3}/_{4}$ inches
Sheets of 12	2 x 6 notes	31 x 40 cm	$12^{1}/_{4}$ x $15^{3}/_{4}$ inches
Sheets of 18	3 x 6 notes	47 x 40 cm	$18^{1}/_{2}$ x $15^{3}/_{4}$ inches
Sheets of 32	4 x 8 notes	62 x 54 cm	$24^{1}/_{2}$ x $21^{1}/_{4}$ inches
Sheets of 16	2 x 8 notes	31 x 54 cm	$12^{1}/_{4}$ x $21^{1}/_{4}$ inches
Sheets of 4	1 x 4 notes	16 x 27 cm	$6^{1}/_{4}$ x $11^{1}/_{2}$ inches

Before purchasing any uncut sheets of currency I would strongly suggest that you acquire a wide roll of good quality wrapping paper. Measure and then cut out pieces that match the above sizes for uncut sheets. This will give you a good idea of what you will need to store in a proper fashion. Both the 32-subject and 16-subject sheets that are now being sold by the BEP do pose storage problems, and this is a matter to which I shall return at the end of this chapter.

All uncut sheets of large-size notes are both rare and expensive. Hessler's catalog gives a comprehensive listing of all of the large-size type notes that are known in uncut sheet form. It includes the Series 1896 $1, $2, and $5 Educational notes, Series 1899 $1, $2, and $5 SCs, and $1 Treasury Notes of Series 1890 and 1891. United States Notes are represented by $1, $2, $5, $10, and $20 sheets, all of which have the Elliott-White signature combination. A sheet of Speelman-White Bison notes is also known. There are also five known uncut $5 sheets of a Series 1918 FRBN from Atlanta and one each of the Series 1915 $10 and $20 FRBNs from Chicago. Several of these varieties are unique in uncut sheet form, and all of the others can be regarded as extremely rare.

Cut sheets of large-size type notes are offered with very much greater frequency. Typically the plate letters on large-size notes will be A, B, C, and D, and a set of four of these with their serial numbers in sequence is termed a cut sheet. Since this is the way in which large-size notes were numbered and stacked, any sizable run of consecutively numbered large-size notes will contain at least a few cut sheets. As a consequence, cut sheets of large-size type notes are only worth about four times what the individual notes in the same condition would be worth. If you are interested in collecting plate letter varieties on large-size type notes (But as I have previously noted, very few collectors are.), cut sheets will be quite interesting for you, but most collectors probably just choose to regard these sets as four notes of the same variety and in the same condition.

The vast majority of the known uncut sheets of large-size notes are of national bank notes. In his catalog of NBNs, Don Kelly gives a full census of all the NBN sheets that are known to him. Rather more than 2000 sheets are recorded, and of these 426 are of large-size NBNs. These include 18 First Charter sheets, 68 Second Charter (58 Brown Back, 7 Date Back, and 3 Value Back), and 340 Third Charter (43 Red Seals, 34 Date Backs, and 263 Blue Seal Plain Backs). Several of the sheets in the census have been cut in recent years, and this is a question to which I shall return.

Although the known First Charter sheets include both 5-5-5-5 and 10-10-10-20 items, most of the known examples are 1-1-1-2 sheets. All of these, however, are extremely rare, and are offered for sale only infrequently. The Second Charter sheets include various 5-5-5-5 and 10-10-10-20 items, but the largest single group of these are the sheets of $5 Brown Backs from the Saint Paul NB (3129) in Nebraska. A few of these have now been cut, but an intact sheet from this bank sold for $6050 in a CAA auction held in 1999. There is also a unique 50-100 Brown Back sheet from the Corn Exchange NB of Chicago (5106).

As might be expected, the great majority of large-size uncut sheets are of Third Charter notes. Most of these are either 5-5-5-5 or 10-10-10-20 sheets, but a few 10-10-10-10 sheets are also known. A wide variety of banks are represented, and no one variety is available in large numbers. In my chapter on national bank notes, I wrote in some detail about the $5 Red Seal notes from the FNB of Fairbanks, Alaska (7718). This was one of the more "common" large-size sheets, but a few of these have now been cut, given the extremely high demand for Alaska notes. Two of the great western Red Seal sheets are both unique. These are the 5-5-5-5 sheet of the FNB of Rexburg, Idaho (7133) and the 10-10-10-10 sheet of Saratoga, Wyoming (8961). The former has now been cut, but the latter is still intact.

Whether or not to cut an extremely rare sheet of NBNs poses a major dilemma for the advanced collector or dealer. There is far more demand for individual notes than there is for uncut sheets. Cutting an extremely rare sheet apart may make it easier to sell, but in many cases it does make uncut sheets for that particular variety forever unavailable.

In his catalog Don Kelly lists the serial numbers of about 1600 known Series 1929 NBN sheets. This includes a number of cut sheets, but the vast majority of these are uncut. Including the large-size notes uncut sheets are known from 50 different jurisdictions. Only Hawaii is unrecorded as having uncut sheets of NBNs. The vast majority of uncut 1929 NBN sheets are of the $5, $10, and $20 denominations. Only nine $50 sheets and ten $100 sheets are presently known. All of the $50 sheets are of type 1 notes, but the

$100 sheets include one type 2 note from the Rhode Island Hospital NB of Providence (13901). A few uncut 1929 NBN sheets exist in substantial quantities. I have already discussed the type 2 sheets of the FNB in Reno, Nevada (7038) in some detail. Two other banks that have fairly large numbers of uncut sheets are the FNB of Cassopolis, Michigan (1812), and The Boatmen's NB of Saint Louis (12916). The former are all type 1 $5 notes, while the latter bank has $5, $10, and $20 notes of the same series.

Between 1929 and 1954 uncut sheets for several other types of small-size notes were made available to collectors. Most of these are either SCs or USNs, but very small numbers of FRNs and FRBNs were also released in the early days of small-size notes. The early sheets of small-size FRNs are restricted to Series 1928 and 1928A notes. Sheets were prepared for all 12 districts, and these were issued in denominations of $5, $10, $20, and $50, although not all of these were issued for all districts. Although these sheets were prepared in very small quantities (no more than 12 of a given note per district), regrettably there have been severe losses of these sheets, most likely through cutting. At the present time no $50 FRN uncut sheets are known. The other three denominations do come up for sale occasionally, but just assembling a set of sheets of these three denominations would be a formidable undertaking. Prices would be about $10,000 to $15,000 per sheet for these notes.

Complete sheets of the Series 1929 FRBNs are, if anything, even more challenging. Only six uncut 12-subject sheets are known. The $10 note is known from New York in this form, and there are three known varieties of $20 FRBNs. But given their extreme rarity, uncut sheets of Series 1929 FRBNs are effectively noncollectible.

There are several varieties of uncut sheets of $1, $5, and $10 SCs, and these range from scarce to very rare. For the normal $1 SCs there are ten known varieties of 12-subject sheets (Series 1928, 1928C, 1928D, 1928E, 1934, 1935, 1935A, 1935B, 1935C, and 1935Dw) plus two varieties of 18-subject sheets (1935Dn and 1935E). For the 1935Dw and 1935E sheets a number of different block varieties are known. These are also the most abundant of the uncut sheets with over 50 examples of each being known. At the other end of the rarity scale, only one sheet of 1935A mule notes is known. All of the notes in the normal 12-subject sheets are sequentially numbered, but the notes in the 18-subject sheets show a range of 136,000 in their serial numbers.

The rarity of the $1 SC sheets does not necessarily parallel that of the single notes. The 1928D sheets are significantly more abundant than are uncut sheets of Series 1928 or 1934. The scarcest of the $1 uncut sheets are Series 1928C and 1928E. The value of a 1928E sheet, however, is not greatly in excess of that for a dozen individual CU notes of this issue. A number of these sheets have been cut apart to provide single examples of this rare note. The 1928E $1 SC in my collection was cut from the second complete sheet of this issue to be printed.

A total of 25 examples each of the $1 Hawaii and North Africa notes in uncut sheet form were released. At the present time 20 of the Hawaii sheets and 14 of the North Africa are known. All of the notes in these sheets are from the FC block. As I noted in Chapter 3, these blocks were used very sparingly for the World War II issues, but a fair number of single FC notes of each issue are known. It seems certain that none of the notes from this block were sent out for distribution overseas, as was the case for almost all of the other Hawaii and North Africa issues. Unlike all of the other 12-subject sheets, the uncut sheets of these issues show a different range of numbers in their two columns, the right hand side being about 2000 numbers higher than the left hand side for a given sheet.

Sheet of 12 $1 North Africa notes. Photo courtesy of Lyn Knight Auctions.

Five-dollar SCs exist in sheets of 12 for Series 1934, 1934B, 1934C, and 1934D, while $10 notes of this format exist only for Series 1934. There are also 18-subject sheets of Series 1953 for both $5 and $10 SCs. All of the $10 sheets are very rare. The $5 sheets are also scarce, the least rare of this group being the 1934D and 1953 sheets.

Uncut sheets of $2 USNs in 12-subject form are known for Series 1928, 1928C, 1928E, 1928F, and 1928G, and in 18-subject form this issue is known for Series 1953. There are only two known examples of the Series 1928 notes, and the 1928D sheets are also quite scarce. About 25-30 examples of uncut sheets of each of the other varieties are known. Only a single example of the Series 1928 $5 USN uncut sheet is known. Uncut 12-subject sheets of Series 1928D and 1928E $5 USNs and 18-subject Series 1953 notes of this type are known, but these are less common than are the uncut sheets of the corresponding $2 notes.

The first ten sheets of the enigmatic Series 1928 $1 USNs were left uncut, as were the final dozen notes of this issue. Eight of these sheets are still known. Although this is not the rarest of the sheets of the various issues of small-size notes, it is easily among the most expensive. An example of this sheet would probably sell for well over $10,000 in today's market. In much more recent times a single sheet of Series 1966* $100 USNs was left uncut. Although this sheet is government property, it was loaned to the ANA and may be seen at its museum in Colorado Springs.

Although these sheets have been expensive for many years, there has been less collector demand for them than there has for many other types of Federal currency. The net result is that price rises on these items have been fairly modest for most of the past two decades or so. In 1998 CAA sold a sizable group of 23 examples of these uncut sheets. Among the $1 SCs prices ranged from $550 for one of the 12-subject 1935C sheets to $880 for an 18-subject 1935D sheet. The $1 Hawaii and North Africa sheets are much more expensive, and these sold for $6050 and $8250, respectively. There were also some 12-subject $2 USN sheets that sold for about $940 each on average. A 12-subject 1928E $5 USN sold for $1650, while a 1934C $5 sheet in the same format sold for $1595. Both 18-subject Series 1953 USN and SC sheets were present. These items sold for about $1300 each.

Between 1954 and 1981 the BEP prepared no uncut sheets for sale to the public. It then began to offer a variety of uncut products. First only $1 FRNs were offered, but these were joined within a few years by $2 notes. The sale of $5 sheets only started in 1998. If sales are good, these items may be joined by $10, $20, $50, and $100 notes. All of these notes exist in three different formats - full 32-subject sheets, half sheets of 16 subjects, and small sheets of four in strip form. The two larger sizes are available both in rolled form and in flat form mounted in a cardboard frame. Current sheets may be ordered from the Order Processing Center of the BEP, P. O. Box 371594, Pittsburgh, PA 15250-7594. They are also available for over the counter sales at the Visitor Center of the BEP in Washington at prices that are significantly less than what they cost through the mail. Another place to buy these sheets is at the major coin and paper money shows where the BEP has set up a display. In 1998 the prices (shipped and over the counter) for the various sheet formats are as follows:

	$1	$2	$5
32 note sheets, framed	52.00/46.00	89.00/83.00	200.00/194.00
32 note sheets, rolled	50.00/44.00	85.00/79.00	196.00/190.00
16 note sheets, framed	32.00/26.00	49.00/43.00	108.00/102.00
16 note sheets, rolled	31.00/25.00	48.00/42.00	107.00/101.00
4 note sheets with folder	15.00/11.50	19.00/16.00	36.50/32.50

The framed sheets cannot be sent to Canada due to Canadian postal regulations that forbid the shipment of such bulky items.

Many different series and block varieties exist for the both $1 and $2 sheets. Unfortunately the BEP order forms do not inform the buyer as to which of these varieties are available. The Oakes and Schwartz catalog attempts to list the serial number ranges of the numerous varieties of $1 and $2 sheets that do exist, but their list is not complete. All series of $1 notes from 1981 through 1995 have been printed, and for some series such as 1981 and 1985, sheets exist for all districts. Most of the $2 sheets have been Series 1976 star notes, but the four-note sheets of this denomination have used some non-star blocks of the New York, Richmond, and Minneapolis districts that have not been widely used for regularly issued notes. Thus far all of the uncut sheets of these issues have been printed at the Washington facility of the BEP. It seems possible, however, that uncut sheets from Fort Worth may appear in the near future.

The post-1981 sheets of FRNs strike me as being collectible items whose time has not yet come. Most of the large sheets that are sold as used just as novelty display objects. Thus far there does not seem to have been much serious syngraphic interest in these items. With as many different series, district, and block varieties in existence as is now the case, it seems most likely that several of these may be very uncommon, and some may even be quite rare. The chief drawback on these sheets as true collector's items, of course, is their unwieldy size. A collection of these sheets requires special storage equipment that is not needed for any other types of currency items.

Although the cardboard frames suppled by the BEP are fine for the casual mounting of a sheet or two on a study or parlor wall, they are not really suitable for the long-term storage of sizable numbers of these sheets. For this I would recommend using a couple of large-size Mylar folders per sheet, and the sheets should then be stored in a metal cabinet of the type used for storing maps. Even 18-subject sheets can pose major storage problems when one tries to put them into a bank rental locker or vault, and I feel that this is one major reasons why there has been less interest in the pre-1954 currency sheets than there has been for most other U. S. Federal paper money items.

I would not recommend the long-term storage of currency sheets in rolled form. Rolled sheets can be pressed with no harm whatsoever to the notes, but the absorbent paper on which they are pressed must be at least as large as the sheets themselves, and uniform pressure needs to be applied across the entire area of the sheet. The sheets can then be placed into a locked metal map cabinet or similar container that is designed to hold flat documents of large surface area.

One 32-subject sheet that is closely related to the currency sheets of this format are the uncut sheets of the Magna test notes that were printed in the early 1970s. (See Chapter 14 for more details.) These are even somewhat larger than are the 32-subject currency sheets, since there are ample margins on some of the sides of these sheets. These items are now selling for about $500 per sheet, and you may want to include one in your collection if you decide seriously to collect uncut sheets.

Thus far I have only discussed uncut sheets of U. S. Federal paper money. Aside from the current products that are now being sold by the BEP, by far the most readily available uncut sheets are of obsolete currency of the pre-Civil War period. Almost all of these are sheets of unissued remainders. Usually they are in new condition, but the paper may show some aging, and occasionally there are tears and chinks in the edges of some sheets. The remainder sheets of the Canal Bank of New Orleans and the Citizens Bank of Louisiana are particularly well known, but there are many other varieties. Indeed one could form a sizable collection of state bank notes in which all of the items were in uncut sheet form. Somewhat later than most state bank notes are the South Carolina Revenue Bond Scrip notes that were printed by the American Bank Note Co. in 1872. These are comparable in beauty to First Charter NBNs, but they are vastly less expensive and make beautiful wall display items. Of all the different types of paper money used in the United States, the state bank notes are the most amenable to being collected in uncut sheet format. These notes are almost always in sheets of four, and the sheets are more or less the same size as is an uncut sheet of large-size Federal notes. Thus in storing complete sheets of obsolete currency, one does not run into the problems which are encountered in properly storing and caring for the recent 32-subject sheets.

If instead you would prefer to stick with modern Federal issues, this is a wide open field both for collecting and for research. Despite their recent vintage there is no established rarity scale for the different series, district, and block varieties of the $1 and $2 FRN sheets at the present time. For the most part, these sheets are also inexpensive. Although there is not much serious syngraphic interest in these sheets at the moment, it may develop within the next few years, and the systematic collecting of the numerous varieties of these sheets would doubtless lead to sharp price increases for some of them.

CHAPTER TWELVE

ALTERED AND COUNTERFEIT NOTES

There are very strict Federal laws forbidding the altering and counterfeiting of U. S. paper money, but many persons, including numismatists, misinterpret the word "alter" in the context in which it is used in these statutes. During the era in which state bank notes were in general circulation, the altering and raising of notes were common practices. A note from a broken bank could be altered to that of a good one by changing some of the logos or titles to match those of the good bank, and these design features could often be obtained by clipping them from low denomination notes of good banks and attaching them to the altered note. Another practice was to "raise" a low denomination note of a good bank to a higher denomination of that same bank. With so many designs in circulation at the same time, both of these practices frequently occurred. In contrast Federal paper money uses only a few designs, and these are familiar to most persons who handle money. Thus the altering and raising of Federal currency are virtually impossible in the sense in which they are defined in the anti-counterfeiting statutes. Printing fake red "R" or "S" letters, for instance, on Series 1935A $1 SCs is not an ethical practice, but in doing this no attempt is made to change the face value of the notes, and so this does not constitute alteration in the sense in which that term is used in the anti-counterfeiting statutes.

For the purposes of paper money collecting I would define altered notes as any in which changes have been made after the note has been issued to the public. In most cases this would include any modifications to the notes after they have left the printers, but one must remember that large-size national bank notes were generally shipped to their respective banks without bank signatures. Properly signed large-size NBNs, of course, are not considered as altered notes. In light of what I have stated above, almost all altered notes are perfectly legal to hold and collect. In my opinion there are three different major categories of altered Federal notes. These are notes with courtesy autographs, novelty alterations, and fraudulent alterations that are designed to deceive numismatists. We shall examine each of these categories in some detail, but let me first refer again to one of the classic rarities of Fractional Currency that is in fact an altered note.

In about 1890 the stamp and coin dealer Harlan P. Smith is believed to have privately perforated a few 50¢ First Issue fractional notes. His products were perforated 14 rather than 12 as was used on the government-issued notes of 1862. These notes are almost always found in choice condition, and several of them have their sheet margins still attached. Although only about a dozen of these notes are now known, it is believed that two sheets or 32 notes were originally privately perforated. Despite the fact that these notes are purely private alterations, they have been assigned numbers in the standard paper money catalogs (Fr. 1310a, H-1575a), and they sell for high prices on the rare occasions when they are offered for sale. As an unofficial issue, however, the perf. 14 First Issue 50¢ note is not needed for a "complete" set of fractional notes. This is the only private alteration of Federal paper money that has been awarded "full honors" in the catalogs, but these are very rare items that only a few specialists can hope to acquire.

Courtesy Autographs

Without doubt the most popular types of altered paper money are notes with courtesy autographs. Autographed signatures are found on all Demand Notes and on several types of Fractional Currency, but in these cases the signatures were applied as part of the manufacturing process. Courtesy autographs were applied after a note had been issued to the public, and in some cases many decades after this note had been originally issued. Putting a signature onto a bank note does not affect its legal tender status, but almost all interest in courtesy autographs focuses on the signatures of those Treasury officials whose facsimile signatures have appeared on Federal paper money. Let us first consider small-size notes.

The tradition of courtesy autographs continues. This Series 1996 $100 Federal Reserve note has manuscript autographs of T. R. Hipschen (portrait engraver, upper left), Mary Ellen Withrow (Treasurer, lower right), V. James Ruther (designer, upper right), and Len Buckley (design director, lower right).

Most small-size notes bear the facsimile signatures of the Secretary of the Treasury and the Treasurer of the United States. Although the former is an important cabinet official, the position of Treasurer has declined immensely in importance since the days when Francis Spinner served in this role. Since 1949 all Treasurers have been women who have been selected primarily for their work in party politics, either Democratic or Republican, as the case may be. As long as silver certificates and United States Notes were still in circulation, the Treasurer had some function in the disbursement of currency to the banks, but now all of that is handled by the Federal Reserve System. At the present time it seems that one of the major functions of the Treasurer is to sign bank notes at large coin and paper money shows. Thus recent FRNs that have been signed only by the Treasurer are not rarities at all. You supply the note at a show where the Treasurer is in attendance, and she signs it. I doubt that you could get a pack of 100 notes autographed in this fashion, but if business is slow you can certainly obtain a few signed notes at the same time. Typically recent $1 FRNs autographed by the Treasurer retail for $4 or $5 each, but if you attend shows at which the Treasurer appears, you should have little difficulty in obtaining a number of these at face value.

Notes that have been signed by the Secretary of the Treasury or by both officials are a good deal more difficult to acquire. Typically $1 or $2 FRNs with these signatures sell for prices in the $20 to $50 range. Older notes such as $1 SCs or $2 USNs are encountered with courtesy autographs less often than are contemporary FRNs. These notes with the signatures of recent Treasurers would not be of much interest, but notes signed in the 1940s or 1950s would probably be worth at least $25 each or more. Recently a CAA auction featured a collection of 29 mostly different autographed small-size notes ranging from the 1940s to the 1990s. Many had both signatures, and some had very low serial numbers. Despite the fact that the face value of this lot was only $35, it sold for $1980. This was well above estimate for this lot, and it indicates that there is a strong interest these days in at least some of the courtesy autographs that are to be found on small-size notes.

This same auction also featured two major small-size rarities with courtesy autographs. These notes in question were gem CU examples of the rare Series 1928E $1 SC, one of which bore the signature of Henry Morganthau Jr. while the other had that of W. A. Julian. The "Morganthau" note sold for $1760, while the "Julian" note sold for $2200. Non-autographed examples of these notes in gem CU sell for about $1250 each, so the autographs in this case (doubtless extremely rare if not actually unique) substantially enhanced their value.

I do not collect courtesy autographs at all, and thus I do not claim to have a very good feeling for the relative demand for these on different types of Federal notes, but I think that there is probably greater interest for these items on small-size notes than on large-size notes, in part because of the lower cost and the much greater availability of the more recent items. On small-size notes most collectors desire items that are autographed by one or both of the individuals whose facsimile signatures appear on the note in question. On large-size notes some of the autographs are contemporary, but many were prepared years after the notes were issued. Without doubt the most common autograph found on these notes is that of John Burke, who was Treasurer from 1913 to 1921. He often signed notes that had been issued decades before his term of office. Another official whose autograph is frequently found on large-size notes is Carmi Thompson, who was Treasurer only briefly in late 1912 and early 1913. Although the Napier-Thompson signature combination is one of the scarcest ones to be found on issued notes, Thompson autographed many notes after he left office. The practice of courtesy autographs became more common in the early 20th century than it had been during the 19th, and consequently the autographs of some of the earlier Treasury officials are rarely encountered on notes. The elaborate signature of Francis Spinner appearing as a courtesy autograph on any note of the 1860s or early 1870s would considerably enhance its value, but such items are quite rare.

The following should give you some idea of what large-size notes with courtesy autographs are selling for at auction these days. In auctions held between 1992 and 1997 typical realizations for notes autographed by officials whose facsimile signatures appear on the notes were as follows. A Series 1880 $2 USN (Fr. 52, H-162) in CU signed by A. U. Wyman brought $633, three notes signed by D. N. Morgan (an 1891 $1 SC in CU, an 1891 $1 Treasury Note in VF, and an 1880 $20 USN in CU sold for $632, $385, and $1320, respectively, while an 1886 $1 SC (Fr. 218, H-39) in CU signed by J. N. Huston brought $1320 and an 1899 $1 SC (Fr. 226a or H-48) in CU signed by E. H. Roberts sold for $385. The notes signed by Wyman and by Morgan sold for prices that were only slightly more than what would be expected for non-autographed notes in the same condition, but the Huston and Roberts notes were sold at a substantial premium. A very high price of $1045 was achieved for a CU example of a Blue Seal $5 FRN (Fr. 871, H-381G4) that had been autographed by the famous A. W. Mellon. If you want to assemble a sizable collection of autographed large-size notes, considerable patience as well as substantial funds are necessary.

National bank notes sometimes are found with courtesy autographs in addition to the normal signatures of the president and cashier that one expects to find on these notes. It does not seem to me that such notes sell at prices that are very much more than similar notes without courtesy autographs, but such notes, of course, would be of enormous interest to a collector who is interested in the signature of a particular bank officer.

The highly comprehensive collection of Fractional Currency that had been formed by Milton Friedberg was sold by CAA in January, 1997. It included about 120 fractional notes with courtesy autographs including a full sheet of 20 Second Issue 5¢ notes that had been signed (15 times) by John Burke. This sheet brought $1540 in this sale. Another interesting group as a set of the four perforated First Issue notes in CU condition that bore the autographs of James Gilfillan, who was Treasurer from 1877 to 1883. It sold for $825, a price that was about twice what an unautographed set of these notes in similar condition would bring. The two highest prices in this group were for notes that had been signed on their backs by the two individuals most involved with the production and issuance of Fractional Currency, viz., Spencer Clark and Francis Spinner. A 5¢ Third Issue note with Clark's signature sold for $2640, while a 25¢ note of the same issue with Spinner's autograph brought $2090. The high price for the note with Clark's autograph can be attributed to the fact that his signature is extremely rare on paper money. Common notes (usually 10 cent notes) of the Fourth and Fifth Issues that had been autographed either by John Burke or by Carmi Thompson did very well in this sale. Typically they sold for about $100 to $150 each, which is far above what normal issues of these series would sell for.

One other category of autographed notes are the so-called "short snorters" that became popular with airmen and other military personnel during World War II. Often the members of a flight crew would each put their signatures on a single bank note. Typically these would be normal $1 SCs, but $1 Hawaii and North Africa notes were also frequently used. Often "short snorters' were prepared on foreign notes, and I have seen a number of Chinese notes of the 1930s or 1940s that were signed by flight crews involved with supplying Chungking from India or Burma. The custom predates World War II, and large-size notes were sometimes signed in this fashion. A few years ago one auction even offered a Series 1922 $100 gold certificate that had been signed in this fashion. More typically, however, the notes were $1 bills that were prepared in a quantity sufficient to allow every member of the crew to have at least one copy. These items are of great interest to collectors of aviation and World War II memorabilia, but they are infrequently seen in most paper money auctions.

Novelty Alterations

I use the term novelty alteration to identify paper money that has been altered either by having artwork done on it or by having attachments placed on it. Included in this category are the satirical fractional notes, postally canceled $2 FRNs, and notes with attached decals. The satirical fractional notes are much the oldest and most interesting of these alterations. During the late 19th century numerous artistic liberties were taken with some of the fractional notes. By far the most popular for these endeavors were the common 10 cent notes of the Fifth Issue. Although many persons might have considered it disrespectful to make caricatures out of engraved portraits of Washington or Lincoln, few had any qualms about modifying the somber portrait of the obscure William Meredith who appeared on these notes.

Milton Friedberg, who collected all forms of Fractional Currency, also had about 200 satirical notes in his collection. Most of these were from the late 19th century, but some were of more recent origin. On most notes additional features (such as beards, moustaches, pipes, hats, etc.) were drawn in, but in a number of cases some of the engraving was removed by scraping out some of the portrait. By the early 20th century several colors were often used. Each note is in effect, unique, and its value depends as much on its artistic quality as on its grade. The better quality notes sold for about $50 each, while notes with less artistic merit sold for more like $20 each. Since a normal red seal Meredith note in XF-AU condition sells for only about $12 to $15, these items do have a premium value, but no one seems willing to pay big sums for any of them. Although the great majority of the satirical items use the 10 cent Fifth Issue note as their base, a few other fractional notes were used as well, most notably the 25 cent notes of the same issue.

When the $2 Federal Reserve Notes were first issued in 1976, there was quite a bit of interest in obtaining these notes with postal cancellations indicating the first day of issue. Such notes would have a postage stamp attached (usually a 13 cent stamp, since this was the letter rate at that time), and they would be canceled in the normal fashion. The presence of a postal cancellation did not affect the legal tender status of the notes. These items are available as single notes or as district sets of 12. Some enterprising individuals even prepared sets that had been canceled in all 50 states. Despite the promotion of these items in the 1970s, they proved to be a fad that never really caught on. Today individual notes are available for about $4 or $5 each, and they sell for even less than this when offered in bulk lots. Postally canceled notes seem to be restricted almost exclusively to Series 1976 $2 FRNs. I have not seen $1 FRNs treated in this fashion, although a few may have been prepared. It seems likely that the persons who prepared these items found that they generated little serious collector interest, and so no further large-scale attempts were made to produce other types of postally canceled Federal Reserve Notes.

A third category of novelty alterations are notes with decals. The issuance of Series 1963 $1 FRNs occurred almost at the same time as the assassination of John F. Kennedy in November, 1963. Kennedy half dollars were soon issued, and the appearance of an entirely new type of $1 bill led some entrepreneurs to attach decals of John Kennedy to the space where the portrait of George Washington appeared on these notes. Soon these were followed by $1 FRNs depicting Jackie Kennedy, Lyndon Johnson, Barry Goldwater, Marilyn Monroe, Elvis Presley, etc. In the mid- to late 1960s there were numerous ads for these items in coin magazines and elsewhere. Typically they were sold for about $2.50

each. Although not illegal to make, I doubt that the Treasury Department or the Federal Reserve Board was ever very much impressed with these efforts, and some cold water from official sources was most likely poured on their increased production. They never were more than a fad that seems to have died out during the 1970s. Recently, however, I note that one dealer is again offering more contemporary designs on current $1 FRNs. If you are interested in "kitsch" of the 1960s, you might want a few of these items for a nostalgia collection, but in my opinion they do not deserve a place in a serious collection of U. S. Federal paper money.

Fraudulent Alterations

As I have already noted, U. S. Federal paper money is essentially immune from any alterations designed to raise the face value of a note, aside from occasional very crude paste-ups that are capable of fooling no one when properly examined. Thus the fraudulent alterations of Federal currency fall into the much milder (from a legal point of view) category of fraud rather than counterfeiting. Fortunately there are not many of them.

In their book on the numismatics of World War II Fred Schwan and Joseph Boling describe a most unusual altered note. It is a Series 1934A $10 North Africa note that was altered to resemble a $10 Federal Reserve Note of the same series. From a numismatic point of view, this is absurd. Why would anyone attempt to transform a common Series 1934A North Africa note into an equally common FRN of the same series? Whoever did this was under the impression that North Africa notes either had been demonetized or could not be used in the United States. Both of these assumptions are quite wrong. Although such an alteration might be of little interest to collectors, it would be fully legal to own (since no attempt was made to raise its face value) and it would be of great interest to collectors of World War II nostalgia items.

The fraudulent alterations that are of interest to syngraphists are those that are designed to deceive collectors, but U. S. Federal money has very few of these, especially in comparison with either coins or stamps. In purchasing a 1914D cent, a 1916D dime, or an 1893S silver dollar great care must be exercised to make sure that the item in question is genuine. Numerous 1944D cents have been filed down, and many 1916 dimes have had fake D's attached. In stamps there are all sorts of problems involving fake overprints on genuine stamps, fake cancels, outright counterfeit stamps, etc. Fortunately collectors of U. S. paper money have much less to worry about.

In my various detailed commentaries I have already mentioned some of the notes for which these problems might arise. The experimental notes of 1944 have the letters "R" or "S" surface printed on the very common Series 1935A $1 SCs. But the 1944 experimentals are all from the SC block, and the first digit of the serial number always is a "7." Refer to my chapter on small-size notes for the serial number ranges of these issues. The star note varieties of these items are very rare. Their serial numbers always begin with 911 and the fourth digit is either a 7, 8, or 9. In the days when specialized catalogs of small-size notes were not available, a few fraudulently overprinted 1944 experimental notes might have been passed onto unsuspecting customers, but no informed person should be fooled by them. It is perfectly legal to collect fake 1944 experimental notes (provided, of course, that the Series 1935A $1 SCs from which they were made are genuine), but they do not deserve a place in a serious holding of small-size notes.

The Series 1934 $10 North Africa note is a major rarity, while the Series 1934A note of this issue is quite common. Doubtless some "A's" have been scraped off of examples of the latter note, but this should fool no one. All Series 1934 North Africa notes are mules, while all 1934A notes are non-mules. In my chapter on small-size notes I also listed the check numbers that are found on the Series 1934 notes. The differences are obvious, and no informed collectors should be fooled by fake Series 1934 notes, if any are to be had these days.

For small-size notes much greater problems with fraudulent alterations arise with paper money errors. These I have already discussed in some detail in Chapter 9. If you collect these items, it is extremely important to know what the real stuff looks like. Some errors such as smears are relatively easy to fake, and doubtless many such fabrications are being made at the present time. As long as no attempt is made to change the face values of the notes, the anti-counterfeiting laws are not being violated when any types of fake error notes are manufactured. Your best defense is to have a good idea as to the look and feel of genuine paper money errors and to deal only with persons of integrity who are highly knowledgeable in this field.

Aside from errors, the most serious problems with fraudulent alterations arise with fractional notes, but even here the problems are minor compared to what awaits the unwary in coins or stamps. Undoubtedly the most famous of the altered fractional notes is the 50 cent note of the Second Issue without any corner overprints on its back. This is listed as Fr. 1314 or H-1579. For many years it was assumed that this variety existed as a genuine note, but all items purporting to be this note appear to be either fraudulent alterations or notes in which the back overprint has faded out. No longer is this variety listed at high prices in the standard catalogs. If you desire one for your collection, a few are floating around, but they are almost certainly alterations of one of the three other varieties of 50 cent Second Issue notes (Fr. 1316, 1317, or 1318) that were printed on plain paper. Thus this note should be worth at best little more than what an example of one of these three notes would bring (about $50 to $75 in XF-AU condition), a far cry from the prices that were sometimes once asked for the "extremely rare" Fr. 1314 note.

Another Second Issue fractional note to be careful with is the 10 cent note with the overprint "O - 63" on its back (Fr. 1248, H-1522). Only about 30 genuine examples of this note are known, and these sell for a minimum of several hundred dollars each. Although I have not heard about any fake overprints, they could be produced by fraudulently overprinting the very common Fr. 1244 (H-1518) with these characters. If there is even the slightest question as to the authenticity of a note being sold as Fr. 1248, I would check with an expert on Fractional Currency such as Martin Gengerke (of R. M. Smythe) or Leonard Glazer (of Currency Auctions of America).

Since the "1a" varieties of the Third Issue 50 cent notes are more valuable than are the "1, "a," or plain notes of the same types, a few attempts may have been made over the years to add either a "1" or an "a" or both to another note, but this does not seem to be a problem. As I mentioned in my chapter on Fractional Currency, there is quite a range of sizes and fonts on these characters, and thus comparisons should always be made with authentic notes of the same issue.

Counterfeit Notes

Counterfeit U. S. paper money is not legal to possess or to collect, but a rather sharp distinction has been drawn between small-size notes on the one hand and the other varieties (large-size notes, fractionals, and MPCs) on the other. Although the major paper money auctioneers will not handle large-size or fractional counterfeits, these items are occasionally seen at large shows, and there seems to be little effort made by government officials to seize them. Small-size counterfeit notes, however, are strictly illegal, and under no circumstances should you attempt to collect or sell them. Mere possession of such items may be treated as a serious Federal crime under the present anti-counterfeiting statues.

The U. S. Secret Service is charged with the enforcement of our nation's anti-counterfeiting laws. Although their agents are trained to detect and intercept counterfeits of contemporary U. S. paper money, my casual contacts with them have led me to believe that most agents are not well informed about earlier types of Federal paper money such as large-size notes, Fractional Currency, MPCs, etc. If you have a questionable note from the 1860s, the Secret Service is most definitely not the place to contact about whether or not the note is genuine. As for more recent issues, neither Fred Schwan nor I are clear about the exact legal status of counterfeit MPCs. Since all MPCs have been demonetized, it may well be that counterfeits of them are perfectly legal to own as is the case with fake state bank notes, Confederate notes, Continental Currency, etc. On the other hand, they are issues of the United States government, and thus fakes of these issues may still be regarded as illegal. When I contacted the Secret Service about the legality of fake MPCs, I had to explain to the agent with whom I spoke what Military Payment Certificates were. He then suggested that I contact the Federal Reserve about them! Since the Federal Reserve System was never involved with the issuance of MPCs, it is clear that the Secret Service these days neither knows no cares about whether collectors may or may not possess a few counterfeit MPCs.

Most available counterfeits of large-size notes date from the 1860s or early 1870s. At that time the custom was to mutilate a fake note and return to the sender much as what one would do today with a bad check. After about 1875, however, counterfeit notes were confiscated whenever they fell into the hands of government agents. Thus counterfeits of large-size notes printed between about 1875 and 1928 are rarely encountered. Earlier ones are sometimes available in canceled form, and there are also a few fake notes that escaped detection as counterfeits and remained uncanceled. For many years the illustration of the Series 1863 $50 USN that appeared in the Friedberg catalog was of a counterfeit that had escaped detection. In the current edition this illustration has been replaced with that of the genuine Series 1862 $50 note that is in my collection. The fake Series 1863 $50 USN was a very good copy, but if you own an earlier Friedberg catalog, flip several times between the $50 illustration and that of a genuine Series 1862 $2 note. Note how much better Alexander Hamilton appears on the $2 note than he does on the $50 note!

Of the three standard paper money catalogs only the Krause-Lemke catalog provides a detailed survey of counterfeit large-size type notes and NBNs. In Don Kelly's catalog of national bank notes there is also a detailed survey of counterfeit NBNs. The Krause-Lemke catalog lists about 350 known varieties of fake large-size type notes and about 250 varieties of counterfeit large-size NBNs. Kelly's catalog lists about 290 varieties of fake large-size NBNs, and there are numerous differences in the listings of these notes provided in these two catalogs. In the listings of rare large-size notes compiled by Martin Gengerke serial number data are provided for a number of counterfeits of some of the rarest type notes.

During the 1850s and early 1860s numerous talented, but dishonest, individuals were involved in the counterfeiting of state bank notes. State bank notes, however, ceased to circulate to any extent after 1866, and this induced many of them to apply their talents to the counterfeiting of the various forms of Federal paper money that was just then coming into circulation. The counterfeiting of this currency (but not of state bank notes) was made a Federal crime, and in 1865 the Secret Service was established with its dual missions of combating counterfeiting and protecting the president.

Since counterfeits of U. S. Federal money were returned like bad checks prior to 1875, far more counterfeits are known to collectors for notes issued between 1862 and 1875 than are known for the later issues of 1875 to 1928 when all detected fake notes were destroyed or at least retained in government custody. Interestingly enough, there are virtually no known counterfeits of the Demand Notes of 1861. These were already largely out of circulation before counterfeiters could come up with good copies of these ephemeral issues.

A number of the counterfeits of the 1860s are well-known and are worthy of some comment here. There were three very good fakes of the $50 USNs, one of the Series 1862 notes and another in New Series 1 of the 1863 issue. Both of these feature very good portraits of Alexander Hamilton. Another example of Series 1863 (but in New Series 2) features a slightly inferior portrait of Hamilton, but its lathe work is superb. This is the one that appeared in earlier editions of the Friedberg catalog. Another note of this vintage that was superbly counterfeited was the $1000 USN with the Second Obligation back. These exist with dates of both March 10, 1862 and March 10, 1863, as do examples of the excessively rare genuine notes.

At shows I have seen an example of a fairly good counterfeit of a Series 1862 $100 USN that had been neatly canceled at the Treasury and returned together with a detailed letter handwritten and signed by Francis Spinner. A less well done note that I have seen is a Series 1863 $20 USN that uses the First Obligation back which appears only (for notes genuinely issued) on Series 1862 notes of this type. There are also Series 1863 $10 USNs that are fairly well done, but the counterfeiter for some reason used the signature of John New, which was not used on this issue, rather than that of Francis Spinner.

The $50 and $100 Compound Interest Treasury Notes of 1864 and 1865 were extensively counterfeited, and more counterfeits are presently known for these notes than are genuine copies. All $50 notes dated July 15, 1864 are believed to be counterfeit. Although the illustration of a genuine (but damaged at the left end) note was used in earlier editions of the Friedberg catalog, the current edition illustrates a counterfeit note instead. (Both the Hessler and Krause-Lemke catalogs illustrate genuine notes for this rare type.) Several counterfeits are also known for the $100 notes of these issue, but all three of the standard paper money catalogs do illustrate genuine copies in this case. The Friedberg catalog, however, illustrates a counterfeit of the Series 1865 $1000 Three-Year Note (Fr. 212g, H-1401).

Two famous counterfeits from the end of this decade are the fake Series 1869 $50 and $500 USNs. The production of these counterfeits led to entirely new designs for these denominations in 1874. The fake $50 notes always have a plate letter B, and there are a few distinguishing features, although the lathe work in general is superb. The $500 counterfeit is even closer to its genuine counterpart than is the $50 note, but the Series 1869 $500 USN is excessively rare either in genuine or in counterfeit form.

Most counterfeit national bank notes that are known to collectors are of the First Charter period. Oddly enough, however, there are no known counterfeits of the National Gold Bank Notes of California. Some of the counterfeits are from spurious banks, and a number have incorrect charter numbers, but some very good fakes are known of the $5 through $100 denominations of First Charter notes. At the right ends of First and Second Charter $100 notes there is an allegorical vignette representing the Union with the slogan "Maintain It." On the early versions of the counterfeits, which are known from six different banks, this slogan appears as "Mainiain It." The best of the $100 NBN counterfeits is a later version of these notes from the Pittsburgh National Bank of Commerce (668). The spelling error has been corrected, and the note is on fiber paper that closely approximates the paper that was used for the authentic notes of that era. There are also a number of good counterfeits of $50 Original Series notes, almost all of which are from New York. Most of these have engraved signatures for the bank officers, a practice that was not used on any First Charter notes. First Charter $5, $10, and $20 notes were counterfeited in larger quantities that were the $50s and $100s, and some of these are deceptive. For about a year (during 1873-74) the production of Original Series $10 notes was halted due to presence of numerous counterfeits of this type,

If you are seeking genuine examples of any of these rarities, extreme caution must be used. Although the fakes are worth far more than their face value, they are worth far less than the values for the corresponding genuine notes. Although no major paper money auctioneers will handle these items, they do appear from time to time in large shows.

As I have already noted, you are much less likely to encounter counterfeits of the 1875-1928 period than you are fake notes of the 1860s and earlier 1870s. A fairly large number of fraudulent notes were made in these years, but few of them were of superb quality. The best were probably fake Series 1891 $100 SCs (Fr. 344, H-1221) bearing the Tillman-Morgan signature combination. All of these bear plate letter D and plate number 1. The existence of these notes led to the removal of $100 SCs from circulation in the late 1890s. Although there were new issues with blue seals for the $10, $20, and $50 SCs printed during the years 1908-16, no $100 SCs were made after the mid-1890s.

A number of counterfeit Fractional Currency notes are seen from time to time. Generally these are not seen in canceled form. Typically fake fractionals saw extensive circulation, and the ones available today are generally well-worn. Since fractional notes were of small size, bore no serial numbers, and passed rapidly from hand to hand, they were favorites with counterfeiters during the 1860s and 1870s. As I noted in my chapter on Fractional Currency, the first 50 cent note of the Fourth Issue (depicting Lincoln) was soon replaced by one depicting Edwin Stanton, and within a fairly short amount of time the Stanton note was replaced by one depicting Samuel Dexter. These changes in design were due to the fact that good-quality counterfeits were prepared of both the Lincoln and Stanton notes.

Although it is not officially legal to collect counterfeit large-size or fractional notes, a number of collectors do own them and a few dealers occasionally handle them. At the present time, it does not seem that the Secret Service is making any serious attempt to confiscate them. Although almost all counterfeit large-size notes are worth far less than are their genuine counterparts, they are in every case worth far more than their face value. Counterfeit fractional notes are rarely encountered in nice condition, and in most cases counterfeit fractionals are worth substantially more than are their genuine counterparts when the latter are in the same condition as are the fake fractionals. Thus these items do not constitute any threat whatsoever to our nation's currency. Perhaps the collecting of these notes will one day be formally legalized, but for the time being one should exercise a fair amount of discretion in buying, selling, or exhibiting counterfeits of the earlier forms of Federal paper money.

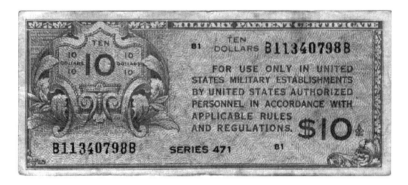

Both of these MPC counterfeits are fairly good with the serial numbers being the most obvious tip. There is also a very subtle and egregious error on the Series 471 (top), one that a collector might spot. The position number 81 is incorrect for this denomination. The highest number used was 50! The counterfeiter had not added the serial numbers to the Series 641 note when it was seized.

If you are concerned about the genuineness of a Federal large-size note, fractional note, or MPC, I would most definitely not advise contacting any government agency. Most government officials, in fact, are not well qualified to pass judgment on the genuineness of the earlier forms of Federal paper money. If the note in question is deemed counterfeit, it will be confiscated and no compensation will be offered. By all means do check the detailed listings given in the Krause-Lemke catalog or in Don Kelly's catalog of national bank notes. I would also consult with an expert on large-size notes. Fred Schwan's book on MPCs lists the best-known counterfeit MPCs, and I would study this work should you acquire a questionable note of this type.

Although you may wish to acquire a few counterfeit large-size or fractional notes, when it comes to small-size notes my advice is quite simple, DON'T! During the past 70 years, large numbers of fake small-size notes have been made by a wide variety of processes both here and abroad. In past decades most counterfeit notes were printed from hand-engraved plates. Today, however, color copiers are capable of producing passable fakes, and devices such as ink jet printers can also be utilized to produce reasonably good copies. In recent years very good intaglio-printed $100 FRNs have been manufactured in the Middle East. These have been deemed the "super hundreds," and sizable numbers of these notes are in circulation abroad. I have not handled or seen any "super hundreds," but they are said to be quite deceptive, even to persons well familiar with the design and paper characteristics of contemporary Federal currency. These notes, however, use the designs of notes issued prior to Series 1996, and thus far no dangerous counterfeits of any of the Series 1996 FRNs have yet appeared in circulation. There have already been some counterfeits of Series 1996 notes, but the ones that I have heard about lack the watermarks, dichroic inks, and plastic threads that are characteristic of the genuine notes.

If you are a member of a coin club or other numismatic organization, the Secret Service will sometimes provide speakers for society meetings. Often these talks include exhibits of "real" contemporary counterfeit paper money. This is one way in which you can become familiar with the look and feel of modern fakes. If you should ever come into possession of any dubious small-size notes, it is probably best to follow the standard procedures. The Secret Service should be contacted, and they will pass judgment on your notes. If deemed counterfeit, they will be confiscated without compensation but also without any criminal charges filed against you. If you have been given a fake note (especially a $20, $50, or $100 note), it might be tempting to pass it on, but in British legal parlance this is termed "uttering" a counterfeit note, and such an action does constitute a serious criminal offense. As a syngraphist, however, it is unlikely that you will be fooled by any but the very best of contemporary counterfeit notes. When traveling in some parts of eastern Europe or the Middle East, however, I would be very cautious about accepting $100 FRNs of Series 1974 through 1993. One group of notes that you will almost never have to worry about, however, are fake $500 or $1000 notes. Due to their limited circulation, these denominations were almost never counterfeited.

CHAPTER THIRTEEN

NON-FEDERAL TYPES OF AMERICAN PAPER MONEY

As I explained in the preface of this book, this is a work on the collecting of U. S. Federal paper money, the regular issue of which began only in 1861. In this chapter I wish to survey in a cursory fashion the other types of paper currency that have been used in the territory of the United States. Perhaps we should begin our discussion, however, with the earliest series of Federal paper money, viz., the notes of 1812-15, which are often go unrecognized by collectors solely because they are not listed in some of the standard catalogs of U. S. paper money.

During the War of 1812 the Treasury Department issued a number of distinct series of bank notes. The issues of 1812-14 bore interest at 5.4% per annum and were issued in denominations of $20, $50, and $100. The issue of February 24, 1815 included an interest bearing $100 note, but it also included non-interest bearing notes for $3, $5, $10, $20, and $50. Although none of these notes were legal tender, they did circulate to some extent during this period. There are still a number of survivors, and these exist in issued, canceled (usually with a single large hole), or unissued (i. e., unsigned) form. The $3 note is of special interest, since it is the only Federally-issued note of this denomination. These notes are expensive (typically $3000 or more in decent condition), but enough examples are known to make them collectible at least for dedicated syngraphists.

Of the standard currency catalogs both the Hessler and Krause-Lemke books list these notes in some detail. It is possible that collector demand would be much higher for these items had the Friedberg catalog (which predates the other two standard catalogs by many years) begun its numbering system with these issues rather than with the Demand Notes of 1861. Unlike later Federal issues, however, these notes are probably not redeemable. An act passed in 1817 provided for the recall of the notes of 1812-15, and it also prohibited the further issue of such notes. There were a few other issues of Federal notes between 1837 and 1860 (all interest bearing and mostly of fairly high denominations), but almost none of these are available to collectors as are some of the notes of 1812-15. Prior to 1861 the U. S. government viewed the its issuance of paper money solely as a means of raising short-term capital or of temporarily deferring payment of debts. It was only the crisis of the Civil War that led to permanent issues of this form of money.

Early Paper Money

Although the permanent issue of Federal paper money began only in 1861, paper currency was issued as much as 170 years earlier in what was to become the United States. Although the history of paper money goes back more than 1000 years in China, in the Western world it began only in 1661 in Sweden. The second jurisdiction in this half of the world to issue paper money, in fact, was the Massachusetts Bay Colony in 1690. The

Bank of England issued its first notes only in 1694, and so in the British Empire colonial issues preceded those of the mother country by a few years.

If you plan to collect early paper money, it is essential to obtain a copy of *The Early Paper Money of America* by Eric P. Newman. This definitive catalog is now in its fourth edition. It is a relatively expensive book (retail price $75.00), but it provides information on these notes that is found nowhere else. The recent editions of the Friedberg catalog do include a pricelist for most of the issues of early paper money, but few illustrations are provided and far more information is needed if you are to get seriously into this area of syngraphics. In contrast the Newman catalog provides full-size illustrations of nearly all of the various issues together with data about the numbers issued and the signatures that are found on many of these notes. Included are listings of all notes from the 1690 issue of Massachusetts to the earliest of the private bank notes that were issued in the 1780s and 1790s.

By the 1750s all of the 13 original colonies had issued paper money. In Virginia tobacco receipts were frequently used *in lieu* of money, and for this reason Virginia was rather sluggish about the issue of paper money (or Bills of Credit as they were more frequently termed) and it delayed doing this until 1755, which is more than two decades after all of the other colonies had begun to print this form of currency. Many of the colonial issues were very temporary in nature, and most soon were recalled or become badly inflated. A very wide array of denominations was used, and the values were expressed both in the British and Spanish systems. It should be noted that in the 18th century the pound (along with the shilling and the penny) were largely used as a money of account in the colonies. British gold and silver coins circulated only to a very limited extent. Spanish milled dollars (i. e., 8 reales pieces from the Spanish American mints) were in wider use, and these were tariffed at different rates (typically from 4s6d to 7s6d per dollar) in different colonies and at different times. In the inflated 1779 issue of South Carolina, however, the Spanish dollar was tariffed at 32s6d in paper currency.

There were numerous factors that prevented paper money from being widely circulated or accepted in the 18th century. The process of transferring an impression from a master die to an engraving plate did not come into general use until the 1820s. Thus notes of this period had to be printed from hand cut copper plates or from typeset forms. A large range of denominations was used, since it was not possible to make identical impressions on a hand cut plate. A skilled counterfeiter could make notes that were about as good in appearance as were the genuine notes. Despite severe penalties against the counterfeiting of notes, almost all of the issues that remained in circulation for extended periods of time were counterfeited. For the most part, however, the issuance of paper money was viewed only as a temporary expedient by the government that issued it. Indeed the first issue of notes by Massachusetts in 1690 was made to pay off soldiers who had failed to return with any loot from an expedition to French Canada in that year. This money could be used to pay local taxes, but it generally did not carry legal tender status. Of all the regions of the Western world in the 18th century the American colonies were the most prone to the issuance of paper money to cover government debts, but such issues were far from being a complete success. At various times the British governors of these colonies suppressed the issues of paper money, but by the mid-1770s most colonies were ignoring British authority and produced ever larger amounts of paper money. Since a colony almost never had enough specie on hand to honor its notes, inevitably all of them became badly inflated.

If you plan to get into the collecting of early paper money, I would suggest that you examine a number of pieces to see how the real stuff looks and feels. For the most part these notes are printed on what is better described as thin cardboard rather than thick paper. Notes that are worn will show a major lack of detail, since the surface-printed impressions will be partially worn off. Notes were often folded in half or quarter-folded, and these folds often can be quite heavy. Sometimes such notes have been repaired with heavy paper tape. Such repairs may well have been made at the times when the notes were in circulation. For some issues notes cut be cut in half or into four pieces, and these pieces could then be used individually at a value equal to one half or one quarter the value of the original note. For the most part early paper money is rather drab and colorless in appearance. The most colorful notes are probably the £3 and £6 notes that were issued by New Jersey in 1776 (bright red and blue on their faces), but for the most part early paper money is printed solely in black. Compared to such Federal issues as the silver certificates of Series 1886 or 1896 or the Treasury Notes of Series 1890, no piece of early paper money can be described as beautiful. Indeed 18th century printers would no more have been able to produce an accurate copy of a Series 1896 Educational note than they would have been capable of making a modern pocket calculator or television set.

Nonetheless most early paper money is of very great historical interest. Benjamin Franklin actually printed many of the Pennsylvania notes of the 1740s to 1760s, while Paul Revere is responsible for several of the designs used on Massachusetts notes in the 1770s. The signers of Continental Currency have been very well researched, and they include signers of the Declaration of Independence. Most of the paper money issued prior to about 1740 was indented, i. e., it was given an irregular cut at one end that could be compared with a stub that was retained by the government. When the note was presented for redemption, the two pieces would have to fit together. Almost all notes have handwritten serial numbers, and most carry either two or three signatures. The latter were often made in different colors of ink. These procedures helped to deter counterfeiting, but this was always a problem for most issues.

The various issues of the 13 original colonies (or states after 1776) are described in great detail in the Newman catalog, and so I shall not go into details here. One interesting project is to collect one note from each of these colonies, and this is not especially difficult to do. At the present time early paper money in decent condition starts at about $30 per note, but many notes are much more expensive than this. Canceled notes exist for a number of issues, most notably for the various state issues of 1780. For these notes a large hole cancellation was used. Although Vermont did not become a state until 1791, there was a single issue of Vermont notes in 1781. These are extremely rare. In addition to these jurisdictions the Newman catalog also lists the issues of La Banque Royale of 1719-20. Although listed under Louisiana, their circulation was in France itself. Within a short period of time, however, they became badly inflated, a fate that befell almost all 18th century paper money.

Most of the issues of early paper money were by the respective colonies or states, but there were other issuers as well. The Water Works notes of 1774-76 were issued by the City rather than the Colony of New York. The Bank of North America in Philadelphia and the Bank of New York commenced the issue of notes in 1782 and 1784, respectively. Many decades later these successful institutions issued national bank notes. There were also a few other private issuers of paper money by the 1790s. These included numerous small-change notes, especially from New York. The earliest issues of private money were made in New London, Connecticut in 1732, but these were soon suppressed and most colonial or state governments tended to retain a monopoly on the issue of paper money until well after independence was declared.

Under the Articles of Confederation the individual states were permitted to issue their own money. By the 1780s, however, almost all of this money was very badly inflated, and the rate of inflation varied from state to state. In 1781 Virginia notes were issued in denominations as high as $2000, but these were declared worthless in the following year. At that time the rate of redemption was $1000 in notes for $1 in silver. In North Carolina notes remained in circulation for a much longer period of time. The notes of 1780 included values as high as $600, and these stated that they were payable in gold or silver. In actual fact they were payable in silver for a few years but at an exchange rate of $800 to $1, and thus a $600 note was tariffed at only 75¢ or six reales in silver.

By far the most famous forms of early paper money are the eleven series of Continental Currency that were issued between May 10, 1775 and January 14, 1779. These were generally printed in sheets of eight and were issued in numerous denominations from $1/6 to $80. Oddly enough there were no $10 Continental notes. Nine of these issues were from Philadelphia, but the February 26, 1777 issue was from Baltimore and the April 11, 1778 issue from Yorktown (i. e., York, Penna.). Only the issue of February 17, 1776 included fractional notes (for $1/6, $1/3, $1/2, and $2/3). There are three different plate varieties for each of these notes, and they differ so radically from one another that they really constitute distinct types. A complete collection thus defined would consist of 110 different notes, and it is possible to form such a collection since none of these notes are excessively rare. The first issue did include an oddly-sized $20 note that was printed on thin marbled paper, and this is probably the most difficult of these notes to find in decent condition. The Yorktown issue was very extensively counterfeited, and this led to its recall. As a result, all Yorktown notes are scarce including the contemporary counterfeits.

Counterfeits of early paper money are all perfectly legal to own, and typically they are worth about the same as are the equivalent genuine notes. For Continental Currency there are also special detector notes that exist for all issues aside from the fractionals of 1776. These were printed on blue paper and were not signed. These are also worth about as much as the regularly issued notes. A typical Continental note sells for about $100 in choice CU condition, but in F-VF condition they can be obtained for as little as $30 or thereabouts. The 1775 $20 note and the Yorktown notes are much more expensive, but only a few Continental notes approach $1000 in price even in very choice condition. These notes also exist in complete sheet form either as issued notes or as blue counterfeit detectors. If you decide to collect early paper money, you will definitely want a few of the Continental issues.

Why is Continental Currency not regarded as Federal currency? That question is very easy to answer. The Federal form of government did not exist until after the Constitution was ratified in 1787, and thus no Federal currency could exist before that date. The

Continental notes were issued under the authority of the Continental Congress, a body that lacked the ability to raise funds through taxation. Under the Articles of Confederation monetary policies were left largely in the hands of the individual states, and the situation soon became utterly chaotic. By 1780 Continental Currency was severely inflated, the exchange rate at that time being about $40 in paper for $1 in silver. By the late 1780s it was traded for as high as $250 for $1 in silver. Finally in 1790 it was agreed that all outstanding Continental Currency would be redeemed for 20-year bonds at the rate of $100 to $1. These bonds were eventually paid in real money, but conservatives such as Alexander Hamilton were strongly opposed to any further government experiments with "funny money." Under the Constitution the states were expressly forbidden from issuing money of any type, and until 1861 the Federal government almost exclusively issued only coins. Between 1788 and 1861 almost all paper money was private in nature.

Although I have not collected early paper money, I did act as agent for a fairly sizable collection of this material that was sold in a CAA auction. It is fun to work out the signatures on Continental notes and compare them with the listings in the Newman catalog, but as I have already noted, early paper money lacks the great beauty that is found on many of the large-size Federal notes. Substantial funds are needed to collect the early notes in depth, but there are many varieties that are available in the $30 - $100 price range, and so it is possible to form at least a representative collection of these items without too great an expenditure of money. Most notes issued before 1740, however, are very rare in any condition, and the private notes of such issuers as the Bank of New York or the Bank of North America are unobtainable for their earlier years. Sound banks such as these would have redeemed all of their outstanding notes, and the only notes of such banks that exist for this vintage are counterfeits, which were sometimes retained as court evidence. Although fake private bank notes of this period are very much collector's items, they are also very rare and valuable. A number of years ago there were a number of poor-quality replicas of Continental notes on pseudo-parchment paper that were being sold at souvenir shops. These items are basically beneath contempt, but recently I have seen a rather attractive set of photographically produced replicas of Continental notes (marked COPY) that are being sold quite inexpensively at various historic sites. I would recommend the purchase of a set or two of these items, if you are unfamiliar with the look and feel of the real notes. Early paper money is of very great historic interest, but in my opinion its chief drawback is its general lack of aesthetic appeal.

State Bank Notes

The term state bank notes is a bit confusing, since these notes were not issued by the states but rather by private firms that held charters from the states to do business as banks. Some of the canal and railroad companies issued similar money, and virtually all of the paper money (aside from a wide variety of private small-change notes) issued between 1790 and 1860 was of this type. State bank notes continued into the Civil War years, but amendments to the National Banking Act in 1864 placed a 10% tax on the further circulation of these notes. That proved to be the death knell for these notes, and they ceased to circulate in any numbers after 1866. State bank notes were purely obligations of the bank that issued them. The first two banks to receive state charters (the Bank of New York and the Bank of North America) proved to be well managed institutions of impeccable integrity, but this was not the case for many state chartered banks. When a bank failed, its notes became worthless. Later on there were also institutions founded by disreputable individuals whose main purpose was to circulate notes of dubious quality. These have been termed "wildcat" banks. Michigan was a state that was especially notorious for its loose banking laws in the 1830s and 1840s, and it harbored several such banks. With thousands of different varieties of bank notes in circulation by the mid-19th Century, it was often possible to pass off worthless notes from dubious banks. In addition there were numerous counterfeit, altered, and raised notes.

A counterfeit note is a clandestinely manufactured note that is designed to closely resemble a genuine note. A raised note is a genuine note that has been clandestinely changed in denomination. With so many different designs in use, it was often possible to convert a $1 or $2 note into a $5, $10, or $20 note of the same bank and pass it to persons unfamiliar with the appearance of the higher-value notes. Such notes can also be termed altered notes, but for state bank notes that term is generally used for notes of a broken bank that have been altered to resemble notes of a good bank by substituting logos and other design devices. Examples of all of these types of fraudulent notes are still encountered, and as is the case with early paper money, such items are completely legal to possess and collect.

State bank notes occur in a wide variety of forms. Issued notes from good quality banks that survived at least into the 1860s tend to be extremely rare. No legitimate bank sought to circulate its private money much after 1864, and it would have tried to redeem as much of it as possible in order to avoid paying a 10% tax on its circulation. Such notes, however, can be found unissued, canceled, or in proof form. State bank notes were usually destroyed after being redeemed, but sometimes they were canceled, usually rather brutally by cutting out signature blocks or other elements of their designs. Most printers of state bank notes were located in New York or Philadelphia, and they supplied notes to the banks in unissued form. These would become obligations of the banks only when they were signed and dated by two or more officers of the bank. There are, of course, also genuine notes that have fraudulent signatures, and these are eagerly sought by collectors today. In the 1840s or 1850s, however, one would have to be very careful about accepting a note if there were any question about the genuineness of the signatures on it. Proof notes were also often supplied to the banks by the printers. They usually have a few small holes drilled into the signature blocks and frequently are mounted on cardboard. Since they were never placed into circulation, they are typically in choice condition. Although a wide variety of proof notes still are in existence, no individual varieties of proofs were ever issued in large numbers since they were intended for the exclusive use (usually as counterfeit detectors) of the issuing bank itself. Although there are many extreme rarities among state bank notes, the most common of these notes are generally uncirculated remainders. These are notes that were sent to the banks by the printers but that were never signed or placed into circulation. Often these notes exist as full sheets, and such items are generally available in choice condition. Almost without exception these notes were issued in sheets of four subjects. Although there is some variation in size, typically they are about the size of large-size Federal currency. Perhaps the most famous of such items are the remainder notes of two New Orleans Banks, the Canal Bank of New Orleans and the Citizens Bank of Louisiana, but many other unissued remainder notes do exist.

State bank notes are a huge area for which there is a great deal of syngraphic interest. In 1991 a definitive catalog on these issues was finally published. This is the *Standard Catalog of United States Obsolete Bank Notes, 1782 - 1866* by James A. Haxby. This is a four-volume work that totals almost 2800 pages. The retail price of this set was $195.00, but you will want it if you plan to get seriously into this area of collecting. This work is no longer in print, and getting secondhand copies of this major work may prove to be a bit difficult. The Society of Paper Money collectors has also published a series of catalogs of obsolete currency for individual states. These list items other than just state bank notes, since merchant scrip and small-change notes are also included. Catalogs of national bank notes have the advantage of not needing huge numbers of illustrations, since the designs are uniform and well known to serious collectors. For state bank notes, however, huge numbers of illustrations are needed. In the Haxby catalog there are more than 15,000 of these. Listings are provided for over 77,000 notes from about 3100 different banks. Clearly a monumental amount of research went into this effort. Many notes listed as "not confirmed" in this catalog have subsequently turned up, and doubtless there are numerous errors in an original work of this magnitude, but this is a major effort in consolidating our knowledge of this field of paper money.

State bank notes are largely confined to the eastern, southern, and Midwestern states, since few charters existed among the western states prior to 1866. Although California became a state in 1850, there was little interest in paper money in the Gold Rush days since all residents there demanded immediate convertibility of any fiat money into gold. Notes do exist for states or territories as far west as Kansas, Nebraska, and Texas, but few were issued for West Virginia *per se*, since that state seceded from Virginia only during the Civil War. Just as there were thousands of different designs, there were also many different denominations for state bank notes. The most standard were $1, $2, $3, $5, $10, $20, $50, and $100. All were subsequently used on Federal notes with the exception of the $3 notes. Plans were made for issuing $3 USNs and NBNs in the 1860s, but for some reason these were never issued despite the fact that $3 state bank notes are very common. Some collectors specialize in notes of a given denomination, and $3 is probably the most popular of all. Far more exotic denominations were also issued. Notes for $4 are found with some frequency, and one of the most popular state bank items are the remainder sheets of the Peoples' Bank of Paterson, New Jersey that contain $6, $7, $8, and $9 notes. There were also a few $12 and $13 notes. On the low side state bank notes were occasionally issued in denominations of $1.25, $1.50, $1.75, and $2.50. On the high side numerous banks issued $500 and $1000 notes, and the Bank of the United States in Philadelphia issued a few notes in denominations of multiple thousands of dollars. These were issued in the 1830s at the time when this bank was operating under a charter from Pennsylvania. Whether or not to charter or recharter the Bank of the United States was a major political question in the early 19th century, and Andrew Jackson refused to utilize the Bank of the United States for government banking after 1833. Although it operated under a charter from Pennsylvania for a few years, it failed in 1837. This bank had been in existence for about 20 years, but the idea of central banking was entirely alien to American political thought at that time, and it was almost a century before the Federal Reserve System finally came into existence.

A good piece of advice in all fields of numismatics is to first buy the book and study it carefully before getting much involved in the collecting of a given area, but some modification to this sound principle may be needed for state bank notes if the definitive book costs well over $200 and is 2800 pages long. If you plan to concentrate exclusively on Federal paper money, then you will not become much involved with state notes. On the other hand these issues may prove to be most interesting to you. There is an enormous range in the relative abundances of the different issues of state bank notes. It is still possible to buy complete sheets of several varieties of notes from the Canal Bank of New Orleans in choice condition at modest prices, although the days when these were less than $20 per sheet have passed. The firm NASCA, which has since been absorbed by R. M. Smythe and Co., used to offer large numbers of different varieties of complete sheets of state bank note remainders in its sales. By all means attend a large currency convention and see what is available.

It should be borne in mind that the conditions for state bank notes vary widely from issue to issue. These notes were printed on thin paper that did not hold up very well with extensive circulation. Most issued notes, especially from legitimate banks, are generally not available in better than VG-F condition. Issued notes for some of the wildcat banks may be quite a bit better, since these notes often failed to circulate to any extent. On the other hand, remainder notes are generally in new condition. They may show aging, and there may a few edge chinks in the full sheets, but most of these items are of attractive appearance. In addition to the notes of the Canal Bank of New Orleans, one of the most readily available of all similar items are the notes prepared for the Hungarian patriot Lajos Kussoth in 1852. These were printed in denominations of 1, 2, and 5 forint and are inscribed entirely in Magyar, but they were printed in Philadelphia and closely resemble typical state bank notes of that vintage in their designs. These can be obtained in perfect condition for not much more than $10 per sheet. Nearly all other remainder sheets cost significantly more than this, but there is still a wide variety of these available at reasonable prices. The previously mentioned Paterson, NJ sheet that features $6, $7, $8, and $9 notes presently sells for about $200. Notes from the 1830s and 1840s tend to be uniface and printed only in black, but by the 1850s and 1860s colored underprints or design features are often used. Often these notes also feature colored backs, but the back designs are generally rather simple in comparison with the designs of their faces. Typically these are colored with red, orange, green, and blue being the most frequently encountered colors for currency backs of this period. Sheets of state bank notes are also interesting to view when framed and mounted on walls in one's home. Although this procedure is not recommended for rare items, there are enough varieties of inexpensive state bank notes around to provide for some very attractive displays of authentic 19th Century engraving art.

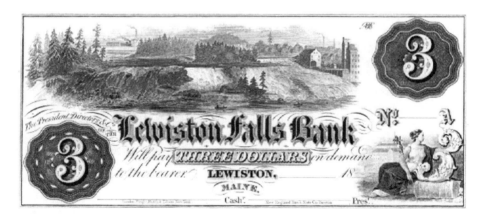

As I have already noted, issued state bank notes can be an entirely different matter. I acted as agent for the sale of a small group of state bank notes that included three canceled notes of the Bank of Saugerties in Saugerties, NY. In addition to large cutout cancels in their signature blocks, these notes also suffered in terms of wear in being no better than in VG condition. Overall they were of wretched appearance. But these items sold for about $150 to $250 each in a CAA auction that was held in 1996. According to Haxby, these were the only non-proof notes known for this bank, but only a truly dedicated collector of state bank notes would find them highly attractive. Aside from owning a few remainder sheets I do not collect state bank notes. A few years ago I made the mistake of passing up a most unusual item of this category. From a private individual I purchased a $1 Original Series NBN from the National Bank of Rutland, Vermont (charter 1450). This person also had a $10 state note from its predecessor, the Bank of Rutland, that was signed by the same president whose signature appeared on the First Charter note. As was already noted, issued state notes from banks that survived into the 1860s are quite uncommon and it is most unusual to find a state note paired with a national note by the same bank signatures. Although state bank notes are fundamentally different from NBNs, this is a case of most unusual pair of notes that do belong together in the same collection.

Proofs of state bank notes are generally found in attractive condition, but almost all of them are rare and typically they sell for at least $200 to $500 each. For many issues of state bank notes, however, proofs are the only form in which such notes can be collected. Issued notes from reputable banks in decent condition typically sell for about the same prices, but a few state bank notes have sold for as much as four or five thousand dollars each in recent years.

In discussing NBNs I pointed out that it utterly impossible to obtain a "complete" collection of these items, and this statement is even more true for state bank notes. If you develop a serious interest in these notes, you will probably want to specialize on notes of a given state, city, or denomination, etc. If you plan to collect issued notes, you will have to settle for many notes that are in no better than VG or fine condition and many that are in even lower grades. On the other hand, remainder notes can generally be found in choice condition, and these items are more amenable to being collected in complete sheet form than are almost any other types of paper money.

Confederate Treasury Notes

By far the best known, best documented, and most popular of all forms of obsolete paper money are the Confederate Treasury Notes. During the past 20 years or so, there have also been huge increases in the values of most Confederate notes. Of the 70 major type varieties of Confederate notes only about half a dozen now sell for less than their face value when in decent condition. Within a few years all of the various Confederate notes will sell for more than face value when in choice condition despite the fact that all such currency was declared "worthless" in 1865.

If you plan to collect Confederate notes at all, by all means obtain both the current editions of the catalogs by Grover Criswell and by Arlie Slabaugh. The latter is a fairly thin book, but it packs much useful detail into its pages. The former employs the definitive numbering system used for Confederate notes. It also includes listings of all of the minor varieties of these items, and the earlier editions contain a thorough listing of the Southern states issues during the Civil War and Reconstruction periods. Also included in those editions of this book is a complete listing of the notes and warrants of the Republic of Texas issued between 1836 and 1845. The latest edition of Criswell's catalog lists only Confederate notes, but this is also an excellent reference since it includes much new material on contemporary counterfeits and other items. The recent most edition of Slabaugh's catalog includes a listing of the notes issued by the Southern states. Recent editions of the Friedberg catalog have also listed the major types of Confederate notes, but their listings are inadequate for this series. The articles by Brent Hughes that have appeared in the *Bank Note Reporter* in recent years also have provided much useful information on Confederate bank notes, and anyone interested in the collecting of these issues should look into these writings.

Most syngraphists consider that there are 70 major types of Confederate paper money that were printed in seven distinct issues. Two additional types are often considered along with these, but it is now fairly well established that they were bogus counterfeits that were introduced into eastern Tennessee in 1862. These are the so-called $10 and $20 "essay" notes that were printed by "Keatings and Ball" of "Columbus," SC. Since Columbia is the capital city of South Carolina where the largest printer of Confederate notes, Keatinge & Ball, had its headquarters, it is not clear why errors so blatant were overlooked, but for many years these notes were considered to be legitimate trial notes of one of the other printers. They did circulate in the South in the 1860s, but these notes need not be considered as legitimate Confederate notes by persons requiring only the genuine issues for their collections. About 60 of the $10 notes and about 80 of the $20 notes are presently known.

Since there are only 70 major types of Confederate notes, a logical approach would be to obtain a note for each of the major types. Although such a project is easy to begin, it is difficult and very expensive to complete such a set given today's market conditions. Several of the notes are very rare. Although the Montgomery notes of 1861 (beautifully printed by the National Bank Note Company in New York) are not actually extreme rarities, they have become extremely expensive. At the present time 96 of the $500 and 109 of the $1000 notes of this issue (out of 607 issued for each denomination) are presently known, and choice examples of these notes now sell for more than $20,000 each. The equally attractive $50 and $100 notes of this issue (of which 142 and 144 examples, respectively, are currently known) sell for prices only slightly inferior to those of their $500 and $1000 counterparts. Other major rarities are the $5 Indian Princess and

$10 Eagle and Shield notes that were printed by Hoyer & Ludwig as part of the Third Issue in 1861. The $20 and $50 notes printed for this issue by the Southern Bank Note Co. of New Orleans are also very rare, and the two different $5 notes of the Second Issue (i. e., those printed by J. Manouvrier and by Hoyer & Ludwig) are extreme rarities when in choice condition. Another very scarce note is the little $2 note printed by B. Duncan with an erroneous September 2, 1861 date. As a note of the Fourth Issue it should have had a June 2, 1862 date. There are also several other Confederate notes that are major challenges to obtain in choice condition. Most of the notes printed by B. Duncan and by the other lithographers such as Hoyer & Ludwig were crudely printed on rather poor quality paper which didn't hold up very well while these notes were in circulation.

Many Confederate notes (other than the interest bearing $100 notes of 1862 and the common Seventh Issue of 1864) exist in canceled form. Some of the cancels consist of neat handstamps, but cut or punch cancellations are more typical. The hammer cancellations generally break the paper with a cross-like pattern. The most frequently encountered form of punch cancellations consists of large holes, and sometimes the signature blocks were cut out as was a common practice with state bank notes. Notes with such problems are clearly worth far less than are uncanceled notes. Restoration work is often done on rarer notes, but don't attempt it yourself unless you really know what you are doing.

Almost all Confederate notes (the only two exceptions being the 50¢ notes of 1863 and 1864) were handsigned. With the exception of the First Issue notes, nearly all of these were signed by persons employed for the purpose. Although a few specialists are interested in different signatures (their relations perhaps?) or signature combinations, there are far too many possibilities for most collectors to become involved in this field. The current edition of Criswell's catalog does include a full list of the known signers of these notes, so it is possible for CSA specialists to collect these in a systematic fashion. Unsigned notes are often found for the last couple of issues of Confederate currency, and these usually sell for about what the corresponding signed notes are worth. Uncut sheets exist for a few of these issues, most notably the $10 note of the 1864 series.

The Criswell catalog lists all of the different minor varieties that are recorded for Confederate notes, but not very many collectors seek most of them out. For instance, there are 120 different minor non-error varieties for the very common $10 note of 1864. These notes were printed in sheets of eight, and thus eight different plate position letters (A through H) were used. These notes exist in 15 different "series" varieties, but in this case the term refers to a serial number block (much as is the case with the United States Notes of 1862-63) and not to a distinct issue of notes in the sense that this term is used for Federal currency issued in 1869 and later years. Even more numerous are the monthly overprints that appear on the $5 through $100 notes of the Sixth Issue of 1863. If one considers all possibilities, several thousand combinations are possible for the Sixth Issue notes.

A few subtypes are worthy of serious consideration, however. The more common designs of the $5, $10, and $20 notes of the Third Issue as well as the first type of the $100 interest bearing notes of 1862 were printed both by Hoyer & Ludwig and by J. T. Paterson, and both varieties of these imprints are more or less equally abundant. A $10 note of the Third Issue that was printed by Keatinge & Ball features two large "X's" that exist in three quite different styles, and the $5 and $20 notes of this issue that were printed by this firm exist both with blue-green and yellow-green ornamentations. The $500 note of the 1864 issue occurs both with bright red and with dull pink background coloring.

The interest bearing $100 notes of 1862 were often held by banks, and the interest on them was collected on an annual basis. Different handstamps indicating the city of payment for these notes can be found on these issues, and some collectors are interested in seeking out the varieties that occur. Since these notes were often held as reserves by banks, they did not circulate as much as did many of the other types of Confederate notes, and thus they can be easily found in choice condition. Choice condition is also the norm for the Seventh Issue notes of 1864, since many of them never actually entered circulation.

Contemporary counterfeits of Confederate notes are also of great interest to collectors. Especially well known are the facsimile notes of S. C. Upham of Philadelphia. When originally issued most of these had a narrow tab at their bottom edges. These notes are worth significantly more in today's market with these features intact than with their edges trimmed. The "Havana counterfeits" were very good imitations of the $50, $100, and $500 notes of the Seventh Issue that were introduced into the South from Cuba late in the war. The "Female Riding Deer" design purports to be a $20 note of the Second Issue. Unlike the two rare "essay" notes, this note was acknowledged to be bogus during the war, but several varieties of this design were printed. Some counterfeits were detected and stamped by Confederate officials during the war. In many cases these notes are worth substantially more than are their genuine counterparts. Not to be confused with contemporary counterfeits are the very numerous replicas of Confederate notes that have been produced in recent years. Most of these are of very little interest to serious collectors. An exception to this rule, however, is an attractive set of authentic replicas of all 70 major types that is being marketed by The Confederate Treasury of Tennessee Ridge, TN. These cost about $140 per set, or $2 per note. This is a far cry from the $100,000 or more that is now required for a complete type set of genuine Confederate notes in decent condition.

The largest collection and accumulation of Confederate paper money ever formed in recent years was assembled by Grover Criswell in the 1950s and 1960s. Much of this was sold in a series of auctions conducted in the late 1970s by NASCA. Today bulk lots of Confederate notes are not commonly seen, and even the most abundant of these notes typically sell for about $20 to $25 each in nice condition. Over the past two decades most Confederate notes have typically increased in value by a factor of about five or six. Prices in the 1970s were already very much higher than they had been in the 1950s or early 1960s, and thus over the years Confederate notes have proven to have been one of the very best of currency investments. Interestingly enough two of the rarities that have shown less spectacular rises in value are the $10 and $20 "essay" notes that are now known to be bogus counterfeits. Although contemporary counterfeits of Confederate notes are avidly collected, these two items are no longer required for type sets of the genuine notes. Also it happens that the numbers of examples known for these notes have more than doubled in the past two decades due to new discoveries.

Although Confederate notes are avidly collected, there is a certain aspect of reinventing the wheel with these items. Complete type set collections have been formed in the past, but a obtaining a full set of all 70 notes in decent condition presents a formidable challenge in today's market. A couple of decades ago it was also possible to purchase at auction lots of 100 or more notes each of single types such as the common $5, $10, or $20 notes of the 1864 issue or the $100 interest bearing notes of 1862. These were great for dealers or for collectors seeking different minor varieties, but today such lots would be broken down into much smaller units. Confederate notes are reminders of one of the most significant eras in our nation's history, and they will continue to remain immensely popular as collector's items for many years to come.

Paper Money of the States

I am using this somewhat confusing term to distinguish paper money that was issued by state governments from that issued by private banks that were chartered by the states, i. e., the state bank notes. Under the U. S. Constitution the states are expressly forbidden from issuing currency, and so all such notes were issued either when these states did not recognize Federal authority or when they were under Union military occupation. Almost all of the latter issues would have been ruled unconstitutional, but there are a large number of survivors. Also included in this category are the issues of the Republic of Texas and of the Kingdom or Republic of Hawaii. As independent nations, both Texas and Hawaii issued their own paper money.

Most of the state paper money was issued by the various Southern states that had seceded from the Union. The Confederate constitution did not forbid states from issuing their own money, and all of the Southern states with the exceptions of South Carolina and Tennessee issued several series of notes. They were also joined in these efforts by the secessionist government of C. F. Jackson of Missouri, where state paper money was in use in the southwest portion of that state in late 1861 and early 1862. All of these notes are thoroughly treated in earlier editions of the Criswell catalog of Confederate currency and in the current edition of Slabaugh's catalog, so I shall not discuss them in detail here. Almost all of the state notes were payable in Confederate Treasury Notes, and thus they served as supplemental currency to that of the national government. Although they too became badly inflated, it seems that the notes of the various states could be exchanged at par with other forms of Southern currency, and thus the South at least did not have the problem faced by the United States in the early 1780s under the Articles of Confederation where the currency issues of one state were tariffed at a rate that was often quite different from those of other states.

A large variety of notes were issued by the ten Southern states (including secessionist Missouri) that regularly issued currency during the Confederate period. Much of this was printed by the same firms (Keatinge & Ball, J. T. Paterson, Hoyer & Ludwig, J. Manouvrier, or B. Duncan) that printed Confederate currency, but much was also printed by more local firms. Several states issued supplemental fractional currency in denominations as low as 5¢. Notes for $50 and $100 were issued by many states, and Georgia also circulated a $500 note. This denomination was also issued very late in the war by the Florida state government, and these notes are one of the best known rarities among the Southern state notes. The secessionist Missouri government issued a note for $4.50, a denomination unusual even by the standards of state bank notes. The state of Texas issued an extensive series of treasury warrants, most of which were made payable to designated payees. Thus these items were essentially state-issued checks, and some of these were not even in fixed denominations. In 1864 Georgia issued a series of ultrahigh-value notes (for

$5000, $10,000, and $20,000). These items were not intended for general circulation, but rather to consolidate the circulation of other Georgia currency, the issue of which was already getting out of hand by this date. In 1865 all Southern state currency suffered the fate of the Confederate paper money that it supplemented.

During the Reconstruction period some currency was printed for Arkansas, Louisiana, Mississippi, and South Carolina. Most of these were in the form of warrants made payable to a designated payee, or else the notes were made receivable for state taxes. The first issue of South Carolina notes (in 1866) was apparently suppressed due to the Constitutional ban on state-issued money, but in 1872 South Carolina printed Revenue Bond Scrip in various denominations. Some of this was typeset, but a series of six notes was printed by the American Bank Note Co. in New York. These were never regularly issued, and they still exist in uncut sheets of $1-1-2-2, $5-5-10-10, and $20-20-50-50. These are among the most beautiful of all obsolete notes. Although these items never served any purpose as currency, they are readily available and very popular with collectors. A complete set of the three sheets now sells for about $200, while a set of the six notes sells for about half this figure in new condition (the only way these notes usually come). Even if you don't collect obsolete notes, this issue is worth picking up for its aesthetic appeal.

In the post-Reconstruction period there were a few issues of treasury warrants that were released. Included was a set of notes from Tennessee that was issued in 1875. By far the best known of the later Southern issues, however, are the so-called "Baby Bonds" of Louisiana. The were $5 notes (inscribed "Bond") that were printed in 1880 and included eleven attached coupons. They were the size of normal large-size notes, however, and they were soon suppressed by the Federal authorities, because it became clear that these items were intended to circulate as currency. In recent years a large hoard of these notes in full sheets has come onto the market, and so they are readily obtainable today. A much earlier issue of notes were the warrants issued by the Territory of Florida in 1828-31. The collectible notes of this issue were endorsed to a specified payee and were made payable at a future date. It seems that this sort of item may or may not have been permissible under Federal law, but Florida in 1830 was very much a wild frontier region and the Constitutional provisions concerning officially issued paper money were not necessarily acknowledged. A set of the $1, $2, $3, and $5 notes of this issue in choice condition sold for $9900 in a Lyn Knight auction in 1996, and thus these early items are among the rarest and most expensive of all Southern state or territorial notes.

Southern state currency has not appreciated at anything like the rate that has been enjoyed by Confederate paper money in recent years, and it is still possible to obtain a significant collection of these items without a large outlay of funds. Many of the fractional notes are downright cheap, as some of these cost only a couple of dollars each. Most Southern fractional notes, of course, have extremely simple designs. Most of the state notes of the $1 - $100 denominations are about on a par with the corresponding Confederate notes in terms of quality of printing. Such notes as the $50 and $100 notes of Virginia of 1861, the $500 note of Georgia of 1864, and the $50 and $100 notes of Florida of 1862, as well as the 1865 provisional issue of that state are decidedly scarce to rare. Needless to say, the ultrahigh denomination notes of Georgia are extremely rare. But there is a wide variety of Southern state notes to satisfy the collecting interests and budgets of most syngraphists interested in material of the Civil War period. Before plunging into this area, however, I would suggest a thorough study of the Criswell's and Slabaugh's listings of these notes, since they provide an excellent and highly detailed account of these issues.

The Republic of Texas issued several series of notes during its nine-year history as an independent nation. These issues are also thoroughly covered in earlier editions of the Criswell catalog. In addition to paper currency there were also treasury warrants (i. e., officially issued checks) and issues of the Consolidated Fund of Texas (a type of stock certificate). There were five different issues of notes, but the last (issued in 1842) is excessively rare. The most frequently encountered notes are of the Fourth Issue. These were issued in 1839-41 in denominations of $1, $2, $3, $5, $10, $20, $50, $100, and $500. A fair number of these items along with a significant quantity of notes of the Third Issue have survived, and many examples are still on file in the state archives in Austin. Most Texas notes have been canceled with punch cancellations, and substantial effort is needed to find notes that are free of this form of mutilation. A set of eight of the 1839-41 notes ($1 - $100) sells for about $1000 in uncanceled VF condition, but these notes are much less expensive with cutout cancellations. The $500 note sells for about $200 in this form, but it is decidedly rare in uncanceled form.

The Republic of Texas notes resemble typical state bank notes of the 1830s and 1840s. They are printed on very thin paper in black only on their faces, but most of the Fourth Issue notes also have orange backs. The Third and Fourth Issues bear the signatures either of Mirabeau Lamar or Sam Houston as President, and the notes of the scarcer First Issue all feature an elaborate signature of Sam Houston as President. It is believed that many of these notes were actually signed by his secretary, since Sam Houston had an injured hand at the time that these notes were being issued, but in any case they are also treasured by autograph collectors desiring an authentic signature of this famous Texas leader. The notes of low denominations were all signed by the Treasurer instead, and most of the warrants were only signed by an auditor. The Consolidated Fund certificates were signed by two administrators of that fund, and so only the higher denomination notes carry the signatures of famous Texans.

There are a total of 25 different major types of notes for the first four issues of notes of the Republic of Texas, although specialists would recognize several additional varieties, especially of the typeset First Issue. Completing such a collection would be a major challenge, but it is not an impossible one. One might wonder why have $500 notes of this ephemeral republic survived at all? They have not survived in substantial quantities, but some do remain since shortly after their issue they nose dived in value. The Republic of Texas had virtually no specie on hand, and it was constantly plagued by financial problems. It never issued any coins despite the fact that Mexican silver coins would have probably been the only acceptable form of money to many of its inhabitants at that time. All of the Texas notes carried a promise to be payable to the bearer at 12 months after issue. The first two issues carry interest at 10% per annum, but the latter two issues only carry a promise to be paid. On none of these notes is it stated that they will be paid in specie. Presumably the earlier issues of notes were paid with later issues, and it was the Fourth Issue that had by far the largest total face value of the various emissions. It is rumored that the Fifth Issue was actually paid in silver (It included notes for 1, 2, 4, and 6 reales as well as for dollar amounts.), and this may account for its excessive rarity today.

The only notes of independent Hawaii that circulated as a national currency are the notes that were issued for the Kingdom of Hawaii in 1879 and the issues of Gold and silver certificates that were issued for the Republic of Hawaii in 1895. All of these notes were beautifully printed by the American Bank Note Co., although some of the scenes depicted would be much more appropriate for Latin America than for Hawaii. Unlike the notes of independent Texas, these notes were "good money" that remained fully redeemable in silver or in gold coins. The 1879 issue was redeemable specifically in silver coins, and the issue of these notes may have been prompted by the decision of the U. S. government to make its paper money fully convertible to gold at par in that year. For the most part the currency of Hawaii during the monarchy period consisted of silver coins (both U. S. silver dollars and Latin American pesos), but there would have been some problems with convertibility to gold at par once the two metals separated from their 16 to 1 ratio in 1873. After 1883 Hawaii also had its own silver coinage. All Hawaii coins and banknotes were called in and demonetized in 1904, and this partially accounts for the excessive rarity of these notes today.

For all intents and purposes Hawaii notes are noncollectible in original form. A few canceled notes of various denominations are known, but in issued form only the $5 silver and gold notes of the 1895 series have shown up for sale in recent years. Even in only fine condition these sell for several thousand dollars each. A set of five original proofs of the 1879 series sold for $38,000 at a Christie's auction in 1990. Fortunately most collectors can afford the souvenir cards that were prepared by the American Bank Note Co. between 1981 and 1995 using the original plates used to print the notes. The face impressions of all of the Series 1879 notes and the Series 1895 silver notes together with the $5, $10, and $20 gold notes of the latter year are available. It was planned also to issue the $50 and $100 gold notes in this form, but the ABNCo officials were unable to locate the original dies for these values.

An earlier non-government Hawaii currency item of considerable interest is a pair of $3 and $5 proof notes for Ladd & Co. that were printed in 1837 in Boston but with texts entirely in the Hawaiian language. This pair sold for $17,600 at a Christie's auction in 1994. If you desire some numismatic items from old Hawaii, the five coins issued either in 1847 or 1883 are still available and you can obtain the 13 different ABNCo souvenir cards depicting Hawaiian notes, but about the only paper money that you can expect to obtain is from the American period, i. e., the NBNs from the big Honolulu bank (charter 5550) and the Hawaii notes issued during World War II.

Small-Change Notes and Merchant Scrip

Small-change notes have a long history in the United States, and several of the earliest issues of these items are listed in the Newman catalog of early paper money. In order to issue private bank notes legitimately between the 1790s and the 1860s it was necessary to have a charter from the state in which the bank was located. But almost anyone could issue small-change notes. For the most part these were issued by retail firms and private individuals. Numerous municipalities also issued small-change notes particularly at the beginning of the Civil War when silver coins disappeared from circulation. In the North small-change notes that were payable in cash soon were suppressed after Fractional Currency was first issued in 1862, but in the South numerous forms of small-change notes continued throughout the war years. Although the further issue of small-change notes was banned in the Northern states after 1862, notes payable in goods or services could still be legally issued and they continued in use for many more years.

If there was little regulation on the issue of these notes, one might ask why would they be accepted at all? It should be noted that a specific small-change note circulated only in a very restricted area. The notes issued by a firm would be used almost entirely by the customers of that firm, the notes issued by a town or city would be used only in that town or city, etc. If the agency that issued these notes was always prepared to redeem them in lawful money, the public was generally quite willing to accept them in lieu of silver coins. Anyone who refused to redeem his notes would soon be out of the note-issuing business, and because of their restricted circulation there was little hope of passing sizable amounts of a dubious issue of small-change notes in a distant state. During the Civil War years small-change notes of good repute would not have been redeemable for silver coins at par, but they would have been redeemable for U. S. government paper money when presented in adequate amounts such as $5 or more. In the South, of course, customers often had no choice about accepting them, but it soon made little difference whether payment was made in private notes, state notes, or Confederate notes, since all were soon severely inflated.

Although Fractional Currency was issued mostly in denominations of 5¢, 10¢, 25, and 50¢, the two lower denominations of this series were not so common among the earlier small-change notes. Half dimes were minted only in very limited quantities between 1794 and 1805, and then none at all were minted until 1829. Dimes were minted more continuously and in larger quantities, but Spanish reales and medio reales were in much wider circulation in the United States prior to the 1830s. The real was tariffed at 12 1/2 cents, while the medio real was valued at 6 1/4 cents. Although these denominations seem strange today, they would have been quite standard in the United States in the early 1800s. Thus small-change notes for these denominations are quite common, and notes for 18 3/4, 37 1/2, and 75 cents are also encountered. There were also notes for 5¢ and 10¢, but in the 1810s and 1820s medio reales of Mexican mintage would have been vastly more common in circulation than would half dimes minted in Philadelphia. Foreign gold and silver coins ceased to be legal tender in the United States in 1857, and that would have put an end to the circulation of the small Mexican silver coins. Although notes for 6 1/4 and 12 1/2 cents were very common in the 1820s, but by the 1850s their usefulness would have been severely limited.

A major problem facing a collector of small-change notes and merchant scrip in general is the lack of a comprehensive catalog that attempts to list all known issues. Thorough listings of the obsolete currency of a number of states have been prepared under the sponsorship of the Society of Paper Money Collectors, but these handbooks are not available for all states. A catalog similar to that of Haxby's but on small-change notes and merchant scrip rather than state bank notes is badly needed, but much research needs yet to be done.

Although I have implied that most of these items were exclusively fractional notes, higher-denomination notes were also issued. Private merchants, however, were much more likely to issue notes for $1, $2, $3, or $5 than notes for $10, $20, $50, and $100. In any case there are very large numbers of different varieties of these notes. Unissued remainder sheets similar to those that are found for many state bank notes are not commonly found for these issues. Most of these items were produced by local printers, and thus a firm did not need to keep a substantial supply of its unissued notes on hand. When issued many of these notes were unsigned and undated, and thus no merchant would want to keep a large reserve supply of these notes since he might be expected to redeem stolen notes. Most small-change notes that presently exist in CU condition, however, are unissued remainders that were intended to be signed and dated when issued. Small-change notes and private scrip suffered less from counterfeiting, raising, and altering than did most state bank issues. The extremely local range over which a specific issue was used proved to be the best security feature for these notes.

Prior to 1862 these notes were usually redeemable in cash, at least when presented in totals of some specified sum. After that date all such notes were redeemable only in goods or services. That made for a major change in the nature of these items, but in appearance they continue much as before. Very few of these notes can be described as beautiful, but they are avidly sought by specialist collectors and some issues can sell for hundreds of dollars each. Before buying any notes of this type I would recommend attending a major currency show and examining the material that is for sale. The absence of a comprehensive reference work on these items makes it difficult for a novice collector to become familiar with these notes, but by all means talk things over with dealers and collectors who have experience in this field.

A few items related to this type of private money should be mentioned here. During the Civil War there were numerous suttlers, who supplied troops with auxiliary items such as extra rations. Many of these persons issued their own private money that could be redeemed for the goods that they sold. Today suttler currency is very much in demand. Another type of currency that was in use at about the same time were the small-change notes that were used among the various tribes and trading posts in the Oklahoma and Indian Territories. Most of these notes are very rare, and they typically bring high prices when offered for sale.

During the 19th century the Mormons issued several types of paper currency as well as the famous gold coins that were minted between 1849 and 1860. In the 1830s notes were printed for the Kirtland Safety Society in Ohio. These closely resemble state bank notes in appearance, but this organization was unable to obtain a bank charter from the Ohio government, and so these items fall more into the category of private money rather than state bank notes. Some of these notes were taken to Utah in the 1840s, where they were reissued after being signed by Brigham Young. During the 1840s there were also several issues of the Nauvoo House Association in Illinois. These items were more like small-size circulating stock certificates than state bank notes, but they tend to be more abundant that are the Kirtland notes. During the 1850s small-change notes were issued in Utah by the Mormons to supplement their gold coinage. The latter was deliberately kept underweight to discourage its export from Utah. Later on, of course, there were the National Bank issues of the Deseret NB (charter 2059). In addition to this Federal paper money, there were also a variety of merchant scrip items from the Bishop's General Store in Salt Lake City. This continued at least until the turn of the century, and these notes are by far the least expensive of the various Mormon issues.

Merchant scrip of various types continued well into the 20th century. As long as it was redeemable only for goods and services, private firms and organizations of various sorts were permitted to issue this type of currency for many years. Some of the issues were exploitative in nature. Workers could be paid in scrip that would only be redeemed at a "company store" where goods were sold at inflated prices. Abuses such as this continued well into the 1930s in some regions of our nation. A huge amount of material is available for collectors who are interested in these items.

In recent years the Treasury Department has become less tolerant of most forms of private money. During the coin shortage in the 1960s the Jewel Tea Co., a major supermarket chain on the West Coast, planned to issue paper scrip for 1¢, 5¢, 10¢, and 25¢, but the Treasury intervened before these items could be put into wide use. One recent form of private paper money that is permitted are the so-called Disney Dollars. These are issued in denominations of $1, $5, and $10. Different serial number blocks are used for Disneyland in California and Walt Disney World in Florida, and a new series appears each year. These notes remain fully redeemable at either site, and there is definitely some collector interest in these notes. It is still possible to form a complete set of all these items for a fairly modest outlay of cash, and so if modern private money is of interest, you might consider collecting these colorful notes.

Clearing House Certificates, Municipal Scrip, etc.

Closely related to private forms of money are some of the substitute money items that were issued under emergency circumstances in the post-Civil War years when only U. S. government paper money and coins served as lawful currency. The clearing house certificates were in effect circulating bearer checks. They were issued by clearing house associations in various cities. These were consortia of banks that cleared (i. e., paid) each others' checks. In times of acute cash shortages certificates were issued *in lieu* of the cash that was temporarily not available. There was usually a guarantee to pay the certificate by a specific date, but in the meantime it could circulate as a bearer check with or without multiple endorsements. Most of the members of a clearing house association were large banks that were not likely to fail during a financial panic, and usually these items were indeed honored once the liquidity crisis had ended. To facilitate commerce these certificates were issued in convenient denominations such as $1, $5, $10, $20, etc., and while they were outstanding these notes functioned as temporary emergency currency. The first major issue of clearing house certificates appeared during the so-called Panic of 1893. I have already discussed the effects of this episode in the chapter on large-size type notes. It resulted in the repeal of the Sherman Silver Purchase Act and in the cessation of the further printing of the Treasury Notes of 1890.

The Panic of 1893 was largely restricted to major cities, but the Panic of 1907 was more widespread. The Aldrich-Vreeland Act of 1908 (see my chapter on national bank notes) was designed to lessen its consequences, and it led Senator Aldrich and other influential persons to think very strongly about setting up a central bank for the United

States, an action that took place only a few years later when the Federal Reserve Act was passed in 1913. Numerous clearing houses issued certificates during 1907, and not all of these were in large cities. Among the most desirable issues are those from Rhyolite, Nevada, a town that had a note-issuing National Bank but for which no NBNs are known. Clearing house certificates from Rhyolite are quite scarce, however, and a $1 certificate in choice condition from this town sold for $3740 in a 1998 CAA auction. Almost all other clearing house certificates, however, are vastly cheaper than this.

Are clearing house certificates to be regarded as emergency money or as checks? They have aspects of both, but they fall into a distinct category of fiscal items. Like currency, but unlike normal checks, they are bearer items that could be used by anyone who possessed them. They were also transferable from one party to another usually without further endorsement. Also like currency, but unlike most checks, they came in convenient denominations. But they were obligations solely of the member banks of a clearing house, and they were most definitely not legal tender. They also were to be redeemed for lawful money within a short period of time. The certificates available to collectors are almost always either canceled, unissued, or specimen notes. Since they were purely temporary in nature, no clearing house certificates remain valid money today.

The Great Depression of the 1930s produced far greater hardships than did the liquidity crises of 1893 and 1907, and it also resulted in the production of far more varieties of substitute money. In 1984 Neil Shafer and Ralph Mitchell published a book on depression scrip, and this book is essential reading for anyone planning to form a collection of the emergency money of the 1930s. There were numerous clearing house certificates, but there were several other forms of emergency money some of which had not been seen in previous fiscal crises. Some towns and merchants' associations issued a form of scrip that lost value if it was not kept in circulation. A note could be issued that would lose 2% of its value per week and thus would be worthless by the end of the year. This would encourage the frequent use of such an item and it would discourage hoarding. There were so many bank failures during the Great Depression that many persons distrusted all banks and kept their money in private hoards. So different schemes, including this one, were designed to keep money in constant circulation.

Although no state bank notes were issued after 1866, municipalities did issue some forms of currency from time to time. Usually these were warrants that were made payable to a specified individual, or to the bearer, or to a specified individual or a later bearer. The latter would allow the warrant to be transferred without additional endorsements. Normally these warrants were to be paid 12 months after date of issue, sometimes with interest and sometimes without. City governments that were strapped for funds found warrants a convenient method of paying their employees. Local taxes could be paid with these items, and some banks and merchants were prepared to accept them. Essentially they were IOU's, and most of them were honored when they were expected to be paid. Often municipal employees had no choice but to accept city warrants in their pay. It was much better than being laid off in a time of hard economic conditions.

Many of these warrants were well printed in intaglio by the American Bank Note Co. or other securities printing firms, and they are actively collected today. The use of this type of substitute money reached its zenith in 1932 and 1933, but notes of this type were issued as early as the 1860s. Several of the most beautiful of the souvenir cards printed by the ABNCo depict intaglio replicas of notes of this type.

Encased Postage Stamps, etc.

In my opinion encased postage stamps resemble metallic tokens much more than they do paper currency, but they were briefly used as money during the Civil War years and they have been very well researched. All three of the standard currency catalogs (Friedberg, Hessler, and Krause-Lemke) discuss them at length, and they are also listed in Scott's U. S. Specialized Stamp Catalog. In addition there are specialized books by Fred Reed and by M. J. Hodder and Q. David Bowers that give the full details of this form of provisional currency.

Encased postage stamps are an invention of J. Gault, who conceived of placing a mint U. S. postage stamp inside a brass disk. The stamp could be viewed through a mica window. In more recent times plastic would have been used, but in the 1860s only mica or thin glass were available. The other sides of the brass disks were imprinted with advertising logos, and Gault made money by selling advertising space on these items. All of the disks for these tokens were produced by the Scovill Button Works in Waterbury, Conn. If both company logos and stamp denominations are taken into account, there are about 200 different varieties of these items, and this number is even greater if minor variations of design in the logos are taken into account. There is also an "unofficial" frame that was designed to hold three 3¢ stamps.

Stamps of the 1861 issue were printed in denominations of 1¢, 3¢, 5¢, 10¢, 12¢, 24¢, 30¢, and 90¢. All of these were used, although the four higher denominations are much rarer than are the four lower values, and they were used by far fewer firms. Aside from values such as 5¢ and 10¢, most of these denominations were not particularly suited for use as circulating currency. There were two additional values of the 1861 type stamps. In 1863 a 2¢ stamp depicting Andrew Jackson was issued, and in 1866 a 15¢ stamp honoring Abraham Lincoln was added. J. Gault produced a very small number of 2¢ items that used his logo, but the 15¢ stamps were never used for these tokens. Encased postage stamps were used fairly widely for about a year in late 1862 and early 1863, but Fractional Currency proved to be much more practical. These tokens never had any official sanction, and Mr. Gault sometimes encountered difficulties in purchasing postage stamps in sufficient quantities to mount in his frames.

Although I do not have detailed censuses for encased postage stamps, it seems likely that a substantial portion of these unusual items were saved. That would have been particularly true of the lower denomination tokens that constituted the vast majority of what was issued. In January, 1998 a CAA auction featured 22 of these items. Prices ranged from $110 to $935 each.

It is really a bit difficult to classify encased postage stamps. They appear much more frequently in coin and paper money auctions than they do in stamp auctions, and thus there seems to be far more interest in these things as numismatic or syngraphic items than as philatelic collectibles. In my opinion they resemble metallic tokens much more than paper currency, and thus I would put them in with the Civil War tokens and other forms of provisional metallic currency that were minted at this time.

Although encased postage stamps were purely a private fabrication, there have been a few official uses of postage stamps for currency. In 1915 Russia printed stamps on thin cardboard in values of 10, 15, and 20 kopecks to replace the subsidiary silver coins of those denominations. In the following year there were also similar items for 1, 2, and 3 kopecks to replace the copper coins that also disappeared from circulation in the harsh economic climate that Russia experienced during World War I. In the South during the Civil War Confederate postage stamps (mostly for 10¢ or 20¢) circulated together with fractional notes of the states and private small-change notes. By 1864 inflation was so bad that the Confederate notes for 50¢, $1, and $2 were themselves mere small-change items.

One other type of item related to Civil War currency are the postage stamp envelopes. These were small paper envelopes that were designed to hold fixed amounts (10¢, 15¢, 20¢, 25¢, 50¢, or 75¢) of mint postage stamps. These were printed by various stationers (almost all of whom were located in New York) and carried logos or advertising from a wide variety of firms. At least 100 different varieties are known, but the total census of all such items is not greatly in excess of 500. Both the Hessler and Krause-Lemke catalogs provide listings of these items. The largest holding of these envelopes are sold by CAA in their January, 1998 auction. It included 49 different envelopes from the Civil War years, and the prices realized for these ranged from $99 to $990.

Unlike the encased postage stamps the survival rate for postage stamp envelopes was undoubtedly very low. Once Fractional Currency came into general circulation, there was no need to deal with this awkward method of making small purchases. The stamps would have been removed and used for postage. In all likelihood the flimsy little envelopes were then discarded in the vast majority of cases. These envelopes are of interest as collateral items for specialists in Fractional Currency, but in this case the collateral items usually cost far more than do many of the fractional notes themselves.

U. S. - Related Foreign Paper Money

Although this book is devoted to the collecting of American paper money, there are two series of foreign paper currency that are closely related to U. S. currency. These are the issues of the American administration in the Philippines that were used between 1903 and 1949 and the various series of Allied Military Currency that were used between 1943 and 1958.

It has often been said that the Spanish-American War itself was almost comic opera, but its consequences were not. As a result of this little war the United States acquired Guam, Puerto Rico, and the Philippine Islands, and it soon also annexed Hawaii and Eastern Samoa. For several years after 1898, the U. S. also exercised a very strong presence in Cuba. Unlike colonial nations such as Great Britain or France, however, the U. S. largely replaced the currency in use in these territories with its own money. As I have noted, Hawaiian currency was demonetized in 1904. Puerto Rican silver coins minted by the Spanish in the 1890s were also soon removed from circulation, although paper money issues of the Banco de Puerto Rico continued until 1909. In Cuba American paper money was used exclusively until 1934.

The one exception to this pattern was the Philippines. In 1903 the U. S. began to circulate distinctive coins and paper money for this territory. These were denominated in Philippine pesos, the value of which was fixed at 50¢ in U. S. currency. In order to avoid confusing the Philippine currency with regular American paper money, the former notes were smaller in size, and this was the size which was to be adopted 25 years later for all U. S. paper money. Except for the major interruption during World War II, the paper money which circulated in the Philippines from 1903 to 1949 was of this type.

There are several different series of Philippine notes. silver certificates were printed between 1903 and 1916, and they were replaced by Treasury Certificates that were first issued in 1918. The first BEP-printed notes of the Banco Espanol Filipino (after 1912 the Bank of the Philippine Islands) appear in 1908, and these continued into the 1930s. The notes of the Philippine National Bank first appeared in 1916, and these also continued into the 1930s. There was also an emergency issue of these notes in 1917 that included locally printed fractional notes, the only currency of this period not to be printed by the BEP. In 1935 the Philippines gained a much greater degree of autonomy, and in 1936 notes of the Commonwealth of the Philippines appeared. These types of notes were reissued in 1944 with Victory overprints on both sides. The first issue (in 1949) of the independent Philippines was produced by overprinting the 1944 series with Central Bank of the Philippines on their back sides.

Including the different series of these notes there are a total of 105 different major varieties of Philippine notes for the American period from 1903 through 1944. There are also a number of additional signature varieties for a number of these issues. Although some of these notes are quite common, several are excessively rare. By far the finest collection of Philippine paper money to come on the market in recent years was that originally formed by Amon Carter, Jr. It was sold by Spink America in 1997. Included were about 950 notes, of which almost half were of the American period. Prices on some of these notes were very high. For instance, a 100 pesos silver certificate of 1905 sold for $5280 in VG, an overprinted 10 pesos note from 1917 of the Philippine NB in VF also fetched $5280, while a Series 1920 100 pesos note of this bank in VG-F condition brought $3520. Many notes of the American period sell at much lower prices, but there is no possibility of forming a "complete" collection despite the relatively small number of possible varieties for these notes.

The Hessler catalog briefly touches on Philippine currency of the American period, but the Krause-Lemke catalog provides a thorough listing. This has been extracted from the listings given in volume 2 of the Pick catalog of world paper money. I should note that during the period of American rule in the Philippines from 1898 to 1946 there were also four additional series of notes that were not printed in the United States. In 1898 and 1899 there were some issues of the ephemeral Republica Filipina that was suppressed by the U. S. military after an extensive campaign. In 1904 the Banco Espanol Filipina issued a series of notes (now extremely rare) that were of the old Spanish-era types. Vastly more common are the Japanese occupation issues of 1942-45. There were also numerous issues of crudely printed notes that were produced by different anti-Japanese groups in the Philippines. These are the famous Philippine guerrilla notes, most of which are listed in detail in volume 1 of the Pick catalog.

The other series of foreign notes that are closely related to American currency are the Allied Military Currency (AMC) issues that were produced for circulation in Italy, France, Germany, Austria, and Japan. Most of the U. S.-printed notes were produced either by the Forbes Lithograph Co. of Boston or by the BEP. The Japanese series, however, were printed by the Stecher-Traung Lithograph Corp. of San Francisco. Most of the Austrian notes were printed in Great Britain, and a high percentage of the German notes were printed in the Soviet Union.

At first glance an unlikely Bureau of Engraving and Printing product.

The AMC issues for Italy were the first to enter circulation. The Series 1943 notes were printed both by Forbes and by the BEP. The former have a small "F" secret mark. There were eight denominations from 1 lira to 1000 lire. The four lower ones were almost square, while the four higher ones were of the usual small-size currency format (156 x 66 mm). The six lower values (i. e., up though 100 lire) are extremely common in circulated condition. The 500 and 1000 lire notes are scarcer, but they are far from being rarities even in CU condition. The Forbes and the BEP printings are about equally abundant. The Series 1943A notes were printed only by Forbes, and this issue included only 5 lire through 1000 lire notes. These notes are also easily obtained, although the 500 and

1000 lire notes are once again a bit scarce in CU condition. Different serial number block varieties are known for the four lower values of this series, but all of these are common. Replacement notes were indicated by stars, and these exist for most of the Series 1943 and 1943A notes. All of these varieties, however, are scarce and some are very rare.

There were also two different series of AMC issues for France, but all of these were printed by Forbes. Notes of the first series depicted a French flag on their backs. These were issued in seven values from 2 to 1000 francs, and there was also an unissued 5000 franc note. The second series (with FRANCE on their backs) was issued only in values of 50, 100, and 1000 francs, but there were also unissued notes for 500 and 5000 francs. The notes for 2, 5, and 10 francs were the same size as the smaller Italian notes, while the higher notes were in the standard small-size currency format. All of the regular 2 - 100 franc notes are very common, but the 500 and 1000 franc notes are fairly scarce. Both varieties of 5000 franc notes as well as the unissued 500 franc note of the second series are rare. These were released only in specimen booklets, and all are perforated SPECIMEN. Numerous block varieties exist, especially for the 100 franc note of the second series. These are indicated by a bold numeral that appears fairly close to the serial number. Replacement notes were designated with the letter "X," and all of these are very scarce to rare.

The AMC issues for Austria were designed in Great Britain, and they look much less like American military currency than do the French and Italian notes. There were ten different values from 50 groschen to 1000 schilling. Some of the 50 g, 1 sch, and 2 sch notes were printed by Forbes, and all of the 25 sch notes were printed by the BEP. The bulk of this issue, however, was printed in Great Britain. The Forbes printings of the three lowest values can be distinguished by their watermarks. The 25 sch note is the only value of this issue for which replacement notes are possible. The regular 25 sch notes are scarce, and the replacement notes are quite rare. The 1000 sch notes are also fairly scarce, but the other values of this issue are very common.

The AMC issue for Germany were printed in eight values from 1/2 mark to 1000 marks. The notes issued by the American and British forces were printed by Forbes, but the plates for these issues were turned over to the Soviet Union where huge numbers of additional notes were printed. The four higher denominations are of standard small-size currency format, while the lower value notes are considerably shorter. The 10M note in fact is the same size as are all $1 MPCs. All of the Forbes printings have a small script "F" as a secret mark. This is lacking on the Soviet printings. All of the regular 1/2 M through 100 M notes are quite common, although the 1000 M notes are scarce. Replacement notes for the Forbes printings were indicated with an initial dash in their serial numbers, and samples of these notes were supplied to the Russians. Thus the earlier Soviet printings also have this feature, but they can be distinguished since they do not have the "F" secret mark. The Forbes replacement notes are fairly scarce, but none are extremely rare. They are very much scarcer than are the Soviet-printed notes, however, so one must be careful about purchasing any AMC notes for Germany that are reported to be replacements. The Soviet printings were very large, and later on serial number blocks were used that were not utilized for the Forbes printings. The excess Soviet printings caused numerous difficulties in the western zone of Germany, and these complications in large part led to the currency reform of 1948, at which time the AMC marks ceased to be legal tender.

The AMC issues for Japan were printed in two different series, A and B. The A series was issued in seven values from 10 sen to 100 yen. It was used in Korea during 1945-46, and then it was briefly used in Japan during 1946 exclusively for American military personnel. These notes are sometimes considered as the immediate predecessors of the MPCs. The A series notes are fairly scarce in choice condition, and the 20 and 100 yen notes of this issue are actually rare in this form. All of the regular notes use the AA block, but the replacement notes for this series used the HA block. Examples are known for all seven of the denominations, but these are rare.

The B series of these notes was used in Japan proper from 1945-48, but its use continued in the Ryukyu Islands until 1958. At that time the so-called B yen were replaced with U. S. currency at the rate of 120 yen per dollar. Since the exchange rate for the normal Japanese yen was 360 per dollar at that time, one B yen was worth 3 regular yen. There were eight different values from 10 sen to 1000 yen. The sizes and color schemes for the A series and B series notes were the same. The three higher values were the size of normal U. S. currency, while the 5 and 10 yen notes were the size of $1 MPCs, and the three lower values had the "square" format used for the low-denomination notes in Europe. The seven lower values of the B series are fairly common in normal form, but the replacement notes designated by the serial number block HA are scarce. The 1000 yen note is scarce, but it exists in five different serial number blocks. The use of different blocks for this denomination was done as a control measure, since this note was printed in much smaller quantities than were any other of the series B notes.

Although all of the AMC issues are essentially foreign currency, they closely resemble the earlier series of MPCs in their physical appearance. Many collectors of MPCs will want to include these notes in their collections. Although many of the replacement notes and some of the high value notes are scarce, most AMC issues are common and can be obtained for very reasonable prices.

Summary

In this chapter I have surveyed in a cursory manner a wide variety of the forms of paper money that were not issues of the Federal government. During the period 1690-1790 there was generally very little coined money in circulation, and the colonial and state governments were forced to issue Bills of Credit to meet their expenses. One other approach was to use commodities for currency, and in Virginia receipts for wholesale amounts of tobacco were sometimes used *in lieu* of cash. The widespread use of tobacco receipts was the major reason for the tardiness of Virginia in issuing paper money. Almost all of the early paper money suffered both from rampant inflation and from rampant counterfeiting. It found reluctant acceptance only because there was nothing else to use. The experience with Continental Currency was enough to discourage many American political personages (most notably Alexander Hamilton) to desire the complete cessation of the issue of all forms of government-printed paper money.

In the period from 1790 to 1860 almost all paper money in circulation was of private origin. It was tolerated only so long as the populace believed that it was convertible into specie on demand. Any failure of a bank to redeem their notes into specie would result in the rapid demise of that bank. Although many state bank notes were of good quality, they also suffered from altering and from counterfeiting. The rampant inflation experienced in the 1780s did not reappear, since these notes could either be redeemed in specie or they couldn't be. Today we accept a check either as being good (i. e., redeemable into FRNs) or bad (i. e., not payable at all). Prior to 1861 a person faced the same choice when it came to accepting state bank notes. Even good quality state bank notes, however, were often discounted when they were presented for payment at any distance from their bank of issue. Small-change notes that were used in a supplemental fashion with state bank notes suffered from the same problems, but their limited circulation gave them a degree of credibility since the source of issue was never very far away.

Although permanent Federal paper money only appeared in 1861, it soon displaced all other forms of fiat money. Private or municipal small-change notes were banned by 1863, and state bank notes ceased to circulate after 1866. From that time on the only lawful money has been U. S. government coins and paper money. Thus all more recent non-Federal currency items have been substitute money. The private scrip that circulated for decades could only be redeemed in goods or services, and the various municipal notes and warrants as well as the clearing house certificates were short-lived obligations that were to be paid in real money, i. e., U. S. Federal money, within a specified amount of time.

You may choose to collect several of these areas in depth, or you may decide to focus entirely on Federal paper money. Confederate paper money is extremely popular, and there are many collectors both of early paper money (especially Continental Currency) and state bank notes. There are fewer collectors of early small-change notes, merchant scrip, and the various forms of Depression notes, but each of these has an enthusiastic if fairly limited following. Items such as the postage stamp envelopes of the early 1860s clearly are sought by only a small number of specialists. There is a huge range of dates of issue for what I have covered in this chapter, from the first issue of colonial paper money in 1690 to the contemporary Disney Dollars that were first printed only in 1987. It is most unlikely that all of these items will appeal to you, but a wide array of issues awaits you if you decide to become involved with their acquisition.

CHAPTER FOURTEEN

OTHER TYPES OF FISCAL PAPER

In addition to items issued and used as currency, syngraphists often include other types of fiscal paper in their collections. Foremost among these are stocks, bonds, and checks, all of which play vital roles in today's economy. But we can also include such highly collectible items as souvenir cards, test notes, advertising notes, and college notes among these issues. Technically speaking none of the latter items are fiscal paper, but they are currency-related issues that often use designs that are found on regularly issued forms of Federal paper money.

Souvenir Cards

Souvenir cards straddle the fields of philately and numismatics, and it is my feeling that the collecting of these items has been more an outgrowth of philately than of syngraphics, but if you collect large-size notes there are many beautiful souvenir cards that should be most appealing to you. The earliest souvenir "card" that is normally seen is the so-called Philatelic Truck sheet, which was issued in 1939. It is printed on stamp paper and resembles in size and appearance the postally valid souvenir sheets that were issued in the late 1930s. The BEP did not issue another item of this type until 1954, when a very rare card depicting four Washington scenes was released in limited quantities.

Government-issued souvenir cards have been distributed by two different agencies, the BEP itself and the U. S. Postal Service (previously the Post Office Department). All of these are printed by intaglio on thin cardboard, and in most cases they bear authentic reproductions of U. S. postage stamps or paper money. All of the cards that have been distributed by the Postal Service are purely philatelic in nature, but the BEP cards feature both philatelic and numismatic themes. Since 1984 the BEP has also produced intaglio prints for sale at premium prices. Usually these are more in the nature of art prints rather than philatelic or numismatic items. Between 1960 and 1990 the USPS produced about 70 different souvenir cards, but it ceased to distribute these items in the latter year. The BEP continues to sell souvenir cards both at its Washington headquarters and at various stamp and coin shows.

From 1969 through 1999 the BEP has produced a total of 100 different currency-related souvenir cards. Most of these display full-size reproductions of large-size notes, and they were prepared from the original dies or plates. Thus far only designs prepared at the Bureau have been utilized, and thus no vignettes prepared for U. S. currency by the printers in New York in the 1860s have been used. Two of the designs used on souvenir cards, however, date from the early 1860s. These are a card distributed by the Plate Printers Union in 1981 that depicts an unissued face design for a $2 USN and a card issued in 1992 which depicts a $1 design intended for the same series. Both of these designs (the *Embarkation of the Pilgrims* and the *Landing of Columbus*) were subsequently used on First Charter NBNs.

Two other BEP cards also depict currency from this period. The card sold in Long Beach in 1985 shows the back of a Series 1865 $20 gold certificate, but this is surface-printed and serves only as a background design for an intaglio printing of stamps. It appears that the original plates for this excessively rare note have been lost. A somewhat similar card is the one issued in 1986 that depicts only portions of a 5¢ Second Issue fractional note in intaglio. The Long Beach item is an example of the so-called philatelic-numismatic cards. These depict both paper money and stamps, but for nearly all of these the currency design is the dominant feature on the card. A few of the BEP currency cards depict vignettes only from BEP-produced bank notes and a couple depict collages of several notes.

All seven major categories of large-size notes produced at the BEP from the 1870s to the 1920s have been reproduced on these cards, and all denominations from $1 through $10,000 have been included. The inclusion of large-size $5000 and $10,000 USN and FRN designs among these cards enables collectors to obtain samples of notes that are quite noncollectible in issued form. In 1987 there was also a card depicting a $500-million Interest Bearing Treasury Note. Thus far there have been only three cards with Fractional Currency themes, and small-size notes have been represented only as collages or vignettes on two of these items.

Many of the issued currency designs have yet to appear on souvenir cards, however, and so the BEP will be able to continue this series for quite a while before it has to start repeating itself. In recent years it has also produced a number of cards with unissued designs, and all of the cards issue in 1994 were of this type. In 1995 the regular souvenir cards from the BEP were issued in folded form. Hopefully this format will not be repeated.

Although the BEP undoubtedly takes great care in the production of its cards, errors of description have occurred on a few of them. The ANA card of 1969 has three vignettes that it describes as having been used on "Jackass" notes, i. e., the $10 USNs of Series 1869-80. Actually only the two side vignettes were used on these notes. The large central vignette was used instead on $50 Three-Year Interest Bearing Notes of the Civil War years. The El Paso card issued in 1985 depicts the back of a $50 Third Charter NBN. The description implies that this design was used only on Red Seal notes, but it was also used on the much more common Blue Seal Plain Back notes issued between 1916 and 1929. The ANA card of 1989 depicts the unfinished back of the Series 1878 $5000 USN. The description on the back of this card states that these notes bore interest, but in fact USNs never paid interest.

The BEP series of currency cards contains no rarities, and the relatively scarce ANA cards of 1969 and 1970 are now much cheaper than they were 20 years ago. During the 1970s there was a speculative market in many souvenir cards, and prices briefly rose to levels that haven't been seen since. The complete set of 100 numismatic cards to date (i. e., the BEP currency cards for 1969 through 1998 plus the 1981 PPU card) should be obtainable for about $900 to $1000.

A few other cards produced by the BEP are sometimes included with these issues. In 1976 the BEP produced an intaglio interleaf on stamp paper that depicts the vignette used on the backs of small-size $100 notes. Very much scarcer are the cards issued for a stamp exhibition in Barcelona in 1960 and for a coin show in Fresno, Calif. in

1969. The former (a U. S. P. O. Dept. card) depicts the Landfall of Columbus and states (in Spanish) that this design was used on the 15¢ stamp issue in 1869 and the 2¢ Columbian stamp issued in 1893. No mention is made of the fact that this vignette was also used on the backs of $5 First Charter NBNs. The Fresno card depicts three views of Washington, and it closely resembles cards issued for the 1966 Sipex and 1969 Sandipex stamp shows.

There are also two other sets of BEP souvenir cards that are related to numismatics. In 1987 the BEP issued a special card depicting the cherry blossoms of Washington. One thousand each of these cards were subsequently embossed for six different coin or currency shows that took place during 1987. In 1988 the special intaglio prints for that year depicted a collage of the 45 state seals used on First Charter NBNs and on Brown Backs. There are three cards in this set, since the same design was printed in brown, green, and blue for three different shows. These three items have a very different format from the regular cards, but they are often included in collections of currency-related souvenir cards. The BEP is currently also issuing one card each year to publicize U. S. Savings Bonds. Sometimes the bonds themselves are depicted, and thus syngraphists who are interested in bond collecting may also find these items of interest. Another series that the BEP produces on an annual basis are the souvenir cards that depict the current issues of migratory waterfowl revenue stamps. These are sold together with a mint or canceled copy of the stamp in question.

The BEP sells its cards both individually and on a subscription basis. Subscriptions include both numismatic and philatelic cards for a given year, but special issues such as intaglio prints or the bond cards are not included. Typically there are six or seven cards in a given subscription. Only cards printed in the current year are available. Although these cards once sold for only $1 each, today the price is $5 at shows or $6.50 by mail. The special intaglio prints are being sold for $22.50 each. For further information contact BEP Mail Order Sales, Room 515M, 14th and C Streets SW, Washington, DC 20228.

The BEP is not the only agency that has printed cards. The American Bank Note Company began printing numismatic cards in 1975, but it ceased to issued them after 1996. There are about 70 different ABNCo cards that depict obsolete currency or currency-related vignettes. It also issued a number of philatelic cards as well as a set that depicted reproductions of the tickets used at the Columbian Exposition in 1893. Typically it would issue a card depicting a state bank note from the state in which the numismatic show for which the card was prepared was being held. For a few western states, however, it had to resort to reproductions of bank drafts or merchant scrip. Perhaps the most interesting of the ABNCo cards are those that depict the faces of the various Hawaiian notes that were issued between 1879 and 1895, all of which are excessively rare or nonexistent in issued form.

The Plate Printers Union holds periodic conventions, and some of the special cards that it has produced for these events are of interest to syngraphists. In 1996 the ANA issued a set of eight different cards to commemorate the 50th anniversary of MPCs. These featured replicas of MPCs, but the size wasn't right, the color fidelity wasn't very good, and they were on heavy paper rather than thin cardboard. I bought a set of these at the issue price of $30, but I don't feel that these cards are up to the standards of the BEP and ABNCo products.

Although most numismatists will want their cards in mint (i. e., uncanceled) form, some persons collect these items with show cancels. For issues of the past two decades or so, there is not much difference in price between these forms for a given card, but for cards issued during the 1970s the canceled varieties are frequently very much rarer than are their mint counterparts.

If you have few souvenir cards but want to form a substantial holding of these items, I would suggest purchasing a collection lot at an auction. There are a few dealers who specialize in these items and they can help you will filling in cards that you lack, but the markups on individual cards tend to be fairly high. All of the collection lots of souvenir cards that I have purchased, however, have been from stamp auctions rather than currency auctions. If will definitely be easier and less expensive to locate scarce souvenir cards if you are a subscriber or have access to catalogs of some of the major stamp auction firms.

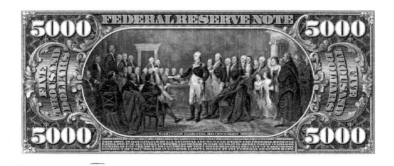

Souvenir cards give the collector the opportunity to obtain authentic engravings of notes that cannot be purchased in original form. Among these are the Series 1918 $5000 and $10,000 Federal Reserve Notes.

At the present time demand for souvenir cards is fairly limited, and only about 8000 examples are sold for each of the current BEP regular issues. The intaglio prints are currently being produced in editions of only about 2500 each. The last two series of cards produced by the ABNCo were released in editions of only about 300 to 400 copies, and if demand for these items picks up, so could prices. At auction the scarce Barcelona card of 1960 and the Fresno card of 1969 sell for about $150 each, but no cards should be more expensive than this aside from the very rare philatelic card printed by the BEP in 1954. Although the ANA cards of 1969 and 1970 have rather high catalog prices, they now sell in the $30 - $40 price range per card. If you decide to become further involved with the collecting of souvenir cards, there is also a Souvenir Card Collectors' Society.

Test Notes

The Magna test notes were printed in Geneva, New York in the 1970s. They are uniface and printed entirely in green. Much scarcer are the Giori test notes that were printed in Germany in the early 1970s. The faces of the Giori test notes are printed in maroon and brown as well as green, and unlike the Magna test notes, they have backs printed in black.

Test notes are items that were produced while checking out the production characteristics of printing presses for currency. Most of these have been printed in recent years, and thus they are of the same size as is normal small-size currency. By far the most frequently encountered of these are the Magna test notes that were printed in upstate New York in the 1970s. These were produced on the Magna presses that were subsequently acquired by the BEP for the first and second printings of nearly all of its currency. The

Magna test notes were printed in sheets of 32 subjects with 16 face impressions and 16 back impressions arranged in a *tete-beche* fashion. These notes are uniface and printed in green ink. The portraits used on the face designs are those of Lincoln, Washington, and Grant, all of these being the same as those used on normal small-size notes. The back design features the Lincoln Memorial, but it also includes logos used on other denominations of small-size notes.

Although the Magna test notes were not intended for public distribution, quite a few of them did leak out and they are legal to possess. Needless to say, they have no legal tender value. A pair of these notes typically sells for about $40 or so, but the value depends somewhat on the degree of smudging. Notes without any degree of smudging sell at higher prices, and heavily smudged notes also are of interest to specialists. Lightly smudged notes (the most frequent way these notes are found) tend to sell for less than do either of the extremes. Occasionally full sheets of 32 subjects are offered. These bring about $500 each. If you collect currency in sheets, you may want to include one of these items. They do have, however, the problem common to all 32-subject sheets, viz., their extremely large size. I would suggest storing these sheets in flat form, but this requires a special storage cabinet, an item that is most definitely needed for all collectors of 32-subject sheets of any type.

The Magna test notes are occasionally referred to as Giori test notes, but this is a misnomer. The true Giori test notes were printed in Germany at the beginning of the 1970s. The face design features Lincoln, Jefferson (not Washington), and Grant, and this is the design which is most often seen for these notes. In 1995 CAA offered a group of these notes with one side printed in green, maroon, or brown, while the back sides were identical but printed in black in each case. These sold for about $200 each. A modified version of the Lincoln Memorial back design was also used for test notes prepared with the Giori press, but all of the Giori test notes are encountered much less frequently than are the Magna test notes. Another set of test notes that resemble small-size U. S. currency was produced while checking out the web press. These are inscribed "Test Plate" and carry a portrait of Abraham Lincoln. A set of four different varieties of these notes sold for about $250 in the same CAA auction.

Closely related to test notes are the sample notes that some of the securities printers distribute to prospective clients and to attendees at major conventions. Several of the British printers, mostly notably Thomas De La Rue and Bradbury Wilkinson have prepared numerous versions over the years. The BEP does not make sample notes for complimentary distribution, and so such items are of greater interest to collectors of foreign bank notes, but the progressive proofs of Series 641 and 661 MPCs that I previously discussed could also be viewed as test notes. In this case, however, they were produced to check out the various stages in the printing for the issued notes instead of whether or not the presses involved could be used satisfactorily for their production.

Stock Certificates

Although it is possible to obtain current stock certificates from brokerage firms, almost all syngraphic interest in these items focuses on canceled certificates or on those of firms that are no longer in business. The collecting of stocks, bonds, checks, and other related types of fiscal paper has been termed scripophily. There is a vast amount of material that can be collected, and so you should be selective as to what you want to collect. As I have previously noted, it is not possible to collect large-size type notes in depth without substantial funds. Contemporary canceled stock certificates, however, are often very inexpensive. In a recent issue of the *Bank Note Reporter* one dealer is offering 40 different certificates for $20, while another offers 50 different for $19. If you are thinking about getting into collecting stock certificates, by all means buy a lot or two of these items. Since thousands of varieties are possible, you may choose to limit yourself to stocks of a given industry such as mining, railroads, automobiles, oil, etc., but the expenditure of only a few hundred dollars can result in an intriguing collection of numerous varieties of these items.

Not all stock certificates are this inexpensive, of course. There is a great deal of interest in 19th Century stocks, particularly those of major firms or those signed by famous individuals such as John D. Rockefeller, Thomas A. Edison, Andrew Carnegie, etc. By far the largest auctioneer of old stock certificates is R. M. Smythe Inc. of New York, and you will want to obtain their catalogs if you plan to seriously venture into this field. I would also strongly recommend attending one or more of the large currency shows. You can then sort through large piles of stock certificates that are offered for sale at such exhibitions. One of the best for scripophilists is the annual stock and bond show held each January in Strasburg, Penna. Unlike the major numismatic and currency shows that focus heavily either on coins or paper money, this show concentrates exclusively on stocks, bonds, and related fiscal items such as old checks. I think that it is best to begin with inexpensive stocks until you have a fairly good feel for what rarer items are selling for. Although a few older stock certificates do sell at prices well over $1000, the vast majority of these items sell for prices that are far below this figure.

As I have already noted, all territorial and many western national bank notes are extremely expensive. It is possible, however, to collect western mining stocks from the frontier days of the Rocky Mountain states, and many of these are available at fairly modest prices. As a typical example, let us consider the state of Nevada. The discovery of the Comstock Lode in 1858 resulted in a huge growth in the then Nevada Territory, and Virginia City soon became a major boom town. There are no NBNs available from this era, but stock certificates are available, and some of these even predate Nevada becoming a state in 1864. A less famous mining boom occurred at the turn of the century, and it resulted in the development of such towns as Goldfield, Rhyolite, and Tonopah. Although NBNs were issued from each of these towns, no notes are known from Rhyolite, the Goldfield note is unique, and a Series 1902 $10 note from Tonopah sold for the "modest" price of $15,950 in the sale of the Harvey's collection of Nevada notes in 1995. Forming a collection of NBNs from this epoch is obviously impossible, but stock certificates of numerous mining firms in this district are available including several from the intriguingly named Bullfrog mining district. Typically such items sell for only about $100 each, a far cry from the huge prices asked for most Nevada national bank notes.

If you become seriously interested in the collecting of stock certificates, you should definitely develop some selectivity. Otherwise you will need a lot of storage space for these items. You will also need to have some plan for selling off or trading in your surplus stocks. A substantial collection of stock certificates could grow in time to many thousands of items. This is clearly an area that offers much of interest to many collectors of fiscal items, but there are far too many stock certificates available for a collector just to hold on to whatever falls into his hands.

Obsolete Bonds

In contemporary securities markets it is possible to purchase a wide variety of bonds. State and municipal bonds (the so-called "munis") are popular with many investors, since the income from these bonds carries no Federal tax and they are also untaxed in the states in which they are issued. There are also the corporate bonds which do have taxable income. A wide variety of U. S. government bonds and interest bearing paper is also available. U. S. Savings Bonds are the most familiar to small investors, but there are also 30-year bonds as well as Treasury Bills and Notes (the latter not to be confused with the Treasury Notes of 1890, of course). Some of these Federal debt instruments have minimum face values as high as $100,000. Many of these securities are available in coupon form, but others are sold in zero coupon form. The former are usually sold at prices that are fairly close to their face value, and the interest is paid by redeeming the coupons in a periodic fashion. The latter are sold at a deep discount from their face value, but the bond can be redeemed at its full value at a future specified date. Despite the wide variety of interest bearing securities that are available, there is relatively little syngraphic interest in these items. Most municipal and corporate bonds have minimum face values of $5000, and many are not transferable once they are issued to a given individual. Although these bonds often do make good investments, they are not collectors' items. Collector interest in bonds is focused almost entirely on bonds that are "worthless," i.e., ones that have been canceled, gone into default, or rendered useless through hyperinflation or the failure of the government that issued them. A few canceled state and municipal bonds do become available from time to time, but usually they are destroyed after being redeemed and this leaves few for collectors. Another problem that the would be collector of government bonds has is that there is very little literature available detailing the available issues and other relevant details.

Although there is a huge interest in U. S. paper money, there is very little interest at the present time in U. S. government bonds as collectors' items. Most of these items are still valid, and many series of bonds continue to accrue interest. Although bonds that are issued in the name of a specified individual can usually be transferred after some paperwork, these documents are not bearer instruments as are all forms of paper money. If canceled government bonds were readily available, there would doubtless be much interest in these items, but nearly all U. S. bonds are destroyed after they are redeemed. A few older Federal bonds do occasionally come up for sale in auctions by R. M. Smythe or other firms, but Series E bonds of World War II vintage generally do not fetch much above their redemption value in these sales. One exception are the Series E $10 bonds that were sold exclusively to military personnel during World War II. The low face value of these items coupled with the special circumstances for their issue results in these bonds fetching prices well above their redemption value in today's market Collector interest in older U. S. government bonds may be starting to pick up. In a CAA auction held in May, 1999 there were two $50 and five $100 Liberty Bonds of 1918 or 1919. These World War I items sold for between $800 and $1050 each. Following this auction R. M. Smythe sold another attractive group of the Liberty Loan bonds in Memphis. Unlike the later Series E bonds, the Liberty Loan bonds were coupon bonds that did not continue to accrue interest. Recent price realizations are now far in excess of their redemption values.

One other related item that is actively collected is the $10 Refunding Certificate of 1879. In effect this was a circulating bearer bond, but all of the standard currency catalogs have treated it as a form of paper money, and it is actively sought by most collectors of large-size type notes. Further details on this note are given in Chapter 6 of this book.

Although contemporary canceled stock certificates are readily available in large quantities at low prices, canceled bonds of recent issue are not nearly as easy to come by. Older bonds from defunct mining firms as well as railroad companies and other organizations are available from time to time. Canceled corporate bonds of more recent vintage are also available, but they are generally not found in the huge quantities that are often the case with canceled stock certificates. One area that is very well documented and avidly collected is that of Confederate bonds. If you have an interest in Confederate bonds, you will most definitely want to obtain a copy of the new catalog of these items by Douglas Ball. Most of these were coupon bonds, and thus some are very large in size. The generally fragile nature of the paper on which they were printed coupled with their often very large size poses some problems for the collector of Confederate bonds, but this is an area in which there is a well-defined market. Many Confederate bonds were sold in Europe, and a huge holding of these items turned up in London a few years ago. The least expensive Confederate bonds cost about $35 each, but there are quite a few rarities among these issues. One of the scarcer (but not extremely rare) issues were the Erlanger bonds that were issued by a French banking house and sold exclusively in Europe. They were denominated in British pounds, French francs, and in cotton at an advantageous price. Payments on Confederate bonds held in Europe were made as late as the early autumn of 1865, but all payments ceased before the end of that year. Without a Trans-Atlantic cable major news events could remain unreported for some weeks. Unsuccessful attempts were frequently made by their holders to have them paid by the United States government, but like Confederate money, of course, these bonds cannot be redeemed and have value only to persons who collect them.

Although far removed from the field of U. S. paper money, some of the foreign bonds are of great historical interest. Included among these are the bonds of the Panama Canal Co. that was headed by Ferdinand De Lesseps. The bankruptcy of this firm in the 1889 severely hurt many French investors. Other obsolete bonds of great interest include the numerous issues of Tsarist Russian bonds that were sold to British, French, and German investors at the turn of the century. The new Soviet government repudiated these issues in 1918, and that caused greater consternation among many British and French officials at that time than did the radical social policies of the new Soviet regime.

Old Checks

All of us are familiar with the use of checks as monetary transfer instruments. I do not collect old checks *per se*, but I do save the canceled checks that are returned to me from my bank. Almost by definition, all checks that are collectible are canceled checks. One could, of course, write out checks for low denominations on forms that are aesthetically appealing, but there is little interest in collecting huge numbers of modern checks. As a collector's item a check will be of serious interest if it is signed by or made payable to a famous person, if it is from an exotic location, if it is written on a very unusual form or in a very high denomination, or if it is very old (generally pre-1850 or so).

Beginning in 1862 bank checks were taxed at 2 cents each, and checks from the 1860s and 1870s often bear canceled 2¢ revenue stamps. Revenue stamped paper was also issued from the 1860s to the 1880s. In this case a government stamp was printed directly onto the check form. Several styles of these issues exist, and collectors of revenue stamps are very much interested in the rarer varieties. Syngraphists, however, will probably be more interested in where the check is from. Collectors of national bank notes may want to acquire checks from some of the banks from which they have NBNs. Although a few checks may be expensive, for the most part bank checks of the late 19th Century can be obtained without much expenditure of funds. Some selectivity is necessary unless you want your collection to grow to many thousands of items. Pre-Civil War checks tended to be written on much simpler blanks, but even these remain relatively inexpensive unless you go back well before 1830 or so.

Checks are good items to supplement a collection of national bank notes, especially from the smaller western states. Recently a CAA auction featured a group of check blanks from a bank in Carson City, Nevada, a town for which NBNs were issued but are presently unknown. As I have already noted, NBNs are generally far too rare and much too expensive to collect in depth for most areas of the frontier West. But checks, along with stock certificates of mining companies, often make very good but vastly cheaper substitutes.

Canceled traveler's checks are not generally available, but unissued or specimen examples of these occasionally appear on the market. Some of the most interesting are the pre-1914 checks of the American Express Co. These are denominated not just in dollars, but also (on the same check) in all of the leading European currencies since the Gold Standard in use at that time rigidly fixed the exchange rates. Prior to 1933 one could write a check to be payable exclusively in gold coins, and prior to 1879 there were checks that specified payment only in United States Notes. Another group of checks that are of interest are ones made payable exclusively in MPCs. These were used in branch banks set up for military personnel in foreign nations where MPCs were in use. Although there are probably not very many syngraphists who collect checks exclusively, canceled checks that relate directly to MPCs, gold coins, or NBNs are certainly of interest of many collectors of these items. The most expensive canceled checks are those written by or made payable to very famous persons. These, however, are treated as autograph items, and thus they are far removed from the fields of syngraphics or numismatics.

College and Advertising Notes, Etc.

Although these items are often included with obsolete currency, they were never intended as currency *per se*. Thus advertising notes are not to be confused with merchant scrip that was usually redeemable in merchandise, if not so often in cash. College "currency" was actually play money or training money that was used by various business schools in the late 19th Century. Also to be included among these issues are various political handbills that resembled real money in their designs, but that were often produced to ridicule the monetary policies of such groups as the Greenback Party of the 1870s.

The advertising notes that are of greatest interest to syngraphists are those that were issued in the 1860s, 1870s, and 1880s. Not infrequently these items resembled United States Notes of Series 1862 and 1863, usually of the $1 and $5 denominations. I have also seen a note from Pennsylvania that resembles the extremely rare $100 Interest Bearing Note of Series 1865. A variety of Fractional Currency lookalikes were also printed and distributed by various firms. Some of these were true advertising notes (i. e., nonnegotiable items with no redemption value) while others functioned as merchant scrip. One common practice in the late 19th Century was to overprint genuine Confederate notes (usually of the common 1864 issue) with the name and address of the firm in question.

The most common of the Confederate notes were so inexpensive at this time that they could be used for handbills or other items prepared for public distribution.

College "currency" is also actively collected by a few specialists. These items were nonnegotiable "play money" that was used for training purposes at numerous business colleges and similar establishments during the second half of the 19th century. The denominations almost always included $1 through $100, but fractional and high-value notes were sometimes also printed. The name of the school in question is always prominently featured on these notes. Some college notes sell for substantial prices despite the fact that they were intended solely for educational and training purposes. Related somewhat to the college currency are the school certificates of merit. These are almost always from the pre-Civil War years, and typically they were in denominations of 50¢ or $1. They were awarded to school pupils, whose names were often filled in on these notes. They were negotiable, and in the 1840s or 1850s a sum such as 50¢ or $1 represented a serious amount of money to the school children to whom these items were presented.

Another category of currency-like items are the political satire notes. During the 1870s and 1880s the so-called Greenback Party advocated a great increase in the volume of United States Notes in circulation. Political opponents of this movement produced "absolute currency" notes and other satirical items. These were usually high denomination notes with absurdly high serial numbers. The political message carried on these notes indicated that hyperinflation and worthless money were inevitable if the Greenback Party should come into office. The satirical notes of the last century are actively collected, but in recent years many handbills have been made that feature a replica of an old state bank note on one side and a political message on the other. Although these modern replicas may be of some interest, they have virtually no value to serious collectors.

During 1928 and 1929 numerous handbills were prepared by a variety of private firms showing the size of the new currency then in preparation. The faces of these items typically gave a few of the design details that were to be found on the different denominations of the new notes, while their back sides often featured an advertisement from a bank or other firm. Despite the fact that many millions of these items were printed, most were discarded once the public became familiar with the new currency, and today these interesting mementos of our monetary history are seen only infrequently.

Food Coupons

Food Coupons were initially issued by the Roosevelt administration between 1939 and 1943. This issue consisted of two different types of 25¢ stamps that were issued in panes of four stamps each. Like postage stamps these items had gum on their backs, and they were thus quite appropriately termed Food Stamps, a name that has stuck with the later issues as well despite the fact that fact that all of the more recent issues physically resemble bank notes much more than they do postage stamps. The Food Stamps of 1939-43 are sometimes available in canceled form, but all of the later issues are destroyed after having been spent.

In actual fact Food Coupons can be considered as government-issued supplemental currency. They resemble MPCs in that they are issued only to authorized persons, and they are intended for the exclusive use of those persons authorized to use them. Unlike the MPCs, however, almost all of the Food Coupons issued after 1961 remain valid for purchases, and thus these issues have not been subject to the hasty recalls that have characterized most of the issues of MPCs. For Food Coupons the issuer is the Dept. of Agriculture rather than the Dept. of Defense, as was the case with all MPCs.

The modern period of Food Coupon issues began in 1961. Coupons of 25¢ and $1 denominations were issued, and by 1971 these had been joined by 50¢, $2, and $5 notes bearing serial numbers, this feature having been lacking on the earlier notes. There was also a special issue of 25¢ coupons that were used exclusively for milk purchases, and these were used between 1970 and 1976. All of these items were issued in booklets, and beginning in 1967 the series date was included on most coupons.

Beginning in 1975 entirely new designs for Food Coupons of the $1, $5, and $10 denominations were introduced, and these have been used exclusively since 1976 with only relatively minor variations in design. The colors have also remained consistent with the $1 printed in brown, the $5 in blue-violet, and the $10 in green. Not all of these notes have been printed by the BEP, since the American Bank Note Co. and the U. S. Bank Note Co. have also been active in their production. Although these notes carry no facsimile signatures, there are numerous series and serial number block varieties. Replacement notes have also been issued for all issues beginning with Series 1975.

All Food Coupons are issued in booklets, and a wide variety of total values (for the booklets) and denomination combinations are possible. The different types of booklets use different serial number blocks, and thus there is much of interest for the specialist. A potential collector would also have to decide whether to collect Food Coupons as single notes or in complete booklets.

Unfortunately there is one serious impediment to all of this. Food Coupons are not officially legal to collect for persons unauthorized to use them. These items are intended only for low income individuals and families. They are not transferable, and that fact is stated on each coupon. In many cities there is an active black market in Food Coupons in which persons owning them sell them for cash to others at a substantial discount.

I doubt that the prohibition on trading in Food Coupons would be tightly enforced for affluent persons who would be willing to pay face value for these items, but I haven't seen them at currency shows. It goes without saying that the persons who are officially authorized to use them are almost never currency collectors. Although Food Coupons are given or sold to low income persons at large discounts, the Dept. of Agriculture would have nothing to lose by selling them to interested syngraphists at full face value. Although an example of each of the three current denominations of these items can be obtained without much difficulty, there are doubtless many actual and potential rarities when the different series and booklet combinations are taken into account.

The earlier editions of Hessler's catalog included a brief listing of this interesting form of supplemental currency, but there are no up-to-date listings on what is currently being issued. If collecting Food Coupons becomes fully legal and if more thorough listings become available, these issues might take on a popularity comparable to that presently enjoyed by Military Payment Certificates.

Some collectors become very specialized and collect a given area in great depth, while others go in for more breadth and less depth. In this chapter I have touched on only some of the major items related to paper money. There are many other items that can be collected, however. Lottery tickets from the late 18th and early 19th Centuries are popular with collectors of early paper money. During the 1870s to 1890s there were special postal note forms that were used to facilitate the transfer of small sums of money. These were bearer instruments that could be redeemed at any post office. Such items would obviously appeal to some collectors of Fractional Currency. Although the collecting of old picture post cards seems far removed from any branch of numismatics, these cards often depicted bank buildings in numerous cities and towns. Collectors of national bank notes sometimes try to obtain such cards or advertising handbills from banks that are of particular interest to them. Obviously checks drawn on specific national banks are also good supplemental items for any collection of NBNs.

Other items that are of great interest to some collectors are engraved vignettes that feature design elements used on actual currency. Both the BEP and the ABNCo have released a number of these over the years, and so most of the portraits and allegorical scenes that appear on U. S. currency from the 1860s, 1870s, and 1880s are available in this form. Typically these were printed on very thin India paper but subsequently mounted on cardboard, as was the case with many proofs. Most of these vignettes tend to be fairly inexpensive, typically costing about $50 to $100 each. If you are interested in currency designs, these vignettes are a way of obtaining engravings that are the same as those used on the actual notes, some of which are excessively rare and expensive in issued form.

Finally I should briefly touch on the creations of J. S. G. Boggs. Mr. Boggs is a very talented artist who likes to paint bank notes and other fiscal items. If he painted these in oil on canvas there would be few problems, but he prefers to work in ink on paper. For a few years the *Bank Note Reporter* was running a few too many articles (in my opinion) on his artistic efforts, but many of his creations are doubtless of interest to syngraphists. He has had to face arrest and other forms of harassment from the U. S. Secret Service and other anti-counterfeiting agencies, but all courts have ruled in his favor. He is not a counterfeiter, and his products cannot be treated as counterfeits. At the moment he is suing to recover the fairly large cache of his art works that are still in government custody. The government has offered to return some of them, but he may have difficulty getting all of them back. Mr. Boggs often appears at major currency shows, and if you want *objets d'art* that closely resemble currency, you might want to acquire a "Boggs bill." These are, however, most definitely original art works and not forms of printed currency.

It is unlikely that you will choose to collect all of the various types of items that I have discussed in this chapter, but you may find some of them to be interesting supplements to a collection of paper money. The only non-currency items discussed in this chapter that I collect in depth are souvenir cards, but any collection of Federal paper money can doubtless be enhanced by the inclusion of a number of related items that are supplemental to it.

CHAPTER FIFTEEN

SOURCES OF U. S. PAPER MONEY

Numerous sources are available for paper money. Although I do not recommend buying notes at auction to start with, the bulk of my purchases are now made in this manner. Individual dealers can also be very good sources for the notes that you need, and not infrequently notes may become available from private collectors. By all means try to attend one of the major currency shows that take place in various parts of the country. There are also a number of societies that specialize in various aspects of syngraphics, and these can offer services to their members who are interested in acquiring notes. The number of auction firms that specialize in paper money is fairly limited, so let us begin this chapter with a detailed discussion of these.

PAPER MONEY AUCTIONS

Currency Auctions of America, Inc.
Allen Mincho, P. O. Box 700, Spicewood, Texas 78669
Leonard Glazer, P. O. Box 111, Forest Hills, New York 11375
  CAA is a partnership of these two professionals, and in former years Kevin Foley of Milwaukee was also a principal of the firm. CAA is presently the largest auction firm for U. S. paper money in the country. They conduct at least three or four large auctions every year, and these are always held in conjunction with major currency or coin shows. Typically a CAA auction will contain about 3000 lots and will be spaced over two days. In such a sale there will always be a selection (typically 150 lots or so) of early paper money. Almost every CAA auction features a good selection of Fractional Currency (typically 200 lots), and nearly every one of the major varieties of this type of currency will be represented. CAA has handled both the Martin Gengerke collection of fractionals (in 1995) and the enormous collection formed by Milton Friedberg (in 1997). A special catalog was prepared for the latter sale, and this is in itself a valuable reference work on all aspects of Fractional Currency.
  CAA always has at least a couple hundred lots of what it terms obsolete currency. In addition to state bank notes this is apt to include merchant scrip, advertising notes, currency-related handbills, and other such items. Such currency items as Confederate notes and MPCs are also often included in these sales, but CAA handles very few foreign bank notes. There is always a good selection of currency errors (typically 150 lots), and these are followed by the regular small-size note issues (typically 500 lots or so). Sheets of these items and notes with fancy serial numbers are generally included in this section unless the assortment of these specialty items is unusually large. In 1998 CAA sold the most expensive small-size note thus far, a Series 1928 $10,000 FRN from the Richmond district in CU. It sold for $126,500.

The second day of a CAA auction is typically devoted to large-size type notes (ca. 700 lots or so) and to National Bank Notes (typically about 800 lots). The arrangement of large-size type notes in a CAA auction follows the listing sequence used in the Friedberg catalog. National Bank Notes are arranged by state, and Series 1929 NBNs are included together with the large-size Nationals. Within a given state the notes are listed in order by town or city rather than by charter number.

Although there will always be a few individual large-size notes that will sell for more than $10,000 each in almost every CAA auction, most lots are far less expensive and there will be many in which the hammer price is less than $100. CAA uses the standard 10%/10% scheme that is used by most numismatic auction firms. The buyer pays 10% more than the hammer price, while this price minus 10% is returned to the vendor. If you become seriously involved with collecting paper money, you will most definitely be submitting bids to various CAA auctions.

Lyn F. Knight, Inc., P. O. Box 7364, Overland, Park, Kansas 66207

Lyn Knight used to run a retail business in U. S. paper money, but he now concentrates almost exclusively on currency auctions. He has handled some very significant collections of paper money including many of the notes that were in the collection of Amon Carter Jr., who died in 1982. A typical Lyn Knight sale will consist of about 1000 lots, and generally this is held on one day, although Mr. Knight has also run a number of two-day sales.

In December, 1998 Lyn Knight conducted the auction of the Levitan collection of U. S. Federal paper money. Although the sale contained only 400 lots, the total realization was almost $6 million. Included was a "Grand Watermelon" note that sold for almost $800,000, which is by far the highest price achieved thus far for a paper money item in any public auction.

In most Lyn Knight auctions there is generally a good selection of small-size notes and currency errors. There are usually a few early notes, MPCs, fractionals, and obsoletes, and Mr. Knight often includes a nice selection of Canadian notes in his sales. There is always a very good selection of large-size type notes, and frequently this includes some of the great rarities. Several of the most valuable large-size notes in my collection have come from various Lyn Knight sales.

Lyn Knight's finest offerings are very often National Bank Notes. He has handled some of the largest and best state collections of NBNs that have been formed. Included among these are the C. Dale Lyon collection of Kansas notes, and the collections of Texas NBNs and of Territorial NBNs formed by J. L. Irish. The catalogs for these sales are beautifully prepared. Much information is given about the towns and the banks, and the illustrations often include old photos from these towns that were taken during the period when NBNs were in circulation. These catalogs, of course, are also excellent reference works for the NBNs and banking history of the state or territory in question.

An estimated value (e. g., $300 - $500) is included for each lot in a Lyn Knight sale. For such a lot $180 (i. e., 60% of the low estimate price) would be the minimum bid that would be accepted. Often a Lyn Knight public auction will be accompanied by a mail sale portion that will largely consist of less expensive lots. Although notes in a Lyn Knight auction can sell for as much as $50,000 each (e. g., the two Brown Backs from Idaho and

Washington Territories that were part of the J. L. Irish collection) or even higher than this for some of the lots in the Levitan sale, many lots in his main sales go for well under $100 each. All lots are sold to the buyer at the hammer price plus 10%. If you collect any aspect of Federal currency in some depth, you will most definitely want to be on Lyn Knight's mailing list.

R. M. Smythe & Co., Inc., 26 Broadway, Suite 271, New York, New York 10004-1701

R. M. Smythe & Co. has been in business for many years as a dealer in autographs and various forms of fiscal paper. A few years ago they took over the NASCA numismatic firm of Rockville Centre, Long Island. Until fairly recently R. M. Smythe auctions concentrated much more heavily in early stocks and bonds plus obsolete paper money than they did on U. S. Federal issues. Recently Martin Gengerke, a leading expert on large-size type notes, has joined the firm, and it appears likely that the offerings of Federal currency are becoming much larger. A sale of this firm that was held in conjunction with the International Paper Money Show in Memphis in June, 1998 also featured one of the finest offerings of Confederate paper money that has appeared on the auction scene for many years. Additional sales of Confederate notes and bonds are planned, and without doubt R. M. Smythe is the foremost auctioneer of Confederate items in the nation. Numerous foreign notes have also been offered, and this firm may well choose to get more deeply into this area since CAA and Lyn Knight do very little with foreign notes aside from selections of Canadian notes that Lyn Knight sells with some regularity.

If you collect fiscal paper, most notably old stocks and bonds, you will find that R. M. Smythe & Co. has by far the finest offering of these items of any firm in its auctions. It would almost be fair to say that they have a near monopoly on the sale of these items by public auction, and these sales are held in conjunction with stock and bond shows where many other vendors of these items are also present. Although R. M. Smythe & Co. used to have comparatively small offerings of U. S. Federal currency in its auctions, this aspect of its sales program is now growing rapidly. R. M. Smythe public auctions are often accompanied by mail sales of less expensive, but similar material. If you collect fiscal paper, you will find R. M. Smythe catalogs to be essential. They are also now becoming good sources for a wide variety of notes, and if you collect only Federal paper money, the sections in their catalogs on fiscal paper still make for very interesting reading.

Spink America, 55 East 59th Street, New York, New York 10022

Spink is a numismatic firm of many years' standing in the United Kingdom. Fairly recently they were taken over by Christie's, which together with its rival Sotheby's, is one of the largest art auction firms in the world. Numismatic customers of Spink America will be invited to subscribe to the various Christie's catalogs, but one can just be put on the mailing list for only numismatic items. Christie's is a very large firm with many branch offices, but customers of Spink America who do not have resale certificates for state sales tax exemptions are tax free except for delivery of lots in New York, New Jersey, Connecticut and California.

Spink America is a newcomer to the paper money auction scene in the United States, but already they have conducted a number of sales very high quality material. One of the best was the collection of bank notes formed by Andrew Shiva that was sold in 1995. Although Mr. Shiva was himself a newcomer to syngraphics, his collection included by far the best selection of Series 1878-80 countersigned silver certificates that have been seen on the market for many decades. Spink America catalogs are fairly thin, since generally only a relatively small number of lots are featured in each auction, but many great rarities are now turning up in their sales.

Stack's, 123 West 57th Street, New York, New York 10019-2280
    Stack's is one of the largest numismatic auction firms in the United States. All aspects of numismatics are sold in its auctions. There is heavy emphasis on United States coins, ancient coins, foreign coins of all vintages, medals, etc. Despite the heavy emphasis on coin sales, Stack's has also conducted major sales of U. S. paper money. Some of the best currency sales that Stack's has conducted over the past few years have included the collections formed by Herman Halperin, Bernard Schaaf, and James Thompson. The currency sold by Stack's is very largely restricted to U. S. Federal paper money (large-size, small-size, fractionals, and some MPCs), but it occasionally also has nice selections of Confederate paper money.

    If you buy a fair number of bank notes from Stack's, you will also be mailed all of its coin auction catalogs. Prices realized are always mailed out a few weeks after each sale. Only a very small portion of the coins sold by Stack's are slabbed, and so if you like un-slabbed coins (as I do) this is also a good firm from which to buy coins before an increasingly high percentage wind up encased in hard plastic.

    A few other numismatic auction firms offer more specialized types of paper money. Aside from some Fractional Currency, Early American History Auctions, Inc. (P. O. Box 3341, La Jolla, California 92038) does not include much U. S. Federal paper money in its sales. It has excellent selections of early paper money, however, and these are often accompanied by good offerings of obsolete bank notes. Their auctions also feature very good selections of early American coins and tokens and a wide variety of collateral material related to the early history of the United States. Another numismatic auction firm with relatively specialized offerings is Ponterio & Associates, Inc. (1818 Robinson Avenue, San Diego, California 92103). Here the emphasis is very much on foreign paper money, especially that of Mexico.

    Bowers and Merena, Inc. of Wolfeboro, New Hampshire and Heritage Numismatic Auctions, Inc. of Dallas, Texas are two of the largest numismatic auction firms in the United States. In both cases the emphasis is heavily on United States coins, but each firm also handles large numbers of foreign coins as well. Both Bowers and Merena and Heritage have handled important collections of paper money, but for each of these firms paper money is a very small fraction of their total business. Although important sales of paper money by these firms are sporadic, they do advertise in publications such as the *Bank Note Reporter* whenever they have a significant consignment for sale. A recent paper money sale by Bowers and Merena was of the collection formed by Harry W. Bass, Jr. which included the finest collection of Demand Notes offered for many decades. It would be nice if these firms put out separate catalogs for their currency sales. If you do not actively collect United States coins as well, it may not be possible to be maintained on their complementary mailing lists for long, since their relatively limited offerings of paper money are usually inundated by their frequently enormous offerings of coins.

Many smaller numismatic auction firms also have offerings of paper money from time to time. The best way of keeping track of these is to subscribe to a journal such as the *Bank Note Reporter*. If a sizable amount of paper money is being sold in an auction, there will probably be an announcement in this paper concerning it.

All auction firms accept bids by mail. When sending in a bid sheet, be sure to check for any numbering or bid errors and always be sure to sign the bid sheet, which is then taken to be a valid legal contract. Auctioneers usually also will accept bids by telephone or by FAX. A question arises as to whether you should do all your bidding by mail, or should you try to attend some of the sales and participate as a floor bidder. As a floor bidder you have a better feel for the auction, but it is very important that you carefully inspect every lot that you intend to bid on. In almost all cases lots purchased by floor bidders are not returnable. In cases where there are a number of identical or very similar lots, a mail bidder may actually have an advantage over a floor bidder. The mail bidder can submit bids on each of these lots with the word "OR" between each of them. As long as one of them sells for no higher than his maximum, he will get that lot. A floor bidder might buy the first lot, but then find to his dismay that the next two or three identical lots could sell for significantly lower prices. In any legitimate auction, if you submit a bid of $500 by mail for a certain lot and the next highest bid on that lot is $400, then you will be awarded that lot for $425 if there is no floor action and if $25 is the unit increment in that range. This lot would open on the floor at $425, but a floor bidder would have to pay $525 to top your mail bid. If you are a floor bidder, do keep track of how much money you are spending - don't get carried away! If you are a mail bidder, you are normally permitted to submit a maximum total amount that you are willing to spend in that auction. Some auction firms require that you send them an advance deposit equal to a certain percentage of the total amount of the bids that you are submitting, but once you have established credit with the firm that is no longer necessary.

PAPER MONEY DEALERS

I do not intend in this book to provide a comprehensive list of dealers who specialize in paper money. Such a list would be a long one, and many currency dealers concentrate on forms of paper money that are outside the scope of this book. I would very strongly suggest that you consult the pages of a currency journal such as the *Bank Note Reporter*. In a typical issue there will be display advertisements from about 150 different dealers. There will also be numerous additional ads in the classified section of such a journal.

It strikes me that the mutual level of trust in syngraphics is substantially higher than it is in either coin or stamp collecting. Most currency dealers expect that their customers have a fairly good knowledge of the field and of the prices that one should pay for numerous items, and there seem to be few attempts to take advantage of a novice collector's lack of knowledge of the items he is buying by price gouging, overgrading, and other unethical practices. As a rule, I would say that currency dealers are generally very much interested in the material that they are selling. This is not always the case with persons who sell either coins or stamps. As I noted in the preface of this book, both coin and stamp collecting are presently experiencing a number of problems. The number of active stamp collectors is far less today than it was a few decades ago, and the diminishing numbers of potential customers in this field has led to a number of business practices that are questionable at best. This I do not find at all in currency dealing, at least in the area of U. S. Federal paper money that I collect.

Large currency dealers often issue extensive price lists that appear in ad form in the Bank Note Reporter. Typical of such individuals are Tom Denly (Denly's of Boston) and William Youngerman of Boca Raton, Florida. Other dealers issue annual price lists that are of great interest. Typical of these are Dean Oakes Currency of Iowa City, Iowa and Mid American Currency (David Koble) of Bartlesville, Oklahoma. Allen's Coin Shop of Westerville, Ohio issues a large price list every month. Although much of this list is concerned with coins and medals, copious amounts of U. S. Federal paper money are also listed. Some dealers list only a few notes in their ads, but there are several others who regularly take out full-page ads in the *Bank Note Reporter* or other journals. Private collectors and small dealers often advertise in the classified sections of such publications. By all means check out these sections for possible bargains on items that you are seeking.

If you are just beginning the collecting of small-size notes I would first check out dealers in these items rather than wait for the appropriate lots to come up in currency auctions. For instance, if you want a set by series of the 18 "common" small-size $1 silver certificates, I would check out the dealers who regularly stock these items. Usually these notes are not sold as sets, and one dealer many have better prices on some of them but poorer prices on some others. Decide what conditions you want. You may choose to get well centered CU notes for all series, but substantial savings can be had if you settle for XF or AU condition on the first four of these notes. If you want to complete this set by adding the 1928C, 1928D, and 1928E issues, should these be purchased at auction? Not necessarily.

Often dealers will have good buys on items that are decidedly rare. Some of the rare small-size notes in my collection such as my Series 1928 USN $1 star note and my pair of 1944 experimental star notes have come from dealers rather than through auctions. I have generally found that dealers can supply nice quality small-size $500 and $1000 FRNs at prices that are lower than what you are apt of pay for these notes in most auctions. Several of my rare large-size type notes and many of the national bank notes in my collection were also purchased directly from dealers rather than from auctions. As examples of the former category, I have recently acquired a pair of the rare Series 1880 $50 and $100 silver certificates from dealers at shows rather than auctions.

Most rare notes and NBNs that are in a dealer's stock are probably only one-of-a-kind. By all means use the telephone for ordering such items, and I would recommend getting on the line immediately for an item that you really want once you know that a given dealer has it in stock. Although I do not collect fancy serial numbers, this is an area where it will pay to develop a good working relationship with one or more specialists in this field. Even quite inexpensive notes may be only one-of-a-kind. On the other hand, I would not consider every possible different numbering scheme for radar or repeater notes as major varieties that must be collected. You would soon find yourself with a substantial number of rather similar notes.

Overgrading is nothing like the problem in paper money that it is in coins. If you find that a certain dealer systematically overgrades, however, I would not hesitate to drop him from your list. Items purchased through the mail are generally returnable, and this also applies to auction lots in which there are clearly problems with the description. If you are just starting relationships with a dealer or auctioneer, however, do not make any frivolous returns. One should not do this anyway, but it is particularly important that you not engage in this practice at the beginning of a business relationship. If an item is fairly graded as XF and it was described as XF, by all means keep it. Do not claim that it was only a weak VF just because you saw an ad for a similar note that was a couple of dollars less. Frivolous returns will soon cause a dealer or auctioneer to drop you from his mailing lists. Early in my collecting career in paper money I once made such a return, and the dealer soon refused to make any additional mailings to me. In this case the mistake was clearly mine. I have made a fair number of returns of auction lots, but I always state reasons for returning each lot. I have never had any problems with any of the major auctioneers or currency dealers. Although there are a fairly large number of dealers in paper money, there are only about half a dozen large auctioneers in this field. If you plan to collect paper money on a large scale, you will probably be dealing with all of them at one time or other. Do not do anything that would needlessly sour your relations with any of these firms.

If you do return a note or are selling notes to other customers, use the proper postage for these items. Paper money is easier to ship by mail than are bulky coin lots or stamps in large albums, but often it does have considerable value. For inexpensive items insured mail for $50 or less can be used. This costs only 75 cents, and one receives a green receipt. For this type of mail the recipient does not need to sign for the insured letter. Insured mail for $50 to $200 or more uses a different type of receipt that is blue and white in color, and the recipient does need to sign for the insured letter. Naturally the fee for this type of mail is higher. Registered mail creates a paper trail that makes it easy to trace at every stage of the delivery process. Although it is an expensive service, it should always be used for shipments of $500 or more. By paying additional funds it can be used to insure letters up to many thousands of dollars in value. There are problems, however, with sending registered letters abroad. For most nations these letters can only be insured for fairly modest amounts.

PAPER MONEY SHOWS

Without doubt one of the best ways of becoming familiar with dealers in paper money, currency auctions, and fellow collectors is to attend one or more of the major paper money shows that take place in various parts of the United States. Detailed previews of each of the major shows are given in publications such as the *Bank Note Reporter*, *Coin World*, or *Numismatic News*. Let us consider a few of these in some detail.

The largest and best known of the various annual currency shows is the International Paper Money Show that is held in Memphis, Tennessee every June. It is jointly sponsored by the Memphis Coin Club and the Society of Paper Money Collectors and has been held every year since 1977. The show runs for three days, and more than 150 dealers are in attendance. Several exhibits of top quality currency items are shown, and the BEP always brings along its display. The auctions are held on Friday and Saturday nights. Under the present arrangement Currency Auctions of America holds its Memphis auction in even years, while Lyn Knight and R. M. Smythe hold their auctions in odd years. The emphasis is on U. S. paper money of all types, but much foreign currency is also available.

The bourse area at a small paper money show.

Another very large show is the Pcda Convention held in St. Louis every year either in October or November. This show is sponsored by the Professional Currency Dealers Association and has been held every year since 1986. This show also runs for three or four days, and a major auction that typically lasts two days is a feature of each show. Usually about 100 dealers are in attendance.

The Chicago Paper Money Expo has more recently become another of the major currency shows. It is under the sponsorship of Krause Publications, and is held annually in suburban Rosemont, Illinois in the month of February. Like the other two big paper money shows the CPMX features a major auction that is conducted by CAA or one of the other major currency auctioneers. Usually about 100 dealers have booths at this midwinter event.

The Historic Strasburg Inn is located in this small town which is situated near Lancaster, Pennsylvania. A principal of R. M. Smythe & Co. has an interest in this hotel, and this has resulted in having two different collectibles shows held at the inn each year. In September there is a paper money collectors show, which is a miniature version of the Memphis, St. Louis, or Chicago shows. In January there is the annual stock and bond show. If you are interested in old stocks, bonds, or other types of scripophily items, this show is an absolute must. There are auctions at both of these shows. Needless to say, R. M. Smythe & Co. is the auctioneer. Although the September auction features quite a bit of paper money, the January auction is devoted almost exclusively to stocks, bonds, and related items.

Paper money is also featured at many other numismatic shows where items such as coins may get top billing. The FUN (Florida United Numismatists) show in Orlando in January has often included major auctions of paper money. The ANA (American Numismatic Association) sponsors two large conventions each year, one in the early spring and one in late summer. Although the emphasis at ANA conventions is on coins, paper money is increasingly significant at these shows. ANA conventions are held in a wide variety of cities throughout the United States. Over 400 dealers have tables at a typical ANA show, and these are the largest of all the numismatic shows held in this country.

Much smaller numismatic shows are being held all the time in all parts of the country. A typical show may last only one day, but some of the smaller shows cover the weekend. The basics of each show are given in the various numismatic publications. A very small show may combine other collectibles such as stamps or sports cards with coins and paper money. Often such shows do not feature an auction, but they usually try to include a few exhibits from various collectors.

One big show began only in 1997, and it may turn out to be yet another of the major shows for paper money. It is the National Paper Money & Historical Artifacts Show that is held in Dallas in late August. In 1997 this show featured Lyn Knight's auction of the J. L. Irish collection of Texas National Bank Notes, which was by far the largest collection of Texas NBNs that has ever been formed. At the 1998 show Mr. Knight auctioned an exceptionally strong selection of small-size notes. Stay tuned to see whether the Dallas meeting develops into the fourth major show for paper money in this country. Since this show is held in Dallas, I am surprised that the sponsors have chosen late August as a time for holding their show. Dallas can still be fiercely hot in late summer, but rentals on exhibition halls are probably much cheaper then than they may be at some other times of the year.

PAPER MONEY PRICE TRENDS

In Chapter 6 I provided numerous price data for large-size type notes. Prices on other types of notes have also been provided extensively in this book. Many of these price data concern auction realizations for rare items, but I also feel that it is useful to survey price trends for a few popular large-size notes for the past decade or so. In order to make meaningful comparisons, it is necessary to compare the same varieties of notes on a grading scale that is quite consistent. One could use the Currency Dealers' Newsletter (the Green Sheet) for this, but I have used the annual price lists of Dean Oakes as my data base. Currency prices in the early 1980s were affected by a sharp correction that took place in most collector markets in mid-1981. Although this correction was moderately severe in paper money, the market was not affected nearly as badly as were the markets for most coins and postage stamps. The paper money market bottomed out in 1983-84, but many stamps of the United States and several British Empire countries have yet to return to the prices that they sold for in the late 1970s or the very beginning of the 1980s.

The data I am presenting here are based on the selling prices of Dean Oakes Currency (Iowa City, Iowa) for various popular large-size notes. In doing price comparisons it is important to work with consistent grading standards and not to compare apples with oranges, so to speak. I have compared sales prices for several years between 1987 and 1998 in fine, XF, and CU condition. The prices for uncirculated notes are for notes that are in choice condition but not in a full gem CU grade. For each variety the 1987 and the 1998 prices are given together with the average annual growth rate, compounded annually, for the 11-year period under consideration.

	F		XF		CU	
USN $1 1917	$14./27.	6.2%	$26./55.	7.0%	$80./155	6.2%
USN $5 1907	20./62.	10.9	43./110.	9.0	150./275.	5.5
USN $10 1901	75./330.	14.4	275./750.	9.5	675./1750.	9.0
SC $1 1896	60./175.	10.2	150./400.	9.3	425./1100.	9.0
SC $1 1899	16./40.	8.7	30./75.	8.7	85./150.	5.3
SC $1 1923	9./16.	5.4	15./34.	7.7	30./60.	6.5
SC $5 1896	325./675.	6.9	575./1650.	11.4	1675./5500.	10.1
SC $5 1899	67./250.	12.7	225./585.	9.1	650./1100.	4.9
Gold $10 1922	31./70.	7.7	55./160.	10.2	190./350.	5.7
Gold $20 1922	36./115.	11.1	85./260.	10.7	250./475.	6.0
FRBN $1 1918	18./40.	7.5	28./68.	8.3	95./175.	5.7
FRN $5 1914BS	12./32.	9.3	20./45.	7.6	45./80.	5.4

It is often stated that items in top condition will always increase in value at a faster rate than will the same items in lower grades. These data prove that this statement is most definitely not true, at least for large-size type notes. If one takes averages for these 12 note types - an admittedly risky procedure - the mean growth annual rates are 9.6% for these notes in fine condition, 9.1% in XF, and 6.7% in CU. In terms of percentage appreciation the highest growth rates have been achieved by the $10 Bison and $5 Indian notes in fine condition. In the early 1980s one could readily find F-VF examples of these notes priced at well under $100 each, but today Indian notes in that grade would sell for at least $300 while similar Bison notes would be more like $400 each. In my opinion there is a very good reason for the increased popularity of these notes in fine condition. High grade examples of either type are now so expensive that many collectors have decided to settle for lesser grades. The $5 Educational note seems to show the opposite tendency, but this note has always been expensive in most of the better grades. In this survey the slowest growth rates have been achieved for the most common of large-size notes, the Series 1923 $1 SCs. These notes are readily available in all grades, and most collectors can easily afford to purchase top grade examples of these notes. Overall a mean annual growth rate of about 9.0% is indicated for all of these large-size type notes over the period 1987-98. This would imply that these notes would double in value in about eight years.

We could look at statistics for other series of notes, and I think that similar price trends would be found. Some types of issues, such as small-size currency in uncut sheets, have lagged behind the other items. In Fractional Currency there is now a very wide spread between notes that are just in new condition and those that are in gem CU condition. The former, as well as most circulated fractional notes, have also lagged in price in comparison with most large-size notes. Most common small-size notes have fallen behind in their growth rate in comparison with the scarcer small-size notes. The true rarity of several of the small-size star notes has been realized only in the past decade or so, and this has led to very large price increases on many of these.

In the past few years there has developed almost an obsessive emphasis on the exact condition of uncirculated coins. Although it is possible to buy a complete set (35 coins) of Franklin half dollars in MS-60 for about $300 or in MS-62 for about $500, prices exceeding $1000 per coin are now being asked for some of these coins in MS-65 to MS-67 with full bell lines. A typical uncirculated Series 1923 $1 silver certificate sells for about $65, and an especially attractive note of this series in gem CU but with uninteresting serial numbers may sell for as much as $100 or so. But it is hard for me to imagine anyone paying several hundred dollars for one of these just because it is in superb gem CU condition. The fact that the PCDA (Professional Currency Dealers Association) has recently come out against the third-party grading and slabbing of U. S. paper money, should help to throw some cold water on a situation that with time could lead to the absurdities that in my opinion have already been achieved with certain series of U. S. coins.

Throughout this book I have emphasized auction sales, and I have quoted numerous price realizations for notes that have been sold by this method. At the end of the 1990s there appears to be a major new trend on the prices realized for the rarest items. It was in 1989 that an auction sale broke the $100,000 barrier for a single note (a Series 1890 Treasury Notes) for the first time. It was not until the beginning of 1998 that the $200,000 barrier was broken with the sale of a Series 1863 $500 USN. The end of 1998 however, saw the sale of the fabulous Levitan collection which yielded numerous prices never before seen. The same $1000 Treasury Note that sold for $121,000 in 1989 now brought almost $800,000 and no fewer than six notes in this auction sold at prices that exceeded the record height of $233,750 that had been achieved only a few months earlier.

What does this portend? As the popularity of paper money collecting grows, it seems almost certain that the prices achieved for the rarest bank notes will soon match those of the most expensive coin or stamp items. Thus we should except to see price realizations as high as $2 million in the near future for the rarest and most desirable types of paper money. Indeed a price exceeding $1,000,000 has already been reported for the ultra-rare Series 1890 $100 Treasury Note (grand watermelon) with a small red seal. (Fr. 379b or H-1426).

With the expectation of a few Series 1918 FRNs and a number of Series 1882, 1907, or 1922 gold notes, almost all large-size $500 and $1000 notes are now "off limits" to all but the most affluent of collectors. This also applies to such extreme rarities as $20 Demand Notes, all Interest Bearing Notes of $50 or higher, most countersigned silver and gold notes, the $50 and $100 Treasury Notes, and the great majority of territorial national bank notes. It is unfortunate that most collectors will have to forego attempts to acquire these items, but I do not anticipate any diminution in the prices for the rarest notes regardless of whatever ups and downs there are in the price structure of the less expensive items. Multimillionaires are capable of paying whatever they want for items that they desire, and consequently the prices realized for the rarest notes will probably move quite independently of the prices achieved for the more mundane items.

The highest prices achieved will almost certainly be for the major rarities in large-size type notes and in a few cases for the rarest of the large-size national bank notes. Other types of U. S. paper money are probably less subject to these extremes of price inflation. The four rarest issues of normal small-size type notes (viz., the 1933 $10 SC, the 1934 $10 North Africa notes, and the 1928 $500 and $1000 gold notes) are all available at something like $10,000 each in choice condition, and prices at about this level should remain reasonably stable since there are roughly 75 known examples for each of these rarities. Rare star notes, of course, could go much higher if a large number of small-size currency collectors should decide to obtain all the verities possible for these items. Very high prices have been obtained in the past few years for $5000 and $10,000 FRNs, but the prices for these notes are always subject to new supplies coming onto the market (from Las Vegas, Nevada, perhaps??) and to the whims of wealthy persons who are not true collectors.

Although prices exceeding $20,000 have been obtained for a few extremely rare Fractional Currency items, all of these have been for special varieties of notes that are reasonably common in there basic type forms. It is quite possible to assemble an extensive and comprehensive collection of fractional notes without a huge outlay of funds. The same can be said for MPCs. The most expensive MPCs sold thus far have fetched rather more than $5000 each. The very rarest MPC replacement noes, if they exist at all, would undoubtedly bring more than this in today's market, but extremely high prices do not appear to be the rule for scarce notes of this series in what is an admittedly thin market.

The present very strong market for Confederate notes can be expected to continue, but an important mitigating factor in all of this is the fact that the most expensive of the Confederate notes are actually not extreme rarities. There are roughly 100 examples each of the $500 and $1000 Montgomery notes, and at least a few dozen examples are known for each of the other celebrated Confederate rarities. In no way do these note compare in scarcity with the rarest and most expensive types of U. S. large-size notes. A few realizations in excess of $10,000 have already been obtained for a few extremely rare examples of state bank notes and other forms of obsolete paper money, but this is a fairly thin market with relatively low demand for specific, rare notes. Thus I expect that it will be many years before an individual non-governmental obsolete bank note sells for as much as $100,000.

Hopefully this discussion will not discourage you in any way from getting into the field of large-size currency collecting. The fact that a number of large-size Federal notes are effectively noncollectible for nearly all syngraphists should not preclude anyone from becoming involved with this field. It is still possible to assemble an attractive and comprehensive collection of large-size notes with an outlay of no more than a few thousand dollars, and so I would encourage anyone who collects Federal paper money at all to acquire at least a number of large-size notes.

SELLING YOUR PAPER MONEY

This book is mostly about forming a collection of paper money rather than disposing of one, but from time to time you may wish to sell off a number of your surplus items, and financial necessity may require that you occasionally liquidate a large portion or even all of your collection.

The Levitan Grand Watermelon is being sold at auction.

I have done far more buying than selling of scarce bank notes, but my sales have included some decidedly rare items, so let us consider these first. Auction sales are certainly a good way of selling your more valuable notes. In currency auctions almost all bids are handled on a 10%/10% basis. If you are the buyer and the price of a lot is $100, you will pay $110, while the vendor will receive $90, the auctioneer splitting the difference. This 20% spread is reasonably low for moderately priced items, but it does become rather high for rarities. Currency auctions, however, seem to have many advantages over what is taking place in most large stamp auctions. I have both bought and sold a fair number of stamp collection lots at auction in recent years. In the largest such auctions almost all of the buyers seem to be dealers, who will then be trying to sell the lots they buy for even higher prices. Some may be acting as agents for individual clients, but if the large lots that are purchased at auction are to be broken down and resold, there will have to be a very large difference in price between what the vendor receives and what these stamps are eventually sold for at retail. Also it seems that the majority of stamp auctioneers are now using a 10%/15% basis for their sales, i. e., the buyer pays 115% of the hammer price while the vendor still receives only 90% of this amount. This makes for about a 25% spread between the buyer and seller. In currency auctions, a great many of the rare lots will be sold either to private collectors or to dealers acting as agents for individual collectors. In the large stamp auctions that I attend, most of the buyers are dealers who are acting for their own accounts. One other facet concerns minimum consignment size. The largest stamp auctioneers usually want a minimum of $5000 in estimated cash value for an individual consignment. Even the largest currency auctioneers are willing to take much smaller minimum consignments. One problem with all auction selling, of course, is that there is a delay of several months between the time you consign the material and the time you receive settlement from the auctioneer. With most auction firms this takes place about 45 days after the date of the sale.

    National bank notes, especially, are sometimes subject to what I would call runaway bids, and these can become hugely advantageous to the vendor. As I have noted on several occasions, a given collector may have been waiting for years or even decades to buy the note of a particular bank that is of great interest to him. The price at auction for such a note can rise to very high levels, provided there is at least one other person at the sale who is also very much interested in that note. I have already noted my own experience with a note from the FNB of Cheraw, South Carolina (9342). A more extreme case occurred in a CAA sale in 1998 with a $10 Third Charter Blue Seal from the Pokomoke City NB of Maryland (4191). Despite the fact that this note was only in F-VF condition, it sold for the amazing price of $15,400. Although this note is apparently unique, so are many other NBNs including several in my own collection. If you have a fair number of NBNs from small towns and you put them in a large auction, it is entirely possible that at least one or two of them will fetch prices that are vastly higher than what either you are the auctioneer would expect. In this case of the Pokomoke City note, CAA estimated a value of $2000-4000 for this lot. Both they and the vendor were pleasantly surprised by the end result.

    In buying at auctions never submit a buy bid on a lot. Most auctioneers will not accept buy bids, but they are particularly inappropriate on scarce NBNs. You might find yourself reaching for the stars against a determined floor bidder. Runaway bids are hugely advantageous for the vendor, but you don't want to be a buyer unless you really are desperate to get that particular note. If you consign material to auction, you do have the right to buy it back, but you must pay the spread if your bid is successful. If you have an item of yours in an auction and you feel that it is worth at least $200, but you also find that the highest bid for the lot is only $95, you can submit a bid of $100 and win this lot. This will cost you $20, but it will prevent your $200 item from being "stolen" for less than half what you think that it is worth. Almost all auctioneers will let you know the prices on their book for the lots that you have consigned to them. There is no need to attend the auction in person; you can do this by telephone. It is then up to you to decide whether or not to submit protective bids.

I have sold a few expensive notes from my collection through dealers on a consignment basis. This is particularly useful for valuable notes that are worth at least $1000 or more each. In such a transaction I consign the note to the dealer. He agrees to sell it for me for a commission, usually 10% or so for a note that is worth at least $500 or more. If we agree that I am to receive $2000 for a particular note, then he sells it to a client for $2200, and I receive $2000 once the sale is concluded. Since the dealer doesn't tie up any of his capital, he can easily operate on a markup of only 10% or so. On a less expensive item, such as a note that is worth only $100 or so, the commission will probably be more like 15% of the sale price. On an extremely valuable note, however, let us say $10,000 or more, a commission as low as 5% might be negotiated. Real estate brokers in my state operate on a commission of 6%. If no money changes hands prior to the time that the deal is actually finalized, the commission on a very expensive note can even be significantly less than this. The dealer may have a client who has been after that particular note for years. With a rare bank note there is no elaborate legal contract that has to be drawn up, and the note does not need to be shown to numerous prospective buyers. In the case of buyers of houses, many people who would like to buy cannot obtain a mortgage from a bank. If you have to mortgage your house in order to purchase a bank note worth $20,000 or more, don't even consider it!

At the other end of the scale you will find that almost all of the more common large-size notes in fairly decent condition are very readily marketable. For instance, the very common Series 1923 $1 SCs that retail for about $22-25 each in VF condition can be easily sold for about $16-18 each, or about 70% of their retail price. The common old back $1 SCs of Series 1928, 1928A, 1928B, and 1934 are also extremely easy to sell at fair prices in all decent grades from fine to CU. Although there still is not much demand for well-circulated $1 SCs and $2 USNs of later series, CU examples of these issues are always marketable and packs of 100 CU notes of these types are hugely in demand. In a publication such as the *Bank Note Reporter* there are usually numerous buy ads from various dealers for all sorts of notes. Paper money shows are also excellent places to sell notes. Of course you should always have some idea of what you want for the notes that you have on hand.

Although popular inexpensive notes can usually be sold at something like 70% of their retail prices, do not expect a dealer in U. S. Federal paper money to offer you anything like that much for a randomly arranged cigar box full of well circulated German Notgeld or Japanese Invasion Money. As I noted way back in the preface of this book, the "gouge factor" seems already to be much too high for many postage stamps and some coins. Regrettably souvenir cards also suffer from this problem. Dealers in these items may often try to buy them for less than a third what they want to sell them for. When it comes to the more exotic material, you definitely need to consult with someone who is an expert in the field. I am very knowledgeable in most aspects of U. S. Federal paper money, but I do not claim to know much about state bank notes. Some have little value, but others that are ragged and basically ugly in appearance may be of substantial worth. Note the comments that I made in Chapter 13 on the canceled notes of the Bank of Saugerties that I sold in a CAA auction. Extremely rare notes can sell for good money even if they are very unattractive in appearance.

Another approach to selling bank notes is the direct one. At a large currency show you will meet collectors or dealers who are especially interested in purchasing just what you might have. This may be especially true of collectors of National Bank Notes who are searching for particular banks. If they are really anxious, be prepared to negotiate for a somewhat higher price. You can also advertise in currency publications what you want to sell. I have done this more with stamps and coins than I have with paper money, but ads in these publications are not very expensive and they may be highly productive. If you have scarce NBNs, I would very carefully research the scarcities of the banks in question. You should want to sell your notes at fair prices, but you could wind up selling a scarce note for a good deal less than it would bring in a major auction.

Unless you have had substantial prior experience in selling in smaller shows, I would not recommend that you rent a table or booth and try selling at a major show. You would then have to decide whether or not to accept personal checks from persons you do not know, and very likely you would wind up on a weekend with far more loose cash than you would like to carry on your person. You should always have a friend or partner to work at your table. Unfortunately thefts from dealers do take place at these shows. Remember that thieves often work in pairs. One attracts your attention, while the other rips off your stuff. In the 1997 FUN show in Orlando the Boston dealer Tom Denly, who has had many years of experience in selling at large shows, was robbed of more than $50,000 worth of notes, and he was not the only person at that show to have lost merchandise through theft. Some persons have also had currency stolen from their cars while attending major shows. Although I do buy and take possession of books and some inexpensive notes at currency shows, I do not take delivery on the notes that I buy at show auctions or on expensive notes that I buy from dealers in the bourse. By placing a deposit I can reserve the note, which can be sent to me when I am ready to receive it at my home which is always many hundreds of miles from any of the major show venues. Although security is fairly tight at a major currency show, one should always exercise both discretion and caution any time that items of considerable value are being handled or are on public view.

PAPER MONEY SOCIETIES

Let us conclude this chapter with a brief discussion of some of the various paper money societies that you might want to join. Foremost among these is the Society of Paper Money Collectors, Inc. This society publishes a bimonthly journal, *Paper Money*, which is discussed in greater detail in the bibliography. The SPMC is also responsible for the publication of numerous handbooks on the obsolete currency of various states. About 20 states have been thoroughly documented thus far. The latest effort in this project concerns the currency of Kentucky. These handbooks list both the state bank notes and the various forms of merchant scrip and small-change notes that circulated in the state in question during the 19th Century. For further information contact Robert Cochran, P. O. Box 1085, Florissant, Missouri 63031.

The secretaries of nonprofit societies have a habit of changing every two years or so, and thus I am not going to put down any more specific names and addresses. Some of them may well be obsolete before you try to get in touch with them. I think that you may find the following societies to be of interest if you decide to specialize in any of these specific areas of syngraphics.

The current address for most of these organizations may be obtained from the American Numismatic Association which is itself a worthwhile organization. As the name implies, the ANA deals with all types of money, not just paper money. You may contact the ANA at 818 North Cascade Avenue, Colorado Springs, CO 80903-3279, or phone the headquarters at (719) 632-2646, or e-mail at ana@money.org. Its web site is www.money.org.

Fractional Currency Collectors Board

Military Money Collectors Club

International Bank Note Society

Latin American Paper Money Society

Canadian Paper Money Society

Souvenir Card Collectors Society

Civil War Numismatic Society

Currency Club of Chester County (PA)

There are also societies for collectors of old stocks and bonds, merchant and municipal scrip, and old checks. All of these societies publish journals or newsletters that contain articles and ads of interest to their members. When a person joins the Fractional Currency Collectors Board, he receives a copy of Milton Friedberg's Fractional Currency encyclopedia that I describe in the bibliography. Members in the Canadian Paper Money Society are given the option of purchasing a matched number set of current Canadian bank notes from the Bank of Canada. All of these societies also encourage members to write articles for their journals, and joining a specialized collectors' society is a good way of learning to know of other people with similar interests.

CHAPTER SIXTEEN

STORAGE AND CARE OF PAPER MONEY

We now turn to the important topic of storage and care of your collection of paper money. As I noted very early in this book, U. S. Federal paper money is basically a fairly expensive area to collect. Furthermore it is to a very large extent fully negotiable. Although you might chose to keep a collection of such inexpensive currency items as German Notgeld or Japanese Invasion Money in your home, I would strongly advise that you not store a collection of U. S. Federal paper money in this fashion. Some banks offer vaults or lockers that are significantly larger in size than are the more standard safety deposit boxes. Either can be used, but I would try to rent a box or locker that is as large as possible. Full sheets can pose major problems for their storage, and this is one of the reasons why I have not ventured into this field. As I noted in Chapter 11, special storage equipment may been necessary if you plan to become seriously involved with the collecting of full sheets. Sheets of four large-size or obsolete notes or sheets of six Series 1929 NBNs will not present any problems in most bank rental boxes, but almost all currency sheets that are substantially larger or wider than these will pose major problems for most of the boxes or lockers that banks are prepared to rent to you.

I was a stamp collector long before I got into U. S. paper money collecting, and a large proportion of my stamps are mounted into albums. Various attempts have been made over the years to produce printed pages for U. S. currency, but most of these have been failures. Although it is possible to mount district sets of $1 FRNs in albums, the monotony of their designs does not lend itself to a very exciting display. Album pages have also been prepared for other series such as $1 SCs, but do you really want to leave your Series 1928E $1 SC sitting in an album in a bookshelf standing in your study? Albums may be fine for many types of stamp and coin collections, but they are ill-suited for most types of Federal paper money.

Recently an album for web notes has been produced and marketed. This book has spaces for all 227 printing run and plate number varieties of these issues, at least three of which are acknowledged to be extreme rarities. It would be extremely difficult to fill all of the space of this album and it remains to be seen whether this mode of collecting web notes will catch on with collectors.

Each of us can choose our own methods for storing and displaying our collections, but for U. S. paper money I favor putting the notes into plastic currency holders. I place these in turn into large-size paper envelopes which I then put into cardboard boxes. The boxes I use are capable of each handling a few dozens of filled paper envelopes. Despite the fact that my collection of U. S. Federal paper currency now contains well over 3000 individual notes, only about seven medium-size cardboard boxes are needed, and all of these can be put into a single large locker that I rent from a bank that is within convenient walking distance of both my home and my office.

I strongly recommend the use of Mylar plastic holders for storing currency. These come in a variety of sizes that can accommodate all types of U. S. Federal paper money. Never store currency long-term in plastic holders that are made of polyvinyl chloride. With time this can react with the notes themselves and cause serious damage. If there is any question as to the chemical composition of the plastic holders that you are using, discard the dubious ones and buy new Mylar holders. Although these holders come in sizes that are suitable for storing individual small-size or fractional notes, I do not use these for storing my collection. Almost all of my notes are in holders designed for large-size notes. A few of my notes are in holders of the so-called auction size (which is even larger), I find it vastly more sensible to store small-size notes a dozen or so at a time in large-size holders rather than individually in holders designed specifically for small-size notes.

Almost all of my collection of small-size notes (together with my collection of MPCs) will fit into a single moderately large cardboard box. Since 10 or 12 small-size notes will comfortably fit into a single large-size currency holder, these holders are superb for $1 or $2 FRN district sets. The 18 common varieties of $1 SCs fit into two holders, while the 12 $5 USNs fit into just one. I give rare notes a "place of honor." Thus my Series 1928C, 1928D, and 1928E $1 SCs are put into a third holder for my collection of $1 SC's. My sets of 1932-33 and 1937 experimental notes are also each in separate holders. My Series 1933 $10 SC, of course, gets its own holder, while my other eight $10 SCs are in a second holder. I can put two or three of these holders into each long paper envelope, and thus all of my normal $1 SCs are in one envelope, all of the $5 and $10 SCs are in a second, and all of the normal USNs are in a third, etc.

The star notes for these series are stored in a similar fashion. All of the SC star notes in my collection fit into five holders, and these again can be put into a single long envelope. The same procedure is used for both the normal and the star varieties of the other types of non-current small-size notes. One long envelope each is sufficient to store my series sets of $5 - $100 FRNs for a given denomination. Therefore all my small-size FRNs (except for the numerous $1 and $2 district sets) fit into just five long envelopes with the $500s and $1000s going into the sixth. I put all of my normal MPCs of a given series into a single large-size currency holder, and I can put four of these into a single long envelope. Thus all of my normal MPCs fit into just three long paper envelopes, with my collection of MPC replacements filling up a fourth.

Although most syngraphists collect NBNs by state, I store them by type and denomination. For Series 1929 NBNs I store all of my $5 notes together, etc. I do put type 1 and type 2 notes in the same holders, however. I have over 900 Series 1929 Nationals in my collection, but they are very systematically arranged. All of the notes for a given denomination are arranged by state in an alphabetical fashion. Within a given state they are arranged in an alphabetical fashion by cities and towns. For a given city I then arrange the notes by bank charter number. Usually there are 10 to 12 notes in each large-size currency holder. As new notes are added, I reshuffle these and add additional plastic holders or long envelopes where necessary. I write on each long envelope the denomination and a number sequence for that denomination. I do not put down the exact sequence of towns or cities, since these will change with time. With this system it is very easy to locate a given note, even if that specific note may be moved from one holder to another as my collection grows.

Many collectors might be tempted to use small-size currency holders for their small-size notes. If you have only a few dozen 1929 Nationals, this might be OK, but what if you have several hundred? Why pay a bank extra money for storing lots of cheap plastic? I have numerous small-size holders on hand, and if I want to send a small-size note out, I can always just put that note into a small-size holder of its own. As I have already noted, my entire collection of small-size notes fits easily into a medium size cardboard box. This would not be the case if there were 1500 individual small-size plastic holders for me to contend with.

The procedure I use for storing my collection of Fractional Currency is a bit different. I put each fractional note into its own glassine envelope. These I mark with the catalog number for that note. Contrary to what one writer (Barry Krause) states, glassine envelopes are entirely safe for the storage of either postage stamps or paper money. A dozen or so of these can be stored in a single large-currency holder. Two or three of these in turn go into a single long envelope, and these I arrange by issue. Special notes such as the 15 cent specimens of the Third Issue go into a separate envelope. I also have a few odd items such as experimental notes, counterfeit detectors, and other specimen notes. These go into yet another long envelope, but my entire Fractional Currency collection fits into about a half dozen long paper envelopes. I do not own a Fractional Currency shield, and frankly I have no plans for acquiring one. Storing one of these securely would pose major problems.

Large-size notes require much more storage volume for me than do the other categories of Federal paper money in my collection. I put either one or two large-size notes into each currency holder. About six or seven of these can be put into a single long envelope, and thus each envelope typically contains about ten to twelve large-size notes. My collection of large-size type notes fits into three moderately large cardboard boxes. I arrange the large-size Nationals by type, but for First Charter notes I mix the Original Series and the Series 1875 notes for a given denomination. These are then arranged in alphabetical order by state and by city or town. My largest holdings of large-size NBNs, of course, are of Third Charter Blue Seals. These I have segregated by denomination and as to whether they are Date Backs or Plain Backs. Within each of these categories I then arrange the notes alphabetically by state and then by city or town. I have so many $5, $10, and $20 Blue Seals that they have now filled one large cardboard box. Thus my collection of $50 and $100 Blue Seals has been put in with my NBNs of earlier types. I have more than 700 large-size NBNs, but all of these still fit into two medium large cardboard boxes.

Everyone has his or her way of arranging a collection, but that is how I do mine. One of the beauties of U. S. Federal money is that it is compact. All of this will still fit into a small bank vault that I can rent from my local bank for only about $125 per year. Imagine trying to do this with a mounted stamp collection or coin collection of comparable value! You may want to follow an entirely different approach for storing your collection, but the method I use is highly systematic. I can locate any single item in this collection within just a couple of minutes after opening the bank vault.

Safe storage is only one aspect to maintaining a large collection of paper money or other collectibles. Good record keeping is also very important. I have a complete set of

3" x 5" file cards on the notes that are in my collection. Every single note gets its own card except for the $1 and $2 FRN district sets for which I record all notes of a given set on one card. For large-size type notes I record the catalog number, the type and description of the note, the serial number plus the plate letter, the condition (sometimes augmented by comments such as close cut at bottom, two pinholes, extra wide margins, etc.), the date of acquisition of the note, and the price I paid. For type notes the plate letter is redundant, but this is not true for large-size NBNs. On the back sides of these cards I have been recording the prices realized for notes of that same variety in similar condition in auctions. I note the month and year of the auction in all cases. Not only does this give me a good idea of the current market value of my note, but it also tells me at a glance how often a given note comes up for sale. For instance, one readily sees that Series 1869 $1, $2, $5, and $10 USNs are sold much more frequently than are most of their counterparts of the various individual varieties of the 1874-1880 period. On very common large-size notes, such as most Series 1899 or 1923 $1 SCs, etc., I only record a few sample prices.

For large-size NBNs I follow a similar procedure. Naturally this includes the bank's name and its charter number. Original series notes that lack charter numbers are noted, and whether or not a regional letter prefix is used is also recorded. On the backs of these cards I record the total number of notes issued for that particular variety and the rarity class according to the Hickman-Oakes catalog. The total dollar amount outstanding in 1935 can be useful for a large-size issue, but this sort of information is generally of no interest for a bank that went out of business prior to 1930. For Fractional Currency I record the catalog number, the description, and the condition of the note as well as its date and price of acquisition. That is about as far as one can go for items that do not have serial numbers. I try to record auction realizations for the scarcer varieties of fractionals, but this is not usually practical for specific varieties of National Bank Notes.

For small-size notes I record the type of currency, the denomination, and the series. Both the serial number and the condition, of course, are also recorded, as are the date and price of acquisition. Occasionally I will put an auction realization or two on the back sides of these cards, but I do not do it for common notes. Although I do not collect mule varieties *per se*, I sometimes also record whether my note is a mule or a non-mule. For Series 1929 NBNs I do record on their back sides the numbers of a given note that were issued as well as their rarity class from the Hickman-Oakes catalog. I have also done extensive research on the check numbers to be found on both the faces and backs of Series 1929 NBNs, and these data are also recorded on my cards. For normal MPCs I record both the sheet position number as well as the serial number of each note. For MPC replacements I also record how many of that particular variety have been verified by Fred Schwan. As I previously noted, I put all the notes of a given $1 or $2 FRN district set on a single card, but I do record their individual serial numbers. The web notes in my collection, however, each rate an individual card.

In addition to this card system, I also have put onto computer disks most of these data for each of these notes. My computer listings, however, do not include the dates and prices at acquisition, and I have not included any of the data that I have written down on the back sides of the cards on the computer listings. When one has a very large collection that is worth many hundreds of thousands of dollars, it is really quite important to know just what is in it.

I have also been working on yet another method of recording the notes in my collection. Using a high resolution photocopier, I have made copies of many of these notes. I then cut these up and store them in envelopes. For most small-size notes and MPCs I copy only the faces, but for many of the large-size notes I do both the face and back. It is quite time-consuming, however, to make photocopies for a collection as large as mine. To be of much use, the resolution needs to be sufficient to read the check numbers that appear on the small-size notes. This procedure is perfectly legal provided the copies are either larger by 25% or smaller by 25% of the real notes. The late John Hickman assembled a huge collection of "play money," since he photocopied all of the many thousands of NBNs that passed through his hands. A lot of information about a note can be conveyed with a good copy of it.

Notes that are damaged or defaced can sometimes be "corrected." This is one of the most controversial aspects to paper money collecting. When such techniques are criticized, they are called doctoring. When supported, restoration is the term of choice. Doctoring and restoration. The line between these can be very fine. During the preparation of this manuscript, I received several inquiries from some dealers and the publisher about what I was going to say on this subject.

The careful inspection of the Grecian vases in any art museum that features them will reveal that many of the vases on display have been put together from fragments. In the art world repair work of this sort is done all the time. Repair and restoration work on rare bank notes can also be a perfectly ethical activity.

Generally the most important ethical consideration is disclosure to prospective buyers of repairs. Even this philosophy has pitfalls, because it is possible that subsequent buyers might be uninformed and deceived. If the repair work that is required is anything other than trivial, do not try it yourself. There are techniques for sewing tears, filling in pinholes, and restoring lost corners on notes, but these are matters that should be handled by a professional who is capable of undertaking the very fine hand work that is required. One person I know who can do this work is the proprietor of Bank Notes Northwest, P. O. Box 406, Wilsonville, Oregon 97070. He charges a fair price for doing repair work, but his work is of excellent quality and well worth it provided the note in question is worth at least a few hundred dollars. If a note with an obvious edge tear is only worth $30 or $40 when sound, however, do not bother with trying to get professional help on having the tear sewn back. Nancy Poli is a very skillful restorer who is highly regarded for the quality of her work. I have never used her services, but have spoken with some who have. A note must have substantial value, however, in order to justify the cost of having some minor damage effectively removed.

There are those who say that one should never tamper with bank notes, but I do not follow this advice in all cases. It is not possible to press out heavy folds or to make a limp note have the feel of a crisp one, but some procedures can definitely improve the appearance of a note and cause it no harm in the process. Even the BEP laundered notes that were considered too dirty for circulation, but too good for destruction in the late 1800s.

BEP employees launder 19th Century notes in order to return them to circulation.

Certain things and substances can be regarded as complete "no-no's" as far as paper money is concerned. Although cellophane tape has been improved quite a bit over the past quarter century or so, it is capable of leaving very nasty and difficult-to-remove stains. Never allow it to come into contact with your bank notes. There may be some organic solvents that are capable of reducing the effects of tape stains, but I do not known exactly which ones these are. I avoid notes with tape stains like the plague. Rubber bands decay with time, and they are capable of producing nasty stains after several decades. Occasionally a pack of notes will turn up in which the top and bottom notes each have nasty stains from rubber bands. Fortunately the other notes in such a pack are usually not affected. The well known rust remover oxalic acid and its salts are not the only substances that turn green inks blue. Other strong acids such as hydrochloric can also do this. Never allow anything that contains sulfuric acid to come into contact with your notes. Concentrated sulfuric acid will immediately destroy any paper or cloth product, and even when strongly diluted it must never be used with anything made of paper. Strong laundry detergents should never be used for cleaning dirty bank notes. They are easily capable of removing the black overprints that are found on Series 1929 NBNs and FRBNs.

As I cautioned in the chapter on errors, certain so-called "errors" must be treated with great skepticism. Never pay more than a nominal price for a circulated 1929 National that is lacking its black overprint. If you want to make one of these, take a 1929 NBN or FRBN that you do not care for very much and hand rub it vigorously with a full-strength laundry detergent. The brown seal and serial numbers will still be there, but the black overprint will mysteriously disappear. Basic ethical considerations, however, dictate that you not attempt to sell such as note as an "error."

If you would like a Federal Reserve Note with a blue seal and serial numbers, just use a little oxalic acid. It will not affect the black district seal, however. The back may or may not be turned blue depending on the vintage of the note - the ink compositions used by the BEP have changed many times. I do not know just which chemicals can be used to change the red seals and serials on small-size USNs from red to various shades of orange or yellow, but they are out there, and never pay serious money for one of these notes with weird colored seals and serial numbers. Strong bleach is adequate enough to remove the red overprints from some of the notes printed in the 19th Century, so watch out for Fourth and Fifth Issue fractionals that lack their seals. With some effort it is also possible to concoct such items. This can also be done on the USNs of the same vintage, although the cost of these would preclude anyone in his right mind from creating such "errors." As I stated in Chapter 9, almost all "errors of color" are not errors at all. They are merely chemical changelings.

Trimming is a process that should be avoided. Occasionally one will find a National Bank Note that has an ugly appendage that can be easily removed, but this is a practice that should be used only very sparingly. Unfortunately bankers in the old days were not always very careful about they ways they cut their notes. NBNs occasionally are found with trims that can be described as downright ugly. All such notes sell at prices that are much lower than what similar notes with normal margins.

Starching is a technique that has been occasionally used to make a limp note appear to have the strength and texture of a much fresher note. By this procedure one might attempt to upgrade a note in fine condition to XF or AU. When placed into water and soaked for some time, the starch in the note will come out. Starched notes will feel as though they were printed on very heavy, stiff paper that shows no sign of crispness. The best thing to do is to avoid buying such a note unless it is described as being starched. A starched note will fail the soaking test, but then the vendor of the note could say that it was altered after the sale. If you are permitted to do this with a questionable note, go ahead and make the test. If not, pass up any apparently high grade note that has the appearance of being starched.

Never do any experiments including erasures on notes until after you have purchased them. Under no circumstances should you ever laminate a note with the intention of preserving it or improving its appearance. Many of the notes in the collection of King Farouk of Egypt were silked, i. e., laminated between two layers of thin silk. These notes reached the market after the overthrow of Farouk in 1954 and the subsequent sale of his collections by the Egyptian government. A fair number of these silked notes have turned up for sale in the United States in more recent years, and this process has in every case resulted in a serious deterioration of the condition of the note that has been subjected to this treatment. In a few cases this silking has been successfully removed, but in at least one case, the entire note disappeared in the process!

Today it would be possible to laminate a note between sheets of thin plastic, but although such a procedure would not appear to further degrade a note, this is not correct. A laminated note is cut off from air and will change over time because it cannot breathe. On the other hand this this might be irrelevant since it would be virtually impossible to remove a note one it was so encased in plastic. I make it a practice never to purchase laminated notes and of course would not do it myself, and I would strongly recommend that you follow this policy as well.

On a couple of occasions I was successful on bids with two different auctioneers for expensive notes that proved to have small edge tears. Since these features were not described in the auction catalogs, I felt perfectly justified in returning the lots. One was a Series 1880 $100 USN (Fr. 181, H-1135) in AU with serial A643910, and the other was a Series 1907 $1000 gold note (Fr. 1219e, H-1423e) in XF-AU with serial D82926. Both would be capable of easy restoration, and I now regret returning them, especially the latter note, but at the time I was not aware of the types of professional services that are available for dealing with such problems. More than likely both of these notes have since been repaired.

In 1995 an auction held by Stack's featured a $100 Red Seal of the Continental NB of Chicago (2894), bank serial #751 that was graded as XF+. It sold for only $1650 to a floor bidder. My mail bid had been for more than twice this amount, and I wondered why such a high grade $100 Red Seal would sell for a price that was so absurdly low. It turned out that the note had been seriously damaged, but that it had been carefully restored. This repair work had failed to catch the eye of the cataloger, and so bidding was reopened to floor bidders only who were not given the right of returning the note. Any note in an auction that has significant repair work should be so described. Really good repair work, however, can sometimes be difficult to detect.

Some of the rarities have had repair work done on them. In the chapter on large-size type notes, I mentioned a certain $100 Watermelon note that has a rather interesting pedigree. The serial number of this note is A93800. In 1974 it was described as well circulated, soiled, laundered, and with pinholes. In 1975 it was described as VF, but with pinholes, rounded corners, and a light stain. In 1979 it was described as being crisp AU and free of pinholes. It seems that this note has been "improved" more than once over the past few years. Martin Gengerke in his book on currency records now describes it as VF but with pinholes. Fortunately great rarities such as the Watermelon notes now usually come with full pedigrees. If you plan to spend big bucks on rare large-size type notes, Gengerke's book on currency records is an absolute essential.

One type of problem that is not encountered with U. S. Federal paper money but which is very much a problem with Confederate paper money is the hammer cancellation. These were applied to many series of CSA notes, and they will leave a series of horizontal and vertical cuts in the paper. For a typical hammer cancellation no paper will be removed from the note, but it will be left with a series of long cuts. Some collectors chose to leave them "as is," but stamp hinges can be used on the back side of a note to secure the cut.

These cause no harm whatsoever, and they can always be removed with a damp swab or by soaking the note if necessary. It may be desirable to get an expensive note with this type of cancellation professionally restored depending upon how much the repair will cost versus how much the note is worth.

I know of two major rarities that have serious defects, and considerable restoration work will be needed to give them an attractive appearance. One is a $20 Demand Note from New York (Fr. 11, H-700B), serial number 24476 that has a large section of its upper left corner gone. Aside from that, this note is in VG-F condition. The restoration of this note will probably require the attachment of a portion of the upper left section from a much more common $20 USN of Series 1862-63 that is in similar condition. The expense for such a repair will involve not only labor but also the difficulty and cost of finding a low grade $20 USN that has a sound and intact upper left corner. A $20 Demand Note thus restored is much less desirable than is a completely sound note, but these notes are so rare that there would be substantial demand for such a product.

I also know that one of the very few Series 1928E $1 SC star notes that exist is badly damaged. It has serial number *36521510A and has been severely damaged by burning on all four corners. About 10-15% of the area of the note has been eroded away. Very careful attachment work will be needed, but in this case only corners from any of the common 1928 series $1 SCs will do. Should this work be done? The answer is definitely yes. What is today a note in an almost repulsive state of preservation will need such repairs before it can take its place of honor in a collection that has all of the other $1 SC star notes.

Fortunately I do not think that there will be any attempts to pass these two very rare notes off as original, undamaged items. Nonetheless caution should always be undertaken when buying expensive paper money rarities. As I indicated in the introduction of this book, I am not favorably inclined to the establishment of third-party grading services. They could perform a valuable service, however, by recognizing restoration work that has been done, but not acknowledged, on a rare note. In the currency field we certainly do not need such grades as AU-52, AU-55, and AU-58 together with sharp price differentials between these variants, but it is extremely important to know that a note purchased as AU is just that (or at least a minimum of XF+) and not a note that was in fine condition and subsequently "improved" by starching, bleaching, pressing, or other techniques.

CHAPTER SEVENTEEN

AN ANNOTATED BIBLIOGRAPHY

In this section I wish to comment in some detail on the more important books that are presently available concerning the collecting of U. S. paper money. If you plan to collect in this field at all, several of these are absolute essentials for your library. I have also included brief reviews of a number of books that deal in topics that are more peripherally related to U. S. government paper money. There are so many different discounts and special offers associated with numismatic books that in general I am not quoting prices for these books. The exceptions are for the more expensive books that might be of interest in this field.

GENERAL CATALOGS

Paper Money of the United States, Fourteenth Edition, Robert Friedberg with additions and revisions by Ira S. and Arthur L. Friedberg, Coin & Currency Institute, Clifton, NJ, 1995, 304 pp.

The first edition of this definitive catalog was published in 1953, and it has set the standard for catalogs of United States paper money ever since. Even if you prefer one of the other standard catalogs, the numbering system that is used in this book, at least for large-size notes and for Fractional Currency, is standard for all collectors, dealers, and auctioneers. In very many places in my book, I have quoted Friedberg numbers for these items. I do not find the Friedberg numbering system for small-size notes so convenient or necessary, however, and I have refrained from using it in my book. I should note that Robert Friedberg himself is long deceased, but his name is permanently attached to the numbering system that is used by almost everyone in the syngraphic field.

This catalog lists the various issues of large-size notes from 1861 to 1929 by categories rather than by denominations, as some of the other catalogs do. Compound Interest Treasury Notes are put in a section distinct from the other Interest Bearing Notes, although they are really just one more series of these emergency Civil War issues. Gold certificates are put at the end of the section on large-size notes, although they should be more properly placed near the silver certificate and Treasury Note listings. The reason for this is that these notes were not officially legal to collect at the time that the first edition of this catalog was published. The National Gold Bank Notes of California are given a very separate listing, although they are essentially just another type of national bank notes.

Friedberg's catalog has set the standard as to what constitutes a major variety and what does not for most forms of U. S. Federal currency. Over the years there have been a few minor changes in the listings, and these I have noted in my extensive chapter on large-size type notes. The catalog is well illustrated, but the quality of the illustrations for many photos that have been added in recent editions could stand some improvement. The $50 USNs of 1862-63 are now represented by a photo of the genuine note that is in my collection rather than the counterfeit that was in earlier editions of this book for several decades, but this photo is too dark. The photo of the Series 1922 $1000 gold note that is in the catalog is of a low grade specimen. I supplied them with a good quality photograph of the XF-AU example of this note that is in my collection, but they are still using the photo of an inferior note to illustrate this type. When listings of Confederate States notes were added, many of the photos were also too dark to show proper detail.

Small-size notes are covered in good detail for a general catalog, and prices for both regular and star notes are given for most issues. Numbers printed are also given for both regular and star notes in many cases. A few listings could stand improvement, e. g., Series 1933A $10 SCs aren't just rare; they are nonexistent. It took years for them to admit there were no Series 1929 $20 NBNs from Hawaii or that type 2 $50 and $100 NBNs were issued from Arkansas, but these changes have been made. The catalog continues to list the absurd number of 51,300 Series 1928 $5000 FRNs as having been issued from San Francisco, whereas this number should have been 1,300, but typos are few and far between in the present edition.

I have been a consultant on this catalog for several of the more recent editions, and I expect that I will continue in that capacity in the future. One feature that is new to the 14th edition is lists of the numbers of National Banks in a given state that issued a particular type of NBN. Doubtless there are some errors, but these listings give the reader a good idea as to how many different varieties of NBNs could conceivably exist for a given type or for a given state. As is typical of most paper money catalogs, a complete listing of all national banks chartered between 1863 and 1935 is provided.

In addition to U. S. paper money the Friedberg catalog also lists encased postage stamps, early paper money (1690 - 1788), and Confederate States paper money. It does not list either MPCs or small-size notes in sheets, although I have suggested to the publishers that listings of both of these would be useful. The listing of early American and CSA paper money in a book on U. S. government paper money is far more questionable. The listings are not thorough enough to be of much use, and much more definitive information on these items are given in the catalogs by Newman for the former category and by Criswell and Slabaugh for the latter. In my opinion listings of these two important classes of non-Federal paper money should be deleted from the Friedberg catalog, since all collectors of these notes would use the Newman and the Criswell and/or Slabaugh catalogs for these two different widely collected series of paper money.

It is my feeling that the prices quoted in the Friedberg catalog for U. S. Federal paper money are about as accurate as one can expect for a catalog that is published in a new edition every three or four years. A few of the prices in some of the earlier editions seemed way out of line to me, and I gave them suggestions for revisions, as did several of the other editorial consultants. For some odd reason they have lowered the condition for quoting prices of Series 1929 NBNs by states to only fine, a rather low grade for notes of such recent vintage. Most prices seem fairly realistic for this grade, but there is no possibility that one can purchase NBNs from Alaska in any acceptable grade for only $2000 each. This price should be at least $7500, even for notes in only fine condition.

There is no question that the Friedberg catalog has had an immense influence on what collectors of U. S. Federal paper money choose to collect. The four different plate letter varieties for most types of Third Issue 50¢ fractional notes are actually fairly minor variants, but since they were all given major number status in the Friedberg catalog, most Fractional Currency collectors try to get as many of them as is possible. This catalog lists small-size star notes, but it does not list these varieties for large-size notes. As a result, small-size star notes are vastly more popular than are large-size replacement notes. Since the Friedberg catalog chose not to list the earliest issues of U. S. Federal paper money (i. e., the issues of 1812 - 60), few collectors are interested in them, whereas the ephemeral issues of the Civil War years (i. e., the Demand Notes and the various Interest Bearing Notes) that are listed by Friedberg are extremely popular with affluent collectors. The Refunding Certificate of 1879 is collected as a currency item in large part because the Friedberg catalog chose to list it, despite the fact that it was in effect a circulating bearer bond. The absence of listings of MPCs in the Friedberg catalog is a bit peculiar, but there are other good references for this series.

While my book was in production the fifteenth edition of the Friedberg catalog appeared in print. The authors of this book are Arthur L. Friedberg and Ira S. Friedberg, since Robert Friedberg is long deceased. The new edition was published late in 1998, and it is 336 pages long.

The listings in the new edition are very similar to those in previous editions. Several improvements are needed in the pricing of recent notes. Some items such as the F* $1 FRN of Series 1988 are prices much too low, whereas others such as the Chicago web notes of Series 1988A are priced too high. The errors that I noted for the 14th edition mostly seem to continue for this version.

The major changes between these two editions are in the illustrations. The 15th edition uses many photographs obtained from the collection of the Federal Reserve Bank of San Francisco, and it also includes 16 pages of color reproductions of notes from the same source. Some of the photos, however, are of notes that are decidedly inferior condition, and the color fidelity of the last section of the book is not as good as it might be in many cases.

Comprehensive Catalog of U. S. Paper Money, Sixth Edition, Gene Hessler, BNR Press, Port Clinton, Ohio, 1997, 505+ pp.

The first edition of this catalog was published in 1974, and the present edition is a thorough revision of earlier versions of this book. It is now available in both hardbound and paper bound editions. Hessler's book includes a much more extensive introduction to the collecting of paper money (52 pages) than does the Friedberg catalog. He next lists the early American Federal paper money that was issued between 1812 and 1860. Much of this is quite noncollectible, but numerous illustrations are provided.

The next 285 pages are devoted to a listing of U. S. Federal paper money from 1861 to date. The notes are listed by denomination, and small-size notes are listed together with the large-size notes. Hessler does consider all types of large-size notes of a given denomination, however, before listing the small-size notes of that same denomination. Unlike the Friedberg catalog, Hessler's book attempts to list the numbers of large-size notes issued for each signature variety. There are a few obvious mistakes in these listings (duly noted in my chapter on large-size type notes), but these data are generally quite useful. Particularly interesting are Hessler's listings of the numbers of large-size star notes that have been recorded for each variety. These data have been taken from the work of Douglas Murray. These notes are left unpriced for all large-size examples. Prices are given for many small-size star notes, but some of these are inaccurate. For instance, a price of $2000 for a Series 1928 $1 USN star note in CU is low by a factor of at least five or six.

Hessler does a good job of listing large-size Federal Reserve Notes. The research that has largely been undertaken by Martin Gengerke has now determined which notes were issued and which varieties should exist. The latest edition of the Friedberg catalog also lists the realities for these issues, as any up-to-date catalog of U. S. paper money should do. Hessler attempts to give the numbers known of all very rare large-size notes. His coverage of large-size $500 and $1000 notes is very much more thorough than is that of Friedberg for these issues. Prices are not quoted for these notes, although they would be useful for some of the more available issues such as the $500 gold notes of 1882 and 1922, $1000 gold notes of 1907 and 1922, and $500 and $1000 FRNs of Series 1918. Prices are quoted for almost all normal notes of the $1 through $100 denominations, and most of them seem realistic to me.

The next section of Hessler's catalog is devoted to Fractional Currency. A couple of pages are given over to listing the small envelopes that were used for holding postage stamps in the early 1860s, and the last page of this section lists the known varieties of Fractional Currency invert errors. Listings of the specimen notes and Fractional Currency shields, of course, are provided. A few consolidations in the listings of specimen backs for fractional notes would be useful. For instance, for the unissued 15¢ note of the Third Issue there is only one type of red back with narrow margins, yet Hessler quotes two different prices depending upon how this same item is paired with the various faces of this issue. Hessler could also be more consistent than he is about his listings for the so-called brown seal varieties of the Fourth Issue. He lists these for the 25¢ and 50¢ notes, but he ignores them for the 10¢ and 15¢ notes. Today these are generally regarded only as chemical changelings. The section on emergency small money of the Civil War era is concluded with a very thorough listing of encased postage stamps. He also briefly describes Postal Notes, another form of small money that was used in the 1880s and 1890s.

Hessler's catalog provides a good listing of complete sheets of the U. S. Federal issues. The issues up to 1954 are listed and priced in detail, but the treatment of the issues since 1981 is cursory. He then gives a brief survey of paper money errors. Far more detail would be needed, however, for anyone who plans to get seriously into error collecting.

Hessler's book is unique among the general paper money catalogs in giving a good listing of BEP numismatic souvenir cards. His list of which cards collectors should regard as specifically currency-related differs somewhat from mine, but his data on the numbers of cards sold are most revealing. In recent years all of these have only been between 5000 and 10,000 each per issue. I think that there are some real sleepers among these items.

This book then gives a fairly cursory listing of the paper money used in U. S. territories and possessions (most notably the Philippine Islands), but it concludes its listings with a thorough treatment of MPCs. Included in these data are the census data for all known MPC replacement notes that have been compiled by Fred Schwan. For the most part his price data are fairly realistic, but a few are too low (e. g., the Series 541 $5 note in circulated grades) while others are too high (e. g., the Series 651 fractional notes).

Hessler concludes his catalog with a cross reference of his numbers with those given in the Friedberg catalog for large-size notes. Some additional data on national bank notes are given, but this catalog lacks a complete listing of the banks or prices of the different types of NBNs by states. In the latest edition there is also a set of color photographs of various types of U. S. currency. Included are such ultra-rarities as gold certificates of 1865-78, Series 1928 gold notes for $5000 and $10,000, and Series 1934 gold certificates. All of these have been taken from government archives, of course, since these items are all quite noncollectible. Earlier editions of Hessler's catalog used to list the Food Coupons issued by the Department of Agriculture, but these listings have been dropped from the present edition.

Standard Catalog of United States Paper Money, 17th Edition, Chester L. Krause and Robert F. Lemke, with Robert E. Wilhite, Editor, Krause Publications, Iola, Wisconsin, 1998, 214 pp.

This catalog, which is the third of the widely used general catalogs of U. S. Federal currency, begins with a brief introduction to the various types of U. S. paper money that is similar to that given in the Friedberg catalog. The next section contains a listing of large-size type notes arranged by denomination. The National Gold Bank Notes are included in this section, but the other types of NBNs are not. The Krause-Lemke number and the Friedberg number for a given note are given in parallel columns. Listings for many of the large-size high denomination notes could stand some improvement. For instance, all varieties of Series 1882 $5000 and $10,000 gold certificates are unknown except for those with the Tehee-Burke signatures, of which two are known for each denomination. The Krause-Lemke catalog lists numerous nonexistent varieties only as "extremely rare." It also lists only one note each as being known for the Series 1918 $5000 and $10,000 FRNs. In actual fact, five of each are known, although all of these are in government custody.

The new 17th edition has corrected a number of problems that occurred in previous versions of this catalog. This book no longer lists signature varieties of large-size Federal Reserve Notes that do not exist, but it still does not distinguish the two varieties that exist for most Seal 1914 red seal FRNs or the three different signature varieties that exist for a number of blue seal notes of this series that have the White-Mellon signature combination. A few spurious notes are also listed. An example is KL-959, a Series 1918 $500 FRN with the Burke-McAdoo signature combination. This variety cannot exist, since the earliest Series 1918 notes were printed with the Buke-Glass combination.

The Krause-Lemke catalog then provides a listing of small-size notes by denomination. For the most part the prices quoted are realistic, although some of the rarer star notes would sell at much higher prices in today's market than what is quoted. This catalog lists the plate #129 notes for Series 1981A and 1985 as major varieties, but they really special variants more deserving in a place in a specialized catalog of small-size notes than in a general catalog. It is far from clear that all of the #129 varieties listed in the K-L catalog actually exist. This catalog does list web notes by district. Eventually I hope that all of the general catalogs will list these notes by block varieties, since they are only a total of 22 of these and that is the way to most web note collectors chose to acquire them. This catalog lists all possible star varieties for the Series 1929 FRBNs, although four of these are not recorded as presently known in collections.

The Krause-Lemke catalog does a very thorough job of listing national bank notes. These are first listed by types (including the various Treasury signature varieties) and then by state for a given type. All notes are priced in three grades - VG, VF, and AU. Much improvement could be made in the pricing of many of the rare notes, however. For instance, First Charter $1 NBNs from Texas are quoted at $600 in VF and $1000 in AU. Ten times these prices would be much closer to reality. For more common notes, however, the prices tend to be much more realistic. The catalog then includes a very extensive listing of all the note-issuing National Banks arranged by state that includes their relative rarities for large- and small-size notes. These data are taken from the Hickman-Oakes catalog of national bank notes, but they do present the rarity estimates of these researchers in a compact, and therefore readily useful, form.

The next three sections of the catalog are devoted to early U. S. Federal paper money (1812-60), postage stamp envelopes of the 1860s, and encased postage stamps. The listings of Fractional Currency include parallel columns of KL numbers and Friedberg numbers, but the Krause-Lemke catalog uses a modified system for listing the proof and specimen notes. Basically the listings of all Fractional Currency items closely parallel those given in the Friedberg catalog.

The following section of this catalog gives a fairly good summary of errors. This is followed by detailed listings of counterfeit large-size type notes and national bank notes. The Krause-Lemke catalog is thus the only one of the general catalogs to provide a detailed listing of large-size counterfeits. It does not include, however, counterfeit Fractional Currency, although these are also seen with some regularity at coin and paper money shows and other places where numismatists and syngraphists gather.

This catalog concludes its listings with sections on MPCs and on the paper money issued by the U. S. administration of the Philippines. The former includes price estimates for replacement MPCs, and these seem to be fairly realistic. The Philippine listings are extracted from the Pick catalog of world paper money that is also produced by Krause Publications.

Although some of the pricing in this catalog is not as accurate as might be hoped, the Krause-Lemke catalog does provide a great deal of information. Of the three general catalogs of United States paper money it provides the most thorough coverage of national bank notes, and it is the only one to provide any listings of counterfeit Federal notes.

SMALL-SIZE NOTES

Standard Guide to Small-Size U. S. Paper Money, 1928 to Date, 2nd Edition, Dean Oakes and John Schwartz, Krause Publications, Iola, Wisconsin, 1997, 339 pp.

This definitive catalog of small-size U. S. paper money is now in its second edition, but plans for a third edition are now already underway. In a certain sense the Oakes-Schwartz catalog is a remake of the former *Standard Handbook of Modern United States Paper Money* by the late Chuck O'Donnell. This catalog is devoted exclusively to non-error small-size note issues from Series 1928 to date. There is some discussion of Series 1929 Nationals, but these are listed with much greater thoroughness in the definitive catalogs on national bank notes.

This catalog begins with a fairly thorough introduction to small-size notes. The basic types of these notes are described, and the reader is introduced to the serial numbering of the notes as well as blocks, groups, check numbers, mules, late finished plates, minor design changes in the backs of these notes, and several other features.

The vast bulk of this book (pages 25 through 311 in the current edition) is devoted to a complete listing of all small-size notes on a denomination basis. The different categories of notes are listed separately within a given denomination, but the World War II issues are included among either the contemporary SCs or FRNs, whichever the case may be. This catalog attempts to give all block and mule data that are known for each issue. Full serial number ranges are presented in all cases. On notes with many blocks (e. g., the more common

$1 SCs) prices are given for each of the blocks. Attempts are made to be as realistic as possible on valuations on the notes, but there are a few with which I would sharply disagree. For instance, the extremely rare Series 1928B $2 USN star note is listed at only $3500 in CU. It is unlikely that this note exists in this grade, but if one were to come to light in such condition, it would certainly sell for well over $20,000 in today's market.

On current $1 FRNs the catalog could be much clearer as to which blocks were printed in Washington and which were printed in Fort Worth. There are obvious differences between the notes from the two BEP facilities, and they should be given separate listings in this catalog. They are certainly as important as the differences between mules and non-mules or the various shades of green for Treasury seals and serial numbers on earlier series of FRNs. Perhaps the Oakes-Schwartz catalog also should attempt to list the check #129 varieties on Series 1981A and 1985 $1 FRNs, but the authors may have chosen to regard these variants as error notes. As I have already noted, this catalog does not deal at all with error notes.

There are doubtless still problems concerning the cataloging of some of the $5 - $100 FRNs. For instance, I have trouble believing that all of the Series 1934A through Series 1950 $50 FRNs were mules, but further research should be able to clarify such questions. I feel quite certain that all listings of regularly issued high denomination notes later than Series 1934A (for $500s and $1000s) or later than Series 1934 (for $5000s and $10,000s) are utterly spurious, and thus I think that all the listings for these later issues of these notes (i. e., 1934B and 1934C on $500s and $1000s and 1934A and 1934B on $5000s and $10,000s) should be deleted from the next edition. My own research indicates that only micro check numbers were used on the backs of $500s, whereas $1000s used both micro and macro check numbers. Thus all Series 1934 $500s are non-mules, while all Series 1934A $500s are mules. For $1000s both Series 1934 and 1934A exist in mule and in non-mule form. This is another topic that could be dealt with more clearly in this catalog.

The last 25 to 30 pages of this book are devoted to a study of uncut sheets, changeover pairs, and fancy serial numbers. The serial numbers of the known uncut sheets of Series 1928 to 1953 notes (excluding 1929 NBNs) are given, and there are also substantial data on the various post-1981 uncut products. Future editions of this catalog will need to expand their discussion of the latter, so that the collector can be quite certain as to just what exists by series, district, and block of the various 32-, 16-, and 4-subject sheets. The discussion of fancy serial numbers that finishes the book is rather cursory, but this is a very specialized collecting topic that is difficult to deal with in a catalog such as this.

If you plan to collect small-size notes in any depth, very careful study of this book is mandatory. This is especially true if you plan to venture into block and mule collecting. No other catalog gives anything like the detail that this book provides on these issues. Since small-size notes are by far the most readily available of all forms of Federal currency, it seems likely that you will want to explore the details of these notes in any case. It is most unlikely, however, that you will want to attempt to acquire all of the almost innumerable district, block, and mule varieties that are listed in this definitive work.

LARGE-SIZE NOTES

United States Paper Money Records, 1997 Edition, Martin Gengerke, 1997, 216 pp.

This book is a compilation of serial number and condition data for all of the individual rarer large-size type notes. It is available directly from the author or from R. M. Smythe and Co. Although expensive (retail price: $100.00), this book gives extremely useful data on rare large-size notes, and I would most strongly recommend its purchase for anyone who plans to acquire any of the rarer notes. This book is actually the ninth such compilation that Mr. Gengerke has produced, the first going back to 1984. The conditions for the notes quoted in this work are taken directly from the original sources, and the author notes that there may be numerous inconsistencies in these data. All notes that are in government, institutional, or private hands are noted, but proofs and other unissued items are generally not included in these listings. Several individual notes are provided with detailed pedigrees, and in some cases these indicate that a few of these notes have been "improved" over the years. Counterfeits are listed for a few of the very rare types of the 1860s. At the end of this book a rarity scale is given for most major varieties of large-size type notes. All such notes excluding the national bank notes and the Series 1914 blue seal FRNs are included in this list. All large-size star notes are rated as to their rarity, however, and this rating does include the FRN star notes.

While this book was being edited, a 1998 edition was released. Priced at $125 this book contains additional data from Mr. Gengerke's ongoing research on large-size notes. Anyone who is seriously involved with the scarcer varieties of large-size type notes should get the latest version of this book. In many cases detailed pedigrees are given for individual notes including various opinions of the grades of a specific item. Before buying an expensive note or bidding on one in an auction, you should check what this reference says about the note in question. The data supporting this book are available on CD rom.

The Encyclopedia of United States Large Size Currency, Martin Gengerke and Douglas Murray, 1995, 70 pp.

This work is not yet available in published form, although it can be obtained in preprint form directly from the authors. All types of large-size notes including national bank notes are listed in the tabulations that are given. This is another extremely useful work for persons seriously interested in large-size notes, since it gives data on these issues that are found nowhere else. Complete serial number data are given for nearly all issues. These include the series numbers for the Demand Notes and USNs of 1862-63. The latter issues are listed in a more detailed fashion than is found in any of the standard catalogs. A strong case can be made for the complete renumbering of the Series 1862 and 1863 United States Notes in the standard catalogs. On the later issues of large-size notes full data on the serial number blocks for each issue are given, and in all cases the total number of notes printed and issued for a given variety is listed. This work uses the Friedberg numbers, but eventually the authors may develop a numbering scheme of their own for large-size notes.

As I have noted in my commentary on the Friedberg catalog, the numbering scheme for large-size notes originally devised by Robert Friedberg has been the one accepted by nearly all syngraphists ever since. The research undertaken by Gengerke and Murray may change that in future years. For instance on USNs of the 1870s to the 1890s there are examples of the same major variety that are found with or without watermarks, with or without localized blue stains, with two horizontal silk threads or with vertically distributed silk fibers, and with backs that were printed either by the BEP or by the Columbian Bank Note Co. The Friedberg catalog does not acknowledge these differences even as minor varieties in its listings, but there are numerous notes in which such differences do exist. Were these varieties given major number statues, collecting patterns for many of the large-size type notes would undergo significant change.

When this important work is published in final form, it may revolutionize our thinking as to what constitutes a major variety for the various issues of large-size notes. If it includes a new numbering system, this new system may replace the Friedberg numbers that are now used by almost everyone for the past 45 years when describing large-size or fractional notes.

Comprehensive Catalog of U. S. Large Size Star Notes, Doug Murray, BNR Press, Port Clinton, Ohio, 1996, 128 pp.

This is by far the most thorough survey of large-size replacement notes, an area that has thus far not been collected to anything like the extent that has been the case for small-size star notes. The basic statistics on all of the known types of large-size star notes are included in the current edition of Hessler's catalog, but if you are interested in price estimates or the serial numbers for all of the known notes, you will definitely want a copy of Murray's book.

NATIONAL BANK NOTES

Standard Catalog of National Bank Notes, 2nd Edition, Dean Oakes and John Hickman, Krause Publications, Iola, Wisconsin, 1990, 1249 pp.

This is the second edition of a major work on national bank notes, the first edition of which had appeared in 1982. Now that John Hickman is deceased, there may never be a third edition. The fact that this book is almost 1250 pages long gives some idea of the scope and depth of this work. The first 37 pages is devoted to a general introduction to NBNs and to the terminology employed in the catalog. Hickman and Oakes used a rarity scale ranging from R1 (50 or more examples known) to R6 (unknown or only one or two known). Small-size and large-size NBNs are given separate rarity ratings for each bank. If uncut sheets are known for a given bank, these are acknowledged.

John Hickman was very much interested in minor changes in bank titles, and all possibilities known to him are recorded in this book. Sometimes the difference is only whether or not the word "The" appears at the beginning of a title. The numbers of notes issued and the sheet arrangements for all issued notes are given. The listings are by state, and within a given state they are by town or city in alphabetical order. Territorial notes and the National Gold Bank Notes of California are given separate listings. For a given city, the banks are listed in order of their names rather than their charter numbers. For major cities such as New York, one may have to jump around a bit for certain banks due to mergers, changes of titles or charter numbers, etc. Occasionally typos do creep in. An example is for the confused listings from the FNB of Salem, Ohio, which used both charter numbers of 43 and 2691. Given the size of the work, however, this definitive catalog is remarkably free of errors.

For every state or territory a listing is given of the banks for which no notes are presently known. These listings are given separately for both large-size and small-size notes. At the end of the book there are illustrations of the different note types and the numbers of NBNs issued by type for each state or territory. Unfortunately there are a number of errors in these totals for several of the larger states.

All notes are assigned collector values in VG, VF, and AU condition. These data are computer-generated, and they are not to be relied upon for much precision. The values quoted for Series 1929 notes seem always to be systematically much too low. Very high prices were often quoted for large-size notes in the first edition of this book, but they have been cut back quite a bit in the second edition. In any case one should not rely on catalogs to provide accurate prices for specific NBNs. Substantial experience coupled with careful study of price lists and auction realizations plus attendances at large paper money shows are the best ways of developing a feeling for the values of national bank notes.

National Bank Notes, A Guide with Prices, Third Edition, Don C. Kelly, The Paper Money Institute, Oxford, Ohio, 1997, 596 pp.

The other complete catalog of national bank notes is the one compiled by Don Kelly. The first 56 pages of this book give a thorough introduction to the subject of national bank notes including a discussion of the various pieces of legislation that were responsible for the various issues of this currency. A "history" of the fictitious Smokey Hollow National Bank in Ohio is included to give the reader a good idea of how a national bank functioned during the note-issuing period. Detailed descriptions are given of all of the different types of NBNs including a full history of the ultrarare or nonexistent $500 and $1000 First Charter NBNs.

Dr. Kelly then lists all of the NBN issues on a state by state basis. The territorial issues of a state that had them are included in with the listings of that state. For the listings of Oklahoma mention is made of whether the notes were from Indian Territory or Oklahoma Territory. The listings of Dakota Territory are given under their respective states. For each state a map is provided that shows the locations of the issuing towns and well as the country lines. The notes are listed by alphabetical order, and the banks of a given city or town are listed again by alphabetical order. For each bank the numbers of known large-size and small-size NBNs are given. If more than 50 are known of either class, these are given as 50+. Banks for which no notes are presently known are acknowledged in the text. Notes in uncut sheets are separately acknowledged in these listings. Prices are estimated in fine condition in the bank listings. At the end of the introductory section Kelly provides a more detailed listing of estimated values of NBNs both by type and condition, but it is not possible to include such a list for thousands of individual banks.

The listings by states take up more than 470 pages of this book. The next section is devoted to uncut sheets of NBNs, and this is by far the most thorough listing and discussion to appear for these items in any general work. All of the relatively few errors that are known for NBNs are then described in detail. Included are photographs of both sides of the incredible $100/$50 and $50/$100 Brown Back error pair from the FNB of Albuquerque, New Mexico Territory. The next section discusses stolen and counterfeit NBNs. A complete listing of the known counterfeits of the earlier NBNs is given. The chapter on NBN errors was written in conjunction with Harry E. Jones, while that on stolen and counterfeit NBNs was done with the assistance of Bob Cochran.

The next chapter gives a listing of all towns that had note-issuing banks. These are given in alphabetical order from Abbeville, Alabama to Zillah, Washington. The final chapter of this book gives the charter number of every note-issuing bank in numerical order. Only banks that actually issued notes are included. The last of these, of course, is the Liberty NB and TC of Louisville, KY (14320), while the next to last was the Keokuk NB in Iowa (14309), as charters numbered 14310 through 14319 declined to issue notes and thus are not listed.

The census data that Dr. Kelly uses in his catalog are based on about 200,000 known NBNs. Despite the vast scope of this work, it is almost totally free of typographical errors, a remarkable achievement for so large a project.

Which of these two monumental books should you buy if you plan to collect national bank notes in depth? My advice is to buy them both. Neither is cheap - both list at $100.00, but the Kelly book is often available at a discount while the Hickman-Oakes catalog is becoming increasingly hard to find. Both are well worth the price, but if you can only afford one of these books, I would suggest the Kelly book. Its census data are somewhat more current, and it discusses a few things not mentioned in the Hickman-Oakes catalog. But both books are extremely important works that deserve a place on your bookshelf.

United States Large Size National Bank Notes, Peter Huntoon, The Society of Paper Money Collectors, Laramie, Wyoming, 1995, 283 pp.

This book is entirely different in concept from the Hickman-Oakes and the Kelly catalogs. It consists of 33 chapters, each which is a detailed investigation of some particular aspect of large-size NBNs. Dr. Huntoon is a professional geologist, who researches his work with amazing thoroughness. He also holds major collections of NBNs from Arizona and from Wyoming. He is a frequent contributor to the SPMC journal *Paper Money,* and many of the chapters of this book had been previously published in that journal.

The chapter titles in this book give some idea of the scope of this work. Included are "The rise and fall of $1 and $2 national bank notes," "The United States $500 and $1000 national bank notes," and "$50 and $100 Series of 1882 Value Back national bank notes," etc. A few chapters are downright esoteric including such items as "Stars on reentered Series of 1875 and 1882 national bank note plates" and "The conversion from stacked to in-line Treasury signatures on $5 Series of 1882 notes in 1886," but Dr. Huntoon provides thorough explanations for everything he writes about. Many illustrations are included, and most of these are of archival material that is held by the Smithsonian Institution. If you get deeply involved with the collecting of NBNs, you will want to own a copy of this book.

There are several other useful books that have been written about national bank notes. Two good ones, that are no longer in print, are *National Banks of the Note Issuing Period, 1863-1935* by Louis Van Belkum and *The National Bank Note Issues of 1929-1935* by Peter Huntoon and Louis Van Belkum, edited by M. Owen Warns. The former was published in 1968, while the latter dates from 1970. Louis Van Belkum is the person responsible for much of the research work that was done in the National Archives on the records from the office of the Comptroller of Currency. The data from these records enabled syngraphists to determine just what notes were issued by which banks. A more recent book, *United States National Banks and Their Shields* by Dewitt Prather, provides much beautiful artwork including illustrations of all the state shield designs used on First Charter notes and on Second Charter Brown Backs.

FRACTIONAL CURRENCY

The Encyclopedia of United States Fractional & Postal Currency, Milton R. Friedberg, edited by Martin Gengerke, NASCA, Rockville Centre, New York, 1978, 158 pp.
    This book was published in 1978 by the now-defunct NASCA numismatic auction firm. In the meantime NASCA has been absorbed by R. M. Smythe and Co., and this extremely useful book has gone out of print, but the Fractional Currency Collectors Board does have a number of these books on hand and these are made available to new members. As I have noted in my chapter on Fractional Currency, Milton Friedberg, the collector of Fractional Currency, is not to be confused with the late Robert Friedberg, the original author of the well-known paper money catalog that is now in its 14th edition.
    If you plan to collect Fractional Currency in any depth, I would strongly recommend that you try to acquire a copy of this book. Especially valuable are the listings of Fractional Currency items that are not included in the standard catalogs. The most prominent of these are the various experimental notes of the Second Issue, but also listed are errors, blocks and sheets, die proofs, counterfeits and counterfeit detectors, artists' sketches, unfinished notes, etc. Milton Friedberg uses his own numbering system that includes a letter designator such as R (regular issues), P (wide margin specimens), S (narrow margin specimens), or E (experimental notes). He assigns a number to every Fractional Currency item, but his numbering system is quite complex and cumbersome. Fortunately it is cross-referenced to the much more familiar Robert Friedberg numbering system for those items that are listed in the latter catalog.

Catalog of the Milton R. Friedberg Collection, sold by Currency Auctions of America, January 10, 1997, 198 pp.
    This is the auction catalog that CAA prepared for its sale of the Milton Friedberg collection of fractional notes in 1997. The scale of this collection speaks for itself; the catalog is 198 pages long! Every conceivable variety of Fractional Currency and items related to fractional notes are included. Especially significant are the listings of the various experimental issues. The Milton Friedberg collection contained by far the largest supply of these that has ever been assembled. As a regular CAA customer, I obtained my copy of this catalog by mail prior to the sale. Hopefully this firm still has retained a number of copies for sale of this most significant auction of fractional notes. It is an invaluable reference for anyone planning to collect Fractional Currency in depth.

MILITARY PAYMENT CERTIFICATES

Comprehensive Catalog of Military Payment Certificates, Fred Schwan, BNR Press, Port Clinton, Ohio, 1997, 256 pp.
    This book is third edition of a catalog of MPCs that was originally published in 1981. It is now a hardbound book with a beautifully designed cover. It includes a full coverage of all aspects of U. S. military currency items. Details are given on the production characteristics, sheet configurations, numbering systems, design sources, and other aspects of MPCs. Specimen and proof notes, MPC errors, and counterfeits are all dis-

cussed. Designs are also shown for the unissued Series 691 and 701 notes. The second section contains a detailed catalog of MPCs complete with current prices. Both regular and replacement notes along with specimen booklets and progressive proofs are included. The price compilation is basically reliable, although Series 651 fractionals are quoted at higher prices than they are now fetching in auction. This listing also includes the so-called A yen notes of Japan that were briefly used as experimental MPCs for U. S. forces stationed in Japan and Korea in 1946.

Fred Schwan has become the world's foremost authority on MPC replacement notes, and his book contains a complete listing of all of these notes (about 2000 examples) known to him at the time of publication. Full details of each note (serial number, sheet position number, and condition) are given in almost every case, and these listings alone take up 30 pages of the book. If you plan to collect MPC replacement notes, this book is absolutely essential.

Schwan's book also discusses in detail a variety of auxiliary items that are related to MPCs. Included are the special coupons that were used by Korean and Thai soldiers in Vietnam, MPC training money, military gasoline ration coupons, and checks denominated in MPCs. No serious collector of MPCs should be without a copy of this book.

PAPER MONEY ERRORS

Comprehensive Catalog of United States Paper Money Errors, Frederick J. Bart, BNR Press, Port Clinton, Ohio, 1994, 190 pp.

This book covers all aspects of the errors found on U. S. Federal paper money. It provides some coverage on the errors found on large-size notes, Fractional Currency, and MPCs, but the great emphasis, of course, is on small-size notes. An overview of contemporary paper money production is given, and Dr. Bart then describes a rarity scale which he grades from R1 (very common) to R9 (extremely rare). He classifies errors into three major groups - first and second printing errors, overprinting errors, and folds and other errors. Thus each group includes both fairly minor errors as well as much more significant errors.

This catalog is profusely illustrated, and these illustrations help clarify any confusion that can arise over the different types of errors. For instance, board brakes can become confused with some cases of underinking or obstructed printing. Valuations are given for each note. Although these are merely approximations, they give the reader some idea as to how the value of a given note is enhanced by a particular type of error. All known varieties of large-size notes with inverted backs are listed, as are all known double denomination notes. The known cases of mismatched serial numbers are also listed with considerable thoroughness. Cutting errors of numerous types are illustrated and priced.

The first edition of this book is not quite new enough to cover some of the most recent errors such as those concerned with incorrectly placed plastic strips, misplaced or inverted watermarks, or missing magnetic ink. A few of the prices that Dr. Bart suggests are also going to need substantial revision in the second edition. On page 146 he prices a Series 1928 gold certificate with its entire third printing missing at $850 in CU. In a 1998 CAA auction one of these sold for $17,600 in this condition. Nonetheless this is a book that everyone interested in errors should have in his library and the publisher reports that a second edition is in preparation. It is scheduled for release within a few months of this book so it will be the edition most likely available when you inquire.

U. S. Error Note Encyclopedia, Stephen M. Sullivan, Capital Currency Inc., Melbourne, Florida, 1997, 431 pp.

This is another book that provides much useful information on errors. It is concerned entirely with large-size and small-size notes, and thus the errors found on Fractional Currency and on MPCs are ignored. The first 53 pages are devoted to a discussion of how currency is printed, and numerous illustrations are provided in this review. Sullivan then discusses the function of star notes. In it he presents a table of the known notes with serial number 100000000 at the end of a 100 million note block. These are regarded as fancy serial numbers rather than error notes by most syngraphists, but listing of these major rarities is most useful since it is not frequently seen.

Sullivan divides errors into eleven different groups, and Sullivan's arrangement of these differs considerably from the way that Bart does in his book. For instance, all misalignment errors are treated in the same section regardless of which of the three printings is affected by the error. Notes with inverted faces (Sullivan's terminology as compared with Bart's inverted backs) are treated as a type of alignment error. Unlike Bart's catalog, Sullivan's provides full serial number and condition data for the known notes, at least for the large-size notes where this is a particularly important type of error.

The engraving errors that Sullivan describes are not always described as errors, but the data he gives are useful. He lists fewer cases of back plate #129 "errors" on Series 1981A and 1985 $1 FRNs than does the Krause-Lemke catalog, but I expect that Sullivan's data are more accurate than is the latter source. In addition to the famous Burke-Elliott Series 1917 $1 USN (Fr. 37a, H-25) Sullivan also mentions the Series 1918 $5 FRBNs from San Francisco dated May 18, 1914 (Fr. 809a, H-382L3). He incorrectly gives this date as May 16, 1914, but he notes that this item is not usually considered to be an error note.

The next section of his book concerns extra prints (including both offsets and double impressions). A detailed discussion of folds and tears is followed by a section on ink smears and solvent smears. Board breaks, underinking errors, and magnetic ink problems are then discussed. Obstructed prints and notes with missing faces or backs are then discussed. Mismatched serial numbers and misaligned digits are discussed in a section entirely different from that devoted to inverted overprints. The problems with the new notes (improperly placed plastic threads and watermarks) are then discussed. Double denomination notes are placed near the end of Sullivan's book together with wrong overprint errors, both of which he refers to as process errors. He classifies the Series 1988A F* web note as a wrong overprint error, but it is not usually put into this class by most syngraphists.

Sullivan's book concludes with a discussion of counterfeit errors. He is quite wrong in stating (on page 428) that making a fake error violates the counterfeiting statues. This would be true only if an attempt is made to alter the face value of the note. Adding fake ink smears, offsets, or other features does not do this. Such fabrications should be termed fakes, not counterfeits. They are perfectly legal to collect, but you do not want to pay inflated prices for them.

Sullivan's work provides much useful data, so I would also strongly recommend its purchase if you plan to collect errors. Like Bart's book it is also well stocked with illustrations.

OTHER FORMS OF PAPER MONEY

There are numerous books on paper money that are devoted to other aspects of this field. A detailed discussion of the paper money of foreign nations is beyond the scope of this book, but I have referred on numerous occasions to non-Federal forms of paper money that have been used in the United States or what was to become the United States. A brief overview of some of the most important titles seems in order.

Early Paper Money of America, Fourth Edition, Eric P. Newman, Krause Publications, Iola, Wisconsin, 1998, 480 pp.
     This is by far the most important work on the early paper money of America, the first edition of this book having been published in 1967. All issues of the American colonies and states from the first issue of Massachusetts in 1690 up to the earliest issues of state bank notes in the 1790s are included. It is not very likely that notes of La Banque Royale of 1719-20 actually circulated in Louisiana, but this famous issue is included among the listings. Many hundreds of life size illustrations are provided, and in the fourth edition a sizable number are in color. Priced at $75.00, it is fairly expensive, but no collector of early paper money should be without this book.

Standard Catalog of United States Obsolete Bank Notes, 1782-1866, James A. Haxby, Krause Publications, Iola, Wisconsin, 1991, Four Volumes, 2784 pp.
     This is the definitive work on state chartered bank notes. Despite its enormous coverage, it does not cover small-change notes or notes of non-banking corporations that circulated together with state bank notes in the pre-Civil War era. The notes of the Bank of the United States, which for the most part were issued when this bank held a charter from the state of Pennsylvania, are included in the fourth volume of this work. The set lists over 77,000 different notes from more than 3100 different banks. Many thousands of illustrations are provided. Also included is much information on counterfeit, altered, and spurious notes. The work was originally priced at $195.00 for the set of four volumes, but all are now out of print. If you want this book, you will probably have to pay almost double this price to one of the few persons who can supply it.

     Collecting obsolete paper money does pose major challenges. Almost all persons who collect state bank notes are also interested in small-change notes and the other forms of private money that characterized the 1800-60 period. Aside from the definitive work by Haxby, the other sources on these types of currency are the books that have been prepared for individual states under the sponsorship of the Society of Paper Money Collectors (SPMC). The book entitled *Wisconsin Obsolete Bank Notes and Scrip* by Chester Krause is currently being printed by Krause Publications and is available from them. A similarly titled book on *Kentucky Obsolete Notes and Scrip* by Earl Hughes and edited by Steven K. Whitfield has recently been published through the SPMC. Similar books for about 20 other states have been published over the years, and they are frequently available from dealers in numismatic literature.

Comprehensive Catalog of Confederate Paper Money, Grover C. Criswell, BNR Press, Port Clinton, Ohio, 1996, 352 pp.

This is the latest version of Criswell's catalog of Confederate paper money. The earlier versions were titled *Confederate and Southern States Currency,* and the different editions with this title were published in 1957, 1964, 1976, and 1992. Criswell's latest catalog includes much additional material on Confederate notes, but the listings of all of the notes of the Southern states plus the Republic of Texas have been dropped. A new book on these forms of paper money will be forthcoming, but the earlier versions of his catalog have excellent listings of this material.

If you plan to collect Confederate Treasury Notes, this book is an absolute must. In addition to an extremely thorough listing of the genuine items, the current edition also contains a very detailed treatment of the known varieties of contemporary counterfeit Confederate notes. A great deal of information is also given about the signatures which appear on Confederate notes.

Confederate States Paper Money, 9th Edition, Arlie R. Slabaugh, Krause Publications, Iola, Wisconsin, 1998, 246 pp.

The first edition of Slabaugh's catalog was published in 1958, and up through the 8th edition (published in 1993) these books listed only CSA notes. The current edition, however, devotes more than 110 pages to a listing by type of the paper money issued by the Southern states during the Civil War and Reconstruction periods. Although this book is fairly slender, it packs a huge amount of information about CSA currency into its pages. It lists Confederate and Southern state notes by major types only and thus does not include listings of the large number of plate varieties that are included in Criswell's catalogs, but all of the essential information for the type collector of these notes is present. Much auxiliary material is also provided, including a good discussion of bogus and facsimile notes. A comparison of the 1993 and the 1998 editions of Slabaugh's catalog will demonstrate the radical increases in prices that have occurred for CSA notes in recent years. No Confederate collector should be without it.

An Illustrated History of U. S. Loans, 1775-1898, Gene Hessler, BNR Press, Port Clinton, Ohio, 1988, 378 pp.

Although some of the material covered in this book goes back to the Revolutionary War period, the most interesting coverage is for U. S. government securities of the 1812 to 1870 period. The paper money issues of 1812-15 could well be considered the earliest forms of U. S. Federal paper money. As I have already noted the catalog of Robert Friedberg first published in 1953 set the tone as to what was and what was not to be regarded as U. S. government paper money. He chose to ignore the War of 1812 issues, and so most collectors today feel that U. S. Federal paper money begins only with the Demand Notes of 1861.

Numerous illustrations and a rarity guide are provided for each of the issues, many of which are noncollectible. Currency collectors will be familiar with the various issues of Interest Bearing Notes during the Civil War years and with the Refunding Certificates of 1879. As Hessler points out in this book, the dividing line between bonds and paper money was not always very clearly drawn until about 1870.

U. S. Essay, Proof and Specimen Notes, Gene Hessler, BNR Press, Port Clinton, Ohio, 1979, 224 pp.

This book provides excellent coverage of the various forms of U. S. paper money that were never issued. Most fall into the era of large-size notes, and thus this is a good auxiliary reference work for collectors of these notes. Although a few of the unissued designs are familiar to collectors of souvenir cards, for the most part the unissued proofs, like the pre-Civil War securities listed in Hessler's 1988 book, are noncollectible. Anyone who collects U. S. large-size type notes in any depth should not be without a copy of this book. It should be noted that Grover Criswell died in 1999, but the research the Criswell promoted will continue to be published by the BNR Press.

Standard Catalog of Depression Scrip of the United States, Ralph A. Mitchell and Neil Shafer, Krause Publications, 1984, 318 pp.

This book covers the substitute money issued by various local governments during the years of the Great Depression. As is well known, this economic disaster did not end in 1933, and items issued as late as 1939 are included in this work. Not everything listed is on paper. In addition to a few metallic tokens, several weird items such as "clamshell currency" are included. This book was originally published by Krause at $27.50, but it is now available at a substantial discount from this price through various dealers. Even if you are not turned on by municipal scrip or clearing house certificates, this is an excellent guide as to what was issued as money substitutes by many different administrations during the 1930s. Depression scrip in Canada and in Mexico is also briefly discussed in this work.

FOREIGN PAPER MONEY

There is obviously a huge amount of literature available on the various issues of world paper money. I wish here to comment just on the standard catalogs for the paper money of Canada and on the available references for world paper money in general.

The Charlton Standard Catalogue of Canadian Government Paper Money, 11th Edition, The Charlton Press, Toronto, Ontario, 1998, 304 pp.
The Charlton Standard Catalogue of Canadian Bank Notes, 3rd Edition,
The Charlton Press, Toronto, Ontario, 1996, 524 pp.

The Charlton Press has for several decades published the standard catalogue for Canadian coins. In earlier editions of that book, a section on Canadian paper money was included. In 1980 they published the First Edition of a standard catalogue on this subject. It was 820 pages long and included both government and private bank issues.

This book is now published as a two separate volumes. The first volume needs more frequent updating, since the Bank of Canada, of course, still issues notes. The current edition devotes about 130 pages to these issues (1935 to date), and 95 pages discuss the Dominion of Canada issues (1870-1925), while the other 80 pages are devoted to the various colonial and provincial issues including the 1866 issues of the Province of Canada.

The second volume of this definitive work on Canadian paper money is devoted to the issues of the Canadian chartered banks and the other private bank issues in Canada. Chartered bank notes were issued as late as 1945, and until 1935 all of the $10, $20, $50, and $100 notes plus most of the $5 notes were issues of these banks and not of the Dominion government. About 165 different banks are included in the listings, and these include numerous banks that failed and whose notes are no longer redeemable. This catalog also lists the notes issued by Canadian banks that were for exclusive use in the British West Indies.

Despite the fact that American and Canadian paper money were often at par with each other, there are many fundamental differences in their paper money issues. If you plan to collect Canadian paper money at all, these books are an absolute must.

Standard Catalog of World Paper Money, Volume I, Specialized Issues, 8th Edition, edited by Colin R. Bruce III and Neil Shafer, Krause Publications, Iola, Wisconsin, 1998, 1184 pp.
Standard Catalog of World Paper Money, Volume II, General Issues, 8th Edition, Albert Pick, Krause Publications, Iola, Wisconsin, 1997, 1232 pp.
Standard Catalog of World Paper Money, Volume III, Modern Issues, 4th Edition, edited by Colin R. Bruce III and Neil Shafer, Krause Publications, Iola, Wisconsin, 1998, 768 pp.

This standard work on world paper money has undergone numerous modifications over the past decade or so. Volume II is now concentrating on the pre-1960 issues of government-issued paper money, since Volume III is devoted entirely to paper money issued since 1960. Volume III is being revised almost on an annual basis, since new issues are always coming up. It would seem that the other two volumes would require less frequent revisions, but these two volumes are also being frequently revised.

Volume I concentrates on the private bank and regional issues of various nations. Most of the Latin American countries, especially Argentina, Brazil, Colombia, and Mexico, are covered in very great detail. There are also very extensive listings of Canada, China, and Germany. The Philippine Guerrilla Currency of the World War II period is covered in great depth, and the various state issues of the Southern states during the Civil War period are thoroughly listed. Early paper money of the United States is also covered, but there are no listings for the enormous numbers of state bank notes. Likewise this catalog does not cover the enormous number of Notgeld issues of Germany and Austria during the 1914-24 period, nor does it cover the more recent small-change notes issued by the Italian banks in the 1960s.

Volume II focuses on official government issues of all nations that issued paper money from the 18th century up to the 1960s. The issues of the United States include both Fractional Currency and MPCs, but oddly enough, NBNs are not listed by type. This is all right for someone who has a standard U. S. paper money catalog at his side, but for a person abroad, I feel that a type listing at least of this important form of Federal paper money should be included. Confederate notes are listed in substantial detail under the letter "C." Specialists in U. S. paper money will not need this book as a general reference, but it does cover the official issues of every other nation as well.

Volume III was first issued only in 1995, if sales remain high, this book may be reissued on an annual basis. It covers only issues of paper money from 1961 to date, or from the late 1950s at the earliest. The private bank issues of Hong Kong, Northern Ireland, and Scotland that fall into this era are covered as well as all government issues. New currency-issuing entities are being added with each new edition, since all of the ex-Soviet republics and parts of the former Yugoslavia are now each issuing their own paper money.

Even if you don't collect world paper money, you will find these books useful guides as to what is out there. Prices are given for most notes, but doubtless some are not very reliable. The earlier notes of heavily collected countries are often priced much too low, but inflation may have reduced the values substantially for many recent notes for some of the Third World countries or other nations with unstable currencies.

OTHER BOOKS

Collecting Paper Money for Pleasure & Profit, Barry Krause, Betterway Books, Cincinnati, Ohio, 1992, 256 pp.

Barry Krause (no relation to the Wisconsin numismatic publisher) has written an attractive book for hobbyists who are beginning the collecting of paper money. It would be fair to state that Mr. Krause is a collector in breadth rather than depth, but his book is attractively printed and has much to recommend it. I differ with him on several points, but there is a lot of information packed into this book. As a stamp collector with literally decades of experience, I can state that glassine envelopes are perfectly safe for the storage of stamps with gum over many years. They are also fine for the storage of bank notes, and I use then for my Fractional Currency collection. Mr. Krause seems to think otherwise - apparently he doesn't collect stamps. One could do a lot of nitpicking on a book like this, but the fact is that it does contain a lot of useful information, and not all of it is just for beginners. Numerous addresses are given for museums, numismatic societies, and the various major paper money shows are discussed. Although some of this book shows a degree of naivete, I would heartily recommend its purchase by any paper money collector.

PUBLICATIONS

Bank Note Reporter, published by Krause Publications, 700 East State Street, Iola, Wisconsin 54990, edited by David C. Harper

This journal is subtitled the Complete Monthly Guide for Paper Money Collectors, and that provides a good idea of what this tabloid-size publication is all about. It is the only commercial publication devoted exclusively to syngraphics. A typical issue is about 75 pages long. Included are numerous advertisements from many dealers, but articles covering a wide range of topics in paper money collecting are always included. Although the emphasis is on U. S. paper money, each issue includes a world paper money section that includes new issues of paper money from all nations. Up-to-date foreign exchange rates are given in each issue, and there are monthly reports on production data of the Washington and Fort Worth facilities of the BEP. The reader is also kept informed on all of the upcoming paper money shows both in the United States and abroad. If you collect paper money at all, you will want to subscribe to this journal. For current subscription information the telephone number 1-800-258-0929 can be used.

Paper Money, published by The Society of Paper Money Collectors Inc., edited by Gene Hessler, P. O. Box 31144, Cincinnati, Ohio 45231.

    This journal is published bimonthly (i. e., six times per year) by the SPMC, and a subscription is included as a part of membership in this society. Persons wishing to join the SPMC should contact Robert Cochran, P. O. Box 1085, Florissant, Missouri 63031. A wide variety of articles appear in each of these journals, which are usually about 40 pages long per issue. Especially useful to collectors of national bank notes are various ongoing census data projects on known NBNs and on which note-issuing National Banks are still unrecorded.

    The SPMC has also greatly assisted syngraphic research through its sponsorship of the publication of handbooks on the obsolete paper money and scrip of numerous states. The latest such book to be published concerns the obsolete notes of Kentucky, but thus far these handbooks have been published for about two dozen states. The SPMC journal also includes book reviews for all of the significant works in syngraphics that are being published.

    In addition to these two journals articles on paper money frequently appear in *Numismatic News* and in *Coin World*. Both are weekly tabloid-size journals largely devoted to coins (especially U. S. coins), but each covers developments in the paper money field as well. *Numismatic News,* which is published by Krause Publications of Iola, Wisconsin, usually contains a feature termed "Paper View" in each issue. It is particularly aimed at introducing coin collectors to paper money collecting. *Coin World,* which is published by Amos Press of Sidney, Ohio, also has frequent coverage of developments in the field of paper money collecting.

Currency Dealer Newsletter, published by Ron Downing, P. O. Box 11099, Torrance, California 90510

    This monthly newsletter is often referred to as the "Green Sheet" because of its color. It lists current bid and ask prices for all the normally collected types of large-size notes and Fractional Currency. All series of small-size notes are also included in each issue. Prices are listed in a wide range of conditions, typically from VG to Gem CU. For uncirculated notes three different subgrades are used for pricing - CU, Choice CU, and Gem CU. Prices for MPCs and for early paper money are also updated on a fairly regular basis. Many back issues of this publication are also available from the publisher.

CHAPTER EIGHTEEN

COLLECTIONS AND DISPLAYS OF PAPER MONEY

At various places in this book I have referred to some of the more famous collections of U. S. paper money that have been formed by various syngraphists. In recent years one of the best known was that of Amon Carter Jr., who died in 1982. Some of others are the collections formed by James Thompson and by J. L. Irish. The former contained by far the finest holding of large-size Federal Reserve Notes that has ever been formed, while the latter was renowned for its holdings of Texas and of territorial national bank notes.

Several very significant collections of U. S. paper money have come onto the market in recent years. The collection formed by Frank Levitan was basically a collection of large-size type notes and double denomination notes. It was sold by Lyn Knight in December, 1998. Six months later the collection formed by the late Harry W. Bass, Jr. was sold by Bowers and Merena. It featured the finest offering of Demand Notes and Interest Bearing Notes to be seen in several decades. One week later the huge collection of the national bank notes of California formed by the late Charles Colver was sold by CAA. Four months earlier this firm sold an extremely fine collection of gold certificates that had been formed by Lawrence Cookson. With the current boom in paper money more outstanding collections can be expected to be offered in upcoming years.

No collection formed in recent years, however, can compare with that assembled several decades ago by Albert A. Grinnell. Although a native of New York State, this prominent businessman also lived for many years in Michigan, and his collections of the NBNs from these two states were especially strong. Grinnell collected almost exclusively U. S. large-size and small-size notes, but these were collected to a depth that would not be possible for anyone to duplicate today. His collection was sold in seven different auctions that were conducted by Barney Bluestone of Syracuse, New York between November, 1944 and November, 1946. In 1971 William T. Anton Jr. and Morey Perlmutter reprinted the original auction catalogs, complete with the prices realized. These were bound into a single book that is almost 700 pages long, and this work should be of great interest to almost all collectors of U. S. Federal currency, most especially large-size type notes and National Bank Notes.

The Grinnell collection was sold almost a decade prior to the publication of the first edition of the Robert Friedberg catalog, and at that time there was no established numbering system for listing paper money. Almost every note is described in detail, since both the signature varieties and seal characteristics needed to be given. Plate number data are also often given, but oddly enough, Barney Bluestone did not record serial number data for the great majority of Grinnell's notes. This makes it a bit difficult to trace pedigrees on many of the Grinnell notes. It is likely, however, that very many currency collectors have at least a note or two from this fabulous collection. One of mine, a $5 Third

Charter Blue Seal from the Dunbar NB of New York (13237), includes a small memo that was handwritten by Mr. Grinnell.

The Grinnell collection helped to set the standard as to what should be included in a collection of U. S. Federal paper money. His collection included no notes prior to the Demand Notes of 1861, but it did include two examples of the Refunding Certificate of 1879. This may be one reason why the first edition of the Friedberg catalog, which was published seven years after the last of the Grinnell sales, begins with the issues of 1861 (rather than 1812) and does include Refunding Certificates in its listings despite the bond-like characteristics of these government securities. Although gold certificates were not officially legal to collect in the 1940s, a nice selection of these was included in the collection, but this did not include any of the canceled Series 1900 $10,000 gold notes that Mr. Grinnell may have chosen to regard only as used government checks. In addition to normal notes the Grinnell collection also included error notes, uncut sheets, and fancy serial numbers. Although this collection was loaded with very many major rarities, one that Mr. Grinnell was especially proud of has more or less faded into obscurity. It is a Series 1899 $1 SC with the Lyons-Treat signatures (Fr. 227, H-49). Under Treat's signature appears the misspelled title "...of the United State." rather than "... of the United States." Although extremely rare, this plate error is little commented on among today's collectors.

By far the largest numbers of notes in Mr. Grinnell's collection were for National Bank Notes. All nine of the National Gold Banks of California were represented, and for NBN types only the $500 First Charter and the $50 and $100 Value Back notes were missing in his collection. All together there were more than 3700 large-size NBNs in the Grinnell collection of which about 30% were First Charter notes (including National Gold Bank Notes), another 30% were Second Charter, and thus only about 40% were Third Charter notes. Today almost any large collection of large-size NBNs will be dominated much more heavily than this in terms of numbers by Third Charter Blue Seals.

In terms of today's market, the prices realized for nearly all of Grinnell's notes would seem utterly absurd. In the 1940s, however, serious collectors of U. S. paper money were few and far between. Even then this collection sold for more than $240,000. In today's market it would doubtless be far in excess of $30 million.

Although Grinnell's collection has been broken up and very widely dispersed, there are a number of institutional collections that are quite large and well worth a visit. Thus let us consider museums that feature good displays of paper money. Although numismatic collections are frequently found in museums, these are very largely devoted to coins and medals. Large exhibits of paper money are uncommon in museums, and most museums that have sizable holdings of paper money do not have very much of it on display at any given time. In all of North America I know of only two museums (one in Iowa and one in Ontario) that are very largely devoted to their displays of paper currency. Let us look at those museums that do have good holdings or displays of paper money.

National Numismatic Collection, Museum of American History
Smithsonian Institution, Washington, DC 20560
tel. 202-357-2700

Without doubt the Smithsonian Institution holds the finest assemblage of paper money anywhere in the United States. In 1978 more that 800 Federal notes were turned over to the Smithsonian from the Treasury Department. The collection also benefited greatly from the acquisition of most of the items in the money collection that the Chase Manhattan Bank had on exhibit for many years. The formation of the national collection of coins goes well back into the 19th century, and in 1968 there was a major addition in the form of the collection of gold coins that had been formed by Josiah K. Lilly. The wealth of the Smithsonian's holdings in paper money can be readily appreciated by looking over the present whereabouts of many of the rare notes that are noted in Martin Gengerke's book on large-size paper money records. For instance, more than two-thirds of the $500 United States Notes of Series 1880 and earlier are in the national collection. Peter Huntoon's book on large-size NBNs is filled with illustrations of unfinished Nationals that are in government hands. The latest edition of Gene Hessler's catalog also includes illustrations of such government-held ultra-rarities as the gold certificates of 1865-78 and the Series 1928 $5000 and $10,000 gold notes.

The big problem with all of this is that only a minuscule fraction of this material is on display. Only a small amount of room in the Museum of American History is allotted to coins and paper money. Perhaps there may be a national numismatic museum at some future date, but for the time being most of the Smithsonian's numismatic treasures are in storage. Provided sufficient arrangements are made in advance, it is possible to make arrangements for the viewing of various items in the collection that are not on exhibit.

American Numismatic Association, 818 North Cascade Avenue, Colorado Springs, Colorado 80903 tel. 303-632-2646

The ANA has a most impressive exhibit of numismatic items at its headquarters in Colorado Springs. Anyone with even the slightest interest in coins should be very much impressed with the $2.05 in "loose change" that are always on exhibit in a single large case, since the coins in question consist of two 1804 silver dollars and one 1913 Liberty Head nickel. Many other rare coins are also on display. The ANA also has very impressive holdings of paper money, and almost all of these have been acquired as donations from various sources. On more than one occasion I have mentioned the unique pair of $50/100 and $100/50 Brown Backs from New Mexico Territory that was donated to the ANA by Omaha coin dealer Aubrey Beebee.

Unfortunately the exhibit space at the ANA headquarters is relatively small, and only a small portion of the currency that the museum holds is on display at any given time. The ANA, however, does make a practice of changing some of its exhibits periodically, and so repeat visits to this museum are recommended.

Higgins Paper Money Museum, P. O. Box 54, Okoboji, Iowa 51355 tel. 712-332-5859

The is the only museum in the United States that is devoted exclusively to U. S. Federal paper money. The emphasis is overwhelmingly on national bank notes, and the museum holds by far the finest holding of Iowa NBNs in existence. Its holdings of notes from Minnesota, South Dakota, Missouri, and Wisconsin are also superb. Numerous unique notes and major rarities among the NBNs are on exhibit in this museum, which is located in a resort community in northwestern Iowa. The Higgins Museum was formerly open only during the summer months, but plans are now underway to have it open for at least a couple of additional months. If you have any interest at all in national bank notes, this museum is an absolute must, even if you have to drive several hundred miles just to get there.

Currency Museum of the Bank of Canada, 245 Sparks Street, Ottawa, Ontario K1A 0G9 tel. 613-782-8914

Without doubt the Currency Museum of the Bank of Canada has one of the finest displays of paper money anywhere in the world. Although the museum has a fair number of coins (including an ultra-rare 1911 Canadian silver dollar) and foreign bank notes, it heavily emphasizes the paper money of Canada, and in this area its collection is without peer. Most of the Canadian notes are on sliding panels, which in my opinion is the best method to mount and exhibit a large collection of paper money.

At the present time all of the colonial, provincial, and Dominion notes have been mounted, and the Bank of Canada notes (from 1935 to date) are kept quite current. The private bank notes are being mounted at a leisurely pace, and several more years will be required before this project has been completed. Most of the mounted notes are issued items, but the Bank of Canada also has an enormous collection of specimen notes and proofs in various stages of completion.

Even if you don't plan to collect Canadian bank notes, this museum is an absolute must. I would also suggest taking along your Charlton catalogue(s) so that you can directly compare the real notes with the item listings.

Federal Reserve Bank of San Francisco, 101 Market Street 94104
Union Bank Money Museum, 400 California Street 94104
Wells Fargo Bank History Museum, 420 Montgomery Street 94104

Downtown San Francisco is home to three different numismatic displays, all of which are of great interest. The Federal Reserve Bank has on exhibit some of the rarest large-size type notes. Included are Series 1882 $5000 and $10,000 gold certificates and Series 1918 $5000 and $10,000 Federal Reserve Notes. The museum in the Union Bank (formerly the Bank of California) features a superb collection of the private gold coins of California. The museum in the Wells Fargo Bank portrays the entire history of banking in the western states in the 19th century. In addition to some coins and paper money there are also exhibits of substantial amounts of collateral material, much of which is of interest both to numismatists and philatelists. All three of these museums are essential stops for any numismatist or syngraphist who visits San Francisco.

Money Museum, Federal Reserve Bank of Richmond, 701 East Byrd Street 23219
Museum of the Confederacy, 1201 East Clay Street 23219 tel. 804-649-1861

Downtown Richmond is also home to two museums that should be of great interest to syngraphists. Like its counterpart in San Francisco, the Federal Reserve Bank of Richmond has also set up a money museum. The Museum of the Confederacy touches on all aspects of Confederate history. Due to a limited space for exhibits the museum is unable to display many of the notes and bonds that it holds, but its holdings of Confederate bonds and paper money together with the paper money of the Southern States is superb. If you are seriously interested in CSA currency or related items, it should be possible to arrange a private viewing of some of this material.

Kutztown Paper Money Collection, Kutztown University, Kutztown, Pennsylvania 19530 tel. 610-683-4484

This is a good place to put in a notice about the collection of paper money that is on permanent exhibit in the Rohrbach Library of Kutztown University. It is the only such collection on public display in Pennsylvania, and to my knowledge the only exhibit of this type in a university library anywhere in the United States. Setting up this exhibit was entirely my idea, and I am responsible for acquiring all of the notes that are on display. Included are about 250 items of U. S. Federal paper money. There are more than 60 large-size notes including a Series 1880 $50 USN, an 1886 $5 SC, an 1890 $10 Treasury Note, and an 1882 $50 gold note. The small-size notes include Series 1934 $500 and $1000 FRNs as well as all major types of small-size notes ($1 to $100) except for the Series 1933 $10 SC. There are also exhibits of Fractional Currency and MPCs. This collection went on exhibit in the autumn of 1998, and it is intended in part as an educational depiction of the monetary history of the United States since 1861.

Binion's Horseshoe Casino, Fremont Street, Las Vegas, Nevada

To gamblers Binion's Casino in downtown Las Vegas is noted for its World Series of Poker, its tenfold odds on craps, and its low vigorish on the banker's hand in baccarat. To syngraphists, however, it is much better known for its million-dollar currency display. This famous collection has been at the casino since the 1950s, and it consists of 100 Series 1934 $10,000 FRNs, all from the New York district. This is probably well over half of all of the small-size $10,000 FRNs of both series and all districts that are in existence. Binion's offers complementary photographs to visitors standing beside this famous collection. Be sure to get one of these souvenirs on your next visit to Las Vegas. After that, cross over Fremont Street to the Golden Nugget Casino, which features an outstanding display of large gold nuggets.

If you are interested in other numismatic museums, an excellent guide on these is to be found in the *Coin World Almanac* that is published by Amos Press Inc. of Sidney, Ohio. Prominent displays of coins are very much more numerous than are large exhibits of paper money, but I expect that most persons who specialize in one of these types of collectibles are usually quite interested in seeing attractive displays of the other.

APPENDIX

On the following pages estimated market prices are given for the most widely collected types and series of U. S. Federal paper money. There are five separate appendices which give prices for normal small-size notes, small-size star notes, large-size type notes, Fractional Currency, and Military Payment Certificates, respectively. A table of prices for web notes is included with the section on star notes. All price data, of course, are time-dependent, and these data refer to midyear 1999. Every attempt has been made to keep these data as current and accurate as is possible, but some variations are to be expected. In general notes are priced in fine, XF, and CU condition. In some instances gem CU notes sell at significantly higher prices than do "normal" CU notes. Many small-size notes have no significant premium over their face value, and no prices are given for these. In a few cases (e. g., Series 1928 $1 USNs with low serial numbers or Series 1953A $10 SCs) notes are rarely encountered in the lower grades, and thus a blank line is given for these notes in fine condition since they are almost never seen in this grade.

In these lists I have avoided extreme rarities. Most of these are discussed in the text in substantial detail, and it makes little sense to list a current price for an item that appears for sale only once or twice a decade in a rapidly changing market. For small-size notes I have omitted prices for the $5000 and $10,000 notes. I have listed almost all of the small-size star notes, but several are very rare and the prices on a number of the scarcest FRN stars are tentative at best. For large-size type notes I have included listings for distinct subtypes where significant price distinctions do occur. In some cases, however, price differences are not significant between the various Treasury seal varieties. This is especially true of the Series 1886 SCs, and for these only one listing is given for each of the five denominations. Listings for national bank notes refer to the most common banks for a given type. The prices for uncirculated fractional notes refer to a normal CU grade. Substantially higher prices are often being asked these days for fractional notes in gem CU condition. The prices quote for MPCs are for the normal varieties. Replacement MPCs always sell for significantly higher prices, but the great rarity of many of these precludes including a similar list for these specialty items. However, the MPC replacement survey summary chart is included with the regular issue values.

A few large-size and fractional notes are listed with an asterisk. This means that one particular variety is substantially more common and less expensive than are other notes of that type. For instance, for imperferate fractional notes of the First Issue, the notes with monograms on their backs are much more common than are those without this feature. Among large-size type notes a single signature variety dominates a given type in a few instances, and this is noted on occasion.

REGULAR SMALL SIZE NOTES

		F	XF	CU
United States Notes				
$1	1928(low serial number)			225
$1	1928	25	60	175
$2	1928	10	15	40
	1928A	12	35	175
	1928B	50	175	700
	1928C	7	12	45
	1928D	4	8	20
	1928E	7	14	40
	1928F	4	8	18
	1928D	4	8	16
	1953		4	8
	1953A		4	7
	1953B		4	7
	1953C		4	8
	1963		3	6
	1963A		3	6
$5	1928	9	15	50
	1928A	10	20	70
	1928B		10	18
	1928C		10	20
	1928D	15	50	75
	1928E		9	30
	1928F		8	15
	1953		7	12
	1953A		7	12
	1953B		7	12
	1953C		7	12
	1963		7	10
$100	1966		140	350
	1966A		325	1100
Silver Certificates				
$1	1928	7	11	25
	1928A	7	11	22
	1928B	7	11	25
	1928C	50	140	450
	1928D	30	85	250
	1928E	175	500	1300
	1934	9	15	40
	1935		4	10
	1935A		3	7
	1935B		3	7
	1935C		3	7
	1935D (both)		3	7
	1935E		2	6
	1935F		2	6
	1935G no motto		2	6
	1935G with motto		4	10
	1935H		2	6
	1957		2	5
	1957A		2	5
	1957B		2	5
$5	1934		8	20
	1934A		8	15
	1934B		10	25
	1934C		8	18
	1934D		8	16
	1953		7	14
	1953A		7	14
	1953B		7	14
$10	1933	1500	5000	12,500
	1934	16	22	60
	1934A	15	30	90
	1934B	40	150	1200
	1934C		18	60
	1934D		25	75
	1953		25	75
	1953A		60	175
	1953B		35	90
Gold Certificates, series 1928				
$10		30	75	350
$20		40	100	400
$50		125	400	1100
$100		200	600	1250
$500		1750	5000	11000
$1000		3250	8000	15000

Guide and Handbook — values\433

		F	XF	CU
World War II Issues				
1944 experimentals				
$1	"R"	20	45	200
$1	"S"	18	40	175
Hawaii				
$1	1935A	11	20	70
$5	1934	30	60	275
$5	1934A	25	50	250
$10	1934A	25	60	350
$20	1934	40	125	800
$20	1934A	30	75	500
North Africa				
$1	1935A	10	20	75
$5	1934A	12	30	90
$10	1934	1000	3000	10,000
$10	1934A	18	30	75
National Bank Notes				
$5 type 1		12	20	55
$5 type 2		15	25	60
$10 type 1		20	30	60
$10 type 2		25	45	65
$20 type 1		30	40	75
$20 type 2		35	45	90
$50 type 1		80	125	200
$50 type 2		175	350	750
$100 type 1		140	200	325
$100 type 2		250	500	1250
Federal Reserve Bank Notes				
$5	"A"	15	30	100
	"B"	15	25	70
	"C"	15	30	90
	"D"	15	25	90
	"F"	15	35	150
	"G"	15	25	150
	"H"	125	300	1250
	"I"	25	40	250
	"J"	15	35	100
	"K"	15	25	90
	"L"	350	900	rare
$10	"A"	15	30	125
	"B"	15	25	75
	"C"	15	30	100
	"D"	15	25	90
	"E"	18	30	125
	"F"	18	35	150
	"G"	15	25	75
	"H"	15	25	90
	"I"	15	30	125
	"J"	15	35	125
	"K"	75	250	1000
	"L"	20	50	175
$20	"A"		40	150
	"B"		35	90
	"C"		45	125
	"D"		40	125
	"E"		45	175
	"F"		40	150
	"G"		35	100
	"H"		50	125
	"I"		45	150
	"J"		45	150
	"K"		50	250
	"L"		45	250
$50	"B"		75	175
	"D"		75	175
	"G"		75	175
	"I"		125	250
	"J"		90	200
	"K"		125	300
	"L"		100	250
$100	"B"		135	250
	"D"		135	250
	"E"		160	300
	"G"		135	250
	"I"		160	350
	"J"		150	325
	"K"		150	325

Federal Reserve Notes		
		CU
$1	1963	3.00
	1963A	3.00
	1963B	3.50
	1969	2.50
	1969A	2.50
	1969B	2.50
	1969C	2.50
	1969D	2.50
	1974	2.00
	1977	2.00
	1977A	2.00
	1981	2.00
	1981A	2.00
	1985	2.00
	1988	2.00
	1988A	2.00
	1993	2.00

	1995	1.50			1963			15
$2	1976	3.00			1963A			12
	1995	2.50			1969			12
		XF	CU		1969A			12
$1	1988A web	10.00	30.00		1969B			20
	1993 web	4.00	9.00		1969C			12
	1995 web	4.00	7.00		1974			12
					1977			10
FRN District Sets (CU)					1977A			10
$1	1963 (12)		30.00		1981			10
	1963A (12)		30.00		1981A			10
	1963B (3)		14.00		1985			10
	1969 (12)		30.00		1988			10
	1969A (12)		30.00		1988A			10
	1969B (12)		30.00		1993			9
	1969C (10)		28.00		1995			7
	1969D (12)		30.00	$10	1928		25	75
	1974 (12)		28.00		1928A		25	50
	1977 (12)		28.00		1928B		18	35
	1977A (12)		28.00		1928C	30	50	150
	1981 (12)		28.00		1934			30
	1981A (12)		28.00		1934A			25
	1985 (12)		26.00		1934B			30
	1988 (12)		28.00		1934C			30
	1988A DC (12)		28.00		1934D			30
	1988A FW (7)		14.00		1950			30
	1993 DC (8)		18.00		1950A			30
	1993 FW (5)		18.00		1950B			28
	1995 DC (8)		16.00		1950C			22
	1995 FW (8)		16.00		1950D			20
$2	1976 DC (12)		42.00		1950E			35
					1963			20
		F	XF	CU	1963A			20
$5	1928		20	60	1969			18
	1928A		20	60	1969A			18
	1928B		15	35	1969B			18
	1928C	125	325	1100	1969C			18
	1928D	175	500	1750	1974			18
	1934		12	30	1977			18
	1934A		12	25	1977A			18
	1934B		12	25	1981			18
	1934C		12	25	1981A			18
	1934D		12	30	1985			16
	1950			18	1988A			15
	1950A			18	1990			15
	1950B			18	1993			15
	1950C			18	1995			13
	1950D			15	$20	1928		35	75
	1950E			18		1928A		40	100

	1928B		30	50		1981			70
	1928C	125	250	500		1981A			70
	1934			40		1985			65
	1934A			40		1988			65
	1934B			45		1990			60
	1934C (old and new)			40		1993			60
	1934D			45		1996			55
	1950			35	$100	1928		140	200
	1950A			35		1928A		130	190
	1950B			35		1934			175
	1950C			35		1934A			175
	1950D			35		1934B			225
	1950E		35	60		1934C			200
	1963			35		1934D		175	300
	1963A			35		1950			175
	1969			33		1950A			175
	1969A			33		1950B			175
	1969B			35		1950C			175
	1969C			33		1950D			175
	1974			30		1950E		250	600
	1977			30		1963A			135
	1981			30		1969			130
	1981A			30		1969A			130
	1985			28		1969C			130
	1988A			28		1974			130
	1990			25		1977			130
	1993			25		1981			125
	1995			24		1981A			125
	1996			22		1985			120
$50	1928		90	120		1988			120
	1928A		90	140		1990			115
	1934			100		1993			115
	1934A			110		1996			110
	1934B			125			F	XF	CU
	1934C			110	$500	1928	600	900	1400
	1934D		150	275		1934	550	700	950
	1950			100		1934A	550	700	950
	1950A			100	$1000	1928	1200	1800	3000
	1950B			100		1934	1100	1350	1850
	1950C			100		1934A	1100	1350	1850
	1950D			100					
	1950E		100	175					
	1963A			75					
	1969			75					
	1969A			75					
	1969B			75					
	1969C			75					
	1974			70					
	1977			70					

STAR (REPLACEMENT) NOTES
United States Note Stars

		F	XF	CU
$1	1928	2000	5000	11,000
$2	1928	75	200	550
	1928A	750	1750	4500
	1928B	4000	rare	
	1928C	150	375	900
	1928D	25	75	200
	1928E	1000	2750	5500
	1928F	20	75	200
	1928G	15	50	175
	1953		8	25
	1953A		10	30
	1953B		8	25
	1953C		10	35
	1963		5	15
	1963A		6	18
$5	1928	25	150	500
	1928A	750	1500	3500
	1928B	20	125	350
	1928C	30	125	350
	1928D	650	1250	2500
	1928E	35	100	350
	1928F	20	50	175
	1953		25	75
	1953A		15	30
	1953B		15	35
	1953C		20	50
	1963		10	20
$100	1966		350	1200

Silver Certificate Stars

		F	XF	CU
$1	1928	20	50	250
	1928A	15	45	225
	1928B	25	75	500
	1928C	1500	3000	8500
	1928D	1250	2500	9000
	1928E	5000	12,500	rare
	1934	40	100	600
	1935	15	40	175
	1935A		6	18
	1935B		18	60
	1935C		8	30
	1935D (wide)		7	20
	1935D (narrow)		7	20
	1935E		3	6
	1935F		3	8
	1935G no motto		3	6
	1935G with motto		6	20
	1935H		5	10
	1957		3	5
	1957A		3	5
	1957B		3	5
$5	1934	20	60	200
	1934A	13	30	125
	1934B	20	50	500
	1934C	13	25	100
	1934D	10	20	60
	1953		15	35
	1953A		10	25
	1953B	1000	2000	6500
$10	1934	40	150	900
	1934A	60	200	750
	1934B	600	1500	12,500
	1934C	25	60	200
	1934D	50	300	900
	1953	20	50	250
	1953A		125	450

Gold Certificate Stars

		F	XF	CU
$10	1928	150	600	1750
$20		175	750	2250
$50		1100	3000	7500
$100		1250	3500	10,000

World War II Issues
1944 Experimental Stars

		F	XF	CU
$1	"R"	500	--	3500
$1	"S"	500	--	3500

Hawaii Stars

		F	XF	CU
$1	1935A	100	250	850
$5	1934	300	750	3250
$5	1934A	4000	8000	rare
$10	1934A	750	2750	7500
$20	1934	425	1750	rare
$20	1934A	375	1500	rare

North Africa Stars

		F	XF	CU
$1	1935A	150	300	1000
$5	1934A	40	150	750
$10	1934A	40	125	400

Guide and Handbook — values\437

Federal Reserve Bank Note (1929) Stars			
$5	175	350	800
$10	150	300	750
$20	125	300	700
$50	150	400	850
$100	250	450	1000

Federal Reserve Note Stars

		CU
$1	1963	3.50
	1963A	3.50
	1963B	4.00
	1969	3.00
	1969A	3.00
	1969B	3.00
	1969C	3.00
	1969D	3.00
	1974	2.50
	1977	2.50
	1977A	2.50
	1981	2.50
	1981A	2.50
	1985	2.50
	1988	3.00
	1988A	2.50
	web	1100.00
	1993	2.50
	1995	2.50
$2	1976	6.00
	1995	8.00

FRN District Star Sets (CU)

$1	1963 (12)	40.00
	1963A (12)	40.00
	1963B (4)	15.00
	1969 (12)	35.00
	1969A (11)	32.00
	1969B (12)	32.00
	1969C (9)	60.00
	1969D (11)	32.00
	1974 (12)	32.00
	1977 (12)	32.00
	1977A (12)	32.00
	1981 (12)	38.00
	1981A (5)	60.00
	1985 (6)	60.00
	1988 (7)	150.00
	1988A DC (7)	20.00
	1988A FW (4)	12.00
	1993 (5)	75.00
	1995 (10)	35.00
$2	1976 (12)	100.00

		F	XF	CU
$5	1928	40	125	500
	1928A	50	125	500
	1928B	40	100	300
	1934	30	60	200
	1934A	25	50	150
	1934B	25	50	250
	1934C	20	60	225
	1934D	25	75	250
	1950		35	100
	1950A		25	60
	1950B		15	40
	1950C		20	40
	1950D		15	30
	1950E		20	40
	1963			20
	1963A			15
	1969			18
	1969A			22
	1969B		35	75
	1969C			22
	1974			15
	1977			15
	1977A			15
	1981			15
	1981A			15
	1985			15
	1988			12
	1988A			10
	1993			10
	1995			10
$10	1928	50	150	500
	1928A	100	300	750
	1928B	40	100	350
	1928C		rare	

	Series					Series			
	1934	25	60	225		1969B			60
	1934A	20	60	200		1969C			40
	1934B	20	60	175		1974			40
	1934C	20	50	175		1977			36
	1934D	20	50	175		1981			35
	1950	20	40	125		1981A			40
	1950A		30	75		1985			35
	1950B		25	60		1988A			35
	1950C		25	60		1990			32
	1950D		25	60		1993			30
	1950E	20	50	125		1995			30
	1963			35		1996			25
	1963A			28	$50	1928	125	400	700
	1969			28		1928A			1500
	1969A			30		1934	100	250	450
	1969B			35		1934A	100	250	550
	1969C			25		1934B		3000	
	1974			22		1934C	200	500	1200
	1977			25		1934D	2000	3000	
	1977A			25		1950	90	175	400
	1981			30		1950A	90	175	400
	1981A			30		1950B	100	200	450
	1985			25		1950C	75	150	350
	1988A			25		1950D	85	175	450
	1990			20		1950E	125	250	600
	1993			18		1963A		100	175
	1995			18		1969		90	150
$20	1928	60	200	600		1969A		90	150
	1928A	500	1000	--		1969B		500	1000
	1928B	50	125	400		1969C		125	250
	1934	45	100	250		1974		100	200
	1934A	40	75	200		1977		100	200
	1934B	40	75	175		1981			125
	1934C (both)		75	200		1981A			125
	1934D	35	60	150		1985			125
	1950	35	75	200		1988			100
	1950A		50	150		1990			75
	1950B		40	100		1993			65
	1950C		40	125		1996			60
	1950D		50	150	$100	1928	200	400	800
	1950E	50	100	225		1928A		2500	
	1963			60		1934	150	250	500
	1963A			45		1934A	150	250	500
	1969			36		1934B		1500	3000
	1969A			45		1934C		2000	

Guide and Handbook

1934D		2000	3500	
1950	150	250	600	
1950A	150	250	600	
1950B	150	250	600	
1950C	175	300	700	
1950D	150	250	600	
1950E	300	600	1250	
1963A			250	
1969			250	
1969A		175	300	
1969C		200	400	
1974			225	
1977			225	
1981			200	
1981A			200	
1985			175	
1988			175	
1990			135	
1993			135	
1996			120	

		F	XF	CU
$500	1928	1500	4000	rare
	1934	1000	2000	4500
	1934A	1000	2000	4500
$1000	1928	3000	8000	rare
	1934	2000	4000	8000
	1934A	2000	4000	8000

Note: several of the earlier FRN stars are very rare, and thus prices quoted here are based on just a few auction realizations. This is particularly true of the $20, $50, and $100 notes for Series 1928A, and the $50 and $100 stars for Series 1934B, 1934C, and 1934D. The Series 1928C $10 note is a special case, since only two examples (both CU) are known.

WEB NOTES

All web notes are $1 Federal Reserve notes that were printed in Washington.

		F	XF	CU
Series	AE	5	10	35
1988A	AF	5	10	30
	AG	5	10	30
	BL	100	300	1500
	CA	5	10	35
	EI	5	10	35
	EK	5	10	35
	FL	20	35	200
	FM	10	20	125
	FN	10	20	110
	FU	5	10	30
	FV	5	10	30
	F*	250	500	1100
	GP	8	20	110
	GQ	8	20	125
Series	BH	3	4	9
1993	CA	3	4	9
Series	AC	3	4	8
1995	AD	4	6	20
	BH	3	4	8
	DC	3	4	7
	FD	3	4	8

LARGE SIZE NOTES

		F	XF	CU
Demand Notes				
$5	1861	1750	4500	--
$10	1861	3500	9000	--
United States Notes				
$1	1862	350	500	1000
$1	1869	300	700	1500
$1	1874-8	100	250	700
$1	1880, brown	80	200	600
$1	1880, sm red	75	150	500
$1	1917	30	60	150
$1	1923	40	90	250
$2	1862	350	900	2250
$2	1869	400	1200	2750
$2	1874-78	225	600	1250
$2	1880, brown	125	300	750
$2	1880, sm red	100	250	600
$2	1917	40	75	225
$5	1862, 1st	250	500	1250
$5	1862-3, 2nd	250	500	1250
$5	1869	250	500	1250
$5	1875-78	175	350	800
$5	1880, brown	150	350	850
$5	1880, lg red	200	450	1100
$5	1880, sm red	150	300	600
$5	1907	60	125	250
$10	1862, 1st	250	1100	2750
$10	1862-3, 2nd	500	1000	2500
$10	1869	500	1000	2750
$10	1875-78	400	900	1200
$10	1880, brn	350	750	1500
$10	1880, lg red	350	750	1500
$10	1880, sm red	300	600	1250
$10	1901	400	900	2000
$10	1923	600	1500	3500
$20	1862, 1st	1250	2250	--
$20	1862-3, 2nd	1250	2250	4500*
$20	1869	1250	2750	7500
$20	1875-78	400	600	1250
$20	1880, brown	400	1000	2500
$20	1880, lg red	400	1000	2250
$20	1880, sm red	250	500	1250*
$50	1880, lg	2500	6000	11,000
$50	1880, sm	1500	4000	8000
$100	1880, lg	5000	11,000	--
$100	1880, sm	4000	9000	--
Interest Bearing Notes				
$10 Compound		2250	6000	--
$20 Compound		2750	8000	--
$10 One-Year		3500	10,000	--
$20 One Year		4000	12,000	--
Refunding Certificates				
$10	1879	1200	2500	6000
Silver Certificates				
$1	1886	200	450	1100
$1	1891	150	350	800
$1	1896	225	400	1000
$1	1899	45	100	200
$1	1923	20	35	70
$2	1886	300	750	1500
$2	1891	250	750	2750
$2	1896	325	800	2500
$2	1899	125	300	550
$5	1886	500	1500	3500
$5	1891	450	9000	2750
$5	1896	700	2000	5500
$5	1899	225	650	1250
$5	1923	250	700	1250
$10	1880	850	2500	5500
$10	1886	600	2000	3750
$10	1891	350	850	2000
$10	1908	359	850	2000
$20	1880	1500	5000	9000
$20	1886	2500	5500	--
$20	1891, rd	700	2000	4500
$20	1891, bl	700	1800	4250
$20	1899	45	100	200
$50	1880	7000	15,000	--
$50	1891, rd	1400	4000	13,500
$50	1891, bl	1250	3500	13,500
$100	1880	10,000	25,000	--
$100	1891	7500	20,000	--

Guide and Handbook values\441

Treasury Notes				
$1	1890	350	750	2000
$1	1891	100	250	700
$2	1890	600	1500	4500
$2	1891	250	700	1750
$5	1890	450	1000	2500
$5	1891	200	450	1200
$10	1890	600	1250	3250
$10	1891	275	750	1750
$20	1890	2500	5000	11,000
$20	1891	2250	4500	9000

Gold Certificates				
$10	1907	80	225	600
$10	1922	80	200	500
$20	1882,brn	1750	4500	--
$20	1882,red	450	1250	3250
$20	1905	750	2750	9000
$20	1906	125	375	850
$50	1882,red	650	2250	5000
$50	1913	425	1250	3500
$50	1922	350	750	2000
$100	1882,red	500	1500	4500
$100	1922	400	1000	3500
$500	1882	5000	14,000	--
$500	1922	5000	14,000	--
$1000	1907	8500	25,000	--
$1000	1922	8500	25,000	--
$10000	1900	400	800	1500

National Bank Notes			
First Charter Period			
$1	225	450	900
$2	700	1500	3500
$5	275	550	1250
$10	400	900	2250
$20	800	2000	4500
$5 gold	3000	9000	--
Second Charter Period			
Brown Backs			
$5	150	350	750
$10	175	350	850
$20	225	450	1100
$50	1250	2500	6500
$100	1500	3000	9000
Date Backs			
$5	150	275	650
$10	175	325	750
$20	225	425	1000
$50	1000	2000	3500
$100	1500	3000	6500

Value Backs			
$5	225	450	1250
$10	250	550	1500
$20	375	750	2250

Third Charter Period			
Red Seals			
$5	175	325	650
$10	225	375	750
$20	300	450	1100
$50	1500	3500	--
$100	1750	4000	--
Blue Seals, Date Back			
$5	45	100	275
$10	50	110	300
$20	60	125	350
$50	325	700	1600
$100	400	850	2000
Blue Seals, Plain Back			
$5	40	90	250
$10	45	100	275
$20	55	110	325
$50	325	700	1600
$100	400	850	2000

Federal Reserve Notes			
Series 1914, Red Seal			
$5	100	250	600
$10	125	300	750
$20	250	650	1500
$50	550	1200	2750
$100	650	1400	3000
Series 1914, Blue Seal			
$5	28	50	125
$10	35	60	175
$20	45	75	250
$50	135	275	1350
$100	225	450	1250
Series 1918			
$500	3500	11,000	--
$1000	4000	12,000	--

Federal Reserve Bank Notes				
$1	1918	35	75	150
$2	1918	150	350	800
$5	1915	75	200	550
$5	1918	75	200	550
$10	1915	300	750	2000
$20	1915	550	1250	3500
$20	1918	550	1250	3500
$50	1918	2750	6000	12,500

Fractional Currency

	F	XF	CU
First Issue			
5¢ perf	15	30	125
5¢ imperf	10	20	50*
10¢ perf	20	35	125*
10¢ imperf	10	20	50*
25¢ perf	25	50	200
25¢ imperf	15	33	100*
50¢ perf	33	60	275
50¢ imperf	25	40	110*
Second Issue			
5¢ reg. paper	7	18	45
5¢ fib. paper	25	60	200
10 reg. paper	7	18	60
10¢ fib. paper	20	45	175
25¢ reg. paper	10	20	90
25¢ fib. paper	20	45	175
50¢ reg. paper	20	45	125
50¢ fib. paper	35	70	200
Third Issue			
3¢ light curtain	12	25	60
3¢ dark curtain	15	30	75
5¢ red back	12	25	100
5¢ green back	10	20	60
10¢ red back	15	28	110
10¢ autographed	20	40	150
10¢ green back	15	20	50
15¢ face, wide			300
15¢ face, nar.			150
15¢ back, wide			200
15¢ back, nar			100
25¢ red back	20	40	125
25¢ green back	12	25	65
25¢ fib. paper	30	60	200
25¢ heavy ovpt	200	500	1500*
50¢ Justice, red	30	70	250
50¢ Just., autog.	35	75	250
50¢ Just., fib. pap.	40	100	350
50¢ Spinner, red	28	60	175
50¢ Spin., autog.	38	80	275
50¢ Spin, green	20	40	125
50¢ Spin., type 2	22	45	150
Fourth Issue			
10¢	10	18	40
15¢	20	40	110
25¢	12	22	50
50¢ Lincoln	40	90	200
50¢ Stanton	20	50	110
50¢ Dexter	20	50	110
Fifth Issue			
10¢ green	10	20	50
10¢ red	6	13	25
25¢	8	15	30
50¢	13	25	60

MILITARY PAYMENT CERTIFICATES

	F	XF	CU
Series 461			
5¢	1.50	12.50	50
10¢	1.50	12.50	50
25¢	4.00	20.00	80
50¢	6.00	20.00	100
$1	3.00	15.00	80
$5	15.00	45.00	200
$10	12.50	40.00	200
Series 471			
5¢	2.50	17.50	75
10¢	2.50	22.50	75
25¢	7.50	40.00	150
50¢	10.00	45.00	200
$1	7.50	45.00	150
$5	400.00	1250.00	5000
$10	150.00	500.00	1250
Series 472			
5¢	.50	1.50	5
10¢	1.50	7.50	40
25¢	2.50	15.00	90
50¢	5.00	25.00	150
$1	5.00	25.00	150
$5	60.00	350.00	1250
$10	30.00	175.00	650
Series 481			
5¢	1.25	5.00	20
10¢	1.25	5.00	25
25¢	3.00	10.00	50
50¢	5.00	15.00	125
$1 R	7.50	30.00	150
$1 L	7.50	30.00	175
$5	35.00	250.00	1100
$10	20.00	150.00	600
Seies 521			
5¢	1.50	6.00	20
10¢	1.50	6.00	20
25¢	3.50	15.00	50
50¢	5.00	25.00	90
$1	4.00	20.00	85
$5	150.00	400.00	1750
$10	50.00	250.00	1000
Series 541			
5¢	.50	2.00	5
10¢	1.50	4.00	13
25¢	2.50	10.00	25
50¢	4.00	15.00	60
$1	6.00	40.00	200
$5	500.00	2000.00	4500
$10	125.00	500.00	1750
Series 591			
5¢	2.00	10.00	40
10¢	3.00	12.50	50
25¢	8.00	35.00	100
50¢	12.50	50.00	175
$1	10.00	50.00	175
$5	350.00	1250.00	3500
$10	100.00	400.00	1500
Series 611			
5¢	.50	2.00	8
10¢	.50	3.00	15
25¢	1.50	5.00	20
50¢	3.00	10.00	50
$1	3.00	10.00	50
$5	40.00	125.00	550
$10	40.00	125.00	525
Series 641			
5¢	.25	1.50	5
10¢	.25	2.00	6
25¢	.75	2.00	6
50¢	1.00	5.00	15
$1	1.50	6.00	16
$5	15.00	45.00	150
$10	8.00	35.00	150
Series 651			
5¢			1100
10¢			1100
25¢			1100
50¢		600.00	1100
$1	1.50	7.50	25
$5	20.00	60.00	125
$10	20.00	60.00	150
Series 661			
5¢	.25	1.00	4
10¢	.25	1.50	4
25¢	.50	2.50	8
50¢	1.00	3.50	8
$1	1.00	3.00	8
$5	1.50	5.00	12
$10	100.00	300.00	1200
$20	75.00	225.00	800
Series 681			
5¢	.25	1.50	5
10¢	.25	1.50	6
25¢	.50	3.00	10
50¢	1.00	5.00	15
$1	1.00	4.00	10
$5	2.00	10.00	30
$10	10.00	35.00	200
$20	10.00	30.00	125
Series 692			
5¢	.50	2.00	6
10¢	1.00	2.50	7
25¢	1.50	4.00	12
50¢	2.50	6.00	20
$1	3.00	8.00	25
$5	35.00	85.00	175
$10	60.00	175.00	550
$20	60.00	150.00	500

MPC replacements reported in collections

	5¢	10¢	25¢	50¢	$1	$5	$10	$20	Total
461	21	21	7	5	19	9	10		92
471	6	9	7	4	12	3	3		44
472	34	25	1	7	19	1	3		90
481	24	38	21	2	11	0	4		100
521	26	18	12	9	10	8	6		89
541	45	70	24	89	20	1	8		257
591	31	6	0	3	7	1	5		53
611	127	145	7	1	170	10	19		479
641	84	22	27	17	16	7	52		225
651	*	*	*	*	1	0	5		6
661	16	59	19	5	66	14	9	14	202
681	38	24	4	32	27	11	17	45	198
692	86	75	29	20	32	3	6	23	274

*not likely
Grand total 2109

Harlan J. Berk, Ltd.

"The Art & Science of Numismatics"

31 N. Clark Street
Chicago, IL 60602
312/609-0016 • Fax 312/609-1305
www.harlanjberk.com
e-mail: info@harlanjberk.com

A Full-Service Numismatic Firm
Your Headquarters for all Your Collecting Needs

PNG   IAPN   ANA   ANS   NLG   PCDA

---

papermoneyworld.com

Confederate States of America notes, bonds, autographs, documents, photographs, and antiquities of the early south

Phillip B. Lamb

1520 Washington Ave (at Prytania St)
Box 15850
New Orleans, LA 70175
(504) 899-7491
fax (504) 891-6826
e-mail lambcsa@aol.com
online catalog at
www.plamb.com
orders (800) 391-0115

Texas

Southern States • Confederate
all type of United States
paper money

bought and sold

John N. Rowe III
Southwest Numismatic Corp.
6301 Gaston Avenue – Suite 650
Dallas, TX 75214
(214) 826-3036
fax (214) 823-1923

Great Lakes Bank Note Company

fine intaglio products
hand crafted souvenirs
custom engraving

Post Office Box 1146
Olney, MD 20832
(800) 793-0683

Leading Dealer in Paper Money for Over 30 Years

I buy most everything
in paper money

Nationals
Type Notes
Uncut Sheets
Error Notes
Serial #1 Notes
Packs
Proof Federal Notes
Obsoletes
Foreign

Please call or write for a
confidential transaction
Life Member
A. N. A.
Pcda
SPMC
PNG

Harry E. Jones

7379 Pearl Road
Middleburg Hts. Ohio 44130
(440) 234-3330

Great paper money books!

The Comprehensive Catalog of United Stares Paper Money by Gene Hessler, the dean of US paper money research, describes, illustrates, and evaluates in detail all types of United States paper money. For the first time in any catalog, color illustrations are featured. This is the best of the catalogs.

The Comprehensive Catalog of U. S. Paper Money, 564 pages, soft bound $25 hard bound $40.

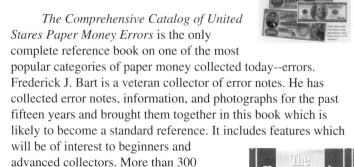

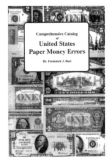

The Comprehensive Catalog of United Stares Paper Money Errors is the only complete reference book on one of the most popular categories of paper money collected today--errors. Frederick J. Bart is a veteran collector of error notes. He has collected error notes, information, and photographs for the past fifteen years and brought them together in this book which is likely to become a standard reference. It includes features which will be of interest to beginners and advanced collectors. More than 300 different notes are listed, described, illustrated and valued. Bob Leuver, former director of the Bureau of Engraving and Printing, provides an insightful foreword for this interesting book, hardbound, $35.00; softbound, $25.00

The Engraver's Line, an Encyclopedia of Paper Money and Postage Stamp Art by Gene Hessler is the first major composite listing of designers and engravers of bank notes and postage stamps; there are over 500 pages and illustrations. For the first time collectors and art lovers will have access to lists of bank notes (and postage stamps) by the artists included here.

The Engraver's Line, regular deluxe hardbound edition $85

Many other titles and subjects available— write for list!

The leader in paper money books—ask for a free list

BNR Press
132 E. Second Street
Port Clinton, Ohio 43452-1115-04

order via voice or fax 800 793-0683
also (419) 732-NOTE (6683)
BNRPress@papermoneyworld.com

American Coins and Collectibles
Always Buying, Selling, Appraising

ACC President Richie Self has purchased over $3,000,000 annually in coins and paper money from people just like you. *"We want your business!"*

- Competitive prices paid on all U. S., Confederate, and obsolete paper money, as well as a wide variety of U. S. coins.

- Over 100 years cumulative experience and a friendly sales staff.

- Financially secure with banking and trade references available on request.

American Coins and Collectibles is always buying and selling

- Confederate currency
- Obsolete currency
- Broken bank notes
- Southern states notes
- Fractional currency
- United States currency
- Historic newspapers
- Rare autographs
- rare maps
- Civil War artifacts
- Confederate bonds
- Early Americana

ANA–R154522　　　　　　　　　　　　　　　　　SPMC–8978
Louisiana Professional Coin Dealers Association

American Coins and Collectibles, Inc.
855 Pierremont Rd., Suite 123 Shreveport, LA 71106 phone (318)-868-9077

1-800-865-3562

R. J. BALBATON.........

BUYS AND SELLS

- CONFEDERATE STATES CURRENCY
- ENCASED POSTAGE STAMPS
- ALLIED MILITARY CURRENCY
- BOOKS ON VARIOUS AREAS OF NUMISMATICS
- COLONIAL AND CONTINENTAL CURRENCY
- EPHEMERA OF DIFFERENT TYPES
- INTERNATIONAL BANKNOTES
- MILITARY PAYMENT CERTIFICATES
- OBSOLETE BANKNOTES AND MERCHANTS SCRIP
- SELECTED WORLD COINS
- UNITED STATES COINS OF ALL TYPES
- U. S. LARGE AND REGULAR SIZE NOTES

We respond best to priced offers. We'll buy one piece or a hoard of an item! Timely FREE price lists or catalogs issued in most of the above listed areas of interest.

We welcome your inquiry whether BUYING or SELLING, contact me now.
Member of: P.C.D.A., A.N.A., S. P. M.C., N.E.N.A., A.P.S., etc.
AUTHORIZED SUBMISSION CENTER FOR :
P.C.G.S., A.N.A.C.S.
*****more than 35 years of service to collectors*****

DORIC COINS & CURRENCY
POB 911
No. Attleboro, MA 02761-0911
508-699-2266 FAX: 508-643-1154

BUYING and SELLING PAPER MONEY

United States, all types Thousands of Nationals, Large and Small, Silver Certificates, U. S. Notes, Gold Certificates, Treasury Notes, Federal Reserve Notes, Fractional, Continental, Colonial, Obsoletes, Depression Scrip, Checks, Stocks, etc. Foreign notes from over 250 countries. Paper Money books and supplies. Send us your want list or ship your material for a fair offer.

LOWELL C. HORWEDEL
P. O. Box 2395
West Lafayette, IN 47996
(765) 583-2748 fax (765) 583-4384

LINDNER CURRENCY ALBUMS

Collecting paper money is a wonderful hobby and most collectors who really work to learn and understand paper seem to make money. One of the true joys of collecting is to take the results of your collecting and display them to other collectors or to friends who would like to see our old money and the stories they tell. One of the finest ways that I know to hold and store a collection is by using our Mylar D® holders and store them in a Lindner album. This is the method I use for my collection, and more collectors use it each and every day. If you want a way to display that is truly the way the top collectors use, the answer is Lindner.

The Lindner Album is an eighteen-ring binder that measures 12 ¾" high, 12" deep and 1 ¾" wide. The high quality textured, scuff-resistant plastic cover comes in your choice of five distinctive colors: wine red, forest green, buckskin tan, ebony black, and dark robin's egg blue. With your album comes twenty currency pages as described in your choice of layout.

Album as described: List Price $76.00 Your Price $66.00

PAGES FOR LINDNER BINDERS

1 pocket to page 9 ½" x 11 ¼"

2 pockets to a page**openings each 9 ½ x 5 ½"

3 pockets to a page**openings each 9 ½ x 3 6/11"

4 pockets to a page**openings each 9 ½ x 2 3/8"

(We recommend the 3 pockets to a page for large and small US currency!
Price per ten pages • $18.00)

SLIPCASES FOR LINDNER BINDERS

Lindner uses the same material used for the binder covers to make a snug fitting slipcase that will protect your album and notes.

List $29.00 • Denly's Discount $25.00

All Lindner orders have a $4.50 postage and handling fee.

**Assorted sizes OK ** 2-, 3-, and 4-pocket pages come with cardboard page interleaves. We can special order any Lindner product at a discount from list. Send stamps, 55¢ legal envelope for their catalog.

MYLAR-D® CURRENCY HOLDERS

These are the best that I know of being made today--what more can I say!

Bank Note and Check Holders

SIZE	INCHES	50	100	500	1000
Fractional	4 ¾ x 2 ¾	16.75	30.50	136.00	235.00
Colonial	5 ½ x 3 1/16	17.25	32.00	144.00	265.00
Small Currency	6 5/8 x 2 7/8	17.75	34.00	150.50	280.00
Large Currency	7 7/8 x 3 ½	20.25	37.00	167.50	310.00
Auction	9 x 3 ¾	21.75	40.00	193.00	339.00
Foreign Currency	8 x 5	25.00	46.00	206.00	360.00
Checks	9 5/8 x 4 ¼	25.00	46.00	206.00	360.00

Sheet Holders

SIZE	INCHES	10	50	100	250
Obsolete Sheet-End Open	8 ¾ x 14 ½	11.20	51.00	82.00	188.00
National Sheet-Side Open	8 ½ x 17 ½	12.00	55.00	90.00	207.50
Stock Certificate-End Open	9 ½ x 12 ½	10.70	48.50	77.00	157.50
Map and Bond Size-End Open	18 x 24	46.50	212.50	342.00	785.00

You may assort note holders for best price (min. 50 pcs one size) you may assort sheet holders for best price (min. 5 pcs one size) (min. 10 pcs total) shipping in the U.S. (Parcel post) free of charge. Mylar-D® is a Registered Trademark of the DuPont Corporation. This also applies to uncoated archival quality Mylar® Type D by the DuPont Corp. or the equivalent materiel by ICI Industries Corp. Melinex Type 516.

SPMC Life Member #1, PNG Member #358
ANA Life Member LM #2849,
PCDA Charter Member

DENLY'S OF BOSTON
BOX 1010
Boston, MA 02205
orders only 1-800-HI-DENLY
617-482-8477 Fax 617-357-8163
e-mail denlys@aol.com

PAPER MONEY • STOCKS AND BONDS
FISCAL DOCUMENTS • AUTOGRAPHS
CIVIL WAR DOCUMENTS • CONFEDERATE BONDS
EXPERIENCE AND LONGEVITY
A COMMITMENT TO THE MARKETPLACE

Since 1985 we have been one of America's largest active buyers and sellers of historical bonds and shares and are recognized as one of the world's leading market makers for good quality American material. We have contributed in large part to the development of many of the finest collections of American material in the world today and understand the needs of both he casual and serious collector.

EXCITING MAIL AND PHONE BID CATALOGS

We conduct some of America's finest mail bid auctions offering a large selection of items in virtually every collecting category imaginable. Our fully illustrated and well researched catalog are an important permanent reference work for serious collectors and dealers alike.

PRIVATE TREATY SALES TO COLLECTORS, DEALERS, AND CORPORATIONS

We maintain a large and diversified inventory of items ranging in price from less than a dollar to in excess of $10,000. Some major categories found in our inventory—
autographs, automotive, aviation, banking, early finance, entertainment, insurance, mining, oil, railroad, shipping, telephone and telegraph, utilities

www.scottwinslow.com
Scott J. Winslow Associates, Inc.

Post Office Box 10240
Bedford, New Hampshire 03110
(800) 255-6233 ~ (603) 641-8292
Fax (603) 641-5583, scott@scottwinslow.com

Society of Paper Money Collectors

It would be to your advantage to join the Society of Paper Money Collectors, organized in 1961 to further the following objectives:
1. Encourage the collecting and study of paper money.
2. Cultivate fraternal collector relations with opportunities for discussion trading, etc.
3. Furnish information and knowledge through experts, particularly through the Society's *PAPER MONEY* magazine.
4. Promote legislation favorable to collectors, providing it is in accord with the general welfare.
6. Advance the prestige of the hobby.
7. Promote exhibits at numismatic and syngraphic meetings.
8. Encourage realistic and consistent market valuations.

PAPER MONEY, the society bimonthly journal, is sent to all members. In addition to informative articles, it lists new members, the collecting specialty of each, and identifies each as a collector or dealer. Members are encouraged to submit articles for publication.
BOOKS that catalog the obsolete currency of individual states are available to members at reduced prices.
DUES are $20 ($30 outside the United States) per year and are payable in U. S. funds. Members who join the Society prior to October 1 receive the magazines already issued in the year in which they join. Members who join after October 1 will have their dues paid through December of the following year. They will also receive, as a bonus, a copy of the magazine issued in November of the year in which they join.
JUNIOR and LIFE MEMBERS, from 12 to 17 years of age, are required to have a parent or guardian sign their application. The "J" that will precede membership numbers will be removed upon notification to the secretary that the member has reached 18 years of age. Life memberships are $300.
MEETINGS, national and regional, take place throughout the year.
Annual dues in US funds: $24 in the U.S.; $29 for Canada and Mexico; $34 for other countries.
To join the SPMC send dues to SPMC, P. O. Box 117060, Carrollton, TX 75011. For a complimentary copy of *PAPER MONEY,* send $2 for postage and handling.

America's Top Buyer of
$500 • $1,000
$5,000 • $10,000

Also Top Buyer: 1928 Gold Certificates
$10.00, $20.00, $50.00, $100.00,
$500.00, $1,000.00

Call for Quote

Harlan White

2425 El Cajon Blvd., San Diego, CA 92104
Ph. 619-298-0137 • FAX: 619-298-7966

MPC

bought and sold, now paying

$10,000.00

for uncirculated replacements:
$5 series 471, 481, 541, 591, 651
also $5,000 or more for others.

Fred Schwan

fred@papermoneyworld.com
voice or fax (419) 732-6683

American Numismatic Association
Application for Membership

☐ **Yes**, I want to be a part of America's Coin Club. I understand that I will receive the association's award winning monthly journal, *The Numismatist;* access to over 40,000 books, videos and slide sets in the world's largest Numismatic library, discounts on numismatic books, the opportunity to be a part of the ANA School of Numismatics and dozens of other member benefits.

Name _____
Address _____
C/S/Z _____
Signature _____
Date of Birth _____ (required for jr. and sr. members)

I herewith make application for membership in the American Numismatic Association, subject to the bylaws of the Association. I also agree to abide by the Code of Ethics adopted by the Association.

❑ **Enclosed is $29 for a 1 yr. membership**
❑ **Enclosed is $26 for a 1 yr. Senior membership (age 65 and over)**
❑ **Enclosed is $11 for a 1 yr Junior Membership (under age 18)**
❑ **Enclosed is $79 for 3 years (Seniors $69)**
❑ **Enclosed is $130 for 5 years (Seniors $110)**

American Numismatic Association
818 N. Cascade Avenue
Colorado Springs, CO 80903-3279
1-800-367-9723

Chartered by Congress in 1912 to promote the hobby and science of numismatics.

In Numismatics, Knowledge Is Power. The American Numismatic Association Is Where You Get Knowledge.

Here Are Just A Few of The Benefits of Membership.

THE NUMISMATIST Every month you will enjoy the hobby's premier magazine. Each issue contains entertaining and informative articles, columns by some the hobby's best known experts, Association news, and ads from dealers pledged to honor and uphold the ANA's Code of Ethics.

EDUCATIONAL PROGRAMS As the world's foremost numismatic educational organization the ANA offers seminars, hundreds of hours of Numismatic Theater presentations, and of course of famous Summer Seminar. For those unable to personally attend seminars the ANA also offers a series of home study courses.

RESOURCE CENTER With over 40,000 titles the ANA Resource Center is the world's largest circulating numismatic library. ANA members can check out books videos and slide programs at no charge. (Members are required to pay the actual postage charges for shipping the material to and from the ANA.) Special research services are also available.

COLLECTOR SERVICES The ANA offers a variety of numismatic services including authentication services, custom photography, consultation, storage and conservation services and grading service submissions. Call 800-467-5725 for complete details.

INSURANCE PROGRAMS In addition to affordable collection insurance, the ANA also offers term life, health, major medical, disability and cancer policies at reasonable group rates.

CAMARADERIE AND REFERRAL Through our conventions and local club representatives we can put you in touch with other people who share your enthusiasm for numismatics. If you are looking for a club in your area, or a group of collectors who share your specialized interests or dealer you can trust; call the ANA Membership Department - we can help.

Call 800-367-9723 to join or request more information.

Chartered by Congress in 1912 to promote the hobby and science of numismatics.

Have Your Collection Featured In A Future

Currency Auctions of America, Inc.

Sale

**Orlando • St. Louis • Chicago
All of the Great Shows**

OUR COMMISSION STRUCTURE IS AMONG THE MOST REASONABLE IN THE TRADE AND IS ALL INCLUSIVE WITH NO ADDITIONAL CHARGES FOR LOTTING, PHOTOGRAPHY, OR INSURANCE.

TO SEE YOUR COLLECTION DISPERSED TO THE COLLECTING FRATERNITY VIA ONE OF OUR PROFUSELY ILLUSTRATED AUCTION CATALOGUES CONTACT ONE OF OUR PRINCIPALS:

ALLEN MINCHO
P. O. Box 700
Spicewood, TX 78669
(830) 693-7590
FAX (830) 693-1283

LEN GLAZER
P. O. Box 111
Forest Hills, NY 11375
(718) 268-3221

U. S. paper money, national bank notes, Confederate and obsolete notes, CSA counterfeits, obsolete notes, error notes, stocks and bonds (especially automotive and aviation)

professional • prompt • reliable service

Lists available please specify areas of interest

Lawrence Falater

50 years in numismatics
Box 81, Allen, MI 49227
toll free 1-888 FALATER
(517) 437-8977 • fax (517) 437-8978
FALATER@papermoneyworld.com

MEMPHIS COIN CLUB'S
INTERNATIONAL PAPER MONEY SHOW
THIRD WEEKEND OF JUNE

COOK CONVENTION CENTER
255 N. Main St., Memphis, TN 38103-0016

Convention Hotel: Holiday Inn-Crowne Plaza
250 N. Main St., Memphis, TN 38103
901-527-7300

Approximately 150 Dealers
Bureau of Engraving and Printing's Billion Dollar Exhibit
Commemorative Souvenir Cards
U. S. P. S. Temporary Postal Station
Fantastic Paper Money Exhibits by Collectors
Society Meetings
Paper Money Auction by leading Auctioneers

free admission

Buy, Sell, Trade, Free Appraisals
Friday & Saturday, 9:00-6:00, Sunday 9:00-
U. S. & World Paper Money, Checks, Stocks & Bonds,
Documents, Autographs, Paper Collectibles, etc.

Information: Mike Crabb
P. O. Box 17871, Memphis, TN 38187-0871
phone 901-754-6118

CSA & OBSOLETE NOTES

ARE MY BUSINESS!!

I have been a full-time dealer in Confederate and obsolete currency for over 20 years. I've helped many collectors assemble complete CSA type sets as well as find rare varieties. I've also helped hundreds of collectors with their obsolete note interests from rare to common. My catalogs are well known in both the dealer and collector fields for their reference value. If you are a serious collector of CSA notes, bonds or obsolete bank notes, I can offer you the following:

1. Thousands of bank notes in the Confederate and obsolete areas.
2. Accurate descriptions, grading and fair prices.
3. Reliable dealings with prompt and friendly service.
4. The knowledge and research capabilities to properly attribute these notes.
5. A want list service that has helped many find notes which they could not locate.
6. Top prices when buying one note or an entire collection. If you are selling, I want to buy your notes!
7. The respect and integrity of dealings that are well known in the hobby.
8. Representation to bid for clients at major auctions.
9. Paying finder's fees on collections referred to me.
10. Appraisal services for reasonable fees.
11. Institutional and museum services for note authentication and valuations.
12. Strong cash decisions and immediate payment for your material.

If you collect, I offer my latest edition 60 page catalog for $5.00, refundable on first order. It features one of the largest CSA note inventories available, an extensive obsolete and scrip section, uncut sheets of notes, U. S. fractional notes, a Continental and colonial section and a reference book section. Whether you are buying or selling, I would be pleased to have you contact me.

Life member
ANA (2851), SPMC (6)
Coin Net SC #18

Hugh Shull

Charter member

Box 761, Camden, SC 29020
PH: (803) 432-8500 FAX (803) 432-9958

If you collect paper money,
you need
PAPER MONEY
the journal of
THE SOCIETY OF PAPER MONEY COLLECTORS
Organized in 1961

Bimonthly *PAPER MONEY* addresses all types of paper money and security documents, however, it specializes in its coverage of United States federal and obsolete notes, Confederate notes, and the artists and engravers of these historic pieces.

PAPER MONEY, is edited by Gene Hessler. This magazine has been recognized by the American Numismatic Association and the Numismatic Literary Guild as the best organizational journal. Hessler is one of the most respected authorities on paper money of all types. He is the author of standard catalogs, articles, and columns. He has received many awards for his writing and was honored with a nomination for a Peabody Broadcasting Award

The SPMC publishes books on obsolete notes and scrip from individual states. The number of books published, including one of the U. S. national banks notes, is approaching two dozen.

The ladies and gentlemen in the SPMC meet annually and hold regional meetings in conjunction with major numismatic conventions in the Untied States.

Annual dues in US funds: $24 in the U.S.; $29 for Canada and Mexico; $34 for other countries.

To join the SPMC send dues to SPMC, P. O. Box 117060, Carrollton, TX 75011. For a complimentary copy of *PAPER MONEY,* send $2 for postage and handling.

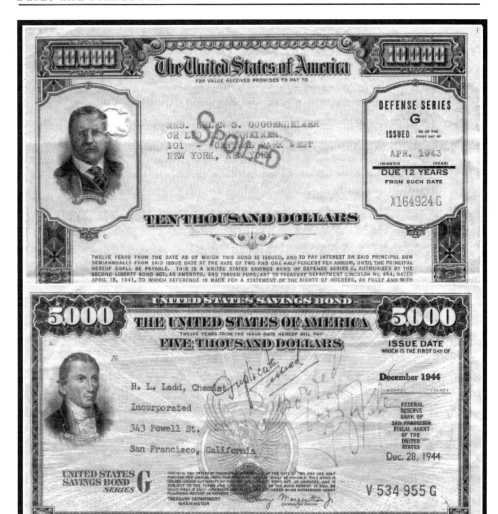

Buying US Government Bonds
All pre 1900 and Liberty Loan Bonds, Series E (especially defense and war bonds), F, G, H, J, K bonds

Fred Schwan

fred@papermoneyworld.com
voice or fax (419) 732-6683
800 793-0683

HERITAGE
Your Source for the Buying and Selling of Currency

Some Recent Highlights

1875 $2, Wisconsin
Denver 1996 ANA, Lot 6071

1875 $5, Colorado Territory
Denver 1996 ANA, Lot 6067

Original Series $1, Colorado Territory
Denver 1996 ANA, Lot 6062

1882 $10 Brown Back, Colorado
Denver 1996 ANA, Lot 6079

**Call
1-800 US COINS
(872-6467)**

Heritage Plaza • 100 Highland Park Village • Dallas, Texas 75205-2788
In Dallas: 214-528-3500 • WATS: 1-800-US COINS (872-6467)
FAX: 214-443-8425

Confederate
Southern States
ObsoleteScrip***
U. S. TypeWorld***
FractionalMPC***
Continental & Colonial

Paper money Lists Available upon Request

David F. Cieniewicz

U. S. and World Currency

Dept. USG
Huntsville, AL 35810-0310

Post Office Box 3310
(256) 852-7015

dave@papermoneyworld.com

The original one-stop shopping place with the most extensive line of numismatic and philatelic supplies available

- we only sell wholesale
- numismatic and philatelic books and supplies
- distributors for BNR Press, Krause Publications and many others

For a complete list of items send a SASE to:

Harry Edelman, Inc.

111-37 Lefferts Blvd
P. O. Box 20040
So. Ozone Park, NY 11420
Ph. 718-641-2710
888-333-6147
Fax 718-641-0737

   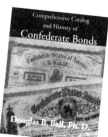

Ian A. Marshall
World Paper Money

c/o Parkway Mall Box 62509
85 Ellesmere Rd. Scarborough
Ontario, Canada M1R 5G8
Ian@papermoneyworld.com
Phone & FAX 416-445-0286

Specialist in

Military payment certificates, Africa, Europe, German and French Notgeld, British Commonwealth & The Americas.

An Extensive Inventory from A to Z. Rarities and bulk modern uncirculated notes always required.

Retail & wholesale lists upon request
Wants lists actively solicited & worked.

Life member ANA
IBNS • CNA • SPMC • NI • CPMS

the CURRENCY DEALER newsletter
"the Greensheet"

... is a Monthly Publication that is the most COMPREHENSIVE and UP-TO-DATE pricing guide available in today's ever-changing field! DEALER-TO-DEALER BID/ASK Charts cover all of the following areas:

LARGE SIZE U.S. NOTES
- DEMAND NOTES
- U.S. NOTES: (LEGAL TENDER)
- COMPOUND INTEREST TREASURY NOTES
- INTEREST BEARING NOTES
- REFUNDING CERTIFICATES
- SILVER CERTIFICATES
- TREASURY NOTES OR COIN NOTES
- NATIONAL BANK NOTES
- FEDERAL RESERVE BANK NOTES
- FEDERAL RESERVE NOTES
- NATIONAL GOLD BANK NOTES
- GOLD CERTIFICATES

SMALL SIZE U.S. NOTES
- LEGAL TENDER NOTES
- SILVER CERTIFICATES
- NATIONAL BANK NOTES
- FEDERAL RESERVE BANK NOTES
- FEDERAL RESERVE NOTES
- GOLD CERTIFICATES
- WW2 EMERGENCY ISSUES

UNCUT SHEETS - SMALL SIZE CURRENCY
- U.S. NOTES (LEGAL TENDER)
- SILVER CERTIFICATES
- WW2 EMERGENCY ISSUES
- NATIONAL CURRENCY

U.S. FRACTIONAL CURRENCY
PROOF & SPECIMEN NOTES
MILITARY PAYMENT CERTIFICATES
COLONIAL NOTES

... **PLUS** IN-DEPTH ARTICLES and analyses, each month, written by the most respected experts in the field!
... **PLUS** AUCTION REPORTS — to give a clear and accurate picture of the most recent activity!
... **PLUS** special ISSUE-BY-ISSUE Charts covering special areas of changing importance!

Subscribe today and get the most comprehensive price guide on the currency market.

The CURRENCY DEALER newsletter
P.O. Box 7939, Torrance, CA 90504 • (310)515-7369 • FAX (310)515-7534

Enter or extend my subscription to the Currency Dealer newsletter for the term checked below. Enclosed is my check/M.O. or MasterCard/Visa # and expiration date.

❑ 1 Year $44   ❑ 2 Years $78

Name _____
Co. Name _____
Address _____
City _____
State _____
Zip _____
Phone _____

The CURRENCY DEALER newsletter
"the Greensheet"

for a complete list of Back-Issue Headlines
http://www.greysheet.com

PAPER MONEY COLLECTORS

the organization that meets your hobby needs is the

INTERNATIONAL BANK NOTE SOCIETY

- promoting the collection of paper money world wide since 1961
- over 2200 members in over 100 nations
- quarterly 64-page award-winning Journal
- 3-4 newsletters annually, including free non-commercial ads for members
- semiannual auctions of thousands of notes
- regional chapters in the USA, UK, Australia, Turkey, BENELUX
- publisher of specialty paper money books (several titles currently in print)
- frequent membership directories
- two comprehensive libraries accessible by mail (Munich and Los Angeles)
- organizer or supporter of many international paper money conventions

Dues and membership categories

	U. S. dollars	U. K. sterling
regular membership	$17.50	£11.00p
family membership	22.50	14.00p
junior membership (to age 18)	9.00	5.50p
life membership	300.00	187.50p

(life membership subject to some restrictions)

To JOIN, send name, address, collecting interests, and payment to:
Milan Alusic   Mrs. Sally Thowney
PO Box 1642   36B, Dartmouth Park Hill
Racine WI 53401, USA   London NW5 1HN, UK

(make check or money order payable to IBNS; send dollars to
Mr. Alusic, Sterling to Mrs. Thowney, EuroCheques, add £.50p)

PAPER MONEY COLLECTORS *ATTENTION !*

We "Make the Market" in Encased Postage Stamps.

CONTACT EAN ABOUT BUYING OR SELLING:

- Fractional Currency
- Colonial Coins & Medals
- United States Coinage
- Colonial Currency
- Fiscal Paper & Bonds
- Civil War Era Photos
- Confederate Currency
- Encased Postage Stamps
- Historic Newspapers
- Ephemera & Prints
- Rare Autographs
- Early Magazines
- Historic Almanacs
- Important & Rare Maps
- Swords & Powder Horns
- Documents & Broadsides
- Colonial Artifacts
- Militaria & Americana
- Antique Playing Cards
- Revolutionary & Civil War militaria

OUR CATALOGS SET THE PACE FOR QUALITY

We Can Sell Your Collection Next !
Contact Dana Linett About Your Important Material.
Call, Fax or Mail us Your Want List Today.

Phone Today - (858) 459-4159 - Subscribe to our Catalogs.
Major Collections of Encased Postage Are Illustrated in Almost Every Auction !

EARLY AMERICAN NUMISMATICS

P.O. BOX 2442 • LA JOLLA, CA 92038 • (858) 459-4159 • FAX (858) 459-4373

www.EarlyAmerican.com   auctions@EarlyAmerican.com

Confederate States of

Civil War Encased Stamps
by Fred Reed

During the Civil War, governments and merchants alike had to be creative in solving financial difficulties. Both sides experienced severe financial difficulties. Gold and silver coinage was hoarded and disappeared from circulation. Both sides then issued paper money. As amazing as that seems today, that was the first successful use of federal paper money. Fractional currency was created and huge quantities of tokens were issued.

Encased postage stamps were perhaps the most interesting and innovative money of them all. Postage stamps were encapsulated so that they could circulate without deteriorating. The denomination was visible to establish the value and the other side was available for advertising. This was the perfect free enterprise solution, but the introduction of fractional currency ended the need for encased stamps.

Fred Reed has studied Civil War encased stamps in a way that few issues have been studied. He has done the traditional things. He studied collections, auction catalogs, old price lists and the like. He has developed pedigrees and lists. Of course he has also cataloged and evaluated each piece and used computer technology to generate emission models for each issue.

You would expect all of the above in a numismatic catalog. However, he went far beyond that. He researched each issuer in detail and in twenty years he had remarkable results. You will love the text and amazing graphics in this book.

Civil War Encased Stamps by Fred Reed is a monumental new reference. It has been TWENTY YEARS in the making: 558 pages, delux hardbound, $60.

America Headquarters

The *Comprehensive Catalog and History of Confederate Bonds* by Douglas B. Ball

This is an innovative new book on the efforts of the Confederate States of America to finance its rebellion. Of course it lists all of the known issues including new emissions never previously cataloged. Beyond that Douglas B. Ball includes a wealth of historic and interesting material that has not been previously published. An insightful and whimsical foreword by John H. Ford rounds out this great new book.

The *Comprehensive Catalog and History of Confederate Bonds* will be of interest to all who are interested in the Civil War and Confederate States of America. Douglas B. Ball is the author of *Financial Failure and Confederate Defeat; Confederate Interim Depository Receipts and Funding Certificates in the Commonwealth of Virginia, 1861-1865;* and numerous articles on Confederate bonds in *The Numismatist* and *Bank Note Reporter.* He holds a B. A., Wooster; M.A., Yale; M.B.A., Columbia; and Ph.D., University of London.

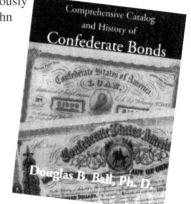

This 288 page, large-format, profusely illustrated work is available directly at $40. Other award winning, interesting, and useful books are also available. Write, call, or fax for a list.

The *Comprehensive Catalog of Confederate Paper Money* by Grover Criswell

This is the standard book for collectors of Confederate paper money by the man who was called the world's richest man in Confederate money. The book includes more varieties than any other catalog and of course uses the standard Criswell numbers. This edition includes many new features including sheets, counterfeits, and counterfeit sheets! Grover Criswell died in the spring of 1999 and will be missed by all. This is the last book created under his supervision although his series of books will continue and be expanded. A very popular book, 358 pages, hardbound, $35. Please add $4 per order (not per book) for shipping.

BNR Press

132 E. Second Street
Port Clinton, Ohio 43452-1115-04
order via voice or fax 800 793-0683
also (419) 732-NOTE (6683)

ALEX PERAKIS COINS & CURRENCY

Serving the collector for over 20 years
Always buying & selling worthwhile material

Specializing in:
- **United States type notes**
- **Large and Small Nationals**
- **Fractional Notes**
- **Obsoletes**

All Want Lists are cheerfully accepted and conscientiously pursued for the beginning, as well as the advanced collector.

Krause Publication Award Recipient
(15 consecutive years)

Member ANA, PCDA, SPMC, FCCB, CCCC

ALEX PERAKIS
P.O. Box 246 • Lima, PA 19037
Phones: (610) 565-1110 • (610) 627-1212
Fax: (610) 891-1466

Everything Else You Need to Know About Federal Currency is in This Book

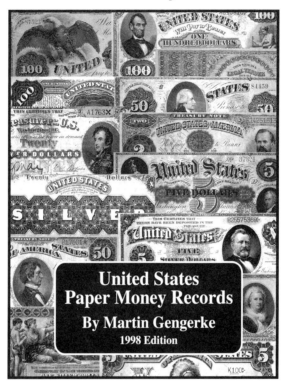

United States Paper Money Records
By Martin Gengerke
1998 Edition

Before you buy a single piece of Federal currency there are several things you really need to know. How many times has a particular note appeared in auction sales or in dealer price lists? How was a specific note graded in its previous appearances? What is the 50-year price history and provenance of that note?

In *United States Paper Money Records,* Martin Gengerke, one of America's leading experts on Federal currency, has compiled an unprecedented data base of facts and figures that every major dealer or collector should have in their own library.

- Close to 10,000 auction or price list appearances are recorded.
- Each note listed is identified by Friedberg number and serial number.
- Gengerke gives "summary" grades when more than one grade has been recorded for a single note.

Special Offer! *The Very Latest Revised Edition of Gengerke's United States Paper Money Records, Autographed by the Author - $125 Postpaid.*

   Stephen Goldsmith Kevin Foley MEMBER

R.M.SMYTHE

26 Broadway, New York, NY 10004 • Toll Free: 800-622-1880
NYS: 212-943-1880 • Fax: 212-908-4047 • www.rm-smythe.com

Don't Miss the Northeast's Most Important Currency Show

The Annual September
Strasburg Paper Money Show & Auction

 at the Historic Strasburg Inn
Route 896, Strasburg, Pennsylvania

For additional show information or to reserve an illustrated catalogue ($20) contact Mary Herzog. To consign material to an upcoming auction contact Stephen Goldsmith or Diana Herzog.

26 Broadway, New York, NY 10004 • Toll Free: 800-622-1880
NYS: 212-943-1880 • Fax: 212-908-4047 • www.rm-smythe.com

Heartland International Trade Shows, Inc., in affiliation with Krause Publications–the world's leading publisher of hobby related periodicals–proudly presents these great numismatic conventions for the collecting fraternity.

6th Annual
Chicago Paper Money Expo

February 18 - 19 - 20, 2000
Ramada Hotel O'Hare
6600 N. Mannheim Road, Rosemont, Illinois

A paper money, stock and bonds speciality event.

25th Annual
Chicago International Coin Fair

April 7 - 8 - 9, 2000
Ramada Hotel O'Hare
6600 N. Mannheim Road, Rosemont, Illinois

A world coin and paper money and ancient coin specialty event.

19th Annual MidAmerica Coin Expo

June 22 - 23 - 24, 2000
Ramada O'Hare Convention Center, Rosemont, Illinois

A national event featuring all aspects of numismatic collecting interest.

For information about these conventions and dates for 2001 and beyond contact:

Kevin Foley
P. O. Box 573
Milwaukee, WI 53201
(414) 421-3498

Fine paper money bought and sold **CARIBBEAN SUN GOLD** John Yasuk P. O. Box 924533 Princeton, FL 33092 305 256 7201 ANA • SPMC • Pcda	Historical Documents Stock Certificates Autographs, Ephemera ## Sam Withers Box 19916 St. Louis, MO 63144 (314) 968-1647
The Coin Shop in Arlington 2229-B W. Park Row Arlington, TX 76013 local (817) 274-5971 Metro (817) 251-9509 fax 274-9992 **Huston Pearson, Jr.** ANA • TNA • SPMC • Pcda • TCDA	Rare Coins and Currency **BOB REED** Box 1162 Gretna. LA 70054 (504) 361-5684 FAX (504) 361-1808 www.rrcoins.net e-mail bobreed@rrcoins.net
US Coins • Paper Money Bought and Sold **Southland Coins and Currency** **Lou Rusera** Box 403 Woodland Hills, CA 91365 phone/fax (818) 348-5275 ANA • Pcda	**Bruce R. Hagen** Buying & Selling U.S. Obsolete Paper Money  Dealer • Auction Agent • Consultant • Appraiser (212) 721-2028 in New York City Member: Pcda • SPMC • ANA • IBNS
PAT BARNES US PAPER MONEY PO Box 25114 Lansing, Mich 48909 (517) 333-9980 patbarnes@voyager.org	BUY • SELL • APPRAISALS • CUNSULTATIONS US Notes & Coins, CSA, Stamps *Colonel's Coins & Stamps* LT. Col. Hudson McDonald Box 7552 Spanish Fort, AL 36577 (334) 937-6580

papermoneyworld.com

MPC • AMC REPLACEMENTS WANTED
Leo May
Box 871
Coral Gables, FL 33124
(305) 343-2429
Leo@papermoneyworld.com

Please see these special advertisments:

inside front cover
Stanely Morycz
Currency Quest

inside back cover
Small Size Shop
Jay Parrino's The Mint L.L.C

back cover
R. M. Smythe Co.

BUYING! SELLING!
World Paper Money
VISIT OUR SHOP
CHAMPION STAMP CO.
ARTHUR H. MOROWITZ
432 WEST 54TH ST, NYC, NY 10019
212/489-8130 FAX 581-8130

Paper Money of
Louisana
Confederate States
Southern States
Clarence Rareshide
Post Office Box 56275
New Orleans, Louisiana 70156
(504) 866-4212 (504) 861-8673

Confederate and
South Carolina
PAPER MONEY
• Bought and Sold •
Carolina Gold and Silver, Inc.
8508-A Two Notch Road
Columbia, SC 29223
(803) 736-0540 or 736-0415
Fax (803) 736-9703
email: kathy@city-online.com
www.carolinacoin.com

U.S. and Foreign Paper Money
Keith and Sue Bauman
Box 250027
Franklin, MI 48025-0027
248/262-1514
TNAsbauman@earthlink.net

ana • ibns • spmc • mspmc • ascc • bbcc • msns

CIGAR LABLES WANTED
HIGHEST PRICES PAID
Darren John Cioffi
Box 393
Newark, DE 19715-0393
phone/fax (302) 235-1698
Darren@GOLD-COAST-TRADING.COM

Last Year Alone...
Littleton Spent More Than $12 Million on U.S. Coins & Paper Money!

Why We Need Your U.S. Paper Money

It's simple. We have lots of customers, and because of their collecting needs, WE NEED YOUR PAPER MONEY! We can afford to pay highly competitive buy prices because we retail all the notes we buy.

Over 150,000+ Customers Want Your Notes!

David Sundman, President
ANA Life Member #4463;
PNG #510; Society of Paper
Money Collectors #LM163;
Member, Professional
Currency Dealers Association

Part of Littleton's experienced team of buyers with some recent purchases.

We welcome the chance to consider your notes!

Wide Range of U.S. Notes Wanted!
- Single notes to entire collections
- Very Good to Gem New
- Early large size notes to high denomination small size notes
- All types including Legal Tender Notes, Silver & Gold Certificates and more

Knowledge and Experience Count – We've Got Both
We've earned our reputation as a nationally recognized leader in the numismatic field. And our buying team – with more than 60 years of combined experience in the grading and buying of coins and paper money – has played a crucial role.

Why You Should Consider Selling to Littleton
- Highly competitive buy prices
- Fair appraisals and offers
- Fast confirmation and settlement
- Finders fees and joint arrangements
- Over 50 years experience buying and selling coins and paper money
- We welcome the opportunity to purchase your paper money

Littleton Coin Company

1309 Mt. Eustis Road
Littleton, N.H. 03561-3735

Buyer Phone: (603) 444-1020
FAX: (603) 444-3501
Teletype: Facts D97,
CoinNet NH07
Or write to our
Chief Buyer Jim Reardon at

**Dept BFS002
1309 Mt. Eustis Rd.
Littleton NH 03561**

Over 50 Years of Friendly Service to Collectors!

☑**YES!** I'm interested in selling paper money to Littleton. Please contact me regarding my collection or holdings.

Name _____

Address _____

City/State/Zip _____

Daytime Phone _____

Best time to call _____

Fill out this coupon (or a photocopy of it) and fax it to (603) 444-3501, or mail it to: Littleton Coin Company, Dept. BFS002, 1309 Mt. Eustis Rd., Littleton, NH 03561

Littleton Coin Company

Guide and Handbook

We are a leading auction house of United States currency. Offering thousands of lots each year, including the greatest rarities and notes for beginning collectors. Our fully illustrated catalogs are for sale in conjunction with regularly scheduled currency shows.

Single Catalogs – $15 • One Year Subscription (4) – $40

CONSIGNMENTS WANTED

If the time has come for you to sale your currency our regular auctions can certainly meet your needs.

Lyn Knight Currency Auctions

Building Collections For Collectors

The Ultimate Collectors Destination™

A CollectorsUniverse Company.

P.O. Box 7364, Overland Park, KS 66207-0364
(800) 243-5211, Fax: (913) 338-4754, E-mail: lynfknight@aol.com, Web Site: lynknight.com

Hot Contact List™

Dealers and resources for collectors [page]

American Coins & Collectibles	(800) 865-3562
[447]	(318) 868-9077
American Numismatic Association	(800) 367-9723
[454, 455] fax	(719) 634-4085
Dick Balbaton [448]	(508) 699-2266
Pat Barnes [476]	(517) 333-9980
	patbarnes@voyager.org
Keith Bauman [477]	(248) 262-1514
	TNAsbauman@earthlink.net
Harlan Berk [444]	(312) 609-0016
fax	(312) 609-1305
BNR Press	(419) 732-6683, 734-6683
[446,470-471] toll free	(800) 793-0683
fax	(419) 732-6683
	bnrpress@papermoneyworld.com
Caribbean Sun Gold [476]	(305) 256-7201
Carolina Gold and Silver, Inc.	(803) 736-0540
[477]	(803) 736-0415
Champion Stamp Co. [477]	(212) 489-8130
fax	(212) 581-8130
Daren J. Cioffi [477] voice/fax	(302) 235-1698
	Darren@GOLD-COAST-TRADING.COM
The Coin Shop in Arlington	(817) 251-9509
[476] fax	(817) 274-9992
David Cieniewicz [464]	(256) 852-7015
	dave@papermoneyworld.com
Currency Dealer Newsletter [467]	(310) 515-7369
Currency Quest [see inside front]	(614) 864-8875
	currencyquest@papermoneyworld.com
Tom Denly [450]	(617) 482-8477
Doric Coins & Currency [448]	(508) 699-2266
fax	(508) 643-1154
Early American Numismatics	(858) 459-4159
[469] fax	(858) 459-4373
Harry Edelman, Inc. [465]	(718) 641-2710
	(888) 333-6147
fax	(718) 641-0737
Lawrence Falater [457]	(517) 437-8977
toll free	(888) FALATER
fax	(517) 437-8978
	FALATER@papermoneyworld.com
Kevin Foley [475]	(414) 481-7287
fax	(414) 481-7297
Len Glazer [456]	(718) 268-3221
Steve Goldsmith [back cover]	(212) 943-1880
Great Lakes Bank Note Company	(800) 793-0683
Cindy Grellman/FUN [462]	(407) 321-8747
Bruce Hagen [476]	(212) 721-2028
Heritage Numismatic Auctions	(800) US COINS
[463]	(800) 872-6467 ext 222
Lowell Horwedel [449]	(765) 583-2748
fax	(765) 583-4384
Harry Jones [445]	(440) 234-3330
Jeff and Janis Jones	(614) 899-1803
[see inside back cover] fax	(614) 899-1557
Lyn Knight auctions [479]	(800) 243-5211
fax	(913) 338-4754
	lynfknight@aol.com
Phillip B. Lamb [444]	(504) 899-7491
fax	(504) 891-6826
	lambcsa@aol.com
Dana Linet [469]	(858) 459-4159
fax	(858) 459-4373

Littleton Coin Company [478]	(603) 444-1020
fax	(603) 444-3501
Ian A. Marshall [466]	(416) 445-0286
	ian@papermoneyworld.com
Leo May [477]	(305) 343-2429
	leo@papermoneyworld.com
Memphis Coin Club [458]	(901) 754-6118
Allan Mincho [456]	(830) 693-7590
fax	(830) 693-1283
The Mint [see inside back cover]	(816) 373-2646
fax	(816) 373-7744
	themint@JP-TheMint.com
Hudson McDonald [476]	(334) 937-6580
Arthur H. Morowitz [477]	(212) 489-8130
fax	(212) 581-8130
Stanley Morycz [inside front]	(937) 898-0114
Jay Parrino [inside back cover]	(816) 373-2646
fax	(816) 373-7744
	themint@JP-TheMint.com
Huston Pearson [476]	(817) 251-9509
fax	(817) 274-9992
Alex Perakis [472]	(610) 565-1110
fax	(610) 891-1466
Clarence Rareshide [477]	(504) 866-4212
Bob Reed [476]	(504) 361-5684
fax	(504) 361-1808
	bobreed@rrcoins.net
John Rowe [445]	(214) 826-3036
fax	(214) 823-1923
Lou Rusera [476] voice/fax	(818) 348-5275
George Schweighofer	(614) 864-8875
[inside front]	currencyquest@papermoneyworld.com
Fred Schwan [453, 461]	(419) 732-6683
Richie Self [447]	(318) 868-9077
Hugh Shull [459]	(803) 432-8500
fax	(803) 432-9958
Small Size Shop [inside back]	(614) 899-1803
fax	(614) 899-1557
R. M. Smythe	(212) 943-1880
[473, 474, back cover]	(800) 622-1880
fax	(212) 908-4047
Southland Coins/Currency [476]	(818) 348-5275
Harlan White [453]	(619) 298-0137
fax	(619) 298-7966
Scott Winslow Associates	(603) 641-8292
[451] fax	(603) 641-5583
	scott@scottwinslow.com
Sam Withers [476]	(314) 968-1647
John Yasuk [476]	(305) 256-7201
Auction companies	
Currency Auctions of America	(830) 693-7590
[456]	(718) 268-3221
fax	(830) 693-1283
Early American Numismatics	(858) 459-4159
[469] fax	(858) 459-4373
Heritage Numismatic Auctions	(800) US COINS
[463]	(800) 872-6467 ext 222
Lyn Knight auctions [479]	(800) 243-5211
fax	(913) 338-4754
	lynfknight@aol.com
R. M. Smythe	(212) 943-1880
[473, 474, back cover]	(800) 622-1880
fax	(212) 908-4047
Scott Winslow Associates	(800) 255-6283
[451] fax	(603) 641-5583
	scott@scottwinslow.com

UNITED STATES CURRENCY

Specialists in small size paper money

For a BIG DEAL

call

The Small Size Shop

Jeff and Janis Jones
Box 2007, Westerville, OH 43086
614/899-1803, fax 614/899-1557
smallsize@papermoneyworld.com